The Richard Strauss Companion

Edited by
MARK-DANIEL SCHMID

 PRAEGER

Westport, Connecticut
London

Library of Congress Cataloging-in-Publishing Data

The Richard Strauss companion / edited by Mark-Daniel Schmid.
    p. cm.
  Includes bibliographical references and indexes.
  ISBN 0-313-27901-2 (alk. paper)
    1. Strauss, Richard, 1864–1949—Criticism and interpretation. I. Schmid,
Mark-Daniel.
  ML410.S93R465   2003
  780'.92—dc21   2002044545
  [B]

British Library Cataloguing in Publication Data is available.

Library of Congress Catalog Card Number: 2002044545
ISBN: 0-313-27901-2

First published in 2003

Praeger Publishers, 88 Post Road West, Westport, CT 06881
An imprint of Greenwood Publishing Group, Inc.
www.praeger.com

Printed in the United States of America

The paper used in this book complies with the
Permanent Paper Standard issued by the National
Information Standards Organization (Z39.48-1984).

10 9 8 7 6 5 4 3 2 1

Copyright Acknowledgments

The editor and publisher gratefully acknowledge permission for use of the following
material:

Heiner Wajemann. "Die Einflüsse: Brahms, Liszt, Wagner, Mozart und andere." *Richard
Strauss-Blätter*, Neue Folge, Heft 43 (June 2000): 149–176. Copyright © Richard Strauss-
Gesellschaft. Used with permission of Dr. Hans Schneider Verlag GmbH.

Richard Strauss and Stefan Zweig. *A Confidential Matter: The Letters of Richard Strauss and
Stefan Zweig: 1931–1935.* Translated by Max Knight. Berkeley: University of California
Press, 1977. Used with permission of the Regents of the University of California.

Contents

Foreword

Bryan Gilliam

As this volume goes to press, it has been a decade since the appearance of two volumes of essays and documents on Richard Strauss. One is the extension of the first major international musicological conference (at Duke University in Durham, North Carolina) on the composer, the other is a part of the Strauss music festival held at Bard College in Annandale-on-Hudson; New York. What has happened in these ten years—in both scholarship and performance—has been utterly remarkable. At least a half-dozen biographies of Strauss, a number of new monographs and dissertations on his work, and a host of newly published correspondence have appeared, and several more conferences have been held on both sides of the Atlantic. Moreover, an international institute for Strauss research opened in Garmisch, Germany, on 8 September 1999.

The music industry has been no less idle during this period. New recordings of his operas have enriched the market beyond the *Salome, Elektra, Der Rosenkavalier,* and *Ariadne* canon. *Die Frau ohne Schatten, Die ägyptische Helena, Friedenstag* (three different versions), and *Die Liebe der Danae* have all appeared during a time when opera recording is generally in a serious decline. A series of recordings called *Der unbekannte Strauss,* which is now in its twelfth volume, feature previously unrecorded chamber music, orchestral music, ballet, and choral works.

In the realm of live performance (beyond the triangle of Vienna, Munich, and Berlin), later Strauss operas have made significant inroads at major opera houses such as Covent Garden, the Metropolitan Opera, the New York City Opera, the Houston Grand Opera, the Chicago Lyric Opera, and the San Francisco Opera, not to mention the various festival opera houses of Salzburg, Glyndebourne, Garsington, Santa Fe, Glimmerglass, and others. It would be foolhardy to propose an all-encompassing explanation for this explosion of interest in Strauss. Certainly some of this activity may have been catalyzed by the fiftieth anniversary of the composer's death in 1999, but, then, how does one explain the fact that the fortieth anniversary went practically unnoticed, especially in the academic community?

At the time of Strauss's birth (1864), his native Bavaria was still a kingdom; when he died (1949), the Federal Republic of Germany had been in existence for four months. A month after his death (September 8), the communist German Democratic Republic was established. Curiously, the year that commemorated the fortieth anniversary of the composer's death also marked the fortieth anniversary of East German socialism, its rapid unraveling, and the opening of the Berlin Wall.

While the political Cold War was rapidly coming to an end, so was a musical one of sorts. To understand better the significance of the musical cold war, one need only look back at the Strauss centennial celebration of 1964. Whereas special concerts and operatic performances took place all over the world, there was a deafening silence among music scholars on the subject of Strauss. Indeed, *Perspectives of New Music,* a major organ for postwar high modernism, broke the silence of 1964 with an English translation of Theodor Adorno's brilliant, polemical essay commemorating the centennial. The intent of *Perspectives* was to create a negative commemoration, to declare that, one hundred years after his birth, the Straussian legacy was essentially moribund.

During that year, the ideas of Darmstadt continued to resonate internationally (though not uniformly) with an ideology of musical style that prized technical progressiveness above all else. During this period of ideological polarization, the discourse on musical modernity centered on the materials of music, and thereby insulated itself from modernist discussions concerning the fields of art and literature, which drew from criticism, aesthetics, and other disciplines. A fundamental emphasis was placed on "value" in a musical work, and value, in turn, was defined by technical progress. The *evolutionary,* triadic compositional narrative of "growth, achievement, and mastery" (rooted in the Beethoven model) continued in the twentieth century, where "mastery" was now equated with serialism.

Strauss's own historical pessimism would not allow for such a linear, unified narrative, which he believed to be incompatible with the modern world. As a result, his musical development was unjustly ignored by most musicologists, specializing in late-nineteenth- and early-twentieth-century modernism. Many textbooks presented a facile triadic narrative that described Strauss's development in metaphorical terms of promise, decline, and a sentimental notion of "Indian summer." For the more orthodox modernists, promise, decline, and irrelevancy characterized a composer they could not equate with the tradition of the so-called Second Viennese School.

It was a highly linear, historicized narrative that could adopt strong, antagonistic modes of thinking, a worldview that would lead René Leibowitz, who taught at the Darmstadt festivals in the late 1940s and mid-1950s, to go so far as to declare (in 1955) that the tonal Jean Sibelius was *le plus mauvais compositeur du monde* (the worst composer in the world). In such a polarized atmosphere composers out of touch with public taste believed that high art could never meet popular art, tonality and atonality must not mix, and the profound and the trivial should remain separate.

Thus, in the biography of Kurt Weill in the first edition of the *New Grove* (1981), the author declared that there was not one but two Weills, the European modernist and the American Broadway sell-out. Adorno supplied labels for these two Weills: "Komponist" (composer) and "Musikregisseur" (musical director). Nothing could have been farther from the thinking of a composer like Richard Strauss, who not only embraced and thematicized the putative binary oppositions cited above (often in a single work) but— as his letters to Hugo von Hofmannsthal, Stefan Zweig, and Joseph Gregor show—he always had the audience clearly in mind as he was composing opera.

In the early decades that followed Strauss's death, musical and social politics overlapped to create a sad and confusing mix as music commentators in opposing camps dug in their heels and assumed unreflective, unyielding positions. For those early defenders of Strauss's legacy, the high modernists were dangerous radicals undermining occidental culture, and, for the high modernists, the Straussians were hopeless, narrow-minded reactionaries. Many early Strauss advocates sought to soft pedal, or even obscure, Strauss's shameful dealings—and early cooperation—with the National Socialist regime, while the composer's detractors indulged in questionable, often erroneous, *ad hominem* polemics against him.

During the 1960s, Glenn Gould stood alone in calling these artificial battle lines into question. In a letter he wrote to Leonard Bernstein in 1961, Gould lauded Schoenberg and Strauss as the two greatest composers of the twentieth century, saying that Strauss's greatness would finally be recognized as such once "the time-style equation, which clutters most judgment of his work" dissolves. The year of that letter was also the year of the Berlin Wall's construction, and both the "time-style" paradigm and the former edifice have, indeed, receded in our memory, especially in the memory of a younger generation of scholars in Europe and the United States.

Many of those younger scholars are represented in this volume, which offers fresh and current insights on one of the most complex composers in modern German history. Hopefully their work will help the layperson and scholar alike to understand the music of the man whose presence in the performance world continues to flourish and, equally important, who has now found a firm place in the discourse of musicology.

Preface

There is no longer any doubt that Richard Strauss has secured his place in the ranks of the most celebrated composers of Western art music. This, however, was not the case just a few decades ago, although the composer had been at the forefront of creative artists during most of his long life. One had to wonder, could the works of Strauss stand the test, and would his ambiguous political association be in the way of his gaining the eternal seal of public approval? Answers to these questions were not immediately at hand. Then in the early 1990s two comprehensive volumes and a series of dissertations indicated a new trend toward a growing interest in Strauss among scholars. The fiftieth anniversary celebration in 1999 not only confirmed this but also provided the definitive answer that interest in Strauss is lasting: his tone poems are staples in many orchestras' repertoires, and his operas appear regularly on stages internationally. At the same time, more and more writers find the composer's works and personal life a challenging area of study, as is obvious from the large number of biographies and studies dealing with musical and philosophical as well as political and sociological aspects of Strauss's music. Apart from accounts of the composer's life—most abundantly furnished by German- and English-speaking scholars—the probing into every aspect of his artistic and personal legacy has also yielded a new body of Strauss scholarship, as a direct result of conferences and festivals organized around the anniversary of the composer's death. The contributions in these publications—by a host of Strauss scholars as well as other scholars—focus frequently on rather specific investigations relating to the composer, ranging from studies of particular works to discussions of ideologies, literary interests, artistic ideas, and musical influences.

What sets *The Richard Strauss Companion* apart from other publications, however, is its content: a blend of predominantly general examinations of entire genres some for which the composer today is well-known, others where he is less-recognized. There are chapters dealing with the early and late instrumental works, the tone poems, the nonoperatic works for chorus, the late operas, and the songs. (A close and exclusive look at Strauss's second opera, *Feuersnot*, is here rather the exception from the rule.) Furthermore, there are chapters that explore his philosophical views and literary interests as well as his poetic imagination. One chapter traces Strauss's musical influences while another probes his political stance. Lastly, one chapter addresses the critical reception of early instrumental Strauss.

Directed at both the layperson and the musically educated reader, *The Richard Strauss Companion* is the sixth in a series of composer studies, which at the time of publication have included Schoenberg, Sibelius, Mendelssohn, Liszt, and Bloch. This most recent *Companion* attempts to provide a comprehensive spectrum of Strauss the man and Strauss the artist. Its goal is to serve as an important step toward solidifying Strauss's place in the canon of Western music and to prove that his personality and oeuvre continue unabatedly to captivate writers, readers, and listeners.

The completion of this book was a long and assiduous process that spanned more than a decade, and no one is happier to see its completion than I am—I have aged several years over it. I would particularly like to thank all the contributors, who were always flexible, dedicated, and enthusiastic. I am especially grateful to Scott Warfield for assisting me with several editorial issues and research questions and to Kathleen Sewright for additional proofreading.

I am also extremely grateful to the editorial staff at Praeger Publishers who has remained helpful, patient, and supportive and thus has allowed me to get this book finally completed. Thanks particularly to Eric Levy for his humor at the most difficult junctures.

I would like to express my thanks to Mansfield University for allowing me to conduct research in Europe through a generous Faculty Research Grant, and for processing my interlibrary loan requests. Furthermore, I would like to thank Evelyne Lüthi-Graf (Archive de Montreux), Christine Roth (Bibliotèque cantonale et l'Universitaire de Lausanne), Jörg Müller (Stadt- und Universitätsbibliothek Bern), and Daniel Fuhrimann for providing me with important sources and lists.

A number of individuals should be singled out who have surrendered their precious time in helping to bring this book to completion. My gratitude goes to two of my colleagues at Mansfield University: Bernard Koloski, professor of English, for reading through drafts of chapters, and Bradley Holtman, professor of languages, for polishing the German and French translations. Thanks also to my music theory colleague Shellie Gregorich for preparing many of the musical examples. I am indebted to Jürgen Thym, professor of music history at the Eastman School of Music, for his insightful suggestions, thorough proofreading, and the hours spent discussing the many aspects one needs to consider as the editor of a book.

More than anyone else, I would like to thank my wife Jennifer who not only took on the lion's share of caring for our daughters Tatiana and Nadia while Daddy was writing and editing, but also found time to type up the work list and index, run a fine-toothed comb through my chapter, keep me motivated, and, in moments of doubt, encourage me to continue my editorship until the *Companion* was on its way to the printer. My love goes to her.

Abbreviations

ADMv	Allgemeiner Deutscher Musikverein
AL	Annotated libretto
BE	Betrachtungen und Erinnerungen
f	Forte
ff	Fortissimo
inc.	Incomplete work
IOC	International Olympic Committee
m.	Measure
mm.	Measures
o. Op.	Without Opus number
Op.	Opus number
Opp.	Opus numbers
P	Particell
p	Piano
pp	Pianissimo
R/reh.	Rehearsal number
RMK	Reichsmusikkammer
RSA	Richard-Strauss-Archiv
SATB	For soprano, alto, tenor, bass choir
S,A,T,B	For soprano, alto, tenor, bass solo
TrV	Trenner number
VS	Vocal score

Part I
Influences

I

The Influences of Richard Strauss

Heiner Wajemann

I.

The sea of music is fed by many tributaries. National schools, formal-historical developments, musicological and aesthetic insights, as well as great composers' personalities fill up the riverbed of music history. This phenomenon can be demonstrated generally for schools and epochs, but also as it relates to individual outstanding musicians. Both the universal, or at least European, music tradition, as well as the appearance on the scene of an individual, who was at once formed by and formative of this tradition, coincide in the person of Richard Strauss. He ingeniously absorbed the most varied currents of music history *and* the great flow of the two-thousand-year evolution of culture and theater, conscious all the while of his own bearings and that he stood at the mouth of a wide and exalted tributary to the sea of music. From the springs, streams, and creeks, across the fluvial plains and great bodies of water to the ocean's coast stretches a single expansive rainbow, at whose end Strauss envisioned himself.[1] Such a perspective implies that Strauss saw himself as an artist who transcended the traditions of the national musical heritage. Flowing into his work, his thinking, and his composing are lines of tradition that can be traced in part back through the centuries, such as the development of piano music and the Lied within the Romantic period; the choral music of the seventeenth and nineteenth centuries; the heated debates over the sonata form and symphonic poem (or the form of the opera, especially that of the French and Italian opera of the eighteenth and nineteenth centuries, or that of the German *Spieloper* and the Wagnerian musical drama); as well as the entire several-thousand-year cultural history of the theater, beginning in ancient Greece and progressing through the classical French theater, through Goethe up to Wilde and Hofmannsthal. In this expansive evolutionary arc, Brahms and Wagner represent only immediate predecessors, as do Liszt and Johann Strauss the younger. All these influences not only can be proved objectively, that is, music-historically and musicologically, but also are apparent in the way Strauss saw himself as an artist. With clear consciousness and sharpened intellect, Strauss contemplated his own musical development, drove it forward, and judged it again and again with admirably objective detachment. In this context, one should recall the well-known statement by Stefan Zweig: "They are perhaps the most alert eyes that I have ever seen in a musician, not demonic, but somehow clairvoyant, the eyes of a man cognizant of the full significance of his task."[2]

The various lines of tradition can be schematized as shown in Figure 1.1. From this figure we can see that many forbearers influenced Strauss, and in the individual creative phases, masters who could hardly be more different from one another. In the end, however, he acknowledged only a few masters, epochs, and music-aesthetic approaches, thereby indicating which compositional objectives were of importance to him, especially with regard to his own work. Yet he also thought about performance practice and large-scale opera festivals. One must keep in mind that Strauss, following Wagner's *Festspiel* idea and Nietzsche's *Birth of Tragedy*, and aware of the Greek cult of tragedy, became a co-founder of the Salzburg Festspiele together with Hugo von Hofmannsthal and Max Reinhardt. Today two composers are the focus of this festival—Mozart and Strauss. Both in his musical writings (see *Betrachtungen und Erinnerungen*) and in his correspondence, he took positions on the musical aesthetics and history of Western culture, trends in music, and his favored composers. Its credo can be reduced to a few names (see Figure 1.2). The names of these five composers indicate that the main influences, and thus the main areas of concern in his work, are to be found in the symphonic poem, the musical drama, and the Mozartian Spieloper. In his essays and work Strauss testifies again and again to these areas of concern within his oeuvre and to his view of himself as an artist. He has gone down in history as a great tone painter and as a musical dramatist, as well as the composer of *Salome* and *Der Rosenkavalier*, and has gained broad public favor through the cultivation and dissemination of the genres he preferred. At the same time, he left behind ambitious works that for the most part have remained reserved only for musical connoisseurs and Straussians, such as the *Couperin* Suites,

FIGURE 1.1

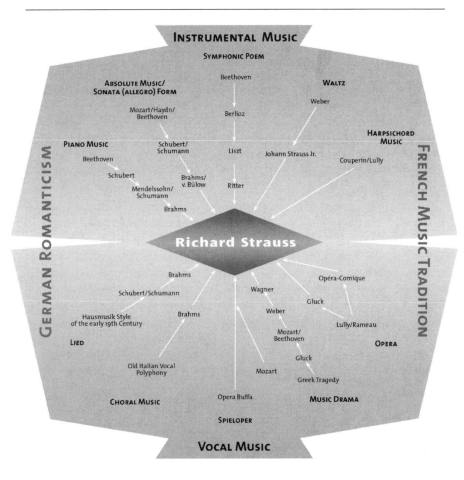

FIGURE 1.2

sixteen-to-twenty-voice choral music, and the later works, including *Capriccio.*

II.

In the biographies of Strauss one frequently learns that he found his own style, in a compositional and instrumental-technical sense, with *Don Juan*, the tone poem after Nikolaus Lenau for large orchestra, written between 1886 and 1888. Even with the problems involved in establishing a clear caesura in the evolution of a composer, it can be asserted that with *Don Juan* the period of searching for clarity of style and an affirmed view of himself as an artist was over. His schooling spanned a period of some eighteen years. At the age of six, shortly after he joined the Cathedral School in Munich, Strauss wrote his first small work, the *Schneiderpolka* for piano (o. Op. 1), and at twenty-four he delivered *Don Juan*. His musical socialization up to this time (1888) can be understood in every detail on the basis of his many statements, letters, and compositions. It can be seen that while Brahms represented a powerful example, other influences also played a role during Strauss's childhood and youth. Of primary importance here were his extended family, particularly the music-loving Pschorrs on the maternal side, and his father Franz Strauss, just as Hans von Bülow and Alexander Ritter were later in his life. The piano pieces and songs of his childhood can be described as his musical "first steps." His father, first horn in the court orchestra, himself a composer and a professor at the Akademie der Tonkunst in Munich, not only supervised the musical development of his son, but also determined its direction. The classical Viennese composers and, in addition, Mendelssohn and Schumann were the favored composers in his early education. Franz Strauss consciously joined the guild of the anti-Wagnerians, even though he was compelled to collaborate as first horn at the Munich premieres of *Tristan und Isolde* and *Die Meistersinger von Nürnberg*. Richard Strauss's first compositions—and this is not surprising in view of his father's musical and pedagogical orientation—breathe the spirit of Mendelssohn and Schumann, both the piano pieces and minor chamber music works as well as the Lieder and the choral pieces. He composed for himself, for the musical exercises in the Pschorr family, and finally also for the amateur orchestra Wilde Gung'l directed by his father. Strauss's studies of counterpoint were completed early. At the age of eleven he began instruction with the Munich court conductor Friedrich Wilhelm Meyer in the theoretical disciplines of harmony, musical form, and instrumentation. When the sixteen-year-old completed this systematic musical education, he had a firm command of simple, double, triple, and quadruple counterpoint, as well as the fugue. It is clear from all these influences that during his young years Strauss particularly cultivated *musical genres* derived from the classical and Mendelssohnian traditions. The following works exemplify this:

Symphony No. 1 in D minor (1880, TrV 94)

String Quartet in A major (1880, Op. 2, TrV 95)

Sonata for Piano in B minor (1881, Op. 5, TrV 103)

Chor aus *Elektra*, based on the tragedy of Sophocles, for men's chorus and orchestra in C minor (?1881, TrV 104)

Fünf Klavierstüke (1881, Op. 3, TrV 105)

Serenade for 13 wind instruments in E-flat major (1881, Op. 7, TrV 105)

Violin Concerto in D minor (1880–82, Op. 8, TrV 110)

Sonata for Violoncello and Piano in F major (1880–83, Op. 6, TrV 115)

Horn Concerto No. 1 in E-flat major (1882–83, Op. 11, TrV 117)

Many further compositions in these genres, as well as songs, trios, variations, overtures, and romances, demonstrate that in those years Strauss was committed to Classicism and Romanticism. A well-formed talent was present, but the typical Straussian style was not yet achieved. The musical craft was learned playing with ease. Not only formally, but also thematically, Strauss was subject to the Classical-Romantic tradition of the masters preferred by his father. For example, the main theme in the Romance in F Major/Andante cantabile for violoncello with orchestra or piano accompaniment, o. Op. 75, written as part of the postlude to the Violoncello Sonata, Op. 6, was composed in just such a spirit; in evidence are two-bar subdivision, rhythmic and melodic repetitions, exchange of major and minor, and simple functional harmonics:

EXAMPLE 1.1

Strauss himself reflected on the musical influences of his youth and wrote them down. The most important documentation for this is the correspondence with Ludwig Thuille (1861–1907), the friend of his youth, who likewise composed. Strauss testifies eloquently to his musical understanding and preference for select genres in the following passages: "I am composing very diligently 1) on a Romance in E-flat major for clarinet and orchestra . . . ; from the pervasive theme there resulted a six-voice orchestral fugato after the first cantilena. 2) again a new gavotte No. IV. 3) . . . for the wedding of my cousin Linda Moralt a comical wedding march . . . , which I'll perform on the wedding day with my ensemble, Hanna and the 4 Pschorr boys . . . 4) . . . the A minor overture . . . : further, I have a quartet [Op. 2] in mind" (22 July 1879).³ Or: "I've already made colossal progress on my symphony [in F minor, Op. 12]! The entire first movement is already finished . . . For a week I've been busy thinking about which key and time the adagio movement should be composed in" (7 March 1882).⁴ The two friends were artistically in agreement with each other. However, Thuille, who came from the Alexander Ritter circle, eventually developed into a moderate progressive within the New German School. When he died in 1907 at the age of 45, the event marked the passing of a member of the "Munich School" of the time, a school in which Richard Strauss—a Munich native—is not to be included.

III.

Johannes Brahms (1833–97) made Strauss's acquaintance during his time in Meiningen; they were introduced by Hans von Bülow (1830–94), who, having turned away from Wagner, at the time supported Brahmsian art and artistic ideology without reservation. Bülow was without question the most important interpreter of Beethoven and Brahms of the time. He befriended Strauss, became his patron, and tried to draw him into the Brahms camp. It was not without skepticism, however, that Strauss delved into the works of this highly Romantic composer. Through his contact with Brahms, Strauss was drawn back once again to the sources of the Classical style, to the composition principles of Haydn and Mozart, and to the symphonic style of Beethoven. In Brahms the architecture, the cultivation, and even more, the preservation of the form predominates. Sonata form remains the deciding and stimulating element in his music.

The relationship between Brahms and Strauss in the years 1884–86 can be described with the words, familiarization—idolization—alienation. In Meiningen, Strauss heard the Third Symphony of Brahms by his own admission four times. He wrote to his father on 6 January 1884: "My head is still throbbing from this vagueness, and I openly confess that I have not yet understood it, yet it [also] has such a lousy and indistinct instrumentation."[5] Strauss reacted like so many who hear Brahms for the first time. He seems inaccessible at first. The power and depth of the scores disclose themselves only with intense study. Thus, it is not surprising that a short time later the following note went out to his father (1 February 1884): "The symphony is really wonderful. Clear in form and structure, splendidly crafted, it has charming themes and a tension and momentum that has something of Beethoven . . . This symphony (F major) belongs to the freshest, most beautiful, and most original that Brahms has created. Under his splendid direction the orchestra was dashing."[6] Strauss's admiration of Brahms then increased when he became acquainted with the Fourth Symphony. Strauss later attributed his enthusiasm of that time to the suggestive influence of von Bülow.[7] This passion for Brahms yielded such works as *Wanderers Sturmlied* (Goethe) for six-part chorus and large orchestra, Op. 14, and the *Burleske* for piano and orchestra, o. Op. 85. The prolonged orchestral prelude to the *Sturmlied* begins with a majestic, dramatic theme modeled on Brahms:

EXAMPLE 1.2

The wanderer Goethe and, correspondingly, the wanderer Strauss suffer through *Sturm und Drang* (Storm and Stress), the highs and lows of life, and finally, reassured and reconciled, extol the muses and charities:

Ihr seid rein, wie das Herz der Wasser,
Ihr seid rein, wie das Mark der Erde,
Ihr umschwebt mich, und ich schwebe
Über Wasser, über Erde,
Göttergleich.

EXAMPLE 1.3

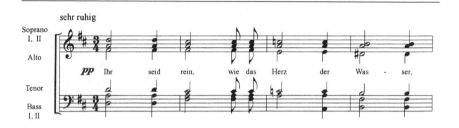

The tempo at the end of the piece is *sehr ruhig* (very quiet). Strauss effortlessly attains the desired mood in the listener: the feeling after a thunderstorm, nature takes a deep breath, the waters subside, the storm has abated. Similar contrasts and developments can be found in Brahms's choral works, such as *Schicksalslied* (Hölderlin), Op. 54, or *Ein Deutsches Requiem*, Op. 45. The negative is followed by the positive, suffering by joy, death by resurrection, the struggle for life by redemption, the tribulations of life by reconciliation. In the *Alto Rhapsodie*, Op. 53, and in the *Gesang der Parzen*, Op. 89, Brahms uses Goethe texts. Thus, as a successor to Brahms, Strauss even goes so far as to emulate his model in his choice of texts.

In Meiningen Brahms gave Strauss some hints on composing. Looking back, Strauss later commented on this: "I am still grateful to him for the suggestion he made to me after he had listened to the F Minor Symphony, which he liked quite well, to do without contrapuntal play built on the triad. This was a valuable guide to me for my entire life."[8] Or:

I was extremely eager to hear his opinion of my symphony. In his taciturn way he said to me only "quite pretty," but added a lesson worth heeding: "Young man, take a close look at Schubert's dances and try your hand at inventing simple eight-bar melodies." I owe it mainly to Johannes Brahms that since then I've no longer scorned the idea of actually incorporating a popular melody (as little as they may be esteemed by the book learning of high criticism nowadays, they nevertheless occur to one very rarely and only at an auspicious hour) into my work.[9]

As examples of this, certainly one could mention the catchy waltz sequences or the love duet at the end of *Der Rosenkavalier*, the Bavarian *Gestampfte* (dance) in *Intermezzo*, or the somersaults of *Till Eulenspiegel*.[10] The influence of and dependence on Brahms during Strauss's maturation period is especially clear in several chamber music works. In addition to the

Lieder Opp. 10, 15, and 17, there are the Quartet for piano, violin, viola, and violoncello in C minor, Op. 13, and the Sonata for Violin and Piano in E-flat major, Op. 18. The piano quartet displays a mixture of Brahmsian influence, which has an impact on the establishment of the themes, and true Strauss, whom we hear in the truncations and strettos and the wide sweeping coda of the first movements. Mendelssohnian style appears in the poetical Andante, a *Song Without Words* with mellow harmony. The finale is virtuosic and, as so often in Strauss, crafted with humor. In the violin sonata he tends once again more to Schumann, especially in the two outer movements, which, with their sonata-allegro form, are rather traditionally and clearly laid out. Themes can be heard that are reminiscent of Schumann's contrasting pair, or Florestan, raging passionately forward, and of the soft, lyrical Eusebius, themes that express passion, chivalry, and romantic rapture. In any case, the choice of key in structurally important locations is striking, as when the third theme in the reprise of the first movement in A major appears, or, similarly, when the coda of the finale modulates to E major. The middle movement, called "Improvisation," brings the broad intervallic jumps and the rather clever harmonic shifts that are so typical of Strauss. One perceives, however, in all the works of his youth a turning away from the strictest Brahmsian formal principles. During the Meiningen period, Alexander Ritter gained gradually more and more influence over Strauss's thinking, philosophizing, and composing, and this paved the way for an inner withdrawal from Brahms. Various circumstances were responsible for Brahms's and Strauss's alienation and estrangement. Later, Strauss commented on Brahms to Cosima Wagner in the context of a discussion of Berlioz's *Requiem* on 26 November 1889: "Next to such a gigantic work, how wretched appears 'Ein Deutsches Requiem' by the musically abstinent temperance society member Brahms."[11] The break was complete. In his later years as a master Strauss looked back to his works of youth and passion for Brahms and regretted that he wrote and published *too many* compositions in strict sonata form, thus committing too many youthful transgressions.

IV.

"New ideas must seek new forms."[12] This thesis had been put forward by Franz Liszt (1811–86), and he proceeded accordingly in the composition of his symphonic poems. As a so-called "New German" he was active not only as an individual creative artist, but also in forming schools by considerably influencing many contemporaries in their musical orientation. The New German School came into being and, with it, the contradictory discussion about content and form in music, program music and sonata form, and tone painting and absolute music.

The antipodes—Liszt and Wagner on the one hand and Brahms on the other—were deployed and played off against each other. Richard Strauss was compelled, especially in the winter of 1885–86 in Meiningen, to confront these problems and deal with both sides. Both Brahms and Alexander Ritter, the glowing representative of the New Germans and admirer of Schopenhauer's philosophy, became the focus of his attention. Feeling that nothing new could be done with the sonata form, he was summoned by Ritter at a favorable moment in his life to continue philosophical and musical-aesthetic insights. He had to confront the problem of content and form as never before in his life. In this context, he remarked to von Bülow that every new work must possess its corresponding form and that purely formal music, such as the Viennese music critic and Brahms's patron Eduard Hanslick had called for, is incompatible with creating the music of the future:

To take up the Beethoven of the *Coriolan*, *Egmont*, and *Leonore* overtures, the *Les Adieux*, or the later Beethoven in general, whose entire creation in my view would probably not have come about without a poetic subject, seems to me to be the only way an independent development of our instrumental music is still possible. If I should lack the artistic energy and talent to achieve something fruitful, then it is probably better to leave it at the great 9 with its 4 famous latecomers [Beethoven's 9 and Brahms's 4 symphonies]; I do not see why, before we have tested whether it is possible for us to create independently and perhaps bring art a small step forwards, we immediately want to meddle in imitativeness and assume this epigonous point of view in advance.[13]

Strauss himself was aware that he had been trained strictly classically until 1885, and that he had just arrived at Brahms from Mendelssohn via Chopin and Schumann. Ritter now opened up for him the music-historical significance of the works and writings of Liszt and Wagner. Strauss owed his understanding and penetration of Schopenhauer's teachings as well to Ritter. He began the expressive, the poetic element in music, and he did this by emulating the examples of Berlioz, Liszt, and Wagner. The meetings in Meiningen and Ritter's advice hence mark the turning point in his life. "New ideas must seek new forms":[14] that is, the poetic idea must at the same time be the formative element. From then on, Strauss became a tone-painter, program musician, and finally, a musical naturalist, if one considers *Eine Alpensinfonie*, Op. 64, in this context. The Saul-Paul conversion had taken place. However, it must not be forgotten that apart from the formal, programmatic dependence there existed a stylistic independence from Liszt. Whereas the virtuosic piano technique developed by Liszt can be heard clearly to be the basis of his symphonic poems, orchestral composition in Strauss is based on a more polyphonic conception.

Program music achieved new momentum through Strauss, and the range of subject matter was expanded. Not only did Strauss not want to remain an imitator of symphonic composition in the Classical-Romantic tradition, he also wanted to move ahead along the path of program music. He was self-assured in the context of German and European music. In many of Beethoven's masterpieces he recognized the poetic idea that imprinted the work—the *Pastoral* Symphony, say, or the piano sonata *Les Adieux*—with the author's own personal stamp. Starting from Beethoven, Berlioz then raised program music to a principle of style. The *idée fixe*, the poetic leitmotif appears in a structurally meaningful way in his symphonie *Fantastique*. The subtitle of this symphony, "Episodes from the Life of an Artist," is indicative of the subject. The orchestra delineates no dramatic course of events; rather, it portrays the spiritual condition of the artist. After the aforementioned turning point in Meiningen, Strauss esteemed the ideas and innovations of Berlioz in program music as well as his teachings on instrumentation. In the end, however, and this is logical from a music-historical perspective, Strauss was placed under the spell of Liszt's symphonic poems in a special way. Liszt had conceived his thirteen poems more generally than had Berlioz. In his case, a program is present that contents itself with an occasional reference to historical material, a dominant character, or a painting. In this way the listener's imagination is steered in a programmatic direction but is not unnecessarily fettered.[15] Different emotions can be bound into the tone-painting process by orchestral effects. Strauss learned much of this technique and transposed it into his tone poems.

The work of the period of change is *Aus Italien*, symphonic fantasy for large orchestra, Op. 16, which, typically enough, is "dedicated to Hans von Bülow in deepest admiration and gratitude." This work was occasioned and influenced on the one hand by Strauss's trip to Italy in 1886 and, on the other, by his critical, systematic and pathbreaking examination of both Liszt's concept of Ausdrucksmusik (expressive music) and Hanslick's notion of music as *tönende Form* (sounding form). None other than Johannes Brahms had spoken with Strauss about Italy and advised him to make his way there so he could familiarize himself with Italian flair, Italian painting, its countryside, and its music. The trip to Italy, nothing more than an entirely normal tourist trip, took the young twenty-two-year-old artist to Bologna, Rome, Naples, Sorrento, Pompeii, Florence, Lake Como and back to Munich. The more relaxed world of the South found expression in pleasant-sounding compositions and offered suggestions and new orientations. Italian expressions and with them for the first time ever within the

Straussian oeuvre, *impressions of nature* are transposed into expressive music. The second influence, upon which Op. 16 is based, can be seen in the situation of radical change in 1886. During the late 1880s, with the nineteenth century drawing to a close, Strauss became aware not only of the musical temper of the time, but also of his own artistic view of himself, which was gradually taking on a character of a religious creed. His juxtaposition of musical-poetic content with the form of the classical sonata underwent a reevaluation that drove him more and more in *one* direction and culminated in statements he made in a letter to his patron, the Siebenburg musician Johann Leopold Bella (1843–1936):

The representation of the local music can indeed be divided into two groups: those for whom music is "expression" and who treat it as just as precise a language as verbal language, but appropriate to things for whose expression the latter has failed; and the others, for whom music is a "sounding form," that is, they impose any general prevailing mood . . . on the work to be composed and develop these themes that arise based on a logic completely external to music for which, since I recognize only poetic logic, I have no understanding at all.

Program music: real music!

Absolute music: its consolidation by means of a certain practice and handicraft technique accessible to everyone with even the slightest musical inclination.

The first:—true art!

The second:—skill![16]

Strauss was aware that all the musicians of his generation, like himself, began with the second manner of composition. They were, however, led to make a crucial decision: Strauss, in any case, decided for the first path. In this context his following statement is of importance: "My symphonic fantasy 'Aus Italien' is the link between old and new method."[17]

Aus Italien is evidence of the fact that program music is possible while observing traditional forms. Influences from Mendelssohn's *Italian* Symphony in A major and Brahmsian creative will united with elements of Strauss's style that would come into force in perfected form in his years as a master. The work is titled a "symphonic fantasy." This genre designation in the subtitle points to the fact that, on the one hand, poetic, programmatic naming has taken the place of the previous practice of formalistic naming and, hence, that the new aesthetic principles find expression already in the title; and, on the other hand, that a symphonic cycle with the character and ordering of the usual four movements is in evidence, similar to the classical sonata, yet in a modified form.[18] In the four movements, the moods of nature are reconciled with poetic and artistic impressions, possibilities of musical expression with technical orchestral arrangement. It is not, however, a matter of pure illustration music. Strauss supplied the individual movements with headings that were to steer the listener's imagination to places and conditions in Italy, but that were not intended to be a musical road map. Moreover, in this orchestral suite with four character pieces—another possible genre designation— there is a displacement of the movements and, in the third movement (Sorrento), a displacement of individual parts of the movement. Strauss himself conducted an analysis that reveals the composer's intentions in those years of radical change:

1. In the Countryside: Andante 4/4 (G major)

This prelude, which reflects the mood the composer felt at the view of the broad Roman countryside bathed in the blazing heat of the sun as seen from the Villa d'Este in Tivoli, has as its basis three main themes (quotations of the three themes: first theme, side theme, coda theme).

2. In Rome's Ruins: Allegro con brio (6/4 3/2) C major

Fantastic pictures of past splendor, feelings of nostalgia and pain in the midst of the sunniest present!

3. On the Beach at Sorrento: Andantino (A major 3/8)

In this movement the attempt is made to represent by tone painting the sweet music of nature, which the inner ear (note quotation: Episode in A minor) hears in the rustling of the wind, in the leaves, in the singing of the birds and all the fine voices of nature, in the distant roar of the sea, from which a lonely song sounds on the shore, and to show the contrast to the human senses taking it in, as expressed in the melodic element of the movement. The interplay achieved by separating and partially unifying these opposites forms the spiritual content of this atmospheric illustration.

4. Neapolitan Folk Life (Allegro molto 2/4)

The main theme is a well-known Neapolitan folk song (quotation), in addition, a tarantella the composer heard in Sorrento is used: (quotation, tarantella and middle themes). After some noisy opening bars the main theme begins, played by violas and cellos, this wild orchestral din that is intended to portray the colorful hustle and bustle in a merry confusion of themes, the tarantella, at the beginning only sounding from afar, gains the upper hand more and more towards the end of the movement and forms the end of this humoresque. Some echoes of the first movement may express the longing for the peacefulness of the countryside."[19]

Aus Italien should be viewed as the point of entry into the world of symphonic poems. Succeeding years saw the mature compositions of this genre such as *Macbeth*, Op. 23, *Don Juan*, Op. 20, *Tod und Verklärung*, Op. 24, all written between 1886 and 1889 and marked as tone poems for large orchestra. In these three, as in other tone poems, the composer struggles with formal laws that vie expression to innovations. As a tone painter and expressive musician he follows literary, individualistic, philosophical, and speculative trends. With respect to the history of his development as an artist, the tone poems of Strauss form an end and climax. His symphonic poems are masterpieces of their genre that are subject to influences from realms external to music. The development and execution of the themes, melodies, and leitmotifs, of the forms and architectures he invented do not happen arbitrarily, but rather reflect those new ideas coined by Liszt. And to which influences or schools does Strauss assign himself at this point? He formulated his response to this question at an advanced age: "I believe neither in schools nor in trends . . . I believe only in music."[20]

V.

Richard Wagner's compositional style, his writings on reform, and his aesthetic demands exerted a great influence on Strauss. His father, Franz Strauss, who played first horn in the Munich premieres of *Tristan* and *Die Meistersinger* and thus had an outstanding knowledge of Wagnerian *Zukunftsmusik* (Music of the Future), lived and made music in open opposition to the Bayreuth musician and raised his son accordingly. In 1878, as a fourteen-year-old, Strauss heard *Siegfried* and *Lohengrin* for the first time, two operas that he found terribly boring.[21] This unfriendly judgment was conditioned by his anti-Wagnerian father. In spite of this, Strauss found his way to Wagner while still in his youth, and particularly through his experience with *Tristan*. In reminiscence of his father he confessed:

In any case, only through forbidden study of the *Tristan* score did I delve into this marvel and later into the *Ring* as well, and I remember quite well how, at around 17, I devoured the pages of the *Tristan* score virtually in a fever and fell into a fit of ecstasy. After this realization I became (despite my old uncle's every warning about the 'fraud of Bayreuth') a 'full Wagnerian', and performing *Lohengrin* (whose marvels of instrumentation constantly delight me), or *Tristan*, or directing an 'improvised' *Ring* with the musicians of the Vienna Philharmonic, which is only half of what I would like to do, are the greatest joys for me still today.[22]

Only after Strauss had attended the Munich performances of *Tristan* as a young man and had finally familiarized himself completely with the score during his first years as conductor in Munich (1886–89) could he collaborate as musical assistant at the *Tristan* rehearsals in 1889 in Bayreuth. Alexander Ritter (1833–96) in particular, whose friendship Strauss made in the Meiningen winter of 1885–86, encouraged Wagner's influence on Strauss as well as Strauss's admiration for Wagner. Ritter awakened the interest in and appreciation of Berlioz's art of instrumentation and his *Symphonie Fantastique,* Liszt's theoretical writings and symphonic poems, and Wagner's musical aesthetics and musical dramas as well as the philosophy of Arthur Schopenhauer. The enthusiastic apostle of *Zukunftsmusik* made Strauss not only into a fan and representative of the New German School, but into an admirer of Wagner par excellence. Ritter finally convinced his friend that it was now time, after already composing many ingenious tone poems for large orchestra, for Strauss to compose an opera in emulation of the Wagnerian symphonic musical drama that would meet the demands of high literary, musical, and aesthetic ideals. Wagner and Ritter *(Der faule Hans, Wem die Krone?)* had written their librettos themselves. Strauss selected as his subject one of the medieval secret religious societies that differentiated themselves from the secular practices of the Minnesingers. Strauss wrote a libretto that rivaled even Wagner, in which the main characters bear names that can be connected directly to the earlier composer,[23] such as Freihild, Guntram, the duke jester, and the four Minnesingers. The action takes place in Germany around the middle of the thirteenth century. The technique of leitmotif, introduced by Berlioz in the *Symphonie fantastique* through the *idée fixe,* further developed by Liszt and Strauss in their tone poems, and systematically adopted as musical drama by Wagner, undergoes a change and expansion already in the first operative work *Guntram,* Op. 25, then in *Feuersnot,* Op. 50, and is intensified in *Salome,* Op. 54, *Elektra,* Op. 58, and the subsequent stage works. Wagner himself had developed progressively in his treatment of the leitmotifs in his major works from *Rienzi* up to the creation of *Die Meistersinger, Tristan,* and the *Ring.* While the musical themes in the operas up to *Lohengrin* can be classified primarily as places and things as well as people and their motivations, no suitable and unambiguous designations can be found any longer for a series of motifs that play a significant role in the *Ring.* Motifs of "flight" or "displeasure" have less the function of characterizing individual things, instead connecting different things in dissimilar contexts and differentiating details in the total course of events.

Wagner referred many times to the ideal of the symphonic as the essential element of his musical dramas and employed the leitmotif technique accordingly. The ambiguity, complexity, and variability of the musical themes can be demonstrated with the motifs that contain a double element, such as the motifs "Spears/Treaty," "Lodge/Fire," "Freia/Youth," etc. The E-flat major triad at the beginning of *Das Rheingold* announces a number of thematic metamorphoses via the following process: Primordial Element ⇒ Becoming and Fading Away ⇒ Rhine ⇒ Erda. The bold procedure of labeling leitmotifs can be applied even less to the musical-dramatic works of Richard Strauss than to those of Wagner. Schematic formulas help in understanding and deciphering the musical-dramatic events, but more often obscure the complex background of meaning behind the characters and their emotions. One further trend relating to the widely varied employment of leitmotifs that can be demonstrated in Wagner in the advanced stages of his creation and especially in *Tristan*, which not without reason was Strauss's favorite work, is intensified more and more from *Guntram* to *Salome*, namely, the leitmotif characterization of human qualities and feelings.

This line of development suggests itself already in *Guntram*, and it became more and more important for Strauss's musical psychologizing to such a degree that, in the end, he advanced to the point of becoming a so-called nervous contrapuntalist. Many textbook commentators have, however questionable or bold this procedure may be, added labels to the individual themes: the theme of goodness, of good works, or youthful enthusiasm, of suffering, etc. The opening theme of the overture to *Guntram* is displayed here as an example. It is connected with four different areas of feeling:[24]

EXAMPLE 1.4

This theme suggests: (1) love, (2) compassion, (3) self-sacrifice, (4) grief.

Strauss did indeed learn and adopt much from Wagner with regard to the treatment of leitmotifs. But he reveals himself already in his first opera to be a musical dramatist who creates psychologically ambiguous motifs and implements them based on clashing emotions. This technique is continued in his next opera, *Feuersnot*, in which he employs a large Wagnerian orchestra and musical references to *Die Meistersinger*. Moreover, the librettist, Ernst von Wolzogen, sets the action on Midsummer's Eve, the same night as Wagner set the second act of *Die Meistersinger*. The score ends with the note "Completed on the birthday and for the higher glory of the 'Almighty', Charlottenburg, May 22, 1901." The next two one-act operas, *Salome* and *Elektra*, in which traumatic and neurotic conflict situations are acted out, as was altogether quite common for many contemporary composers in those years after the turn of the century, intensify yet again the Wagnerian musical apparatus; huge orchestras come into use. *Salome* and *Elektra* are no number operas, but rather total works of art with endless melody, instrumentation that in part employs subtle tone painting and timbre coloration, refined harmony, orientalisms, and avant-garde cacophonies, chromatics and whole-tone ladder technique, elements that in *Elektra* are taken to the most extreme limit of tonality. In this way Strauss strongly influenced the next generation of musicians, the atonal composers. In *Elektra* harmonically contrasting themes, as Strauss had previously found in the *Tristan* score he so admired, are forced into temporary unification,[25] indeed, entire complexes of themes interpenetrate one another contrapuntally, insofar as this is dramaturgically necessary. In this connection one should consider Strauss's confession: "I believe I've learned from Wagner what there actually is to learn. . . . I mean, I've taken everything into account and not made the error of copying."[26] In any case Strauss, like all composers around the turn of the century, had to differentiate himself from Wagner in order not to be an imitator. Strauss expanded Wagner's leitmotif technique in a manner that was simultaneously psychological and psychologizing, insofar as he created a "sort of music-psychoanalysis, a method of obtaining creative inspiration and artistic orientation from the subconscious"[27] with his "modern" orchestra. Wagner's leitmotif is thus further developed to the point of psychologically interpretative music that externalizes spiritual processes, hence bringing them to "expression." Strauss himself characterized this transcendence of Wagner:

Critics who didn't have a clue called *Salome* and *Elektra* 'symphonies with accompanying vocal parts.' That these 'symphonies' put into motion the core of the dramatic contents, that just a symphony orchestra (instead of the one that usually only accompanies the singing in opera) can develop a narrative up to the very end, as in my dramatic biography *Intermezzo*, in which only the 'symphonic interludes' actually manifest what is happening inwardly in the performers, just as in the famous scene between Siegfried and Mime before the latter is killed; a typical example of what is only possible on the stage with the help of musical themes.— All of this will perhaps only be understood fully and completely by our descendants. Hofmannsthal, too, perhaps concluded the same of Renaissance theater and commedia dell'arte at the end of *Ariadne*. And only my so delicately refined orchestra with its subtle 'nervous counterpoint', if the bold expression is permitted, could in the final scene of *Salome*, in Klytämnestra's anxiety states, in the recognition scene between Elektra and Orest, in the second act of *Helena*, and in the Empress's dream (second act of *Frau ohne Schatten*, venture forward into areas that only music was allowed to open up.[28]

Musical psychologizing, nervous counterpoint, and ambiguity of the leitmotifs are drawn to a climax already in *Salome*:

EXAMPLE 1.5

This motif characterizes only *one* person, Salome; however, it characterizes this person in her psychic and dynamic complexity, namely Salome as Self-willed—Reptilian—Untamed and wild—Ecstatic and unrestrained—Connected to life—Doomed to death.

Besides these purely psychologically oriented and psychologically explainable motifs, in *Salome* and in subsequent stage works Strauss employs his typical naturalistic tone paintings that turn up sporadically and abruptly in the score and that rival Wagner in their descriptiveness. The path leads from the High Romantic to musical Naturalism. Some examples of these illustrative tone painting motifs are cited here (Examples 1.6.1–1.6.4).[29]

The use of oversized orchestras make possible Strauss's musical naturalism, psychological motif technique, and art of tone-color illumination of character and spiritual processes. The criticism, often brought up by opponents, of Strauss's work as viscous orchestral gravy that causes the famous

EXAMPLE 1.6.1

The wind, the wings of the angel of death

EXAMPLE 1.6.2

The silver bowl motif

EXAMPLE 1.6.3

The peacock motif

EXAMPLE 1.6.4

The bird-of-prey shrieks of Herodias

and infamous murder of the singer lacks any serious foundation. In Strauss the orchestra becomes more and more the representative of the sensitive and spiritual inner life. The contrapuntal texture of the scores can be best characterized by the term polymelody, which in part implies polyrhythm and polyharmony; and polymelody brings about, among other things, the endless melody, the continuous reciprocal flow of the different emotional states. Strauss's compositional goal is the ideal of a transparent symphonic accompaniment that is characterized by the influence of individual instrumental solos. He learned this procedure from Berlioz's writings on instrumentation. The violin, the viola, the violoncello, the oboe, and the horn are used so that they adapt to the emotional sensibility and atmosphere of the musical-dramatic subject and the programmatic course of events. In this connection, Strauss himself provides suggestions for handling his scores in the preface to *Intermezzo*:

On this occasion one should refer to my rather special manner of noting orchestral dynamics, which often no longer confines itself to calling for *pp, p, f,* or *ff* for the whole orchestra, but rather prescribes the most varied markings to individual groups simultaneously, yes, even to individual instruments, marking whose precise observance—the main requirement for the correct style of orchestrating my scores—requires in any case an orchestral discipline that is still rather unusual today, but the fundamental condition for it is also that my scores really sound as I intended them.[30]

From the triple woodwind parts of the *Lohengrin* score that Strauss so admired during his lifetime, he enlarged the late Romantic orchestra step by step. He added seldom-used instruments such as the oboe d'amore, heckelphone, bass clarinet, saxophone, celesta, organ, and stopped trumpet to his efflorescent and enormous string tone sound and to the subdivided string parts (in *Elektra, Zarathustra,* and *Ariadne,* among others). The requirement in the post-Wagnerian age to push the limits of the individual instruments' technique and range introduced new tone colors to the palette of orchestral possibilities. In this way Strauss could impart fire and radiance to his orchestra. The orchestral part here is not, or at least is seldom, determined by monumentality, but rather by a refined treatment of the late Romantic orchestra, whose enormous size can be shown using the example of the *Die ägyptische Helena*, Op. 75: four flutes (third and fourth also piccolos), two oboes, English horn, three clarinets, bass clarinet, three bassoons (third also contrabassoon), six horns, six trumpets, three trombones, bass tuba, timpani, percussion, two harps, celesta, harpsichord, organ, strings; and as stage music six oboes, six clarinets, four horns, two trumpets, four trombones, timpani, wind machine, and percussion. Incidentally, in the discussions and collaboration on the opera with Hugo von Hofmannsthal, yet another Wagnerian drama of ideas emerged, in which the poet used the technique of alliteration, which he had studied most thoroughly in the *Ring*.

VI.

During his lifetime Strauss admired *Tristan* and Wagnerian *Zukunfts-musik* in general, as well as *Oper und Drama* and other writings of the master. However, Wagner did not always, and certainly did not exclusively, affect Strauss's own work in a stimulating and influential manner. On the contrary, Strauss examined Wagner critically and frequently differentiated himself from him. Thus, for example, he undertook the well-known re-duction in the size of the orchestra in *Ariadne auf Naxos*, Op. 60. From the Wagnerian music drama he found the way to comic opera, to opera buffa, to comedy for music, indeed, almost to operetta. The monumental work *Elektra* forms the turning point within his biography and work theory, and thus within his total compositional and stylistic development. Wagner wrote *Tristan* in the fifth decade of his life, and Strauss produced *Elektra* at approximately the same age. The creative curve of both composers runs about parallel, for both works stand on a previously unattained high point within the total oeuvre of each. Thus, Strauss had composed his most pro-gressive work [*Elektra*], with its difficult, exceptionally condensed, and avant-garde harmonies. After both works a regressive movement began.[31] The *Tristan* chromaticism is followed by the diatonicism of *Meistersinger*, a gloomy subject followed by a gay one. The modernist boldness, melody, and harmony, which are taken to the limits of tonality, as well as the feel-ings of revenge in *Elektra* are replaced by the predominantly harmonious euphony, the waltzes, closed numbers, and humoristic element of *Der Rosenkavalier*. A different and for Strauss very relevant theatrical ideal gradually moves more and more into the foreground: Wolfgang Amadeus Mozart (1756–91). Not only in the compositions, but also in many written attestations of those years, Strauss reconsiders and changes his position, as in that famous letter to Hofmannsthal in which he defines his appreciation of comic opera as well:

Your cry for help against Wagnerian 'music making' has deeply stirred my heart and has pushed open the door to a completely new landscape, in which I, led by 'Ari-adne' and especially the new prelude, hope to expose myself completely to the area of un-Wagnerian comic, emotional and human opera . . . with dialogue, arias, duets, ensembles, witnessed by really competent composers in the manner of the

Marschallin, Ochs, and Barak. In whatever form they want! I promise you that I have now definitely shed the Wagnerian music-making armor.[32]

As he grew older, Strauss obtained ideas for his own work from the works of Mozart; Strauss was receptive to Mozart's gaiety, lightness, and lucidity, without ever becoming hostile to Wagner. He admired both Wagner and Mozart in an identical way until his death at an advanced age in 1949. In later years Strauss often returned to one of his favorite thoughts: "The birth of the Mozartian melody is the revelation of the human soul sought by all philosophers."[33] Or in another version: "The Mozartian melody is—freed of every earthly form—the thing-in-itself, [it] hovers like Plato's Eros between heaven and Earth, between mortal and immortal—freed of 'will,' deepest penetration of the artistic imagination, of the unconscious, into the last secrets, into the realm of 'archetypes.'"[34] It is well known that Strauss perceived, felt, and comprehended the music of the Classical composers profoundly, according to Karl Böhm in his memoirs,[35] and thus was well prepared for Mozart. However, he was not content with aural admiration, but rather transposed, in a practical and compositional sense, Mozart's stylistic features and ideas into the music and conception of many works. The three Da Ponte operas and *Die Zauberflöte* exerted an enduring influence on Strauss's operatic works, especially in the time after completion of *Elektra* (1908), as he set out in search of a new form, a completely different opera style from before. "Next time I'm writing a Mozart opera."[36] His like-minded librettist Hugo von Hofmannsthal began working on the poetic formulation of a comic opera or an opera buffa, and drew up a libretto with the rococo tone of the eighteenth century. Moreover, the nickname of the Rosenkavalier—Quinqui—is that of a Count Franz Esterházy from Mozart's time.[37] *Der Rosenkavalier*, this "comedy of music," contains and preserves music that is modeled on Mozart's lightness and gaiety. Strauss commented: "I have only attempted to adapt the music to the graceful, light character of the Hofmannsthal poetry.... The Mozartian spirit rose up spontaneously before me, but I have nevertheless remained true to myself. The orchestra is not as strong as in *Salome* or *Elektra*, but it is in no way treated according to the newest fashion, which aims at performing Mozart with a small orchestra."[38]

It is thus in no respect a matter of pure stylistic copying or borrowing of Mozartian elements. Rather, Strauss creates a comic opera with a full late-Romantic orchestra, Straussian leitmotif technique, closed numbers, as well as sections trained in Wagnerian *Sprechgesang*, but also with waltzes that were criticized as anachronistic, a genre that did not fit into the age of Maria Theresa but that, however, gladly adopted from his admired namesake, Johann Strauss the younger. A further influence on the *Rosenkavalier* can certainly also be seen in the model of Italian music, whose grace and harmony Strauss always enjoyed. The tenor aria of the "singer" in the first act, "Di rigori armato il seno," fully dedicated to the euphony and silky melody of a Paisiello or Stradella, is based on Italian stylistic models, as is the entire melodic creation. Strauss declares his support for the melody—this credo can be applied to other operas as well—and is subject to the "primacy of the melodic."[39] On the one hand he uses melodies that follow the four-bar phrase construction, as in many of his waltzes: "four bars of a beautiful melody come to me, . . . and I try to spin these four bars out based on their thematic content and other requirements for their development—in short order these four bars develop into an eighteen-bar melody that seems well-suited to my need to express myself.[40]

On the other hand one finds structural principles that deviate decisively from Mozart—such as the widely curving "Frauenmelodik" characteristic of Strauss, adorned with bit intervallic leaps upward and downward, plus the contrapuntal layering of various longer melodies and the mutual embedding of leitmotif lines into each other, hence the so-called polymelody, which often has polyrhythm and polyharmony as a consequence. The scenes of scheming and commotion, but particularly also the burlesque pub scene and the trio in the third act, belong to such contrapuntal networks in the most varied manifestations. In its entire conception the final love duet between Sophie and Octavian is oriented to Mozart—four-bar phrase construction as well as Classical functional harmony and melodic development—as well as to Schubert. Mozart and comic opera occupied Strauss not only during the time of writing *Der Rosenkavalier*. Subjects, titles, and plots come up many times in Strauss's correspondence with his contemporaries. He gladly draws attention to one of his favorite operas, *Così fan tutte*, with its psychological refinements, an opera buffa esteemed as the pearl of all comedic literature before Wagner's *Die Meistersinger*. "One work is not enough to substantiate modern comic opera. This must immediately be constituted within genre and I would venture to write five such operas in the next ten years should I have the necessary poetic materials."[41] And he really did commence to work. With *Ariadne auf Naxos*, Op. 60 (1911/12) he hoped to reveal a new path for the genre of comic opera. *Arabella*, Op. 79, a lyric opera, and *Die schweigsame Frau*, Op. 80, a comic opera, followed later, as did the conversation operas *Intermezzo*, Op. 72, and *Capriccio*, Op. 85, as well as the stage works with a Greek subject. The correspondence between Hofmannsthal and Strauss on the subject of *Arabella* shows itself to be a conscious exercise—beginning with *Ariadne auf Naxos* and its striking secco recitatives in the prelude and the *Intermezzo*—to develop further the lyrical conversation style of *Der Rosenkavalier* as a refinement of parlando. *Arabella* achieves a deep-

ened psychologizing of the melody, a better audibility of the text, and a music
that interprets the text down to the finest emotional nuances.[42] Not only the
two role models Mozart and Wagner, but also the commedia dell'arte,
Baroque theater, the Viennese *Volksstück* and the operetta served as models
for the lyric opera, and they determined the influence on Strauss's compositional and musical conversation style as he approached his last work for the
stage, the conversation piece for music in one act, *Capriccio*. In particular,
the French tradition of Baroque theater with its relevant literary and musical representatives and models for Strauss—Molière as well as Lully and
Rameau—had a stimulating effect on Strauss. Christoph Willibald Gluck
(1714–78), who was strongly influenced by Rameau, should be classified in
this tradition. In 1889 Strauss had revised Gluck's *Iphigenie auf Tauris*, with
text in French, and informed his publisher Fürstner:

> Please permit me now one more comment! I have just finished, based on the ex-
> ample of Richard Wagner's version of Gluck's *Iphigenie in Aulis*, a complete revision
> of *Iphigenie auf Tauris* by the same composer. . . . My revision consists of a com-
> pletely new translation, that especially concerns the first act, whose sequence of
> scenes is completely changed, and the last act, for which I have composed a new
> ending. Changes in the instrumentation, in order for it to suit the requirements of
> the modern age at least to some degree etc., etc.[43]

Strauss not only drew up this adaptation, but also adopted Gluck's approaches in his writing; noteworthy are, among others, Gluck's reduction
of music and plot to simplicity and truth, his reforms regarding excesses
and abuses in theater, and his insistence on strong passions and engaging
situations.

The action in *Capriccio* takes place in eighteenth-century France, hence
in an era with which Strauss, as can be shown, had repeatedly concerned
himself. He had already paid tribute to the art of Lully in the music to *Bürger
als Edelmann*, Op. 60 (III). The fifth movement of the orchestral suite to this
stage work is entitled "Das Menuett des Lully." Other influences and stylistic
characteristics can be heard in the remaining movements. The love of
François Couperin (1688–1733) and his clavichord music accompanied
Strauss for decades. At the premiere of the *Tanzsuite aus Klavierstücken von
F. Couperin*, o. Op. 107, in Vienna in 1923, this ballet was referred to as
"Gesellschafts- und Theatertänze im Stile Ludwigs XV (Society and The-
ater Dances in the Style of Louis XV);" it is a Baroque cycle of suites:
Procession and Ceremonial Dance (Pavane), Courante, Carillon, Sarabande,
Gavotte, Dervish, Allemande and Minuet, March. Strauss felt drawn to
French delicacy, charm, elegance, and grace. In the twentieth century Strauss,

moved by his joy in the ornamental character of these pre-Classical courtly dance pieces, tastefully renewed older arm forms.[44] They were small works in which, however, the sound of the strings in the thirty-member chamber orchestra led to a result completely different from the delicacy of the old harpsichord or clavichord sound. During the Second World War Strauss once again added six new pieces to this dance suite based on Couperin's clavichord pieces and, in emulation of the old French ballet master Le Feuillet, premiered it on 5 April 1941, at the Munich Opera,[45] with the new title "Verklungene Feste, Tanzvisionen aus zwei Jahrhunderten (Faded Festivals, Dance Visions from Two Centuries). Choreography based on historical material by Pia and Pino Mlakar. Music based on François Couperin for small orchestra," o. Op. 128. Stylistically it is a fusion of rococo and modern, of Couperin and Strauss, distinctive, insightful, humorous, and subtle.

A classical particularly Mozartian influence extends to the chamber music and concert works of the last creative phase. Hence, for example, the first and second Sonatinas for 16 Winds (1943 and 1943/45, respectively), the second Concerto for Horn and Orchestra (1942), the Concerto for Oboe and Small Orchestra (1945), the Duet-Concertino for Clarinet and Bassoon with String Orchestra and Harp (1947), the *Metamorphosen*, Study for 23 Solo Strings (1944/45), and other compositions emerged from the "cheerful workshop" or "from the workshop of an invalid," as the two sonatinas for winds are subtitled. He achieves proximity to his beloved Classical composers through the use of unobstructive and moderate forms and orchestration, and through the cheerful play and cool sense of remove[46] that Mozart managed to express in his works. Strauss thus again moves toward Classical forms: sonata, song, and rondo. The melodic development frequently orients itself to the periodization, playful technique, and motif figuration so typical of Strauss as it occurs, significantly, in the main theme, that lightly lilting melody in the first movement of the Oboe Concerto, o. Op. 144 (1945) (here skirting around the target note d":

EXAMPLE I.7

Pieces for winds and concertos, two genres that he had cultivated already as a youth, emerge again in emulation of Mozart, but of course, always with the melodic and harmonic features of the Straussian style. Hence, in the 1940s not only "the last Romantic" but also the last Classical composer has spoken to us through music.

NOTES

1. *Richard Strauss and Joseph Gregor, Briefwechsel,* ed. Roland Tenschert (Salzburg: O. Müller, 1955), 271–72.

2. Stefan Zweig, *Die Welt von Gestern, Erinnerungen eines Europäers* (Frankfurt am Main: Fischer, 1982), 423.

3. *Richard Strauss—Ludwig Thuille: Ein Briefwechsel,* ed. Franz Trenner (Tutzing: Schneider, 1980), 69–70.

4. Ibid., 78.

5. Richard Strauss, *Briefe an die Eltern 1882–1906,* ed. Willi Schuh (Zurich, Freiburg im Breisgau: Atlantis, 1954), 32.

6. Ibid., 38–39.

7. Richard Strauss, *Betrachtungen und Erinnerungen,* ed. Willi Schuh (Zurich, Freiburg im Breisgau: Atlantis, 1981), 207.

8. Ibid.

9. Richard Strauss, *Dokumente seines Lebens und Schaffens,* ed. Franz Trenner (Munich: C. H. Beck, 1954), 34.

10. On the *Volkslied* and *Volkstümlichkeit* in Richard Strauss, see Ernst Krause, *Richard Strauss. Der letzte Romantiker* (Munich: Heyne, 1979), 98–101.

11. *Cosima Wagner—Richard Strauss: Ein Briefwechsel,* ed. Franz Trenner (Tutzing: Schneider, 1978), 11.

12. Strauss, *Betrachtungen und Erinnerungen,* 210.

13. *Richard Strauss—Hans von Bülow: Briefwechsel,* ed. Willi Schuh and Franz Trenner. In: *Richard-Strauss-Jahrbuch 1954* (Bonn: Boosey and Hawkes, 1953), 69.

14. Strauss, *Betrachtungen und Erinnerungen,* 210.

15. Krause, *Der letzte Romantiker,* 207.

16. *Johann Leopold Bella und Richard Strauss: Briefwechsel* in Franz Zagiba, *Johann L. Bella (1843–1936) und das Wiener Musikleben* (Vienna: Verlag des Notringes der wissenschaftlichen Verbände Österreichs, 1955), 57. Letter of 13 March 1890.

17. Strauss, *Dokumente,* Selection and connection text by Franz Trenner, 56.

18. Heinrich Kralik, *Richard Strauss. Weltbürger der Musik* (Vienna, Munich, Basel: Wollzeilen, 1963), 51ff.

19. Willi Schuh: *Richard Strauss. Jugend and frühe Meisterjahre/Lebenschronik 1864–1989* (Zurich, Freiburg im Breisgau: Atlantis, 1976), 145–46.

20. *Strauss and Gregor: Briefwechsel,* 279.

21. *Strauss—Thuille: Ein Briefwechsel,* 46ff, 60.

22. Strauss, *Betrachtungen und Erinnerungen,* 201–2.

23. William Mann, *Richard Strauss. Das Opernwerk* (Munich: C. H. Beck, 1967), 5.

24. Ibid, 5–7. See also Charles Youmans, "Richard Strauss's *Guntram* and the Dismantling of Wagnerian Musical Metaphysics," Ph.D. dissertation, Duke University, 1996.

25. Strauss, *Betrachtungen und Erinnerungen*, 190.

26. Strauss, *Dokumente*, 129.

27. Kralik, *Weltbürger der Musik*, 92.

28. Letter to Joseph Gregor from 8 January 1935. In: *Der Strom der Töne trug mich fort. Die Welt um Richard Strauss in Briefen*, with the cooperation of Franz und Alice Strauss, ed. Franz Grasberger (Tutzing: Schneider, 1967), 360–61.

29. Wolfgang Krebs, *Der Wille zum Rausch. Aspekte der musikalischen Dramaturgie von Richard Strauss' Salome* (Munich: Fink, 1991), 227–30.

30. Richard Strauss: Preface to "Intermezzo" (1924). In: *Betrachtungen und Erinnerungen*, 143–44.

31. Kralik, *Weltbürger der Musik*, 168.

32. *Richard Strauss—Hugo von Hofmannsthal: Briefwechsel*, ed. Willi Schuh (Zurich, Freiburg im Breisgau: Atlantis, 1978), 358–59.

33. Strauss, *Betrachtungen und Erinnerungen*, 69.

34. Ibid., 107.

35. Karl Böhm, *Begegnung mit Richard Strauss*, ed. and introduction by Franz Eugen Dostal (Vienna, Munich: Doblinger, 1964), 30.

36. *Strauss, Dokumente*, 130.

37. Krause, *Der letzte Romantiker*, 314.

38. *Strauss, Dokumente*, 136–37.

39. Cf. Karl Schumann, *Das kleine Richard Strauss-Buch* (Reinbeck bei Hamburg: Rowohlt, 1981), 48.

40. Richard Strauss, *Über mein Schaffen*. In: *Österreichische Musikzeitschrift* 19, No. 5/6, Vienna, 1964, 221.

41. *Meister und Meisterbriefe um Hermann Bahr*, selected and introduced by Joseph Gregor (Vienna: Bauer, 1947), 103.

42. Bernhard Adamy, "hunderfache Bemühung." Zum künstlerischen Selbstverständnis von Richard Strauss. In: *Richard Strauss-Blätter/Neue Folge*, No. 26 (Tutzing: Schneider, 1991), 16–17.

43. *Der Strom der Töne trug mich fort. Die Welt um Richard Strauss in Briefen, in Zusammenarbeit mit Franz und Alice Strauss*. Ed. by Franz Grasberger (Tutzing: Schneider, 1967), 63.

44. Ernst Krause, *Richard Strauss, Gestalt und Werk* (Leipzig: Breitkopf & Härtel, 1970), 458.

45. Ibid.

46. Willi Schuh, *Zum Melodie- und Harmoniestil der Richard Strauss'schen Spätwerke (1949)*. In: Willi Schuh: *Straussiana aus vier Jahrzehnten* (Tutzing: Schneider, 1981), 15–16.

2

Richard Strauss and His Contemporaries: Critical Perspectives

Peter Franklin

Music is the language which unites all people; under its banner we must love and respect one another.

> —Richard Strauss, introducing the Deutsche Komponisten-Tage, Berlin, 1934 (from a German newsreel)

In a 1964 book bearing a similar title to this chapter, Walter Thomas launched uncompromisingly into his subject, which need only have cataloged Richard Strauss's relationships with other composers and critics. Instead, he began by considering the two most powerful contemporaries for whom the composer worked in an official capacity: Kaiser Wilhelm II (as the first *Kapellmeister* [orchestra conductor] at the Berlin Court Opera for ten years, from 1898) and Adolf Hitler (as Präsident [president] of the Reichsmusikkammer, 1933–35, and tacit, if ambivalent, supporter thereafter).[1] It was a provocative move, which I am happy to follow. Such powerful names immediately invoke a Strauss criticism that has become a site for exercising and elaborating conflicting views about the relationship between musical values and music's social and cultural context. Difficult questions about political aims and affiliations are involved. Some would have us accept that Strauss the composer transcended such things in the manner suggested by the famous, possibly apocryphal, Toscanini story that vexed Stefan Zweig in London in 1934: the conductor was reported to have said that he would take his hat off to Strauss the composer but replace it for Strauss the man.[2] Others have found their distaste for his music conclusively reinforced by knowledge of Strauss's activities as a key representative of that conservatively "liberal" bourgeois German culture on which the Third Reich fed.

To what extent did Strauss stand and fall with the movers and shakers of his culture in its apocalyptic phase, leading from Bismarck's Prussia through two world wars? The question must be confronted by any twenty-first-century student of Strauss's relations with his contemporaries, particularly now that classical musicology (whose techniques and aesthetic program were themselves instrumental creations of Strauss's world) has grown more nervous of its underlying assumptions, more ready to confront the work of Marxist critics like Theodor Adorno. One of a younger generation of Strauss's contemporaries, who was articulate in his own condemnation of the composer, Adorno (1903–69) was a philosophical proponent of the kind of modernism in music that would challenge all the aesthetic priorities of Strauss's post-*Elektra* works. Resistance to his particular style of analytical music criticism has fed on sensitivities that we find in Strauss and that are grounded in ideas about music as an "ideal" language that joins rather than divides people—about the impossibility, by definition, of it expressing political partisanship.

Even as recently as 1980, the colossal *New Grove Dictionary of Music and Musicians* omitted Adorno from its Strauss bibliography altogether, making no mention even of his long essay on the composer, which had been published in translation in two parts in *Perspectives of New Music* in 1965–66.[3] That essay provides an exemplary framework within which, or perhaps against which, to reassess Strauss as an active participant, with many others, in a culture we may fear, even detest, with demonstrable justification. Although compromised to a degree by his own involvement with some of that culture's ideological assumptions, Adorno's denunciation of Strauss is remarkable in that it attempts to address the man as manifested in his music. He pulls the music down from Olympus and finds in it the marks of so much that was bad in German culture that other forms of personal accusation become superfluous. Making no direct reference to the composer's activities in the 1930s, Adorno uncompromisingly and uncomfortably seeks to demonstrate why Toscanini might reasonably have preferred to keep his hat firmly on his head in the presence of Strauss's art.

ADORNO'S CRITIQUE

In outline, Adorno's picture was the conventional one of Strauss as a fin de siècle modernist who subsequently defected to the conservatives. First there was the "unbourgeois" bourgeois, a master of the musical "jet-flame" ("music around 1900 liked to turn on the electric light"),[4] whose real potency, Adorno suggests, consisted in his down-to-earth resistance to the bourgeois notion of the artist as elevated and unworldly: "Strauss, who founded the German Musicians' Union, resisted the hocus-pocus of sylvan souls in the midst of an industrial landscape."[5] He suggests that the composer's much-criticized materialism might best be regarded as a refusal to veil "the situation which applies to all music under capitalism."[6] It was nevertheless in the lavishness of means and effects that Adorno recognized the central ambivalence on which Strauss's career turned: "Socially, its meaning is twofold: freedom from narrowness, hypocrisy, and petty prejudice as attacked by Nietzsche; yet also ruthlessness, violence, lack of solidity as the complements to that detestable respectability of the middle *bourgeoisie.*"[7] As the brilliant manufacturer of musical luxury goods, Strauss emerges as the liberal bourgeois who "allows himself much, but not too much . . . one of those sons of rich parents who do not dissociate themselves from their family, or, if so, only temporarily."[8]

Along with many other commentators, Adorno came to see in the prelude to the revised *Ariadne* "the Nachspiel of the great Strauss." *Salome* and *Elektra* represented for him an irrationalism which "presupposes that against which it turns" and "gives the tradition mechanical shocks as therapy."[9] Behind their daring modernism lay a naive attitude toward the implications of consonance and dissonance which divided the musical spirit "into sheep and goats, and the unrest of the dissatisfied . . . is included amongst the at times unavoidable goats."[10] The imbalance between "the progressiveness of the sounds and that of the ideas"[11] Adorno found corrected in *Der Rosenkavalier* in favor of conservatism: in a sort of music Grand Hotel whose restaurant was divided, in the manner of the period, into clearly designated "wine" and "beer" sections. But the counterfeit Grand Hotel was also erected close to the Grand Bazaar, he reminds us, where glittering kitsch is displayed alongside high-style music whose "consiliatory innocence" Adorno likens to the tone of "official speakers with classical citations or a latitudinarian minister at a cremation."[12]

Believing that the late works merely caricatured the early masterpieces, Adorno found in *Capriccio* little more than "garrulous inanity." Strauss had given way to an everything-for-the-best mentality that defined his role as a purveyor who ultimately affirmed precisely what was bad in his culture. Even the élan of the early tone poems is reduced by Adorno to an expression of bourgeois liberality on the point of turning into its opposite: the charismatic irrationalism of the calculating "go-getter" whose home city, Munich, would later be claimed by Hitler as the capital of the National

Socialist movement. The explosive gestures of Strauss's music, too, "dupli-
cate oppression," his guilt hiding behind the technological artifice of it all
and expressing itself only in the "fear that his music will be caught if it does
not get away quickly."[13] Adorno catches it, metaphorically, in the rising
and falling curve of the structure of *Don Juan*, in which he sees a caution-
ary model of Strauss's entire development. Strauss was a great composer
whose all too worldly pragmatism turned him into an embodiment of the
bourgeois values he had once ostensibly rejected. In consequence, his historical importance was as a provoker rather than a creator of what was really
new in music.

Adorno's fireworks-display of invective (at times as confusingly arbitrary in structure as he regarded the composer's development sections)
throws up few pale flares of faint praise to survive the storm of exploding
rockets. "What is untrue in him is the truth about his epoch,"[14] he had observed at the outset of the essay. It concludes with a shocking assessment
of Strauss's "spontaneity produced by technique" (the artificial flower of *Der
Rosenkavalier* is cruelly invoked) as tending toward the "childlike speech of
the dying":

senile and infantile, his music responds through mimesis to the universal domination of the calculated effect in which it became ensnared; it thumbs its nose at
the censors. It does not take part, however, in the process of self-preservation. The
life which celebrates itself in this music is death; to understand Strauss would be to
listen for the murmur beneath the roar, which, inarticulate and questioning, becomes audible in the final measures of *Don Juan* and is its truth-content. Solely in
decline, perhaps, is there a trace of what might be more than mortal: inextinguish-
able experience in disintegration.[15]

THE ROOTS OF THE PROBLEM IN STRAUSS'S EARLY CAREER

As always, after reading Adorno, one pauses for breath before wonder-
ing not so much what his alternative might have been—he tells us that in
his other writings—as what alternatives presented themselves to those who
compared themselves with Strauss as artistic creators and performers in the
1880s and 1890s, for example. Their world still believed in its organic coherence, in the singular of its fundamental values and ideals, however
contested the high ground may have been. North European cultural institutions were sustained by an apolitical, even antipolitical liberal

intelligentsia that might have recognized in Strauss's failed first opera, *Guntram* (1894), an uncomfortable document of its own artistic ideology.

The political reality in which Guntram, the singer-Artist, intervenes in act 2—to the extent of angrily killing the erstwhile villain (Robert) at the climax of a thinly veiled "artistic" denunciation of tyranny—closes ranks on him in the strangest fashion. The "good" king laments the death of his tyrant son and Guntram weakly fails to entice the rebellious peasants into the act's triumphant finale (something a more naive operatic librettist than Strauss might have permitted). We never know what happens to the king or his subjects, since act 3 finds the imprisoned Guntram becoming no more than a function of the idyllic utopianism with which he had earlier challenged his royal host in public song. The denouement seemed dangerously amoral to Strauss's mentor, Alexander Ritter, in its rejection of society. In fact it indulges a high version of the sanctimoniousness that Robert had earlier scorned in Guntram. Musically, Strauss joins forces with the latter in dropping veil after revelatory veil, in the manner of *Parsifal,* although Guntram's words could be interpreted as indicating the extent to which the murdered Robert lived on within him, possibly preparing for his rebirth as a Nietzschean *Übermensch*:

> Träumet ihr fort, ihr Guten, / von der Menschheit Heil!
> [düster] Nie könnt ihr erfassen / was mich bewegt! [*Guntram* III/3]

> [Dream on, good people, / of mankind's well-being!
> (darkly) You will never grasp / what moves me!]

Guntram renounces Freihild (Robert's wife, with whom he has fallen in love) along with the punishment of the Brotherhood that, as a murderer, he fully deserves. In the end, the champion of Love avoids the banality of becoming a pasteboard revolutionary, but remains doubly compromised by both unrepentance and self-delusion in his shirking of any responsibility in the real world. Papering over the world's sorrow with comforting illusion, he consigns himself to Art.

Will he, like Strauss (we might ask in maliciously Adornian fashion), go on to make a fortune from the royalties? Will he become an artistic modernist whose political attitudes move ever nearer to those of the most philistine banker, cleric, or civil servant? Already we can see what Adorno might have meant by describing Strauss's sound as more progressive than his ideas. While that sound appeared to jar against the accepted values of musical taste in the pre–First World War period, the underlying truth of the

matter was more complex. Strauss demonstrated all the underlying seriousness of purpose and intellectual tone that Romantic modernists had
inherited from early-nineteenth-century Classicism; he also shared the
unofficial bourgeois taste for the older popular style of Auber and Donizetti,
of the virtuoso performers with their concertos and dances—all of which
would be subsumed under the general heading of "Classical Music" in our
own culture, in which both Richard and Johann Strauss appropriately merit
"greatest hits" albums.

A majority of social, rather than idealistic, concertgoers for whom Eduard Hanslick had spoken and written often rejected the most advanced
music of the 1890s not least for the fact that it appeared to take itself too seriously by half. Strauss understood them: "boring and always equally
boring," was how the young composer had described Wagner to his friend
Ludwig Thuille in a letter of 1878.[16] The concerns of artistic ladies and fancy
aesthetes who went for such things would be similarly dispensed with as
"merely literature" by Count Leinsdorf in the Austrian novelist Robert
Musil's *A Man without Qualities:* "a conception that for him was bound up
with Jews, newspapers, sensation-seeking booksellers, and the liberalistic
spirit of the impotently wordy, commercially-minded third estate."[17] To pro-
tect himself from such things, Count Leinsdorf would habitually think of
"fields, peasants, little country churches, and that order of things which God
has bound together as firmly as the sheaves on a mown field."[18] Some of the
businessmen with whom he has dealings, however, prove more aware of the
social and economic significance of the ideology to which the count thus
naively commits himself; the mythology of a hierarchical society is most
readily acceptable as natural truth by those who either hold ancestral power
or ignorantly aspire to gain.

Nowhere more than in the realm of art at this time, particularly music,
was social and economic mobility so open a prospect to those of even relatively lowly middle-class origins—as low, perhaps, as those of the musically
talented and powerfully intellectual Moravian Jew Gustav Mahler, who, as
director of the Imperial and Royal Court Opera, would assume one of the
key positions of power in the cultural life of Vienna between 1897 and 1907.
A comparison between Mahler and Strauss, just four years his senior and
later a director of the Vienna Opera in his turn, proves valuable here not
only because of the extent to which they were compared in the period, or of
the evidence of their response to each other in both rivalry and friendship.
Mahler's currently more secure position in early-twenty-first-century European and American cultural life refocuses that image of uncompromising
artistic idealism against which Strauss was measured implicitly by Adorno,
as he was by Mahler, and found wanting.

SOCIETY AND MUSICAL MODERNITY:
THE COMPARISON WITH MAHLER

[W]ith Beethoven, the *new era* of music began: from now on the *fundamentals* are no longer mood—that is to say, mere sadness etc.—but also the transition from one to the other—conflicts—physical nature and its effects on us—humour and poetic ideas—all these have become objects of musical imitation.

—Mahler to Gisela Tolnay-Witt (age 9), 1893

We observe in the history of music, as in the development of the other arts, an evolution from the representation of general and typical concepts to the expression of an orbit of ideas which becomes increasingly more definite, individual and intimate.

—Strauss

It is clear from these two quotations[19] that Strauss and Mahler shared an understanding of their art as "modern" particularly in terms of what we might call the "technology of expression." Their critical detractors frequently cast them as "realists" or even "naturalists" as a result, intending not only to suggest a debasement of music from its proper status as idealistic revelation, but also one that was brought about with a deliberately subversive, even socialist aim (comparison being made with the literary and dramatic naturalism of men like Zola, Ibsen, and Hauptmann). The cultural tensions of this period were not simply reflected in clear-cut creative and critical allegiances, although fuelers of the Brahms–Wagner dispute often succeeded in making it look that way. While the institutions of nineteenth-century culture maintained their broad hegemony, an explosive mixture of conservative idealism, subversive naturalism, and the critical or even political sentiments aroused by both was internalized by artists who sought to maintain such prominent roles as cultural practitioners as did Mahler and Strauss. Both earned their living for a time as court opera conductors, caught symbolically between the Leinsdorfs of their world, the holders of ancient power, and the new power of the bourgeois marketplace. The battle between idealists and naturalists, conservatives and modernists, absolutists and programmaticists was thus waged within individual artists as much as between them.

Social and cultural chemistry nevertheless saw to it that Mahler tended to play the idealist to Strauss's worldly materialist, in their own understanding if not also that of the wider public. Mahler was frequently shocked by Strauss's notorious interest in his financial returns, as after *Feuersnot* in Vienna (1902).[20] Yet Mahler also understood and even anticipated his own characterization as a kind of sensation-seeking musical anarchist in works like the Third Symphony, whose premiere took place in 1902, at Strauss's instigation (as president of the Allgemeiner Deutscher Musikverein).[21] By the same token, Strauss would engage in ever more complex internal negotiations with the artistic values and ideological baggage of idealism that were his birthright, yet whose culturally instituted basis in religion he was to challenge in the diary entry he made after hearing of Mahler's passing in 1911:

The death of this aspiring, idealistic and energetic artist is a heavy loss. Read Wagner's memoirs with emotion. Read German history in the age of the reformation, Leopold Ranke: this confirmed very clearly for me that all the elements that fostered culture at that time have been a spent force for centuries, just as all great political and religious movements can only have a truly fruitful influence for a limited period.

    The Jew Mahler could still find elevation in Christianity.

    The hero Richard Wagner came back to it as an old man through the influence of Schopenhauer.

    It is absolutely clear to me that the German nation can only attain new vigour by freeing itself from Christianity . . . I shall call my *Alpensymphonie* The Antichrist, since it embodies: moral purification through one's own strength, liberation through work, worship of eternal, glorious Nature.[22]

This statement represents a key document of what, following Michael P. Steinberg, we might call Strauss's "spiritual politics."[23] On the one hand there is the language of German nationalism, shadowed by the conventional antisemitism of the period (Mahler the Jew contrasted with Wagner the Hero); on the other hand there is the iconoclastic Nietzscheanism, whose presence in the *Alpensinfonie* has all too infrequently been grasped. Nietzscheanism and the residue of leftist, student pan-Germanism are similarly found in a work like Mahler's Third Symphony—written at that crucial juncture in his life, however, when machinations to secure the directorship of the Vienna Court Opera entailed his converting to Catholicism and beginning to distance himself in public from the more radical aspects of programmatic, "naturalistic" modernism of Strauss's kind. The spiritual–political economy of both men was highly complex, and the prevailing strategy for mediating differences between them was to label both "Nietzschean" modernists or "left-wing Wagnerians." An influential coiner of these terms was Strauss's student friend Arthur Seidl, who in 1901 published four lectures (dedicated to Strauss) under the title *Moderner Geist in der deutschen Tonkunst.*

    What Seidl meant by "left-wing" was really just a readiness to build on Wagner's achievements without bowing the knee in the slavish fashion of more dutiful "right-wing" Wagnerians, for whom the Master represented a point beyond which further progress was inconceivable. "Progress" was interpreted by Seidl in a way that closely echoes the above-quoted statements by Mahler and Strauss on the matter of music's developing expressive facility. Seidl likens Wagner's complex polyphonic textures and "art of transition" in *Tristan und Isolde* to the fantastic constructional spans of modern engineering made possible by the use of iron. He also celebrates what music has gained from an increased scientific progress in the study of the mind, from the psychology of feeling to the physiology of emotion (extending now even to the finest nerve fibers). The artistic analog to this process is presented by music in the far-reaching elaboration of the polyphonic orchestral texture to the point where all these motivic particles divide out into ever more intricately wrought musical structures."[24]

The difficulty Seidl nevertheless had in fully assessing Mahler at that time parallels Strauss's own developing ambivalence about him. In it we might detect intimations of Mahler's subsequent ostracism by official, antisemitic German critical opinion in the late 1920s and early 1930s, whose grounds were already implicit in Strauss's 1911 diary entry. Earlier, he had more unequivocally admired Mahler (who, in a celebrated image, likened himself and Strauss to tunnelers digging into the same mountain from opposite sides.[25]) Instructive in this last respect is Wilhelm Kienzl's story of the 1895 Berlin rehearsal of the first three movements of Mahler's still unpublished Second Symphony. Kienzl had sat between Strauss (age thirty-one) and the conservative conductor Karl Muck (age thirty-six) as the thirty-five-year-old composer had led the orchestra into the crashing, dissonant climax of the first movement's development: "Strauss, sitting on my left, turns to me with enthusiasm in his eyes, 'Believe me, there are no limits to musical expression!' At the same time, to my right, Muck's face is distorted with unmistakable revulsion and the single word 'Horrible!' comes from between his teeth."[26]

The problem that Strauss later had with Mahler was focused not on the iconoclastic technique, but on the extremity and social awkwardness of Mahler's heightened idealism. Conventionally, artistic idealism was intended to reconcile cultural oppositions, whereas Mahler's, for all that he may have aspired to in the politics of his public life, tended to disrupt and unnerve. Reasons might be sought in the different social backgrounds of the two composers. For one thing, Strauss was solidly and unequivocally German where Mahler was decidedly and complicatedly not. Indeed, Strauss's father, rather than Strauss himself, presents a more apt comparison with Mahler. Of relatively humble origins (he appears to have been illegitimate), Franz Strauss rose by his own efforts to high status within the musical profession as a horn player of wide reputation. His son, the composer, was born into a family that was especially conscious of its respectable middle-class standing and suspicious of Johnny-come-lately types like Wagner. Strauss could set out blithely, like any good bourgeois, to make good in what was from the start "his" world. The intensely single-minded idealism of Mahler, the born outsider, was simply not available to Strauss: He did not have to so urgently question his every move as part of a pragmatic sociocultural strategy. Nor had Strauss much use for the self-questioning of someone whose career path was, in the fullest sense, a process of *Bildung* (education): of acquiring culture by painstakingly colonizing it from outside; of assuming its forms while in the process re-creating and redefining them to the end, perhaps, of that "breakthrough"[27] to certainty which was assimilation, power, "redemption." For Strauss the question of form was a "more or less playful" matter[28] of outward appearances.

THE NIETZSCHEAN HERO AS BOURGEOIS GERMAN

The above comparison is intended to be disparaging of neither Strauss nor Mahler, but rather to indicate a tension between them that would find its darkest social manifestation in the antisemitic rejection of Mahler by German culture—something that already quivered at the tip of Strauss's pen in 1911. It is equally intended to point to something deeper about the different networks of complex emotion that both, as modernists, believed to be their proper expressive subject matter. Mahler, of course, would be influentially celebrated by Adorno as a precursor of the avant-garde for the lines of fissure and fracture that articulate his forms, where the creative spirit is in constant battle with the often victorious forces of its own destruction. By comparison, Strauss seemed pugnaciously certain of himself, of the heroic self that celebrated itself in his music which, by implication, therefore, is reckoned to have avoided the Mahlerian struggle with its own identity, its own tradition. In the same way, Strauss himself (in Adorno's already quoted malicious characterization) was "one of those sons of rich parents who do not dissociate themselves from their family, or, if so, only temporarily."

But Adorno had also accepted that Strauss was, for a time at least, a decidedly "unbourgeois bourgeois." That aspect of his modernism, invoked in Seidl's 1901 emphasis on his Nietzscheanism, must be examined more closely, with an eye on the extent and brilliance of his success with audiences. On one level, of course, Adorno's characterization suggests the well-heeled youth who kicks over the traces, only to *re*trace them all the more carefully in later life. At the heart of Strauss's early rebelliousness, however, was something that could shock even a Mahler, precisely in his insistence on some of the bourgeois manners that his music appeared to threaten. Further still, his music drew those same manners into itself as its autobiographical project grew ever bolder. By insisting on its material ability to depict the real, Strauss initially relocated his however un-Mahlerian music well away from the cultural environment of conventional idealism—about which, Musil observed in *A Man without Qualities*, there was, in polite society, "nothing concrete . . . for concreteness suggests craftsmanship, and getting down to craftsmanship means dirtying one's hands, on the contrary, it was reminiscent of the flower-paintings done by archduchesses, for whom models other than flowers are not suitable on grounds of propriety."[29] Strauss was nothing if not a craftsman, and his ideas were anti-intellectual only in the very specific sense that they intended to throw the dirt on his hands deftly back at the sterile propriety that irked him—as it had in the "drone of a professorial voice" in 1883. That voice had made him leave Munich University, despite his interest in the courses on cultural history, aesthetics, and Schopenhauer that he had been attending with Arthur Seidl. In *Moderner Geist in der deutschen Tonkunst* the latter was anxious to lay the premature ghost of Strauss as an intellectual lightweight by recalling the enthusiasm of his reading. Around 1889 he seems to have been absorbed by Dostoyevsky and Gerhart Hauptmann; by 1893 Strauss, like Mahler, was reading Nietzsche.[30]

His enthusiasm for the author of *Also sprach Zarathustra* may have developed, as Willi Schuh has pointed out, only after the completion of *Guntram* in 1893, but it certainly colored the terms in which Strauss later justified his decision to have Guntram shun the brotherhood as well as Freihild. The recipient of this justification was the good Alexander Ritter, who had found the new ending immoral, un-Christian, and, consequently, "unartistic." In Strauss's February 1893 letter to Ritter from Luxor (where he was on the convalescence trip during which he apparently read Nietzsche for the first time), Strauss explained that, in spite of *Parsifal*, ethical art was essentially a utopian fantasy: "[I]n an artist whose works have this strong ethical and religious tendency the religious emotion always outweighs the artistic emotion. So it is with my brotherhood: the men who had those ambitions were better Christians than artists. Perhaps you will object that the two cannot be separated, but I believe that they are separate in principle!"[31] Already here Strauss is outlining a kind of political, or even "ethical," idealism of his own that, as we have seen, defined itself not just as apart from but set specifically *against* Christian practice and dogma. In this respect it is interesting to note how critical scorn of the famous waltz that concludes Strauss's 1896 *Also sprach Zarathustra* tone poem has always been couched in terms of conventional idealistic suspicion of its insufficiently elevated tone and character.

Seidl was more inclined to find in it a lyric, "dithyrambic" style that was authentically Nietzschean in its self-conscious, and in part humorous rejection of the grand manner of Wagner (the parallel with Mahler's Third Symphony is instructively close). The games played by its successor, *Don Quixote*, might even be logical extensions of the Nietzschean critique of Wagner. The metaphysical imagery of Romantic opera that Wagner perfected is teasingly unmasked in a series of visions which are grounded (in one case quite literally) on the knowledge that they are only imaginative fictions—the forces of darkness proving no more than a herd of sheep or priests on mules, our "flight through the air" simply a trick of harmony and orchestration (did anger at Strauss's musical "depiction" of such things harbor a deeper anger at the unmasking of musical illusion?). Strauss's was not the magic of an E. T. A. Hoffmann visionary so much as the work of a domesticated Faust who might be prepared to consult Dr. Freud in the company of Salome and Elektra in order to return to Garmisch a reconstituted, thoroughly secure, and self-confident paterfamilias.

Before that descent into "shock therapy" that Adorno mocked for having revived the tradition it was otherwise reckoned to attack, the influence of Nietzsche had itself been domesticated within Strauss, along with the old Wagnerian Grand Manner, in an ever more strikingly symbolic fashion. *Ein Heldenleben* was to be succeeded by *Symphonia domestica* (1904), in which the cosmic orchestra of the *Ring* cycle snores, laughs, bathes the baby, and makes love with the ideal bourgeois family; indeed Strauss's own family. The tastelessness of the idea reaped much critical opprobrium and mirth, but the composer made it (humorously?) clear that he was, of course, quite serious: "The symphony should present the musical picture of married life. I know that some people believe the work to be a humorous representation of domestic bliss. But I confess that I did not intend to joke while I was composing it. After all, what could be more serious than married life?"[32] Sounding like nothing so much as a Hollywood film score *avant la lettre*, *Symphonia domestica* was already looking toward a new kind of bourgeois opera in which the experience of high romantic passion and the expression of minute psychological nuance were to be appropriated by those who had cherished them for so long in the darkened opera house of idealized Wagnerian heroes and heroines.

As if mindful of Nietzsche's concern about Wagnerian pathology, Strauss was to find in Hugo von Hofmannsthal a most appropriate librettist with whom to create *Der Rosenkavalier* (1910) and *Ariadne auf Naxos* (1912/16). In the latter work, Zerbinetta's comic debunking of high-romantic posturing prepares and accommodates the compromise of bourgeois married life, where both ecstasy and renunciation must somehow come to terms with nappies, jealousy, and the thousand day-to-day misunderstandings that Tristan and Isolde never had to cope with. Certainly Hofmannsthal seemed to grow almost fanatical in his concern for the mystic significance (particularly in *Die Frau ohne Schatten*) of the institution of marriage and childbearing; for what comes after yet does not deny the "grand passion."

Serious music was undergoing a significant transformation in Strauss's hands. From the imperfectly apprehended but thoroughly proper symbolic adornment of middle-class culture it was turning into something more directly accessible: a homely and vernacular performance rather than a learnedly "historical" expression of the bourgeois appropriation and rationalization of aristocratic values. In *Der Rosenkavalier,* the aristocratic (with its favored musical furnishings faithfully evoked) is "seen through" as humorously dreadful in the waltz-drunk Baron Ochs; it is also still the model for all that is ultimately nicest, most reasonable, and most sublime. In the last act the Marschallin brings her soaring and searing music of renunciation down from on high (the "wine" section of Adorno's *Rosenkavalier* restaurant) to a far from socially respectable tavern. Arabella would later descend a staircase into Mandryka's life with nothing more than a glass of water; the orchestra, however, constructs that scene from Mandryka's point of view, magically suffusing it with music that elevates and transports us no less than does the Marschallin's. Or is this to allow ourselves to be snared by the ideology of idealism? Perhaps we should shun that water as irradiated by a music that infects our moral consciousness as it warms our hearts.

That was certainly the message of operas by Franz Schreker, one of the younger-generation composers whom Strauss had initially encouraged. The growing fame and popularity of Schreker in the early 1920s (following *Die Gezeichneten,* 1918, and *Der Schatzgräber,* 1920) must have been disconcerting, as if the ghost of Salome had returned to haunt him in ever more sensationalized guise: stolen pearls cast before eager swine. The image is cruel, but reflects how a part of Strauss came to view the growing mass audience of petit-bourgeois culture consumers whose taste for Puccini, for the prototypical movie-operas of the young Erich Wolfgang Korngold (like *Die tote Stadt,* 1920) and later for Ernst Krenek's jazzy *Zeitoper* (contemporary opera) *Jonny spielt auf* (1927) had been nudging his own works from the repertoire.[33] Strauss's attitude toward popularity had, in fact, always been torn between pragmatic and idealistic impulses whose incompatibility stemmed from fundamental contradictions in the established ideology of art in his culture. Those contradictions might well have seemed on the verge of resolution when the Nazis began to clear the decks of Jewish "decadents" and the modernism for which they were held responsible. The way was open for Strauss, like the Marschallin, to step onto the stage once more to sing a nobler, more elevating, and even more German kind of song.

IDEALISM CONTEXTUALIZED AND COMPROMISED

Someone who had particularly good cause to question the purity of Arabella's glass of water was the conductor Fritz Busch, one of the opera's dedicatees who, Aryan though he was, had been forced to resign his post as musical director at Dresden in March 1933. He had been too open in his contempt for the new National Socialist administration and its informers among his orchestral players. Strauss threatened to take *Arabella* to another opera house if Busch was not permitted to conduct the already planned July premiere; in his autobiography, Busch professed a sad belief in Strauss's sincerity, observing that "the claims of the contracts" must ultimately have taken precedence,[34] for Strauss failed both to keep and to carry out his threat. Clemens Krauss conducted what was thus the first major operatic premiere under the Nazi regime.

At this point questions about the relation between the music and the man become pressing, and can threaten to rebound on those who would attempt an injudiciously "postmodernist" revaluation of this period of Strauss's career.[35] Toscanini's metaphorical hat hovers nervously in midair; more nervously than Toscanini himself, whose withdrawal from the Bayreuth Festival in 1933 led to the vacancy being dangled as an enticing sop to Busch, whom the Nazis still hoped to pacify. He refused and soon left Germany. "Richard Strauss sprang into the breach" was as near as Busch could bring himself to direct criticism of Strauss on the last page of his autobiography.[36]

The path of Strauss, the Bavarian bourgeois, had apparently turned decisively away from that of the outsider Mahler. Had he not returned to the social brotherhood that Guntram had once rejected? The latter's pre-Nietzschean iconoclasm proves secretly to have presaged a post-Nietzschean conservatism of the kind that was to be fanned in a baleful way by the philosopher's sister in her attempts to reconcile her brother's ideas with those of the National Socialists.[37] Whatever is to be said about Strauss's Nazi-period activities and attitudes, it must be clear that the ways in which he sought to exercise his powers as president of Hitler's Reichsmusikkammer (henceforth RMK) in 1933–35 deserve careful consideration. No less do his relations with German composers like his old friend the conservative and antisemitic Max von Schillings (1868–1933), whose rehabilitation by the Nazis was cut short by his death less than a month after he had attended the premiere of *Arabella*. And then there was the edgy, jealously combative Hans Pfitzner (1869–1949), whose writings on music had been denouncing Jewish plots and "cultural bolshevism" in the name of the German soul since the early 1920s. For all the rhetoric about "the dreamed-of goal of all German music" and "our great goal: to unite the German people with their music again!" that filled Strauss's speech at the opening of the RMK's first "working meeting" on 13 February 1934,[38] it is worth recalling that as recently as December of the previous year he had directed Wilhelm Furtwängler to resist party officials' objection to the performance of foreign music like Debussy's *Nocturnes*, or even "any of the symphonies of Mahler."[39]

It is similarly well-known that Strauss dangerously insisted on the retention of Stefan Zweig's name as librettist on the program book for the premiere of *Die schweigsame Frau* in 1935. It is also often pointed out that Strauss's daughter-in-law was Jewish; so too that he justified his acceptance of the decreed presidency of the RKM to Zweig in January 1934 on the grounds that "the goodwill of the new German government in promoting music and theater can really produce a lot of good; and I have, in fact, been able to accomplish some fruitful things and prevent some misfortunes."[40] A month later he would be crazily seeking to improve the quality of entertainment music played by spa orchestras and prevent their desecration of pieces like the *Götterdämmerung* Funeral March.[41] Arguably more important to him was his concern to further press reforms that he had long ago been responsible for initiating, regarding copyright laws and the rights of composers to receive royalties when their works were performed.

Strauss's efforts, reaching back to the 1890s, on behalf of his fellow composers have usually been unambiguously celebrated. As a conductor and as president of the influential Allgemeiner Deutscher Musikverein from 1901 to 1910, Strauss supported composers as unlike each other, and himself, as Gustav Mahler, Max Reger, and the young Arnold Schoenberg (whom he would later refer to simply as "*der wahnsinnige Schönberg*" [the crazy Schoenberg]).[42] Before that, as cofounder with Friedrich Rösch and Hans Sommer of the Genossenschaft deutscher Tonsetzer in 1898, he had begun to form a support base from which to work for the improvement of composers' rights (out of the association grew the 1903 Anstalt für musikalische Aufführungsrechte and subsequently, in 1915, the Gesellschaft für musikalische Aufführungs- und mechanische Verfielfältigungsrechte).[43] Strauss's tangible personal support of individual colleagues certainly does not bear out Alma Mahler's barbed suggestion that he only championed composers who were manifestly less accomplished than he himself.[44]

The real shadow that hovered over all this activity and bears significantly on the question of Strauss's later political character was oddly and approvingly sketched in by Arthur Seidl in his 1912 open letter on "*Strauss als Politiker*," reprinted in his 1913 volume of *Straussiana: Aufsätze zur Richard Strauss-Frage aus drei Jahrzehnten*. The immediate provocation for Seidl's typically spirited and loquacious support of his friend (Strauss sometimes found him rather too much of a good thing[45]) was precisely the opprobrium Strauss had been reaping in parts of the liberal press for his stated position with respect to the copyright debate. This had been re-opened by the issue of Wagner's *Parsifal*, whose copyright (and thus the ban preventing performances outside Bayreuth) was due to expire in 1913. In an open letter of August 1912 to Ludwig Karpath, Strauss would come down on the side of Wahnfried and the embattled Frau Cosima, linking the whole affair with his own 1901 campaign to get an *Urheberrechtsgesetz* (authors' rights law) passed by the German Reichstag in the face of strong opposition from the leader of the Freisinnige Volkspartei (Freethinking People's Party), Eugen Richter (1838–1906).[46]

The controversy is historically fascinating for the insight it offers into what was considered to be ideologically and even politically at stake in this matter. Around 1901, and again in 1912, Strauss's concern for composers' rights represented a major public source of his image as an anti-idealistic, money-grubbing materialist who (as the music publishers were keen to stress, with an eye to their vested interests) was effectively restricting the German nation's access to its cultural heritage through his concern for personal profit. What is particularly interesting is that Strauss, astute in his reading of the publishers' motives, insisted from the outset on maintaining a political standpoint that matched and trumped their ideological ploys blow for blow. In 1901 he had denounced Richter's case against the signatories of the composers' petition as being made on behalf of "200,000 innkeepers and amateur choral singers" and "all simply politics!"—subsequently damning the freethinkers, liberals, and socialists who disagreed with him.[47] In 1912 the *Parsifal* question inspired him to recall the 1901 Reichstag sessions in a manner that blatantly linked the rights of "geniuses" with the suppression of those of lesser mortals:

I personally heard a man by the name of Eugen Richter trample under foot with the most brazen of lies the rights of two hundred German composers, including the heirs of Richard Wagner, in favour of two hundred thousand innkeepers.

These things will not change as long as we have this stupid common suffrage and as long as votes are counted and not weighed, as long as, for example, the vote of a Richard Wagner does not count for 100,000 and those of approximately 10,000 stable boys for one. . . .

We few will protest in vain, and in two year's time the German petit bourgeois will, instead of frequenting the cinema and music halls be able, between lunch and dinner on a Sunday afternoon, to hear *Parsifal* for sixpence.[48]

Adorno had reckoned Strauss's composers'-rights activities to be bound up with the conclusive unmasking of the "sylvan souls" ideology of an economic idealism that permitted industrialists and music publishers to profit from the works of decorously impoverished artists. In going on to note that the composer's celebrated materialism might best be interpreted as a refusal to veil "the situation which applies to all music under capitalism," he failed quite to explain that the situation did indeed apply to all music; certainly to all those musicians of "modernist" persuasion whom he sought to locate in opposition to the conditions of the market place. In a world that might actually reward artists whether they celebrated or scorned the status quo, the rebellious might still erroneously seek to claim the cultural power that their rewards appeared to represent. Such was the delusion of those who relied on the value system derived from an antipluralistic notion of "high" culture—not least the more angrily embattled members of the avant-garde who continued to believe that by contesting what was valued, they might hijack the aura of authenticity that protected the "best" cultural products. The truth, perhaps, was that their radicalism was no more than the fashionable garb of an unconscious conservatism. Adorno might reasonably have been sensitive about the fact that Schoenberg, whom he believed to have been goaded toward the New by Strauss (as a productively negative example), proved far more fanatical and serious about his own antidemocratic, dictatorial promptings. In 1933 these had led him to envisage a "new party, a new sect . . . nationalistic-chauvinistic to the highest degree, in the religious sense, based on the notion of the chosen people, militant, aggressive, against all pacifism, against all internationalism."[49] We may feel that as a Jew at that time Schoenberg had been provoked to a degree that claims our fullest sympathy; his language nevertheless echoes on as a grim reflection of the style and ideas of those whose oppression he fought.

It would be to facile to merely observe that the unoppressed Strauss, even in his official speeches as president of the RMK, rarely used language more aggressive or chauvinistic than that in the open letter to Karpath.

Other commentators, like the humane and admiring Romain Rolland (1866–1944), had long found in him "the typical artist of the new German empire, the powerful reflection of that heroic pride, which is on the verge of becoming delirious, of that contemptuous Nietzscheanism, of that ego-tistical and practical idealism, which makes a cult of power and disdains weakness."[50] The fact that Rolland formed this opinion of Strauss as a "typ-ical" German as early as 1900 only reinforces the impression of the composer as a representative of his culture in a way that excuses nothing but deflects specific personal blame. That was clearly the basis on which Zweig, a fellow older-generation modernist, worked in his dealings with Strauss; indeed, it is Zweig, the Viennese Jew, who offers the most instructive com-parison with the rather younger Schoenberg in this period. Zweig's letters to Strauss during the dark and dangerous period of his collaboration with him, bear witness to his subtly perceptive and sympathetic attempt to per-suade the composer, in a language he understood, the language of art, of the difficulty, if not impossibility, of maintaining a truly apolitical idealism. Zweig tactfully but fruitlessly tried to separate Strauss's artistic ideals from the ideological baggage that was their heritage and was giving birth to so-cial and political evil on a scale that Strauss seems to have bade his con-science to ignore.

During the First World War he had typically taken pride in his rejection of the opportunism of "patriotic" artists "who forget that I wrote my *Heldenleben,* the *Bardengesang,* battle-songs and military marches in peace-time but am now, face to face with the present great events, keeping a respectful silence, whereas they, exploiting the present 'boom' and under the cloak of patriotism, are launching forth the most dilettantish stuff!"[51] His readiness to support his colleagues had, at the beginning of that month (February 1915), brought him into contact with an example of the kind of work he might have been referring to when he permitted Max Reger to con-clude the sixth "symphony-evening" of the Berlin Court Opera (in which Strauss had conducted Schumann's First and Beethoven's Eighth Sym-phonies and Reger had conducted his Op. 132, *Variations and Fugue on a Theme of Mozart*) with the premiere of his *Vaterländische Ouvertüre* (Op. 140). This included references to "*Nun danket alle Gott,*" "*Ich hab mich ergeben,*" and the German national anthem.[52] Such things were not to Strauss's taste; he readily left them to men like Reger and Pfitzner, both of whom he admired as musicians without ever himself producing a work quite like Pfitzner's *Von deutscher Seele* (1921).

Recognizing this, Zweig seems to have attempted in the 1930s to at-tach Strauss's hitherto nonpartisan idealism to more humane and less elitist ideas than its natural "elective affinities" might have allowed. The first projects that Zweig suggested to Strauss in 1931 were a grand, "timeless" ballet pantomime that would be "universally understandable, playable on every stage in the world, in all languages, before any audience high-brow or low-brow, and an entertaining "classical" opera (to become *Die schweigsame Frau*), which would, he politely and deferentially suggested, require a less sophisticatedly symbolic libretto than Hofmannsthal's later work for Strauss, and more practicably performable: "I see works of art in a European, truly universal dimension, not tied, because of their cumbersome apparatus, to a few large cities."[53] Michael Steinberg has valuably invoked Freud's criticism of the pacifist, sentimental universalism that was shared by Zweig and Rolland,[54] but in the context of his developing relationship with Strauss, then still at an early stage, Zweig's intention could be interpreted as a subtle attempt to reconstruct the composer's idealism in a manner that avoided any direct reference to national or party politics.

That repression was in itself symptomatic, of course, of a degree of underlying complicity between Strauss's and Zweig's idealisms that found its monument in *Friedenstag*, whose ostensibly pacifist libretto was fashioned by Joseph Gregor around a detailed scenario by Zweig. Steinberg, as well as others, has convincingly deciphered the repressed and, from Zweig's point of view, unintentional subtext of that opera as curiously open to the spirit of Nazism and more specifically those strategies whereby the Austrian *Anschluss* with Germany was justified (not least by Austrians).[55] Avoidance of the overtly political was a striking feature of the first three years or more of Strauss's correspondence with his new collaborator. It grew particularly interesting when Zweig's judicious self-censorship was matched by Strauss's own more guilty and perhaps shocked refusal, in July 1934, to admit to his friend (who had anticipated it) that his planned visit to Salzburg had been prevented by the Nazis, following the murder of Dollfuss.[56] Officially forbidden to conduct *Fidelio* and an orchestral concert in the Salzburg Festival, Strauss simply informed Zweig that recent exertions had led him to cancel the visit.

Zweig's perhaps overgentle and gentlemanly approach in his dealings with Strauss came nearest to direct political confrontation at the time of the 1935 Furtwängler–Hindemith affair, in the immediate run-up to the planned July premiere of *Die schweigsame Frau*. Protesting his intention to "keep away from politics," while receiving a somewhat disingenuous assurance from Strauss that "Hitler and Goebbels have officially approved,"[57] Zweig set about the difficult task of distancing himself from the composer, who had indicated that any new project between them would "go into a safe that will be opened only when we both consider the time propitious."[58] This gave Zweig the opportunity to withdraw under the veil of flattery (which he might conceivably have hoped that Strauss would penetrate and be stung into a more principled public stance):

Everything you do is destined to be of historic significance. One day, your letters, your decisions will belong to mankind, like those of Wagner and Brahms. For this reason it seems inappropriate to me that something in your life, your art, should be done in secrecy. Even if I were to refrain from ever mentioning that I am writing something for you, later it would come out that I had done it secretly. And this I feel would be beneath you. A Richard Strauss is privileged to take in public what is his right.[59]

The ploy, if such it was, failed and Strauss was soon informing Zweig that Goebbels had vetoed any further collaboration. Zweig can hardly have been surprised and retreated to the point where he began suggesting alternative librettists, for all that he was prepared to advise and guide them. Strauss's annoyance grew to the point where he penned the famous exasperated letter of 1 June 1935, which would be intercepted by the Gestapo and would lead to his effective demise as a figure with any power in the Nazi regime. The irony was that his "apolitical," idealistic anger both at Zweig's "Jewish obstinacy" and the annoying duties of the RMK presidency expressed themselves in terms whose commanding, egocentric self-assertion and accusation of excessive racial solidarity in Zweig's position were sadly much closer to Nazi ideology than either he or the Nazi officials were prepared to recognize.[60] Strauss exposed himself in the very manner of his angry denial of the political self-exposure that Zweig appears at last to have castigated:

Who told you that I have exposed myself politically? Because I have conducted in place of Bruno Walter? That I did for the orchestra's sake. Because I substituted for Toscanini? That I did for the sake of Bayreuth. This has nothing to do with politics. It is none of my business how the boulevard press interprets what I do, and it should not concern you either. Because I ape the president of the Reich's Music Chamber? That I do only for good purposes and to prevent great disasters! I would have accepted this troublesome office under any government, but neither Kaiser Wilhelm nor Herr Rathenau offered it to me. So be a good boy, forget Moses and the other apostles for a few weeks, and work on your two one-act plays. Maybe the Mexican text could become a good opera, but not for me. I cannot be interested in Indians, red or white gods, and Spanish conflicts of conscience.[61]

Here idealism falls to earth with a grim thud. The Berlin Philharmonic Orchestra and Bayreuth are equated directly with "good purposes" and the prevention of "disasters"—all of which is set outside the sphere of politics, even though Bruno Walter had been put to flight by official threats and

Toscanini's withdrawal from Bayreuth in 1933 had been precisely because of the political situation in Germany. The fact was that neither Kaiser Wilhelm's Empire nor Rathenau's Republic desired a powerful *apparatchik* to control musical culture from above (and the puppetlike implications of Strauss's "ape" only further compromise his position). And what, indeed, did interest him if not other races or conflicts of conscience? Of the opera plots that he had recently been discussing with Zweig (although their supervised author was theoretically to have been Gregor), one was a Mexican opera in which Zweig envisaged the "barbarian-aristocratic," "demonic-fascinating" world of the ancient Aztecs as a context against which to present a pure, Christlike stranger in ethical conflict with forces that would ultimately destroy him.[62] The other was *Semiramis*, after Calderon, which celebrated the brutal, world-conquering heroine who, Turandot-like, is finally vanquished only by her male alter ego.[63] Strauss quickly perceived that the Aztec opera would be like recomposing *Salome* with John the Baptist as the hero. Protesting how "passionate an anti-Christ" he remained, he knew which subject he preferred: "I'd rather have the monster Semiramis, who has at least some air of grandeur as general and ruler."[64]

Strauss's fin de siècle Nietzscheanism was clearly threatening to transform itself into a protofascist susceptibility to artistically sanctioned images of power—albeit held at arm's length by being gendered female, like so many patriarchal visions of alluring, libidinous derangement: a Muse turned terrible, turned general. He did not, however, compose either subject. Perhaps for once Zweig's strategy (19 May) of politely insisting on the opposite of what he really believed ("Semiramis remains a priestly figure, spiritually unrelated to our time")[65] had worked. The question that remains, and which might lead us back to Adorno, is how the texts that Strauss did set, the music he did go on to write, might subtly have mediated that grand and monstrous vision that was, of course, all too dangerously related to that time in which *Die schweigsame Frau* received its officially shunned premiere.

THE TWOFOLD MEANING

The notion of a kind of symbiosis—the neighboring growth of different entities that develop a vital interdependence—is implicit in my title formula. Strauss "and" his contemporaries comprise a collective historical subject; the protested innocence of its component individuals (particularly prominent ones) is, from this perspective, overshadowed by a collective guilt. It would certainly appear that the ambivalent, "twofold" meaning detected by Adorno in Strauss's career, initially balanced toward Nietzschean iconoclasm and a violent "lack of solidity," had by the 1930s become weighted rather more in favor of the hypocritical narrowness and "detestable respectability of the middle *bourgeoisie*."[66] Adorno implied that the two meanings had, all along, been complementarily related. Did Strauss musically "get away" once again only by clinging to bourgeois respectability all the more tangibly as the petty prejudice and ruthless violence it kept company with found public political expression? There is, after all, good reason to celebrate the fact that Strauss did not compose a *Semiramis*, that he turned instead to subjects like *Daphne* and what Adorno mocked as the "garrulous inanity" of *Capriccio*.

He did, however, compose *Friedenstag*. Kurt Wilhelm's incomprehension as to why Strauss was so attracted to "its overriding ethos of blind, suicidal obedience to a remote emperor" is revealingly glossed by Strauss's angry direction to librettist Gregor to aim for "Action and character! No 'thoughts'! No Poetry! Theatre!! . . . No weighing of motives, no poetic self-indulgence. Headlines!"[67] Strauss may have come to despise Joseph Goebbels as a "*Bübchen*," but he could clearly muster a not altogether dissimilar conception of what best worked with audiences, who represented for him only the better paying end of the mass of ordinary mortals (we recall the despised innkeepers and stable boys). It was, after all, the proletarian enthusiasm for sport among the masses that had exasperated Strauss, in December 1934, about his commissioned hymn for the 1936 Berlin Olympics—not the political philosophy of those who had commissioned it (along with other opening-celebration music from Carl Orff and Werner Egk): "I kill the boredom of the Advent season by composing an Olympic Hymn for the proletarians—I, of all people, who hate and despise sports. Well, Idleness is the Root of All Evil."[68]

The symbiotic relationship between Strauss and the Nazi regime continued, in fact, throughout the 1930s and into the war years. It is of considerable historiographical interest to consider how commentators and biographers have fixated, in this period above all, on Strauss's lifelong tendency to be humorously scornful of the authorities he served under and on the supposed fall from grace he suffered after the letter to Zweig had been intercepted in 1935. He certainly ceased to be president of the RMK and was edged out of the official limelight, but his works continued to be performed with official sanction. Although he wisely gave 1936 over to foreign tours, he was honored with a Strauss Week in Frankfurt in 1937 and took part in the Munich Festival of that year. The year 1938 saw the premieres of *Friedenstag* and *Daphne* in Dresden, before which there had taken place in Düsseldorf a notorious Reichsmusiktage festival, during which an *Entartete Musik* exhibition opened in which Schoenberg,

Schreker, Krenek, Hindemith, Stravinsky, and a host of others (mostly Jewish) were crassly mocked, as their colleagues in the visual arts had been before them.[69] None of the shorter standard accounts of Strauss's life deal with that festival, at which he conducted a performance of *Arabella* the day after Pfitzner's *Von deutscher Seele* had been presented. A few hours before the curtain rose on *Arabella* there had been a musicological meeting whose welcoming address had been given by Professor Ludwig Schiedermair, oddly enough Mahler's first biographer, after which Friedrich Blume read his subsequently notorious paper "Musik und Rasse."[70] The session was rounded off with the performance of a Handel Concerto Grosso. While Strauss might have taken it as a snub that *Arabella*, unlike *Von deutscher Seele*, was in competition with another more populist attraction (a community-singing event: "Gesellige Musik der NS-Gemeinschaft 'Kraft durch Freude!'") no alternatives were permitted to detract from the following day's (Saturday) 4 P.M. address by Reichsminister Dr. Goebbels, behind whom an impressive bank of orchestral players and singers rose to the large swastika on a typically giant-sized wall hanging. The musicians were there to perform Strauss's *Festliches Präludium* (there were also "Nationalhymnen" after the address). The composer conducted and was photo- graphed on the occasion, both during the performance and seated in the front row of the audience for the address.[71]

Of course, all such collaboration demands careful reading. By the time the war broke out Strauss had undoubtedly tested official patience on many occasions, but with such reckless determination that Michael Kennedy's description of him as "a frightened old man" would seem way off the mark.[72] He had a knack for knowing just how far he could go—after which he was clearly prepared to pay musically, and in public, for the annoyance he often occasioned in private dealings with Nazi officials of all ranks. The persistent success of the balancing act similarly compromises Kennedy's account, typical of others, of the events of 1941: "Late in 1941 Strauss and his family moved to Vienna to reoccupy their Belvedere Schlösschen which they had vacated at the start of the war. In Garmisch their position had become precarious because both Strauss and Pauline made no attempt to disguise their contempt for the Nazi authorities."[73] As if the *Anschluss* had not taken place; as if their friend Baldur von Schirach, Gauleiter and Reich-Commissioner of Vienna, was not himself a Nazi "authority" who in the previous year, had been advised by Hitler of his intention to relocate all the Jews of Vienna in Poland! The same von Schirach was later to report to Hitler, in a notorious telegram, "My Führer I report to you that Vienna has been cleansed of the Jews."[74] Only in 1942 did the composer very nearly go too far in attempting to outface Goebbels in Berlin over the issue of the independence

Strauss had claimed for German musicians as the proper arbiters in matters of comparative artistic value. There was a ghoulish truth in Goebbels's furious denunciation of Strauss's elitism on that occasion, witnessed by Werner Egk:

Be quiet! You have no conception of who you are or of who I am! You dare to refer to Lehar as a street musician?! I can have these outrageous statements of yours published in every newspaper in the world. Do you realize what would happen then? Lehar has the masses and you haven't! Stop your claptrap about the importance of serious music, once and for all. It will not serve to raise your own standing. Tomorrow's art is different from yesterday's! You, Herr Strauss, belong to yesterday![75]

The accusation had a point, yet it is difficult not to feel sympathy for the aging Strauss who certainly shed tears on that occasion. But Goebbels's rebuke of him also holds a lesson for us, as it might have done for Adorno in his condemnation of Strauss for not, in a sense, being idealistic enough.

CONCLUSION (THE LESSON OF THE UNBORN CHILDREN)

At the outset of this chapter I described Strauss criticism as having become a site for exercising conflicting views about the relationship between musical value and music's social and cultural context. That site still remains attractive, richly stocked as it is by the music that survives and retains the power to challenge new speculators in artistic values. It is, of course, our own nervous contemporary relationship with Strauss's music that is at issue here: as we damn it for the reasons that we might damn Strauss as a Nazi collaborator, or as we retrospectively exonerate him for the reason that we still find ourselves moved, shocked, or excited by the music and fear, perhaps, our own involvement in that symbiotic relationship between artistic and social or even political values. Much may be at stake in recent pleas for a postmodernist revaluation of the later operas, for example. After all, Strauss himself claimed to have recognized in 1934 what operatic subjects best suited him: "South German bourgeois sentimental jobs. . . . Must one become seventy years old to recognize that one's greatest strength lies in creating kitsch?"[76]

Precisely the issue, and definition, of kitsch surfaced over ten years ago in a 1990 *Times Literary Supplement* debate over the quality of *Arabella* and *Salome.*[77] It was occasioned by an aggressively anti-Straussian review of books on those operas. (*Salome,* of course, continues to provoke critical interest to the extent that it has been drawn into the center of what might be called "new wave" opera studies.[78]) The camouflage or sugarcoating by orchestral color and lyrical effulgence of something assumed to be repellent was offered as a definition of Strauss's brand of kitsch. It incited a traditionalist analytical plea for the respect of "purely musical" values—which bring us back to idealism and the point at which Adorno started perceiving that Strauss himself, let alone the history of twentieth-century Europe, had conclusively unmasked that idealism as part of the whole "hocus pocus of sylvan souls."

The matter of mediation, to which I alluded earlier, can only return us to the question of Beauty itself as pleasurably, or perhaps tastelessly (or worse) constructed by those passages of seemingly unfettered and yet in fact so carefully controlled lyrical effusion in late Strauss: gentle, possessed (might we admit?) of not a little "nobility" of the kind that causes eyes to close upon inner visions that match Reality so imperfectly as to prompt tears. This private experience is also, of course, a public one that is shared, however furtively, in opera houses—particularly the older ones where gods and goddesses, sculptured supporters of our tiers and boxes (even, as so often with Strauss, on stage before us, as singing representatives of Art), may serve us as they served their world, and perhaps its political regimes, by turning conveniently into trees or countesses meditating on the possible preeminence of music over words.

But this, it will be protested, is in no way a specifically "fascist" or "Nazi" experience. Is it not more universal? Are not Strauss's classical figures, like his countesses and Marschallins, perhaps even the noble, upwardly mobile Arabella, related to symbolic personifications of ideals that haunt all human culture in different ways? The problem is that such protestations could have been made most eloquently (and were) by the most powerful members of Strauss's post-1933 German audiences—by "cultivated" men like Baldur von Schirach, or even Goebbels, to whom Strauss's music was never questioning or insubordinate in the way that Strauss the man might have been. This is where the problem resides, of course, and why comparisons between Strauss and his contemporaries must continue to probe the politics of artistic ideals and choices, not least among the younger representatives of the New whose music, increasingly rejected by Strauss, either compromisingly unmasked the status quo (as in the operas of Schreker) or rejected it (as in the outward manner of Schoenberg or the politicized populism of Weill and Eisler). A more like-mindedly typical contemporary of Strauss, in artistic sensibilities and intellectual preoccupations, was described by John Carey in his 1992 study *The Intellectuals and the Masses*:

Nietzsche was often on his lips, and he could quote Schopenhauer by the page. He admired the works of Cervantes, Defoe, Swift, Goethe and Carlyle. Among musicians his heroes were Mozart, Bruckner, Haydn and Bach, and he idolized Wagner. . . .

[He] also believed . . . in the permanence of aesthetic values . . . he contrasts the all-time greats such as Shakespeare, Schiller and Goethe with the degeneracy of modern culture. The creative spirit of the Periclean age, as manifested in the Parthenon, is one of his touchstones. He venerates the "divine spark" as it flashes forth from the "shining brow" of genius. Art is higher and more valuable, he insists, than science or philosophy and more permanent than politics.[79]

It should be pointed out that Carey is describing Adolf Hitler here, although much of it might fit Strauss. Carey's purpose in *The Intellectuals and the Masses* was not to condemn Hitler as an aberrant individual so much as to draw into the dock most of the prominent English intellectuals of the first half of the twentieth century. There is tendentiousness in his argument, but his point is an uncomfortable one that it was well to make. Although Carey's main concern was with English intellectual life, he correctly notes that Adorno and his Frankfurt School colleagues were possessed of a view of the masses, and the "culture industry" that preyed on them, that was, oddly, as congruent with Strauss's bourgeois, antidemocratic antiproletarianism as it was confirmed by Goebbels's instrumental notions about popular culture and its uses. One might also add that Adorno's conception of authenticity and artistic truth has come to be read as a tortuously rigorous exemplar, in its negativity, of what Strauss aspired to throughout his career, yet came, in spite of himself, to suspect as being both culturally located ("south German, bourgeois sentimental") and perhaps even a kind of kitsch.

That last vestige of subversiveness in Strauss was recognized by Adorno, who struggled to reject and satirize its musical embodiment with a brutality that went well beyond Goebbels's denunciation of Strauss as a has-been. The complex nature of the "collaboration" issue may not have occasioned quite the level and heat of intellectual debate in Strauss studies that Heidegger's Nazism has occasioned among philosophers, but more than just the popular end of musical criticism demonstrates an unspoken assumption that to deal with the later Strauss at all is probably to signal a blanket approval of his music and a desire to exonerate him. Adorno's problem is one that we all inherit. In unmasking the idealist construction of music, Strauss's not least, critical musicology paradoxically reinforces its cultural and historical importance. If anything, the compromised and compromising Strauss—the composer whose works we may secretly love while publicly advertising our modernist scorn of his calculation, political naiveté and subversive honesty—might again become a significant focus of cultural study. We readmit him to a postmodernist pantheon, however, not on grounds of changed aesthetic values or critical sensibilities, but our interest in the conceptualization and relocation of those historical values and sensibilities as diffused among other and very different composers, also into wider categories of pleasure, sexuality, power, politics, social aspiration, and social exclusion that often link Strauss inextricably with those petit-bourgeois innkeepers and lowly stable boys.

A related challenge might no longer simply be to reinterpret the later works as redundantly defined by the earlier, but rather to reinterpret *Salome*, *Elektra*, and the early tone poems as bearing the seeds of *Arabella*, *Daphne*, the *Metamorphosen*, and all that those works signified (or failed to signify) in their own, later cultural context. Confronted squarely, along with the compromising pleasure we may still derive from them, their music seems to rejoice in what we might describe as its shadow. It is that shadow of fruitful, historically factual bourgeois Life that the empress in *Die Frau ohne Schatten* had so eagerly sought, and from which we (perceiving what lurked within it) have understandably become anxious to disentangle ourselves. If music is indeed the language that "unites all people," then Strauss's infuriatingly does so by transporting us back into the Grand Hotel of a historical European High Culture, only to relish our embarrassment as we see it for what it is; as we realize, oddly like the Unborn Children, that we are still as much complicit hosts there as discriminating guests: "*Wäre denn je eine Fest, / Brüder! / Wären nicht insgeheim . . . wir die Geladenen, wir auch die Wirte!*" [Would there ever be a feast, / Brothers! / if we were not secretly . . . at once the guests and also the hosts!][80]

NOTES

The chapter opening epigraph is from a *Ufaton* newsreel extract included in Peter Adams's 1984 television film *Richard Strauss Remembered* (Blakefield Carrington Productions in association with the BBC). Following Strauss's statement was one by Adriano Lualdi on behalf of the "Fascist composers of Italy"; the credits indicate that Wilhelm Kienzl subsequently spoke for Austria. Beside Strauss stood Hans Pfitzner.

1. Walter Thomas, *Richard Strauss und seine Zeitgenossen* (Vienna: Albert Langen–Georg Müller, 1964), 11–13. Thomas's adopted strategy had been influentially explored by Ernst Krause in his Strauss biography (first published in 1955); see Krause's *Richard Strauss: The Man and His Work*, trans. John Coombs (London: Collets, 1964), 24.

2. See Richard Strauss and Stefan Zweig, *A Confidential Matter: The Letters of Richard Strauss and Stefan Zweig, 1931–1935,* trans. Max Knight (Berkeley: University of California Press, 1977), 62, 116n. 41.

3. Theodor Adorno, "Richard Strauss: Born June 11, 1964," trans. Samuel and Shierry Weber, *Perspectives of New Music* 4 (fall–winter 1965): 14–32, concluded in the following edition 5 (spring–summer 1966): 113–29. Although specialist work on Strauss has ceased to ignore Adorno—his youthful sixtieth-birthday Strauss essay is included in Bryan Gilliam, ed., *Richard Strauss and His World* (Princeton, N.J.: Princeton University Press, 1992), 406–15—he was still absent from the Strauss bibliography in the *New Grove Dictionary of Opera* (London: Macmillan, 1993).

4. Adorno, "Richard Strauss," 31.

5. Ibid., 22.

6. Ibid., 15.

7. Ibid., 14.

8. Ibid., 15.

9. Ibid., 26; the comment about the *Ariadne auf Naxos* prelude appears on 32.

10. Ibid., 29.

11. Ibid., 118.

12. Ibid., 122.

13. Ibid., 120.

14. Ibid., 17.

15. Ibid., 128–29.

16. Letter from Strauss to Thuille, summer 1878, translated in Gilliam, *Richard Strauss and His World,* 209. A facsimile of the original can be found in Alfons Ott, ed., *Briefe der Freundschaft: Richard Strauss und Ludwig Thuille (1877–1907)* (Munich: Walter Ricke, 1969), 41–44. The relevant page (43) stresses the ambivalence of Strauss's reaction to Wagner at that time. The "boring" outburst is followed by a full-page "Aber geistreich!!!" (but ingenious!!!) Other comments in that letter are indicative of a growing fascination for Wagner, anxious though Strauss was to disclaim the fact to Thuille.

17. Robert Musil, *A Man without Qualities,* trans. Eithne Wilkins and Ernst Kaiser (London: Pan Books, 1979), 2:25.

18. Ibid., 2:21.

19. The first quote is from Knud Martner, ed., *Selected Letters of Gustav Mahler,* trans. Eithne Wilkins and Ernst Kaiser (London: Faber, 1979), 148. The second quote is from Richard Strauss, *Recollections and Reflections,* ed. Willi Schuh, trans. L. J. Lawrence (London: Boosey and Hawkes, 1953), 9.

20. See Alma Mahler, *Gustav Mahler: Memories and Letters,* ed. Donald Mitchell, trans. Basil Creighton, 3d ed. (London: John Murray, 1973), 28. Following one of her many anecdotes about Pauline's public rudeness to Strauss, Alma notes that the latter "tormented Mahler without ceasing with calculations of the exact royalty on successes great or middling." See also 51, 93.

21. See Natalie Bauer-Lechner, *Recollections of Gustav Mahler,* trans. Dika Newlin, ed. Peter Franklin (London: Faber, 1980), 63–64.

22. See Herta Blaukopf, ed., *Gustav Mahler/Richard Strauss: Correspondence 1888–1911*, trans. Edmund Jephcott (Chicago: University of Chicago Press, 1984), 153.

23. Michael P. Steinberg, "Richard Strauss and the Question," in *Richard Strauss and His World*, ed. Bryan Gilliam (Princeton, N.J.: Princeton University Press, 1992), 165. This valuable essay draws comparisons between Strauss's and Heidegger's relationship to the Nazi regime, taking as its starting point the notion of a "politics of the spirit" from Jacques Derrida's 1987 book *De l'esprit: Heidegger et la question.*

24. Arthur Seidl, *Moderner Geist in der deutschen Tonkunst* (Regensburg: Gustav Bosse, 1913), 63.

25. See Mahler, *Gustav Mahler*, 89.

26. See Blaukopf, *Gustav Mahler/Richard Strauss*, 119.

27. I refer to Adorno's concept of "Durchbruch." See Theodor Adorno, *Mahler: Eine musikalische Physiognomik* (1963, 2d ed.; reprint, Frankfurt am Main: Suhrkamp, 1978), 13.

28. The phrase occurs in the 1903 introduction to *Die Musik*. See Strauss, *Recollections and Reflections,* 10.

29. Musil, *A Man without Qualities*, 2:32.

30. Seidl, *Moderner Geist in der deutschen Tonkunst,* 72–73. Strauss's comment about the droning professor is quoted in Willi Schuh, *Richard Strauss: A Chronicle of the Early Years, 1864–1898,* trans. Mary Whittall (Cambridge: Cambridge University Press, 1982), 57.

31. See Schuh, *Richard Strauss*, 285.

32. See Erich H. Mueller von Asow, *Richard Strauss: Thematisches Verzeichnis* (Vienna: Doblinger, 1959), 1:343.

33. There is already a hint of this attitude in the slightly rueful list of "non-German" composers (including Schreker and Korngold) made by Strauss in his letter to Franz Schalk of 22 September 1921, which he notes the lack of any of his works being performed in Vienna that month. See Günther Brosche, ed., *Richard Strauss–Franz Schalk: Ein Briefwechsel* (Tutzing: Hans Schneider, 1983), 244.

34. Fritz Busch, *Pages from a Musician's Life,* trans. Marjorie Strachey (London: Hogarth Press, 1953), 210.

35. An interesting attempt, orientated toward "postmodernist developments," at a revaluation of Strauss's post-*Elektra* works can be found in Leon Botstein, "The Enigmas of Richard Strauss: A Revisionist View," in *Richard Strauss and His World*, ed. Bryan Gilliam (Princeton, N.J.: Princeton University Press, 1992), 3–32.

36. Busch, *Pages from a Musician's Life,* 218. The best short account of scholarly treatment (and avoidance) of Strauss's Nazi-period activities is Pamela M. Potter's "Strauss and the National Socialists: The Debate and its Relevance," in *Richard Strauss: New Perspectives on the Composer and His Work,* ed. Bryan Gilliam (Durham, N.C.: Duke University Press, 1992), 93–113. The rather blandly "scholarly" conclusions of that essay might nevertheless be reckoned to be as tendentious, in their way, as the polemical work of Fred Prieberg and Gerhand Splitt that is criticized by Potter.

37. Elizabeth Förster-Nietzsche, the editor of her brother's letters and unpublished writings—including *The Will to Power*—encouraged Mussolini and later Hitler to find in Nietzsche a philosophical basis for their own worldviews.

38. The German text of Strauss's speech, as published in the official news sheet *Musik im Zeitbewusstsein* (Berlin, 17 February 1934), is reproduced in facsimile in Albrecht Dümling and Peter Girth, eds., *Entartete Musik: Zur Düsseldorfer Ausstellung von 1938: Eine Kommentierte Rekonstruktion* (Düsseldorf: city of Düsseldorf, 1988), 56–57.

39. Kurt Wilhelm, *Richard Strauss: An Intimate Portrait,* trans. Mary Whittall (London: Thames and Hudson, 1989), 219.

40. Strauss and Zweig, *A Confidential Matter,* 38.

41. Wilhelm, *Richard Strauss,* 220.

42. Strauss's letter to Franz Schalk of 8 June 1920 in Brosche, *Richard Strauss–Franz Schalk,* 164.

43. See Wilhelm, *Richard Strauss,* 85. The names of these two associations would translate respectively as Institute for Musical Performing Rights and Society for Musical Performance and Mechanical Reproduction Rights.

44. See Mahler, *Gustav Mahler,* 101.

45. See Roswitha Schlötterer, ed., *Richard Strauss–Max von Schillings: Ein Briefwechsel* (Pfaffenhofen: W. Ludwig, 1987), 44–45 and elsewhere. Seidl's open letter appears in Arthur Seidl, *Straussiana: Aufsätze zur Richard Strauss-Frage aus drei Jahrzehnten* (Regensburg: Gustav Bosse, n.d. [foreword dated 1913]), 170–91.

46. See Strauss, *Recollections and Reflections,* 67–68. Heinrich Mann's character Diederich Hessling in *Der Untertan* (1918) criticizes the "notorious Eugen Richter" as a dangerous friend of "unpatriotic slackers, at odds with the Government!"—see unattributed translation of *Man of Straw* (London: Penguin, 1984), 76–77.

47. Richard Strauss, *Briefe an die Eltern: 1882–1906,* ed. Willi Schuh (Zurich: Atlantis Verlag, 1954), 245–46.

48. Strauss, *Recollections and Reflections,* 67.

49. Alexander Ringer, *Arnold Schoenberg: The Composer as Jew* (Oxford: Clarendon Press, 1990), 128, 130–31.

50. Rollo Myers, ed., *Richard Strauss and Romain Rolland: Correspondence* (London: Calder and Boyars, 1968), 122.

51. Hanns Hammelmann and Ewald Osers, trans., *A Working Friendship: The Correspondence between Richard Strauss and Hugo von Hofmannsthal* (New York: Random House, 1961), 216.

52. See Eberhard Otto, "Richard Strauss und Max Reger—Antipoden oder Gesinnungsverwandte?" in *Mitteilungen des Max-Reger-Instituts,* ed. Ottmar Schreiber (16 October 1966): 37.

53. Strauss and Zweig, *A Confidential Matter,* 5.

54. Steinberg, "Richard Strauss and the Questions," 176.

55. Ibid., 179.

56. Strauss and Zweig, *A Confidential Matter,* 49, 115n. 32.

57. See Ibid., 65–67.

58. Ibid., 67.

59. Ibid., 67–68.

60. Ibid., 99.

61. Ibid., 100.

62. Ibid., 86.

63. Ibid., 89.

64. Ibid., 90.

65. Ibid., 98.

66. Adorno, "Richard Strauss," 14.

67. Wilhelm, *Richard Strauss*, 241–42.

68. Strauss and Zweig, *A Confidential Matter*, 63.

69. See Dümling and Girth, *Entartete Musik*.

70. See Pamela Potter, *Most German of the Arts: Musicology and Society from the Weimar Republic to the End of Hitler's Reich* (New Haven, Conn.: Yale University Press, 1998), 183ff.

71. Dümling and Girth, *Entartete Musik*, 105–10, where the full program of the "Festfolge" is reproduced in facsimile. The photographs appear there on 113 and 119.

72. Michael Kennedy, *Richard Strauss*, The Master Musicians Series, 2d ed. (London: Dent, 1976), 100.

73. Ibid., 107.

74. See Ivar Oxaal, Michael Pollack, and Gerhard Botz, *Jews, Antisemitism, and Culture in Vienna* (London: Routledge and Kegan Paul, 1987), 200, 238.

75. Wilhelm, *Richard Strauss*, 255.

76. Strauss and Zweig, *A Confidential Matter*, 38.

77. See *Times Literary Supplement* correspondence columns for 22–28 June 1990, 667; 29 June–5 July 1990, 695; 6–12 July 1990, 727; and 13–19 July 1990, 753. The correspondence was provoked by Michael Tanner's composite review "A Master Cosmetician," in the edition for 15–21 June 1990, 642.

78. See, for example, Lawrence Kramer, "Culture and Musical Hermeneutics: The Salome Complex," in *Cambridge Opera Journal* 2, no. 3 (1990): 269–94; Sander L. Gilman, "Strauss and the Pervert," in *Reading Opera*, ed. Arthur Groos and Roger Parker (Princeton, N.J.: Princeton University Press, 1988), 306–27; and Carolyn Abbate, "Opera, or the Envoicing of Women," in *Musicology and Difference: Gender and Sexuality in Music Scholarship*, ed. Ruth Solie (Berkeley: University of California Press, 1993), 225–58.

79. John Carey, *The Intellectuals and the Masses: Pride and Prejudice among the Literary Intelligentsia, 1880–1939* (London: Faber, 1992), 198–99.

80. The end of act 3 in *Die Frau ohne Schatten*. The translation is by Gertrude M. Holland, from the Boosey and Hawkes libretto (London: Boosey and Hawkes/Fürstner, 1964), 49. A model for the projected reinterpretation of Strauss's early works would be James Hepokoski's "Fiery-Pulsed Libertine or Domestic Hero? Strauss's *Don Juan* Reinvestigated," in *Richard Strauss: New Perspectives on the Composer of His Work*, ed. Bryan Gilliam (Durham, N.C.: Duke University Press, 1992), 135–75.

3

The Development of Richard Strauss's Worldview

Charles D. Youmans

At the end of his life, as he endured the self-destruction of his homeland and the inexorable failure of his own body, Richard Strauss consoled himself by rereading classic works of Western intellectual heritage: Homer, Shakespeare, Goethe, Wagner. These great minds, and others like them, embodied a culture to which Strauss had devoted eight decades of creative energy, and through which he hoped to find the only immortality he could imagine. Now they offered shelter, from the realities of age and from the abomination that had become German society. In the writings of Europe's greatest thinkers Strauss found the strength to accept that his charmed existence would end in tragedy.

By looking outside music to literary and philosophical thought, Strauss followed a natural predilection, a habit that went back to his school days. As a youth he had received as thorough a general education as any Austro-German nineteenth-century composer other than Felix Mendelssohn. An enthusiastic autodidact throughout his career, he took pride in his broad knowledge of European culture, believing that intellectual consciousness was a determining feature of his artistic persona. Contemplation was part of Strauss's routine, an activity he pursued assiduously despite the many other demands on his time and energy. His actions in the last years were no act of desperation, then, but a reflex of some seventy years' standing. Neither melodramatic nor pretentious, they followed the usual formula.

As important to the composer as reflection was the privacy of that reflection. Strauss considered his worldview the most personal dimension of his life. His reluctance to discuss serious intellectual matters in public forums, or to make a show of taking intellectual matters seriously, allowed caricatures to flourish, as he knew. These misperceptions cost him little sleep. He made no apologies for his expensive taste in clothing, for his Bavarian accent, or for his relentless battle for composers' financial welfare. But at the center of the man was a thoughtful humanistic outlook—highly informed and surprisingly nuanced, if not quite learned—and a deep concern for his own *Bildung* (education), however hidden that concern might have been from the view of those who knew him only through his music and its reception in the popular press.

The evidence of Strauss's quiet, unwavering engagement with intellectual matters has long been generally available. He was a lifelong history buff, with an impressive range of knowledge; even the negatively disposed Alma Mahler envied her husband the opportunity to hear Strauss's views on the historical foundations of European culture.[1] His command of Goethe was legendary among the educated individuals who knew him. He studied Schopenhauer while still in his teens and Nietzsche soon thereafter, and often returned to them during the next sixty years, most notably toward the end of his life. His taste in poetry ranged widely and sometimes in unfortunate directions (more so during his youth), but fascination with the insipid and the banal gave way to modern voices of social conscience and then increasingly to the rarefied masterworks of the greatest German poets. His interest in Classical culture was rooted in reading knowledge of ancient languages, yet he always treated those works as living documents to be brought into productive contact with the complex aesthetic dilemmas of modern Europe. All things considered, he had impressive credentials as a humanist, perhaps most of all in his cognizance of the lateness of his own historical moment vis-à-vis that tradition. It is a tribute to his private work ethic that he labored on to the end, consistently and tirelessly, attempting in clear-eyed modesty to sustain and extend a worldview that he believed history had outgrown. Only in the context of this project can his oeuvre be fully understood.

What follows is a survey of the most important influences on Strauss's intellectual life: his education, his reception of Goethe, the process by which he came to terms with Schopenhauer and Nietzsche, his choices of poetry for setting as Lieder, and some issues in his relationship with Hofmannsthal. I make no claim to comprehensiveness; my goal is merely to touch on those strains of thought that had the most direct and lasting effect on his worldview. Because most of the issues that occupied him arose first while he was still a young man, I focus on the period during which he very gradually came to maturity—roughly his first forty years. What emerges, however, is a clear sense that the questions occupying him during his youth elicited answers and beliefs that remained central to his worldview throughout the remainder of his life. And for Strauss that process was inseparable from the act of artistic creation.

Though Strauss did not enjoy an extraordinarily privileged youth—he followed a conventional upper-bourgeois path leading to social and financial respectability—he did learn early an appreciation for intellectual balance and broad knowledge. His father always intended for him to become a musician, but Strauss did not attend the local conservatory (where Franz Strauss eventually served as professor), studying instead at the Ludwigsgymnasium and then at the university (if only for a single semester).[2] Musical instruction largely took care of itself in the Strauss home, and what did not could be supplemented with lessons that in any case Strauss had outgrown by his late teens. *Bildung*, however, required systematic guided efforts, and therefore an education no different than if he had been destined for a career in law or theology.[3]

The Gymnasium in the 1870s was a resolutely humanist institution, still grounded in the early nineteenth-century reforms of Wilhelm von Humboldt (1767–1835).[4] As a leader of turn-of the-century New Humanism, Humboldt argued for reforms in the content and goals of the German educational system, and he instituted them with great success and lasting influence. With respect to content, he gave pride of place to the achievements of classical culture, in literature, art, philosophy, and history. Language was central, as the primary mode of perception and communication for any individual; thus training in the classical languages formed the core of instruction. Above all, education focused on the cultivation of the individual, a process seen as imperative if the society were to receive any collective benefits from its educational system.

Humboldt was not alone in his cultural views. Lessing, Schiller (a close friend of Humboldt), and Hegel all advocated the revival of humanism in Germany around 1800, seeking to shore up what they considered a middle ground between science and theology. Collectively they worked to respond to a crisis, confronting the multidetermined collapse of humanism that had begun around the death of Shakespeare. On the level of higher thought, their principal concern was that as modernity came into its own the intellectual world became more and more fragmented, as a result of increasing disciplinary specialization and the disconnection of the humanities from the sciences, on the one hand, and from theology, on the other hand. Similar fragmentation prevailed within the humanities, with philosophy diverging from letters and nationalism encouraging the abandonment of Latin as lingua franca. Into this context stepped Goethe as a marvel and potentially a savior—a living example of the splendidly diverse talents of Renaissance Men such as Leon Battista

Alberti (1404–72), whom Jacob Burckhardt praised for the astounding universality of his mind.[5] In the end, though, Goethe became the exception that proved the rule, an unrepeatable phenomenon marking the beginning of a final period of decline.

Until the era of Wilhelm II, however, Humboldt's nostalgic vision held sway; indeed, its implementation was comprehensive, serious, and one might almost say radical. Beginning in 1834, anyone who hoped to become a scholar, a civil servant, or even simply a university student was required to pass the final examination of the Gymnasium, the *Abitur*. Although students had three available tracks—the classical nine-year Gymnasium, with a curriculum that included Latin, Greek, and a modern language; the Realgymnasium, with Latin, modern languages, natural sciences, and mathematics; and the Realschule or Oberrealschule, with natural sciences and mathematics—only the classical curriculum held the promise of a liberal career. Strauss's attendance at the Gymnasium, then, had as much to do with the entrance requirements of a particular career track as with social respectability or intellectual growth; as Franz Strauss realized, once the opportunity had been missed it could not be recovered. In the end, Strauss's generation was the last to face this requirement. Wilhelm II ever more forcefully emphasized the non-classical institutions, calling a school conference in 1890 and declaring that "it is our duty to educate young men to become young Germans and not young Greeks or Romans."[6] In 1900 the three types of schools were granted equal privileges, significantly loosening humanism's grip on German educational philosophy.

The grade report from Strauss's final year at the Gymnasium confirms his affinity for the classical and historical emphases of the curriculum. Of Latin, Greek, German, French, mathematics, and history, the only subject in which he performed below average was mathematics, while he excelled in history.[7] The teacher's report describes "a mature understanding in the exposition of the classics," a comment that reflects a rather more extensive knowledge of the subject matter than one might imagine. His enthusiasm for classical literature affected his musical activities as well, particularly in a setting (probably from 1881) of the third stasimon (verses 1384–97) of Sophocles's *Elektra*. (The score, for male choir, strings, clarinets, horns, trumpets, and timpani, was lost in the bombing of 1943, but a piano reduction survives.)[8] The overlap of literary and historical study with creative activity was to be the norm for the remainder of Strauss's life, thanks to an early and sensitive awareness that he belonged in a continuum extending back two millennia. Likewise, with those of his friends whom he considered capable of discussing such matters he returned again and again to the contemplation of European culture. Thus the surviving correspondence with

Friedrich Rösch, an unusually gifted student colleague and a lifelong friend, is peppered with classical allusions and Greek words and phrases; for Rösch as for Strauss the classroom concerns of the student years became the daily bread of adulthood.[9]

Looking back on his life at age eighty-one, Strauss regarded his training in the Gymnasium as "the benevolent guardian of European culture," as the determining formative experience of his life.[10] He recognized that without that opportunity he could not have produced his life's work, whatever his musical talent and education. What is more, he realized that later generations, if deprived of that same opportunity, would lack the wherewithal to appreciate either German music or the larger context of European humanism from which it grew—a scenario in which the culture itself would wither. In a passionate plea on behalf of the "humanist Gymnasium," delivered hopefully although from the ashes of postwar Germany, Strauss claimed that the two world wars had exposed the absurdity of the teaching of mathematics and science at the expense of cultural subjects. Calling himself a "German Greek, even to this day," Strauss identified the Greek spirit, tempered by the "moderating influence of the central European climate . . . and landscape," as the source of European cultural achievement from "Michelangelo, Raphael, Grünewald, Shakespeare, Kant, Schopenhauer, and Schiller" to "the greatest of them all, Goethe."[11] Without the systematic training of at least the more gifted members of the society in that tradition, the tradition would come to an end, just as German musical culture, which in Wagner had completed a "cultural development of three thousand years," would lose its audience, its relevance, and its ability to sustain itself. The concern to solidify a new generation of concertgoers who could appreciate the works of Richard Strauss obviously sharpened this rhetoric. At this stage of his life, however, Strauss felt himself about to join the pantheon of fellow creative artists, many of them greater than he, but all of them united by common aesthetic and intellectual principles, and none of them able to survive alone.

The pride that Strauss felt in passing (at the age of eighteen) his matriculation examination reinforced his belief that university study would be superfluous, at least given his disposition for private *Lektüre* (reading). Nevertheless, he attended the University of Munich during the winter semester of 1882–83, mostly to satisfy his father. His courses coincided squarely with his interests—history of philosophy (Schopenhauer), aesthetics, cultural history, and Shakespeare—but he saw no reason that he could not pursue the same program of learning on his own: "I soon opted for the acquisition of that kind of knowledge through reading and making my own choice of teachers!"[12] Indeed, Strauss was far better equipped at eighteen to approach thinkers like Schopenhauer and Goethe than most graduates of the finest twenty-first-century undergraduate institutions. Ironically, in asserting his right to determine his own course of learning Strauss merely adapted principles that he learned in the university, the ideas of *Lernfreiheit* (freedom of the student to study what he wished) and *Lehrfreiheit* (the freedom of the professor from harassment on the basis of the direction and results of his research). In the university itself these principles introduced a fair degree of fragmentation—the natural result of specialization—and Strauss saw no need to pursue, as a member of a bureaucratic institution, something that he could provide for himself. Specialization certainly did not appeal to his catholic tastes. Abandoning the prospect of earning a degree did cost him some suffering, however, which left him only when he gained the privilege of signing his name as "Dr. Richard Strauss" after being granted an honorary doctorate from the University of Heidelberg in 1903.

From his blissful teenage years until the pampered agony of his postwar retirement, Strauss looked to Goethe as the shining example of a modern humanist. Goethe was the only poet Strauss set in every decade of his life from the 1870s to the 1940s. The novels, plays, and longer poems interested Strauss as well, indeed every bit as much as the lyric poetry; according to his elder grandson the only work by Goethe that Strauss read but a single time was the *Farbenlehre* (1810).[13] Once Strauss reached adulthood and assumed the responsibilities of a professional career, any period of free time was sure to bring renewed engagement with Goethe. During a year spent convalescing in Greece and Egypt (1892–93) the first item on his reading list was *Wilhelm Meisters Wanderjahre* (1829). (His travel diary begins with the declaration "the wander-years begin!")[14] When a tour with the Vienna Philharmonic took him to Rio de Janeiro in 1920, he brought along Goethe's literary essays.[15] Thoughts of Goethe seem to have been omnipresent, and always in dialogue with the content of whatever creative project was at hand. During work on *Also sprach Zarathustra* (1896), when Strauss was ostensibly immersed in the ideas of Nietzsche, it was Goethe who came to mind (in a quote of the "Earth Spirit" from *Faust*, part 1 [1808]) as he sketched the shattering collapse midway through the piece.[16] In Hofmannsthal's view, the "Goethean atmosphere" of "purification" in *Der Rosenkavalier* (1910), *Ariadne auf Naxos* (1912; revised, 1916), and *Die Frau ohne Schatten* (1917) stood as one of their principal unifying features.[17] And for his final instrumental masterpiece, the *Metamorphosen* (1945), Strauss returned to Goethe for inspiration, this time to the fourteen-line poem "Niemand wird sich selber kennen" (No One Can Know Himself), with its despairing verdict on the limits of human knowledge.[18] Whatever Strauss's artistic task, Goethe was never far away.

As he grew older, Strauss increasingly saw himself as a Goethean figure, a lonely protector of a dying tradition. In Goethe he found a kindred spirit, albeit one toward whom he always retained the most profound humility. The connection to this supreme modern example of the Western humanist philosophy mattered as much to him as any musical ancestry. Thus when he called himself "the last mountain of a large mountain range," Strauss thought not only of the German musical tradition from Bach to Wagner, but of the German intellectual tradition, which included music as an important element but had reached its apex in the relatively unmusical Goethe.[19] This sentiment became particularly focused in his last days, when he found consolation in reflecting that "when he died, Goethe was never so alive and renowned as he is today."[20] For the atheist Strauss, a position in the pantheon of creative artists in the Western tradition was as close as one could come to genuine immortality.

That thought was of course inherently Goethean, as were many of Strauss's attitudes about life and art. The philosophical commonalities that exist between Goethe and Strauss, and the biographical as well, are in fact quite extensive, far more so than has been noticed in the published literature. Both artists lived long, relentlessly active lives, motivated by a love of hard work and a determination to develop their creative gifts through consistent activity; in Goethe's words, as quoted by Strauss in the essay "On Inspiration in Music," "genius is hard work."[21] Both showed in their works a pronounced, recurring autobiographical tendency, while at the same time censoring outsiders' knowledge of their private views with a carefully constructed public persona. A fascination with the landscape—whether that of the south, with its ties to ancient culture, or of the Alps—exercised a considerable influence on both of them, in each case after a never-to-be-forgotten pilgrimage to Italy during early maturity. A distant, conflicted, and intense relationship with a political figure of world-historical significance had a profound effect on both careers. And not to be underestimated is the importance of profound devotion to an oddball wife, known for her lack of culture, bad manners (or at least innocence of courtly decorum), and preoccupation with domestic details. For Goethe as for Strauss such marital circumstances were a condition of creative production, and both explicitly admitted so.

The noteworthy correspondence between the outward features of these two artists' lives manifests an even deeper connection in terms of artistic philosophy. The creative lives of Goethe and Strauss were shaped early on by a flirtation with Romanticism (in Strauss's case, Wagnerian neo-Romanticism) that gave way to a strong, mature faith in a kind of post-Romantic classicism.

Goethe's flirtation with Romanticism gave birth to *Die Leiden des jungen Werther* (1774), simultaneously one of the principal early documents of the movement in Germany and a sharp critique. (Werther's self-centered adolescent sentimentality ultimately turns on itself, so that he meets the same self-destructive end as the quintessentially Romantic characters of *Wilhelm Meisters Lehrjahre* [1796]: Mignon and the Harper.) Roughly a century later Strauss followed a similar path, discovering Romanticism and then rapidly moving to destroy it; the process can be observed both in the tone poems, where for example the *Tristan* chord turns into the sound of a rogue sticking out his tongue, and in the operas, where Strauss hoped in *Die Frau ohne Schatten* to have written the "last Romantic opera."[22] For both artists, an early fluency in the language of pathetic emotion made later deployment of ironic, overblown pathos all the more effective.

This active rejection of Romanticism contributed to the perception of both artists in their later years as establishment reactionaries. Given the technical innovations of their early works, however, neither could be accused of a conservatism based wholly in the materials of their art. The deciding factor was an intense suspicion of theoretical philosophy, or indeed theory of any kind. The down-to-earth practicality that we find in the art and lives of Goethe and Strauss stemmed from a fundamental distrust of abstract thought, particularly abstraction as reflected in the language of Romantic transcendentalism. Just as Goethe returned again and again in his poetry to embrace the physical at the expense of the metaphysical, so Strauss thematized the distinction by using the idiom of Wagnerian metaphysics to paint the physical experiences of everyday life. Underlying all of this was agnosticism, which arrived at an early age—the teenage years, during the first awareness of the life of the mind—and persisted throughout life, even into very old age, despite the inevitable fears. ("I shall never be converted, and I shall remain true to my old religion of the classics until my life's end," declared Strauss shortly before his death.) Whatever hopes of immortality these men entertained had little to do with traditional religion, and everything to do with the subsequent reception of their art.

Perhaps because of the emotional toll of living out their severe conclusions about life and its meaning, or perhaps because of the ongoing struggle to accept the innate limitations of being human, Goethe and Strauss took on chameleon-like artistic personae, always staying one step ahead of their audience. The constant shifting of approach and perspective from work to work in Strauss's oeuvre is a version of Faust's informed intellectual pessimism, which Strauss considered the defining condition of his own life, however effectively he was able to bring humor to bear on the issue. Nietzsche's healthy influence is easy to see in this context, though one finds it remarkable to survey in Goethe as in Strauss the engagement with "Nietzschean" ideas that predated Nietzsche, most famously the eternal recurrence, an idea that Goethe contemplated on his own and that Strauss unearthed in Schopenhauer.[23] Nietzschean or not, a strong work ethic and a natural joy in existence supplied them with the wherewithal to cope with disturbing philosophical convictions. Wrenching changes of creative direction, when public success might have elicited more of the same (*Werther*, *Till Eulenspiegel*) confirm in both cases that their art was shaped less by public reception than by inwardness and examination of the intellectual interior.

Goethe's reputation as an artist ahead of his time has much to do with the fragmentation of works like *Wilhelm Meisters Wanderjahre*, in which formal problems are created but not solved and competing levels or modes of communication exist in tension, without synthesis. By placing technical questions or conflicts in the foreground, Goethe made artworks self-referential, so that one of the principal functions of artwork became contemplation of its own nature as art. Whether this tendency constitutes an anticipation of modernism, or the birth of modernism, it plays a crucial role in Strauss, where the problem of artistic unity always takes center stage. The disconcerting mixture of high and low art in Strauss (as in the comparable case of Mahler), the deliberate undercutting of artistic unity, has one of its main precedents in *Faust*. And there the hodgepodge reproduces on the level of art one of the central questions of the poem: whether the diversity of experience could add up to a recognizable, universally valid "truth." Clearly, in an era when truth as a concept was fast losing its credibility, art would have difficulty maintaining its prestige, based as it was on the idea of a special relationship with truth. That it should have taken eight decades for these ideas to make the leap from Goethe to Strauss—that is, from poetry to music—is first a testament to Wagner and, second, a statement about the typically sluggish response of music to trends in the philosophy of art. Certainly it may be said of both Goethe and Strauss that they made a Nietzschean transition from viewing art as a mirror of life to viewing life as an "aesthetic phenomenon."

One might expect that a composer so deeply involved with Goethe's thought would have made substantial musical use of Goethe's writings, yet Strauss's output is relatively small: about a dozen Lieder, a work for chorus and orchestra, the *Metamorphosen* (where the connection to Goethe is a private matter), and the unfinished dramatic setting of *Lila*. It is for this reason more than any other that thought on Strauss's relationship to Goethe has remained underdeveloped. Particularly his choices of poems for Lieder have perplexed commentators. For the most part he shied away from acknowledged masterpieces and poems that had received a large number of previous settings. (Only four of the poems Strauss chose had been set previously, in the reckoning of Reinhold Schlötterer, and these included the spurious "Das Bächlein" [The Brooklet].)[24] In form and subject the poems range widely, but they share a certain modesty of intent when taken in the context of Goethe's entire oeuvre. Even the best-known among them, the endlessly interpretable "Der Fischer" (The Fisher), stands as a model of folkish pith and pregnant naiveté.

On the other hand, this tiny sampling of poems offers a strikingly comprehensive survey of those artistic concerns that occupied Strauss consistently, naggingly, across his lifetime. Sensuality, domesticity, self-determination, the individual's relationship with nature, the Dionysian, the relationship between the real and the ideal, the productive destruction of old artistic forms, the human being's insignificance and exaggerated sense of self-importance—all of these themes find treatment in the poems that Strauss selected from Goethe, and all of them played some fundamental constitution role in his conception of the nature of art and the role of the artist. The sheer virtuosity of instinct revealed in the choices, then, bears consideration, for what it reveals about his thoughts on Goethe, but also for what it says about Strauss's ostensibly haphazard method of selecting texts for song composition.

It is not surprising that Strauss initiated his Goethe-Lieder with the well-known folk ballad "Der Fischer" (1877); self-confidence came early to him, and he probably chose it precisely because the poem was recognizable and had been set memorably more than once. Less certain is the breadth with which the thirteen-year-old would have understood the poem's figurative dimensions, above all the menacing sexuality of the water imagery and the implications of such lines as *"Halb zog sie ihn, halb sank er hin"* (partly she pulled him in, partly he sank below). That he paired the song with the more explicitly sexual "Lust und Qual" (Rapture and Torment), however, identifies at least a baseline awareness of the essential metaphorical content, whatever his ability to perceive the nuances. In the latter poem the first two stanzas amount to an introduction to the figurative interpretation of reality, that is, to the art of reading poetry: the first stanza, in which the fisherboy tricks his prey and pulls it wriggling from the water, is mirrored by a second in which the boy sees himself as a fish caught by the shepherdess. The final stanza replays this transition away from the literal, with the boy's confession that each fresh net of squirming fish renews his wish to be caught again in the young woman's arms (terms likely to be understood by an adolescent male).

Sexuality was never an issue that Strauss avoided in his music; indeed, the graphic qualities of an early work like *Don Juan* (1888) represent a veiled but palpable challenge of the repressive atmosphere of Munich, where cen-sorship tied the hands of artists like Ibsen.[25] Sexuality sublimated as redemption—Wagnerian sexuality—however, did not interest him in the slightest, and he delighted in offering a realistic, down-to-earth alternative. Another folk ballad, "Gefunden" (Found), captures the essence of this ap-proach. The setting comes from 1903, just as Strauss stood at the crossroads between opera and tone poem, between *Salome* (1905) and the *Symphonia domestica* (1903). In content the poem reads like an alternate "Heiden-röslein" (Hedge Rose): The speaker wanders through a pastoral scene, encounters a flower, and attempts to pluck it. This time, however, the flower's protests are heeded. It is dug up, roots and all, and replanted in the garden *"am hübschen Haus"* (by my pretty home), where it can thrive and bloom year after year. By 1903 Strauss was fully equipped to read between the lines of fables about flower violence, and to understand the difference between plucking and transplanting. What caught his interest was the cel-ebration of domesticity, the secure, year-after-year warmth *"am stillen Ort"* (in a quiet place), which formed the core of his own existence and of Goethe's. This move did not exclude sexuality by any means, but it did ease it out of the philosophical realm.

The three poems of Op. 67 (1918)—"Hab' ich euch denn je geraten" (Have I Then Ever Advised You), "Wer wird von der Welt verlangen" (Who Will from the World Demand), and "Wanderers Gemütsruhe" (Wanderer's Peace of Mind)—are much more abstract and obscure. Collectively they deal with the issue of selfhood, as measured in the relationships between the self and the world and between the self and others. These questions had dogged Strauss throughout his youth; the personal struggles to which they are connected, in particular the possibility of self-determination in a world that no longer had an objective religious or metaphysical measuring stick, have much to do with the wrenching formal conflicts of the tone poems. And they continued to occupy him during work on the great Hofmannsthal operas, so many of whose main characters confront the crisis of fluid iden-tity in the modern world. If Strauss stands as an unusually eager musical autobiographer, that fact is not unrelated to the crumbling of the self in a world in which fragmentation ruled every dimension of experience from artistic style to European politics.

The centerpiece of the set, "Hab ich euch denn je geraten," blankly asserts the individual's right to self-determination, setting up an oppositional dy-namic (grammatical first and second person) that underscores the boundary between distinct human subjects. In place of interpersonal influence the poet advocates the power of Nature, a force against which no human agency can compete, but which, when used productively, yields the healthy realization of one's potential. The topic brings to mind the more antagonistic relationship between the individual and Nature at the beginning of *Also sprach Zarathustra*, a tone poem that yearns for, but does not achieve, just the sort of synthesis described by Goethe. (The tone poem had other Goethean connections, as I have mentioned.) It was entirely characteristic of Strauss to revisit an issue that he had not been able to settle earlier in his career; just how far he now accepted Goethe's resolution remains uncertain.

The other two poems return to the theme of the individual's relationship to the world, focusing on ethical questions of individual action given a particular external state. As we shall see, this concern took center stage in Strauss's artistic thought shortly after his "conversion" to Wagnerism in the 1880s, and never really subsided. Both poems advocate a kind of stoicism, one suggesting that the individual not make demands on external reality, the other that the individual avoid responding to outside forces. Strauss's own strong conviction that reality, in the philosophical sense, lay outside of the reach of human faculties is echoed in "Wer wird von der Welt verlangen," which counsels the reader/listener not to expect from the world what it cannot give, and not to try to bend it to one's own purposes. Similarly, "Wanderers Gemütsruhe" recommends personal distance from the machinations of the world, here specifically referring to evil, which should be met not with resistance but with detached equanimity. One can easily imagine Strauss returning to such a sentiment two decades later, whether or not it amounted to rationalization. Certainly a more general distance or removal from everything outside his own domestic and creative inner sanctum remained the defining feature of his personal life for close to six decades.

With "Sinnspruch" (Aphorism), composed the year after Op. 67, Strauss again touched on the essential defining qualities of humanity, this time in a poem making a tongue-in-cheek comparison of human beings to insects. In considering the motivation of a choice like this it is essential to remember that despite Strauss's technical flamboyance and uncompromising self-confidence, the defining feature of his artistic character was modesty. Strauss did not believe that his music, or anyone's music, could or should communicate profound philosophical truths, unless it was the truth that music did not have that capacity. Given that view of the art, it goes without saying that Strauss had a more restrained appraisal of the spiritual or intellectual prestige of musical composition than did Beethoven, Wagner, or Schoenberg. With Strauss began a new era in German music, the era of the great composer whose music was just music. In this light, the thrust of "Sinnspruch" for Strauss would have been not just the human-as-spider, bearing itself with absurd pomp, but the broom that sweeps it away—a fate that awaited all humans, whatever the seriousness of their works.

Finally, with the modest "Zugemessne Rhythmen" (Measured Rhythms) we find Strauss working his way in 1935 back to a basic theme of his early work, and to the aesthetic questions that set his career on its unique path. Strauss would have seen in this seven-line miniature a pithy reproduction of his own involvement in the contemporaneous controversies of musical form. Goethe's theme is the maturation process of the creative artist. While young, talent revels in the received forms of artistic tradition, but soon they seem nothing more than "*hohle Masken ohne Blut und Sinn*" (hollow masks with neither blood nor sense).[26] In the long run, "Geist" (Spirit) must conceive new forms and destroy the old. Strauss might easily have set this poem in 1888 when he was lecturing Hans von Bülow on the necessity of new forms to accommodate new content. Fifty years later, as he stood on the verge of an "Indian Summer" that would see a revival of the genres and forms that occupied him during his period of *Talent*, Strauss paid homage to the liberating impulse that was the precondition of all his subsequent work, including his transformed return to his roots.

In another letter to Bülow, written while Strauss spent a full year (1892–93) resting his weak lungs in Italy, Greece, and Egypt, the young composer described what Goethe meant to his creative development. What this great figure offered was precisely the possibility of becoming more than just a young composer—Goethe taught him to open his horizons and to look beyond the narrow perspective of the musician, out to "all of the things of the world." Now he hoped "to put on the magnificent glasses through which the noblest spirits of the world have seen, and indeed to forge my own pair: original artistic production."[27] In fact Strauss was describing a process that had already been underway since the mid-1880s, specifically since the fall of 1885, when he had moved to Meiningen to become Bülow's assistant with the famed Meiningen Court Orchestra. This engagement had marked the beginning of his decade-long transition to intellectual and artistic maturity, a period during which the struggle to come to terms with the complex musical challenges facing young post-Wagnerians forced him to think out his own positions on the nature of music and on music's significance in the cultural context of late-nineteenth-century Europe. The process involved close work with a series of mentors, as well as the near-systematic alienation of each (including Bülow, who was gone from Meiningen by the beginning of 1886 and whose thought, outside of practical questions of music making, Strauss rapidly left behind). That all of these relationships should have ended in some degree of bitterness and distance is perhaps the best testament to the breadth of the relevant issues, that is, their extension beyond music into the sphere of intellectual life and worldview.

Bülow provided Strauss with an extraordinarily successful example of a first-rate musician who also could marshal significant extramusical intellectual powers. The brilliant conductor's razor-sharp letters are famous for their virtuosic literacy, flitting between languages in a barrage of subtle puns and dark wit. At this late stage of his career, however, and given the trials he had endured over the previous three decades, Bülow was an impatient mentor, not given to abstract reflection. Strauss's descriptions of their relationship focus on specific issues of musical technique and interpretation—rehearsal methods, for example—and leave a distinct impression that what he received from Bülow he learned on the fly, rather than from patient personal communication intended to nurture.[28] For Strauss these parameters represented a significant missed opportunity; for instance, it was not until the early 1890s when he actively recognized the importance of Nietzsche, although Bülow had been wildly enthusiastic about *The Birth of Tragedy* from the time of its publication in 1872. By the mid-1880s, however, possibilities for conversing with Bülow along these lines were limited, given his fondness for the efficient discussion-stopping quip.

Alexander Ritter (1833–96), on the other hand, the individual whom Strauss would regard as the single most important figure in his intellectual development, had no such shortage of time. Barely able to eke out a living during some thirty years as composer, violinist, and small-town conductor, he now sat among the violins in the Meiningen Orchestra as Bülow's guest, rewarded for a lifetime of faithful friendship. (The two had grown up together in Dresden.) Yet Ritter was not without a respectable artistic pedigree. His mother, Julie Ritter, had provided monetary support for Wagner during a crucial period of need. Ritter would later recall playing string quartets with his brother as Wagner listened patiently in the family's living room, and the impression of that early contact, along with the experience of witnessing all eighteen performances of the first production of *Tannhäuser*, never left him.[29] For the remainder of his life he proclaimed the deep spiritual significance of Wagnerian art, a mystical Catholicism souped up by the music drama and a species of Platonic idealism. At the age of twenty-one he married Franziska Wagner, Wagner's niece, and dedicated himself to discipleship. By 1885, however, Ritter had not been able to accomplish much for the cause, and time was running out. The arrival of Strauss thus represented an impossibly fortunate opportunity.

At the end of his life Strauss famously described his acquaintance with Ritter as "the greatest event of the winter in Meiningen."[30] Notwithstanding the relationship's significance, however, he would eventually reject everything Ritter taught him (though it took more than a decade) and Ritter would go to his grave believing that Strauss had betrayed him. The crucial service that Ritter performed was to raise questions, not to provide answers. Strauss related that in countless evenings in the elder man's modest home he "found the spiritual stimulus which was the decisive factor in my further development."[31] That comment requires careful interpretation. Ritter did stimulate Strauss's interest in the debates surrounding the spiritual dimension of music. He did introduce Strauss to Wagner's writings and to novel theories of Schopenhauer interpretation (a philosophy that Strauss had already studied to some extent at the University of Munich). And he did make him aware, in detail, of the argument that Liszt and Wagner had drawn from Beethoven the concept of musical "expression," that is, the notion that music had a spiritual content the communication of which was the art's primary responsibility. What he did not accomplish, however, was to convince Strauss that this content was true, that it existed, or even that it was desirable. Indeed, Strauss had great difficulty grasping its precise nature, which he became obsessed with defining. That obsession stimulated the most sustained period of philosophical study of his life, and it produced his only known diary of philosophical reflections. In the end, he unequivocally rejected the idea of metaphysical content in music, and what is more, he devoted his mature orchestral compositions to proving that he was right. Meeting Ritter was a "great event," then, but it was an event of anti-influence (and ultimately a guilt-inducing one; not for nothing did Strauss give his son, born one year to the day after Ritter's death, the middle name of Alexander).

Most of the information about Ritter's own views has to be gleaned from a few emotionally charged letters that he sent to Strauss when their relationship fell apart, during work on Strauss's first opera, *Guntram* (1893). His published writings, however, though by no means numerous, do give a glimpse of his principal concerns insofar as he felt they were publicly relevant. A humorous parody of Hanslick, "Vom Spanisch-Schönen" (On the Spanishly Beautiful) reveals an acerbic wit and a free extension of Wagner's dictum that music should be a means, not an end. The article describes the author's discovery of a Spanish manuscript in which words are arranged not according to their meaning but following principles of symmetry and visual beauty. Complex formal arrangements abound, but sense remains entirely absent. As a theorist of this strange art explains, "[I]n many places this amusement has become a kind of formal pastime. Of course, only people who don't understand Spanish enjoy it."[32] Elsewhere Ritter left humor aside, preaching with the passion of an evangelist. In a major article for the *Bayreuther Blätter*—uninvitingly titled "Three Chapters: On Franz Liszt, On the 'heiligen Elizabeth' in Karlsruhe, and On Our Ethical Defect" (1890)—Ritter explained the fundamentally moral nature of aesthetic choices. All Bayreuthians, if they were true believers, traced their faith back to a moment of *Erkenntnis* (epiphany) when they realized that music existed to convey eternal truths. But pitifully few had the moral strength to retain the sacred memory of that moment, and to remain devoted to it in practical ways, on a daily basis, in their professional lives.[33]

The crux of Ritter's philosophy, then, was the belief that music existed to communicate some sort of religious, or at least spiritual, content. Acceptance of his aesthetic views thus amounted to a moral imperative: Opponents were either evil or ignorant. Curiously, the precise nature of that content came through less clearly in the publications than in the dialogue with Strauss. Ritter seems to have felt that detailed exegesis of this dimension of his views would be too cumbersome, or somehow inappropriate for the general readership of a music journal. Perhaps, on the other hand, he lacked the confidence to attempt a systematic explanation. In any case, what he "reminded" Strauss in early 1893 was that their relationship had been based on Ritter's belief that Strauss was the composer best equipped to "build upon Wagner's achievement in *his sense.*" That ability stemmed from a deep understanding of Wagner's works, an understanding possible only because Strauss recognized the foundation of those works in "Schopenhauerian epistemology and ideal-Christian religiosity." Now, however, Ritter believed that Strauss had rejected that learning, and was moving toward a music that radically disengaged form from content. "[N]othing of Wagner's worldview remains in you. What alone of Wagner has survived in you? The mechanics of his art. But to use this art for the glorification of a world view that directly contradicts the Wagnerian is not to *build upon* Wagner's achievement, but to *undermine it.*"[34]

It is not an exaggeration to say that Alexander Ritter understood the aesthetic basis of Strauss's music better than anyone other than Strauss himself. Few have conceded that point, mostly due to Ritter's reputation as a crackpot and shrill partisan. But a close look at the issues around *Guntram* shows that Ritter was correct in his assessment of the severity of Strauss's critique, as well as in his recognition that this critique would turn into a long-term antagonism of the Wagnerian worldview. What all of this means is that Strauss engaged in a conscious philosophical analysis of Wagnerism relatively early in his career (after composing only his first three tone poems, *Macbeth* [1888; revised 1891], *Don Juan* [1888], and *Tod und Verklärung* [1889]), and that the results determined the course of his future as a composer.

The plot of *Guntram* concerns a young member of the Streiter der Liebe (Champions of Love), a brotherhood of minstrel priests who use music to disseminate spiritual truths. On his first mission Guntram sins by killing an evil duke, albeit in self-defense, and is summoned by his mentor to face the brotherhood for judgment. In the first version of the opera, Guntram was to atone for his transgression by doing penance as decreed by the brotherhood. But in a revision that Strauss made in late 1892, without Ritter's advice, Guntram rejects his mentor's demands and flings his lyre to the ground, announcing that music can play no meaningful role in spiritual *Erlösung* (redemption). This change was the proximate cause of the dispute with Ritter, who understood the implications, notwithstanding Guntram's decision to retire to the woods to live a life of asceticism "in imitation of the Saviour." Strauss had turned his first opera, the work meant to show the world that the Wagnerian music drama could survive the Master's death, into a vehicle for the message that music was an unspiritual art.

What is most fascinating about this revision is that it embodies an informed and literal reading of Schopenhauer, one that attempts to counteract the distortive tradition of Wagnerian readings that began with Wagner's own study of *The World as Will and Representation* in the early 1850s. Contrary to what Wagner and his followers made of it, Schopenhauer's position on music had been ambivalent at best. Among all the arts, music was the only one with the capacity for direct representation of the Will that dark metaphysical essence defined as "endless striving." While other arts imitated or represented objectifications of the Will—people, for example—music's mimesis related directly to the Will itself. With regard to the ultimate goal of human existence, however, the ultimate denial or renunciation of the Will, music had no greater claims to efficacy than any other art. Music could offer moments of "will-less" knowledge, a taste of *Willensverneinung* (denial of the Will), but nothing more. Genuine denial, the final lasting victory over the Will, was only possible through "saintly" renunciation, an ascetic denial of self much like that to which Guntram retires at the end of Strauss's opera.[35]

What the revision accomplished, then, was to dramatically reproduce the basic philosophical argument of the third and fourth books of *The World as Will and Representation*. Strauss said as much in his response to Ritter's plea, calling the union of art and religion "utopian" and citing Schopenhauer as confirmation: "[O]ur friend Schopenhauer also takes this view in book three of *The World as Will and Representation*."[36] At this stage Ritter must have realized that he no longer stood on solid ground; Strauss had uncovered a dimension of Schopenhauer conveniently overlooked by virtually every musician interested in Schopenhauer from Wagner on. What is more, it was no minor issue, in the philosophy or in its implications for the intellectual status of music. Certainly Ritter now felt considerable humiliation as a thinker, for his already clear tendentiousness had been exposed as intellectually irresponsible. His prompt withdrawal as a day-to-day mentor is not surprising, particularly given that Strauss had been proceeding without delay with the composition of the music to the revision, a strong signal that his mind was made up.

Strauss would stick to his guns, but not without losing confidence more than once. Though he never second-guessed his reading of Schopenhauer's final pronouncements about music, Strauss wondered a great deal about the appropriate course of action given this new knowledge. Did it make sense for a convinced Schopenhauerian to pursue a career as a composer? How would one justify such a choice? Clearly, some sort of critique of Schopenhauer would be necessary, because Strauss was by no means prepared simply to disregard the philosopher altogether now that he understood music's unexpectedly modest role in the overall philosophy. These questions dominated Strauss's correspondence in the spring of 1893 with Cosima Wagner, who oddly enough found them tedious, and Friedrich Rösch, an old classmate from the Gymnasium.[37] Rösch, a lawyer who dabbled in conducting and music criticism, had been recognized from youth as one of the most gifted minds in Munich, and he knew Schopenhauer inside and out. Strauss thus expected both sympathy and assistance from him in his new project of refuting Schopenhauerian metaphysics.

What he got, unfortunately, was ridicule. These letters, unfortunately still unpublished, present a litany of complaints from Rösch that Strauss was unfairly attempting to find weak spots where there were none.[38] On 15 March, for example, Rösch quoted Strauss as having suggested that comprehensive denial of the Will was not possible, or it would have been accomplished already. Rösch found this argument absurd, on the grounds that historical evidence had nothing to do with philosophical questions. And aside from that criticism, Rösch pointed out that "millions" had indeed already achieved it, in the East. (The mere fact that he could make such an assertion speaks volumes about the seriousness with which Schopenhauer's metaphysics could be taken in Germany, even in the 1890s.) Elsewhere in this thirty-plus-page letter Rösch willingly conceded that Wagner's character as an artist had prevented him from being a real Schopenhauerian. But Rösch refused to take that as a serious indictment of Schopenhauer's judgment, or a failure to provide special consideration for the powers of artistic genius. Finally, Rösch gave no credence whatsoever to the suggestion that Schopenhauer had insufficiently considered the force of predestination in the lives of individuals who tried and failed to achieve denial.

Philosophical arcana aside, this exchange between Strauss and Rösch shows the composer to have been deeply concerned with a philosophical matter after he had proved to his own satisfaction that music did not figure significantly in that philosophy. Why the continuing concern, then? There are at least two good reasons: First, Strauss seems to have needed reasons other than musical for disavowing Schopenhauer, whose prestige in German musical circles had given no signs of fading; and second, the prestige of his art was at stake; the aesthetic superiority of music in German culture, hard-won over the course of a century, now seemed in jeopardy. To maintain his credibility as a thinking composer, and to maintain the prestige of the art to which he would continue to devote himself no matter what happened, Strauss had to find a way to link music with some sort of post-Schopenhauerian worldview. Only through a philosophy in which music played a leading role in an effective critique of Schopenhauer could Strauss rescue that of which he had deprived himself.

Of course, that philosophy, if one can call it that, stood ready in the later writings of Friedrich Nietzsche. Strauss did know of Nietzsche before the controversy arose with Ritter; he took a copy of *Beyond Good and Evil* (1886) on the trip to the south, and among Strauss's friends and family there was a quiet awareness that his interest in these scandalous writings had begun to rise. To Ritter, however, he denied having any substantial knowledge of them before the revision of *Guntram*, and the contention seems credible.[39] Only with the rise of a pressing critical need vis-à-vis Schopenhauer did Strauss throw himself into Nietzsche.

The crucial factor of Strauss's turn to Nietzsche is that the works he studied came from the middle and late periods of Nietzsche's career, after his break with Wagner. Whereas Mahler, for example, encountered the Nietzsche of *The Birth of Tragedy* (1872), and never reconciled himself to the post-Wagnerian Nietzsche, Strauss found Nietzsche helpful precisely because he had undergone the process through which Strauss was now putting himself: that rejecting Wagnerian/Schopenhauerian musical metaphysics. In working through the Schopenhauerian issues connected with *Guntram*, Strauss had not anticipated that separating music from metaphysics would leave him with further unresolved philosophical issues. As he discovered, however, Nietzsche had been down this path, and had confronted the problem of how to deal with the real Schopenhauer, that is, the Schopenhauer who moved beyond musical metaphysics to a metaphysics of saintly renunciation. Nietzsche's primary significance, as far as Strauss was concerned, lay in his rejection of metaphysics altogether, and his advocacy of a new, postmetaphysical, twentieth-century optimism.

A variety of sources confirms Strauss's interest in the later writings of Nietzsche. Above all, the composition of a tone poem based (however "freely") on *Also sprach Zarathustra* (1883–85) is a confession of faith—*Also sprach Zarathustra* was not just Nietzsche's most artistically inclined work, but his principal positive statement of a postmetaphysical worldview. *Beyond Good and Evil*, which Nietzsche called the critical counterpart of *Also sprach Zarathustra*, may have been among Strauss's reading even before *Also sprach Zarathustra*. By March of 1893 his enthusiasm for that work had reached such a pitch that he even shared it with Cosima Wagner, who of course had observed the estrangement between Wagner and Nietzsche first-hand and had little interest, to say the least, in discussing the philosopher's latest ideas. (In any case he was now insane, as she pointed out to Strauss, who for his part pushed conversation to the height of absurdity by admitting that he found Nietzsche's ideas on women and democracy "highly sympathetic.")[40] Shortly thereafter, Arthur Seidl reported a visit with Strauss in April 1894, during which Strauss read aloud from Nietzsche's "main works" and generally expressed his enthusiasm.[41] The plural *Hauptwerken* (main works) indicates that at least most of the works come from Nietzsche's period of Wagner antagonism (besides *The Birth of Tragedy* only *Richard Wagner in Bayreuth* [1876] would count as a pro-Wagnerian main work), but the precise titles are not known. Seidl does remark elsewhere, however, that while Strauss would take the title of his newest tone poem from *Also sprach Zarathustra*, the subject matter of the work would be drawn from *Human, All Too Human* (1878).

This apparently insignificant remark actually provides perhaps the most important bit of information in the historical record. *Human, All Too Human* embodied the crucial turning point in Nietzsche's life, the moment at which he recognized what he believed to be the fallacy in Wagner's artistic project and rejected Wagnerism unequivocally. Though Wagner is not mentioned in the book, he is evoked by every reference to the "artist," as was perfectly clear to Wagner when he received his copy from Nietzsche and declared that he would do the philosopher the favor of not reading it. Thus the book marked the end of their relationship, and for Strauss it served a similar function. Here Strauss could find, clearly stated and with unparalleled eloquence, precisely those conclusions at which he had only recently arrived through his study of Schopenhauer: "No music is in itself deep and full of meaning. It does not speak of the 'Will' or the 'thing in itself.'" And beyond that recognition, Nietzsche began to show how one could move toward a confident rejection of metaphysics altogether. A person's educational development, in Nietzsche's view, involved moving "beyond superstitious and religious concepts and fears," and ultimately demanded "a last intense effort to overcome metaphysics." In the aftermath of *Guntram*, Strauss saw this effort as his last obstacle to artistic maturity.[42]

In Nietzsche's writings the overcoming of metaphysics elicited a special kind of rhetoric, complete with a jargon designed to focus perception on the *diesseits* (the world of our experience). Not only original Nietzschean terms, such as the *eternal recurrence*, but also specific interpretations of words like *objectivity* and *becoming* hovered around a self-consciously forward-looking worldview in which fulfillment, and even a kind of alternate *Erlösung*, could be found in the here and now. Many of these terms can be found echoing in Strauss's correspondence and personal notes around this time. In a letter to Strauss of 9 April 1893, Rösch quotes Strauss as having praised Nietzsche, at Schopenhauer's expense, for his grasp of the value of objectivity. Though Rösch did not share Strauss's high appraisal of Nietzsche (and claimed to have formed his opinion on substantial experience with Nietzsche's texts, especially "the latest ones"), he did concede that his friend seemed thoroughly convinced, saying "the will to power seems to have had particular success with you." Yet he also noted a certain apprehension in Strauss, who had observed with alarm that (here again Rösch quoted Strauss) "over such objectivity the first trail-blazer, Nietzsche, has gone insane."[43]

The notion of "becoming" also finds a prominent place in notes written by Strauss in early 1893. In a private travel diary in which he voiced his strongest objections to Schopenhauer, Strauss also registered his newfound Nietzschean optimism. Fulfillment was now to be found in "affirmation of the Will," in "the consciousness of *eternal being* in the eternally new, never-ending *becoming*."[44] Though he does not use the phrase *eternal recurrence*, he circles around it closely enough to confirm his engagement with the concept. And in a remarkable display of sensitivity as a reader, Strauss managed to uncover a passage in *The World as Will and Representation* in which Schopenhauer adumbrates the eternal recurrence by imagining the state of mind of an individual who faced a future in which the same circumstances replicated themselves without end.[45] This discovery certainly delighted him, for it provided another instance in which Schopenhauer's own text could be used as a rhetorical weapon against Schopenhauerian philosophy (or Strauss's perception of it).

The Nietzschean musings in this diary also contain a number of strong positive statements regarding sexuality, including the remarkable assertion that "affirmation of the Will must properly be called affirmation of the body."[46] The open, even graphic, sexual tendencies of Strauss's music must have some relationship to these ideas, though what he found in Nietzsche undoubtedly confirmed a predisposition—as *Don Juan*, composed in 1888, makes clear. Much the same could be said about this entire period of philosophical activity, however; at the bottom what he wanted to accomplish was to find intellectual justification or grounding for artistic tendencies that grew from instinct.

One might say the same thing about certain doubts and uncertainties that plagued him as he produced his first new works after the rejection of Schopenhauer. The fear inherent in unmooring oneself from belief in a metaphysical reality became a central theme in the second cycle of tone poems (*Till Eulenspiegel, Also sprach Zarathustra, Don Quixote*, and *Ein Heldenleben*), in several cases taking the Nietzschean label *Ekel* (disgust). In *Also sprach Zarathustra*, Nietzsche had described *Ekel* as a periodic, recurring experience of dread—a kind of failure of optimism, and an unavoidable symptom of being human (as opposed to "superhuman," to use a proper translation of *Übermensch*). This mental state figures explicitly in the programs of *Also sprach Zarathustra* and *Ein Heldenleben*, standing as the principal antagonizing force to be combatted by the protagonists.[47] In both cases it is an "inner enemy," and one senses that it was an enemy that Strauss engaged in his own personal life as well.

What emerges from this detailed survey of the philosophical issues engaged by Strauss as he emerged into maturity is a picture of a young composer determined to find an intellectual position that he deemed adequate to ground a body of musical works in the post-Wagnerian world. He did not study philosophy systematically, and he certainly had no intentions of disseminating his observations, even among his inner circle. But to proceed with his creative activity he felt he had to work through these issues. The creative standstill to which Strauss came in the years 1889 to 1892 shows the seriousness of his dilemma better than any documentary evidence. Though we often assume that Strauss spent the years between *Tod und Verklärung* and *Till Eulenspiegel* (1895) working on *Guntram*—and therefore steadily composing—in fact Strauss did not begin composing the opera until 1892. For some three years, then, he produced no music, aside from a few Lieder, and thus endured one of the longest creative lulls of his career. In a sense, though, that lull made possible all that came after it.

Considered in light of his fundamentally Goethean creative outlook and the narrowly circumscribed intellectual dilemma underlying his interest in Nietzsche, Strauss's choices of poets in his Lieder and choral works seem both thoughtful and coherent. Certainly a process, parallel to that of his other creative and intellectual activity, can be traced in the body of poetry that he chose. Between the 1870s and 1890s his poetic tastes shifted from formal conservatism to experimentation, from abstract Romantic obscurity to preoccupation with the everyday modern world, from nationalist sentimentalism to determined concentration on the future, from cozy lyricism to uncompromising critique. Here, as in the other dimensions of Strauss's life, his activity was defined by a steady process in which critical evaluation of the past yielded a vision of artistic originality.

Strauss's Lieder of the 1870s avoided the major figures of German poetry (with the exceptions of the two early Goethe songs I have already
discussed) in favor of the comfortable conservatism of poet-scholars like
Johann Ludwig Uhland (1787–1862) and August Heinrich Hoffmann von
Fallersleben (1798–1874). Uhland, a professor at Tübingen and an important figure in the development of German medieval studies, kept to the
classical poetic formal ideal established by Goethe and Schiller, and made
use of the full range of Romantic images and idioms. Likewise, Fallersleben,
a philologist and literary historian whose nationalist sentiments found their
most successful expression in the poem "Deutschland, Deutschland über
alles" (Germany, Germany Over All), produced attractive poems in an un-
complicated, traditional Romantic idiom. The idea of "traditional
Romanticism," of course, hints at certain weaknesses. While both poets
showed a sound grasp of the typical themes of Romanticism—the plucking
of a rose; the wanderer going to his grave; the unique, uncorrupted perceptive powers of children; the forlorn lover seeking comfort in nature; the
strange power of dreams (to cite examples from the poems chosen by
Strauss)—they were unable or unwilling to imbue their poems with the
kind of sophistication, the compulsion to figurative interpretation, that is
characteristic of the best Romantic poetry. Indeed, much of this poetry is
ruthlessly flat, seemingly designed to prevent reading at any but the basic
foreground level. And while that feature may have been an advantage for a
precocious teenager trying his hand at song composition for the first time,
it did not satisfy him for long.

Fallersleben's connections with the student movement eventually cost
him his post at the University of Breslau, the immediate cause being the political content of his optimistically titled *Unpolitische Lieder* (Unpolitical
Songs, 1840–41). In that light, Strauss seems almost reactionary in having
turned next to the poetry of Emanuel Geibel (1815–84) and his school of
popular, traditionalist poets based in Munich. In addition to two poems
by Geibel, Strauss set the works of Geibel protégés Adolf Friedrich von
Schack (1815–94), Felix Dahn (1834–1912), Karl Stieler (1842–85), Hermann Lingg (1820–1905), and Friedrich Martin von Bodenstedt (1819–92).
The only member of the circle whose poetry Strauss did not set was Paul
Heyse (1830–1914), whose works would be so important to Hugo Wolf
(1860–1903).[48] Strauss's intense occupation with this school bears witness
to his upper bourgeois roots, and it may confirm his sister's testimony that
his poetic choices were sometimes affected by family members. By any standard the Geibel circle must be regarded as a conservative, palatable
alternative to the ideas of Young Germany, particularly that movement's
radical critique of Romanticism and nationalism in favor of increased

attention to issues of social and political justice. That Strauss could have found himself on the side of banal bourgeois *Spätromantik* (late Romanticism) in the mid-1880s, when by the mid-1890s he would have so thoroughly renounced that position, testifies eloquently to the speed of his intellectual growth during this period.

Strauss's two preferred poets from this group, Dahn and Schack, were accomplished thinkers in their own right. Dahn, having studied law and philosophy in Munich and Berlin, taught jurisprudence at the universities of Munich, Würzburg, Königsberg, and Breslau, where he was appointed rector in 1895. Equally well-known as a novelist, he produced popular historical novels of dubious aesthetic value. Count von Schack too had academic impulses, writing an important introduction to art and culture in Moorish Spain (*Poesie und Kunst der Araber in Spanien und Sicilien* [Arab Poetry and Art in Spain and Sicily, 1872]) and assembling a well-known collection of late Romantic German painting. Despite their scholarly activities, however, for both figures the act of poetic creation, at least in those works chosen by Strauss, seldom aspired to more than the charming. Stanzas such as the following, from Dahn's "Du meines Herzens Krönelein" (You, the Pride of My Heart), leave no doubt that the exclusive goal is a sense of modesty, ease, delightfulness:

> Du meines Herzens Krönelein,
> Du bist von lautrem Golde,
> Wenn andere daneben sein,
> Dann bist du noch viel holde.
>
> [You, the pride of my heart,
> you are of pure gold,
> compared with all others,
> you are still very beautiful.]

The avoidance of pretension can itself be pretentious in this poetry, and perhaps that is the point. In any case, Strauss required nothing more than attractive love poetry, and the music it elicited from him leads one not to question too severely the literature that inspired it. No better evidence of this truth could be found than the Op. 10 set, in which the beauty and inventiveness of the music lifted the sentimental lyricism of Hermann von Gilm (1812–64) far above itself.

With the advent of the 1890s, however, Strauss made an about-face that could hardly have been more radical. The poets that he chose for the Op. 27 set, and those of the bulk of his songs through the beginning of the new century, represented an active and aggressive opposition to the traditionalism and epigonism of the likes of Geibel, Dahn, and Schack. This change in poetic taste is in fact no less extreme than Strauss's almost concurrent transformation from ardent Brahmsian (his "*Brahmsschwärmerei*" [Brahms enthusiasm], as he called it, peaked in the fall of 1885) to young "Musician of the Future." And though the grounds of the poetic controversy lay somewhat outside Strauss's professional area of expertise, he certainly recognized that there existed an area of nexus between the debates, particularly in the area of form. If all of Strauss's favored poets through the end of the 1880s shared a rigorous faith in the continuing viability of classical poetic forms, the poets to whom he now turned agreed that those forms had to be overturned at all costs.

The three poets of Op. 27 (1894), Karl Henckell (1869–1929), John Henry Mackay (1864–1933), and Heinrich Hart (1855–1906), were central figures in the introduction of Naturalism into German literature.[49] They also belonged to Strauss's generation, and like Strauss they argued against a role for moral judgment in art, instead focusing on poetry as a faithful, undifferentiating representation of reality. Hart, along with his brother Julius (1859–1930), was a founding member of the Freie Bühne (Free Stage), whose performances of Ibsen and Hauptmann marked the apex of German Naturalism. Mackay was less known as a poet than as the biographer of the philosopher Max Stirner (1806–56), whose individualist anarchism he attempted to wield in combination with naturalism on behalf of a radical socialism. Henckell too thought of himself as a social revolutionary/poet, though he would later move more aggressively in the direction of German Impressionism than the others.

It is hard to imagine Strauss having much practical sympathy for the socialist agenda of these figures. Likewise, the focus in Naturalism on scientific determinism, on the human as helpless victim of physiology and environment, contained a pessimism antithetical to Strauss's natural disposition. He did share with them, however, a fascination with instinct and with the notion that human lives were lived among, and controlled by, forces belonging distinctly to the physical realm, the here and now. Strauss's choices for Op. 27 reflect as much: Henckell's "Ruhe, meine Seele!" (Rest, My Soul) and Mackay's "Morgen" (Morning) frame the set with references to the sun as a healing power, treating it in much the same way as Nietzsche's *Also sprach Zarathustra*, where for Strauss it symbolized a healthy, optimistic alternative to metaphysical delusion. (Strauss was to begin work on *Also sprach Zarathustra* the following year.) When Strauss met Mackay in 1892 he referred to him in a letter to his father as "the most significant antagonist of Schopenhauer and Christianity";[50] he obviously considered him an intellectual ally of

Nietzsche, then, and would not have overlooked the similarities in their deployment of a prominent symbol of "objectivity." The middle poems, on the other hand—Heinrich Hart's "Cäcilie" and Mackay's "Heimliche Aufforderung" (Secret Invitation)—deal with love, but using a wealth of detail to emphasize its physical, sensual aspects: "burning kisses," "caressing and talking," a "soft mouth," "lips," "breast," "hair," and so forth. The effect is to link the two principal facets of Strauss's private response to his metaphysical crisis, as outlined in the travel diary of 1893: the abandonment of metaphysical spirituality and the celebration of the physical through sexuality.

That a composer theorizing in the 1890s a new form of *Erlösung* in sexual experience would have been interested in Richard Dehmel (1863–1920) almost goes without saying. Dehmel's first collection, *Erlösungen* (1891), dealt with the tension between sexuality and asceticism, and thus treated an issue remarkably close to the fundamental dramatic conflict of *Guntram*. With his sometimes overblown expression of the mystical power of love and sex, and more basically with his frank treatment of sexual issues, Dehmel worked squarely within the aesthetic territory occupied by Strauss. (Dehmel's interest in having Strauss set his poetry may reflect a recognition of this common ground, but it may also simply show his awareness of the meteoric rise of Strauss's reputation.) Strauss's selections from Dehmel tend to focus on the family, however, with such poems as "Der Arbeitsmann" (The Working Man), "Lied an meinen Sohn" (Song to My Son), and "Befreit" (Released). For Strauss, sexuality reached its redemptive potential in the context of a stable family relationship—which is not to say that it disappeared, but that it found liberation within strict containment, as in the love scene from *Symphonia domestica*. Thus Dehmel, like so many other of Strauss's poets, was subjected to a highly idiosyncratic molding process for purposes that only Strauss fully understood.

In the poetry of two other modernists, Detlev von Liliencron (1844–1909) and Otto Julius Bierbaum (1865–1910), Strauss found other aesthetic tendencies sympathetic to his own. In Liliencron, vividness of expression and accuracy of detail formed a complement to the photographic representationalism toward which Strauss was pushing his orchestral idiom. "Ich liebe dich" (I Love You), for example, which Strauss set as Op. 37, No. 2, creates emotional power with details that draw the reader toward the physical level of experience:

> Es bluten die Hände
> Die Füsse sind wund
> Vier trostlose Wände
> Es kennt uns kein Hund

[Our hands are bleeding
our feet are sore
four dreary walls enclose us
no dog knows us]

Materiality comes to the forefront, without compromising expressivity—
indeed, expressivity heightens as the focus becomes more precise. All of
Strauss's choices from Liliencron deal with love, and they all approach it
through a language of hyper-precision, in which the carefully described
detail stands for intensity of experience.

Bierbaum might be called even more of a kindred spirit, and it is not surprising to find his work later inspiring Strauss's collaborator on *Feuersnot*
(1901), Ernst von Wolzogen, whose *Überbrettl* grew from a Bierbaum novel.
Bierbaum's fondness for using old poetic styles (Minnesang, Rococo, Bieder-
meier, *Anakreontik*, the *Volkslied*) while maintaining ironic distance points the
way toward crucial features of Strauss's work in the twentieth century. In flitting back and forth between Naturalism, Impressionism, and Decadence,
rather than moving through them directionally, Bierbaum lived out a new
conception of style that was to become fundamental in Strauss's music at least
from *Der Rosenkavalier* on. As much as the irony, however, Strauss was fascinated, as he was in Liliencron, with the ability of physical details to elicit a
kind of heightened experience, as in "Nachtgang" (A Walk by Night):

Wir gingen durch die stille, milde Nacht,
Dein Arm in meinem, dein Auge in meinem.
Der Mond goss silbernes Licht über dein Angesicht,
Wie auf Goldgrund ruhte dein schönes Haupt.
Und du erschienst mir wie eine Heilge,
Mild, mild und gross und seelenübervoll,
Heilig und rein wie die liebe Sonne.

[We walked through the quiet, mellow night,
your arm in mine and your eyes looking into mine.
The moon poured silver light over your face,
and your fair head seemed to be haloed in gold.
And you seemed to me like a saint,
gentle, gentle and great and brimming soul,
holy and pure as the dear sun.]

This poem once again demonstrates Strauss's highly sensitive attraction to
the sun as a symbol of the heightened physical experience that he saw as a

modern, twentieth-century alternative to the outdated *Erlösung* of Wagner
and his Romantic ancestors. The abatement of Strauss's Lieder composition
shortly after the turn of the century coincided with his wife's retirement
from performance, but also with an apparent relaxation of those creative
tensions that had necessitated association with poetry of revolutionary tendency. Strauss did not stop composing Lieder altogether, and those that he
did write drew more and more on the works of indisputably great German
poets of the nineteenth century, particularly Goethe and Friedrich Rückert (1788–1866). Still, however, the themes that he chose lay squarely within
the concerns that had occupied him during the 1890s, when he had struggled to find a role for music in a world devoid of hope in the kind of
spiritual dimension that was in a sense the raison d'être of nineteenth-century German music. The Rückert songs of 1929, Op. 87, contemplate the
approach of old age, and therefore of death, but build toward a consolation
represented by sunshine. Now, as Strauss looked back on a long, successful
creative life and saw it reaching its natural conclusion, he found comfort
in the image that had given him something positive for which to strive after
he had destroyed his old idols:

> Ich geh, die süsse Müdigkeit des Lebens
> Nun auszuruhn,
> Die Lust, den Gram der Erde nun auszuheilen
> Im Sonnenschein.
>
> [I go, the sweet fatigue of life
> to rest away,
> the joy, the grief of earth to render healed
> in the sunshine.]

The placement of this song, "Im Sonnenschein" (In the Sunshine), as the
fourth in the set suggests that Strauss continued to regard the sun as symbolic of an alternative to traditional religious devotion, a view he had held
since *Also sprach Zarathustra*. In fact he had already explored what he considered Rückert's similar religious disposition before the turn of the century.
In 1898, only two years after producing the sickly sweet, ironic A-flat representation of the *Anbetung* (worship) practiced by the *Hinterweltlern*
(backwoodsmen) in *Also sprach Zarathustra*, Strauss set Rückert's "Anbetung," a poem that reconstrues that term by dwelling on the bodily features
of a beloved woman. Other such Nietzsche–Rückert connections are not
difficult to find among the poems that Strauss selected; for example, Op. 46,
No. 4, "Morgenrot" (Sunrise), draws the metaphysical back down to the

physical ("Die Himmel dreh'n um Liebe sich, / Die Liebe dreht sich nur um dich" [The heavens revolve around love / and love only revolves around you]), in a poem equating redemption with love, symbolized by the sun.

Of Strauss's some fifteen works to texts by Goethe, only four were composed before 1900. The centrality of Goethean ideas to his worldview (as I have discussed) thus manifested itself rather late, after a long period of maturation that engaged poetry of wide-ranging subject matter, technique, and quality. The emergence of Goethe as a principal poetic interest reveals a process of concentration, or one might say purification, in which Strauss recast the nineteenth-century debates about the nature and purpose of music in universal terms, that is, in terms relevant on a fundamental human level. The study of Nietzsche, who could treat Plato, Jesus, and Wagner as though they were contemporaries, had convinced him, perhaps more directly than anything in Goethe, that aesthetic questions of any consequence were relevant across the entire span of European history. Following the example of these two panoramic thinkers, Strauss tried in his maturity, which is to say during his career as a successful opera composer, to address issues of general human concern, and thereby to create art that could stand alone outside any particular historical context. It was this goal that established the mysterious productive intimacy that Strauss shared with Hugo von Hofmannsthal.

Looking back on his creative relationship with Hofmannsthal about a year before the latter's death, Strauss saw a positive trajectory, two decades of "good, continuous progress toward perfection."[51] While others might have pointed to a gradual weakening of their powers, or a failure of will to pursue the more challenging facets of their artistic personalities (after *Elektra* [1909], for example), Strauss believed that they had maintained a consistent direction and had done so with increasing effectiveness. Hofmannsthal agreed, and took responsibility for that consistency; he certainly had the more nuanced conception of their work's unique aesthetic qualities, and he steered the collaboration (if in fact he was steering it) with great subtlety. Even as early as 1912 Hofmannsthal could admit that he had actively starved Strauss's "mastery over the dark savage side of life," in favor of subjects that dealt with "purification," which he identified as a fundamentally Goethean quality.[52]

Whatever the extent to which Hofmannsthal controlled their creative direction, a purifying process runs through their entire oeuvre, uniting remarkably divergent works in pursuit of a common goal. The sense in which *Der Rosenkavalier*, *Ariadne auf Naxos*, and *Die Frau ohne Schatten* could all be Goethean is in their critical attitude toward Romanticism in its specific manifestation as nineteenth-century operatic grandeur. On their most basic level these works attempt to counteract, or at least to bring to an end, the

long domination of music by an overblown and outdated Romantic aesthetic. Strauss considered *Der Rosenkavalier* their starting point because it
brought sentimentality and parody to the foreground.[53] Not only did ironic
modes of expression elicit the strongest response from his talents, they represented the most effective way to make a new start in music while bringing
an element of critical judgment to bear on what had come before. *Die Frau
ohne Schatten* did not go far enough in this respect for Strauss, who famously groused, "[L]et's make up our minds that *Frau ohne Schatten* shall
be the last romantic opera."[54] The truth of the matter, though, may have
been that the subtlety of Hofmannsthal's dramatic conception, which
escaped most audiences, also eluded the composer.

The work that hit the bulls-eye, as far as both artists were concerned,
was *Ariadne*, particularly the 1916 revision, which offered Strauss the opportunity to "move forward wholly into the realm of un-Wagnerian
emotional and human comic opera." During work on this crucial composition Hofmannsthal had left no doubt about his antipathy for Wagnerian
style and its aesthetic motivation, and the success of the result convinced
him that of all their works *Ariadne* had the greatest chance to endure.[55]
Hofmannsthal believed consistently, throughout the collaboration, that
the great problem facing them was a musical one—the necessity for the
composer to "leap over his own shadow, his German nineteenth-century
shadow."[56] Few had the ability to face this challenge, in Hofmannsthal's
view, because of its ubiquity in the nineteenth-century culture in which
early-twentieth-century composers were raised. As the quintessential example of late or neo-Romanticism, for example, Hofmannsthal chose
not *Tristan und Isolde* (1859), but its luminous companion piece *Die Meistersinger von Nürnberg* (1867), the very setting of which had decisively
affected Romantics from Ludwig Tieck (1773–1853) to Wagner, "the man
who rounded off the romantic age."[57] This overpowering example, and
everything that drew from it, contained a distillation of a century of aesthetic baggage, and retained a virtually unbreakable hold on the imag-
inations of German composers.

The most successful opera that took *Die Meistersinger von Nürnberg* as
a model was, of course, *Der Rosenkavalier* but that allusiveness functions
within and draws attention to a critique of the model. Hofmannsthal referred to it as "our *Figaro*," implying that he wanted a direct engagement
with the eighteenth century, an end-run around the intervening era. He
took great care to ensure that Strauss followed him on the level of musical
style, demanding set numbers and secco recitative, that is, something that
would "resemble more closely the older type of opera rather than *Meistersinger* or *Feuersnot*." Instead of "erotic screaming," he wanted a "sweet and

saucy" Viennese waltz, whereby the drama could play out in a pre-Wagner-ian atmosphere while working out issues and concerns of the post-Wagnerian world.[58] Strauss's instincts pushed him in less subtle directions, even toward operetta, but Hofmannsthal had something entirely novel in mind: a work that used historicism to facilitate the juxtaposition of histor-ically nonadjacent eras. Nor would he limit the idea to this particular work; during preliminary planning for *Die Frau ohne Schatten* he described just this sort of approach, envisioning "a romantic opera of the old type and yet something that could have been thought of only today."[59]

Creating a work of the present day involved admitting that certain pos-sibilities no longer existed. Strauss yearned to write operetta for more reasons than simply wanting to make people laugh; he felt that the spirit of operetta might be the only mode of drama that could survive in a world that had rendered dramatic tragedy obsolete. Already during the First World War he concluded as much: "And since my tragic vein is more or less ex-hausted, and since tragedy in the theatre, after this war, strikes me at present as something rather idiotic and childish, I should like to apply this irre-pressible talent of mine—after all, I'm the only composer nowadays with some real humour and a sense of fun and a marked gift for parody."[60] It was in this letter that Strauss made his famous claim to be the "Offenbach of the twentieth century," a wish that once again reflects his solid determination to bring the world of music and musical drama into distinctly new territory. In Offenbach, Strauss saw a composer who had cleverly and deliberately cut grand opera down to size by satirizing its grandiloquence. Now he meant to do the same to Wagner, for the good of music's future and out of a sense of intellectual conviction and responsibility.

The present day for Hofmannsthal demanded historical heterogeneity because nineteenth-century dramatic historicism had rendered obsolete the kind of idealized drama that had been possible in the eighteenth century. Whereas Goethe, for example, had been able to employ the dress and decor of antiquity to evoke an eternal or timeless atmosphere, the nineteenth-cen-tury insistence on historical accuracy had made it impossible for subsequent eras to create the same effect with a unified approach to staging. The answer was to de-historicize historically marked material by undermining its his-torical precision—that is, "to gather together heterogeneous elements and by their combination to suggest remoteness, mystery, grandeur and reli-gious feeling."[61] This crucial function served by heterogeneity in their art led Hofmannsthal to identify their roots not in "(North-German) roman-ticism" but in "the Bavarian Austrian baroque with its mixture of different elements and their fusion in music." Hofmannsthal had little interest in re-lating his work directly to the petty aesthetic debates of the day, however;

what he hoped to accomplish through the process of idealization was to produce art somehow immune to the passage of time and the contextual-izing or limiting force of history.[62] In other words, he meant to bring about a new mode of sacralized art, one appropriate to a world that had seen the collapse of Wagner and all he stood for, and one that had assimilated the thought of Nietzsche.

The closest they came to traditional religious content was in *Josephs-legende* (1914), a work that stretched Strauss's patience to the breaking point. The difficulty he had in identifying with the "God-seeker" Joseph sti-fled his creativity, and though he gave in and managed to bring forth a product, he considered the entire undertaking "atavistic." Hofmannsthal's response shows remarkable imagination and a genuine belief in the survival of sacred feeling in a post-Christian world. As always, he conceived the drama symbolically, with Joseph representing not piety in the traditional sense, or even God, but intellectual purity, which Hofmannsthal compared to a mountain atmosphere. Even Hofmannsthal lacked the language to cap-ture in a few words the quality he intended—though he tried with phrases such as "lone, pure ecstasy," "unattainable brightness," "a little piece of heaven"—but he did succeed in communicating that his idea had nothing to do with an orthodox God, but rather encapsulated something new that could now be called by the old name.[63] Hofmannsthal rightly imagined that *Eine Alpensinfonie* (1915), still some three years from completion and known to him only by title and general subject matter, engaged these same issues. What he envisioned there as an "upward surge, the soaring to-wards?—well, towards 'God'" had not proceeded nearly as far in a process of resacralization, however, as Hofmannsthal believed, at least in the sense that a state of experience toward which the work strove could be called God. Strauss remained devoted in 1912, as he would throughout his collabora-tion with Hofmannsthal, to the physical and the everyday not as a transfigured version of itself, but for its own sake.

Strauss and Hofmannsthal shared a fundamental belief that their best hope for personal immortality lay in the creation of lasting works of art. Hofmannsthal's stated goal for *Die Frau ohne Schatten*—to produce some-thing that "when compared with Da Ponte's, Goethe's, Wagner's output, will prove itself true and genuine"—could stand as a motto for their entire oeu-vre.[64] After his librettist's death, Strauss seems to have recognized that his window of opportunity for reaching that goal was closing. He continued working, and he produced music the high quality of which is only now being fully recognized, but at the bottom his continued output conveys the simple truth that he did not know how to live without working. Always a reflective artist with a keen sense of his own character and historical position, Strauss in his latter years increasingly contemplated his final position in the European tradition, and this speculation ushered in a period of sentimental revisionism in his worldview.

During and after the Second World War, sentimentality was for Strauss both a way of coping with the self-destruction of his homeland and a candid assessment of the state of the culture that had produced him. With a return to the absolute genres through which he learned the craft of composition, Strauss could forget the political present by burying himself in the artistic past. (His characterization of these works as "wrist exercises" is accurate insofar as it confirms that he wrote them for purposes extending beyond musical creation.) That *Capriccio* (1941) more or less explicitly renounced any connection to politics only shows just how deeply troubling Strauss found the everyday realities of his time. But what bothered him most was what he perceived as the end of Western culture, the violent and preventable demise of a period of cultural development spanning millennia. It concerned him enough that he spoke publicly about it in 1944 (at the dress rehearsal of *Die Liebe der Danae* [1940]), with a forthrightness few others would have dared at that historical moment. Such recklessness, from a notoriously cool artist, shows just how deeply he feared that his entire life's work would have been for nothing.

Strauss's assessments of his own importance in the history of Western art always placed modesty in the foreground, as in his description of himself as a "first-class second-rate composer." He did not mind admitting his relative weaknesses, as long as he could be granted his proper place within a tradition grounded by greater figures. The collapse of the culture, however, threatened his own survival, by undermining the artistic and intellectual context in which his work could be understood. Without Bach, without Mozart, without Wagner, the music of Strauss would neither make sense nor matter. Goebbels's harsh verdict—"You, Herr Strauss, are from yesterday!"—seemed an all too accurate prediction of the post-war cultural environment.[65] In response, Strauss returned to the questions of musical idealism that he had opened and answered as a young man. With the *Metamorphosen*, he wrote his first serious, self-consciously profound instrumental work since *Tod und Verklärung*, composing out a grotesque reverse metamorphosis in which humanity gradually descended to the bestial. In fact the *Metamorphosen* might be seen as a deliberate reversal of the earlier work (and in the same key), with the redemption of an ideal artistic vision undone and replaced by agonizing struggles and death. Such was Strauss's view of what the Nazis were doing to the achievement of the great figures of German culture, above all Goethe, in whose works Strauss's spent more and more time.

The gravity of the situation even drew from Strauss a reconsideration of the musical idealism that he had rejected so decisively in the period immediately following *Tod und Verklärung*. Not unlike E. T. A. Hoffmann, Strauss in his old age managed to interpret Mozart in Romantic terms, comparing the expressive power of *Figaro* to the experience of Plato's Ideas, and praising this incomparable music's ability to penetrate "to the realm of the prototypes." Pursuing this line of thought he went so far as to ascribe Schopenhauerian powers to Mozart's music, claiming that it found a plane of communication "between heaven and earth . . . set free from 'the Will.'"[66] One senses remorse here, even guilt, in the futility of trying to prop up ideas that he had attacked with all his might fifty years earlier. Perhaps he wondered if he were not somehow complicit in the madness that surrounded him, by having once made his own attack on the cultural tradition that was now being destroyed in a much more violent and thoughtless way. His conception of education as a "guardian" signals a newly reactionary stance that acknowledges the short life span of revolutionaries; if he hoped for a kind of immortality through his artistic work, his works depended on the survival of Wagner at least as much as Wagner depended on Goethe and Schiller.[67]

What Strauss could not see, because of the immediacy and intensity with which he experienced the destruction that surrounded him, was that the aesthetic positions that he now tried to renounce amounted to more than thoughtless iconoclasm perpetrated by a wild revolutionary. The desacralization that figured so prominently in his early work prefigured and participated in a sea of change in European culture, but it did not destroy that culture itself. By helping to introduce a new conception of music, Strauss altered the direction of European aesthetics without destroying the traditional mechanisms of discussion and interpretation. Those extended beyond his oeuvre and his art; they survived wars and whatever obstacles stood arrayed against them. Unfortunately, Strauss's life span, long though it was, did not allow him sufficient time and perspective to recognize the meaning of his own contribution.

NOTES

1. Strauss regularly exchanged recommendations of historical monographs with Hugo von Hofmannsthal; see Franz Strauss and Alice Strauss, with Willi Schuh, eds., *The Correspondence between Richard Strauss and Hugo von Hofmannsthal*, trans. Hanns Hammelmann and Ewald Osers (Cambridge: Cambridge University Press, 1980), 302, 354, 396. For Alma Mahler's account of a discussion between Gustav Mahler and Strauss of Theodor Mommsen's *Römische Geschichte*,

see Alma Mahler, *Gustav Mahler: Memories and Letters*, ed. Donald Mitchell, trans. Basil Creighton (New York: Viking, 1969), 51.

2. An honest self-assessment of his strengths and weaknesses as a student may be found in the "Letter on the 'Humanistische Gymnasium,'" in Richard Strauss, *Recollections and Reflections*, ed. Willi Schuh, trans. L. J. Lawence (London: Boosey and Hawkes, 1953), 89.

3. *Bildung*, of course, involves much more than formal education; a more appropriate translation might be "personal development," in a broad sense encompassing intellectual, cultural, artistic, and spiritual concerns.

4. On the nineteenth-century history of the Gymnasium, see James C. Albisetti, *Secondary School Reform in Imperial Germany* (Princeton, N.J.: Princeton University Press, 1983), 16–56; Marjorie Lamberti, *State, Society, and the Elementary School in Imperial Germany* (New York: Oxford University Press, 1989), 13–87; and Herwig Blankhertz, *Bildung im Zeitalter der grossen Industrie: Pädagogik, Schule und Berufsbildung im 19. Jahrhundert* (Berlin: Schroedel, 1969).

5. Jacob Burckhardt, *The Civilization of the Renaissance in Italy*, trans. L. Goldscheider (London: Phaidon, 1995), 92–93.

6 Wilhelm's speech appears in edited form in *Schalthess' Europäischer Geschichtskalender* (1890): 174–79.

7. Willi Schuh, *Richard Strauss: A Chronicle of the Early Years, 1864–1898*, trans. Mary Whittall (Cambridge: Cambridge University Press, 1982), 54–56.

8. Ibid., 41, 54.

9. Rösch letters are held at the Richard-Strauss Archiv, Garmisch-Partenkirchen (hereafter RSA).

10. Strauss, "Letter on the 'Humanistische Gymnasium,'" 93.

11. This discussion is based on ibid., 89–93.

12. The topics of his coursework are given by Max Steinitzer, *Richard Strauss* (Berlin: Schuster and Loeffler, 1911), 27. Strauss's comment comes from "Meine Freunde und Förderer meines Werkes," an unpublished manuscript in the RSA.

13. Personal communication, Richard Strauss (Strauss's grandson), Garmisch-Partenkirchen, 24 June 1994.

14. This diary is held at the RSA.

15. Strauss and Strauss, *Richard Strauss und Hugo von Hofmannsthal*, 340.

16. The sketches for this moment quote material from the Earth Spirit's speech. See the discussions in John Williamson, *Strauss: "Also sprach Zarathustra"* (Cambridge: Cambridge University Press, 1993), 64–66; Walter Werbeck, *Die Tondichtungen von Richard Strauss. Dokumente und Studien zu Richard Strauss*, Bd. 2. (Tutzing: Hans Schneider, 1996), 142; and Charles Youmans, "The Private Intellectual Context of Strauss's *Also sprach Zarathustra*," *Nineteenth Century Music* 22 (1998): 117.

17. Strauss and Strauss, *Richard Strauss und Hugo von Hofmannsthal*, 121.

18. See Timothy L. Jackson, "The Metamorphosis of the *Metamorphosen*: New Analytical and Source-Critical Discoveries," in *Richard Strauss: New Perspectives on the Composer and His Work* ed. Bryan Gilliam (Durham, N.C.: Duke University Press, 1992), 93–142.

19. Walter Thomas Anderman, *Bis der Vorhang fiel: Berichtet nach Aufzeich-nungen aus den Jahren 1940 bis 1945* (Dortmund: K. Schwalvenberg, 1947), 241.

20. Bryan Gilliam, *The Life of Richard Strauss* (Cambridge: Cambridge University Press, 1999), 183.

21. Richard Strauss, "On Inspiration in Music," in *Recollections and Reflections,* ed. Willi Schuh, trans. L. J. Lawrence (London: Boosey and Hawkes, 1953), 116.

22. Strauss and Strauss, *Richard Strauss und Hugo von Hofmannsthal,* 259.

23. In his edition of Schopenhauer Strauss highlighted the following passage, from book 4 of *The World as Will and Representation:* "A man . . . who desired, in spite of calm deliberation, that the course of his life as he had hitherto experienced it should be of endless duration or of constant recurrence . . . would stand 'with firm, strong bones on the well-grounded, enduring earth' [a quotation from Goethe's *Grenzen der Menschheit*], and would have nothing to fear." See Arthur Schopenhauer, *The World as Will and Representation,* trans. E. F. J. Payne (New York: Dover, 1969), 4:283–84.

24. Reinhold Schlötterer, *Die Texte der Lieder von Richard Strauss* (Pfaffenhofen: W. Ludwig, 1988), 54–66.

25. On the reception of progressive drama in Munich circa 1890, see Peter Jelavich, *Munich and Theatrical Modernism* (Cambridge: Harvard University Press, 1985), 11–52.

26. Translations of poetry in this chapter are adapted from those by Geoffrey Watkins et al. in *The Songs of Richard Strauss,* E.M.I. Records, ASD 2622–2627, 1968.

27. Steinitzer, *Richard Strauss,* 68.

28. See Richard Strauss, "Reminiscences of Hans von Bülow," in *Recollections and Reflections,* ed. Willi Schuh, trans. L. J. Lawrence (London: Boosey and Hawkes, 1953), 118–26.

29. Siegmund von Hausegger, *Alexander Ritter* (Berlin: Marquardt, 1907), 12–14.

30. Richard Strauss, "Recollections of My Youth and Apprenticeship," in *Recollections and Reflections,* ed. Willi Schuh, trans. L. J. Lawrence (London: Boosey and Hawkes, 1953), 138.

31. Ibid.

32. Alexander Ritter, "Vom Spanisch-Schönen," *Allgemeine Musikzeitung* 18, no. 10 (1891): 128–29.

33. Alexander Ritter, "Drei Kapitel: Von Franz Liszt, von der 'heiligen Elisabeth' in Karlsruhe, und von unserm ethischen Defekt," *Bayreuther Blätter* 13 (1890): 380–88.

34. Emphasis added. This letter is held in the RSA. A full transcription and translation can be found in Charles Youmans, "Richard Strauss's *Guntram* and the Dismantling of Wagnerian Musical Metaphysics" (Ph.D. diss., Duke University, 1996), 383–98.

35. These issues are discussed extensively in ibid., 130–45.

36. Schuh, *Richard Strauss,* 285.

37. Franz Trenner and Gabrielle Strauss, eds., *Cosima Wagner–Richard Strauss: Ein Briefwechsel,* Veröffentlichungen der Richard-Strauss-Gesellschaft München, Bd. 2. (Tutzing: Hans Schneider, 1978), 150.

38. These materials are held at the RSA.

39. Schuh, *Richard Strauss*, 284.

40. See Trenner and Strauss, *Cosima Wagner–Richard Strauss*, 148–55.

41. Arthur Seidl, "Richard Strauss—Eine Charakterskizze (1896)," in *Straussiana: Aufsätze zur Richard Strauss-Frage aus drei Jahrzehnten* (Regensburg: Gustav Bosse, n.d. [foreword dated 1913]).

42. Friedrich Nietzsche, *Menschliches, Allzumenschliches*, vol. 1, *Nietzsche Werke*, ed. Giorgio Colli and Mazzino Montinari, pt. 4, vol. 2 (Berlin: Walter de Gruyter, 1967), 177, 37.

43. This letter is held at the RSA.

44. Emphasis added. Schuh, *Richard Strauss*, 309.

45. See note 22.

46. Schuh, *Richard Strauss*, 313.

47. Werbeck, *Die Tondichtungen*, 135–47, 161–70, especially 164–65. See also the facsimile from the sketches for *Heldenleben*, mis-transcribed by Schuh in his *Richard Strauss*, 479.

48. On the Geibel circle see Hans N. Fügen, "Geibel und Heyse," in *Dichtung in der bürgerlichen Gesellschaft* (Bonn: Bouvier, 1972), 28–50; and Michail Krausnick, *Paul Heyse und der Münchener Dichterkreis* (Bonn: Bouvier, 1974).

49. The literature on Naturalism is vast; good starting points are York-Gothart Mix, *Naturalismus, Fin de siècle, Expressionismus: 1890–1918* (Munich: C. Hanser, 2000); Theo Meyer, *Theorie des Naturalismus* (Stuttgart: P. Reclam, 1997); and Günther Mahal, *Naturalismus* (Munich: W. Fink, 1990).

50. Schuh, *Richard Strauss*, 258.

51. Strauss and Hofmannsthal, *Correspondence*, 484.

52. Ibid., 121.

53. Ibid., 250–51.

54. Ibid., 259.

55. Ibid., 262, 299.

56. Ibid., 496.

57. Ibid., 433–34.

58. Ibid., 20, 26, 30, 49.

59. Ibid., 74.

60. Ibid., 250.

61. Ibid., 323–24.

62. Ibid., 324, 385.

63. Ibid., 142–43.

64. Ibid., 155.

65. Gilliam, *The Life of Richard Strauss*, 167.

66. Richard Strauss, "On Mozart," in *Recollections and Reflections*, ed. Willi Schuh, trans. L. J. Lawrence (London: Boosey and Hawkes, 1953), 74–75.

67. Richard Strauss, "Remarks on Richard Wagner's Work and on the Bayreuth Festival Theater," in *Recollections and Reflections*, ed. Willi Schuh, trans. L. J. Lawrence (London: Boosey and Hawkes, 1953), 69.

Part II
Instrumental Works

4

Richard Strauss's Tone Poems

Walter Werbeck

HISTORICAL BACKGROUND

No composer has captured audiences with large-scale orchestral program music as much as Richard Strauss: with *Macbeth*, then, in particular, with *Don Juan* and *Tod und Verklärung*, but no less with *Till Eulenspiegel, Also sprach Zarathustra, Don Quixote, Ein Heldenleben*, and finally *Symphonia domestica* and *Eine Alpensinfonie*. His nine tone poems, premiered between 1889 and 1915, have, since then, not only enraptured and inspired their listeners, but also shocked and repelled them, generating in turn fanatic admirers as well as passionate enemies. When a tone poem was performed, violent reactions were the result; his pieces never produced indifference. Strauss himself was pleased about the reception. If until the late 1880s he was hardly known beyond the vicinity of his hometown of Munich, his tone poems catapulted him suddenly to the top of the German avant-garde. The positive echo to the first performances of his tone poems—premieres that, after *Tod und Verklärung*, became outright sensational—contributed much to the recognition of Strauss as Germany's preeminent composer, a stature he retained until old age.

Strauss's successes, of course, were anything but predictable. He had begun composing in 1870 at the age of six, but until the mid-1880s had not dared to go further with his works than the style of Johannes Brahms. Piano pieces, numerous songs, chamber music, and orchestral works of smaller and larger size (including two symphonies) prevailed in his oeuvre. Strauss seemed to settle down at the level of *mittlere Musik*,[1] characterized by solid craftsmanship and by being modeled on Schubert, Mendelssohn, Schumann, and Brahms. The presumption that the young Munich composer would limit himself to this area had to be obvious, since Strauss's father Franz, solo horn player in the Munich Court Orchestra, did everything in his power to commit his talented son to a rather conservative mode of composition, anchored in the works of the classical masters, especially Mozart. Beyond that, Strauss captured the attention and support of Hans von Bülow, who had already observed the young composer for quite a while, initially at the request of the Munich publisher Eugen Spitzweg (Joseph Aibl-Verlag), who occasionally asked Bülow for advice on whether Strauss's works deserved to be published. Bülow, at that time the celebrated leader of the Meiningen Hofkapelle and one of the most well-known German conductors, had publicly renounced his former deities Franz Liszt and Richard Wagner and converted to Brahms. One could assume, therefore, that he advised the young Strauss, along the lines of Strauss's father, against joining the party of Liszt and Wagner and that he steered him toward a future career in Brahmsian waterways. Bülow thought that Strauss's compositions were not really original, but just "well-crafted and good-sounding,"[2] and he was not alone in his assessment. In general, critics praised Strauss's surprisingly mature handling of the sound resources chosen, the masterful technique of instrumentation, as well as the stunning command over traditional instrumental forms, especially the most important and demanding, sonata form. Thematic invention and harmonic substance of his music, however, were judged to be commensurate with the gifts of a talent (not a genius), at the most.

How did it happen that Strauss gave the lie to all such verdicts and predictions and transformed himself, all of a sudden, in the late 1880s into a musical revolutionary who no longer composed symphonies but one-movement programmatic tone poems for large orchestra? Pieces of such nature had been introduced to Germany by Franz Liszt in the 1850s. But his symphonic poems (as he called them) remained extremely controversial and found no successful composers, at least not in Germany, continuing the genre. Instead there seemed to be a return of the traditionally grand form of instrumental music, assuming its premier position in the concert hall and finally pushing Liszt aside—at the latest with the advent of the symphonies of Johannes Brahms propagated so strongly by Bülow. Even Strauss did not object, as late as 1884, when his friend Ludwig Thuille denounced Liszt's Piano Concerto No. 1 "as the most unbelievable rubbish imaginable."[3] Six years later the scene had changed drastically. Now Strauss could not praise Liszt enough—a work such as the *Faust* Symphony was "indescribable" and "magnificent" and "by far the most grandiose accomplishment in the symphonic realm since Beethoven—and, at the same time, full of clarity, deepest expression and most flourishing invention."[4]

The person who steered Strauss's career into entirely new avenues was the composer and violinist Alexander Ritter. Only moderately successful as a composer and performer, Ritter influenced Strauss's development to a degree that hardly can be underestimated. It was Ritter who convinced the young Strauss that he was barking up the wrong tree with his Brahmsian orientation, and that only composing in the Wagnerian vein was meaningful. Ritter also won Strauss over to the idea of conquering the new compositional terrain by way of music dramas (or operas) in (initially) purely instrumental guise. Strauss already had proven his mettle in this area, Ritter argued; what was at stake were no longer symphonies, serenades, or concertos, but orchestra works in which the life and works of heroes played a role, just as in a Wagner opera—hence, program music—and the models in this case were, first and foremost, the symphonic poems of Liszt.

Strauss, of course, knew the operas of Wagner already before the encounter with Ritter. His father participated in performances of Wagner's music in Munich and Bayreuth, and, precisely because his father was appalled by Wagner and his music, it might have been tempting for the adolescent son to investigate it. Furthermore, Bülow may have renounced Wagner's music but not Wagnerian principles of musical interpretation, and he decisively imparted that knowledge to the young Strauss, whom he attracted as his assistant to the court in Meiningen. Strauss had to read Wagner's writings, and, of course, there were discussions of Wagner's music. Still, it was the authority of Ritter who ultimately affected Strauss's conversion to Liszt and Wagner. Ritter's personal connections to both may have played a considerable role in this case: he was the son of the Wagner patroness Julie Ritter; he was married to Franziska Wagner, the master's niece; and in the 1850s he was in close contact with Liszt in Weimar together with Bülow, Raff, and others.

Strauss got to know Ritter at the end of the year 1885 in Meiningen (Strauss conducted the Hofkapelle in which Ritter played the violin) and thus began an apprenticeship that Strauss, ten years later, summarized in a biographical sketch as follows:

Acquaintance with *Alexander Ritter* who, through kind efforts and advice over a long time, turned me finally into a *Zukunftsmusiker* (musician of the future). Until then I had been educated in a strictly classical vein; I had grown up with Haydn, Mozart and Beethoven and, progressing via Mendelssohn, Chopin and Schumann, I had just arrived at Brahms. Ritter opened up to me the art-historical significance

of the music and writings of Wagner and Liszt. To him alone I owe the understanding of these two masters, he showed me the path which I am now able to go
on my own.[5]

How decisive Ritter's influence was can be seen not only in Strauss's
compositions but also in numerous letters. On 2 December 1888, for instance, Strauss wrote to the Slovakian composer Johann Leopold Bella:

Let's abolish the desolate four-movement formula which, since Beethoven's Ninth,
was unable to generate any new content; in the future, the musical content needs
to determine the form, and in this matter Liszt, picking up cues from Beethoven's
Coriolan, Leonore III, etc., has been the guide for the younger generation. I also
began composing by utilizing sonata forms, but, recognizing that nothing truly new
is to be expressed in it, I have completely abolished it. In two grand symphonic
poems, namely *Macbeth* and *Don Juan* (the latter composed after Lenau's splendid poem), I turned completely toward one-movement forms, whereby the
musical-poetic content of my work generated its structure. Generating a specific
new structure with each new work (without becoming formless), however, is more
difficult than to write a passable symphony with the help of the old sonata formula,
which has already been stretched in all directions.... In your B minor Sonata I saw
clearly how a wonderful poetic content struggles to take shape and how it could not
develop fully and clearly in the straitjacket of the four-movement sonata formula.
(For Beethoven this formula was predominantly "form," i.e., the only possible way
to express his thoughts.) For that reason, let's resolve to write "program music" (an
invective only for the ill-disposed), for I believe that Beethoven wrote nothing but
program music, even though he only very rarely informed us about the poetic idea
from which his work was generated.[6]

Thanks to Ritter, Strauss had become a committed Lisztian. Tradition—
this seems to be the necessary conclusion—did not count any longer. Works
with musical-poetic content took its place, one-movement works with individual structures instead of empty and worn-out structural formulas.
According to Strauss, the symphony was passé. Only Beethoven (in his
Ninth, as well as in the *Eroica* and the *Pastoral*) and, walking in his footsteps,
Liszt with his symphonic poems had shown how grand instrumental music
for orchestra could be further developed at all.

But Ritter saw the goal of his protégé not in the composition of tone
poems but of music dramas of the Wagnerian kind. As much as Ritter
revered Liszt, he clearly followed Wagner in the belief that music's future
could only be assured in the joining of word and tone in the music drama.
And since Ritter recognized, with reliable instinct, the compositional power
of the young Strauss, he quickly arrived at the conviction that Strauss alone

was the legitimate heir of Wagner's legacy. "My friendship for you," he remarked in a letter of 1893,

is based on confident expectation. I had recognized in Wagner's work the artistic revelation of the highpoint of philosophical and, at the same time, religious culture. Who is able to continue to build from this zenith? For many years I longingly looked in vain for such a person: Should Wagner's work really not be continued, because there was not one person in the entire German nation able to do it? I pondered this question with painful concern and deep anxiety, until I finally recognized *in you*, dearest friend, the potential that, in my opinion, will enable you to continue Wagner's work *in his spirit*. I cannot express in words the deep and heartfelt joy I felt when I saw how you developed, more and more, an understanding of Wagner's *work*, how you absorbed ... Wagner's world view and made it entirely your own.[7]

There is no doubt that Strauss was completely in line with Ritter, not only in his turn toward Liszt, but also on the issue of Wagner's legacy. Already in 1887 he began to occupy himself with a text for his first music drama, *Guntram*; a true Wagnerian, of course, had to be also his own librettist. However, to be generally accepted as a second Wagner in musical terms as well, it was mandatory to change course in orchestral composition and learn the technique and language of the Lisztian symphonic poem. Strauss, according to Ritter, needed to learn to write music to poetic rather than purely formal contents and to express himself musically in such a way that audiences would clearly understand his poetic contents. In other words, he had to compose one-movement programmatic works for orchestra.

THE WORKS AND THEIR ORIGIN

The First Group (1888–90)

"I was quite diligent lately. I was very successful, I think, with my symphonic poem *Macbeth*, with which I began an entirely new path; now I have devised a one-movement work *Don Juan* for orchestra (after Lenau's poem) and, with both works, entered my very own path to which the Italian fantasy was the bridge."[8] Strauss's letter to his uncle Carl Hörburger of 11 June 1888 makes it clear how strongly the composer himself felt the caesura that separated works such as *Macbeth* and *Don Juan* from earlier orchestral compositions, even the symphonic fantasy *Aus Italien*, Op. 16, a multimovement work with programmatic titles for each movement. Under the guidance of Ritter, Strauss had found "his very own path." That the path was initially full of thorns and that *Macbeth* (in a way, the entrance to this path) was any-thing but "very successful" will become clear.

Strauss began work on *Macbeth* possibly as early as 1886, but the bulk of the work falls into the summer of 1887. The choice of a Shakespeare play, of course, was unthinkable without Liszt, who had accepted only mas-terworks of great artists as subject matter. However, when *Macbeth* was completed on 9 January 1888, Strauss experienced a disappointment: Bülow criticized the piece; he was not pleased especially by its conclusion. "A symphonic poem 'Macbeth,'" Bülow felt (as reported by Strauss), "could not end with the triumph of Macduff."[9] *Macbeth* was revised and got a new ending. But when Strauss played the second version to Bülow in the sum-mer of 1888, it was rejected as well because of the numerous dissonances. This was a hard blow for the young composer, especially since he had al-ready begun the next tone poem, *Don Juan*, and probably conceived of a third, *Tod und Verklärung*. Without Bülow's protection—Strauss knew this as well as his father and his publisher—the new path would perhaps not be condemned to failure, but convincing the public of its viability would be much more difficult.

Thus, Strauss had to be content, for the time being, with performances of his Symphony No. 2 in the winter of 1888–89. There were no public per-formances of the tone poems, neither of *Macbeth* nor of *Don Juan* (a piece he completed at the end of September 1888). But Strauss was not put off. The criticism of Bülow had hit him, but it could not distract him from pur-suing his new course. And the conductor did not drop his support for his disciple. Even though he had doubts about Strauss the composer, Bülow paved the way for Strauss the conductor on the path to a new position as Kapellmeister of the Grand Duke of Weimar. (After his Meiningen ap-pointment Strauss had returned to Munich where he did not feel comfortable.) Thus, important decisions had been made for Strauss's fu-ture. For one, Strauss was able to develop freely in Weimar, arranging concert and opera schedules in a "progressive" manner. And two, since the Weimar chief intendant Hans von Bronsart was also the head of the Allge-meiner Deutscher Musikverein (General German Musicians League; ADMv), Strauss had the opportunity not only to participate in this influ-ential institution but also introduce his own works during its annual meetings to the public-at-large.

It was the successful reception that *Aus Italien* encountered at the Tonkünstlerversammlung (Composers' Convention) in Wiesbaden in June 1889 that intensified the interest in Strauss's newest creations. Six months later, on 11 November 1889, *Don Juan* was premiered in Weimar, only a few days before the completion of *Tod und Verklärung*. Subsequent performances of *Don Juan* in Dresden and Berlin, however, made it clear to Strauss that his music still was not easily understood, and this was true for conductors as well as critics and audiences. Only the overwhelming success of *Tod und Verklärung*—the work was premiered in Eisenach in June 1890, again in the context of an ADMv convention—signified the final breakthrough. Conductors fought for getting a score of the piece, reviewers and audiences were impressed. Strauss wrote to Cosima Wagner that he believed "to have made significant progress also in the choice of subject matter suited for artistic treatment,[10] and, in general, critics praised the realistic manner of expression and great precision in the representation of content.[11] The Viennese music critic Eduard Hanslick drew conclusions from that with a veritable prophesy: "The type of talent really directs the composer toward the music drama."[12] Hanslick did not know that his sentiment expressed openly the secret goal of the efforts of both the composer and the composer's mentor Ritter.

With *Tod und Verklärung* Strauss seemed to have reached the first stage on the way to becoming Wagner's successor. Now the second and decisive step could follow. With joyful confidence Strauss wrote to his publisher Spitzweg on 19 November 1890 concerning the publication of the new tone poem that *Tod und Verklärung* "was the best and most mature . . . composition he had written so far," and mentioned that in all likelihood "he would not compose that way any longer . . . as he had turned away from absolute music to search for his salvation in music drama."[13] And this exactly happened: During a long journey to Greece, Egypt, and Italy, Strauss composed the music to his opera *Guntram*, whose text had occupied him for quite some time; already before the piece had been premiered, he intensified his search for new subjects, since he was convinced that in the future he would produce only operas. But *Guntram* was a failure. The piece disappeared from the scene after only five performances between 10 May and 6 June 1894 in Weimar.

This was a heavy blow. Strauss risked being suffocated, as many other composers of opera, by his model Wagner and by not being taken seriously by the public. On the other hand, his career as composer of brilliant tone poems, which would make him famous, had only just begun. Would it not be wise, in view of the circumstances, to return to the trajectory of success, at least for a while longer, and show off new orchestral winning numbers instead of drawing musico-dramatic blanks?

We do not know whether it was difficult for Strauss to revise his compositional career plan, nor do we know whether he consulted others about it. All evidence points to the fact that he did not need advice from others any longer. His decision was probably made soon after the *Guntram* failure.

In the future he still would search for subjects for the stage, but he would not neglect the genre of the tone poem. Certainly this was not what Ritter had in mind, but Strauss did not need him anymore (aside from the fact that he had a falling-out with Ritter during the composition of *Guntram*). And also his other mentors—Bülow who died in 1894, Cosima Wagner, and his father—had little say in his affairs. The private step toward independence (in the form of his marriage to Pauline de Ahna in May 1894) was followed immediately by a compositional one. He began his second phase as a composer of tone poems—a time in which he would leap from success to success.

The Second Group (1895–1915)

Among the operatic subjects with which Strauss was occupied in 1893–94 after completing *Guntram* was one for a fairy-tale opera: *Till Eulenspiegel bei den Schildbürgern* (Till Eulenspiegel among the Philistines). Strauss even completed a draft for the text of the first act. But instead of composing an opera, he wrote, probably beginning at the end of 1894, a new tone poem: *Till Eulenspiegels lustige Streiche: Nach alter Schelmenweise—in Rondeauform—für großes Orchester gesetzt*. It was completed on 6 May 1895 (but more likely on 6 June). It constitutes a new beginning not only in terms of music (I will discuss this shortly), but in terms of publicity and propaganda as well. Several measures were taken to draw the attention of the public to a greater extent than before to Strauss's work, and these measures, from now on, will accompany, like a ritual, all of the composer's tone poems and their paths into concert life:

- The composition and completion of the new work were announced in the appropriate newspapers and magazines. True, no announcements about the beginning and composing of *Till Eulenspiegel* have come down to us, but the interested public could read about its completion at the end of June in the *Neue Musik-Zeitung*: "*Richard Strauss* has just completed the score of his most recent symphonic poem *Till Eulenspiegel*. Originally conceived as a comic opera, the popular figure is treated now symphonically with his pranks, amorous escapes and catastrophes."[14]
- Strauss published his scores immediately after completion: *Till Eulenspiegel*, for instance, appeared in mid-June 1895. The publication process starts—with later tone poems—even before the

composition was completed. The times of uncertainty about whether his pieces would be accepted for publication was now a matter of the past.

- Even first performances are awarded by Strauss during the composition or shortly after completing the work. On 9 June 1895 he wrote to the conductor of the Gürzenich Concerts in Cologne, Franz Wüllner, that, "with great joy" he would make available to him *Till Eulenspiegel* "for the *first performance* in Cologne."[15] Wüllner indeed premiered the piece on 5 November 1895—half a year after its completion. *Macbeth* took two-and-a-half years from completion to premiere, *Don Juan* one year, *Tod und Verklärung* more than half a year. In the future the time lag between completion and premiere of Strauss's tone poems was three months at the most. Only *Eine Alpensinfonie* was an exception.

- The premieres of the first three tone poems had always been linked to the composer: Strauss himself conducted. This now changed, and, in turn, also the cities of first performances. Now they alternated between Cologne (Gürzenich) and Frankfurt/Main (Museum); only then follow Berlin and Munich. The Cologne premieres (*Till Eulenspiegel, Don Quixote*) were always conducted by Wüllner, the Frankfurt premieres (*Also sprach Zarathustra, Ein Heldenleben*) are prepared by Gustav Kogel, with Strauss coming in as a guest conductor. That changed after *Ein Heldenleben*. The premiere of *Symphonia domestica* took place in New York, *Eine Alpensinfonie* in Berlin; both times Strauss conducted.

The next tone poem, *Also sprach Zarathustra*—in contrast to *Till Eulenspiegel*, which replaced an operatic project—was conceived and composed, in part, together with a singspiel project, namely *Lila*, after a Goethe text. But while he got stuck with his work on *Lila* in the fall of 1895, the new tone poem proved to be more attractive. Already in early December 1895 Strauss could begin with the particell, and thus the second compositional stage. (The *particell*, that is, a draft consisting mostly of two to three notated staves, was usually preceded by more or less detailed sketches; then followed the fair copy of the score—a routine matter for Strauss already early on, but it was not unusual that compositional decisions were still made at this stage. As a rule Strauss began the fair copy of the score while working on the particell or even sketches for the conclusion of the piece.) The score of *Also sprach Zarathustra*, begun on 4 February 1896, was completed on 24 August.

A month and a half later, he jotted down during a journey to Italy on 10 October 1896: "First idea for an orchestral piece Don Quichote, crazy free variations on a knightly theme."[16] There were several projects to which Strauss turned after *Also sprach Zarathustra*, including operas. But again the orchestral works turned out to be the most interesting projects. Besides *Don Quixote* (Strauss picked up the spelling "Quixote" from a Cervantes edition in his library) another project emerged in the spring of 1897 with the working title *Held und Welt* (Hero and World), to which *Don Quixote* would relate as a "satyr play" or "humoristic counterpart."[17] For a long while Strauss composed both pieces at the same time—an indication of how closely they were linked. Only beginning in August 1897 did he focus exclusively on *Don Quixote*, which he completed on 29 December.

The counterpart to *Don Quixote* gained shape from the spring of 1898 onward. The title for the project changed often: from *Held und Welt* via *Heroic* Symphony and *Eroica* to *Heldenleben* and, finally, *Ein Heldenleben*. For a while Strauss worked simultaneously on another tone poem with the working title *Im Frühling* (In Spring), but then he focused exclusively on *Ein Heldenleben*. One year after *Don Quixote*, at the end of December 1898, the piece was finished, after Strauss had revised the conclusion.

After *Ein Heldenleben* Strauss succeeded, for the first time in quite a while, in completing an opera (*Feuersnot*), which was well received. But the preoccupation with tone poems had not yet run its course. In 1902–3 Strauss wrote his *Symphonia domestica*. Only the exceptional success of the next work, *Salome*, and of the next two operas, *Elektra* and *Der Rosenkavalier*, turned the tide for Strauss. After that he remained primarily a composer of operas; from now on only works for the musical theater received almost all of his attention. *Eine Alpensinfonie*, Strauss's ninth tone poem, is, no doubt, an afterthought.

That it was written and completed at all had something to do not only with the symbolic number "nine," but also with biographical circumstances. First drafts had been jotted down by Strauss as early as 1899, but they were meant for a tone poem *Künstlertragödie*, to be dedicated to the memory of the Swiss painter Karl Stauffer. The project fizzled, but parts made it into a new four-movement composition with the title *Die Alpen* whose initial movement became the kernel of the later *Eine Alpensinfonie*. After the work lay dormant for a long time, it received new impetus in May 1911 after the death of Gustav Mahler, an event that moved Strauss deeply. But now Strauss planned a two-part work that he wanted to call *Der Antichrist: Eine Alpensinfonie*. But even this concept was altered: The second part of *Antichrist* was never written, and Strauss dropped the Nietzschean title. What was left was a single grand movement with the title *Eine Alpensinfonie*. The score was completed early in February 1915.

PROGRAM MUSIC

Poetic Idea and Program

Strauss wrote program music with enthusiasm. Prepared through Beethoven's symphonies and later continued by Berlioz and, especially, through Liszt's symphonic poems (whose structures were considered particularly progressive), program music performed by large ensembles seemed to him the only possible form of instrumental music after Wagner. A further development—Ritter and Strauss were clear about that—was possible only by including the orchestral language of Richard Wagner, especially his instrumentation and richly nuanced orchestral polyphony. Creating a synthesis of Liszt's daring structures and Wagner's sonorous textures was, in a way, the music historical mission that Strauss considered it his duty to fulfill. That he was able to quickly convince the professionals with such a strategy is evident from the review of the first Berlin performances of *Don Juan* early in 1890, which the Berlin music critic Otto Lessmann published in his *Allgemeine Musikzeitung*. Following is an excerpt:

Whoever did not want to walk around as an epigone of Beethoven needed to generate something new, to find new forms. This was accomplished not by Mendelssohn, Schumann, or Brahms, but by Liszt when he created the genre of the symphonic poem. One may minimize the musical potency of the composer Liszt, but his great deed of music history remains to have pointed to the new goal toward which instrumental composers of the present and future have to aspire. And *Richard Strauss* has understood this clue. The contributions of Liszt's more significant contemporary *Richard Wagner* made to art are absorbed by Strauss as much as Wagner absorbed Beethoven, and Strauss is justified when he considers himself a child of his time, contributing his share in realizing Wagner's legacy in pure instrumental music.[18]

Connecting to Liszt and Wagner meant also writing music in which every theme and motive, every chord and rhythm, every sonority, even every tone should signify something and should "communicate" something to the listener. The musical work was the composer's medium for aiding him in communicating a definite content to his audience. This content, of course, needed to be already present in the composer's mind during the genesis of the work. "If the artwork . . . is to have a concrete effect on the listener," wrote Strauss in a letter to Bülow in the summer of 1888, "then whatever he wants to communicate needs to be clearly envisioned in his mind."[19] The success of the work of art depends on the composer's ability to communicate his message to the listener; the audience's thoughts are to correspond with the composer's ideas. The audience as re-creator of the art-work, in tune with the composer and his intentions—this is an essentially Romantic conception that connects Strauss via Ritter to the early nineteenth century.

Similarly tinged by Romantic thinking is the closer definition of the content to be communicated. Strauss paraphrases it constantly as "poetic idea," an aesthetic category that already had gained currency in Beethoven's circle, later with Schumann, and, finally, with Liszt and Wagner. The issue it circumscribes is basically always the same: Music that is based on a poetic idea is fantastic, original, and novel and, therefore, completely different from merely superficial-virtuoso, mechanical-formal, and, ultimately, empty play with tones reduced to their acoustical-sensual surface.

The poetic idea cannot be described in words. If, as Strauss was convinced, the poetic idea is represented solely in music as the highest manifestation of all the poetic arts, then it escapes any kind of concretization through words—it remains entirely abstract. What can be grasped in words in whatever form—in other words, what can also be communicated without music—is not the poetic idea.

Strauss, like Liszt, linked the poetic idea closely to extramusical contents. The contents are based in the first two groups of tone poems (*Macbeth* and *Don Juan* as well as *Till Eulenspiegel, Also sprach Zarathustra,* and *Don Quixote*) on literary subjects, in the latter groups (*Tod und Verklärung* and *Ein Heldenleben* as well as *Symphonia domestica* and *Eine Alpensinfonie*) on subjects devised by the composer. Before and during the compositional process these subjects are shaped musically for the compositions—the literary subjects more so than those devised by the composer. Strauss uses all his subjects always with an eye on their musical usefulness and their function in serving the poetic idea.

Inasmuch as Strauss adjusts his subjects to music and music's specific needs, he transforms them into the respective programs. Whatever he jots down about the extramusical content of the work during the compositional process are programmatic ideas, generated both from the subject and from musical conceptions. The program develops from the music as well as from the subject transformed into music. It can be formulated and, by dint of being grasped in words, can aid in comprehending the music. In this respect Strauss follows Liszt, who had similar convictions.

Because the program—be it a title, a heading, or a lengthy text—can be written down, it is not to be confused with the poetic idea, which cannot be expressed in words. Strauss himself did not always observe this distinction. Formulations such as "poetic program" (Romain Rolland) or the note (to Bülow) that the poetic idea could be added to a work as program show sufficiently how close the two central categories of Strauss's aesthetics are.

As diverse as Strauss's programs appear to be, they can be reduced in most cases to a central issue of modern thought, namely, the conflict between individual and society. There is always a hero (and he is always male); he has problems with the rules and norms of society, rebels against them, and, in the process, perishes—the domineering Macbeth as well as the libertine Don Juan who despises marital ethics, the anarchic Till Eulenspiegel as well as Don Quichote who inhabits a fantastic dreamworld. In *Tod und Verklärung*, and even more so in *Ein Heldenleben*, the hero is presented as an artist who is in conflict with the narrow-minded world of Philistines and who will be honored appropriately—again a topos of the nineteenth century—only after his death by posterity.

Strauss soon prevailed as composer; his works filled the concert halls. He certainly was not a misunderstood genius whose path was littered with obstacles. Still, critics have always noted autobiographical features in his programs—especially the numerous self-quotations in *Ein Heldenleben*, functioning as symbols of "The Hero's Works of Peace," as well as those in *Symphonia domestica*, which Strauss dedicated to his wife and son, have been marshaled as evidence. It obviously was not difficult for Strauss to let personal events and experiences influence artistic ideas—however, without turning their musical realizations into sonic autobiography. Differently put, there were autobiographical stimuli, but the works developed according to their own laws. Besides, we should not overlook that in *Symphonia domestica* the son and his education toward becoming an autonomous member of society rather than his creative daddy is the protagonist of the tone poem. In *Also sprach Zarathustra* (and, similarly, in *Eine Alpensinfonie*) the issue is the shaping of human beings through changing societal forces and the attendant conflicts without which individuality cannot be won.

The Function of the Program within the Composition

Strauss has been criticized, again and again, that his tone poems were not really "real" music; they should not be taken seriously because they did not follow their own logic, but could be understood only with the help of their programs. Strauss, the critics argued, was guided during the compositional process by a program, with the program serving as a point of departure and foundation of the composition; music had, thereby, become dependent on extramusical subjects and had degenerated into mere illustration. As evidence they cited, for instance, a statement by Strauss passed on by David Ewen: "I have long since learned that in my composition I am unable to write without a program to guide me."[20] Or they quoted those passages in letters that mention the program as the inspiration for composition.

Indeed, there are programmatic texts for all the tone poems, not written by Strauss himself, but initiated and authorized by him. These texts, of course, were written only after the respective pieces had been completed and, indeed, always for the premieres to serve as listening guides for the audience. Beginning with *Till Eulenspiegel*, brochures appeared, so-called analyses, published separately and functioning as explanatory tracts. But sometimes the concert program contained detailed explanations. In general, the programs could be deduced only from the rather scanty information that Strauss added to the scores and piano reductions, respectively, of the tone poems; from titles and subtitles, in some cases amplified by a poem (*Don Juan, Tod und Verklärung*); or from internal section headings or brief cues (*Macbeth, Don Quixote, Symphonia domestica, Eine Alpensinfonie*).

The nature of the program that guided Strauss during the process of composition cannot be inferred from these meager hints. The full title of *Till Eulenspiegel—Till Eulenspiegels lustige Streiche: Nach alter Schelmenweise, in Rondeauform, für großes Orchester gesetzt*—leads us not only to the source of the subject, the folk legend of Till Eulenspiegel; it also provides us with cues about the structure and ensemble of the piece as well as about its rather humorous tone. It says very little about the exact program; it remains open which pranks of his hero Strauss selected from the folk tale. The more detailed explanatory texts are of some help, because themes, motives, sonorities, and entire sections are deciphered programmatically.

Still, a complete determination of the music is out of the question even here. The program by Strauss's friend Wilhelm Mauke for the first 111 measures of *Till Eulenspiegel* is limited to brief entries with short musical illustrations:

EXAMPLE 4.1.1
Prologue: "Once Upon a Time" There Was a Prankster.

EXAMPLE 4.1.2
Called "Till Eulenspiegel."

EXAMPLE 4.1.3.
He Was Quite a "Mischief Maker."

EXAMPLE 4.1.4
"Onward to New Pranks."

(Note: The words enclosed by quotation marks designate the name of the motive.) The explanatory notes state the following:

There he is, a real-life figure: The jolly-good Till with his funny eyes and precocious face! A mischievous leap! A sarcastic smirk with his hand on his nose! Note the painful chord below the g-sharp, the tragic feature in this conflicted character! Note also the rhythmic distortions in the character motive II [Example 4.1.2]. Can the character be more potently grasped than in motive III [Example 4.1.3]? But this was only the introduction, the presentation. Soon he will give you samples of his activities. Cracking a whip and making funny remarks, he rushes past people who are hustling and bustling at the weekly market—he is planning a prank.[21]

More than an interpretation of the musical examples cannot be derived from the text. How Strauss works with his themes is obviously determined solely by musical laws. Norman Del Mar was right when he characterized the beginning of *Till Eulenspiegel* as a "non-programmatic symphonic exposition."[22] And since Mauke got his information, no doubt, from the composer, we must assume that even Strauss did not have a detailed program for the first hundred measures of the piece.

Such observations are not unique. The density of information in the published explanatory notes varies for all the tone poems. Is there perhaps no complete program dominating the music at all times? Or did Strauss reveal it in part and keep mum about certain details? Was he really guided by a program while composing? How can we imagine what was really going on?

Answers to such questions are provided by studying Strauss's sketches, which have come down to us for all of the tone poems. Sketches and particell permit the following conclusions about the relation between programmatic and musical conception of *Till Eulenspiegel*:

- Strauss begins his work with a plan in which the conflict between Till (F major) and Philistines (A minor) plays a major role—in other words, with a plan that evidently is based on the preceding opera project *Till Eulenspiegel bei den Schildbürgern* (Till Eulenspiegel among the Philistines). The principal themes of Eulenspiegel (Examples 4.1.2 and 4.1 3) and the Philistines (mm.293ff) are firmly established (presumably they were intended for the opera). In addition, Strauss drafts the music for the concluding trial to be preceded by a funeral march, which, likewise, is already sketched.

- Till's clarinet theme (Example 4.1.3) inspires Strauss to sketch a fugato and a recitative. In the course of varying the theme metrically (transformation from 6/8 to 2/4 meter with the initial rhythmic figure as in Example 4.1.1), he generates the two episodal themes in B-flat major (mm.179ff) and A-flat major (mm.375ff).

- For the music from approximately m.410 to m.573 there are only verbal notes on compositional procedures to be used: intensification and synthesis.

Initially the conflict between Till and the Philistines culminates in a concluding trial (presumably inspired by Berlioz's *Symphonie fantastique*) and a funeral march, including, possibly, the idea of the recitative. During the process of working with the Till themes Strauss arrives at new drafts that are folded into the music and that clearly augment it thematically, harmonically, and, in turn, in terms of structure. The recitative as well as the funeral march are abandoned. The end is dominated by intensification and synthesis of the material.

Thus, the notion of a preexistent program—fixed from the start and determining the composition—is a chimera. Initially, there is only a programmatic idea linked to certain musical materials: Till's conflict with the Philistines. Then the work proceeds basically by musical laws: Something new is drafted, tried out, or abolished. Strauss can sketch a march or a recitative (both could have easily fit into a program) as well as delete them. What counts are the musical decisions. Once the composer has made the decision, the programmatic interpretation is supplied a posteriori, as it were. Certain sections of the work, it seems, did not even have any more detailed programmatic ideas.

Not until *Till Eulenspiegel* was completed was Strauss able to pass on to his exegete the programmatic information that Mauke, in turn, used for the program we know today. Now, of course, it was easy to assign themes and sections to different personae and pranks of the protagonist. For the thematic development, however, there were no programmatic details, because they never existed in the first place. The music does not depend on the program, but—vice versa—the program on the music.

The freedom of the composer from extramusical influences also included a correspondingly free use of the material. In the folk legend of Till Eulenspiegel there is, for instance, no death by hanging and no ride through the pottery displays of the market women. (The latter motive comes from "King Drosselbart"—a fairy tale by the Grimm brothers.) Strauss took whatever suited his musical concept. It is no surprise, then, that such an unflappable modus operandi led him finally to his own subjects, which, from the start, were governed by musical strategies.

The compositional process in the other tone poems is similar to that which we observed in *Till Eulenspiegel*. As a rule, musical decisions and ideas are the determining factors. The programmatic concepts have to adjust to them. Strauss, of course, liked to rely on extramusical images for musical invention. We often encounter in his sketchbooks drafts for themes and sonorities with programmatic connotations, but programmatic ideas played no role, or only a small role, in the compositional elaboration of such materials.

The sketches also show Strauss, already at the beginning of the composition, making an effort to design a programmatic skeleton that secured at least the direction of the composition, in other words its overall structure. Developing such a skeleton early on, of course, was dependent on a musical and formal surefootedness that Strauss had to acquire through painstaking efforts. Only in his last tone poems had he finally gained such confidence. For *Symphonia domestica* he was able, at the beginning, to notate a skeletal program that proved to be a solid foundation for the entire subsequent compositional process. The musical discourse in all its details was not determined by the program; the advantage of such a program consisted in its very openness to details. It was characterized by a flexibility that was able to withstand, in part, even serious changes in the music.

The often quoted statements about composing under the guidance of a program become more plausible in this context. What guided Strauss was not a detailed program, and certainly not the texts formulated later. What provided him with orientation were a few principal programmatic ideas that, at best, were congruent enough to support a concept sufficiently general to allow him all the freedom he required during composition. The programmatic precepts became more detailed only when the decision was made to compose tone poems solely on his own subjects. In the transition from tone poem to opera, the programmatic skeleton, in a way, was finally succeeded by the libretto.

The Function of the Program for the Reception

Following his model Liszt, Strauss began his series of tone poems with a "masterpiece of literature," namely Shakespeare's *Macbeth*. Even subjects such as the legendary figure of Don Juan or *Tod und Verklärung*, whose attractiveness (in the nineteenth century) is evident in numerous musical (Liszt: *Tasso—Lamento e trionfo*) and literary works, follow in their programs' well-paved avenues.

That changes with the second group. In *Till Eulenspiegel*, the literary palette is amplified by the fairy tale, the musical palette by the humorous. In *Also sprach Zarathustra*, Strauss integrates ideas of the then-fashionable philosopher Nietzsche, in *Symphonia domestica* episodes in the life of a bourgeois artist family. Moreover, the title here hints at a traditional genre in its (lightly disguised) multimovement format, while the subtitles of *Till Eulenspiegel* and *Don Quixote* point to rondo and variation as structural underpinnings of the respective works. All things considered, the conditions were not unfavorable to reach out, programmatically and musically, to audiences with the tone poems through the titles.

Nevertheless, at the beginning Strauss faced misunderstandings. That his first two tone poems, *Macbeth* and *Don Juan*, had been vehemently rejected initially by an authority such as Bülow gave him pause to think. But when Bülow finally conducted *Don Juan* in January 1890 in Berlin, Strauss was horrified: He reported to his parents that Bülow no longer had an "appreciation for poetic music" and, through his mistaken interpretation, had seen to it that the message of the composer "could not have come across."[23] As a remedy Strauss asked to publish his next tone poem, *Tod und Verklärung*, with a lengthy programmatic poem by Ritter; only then did he allow his piece to be performed by conductors other than himself.

Initially, Strauss wanted to forego any detailed explanations for *Till Eulenspiegel*. But very soon detailed analyses emerged, whose dissemination was supported by the composer in order to have available exhaustive answers to questions regarding the program. The poems in the scores (as was the case with *Don Juan* and *Tod und Verklärung*) were replaced, as mentioned earlier, by explanations in prose, which were illustrated by musical examples and published separately. Strauss adapted here to a practice introduced by the Berlin impresario Hermann Wolff for orchestral concerts and also known to audiences through Hermann Kretzschmar's *Führer durch den Konzertsaal* (Guides through the Concert Hall).[24]

As successful as this method seemed to be, very soon it showed fatal flaws. Audiences reduced Strauss's music to a sonorous illustration of the texts—"a picture book fiddled by strings and blown by winds."[25] People heard novel, interesting, and disconcerting sounds, like the bleating sheep in *Don Quixote*, and could read up on what was meant by those sounds, because the authors of the texts always could cite information provided by the composer. The relation between music and program was indeed stood on its head. Strauss's concept of a poetic idea did not play a role; it was forgotten that the texts were only auxiliary means that hardly came close to reaching the expressive quality of the music.

The composer tried to avoid this dilemma, but his attempts remained halfhearted. After the usual explanatory notes had been published, Strauss had another guide written for *Ein Heldenleben*; now a poem paraphrased the content of the work, while Strauss's friend Friedrich Rösch focused in his detailed commentary on the musical elaboration. And in the case of *Symphonia domestica* Strauss proved to be particularly untrustworthy: after refusing initially to publicize a program, he later revealed the content of the work, gradually and in bits and pieces, until finally a separate explanatory brochure was published, confirming the familiar pattern. That Strauss appealed here (speaking through Wilhelm Klatte) to the sentiments and the imagination of the audience and that he warned against the convenient mode of reception, namely, being led by the nose through the program—all these subtleties remained unnoticed.[26]

With his policy to steer the reception of a work through printed programs, Strauss contributed his share, to a considerable degree, to the early misunderstanding of his program music—a misunderstanding that stubbornly refused to go away and that had the most contradictory consequences. True, the illustrative power of music, which no doubt exists, secured the presence of his music in the concert repertory, but it impeded, for a long time, adequate attempts to come to terms with it. Musicology and audiences were in agreement: Musical picture books do not need to be analyzed.

THE MUSIC OF THE TONE POEMS

Strauss turned to tone poems, because, in the long run, he was striving for a career as a composer of operas in the Wagnerian tradition. Guided by a subject matter and by programmatic ideas, he tackled the task of imbuing his music with as much rhetoric, meaning, and expression as possible. The conviction that music was nothing but "expression"—in this respect he was a follower of the philosopher Friedrich von Hausegger—became for him the guiding principle of composition.

"Composing expressively" meant, as mentioned already several times, a thematic and harmonic invention inspired by the music of Liszt and

Wagner and a compositional technique showing mastery of the whole range of homophonic and polyphonic textural nuances. In addition, timbre, for which he had always harbored a particular interest, was elevated by Strauss to a compositional means in its own right. He treated the orchestra not only as a symphony orchestra but also, and with the same confidence and mastery, as an operatic orchestra.

Finally, any musical piece needs to have a form. Here Strauss may have felt especially competent: already early on he was considered to have a mastery of traditional forms. Now, of course, it was no longer sufficient to write sonata forms, scherzos, rondos, and variations. Liszt—as general opinion had it—had considerably expanded, differentiated, and adjusted the forms to make them fit his subjects. And Strauss believed, following Liszt's lead, that each individual subject needed to generate its own specific form. But he also knew about the risks involved: "To generate a new form with each work without becoming formless," he wrote to Bella on 2 December 1888, "is more difficult than to write a passable symphony with the help of the old sonata formula, which already has been stretched in all directions."[27] The trick was to be original in terms of structure without giving the impression of being formless.

Strauss knew the benefits of Liszt's symphonic poems as well as their shortcomings—no surprise, considering that Ritter and Bülow, both close companions of Liszt, were his mentors. Originally a piano virtuoso, Liszt preferred, in his piano as well as orchestral works, monothematic music in which the material was developed by means of variation (*Tasso*, *Mazeppa*, *Les Préludes*), but he also indulged in potpourri-like structures (*Hungaria*, *Festklänge*). In addition, he liked homophonic textures. Following Wagner's lead, Strauss, on the other hand, composed rather polyphonically. But filling his polyphony with "expression" required several themes, and this was meaningful only in connection with subject matters in which different characters are pitted against one another in conflicts. Liszt's subjects and programs are, for the most part, dominated by only one single hero, whereas Strauss never presents his protagonist exclusively. They are pitted against opponents, either alone or, as is the case in *Don Quixote* and *Ein Heldenleben*, together with a sidekick or beloved companion. Sonata form and rondo were natural structures for such constellations. There are two contrasting themes in sonata form—the first often called "masculine" and the second "feminine" in romantic writing about music—followed by a development section full of conflicts as well as a conciliatory recapitulation. In cases in which the number of opponents increased, it was logical to utilize rondo structures, where the programmatic linkage of ritornello (hero) and episode (opponents) was obvious.

Thus, despite his striving for originality, Strauss had every reason not to neglect the old forms in his tone poems. He merely abolished—to recall the letter to Bella cited earlier—form as a formula. But he was aware of the programmatic connotations of musical forms, especially of sonata form. He had been able to study in Liszt's works how one-movement works could benefit from the possibilities of symphonic multimovement structures, in other words, how multimovement forms could be absorbed by one-movement structures. And, last but not least, he had learned to take seriously the psychological implications of the forms in addition to their purely musical logic. He knew that audiences needed formal templates for orientation. But the relation between templates and "poetic" structures was flexible.

If Strauss wanted to be understood by his audience without resorting to formulaic structures, he needed to strive toward adjusting the familiar forms to the subject matters so skillfully that the desires of both parties were satisfied: the audience's for orientation as well as the composer's for expressive, that is, "poetic" music. Strauss never ceased to realize sonata forms, rondo structures, and variations in his tone poems. He even mentions rondo and variation forms in the subtitles of *Till Eulenspiegel* and *Don Quixote*, respectively. But the composer's ironic-humorous undertone signals the liberty with which Strauss treated forms, and not only these two. He never proceeded along formulaic lines. Instead of reproducing formulas, he modified traditional models as a matter of principle and combined them with other structural ideas, both historical and novel. This makes the analysis of his music interesting and difficult at the same time.

Till Eulenspiegel and Form

The subtitle of *Till Eulenspiegel* promises a rondo form to the listener (later Strauss even spoke of a rondo)—that is, a series of sections in which a ritornello alternates with different episodes. The nineteenth century, however, saw the establishment of the so-called sonata rondo characterized by a reduction in the number of episodes: the second episode was imbued with developmental features or, at least, with aspects of a contrasting middle section, while the third episode was transformed into a recapitulation of the first followed by a coda. There were also sections in which developmental and transitional aspects dominated, especially between episode and the following ritornello. The hierarchic principle of sonata form began to intrude on the paratactically organized rondo form, especially when "the rondo scheme was the basis of a movement aspiring to symphonic dimensions."[28]

In *Till Eulenspiegel*, Strauss, rather than mediating between sections, juxtaposed them without transitions. The so-called market scene, for instance, begins as abruptly in m.133 as it ends in m.153. The "Philistines" in m.293 or the "Gassenhauer" (street song) in m.375 make their appearance in a similarly surprising fashion, and the "Gericht" (court or trial scene) interrupts in m.573 the preceding hustle and bustle. Are all of these episodes following the old rondo scheme? Is this perhaps a symphonic form? Things are not that easy: Strauss composes neither an authentic sonata rondo nor a traditional rondo chain.

Indeed, the most important element of a rondo is missing, namely, a closed ritornello repeated several times in the principal key. At the beginning after the short prologue, there is, of course, a lengthy section that begins and ends in F major and that features two distinct themes (in the horn and clarinet—see Examples 4.1.1–4.1.3). But it reveals so many different facets and proceeds so discontinuously that we have difficulty considering it the ritornello of a rondo. In addition, the section never returns in its initial form.

The beginning section is succeeded by four distinct sections: the "market scene" (mm.133–53), the so-called "*Pastorenszene*" (sermon scene) with a brief epilogue (mm.179–208), the "love scene" (mm.230–374) expanded by an introduction, and the scene with the "Philistines" mentioned earlier (mm.294–374). In other words, there are no fewer than four sections contrasting with the ritornello, and all of them could be labeled as episodes, if the term had not become meaningless by the fact that a ritornello separating them is missing.

Only later does the initial section return (mm.429–42), but Strauss limits the recapitulation to presenting the horn theme in F major and D major. Later on, it is briefly continued (mm.465–84 correspond, with a little addition, to mm.63–80). None of the "episodes" is repeated. Instead, Strauss uses the material of the horn theme to compose a huge climax (mm.516ff), culminating in the "sermon" theme now transformed into a blaring march thundered out fortissimo (mm.567ff). The court scene is added as a final episode, before the epilogue rounds off the piece.

Because of the unique, even though incomplete, recapitulation of the first F major section, it is logical to divide *Till Eulenspiegel* into two large parts. After the exposition in F major, Strauss juxtaposes, in the somewhat lengthier first part, several scenes by compressing the episodes, so to speak; in the shorter second part, he utilizes basically the thematic–motivic material introduced earlier/in the first section.

If we understand the rondo's essential character as a representation of more than two themes and an additive structure, then the form just sketched of *Till Eulenspiegel* could be viewed as a variant of a rondo. In that case, Strauss would have merely rearranged the sections by gathering all the episodes in the first part. Such a form is hardly compatible, however, with the notion of a rondo as a paradigm of the structural idea of juxtaposing repetition (ritornello) and contrast (episodes). Even though, in terms of the program, it is always the same hero who commits the pranks, there is no corresponding ritornello in the music. The repetitive element (the Eulenspiegel theme) and the contrasting segments (the individual episodes) are closely linked to each other; it is always the same hero who gets into ever new situations.

This work is reminiscent of a series of variations rather than a rondo. The thematic material of the love scene, in particular, is more easily understood as a variant of the horn theme, whereas in the market scene the clarinet motive dominates. Strauss, however, in the sermon scene as well as in the music of the Philistines utilizes new material. One could easily describe the first part of *Till Eulenspiegel* as a free variation form, or, preferably, as a form in which rondo and variation are combined as follows: A (Exposition); A' (market scene, variation 1); B (sermon scene, episode 1); A'' (love scene, variation 2); and C (Philistines, episode 2).

Still, the mixture of variation and rondo form does not suffice to account for the structure of *Till Eulenspiegel*. Strauss also drew on principles of sonata form. As evidence we might cite especially the emphatic recapitulation of the initial horn theme in m.429 that opens the second part of the piece. In addition, note that the market scene in mm.133ff functions as a harmonic bridge; it begins in D minor and ends in G minor, a key in which Strauss hovers for a while and from which he moves via F major in a genuine transition to B-flat major, the tonality of the sermon scene (m.179). Thus, the initial section in F major is followed by a transition leading to a new section with a new theme, new key (the subdominant), new texture (songlike and homophonic), new meter, and new tempo (even though meter, tempo, and rhythm are foreshadowed already in the introductory prologue). Indeed, we could identify this part as an enlarged sonata exposition with a principal theme (listed above as A), transition (A'), and second theme (B).

Sonata categories remain in effect even in what follows. The love scene with its thematic elaboration has features of a development section, and so does the Philistine scene with its conflicts. The appropriately placed recapitulation has been mentioned already. If we do not limit our understanding of the recapitulation of a sonata form as being merely the repetition of materials of the exposition, if we attribute to it also the function of a resolution of tensions or, expressed in terms of the program, of a victory or triumph after struggle and conflict—then the hymnlike augmentation of the horn theme in mm.485ff would have to be interpreted as a recapitulation or, even more appropriately, as a kind of triumphal closure.

Till Eulenspiegel, no doubt, is more than a rondo. In a compositional tour-de-force, Strauss combines rondo, variations, and sonata form. The forms overlap, even penetrate each other to varying degrees; sometimes the impression of a rondo dominates, at other times that of a set of variations, or of a sonata form. As Till Eulenspiegel, the protagonist of the tone poem, resists societal norms by mocking them with continuous pranks, so does the composer thwart the expectations of those who want to pin him down to the norms of a rondo. Strauss plays with the listener's expectations in general. The beginning (Example 4.1.2) is a case in point with its 7/8 theme in a 6/8 meter, its bravado intensification, and its shocklike slaps in m.49. *Till Eulenspiegel* is also a scherzo—Strauss's first tone poem in which humor, irony, and the grotesque triumph. Liszt never composed anything like this.

Strauss's treatment of traditional forms in *Till Eulenspiegel* can also be observed elsewhere. All tone poems feature hybrid structures. *Don Quixote* is more than a traditional variation movement, and neither *Symphonia domestica* nor *Eine Alpensinfonie* constitute a simple return to the symphony. In general, the principal structurè of the old symphony, that is, the sonata form of the first movement, still plays an important role in Strauss's work. The sonata structures are rendered flexible, to varying degrees, by other structural models, whereby juxtapositions of sections always imply rondo or variation forms. Quite often Strauss combines the juxtaposition of sections with development in a grand two-part structure: the first part is dominated by episodes with individual self-contained sections following each other; the second part develops and intensifies the material of the first part. Only rarely do the tone poems conclude with triumphal climaxes (as in *Tod und Verklärung* or *Symphonia domestica*); more often the protagonists fail, and the music concludes with a slow final section (enlarged since *Also sprach Zarathustra*) in which the principal conflicts can reverberate one more time.

In addition to the overlapping of different structures, Strauss organizes his tone poems, especially those in large-scale proportions (of which *Also sparch Zarathustra* is the first), by composing forms in changing dimensions. The opening section of *Ein Heldenleben*, for instance—the section that in early programs notes was called *Der Held* (The Hero; mm.1–117)—can no doubt be interpreted as a monumental complex of themes corresponding to the principal-theme section of a large-scale sonata form. But Strauss shaped this large-scale principal theme as a symmetrically planned sonata form in miniature with an exposition consisting of principal theme (mm.1–20) and a contrasting second theme (mm.21–45), a development (mm.46–83), and a recapitulation beginning with the second theme (mm.84–93) and climaxing with the principal theme (mm.94–117). Such intertwining requires a long breath from the composer lest the large-scale form spin out of control— especially in works that, like the last two tone poems, are longer than a thousand measures. Strauss solved this difficulty in *Ein Heldenleben* with the confidence of a real master. The composition of *Des Helden Walstatt* (The Hero's Battleground; or, "Krieg [War] in Heldenleben," as Strauss called it in his diary)[29] leaves no doubt that this section is shaped as a grand development, capable of balancing the monumental exposition. And the same is true of *Des Helden Friedenswerke* (The Hero's Works of Peace), composed as a recapitulation on multiple levels. Not only do the themes of the exposition return, but so do the principal themes of some of the composer's earlier works. Programmatic ideas and musical-structural requirements are intertwined.

Don Juan and Élan

With his tone poems Strauss acquired the reputation of an "allegro composer." Slow tempi, sustained over long stretches, were not his forte. We know of his admiration for the Adagio in Mahler's Fourth Symphony: Something like this [he freely admitted] "he could not do."[30] His preference for fast tempi corresponds with the impetus that, over and over again, was attributed to his works—an aspect that was seen as the musical equivalent of Bergson's élan vital and, thereby, as an expression of the *Zeitgeist*, taking off to new shores, at the end of the nineteenth century. Carl Dahlhaus saw in the stormy beginning of *Don Juan* even the upbeat of a new epoch, namely, musical modernism leaving Romanticism behind—once and for all.[31]

Indeed, the piece begins like a musical tornado. Already the first eight measures—a brief introduction—are full of ascents at breakneck speed (Example 4.2). Here is what occurs: a rapid ascent (over more than three octaves) from g to b''' in mm.1–3; an intense crescendo in m.4, consisting of a scalar passage in harp and strings and culminating in a cymbal clash; a trumpet fanfare in m.7; and another ascent following the steep collapse in triplets. The explosive climaxes turn this passage into an event, admired by critics and audiences alike since the premiere of the piece: an effect whose imitation Strauss recommended to his colleague, Igor Stravinsky, that he did not repeat, ever, in any other of his tone poems.

But *Don Juan* does not just start with élan. The entire work consists, to a large degree, of passages in which the music continuously gains in élan, either in the form of accelerations of meter, rhythm, tempo, and harmonic progressions, or through dynamic crescendos, either simple or written out, or through a gradual increase in using the orchestral apparatus. There are no limits to the possibilities of increasing the intensity, and, from the start,

EXAMPLE 4.2
Don Juan
Tondichtung von Rich. Strauss, Op. 20

Strauss preferred this method of composition, perhaps because it did not require an overly subtle approach to polyphonic writing. Not every note was important, only the overall effect of explosively bursting forth. Simple upbeats gained in vividness through rapid scales, as chord repetitions were animated by arpeggios in the harp. Such a modus operandi made *Don Juan* extremely tricky in technical terms, but "not really difficult," as he reported to his parents after the first rehearsals before the premiere; "fifty notes, more or less" did not really matter.[32]

Strauss, of course, recognized quickly the significance of passages of intensification for musical continuity. The compelling force of the protagonist, his immediately irresistible nature, for instance, is not a foregone conclusion in the brief introduction. The rhythm changes continuously, and the meter is uncertain, as is the harmonic center; it is not until m.8 that things become clear. These types of musical gestures, however, cover up such inconsistencies, and because they link even the most disparate elements, they advance to become an important compositional tool not only in *Don Juan*, but also in other tone poems. Strauss consciously developed a variety of such passages as compositional stratagems. Some of them have a theme as a point of departure, others a theme as a goal, and, finally, there are frequently passages of intensification that are open-ended—thus the reason why the composer can use them to lead into almost any kind of material. The latter often function as transitions, whereas passages leading to themes often function as large-scale upbeats. We encounter such types especially at the end of works, when it is time for grand and triumphal closing gestures.

Such passages of intensification become particularly significant when they are juxtaposed with static passages of similar proportions. In this case, Strauss creates contrasts, which are equally important as the traditional differentiation by thematic and harmonic means. In *Don Juan*, for instance, the first theme in E major (mm.9–40) is later succeeded by two large-scale thematic complexes, one in B major (mm.90–160), the other in G major (mm.232–307). If the first theme appears to be the principal theme of a sonata form, the second begins like the typical second theme in the dominant; the third theme then seems to replace the sonata structure with a rondo form. But more important than fighting a futile battle over the structure of *Don Juan* (which, as in the case of *Till Eulenspiegel*, results from the overlapping of several models) is the fact that the B major complex even outdoes the E major theme in intensity, whereas the G major section manages without intensification. It is juxtaposed with the earlier sections as a grand area of repose and, thereby, as a basic contrast. And precisely because music is allowed to come to a complete rest here, it is necessary to introduce a new theme in the horns (mm.314ff) to get things moving again.

Contrasts between areas of intensification and repose determine the remainder of the piece. Strauss, of course, does not compose any more restful themes, but interrupts the music suddenly—at first, very effectively with a collapse in mm.423ff, and, finally, by breaking off, after a long stretto, in m.585, and continuing with a brief and somber coda.

It still matters, of course, how the themes are distributed in these tidal waves and how they are treated by the composer. But *Don Juan* shows, very clearly, that it does not suffice to look at the piece through the prism of traditional forms. They are no longer the exclusive determinants of structure; new models now compete with them. We perhaps could even venture to say that the traditional categories of form have already been subsumed by Strauss's élan, that is, his continuous unleashing of the dynamic dimension on every level. Don Juan is not concerned about traditional rules and laws; he creates his own.

Symphonia domestica and Thematic Elaboration

Among the characteristics of Strauss's tone poems, highlighted over and over again, is the dense web of closely related themes and motives. The composer himself emphasized repeatedly how much he was concerned to exert control over his music as well as secure its coherence through intense thematic–motivic elaboration.

Strauss's position was not new. The increasing attention to thematic relationships, especially in the grand genres of instrumental music, had been an essential characteristic of composition in the nineteenth century. The shaping of themes, originally only of subordinate rank after the all-important harmonic disposition, gained in significance as early as Beethoven and became at least an equal partner. During the course of the century—the era not only of the sonata and the symphony, but also of the character piece and the Wagnerian music drama—themes advanced to become the most important aspect of composition. As the unifying force of harmony declined, a substitute needed to be found; thematic connections took over the function of the harmonic scaffold, which lost its stability because of an ever-increasing supply of chords and the attendant multitude of possibilities of connecting chords through chromatic and enharmonic means. Even in Wagner's music drama, the leitmotivs functioned as elements unifying the music—in addition to advancing to most significant props of the dramaturgy.

The strategy to compensate for the loss of harmonic cohesion with an increase in thematic connections was appropriated by all composers of large-scale genres, not only by Wagner and Liszt but also by Brahms. Thus, there were plenty of models for Strauss in this respect, and he familiarized himself, early on, with the possibilities of thematic elaboration.

The results of his study, and how he placed his trust already quite early in the structural function of thematic–motivic elaboration, can be seen in his First Concerto for Horn and Orchestra, completed in 1883. The fast first and last movements are tightly connected, structurally and thematically, with the Andante directly following without break the preceding Allegro. The conclusions are obvious: The first movement functions as an exposition, the slow movement as a development, and the finale as a recapitulation. Later critics have interpreted such a form as already foreshadowing future developments, namely, the synthesis of multimovement and one-movement structures of the tone poems. This is, no doubt, an exaggeration. But the structural potential of thematic connections would have been known to Strauss by that time.

Strauss could not avoid intensive thematic elaboration in his tone poems because of his polyphonic style of composition. Not only the principal voices—indeed, all voices—needed to be thematically significant; they needed to participate in the discourse, they needed to communicate something. It was, of course, not sufficient simply to distribute the same material to as many voices as possible; what was needed, in addition, was a perpetual variation of themes and motives, depending on the structural and programmatic ideas guiding Strauss's composition. He used a most diverse array of techniques: He varied the melodic and harmonic aspects of the themes as well as their rhythm, meter, and timbre. In addition, he differentiated themes by separating them through continuous variation of their intervals or, vice versa, brought contrasting themes closer to each other by placing them in similar harmonic or sonorous environments.

In addition to the musical advantage of dense thematic elaboration, namely, generating coherence without having to abolish contrasts, there was a programmatic justification. Themes could be treated like characters; they could be developed and shown in different lights depending on the situation. And this was beneficial not only for the dramaturgy of the tone poems, but also for their structure. In some of Strauss's pieces the thematic development becomes the central category of form in general.

The idea of understanding musical form as the development of the history of a theme was not new in the nineteenth century—in fact, it corresponded with the general trend of bringing music close to literature. Especially those composers who also were active as authors tended to relate musical and literary forms and genres; an example is Schumann's paean celebrating the finale of Schubert's Symphony in C major, whose "heavenly length" he compared with a "sprawling novel in four volumes of, say, Jean

Paul."[33] Eduard Hanslick, vociferous opponent of Strauss's tone poems, had used a similar image in his well-known treatise on aesthetics, *Vom Musikalisch-Schönen*.[34] "Like the protagonist of a novel," he wrote, "the composer brings the theme in most diverse locales and environments, subjects it to highly different emotional states—everything else, however contrasting, is conceived and shaped in relation to it."[35] Strauss, who, like Wagner, was concerned that his music be highly comprehensible, eagerly picked up these and similar thoughts, especially since musical and programmatic ideas could be easily related to each other that way. Already in *Tod und Verklärung*, the central structural idea is most closely linked with the evolution of the theme of transfiguration, and Strauss returned to a similar conception with beneficial results in *Symphonia domestica*.

At first glance, *Symphonia domestica* seems to be a conventional symphony with a slightly disguised four-movement structure. (After a kind of introductory movement, follow a Scherzo [9 measures after 18], Adagio [at 55], and Finale [8 measures before 86], and these "movements" are even subtitled as such.) But entirely different structural divisions are possible, because Strauss did not compose the movements as self-contained units (as the appearance might suggest). The introductory movement, which lacks closure, for instance, flows seamlessly into the Scherzo, structured by Strauss by dint of a clear-cut caesura (6 measures after 31) into a coherent first part and a disparate second part with a lullaby at the end. And the conclusion of the Adagio (whose beginning, as the sketches show, posed uncertainties for Strauss for a long time) is shaped as a longish transition, leading, in turn, to the multisectional Finale. The movements obviously are pervaded by other structural ideas. One of these ideas can be deciphered from the relationship between introductory and closing movements. Both sections relate to each other, at least initially, as if they are exposition and recapitulation. The characteristic features of the beginning (voice-leading in unison, low register, F major, lively tempo) return at the beginning of the double fugue (at 87). Even identifying labels such as "I. Thema" and "II. Thema" appear in both places. In summary, thus, one could conclude that the form is a typical "dual function" structure, a synthesis of multimovement symphony and one-movement form.

That the narrative and content of the *Symphonia domestica*, going beyond this conception, is determined by the structural idea of thematic development can be shown, initially, by a more detailed study of the piece from the beginning up to the end of the first half of the Scherzo. The work begins with the principal theme (the theme of the Man). But the theme is really a juxtaposition of no fewer than six motives welded together merely by the key of F major. Not until the exposition of the second theme (of the Woman) has been brought to closure in B major, do we hear a "real" principal theme—motivically coherent and divided by regular periodicity—in the main key of F major (at rehearsal number 8). The principal theme, it seems, must develop from initially amorphous thematic and harmonic surroundings, and this development, characteristically, originates in the juxtaposition with the second theme: The disparate qualities of the Man— this seems to be the obvious programmatic interpretation—will be cast into a meaningful form only by a Woman.

The same idea, now projected on a larger scale, is the basis of the treatment of the third theme (of the Child). Initially (at rehearsal number 14), only intervallic contours are indicated; at their second occurrence clear melodic shapes in D major occur (9 measures after rehearsal number 15). But not until the beginning of the Scherzo does the theme receive its concrete shape, leading, after yet another development (at rehearsal number 29) to a grand, almost heroic and hymnlike climax. Strauss closes off with a subsequent caesura (6 measures after rehearsal number 31). A large first part of the *Symphonia domestica*, encompassing the exposition of three themes as well as the development of the first and the third themes to self-contained shapes, has thus come to an end.

The first main part of the work includes the introductory movement as well as the first half of the Scherzo, because the latter is continuation and conclusion of a thematic process set in motion at the beginning. The second half of the Scherzo, juxtaposing a series of shorter episodic sections, functions as an upbeat to what follows. The reason for overlapping introductory movement and Scherzo, however, is Strauss's idea of realizing structure as thematic development.

The combination of thematic development and formal conventions informs the Finale or recapitulation of the *Symphonia domestica*. Again, the third theme (the theme of the Child) plays the decisive role. In the initial theme of the double fugue Strauss still combines features of the principal theme (F major) and the third theme (melodic shape), but now the music, as is always the case after a grand intensification, returns to the proper key of the Child (D major, 5 measures after 107). But the anticipated breakthrough, already announced in the trumpets, is withheld; instead Strauss lets the music end in a large field of noise and interjects a recapitulation of the principal theme of the exposition (at 121). Only at the end of the reprise, again prepared by a grand intensification, does the hymnlike third theme come back in its proper key of D major, establishing the real climax of the *Symphonia domestica* (at 139).

The double-function form, the combination of sonata form and sonata cycle, is dominated, over long stretches of the work, by the thematic development of the third theme. Strauss organizes his narrative in two large chapters. The first narrative discourse is largely undisturbed, and the second as well cannot be derailed even by interpolated recapitulatory sections.

The programmatic idea—to depict symphonically the education of the Child through the parents and the evolution of the Child from an infant to an adult—was so attractive for Strauss that he even risked the harmonic unity of the piece. In the coda he pulls out all the stops to reaffirm F major as the main key; whether he succeeded is debatable. In the preceding, the music was geared too strongly toward arriving at the dynamic highpoint in D major. The music climaxed here where the structural idea arrived at its goal; Strauss celebrated here one more time, in both musical and programmatic terms, the topos of the theme as symphonic protagonist.

Also sprach Zarathustra and Harmony

Strauss took over a colorful and richly nuanced harmonic language from the music of the Romantic era into which he was born. To appropriate Wagner's and Liszt's achievements in this field had to be one of the first goals of the young composer on his new path. There is no doubt that Strauss reached his goal; moreover, he succeeded in speaking early on in his own distinct harmonic voice. It is also clear that the programmatic ideas of his tone poems aided him in his search for attractive chords and chord successions. But Strauss would not have been true to himself, if he had not utilized the musical means he inherited as well as newly invented, from the very start, in the context of larger musical concepts. And in this endeavor he proceeded with an extraordinary sense of purpose.

In principle, Strauss respected the harmonic system of his time. The sounds of his works are part of the major–minor cadential system of harmony. All his tone poems have a clear principal key or tonality, on which the respective subsidiary keys and modulatory processes are dependent.

Strauss demonstrated his respect for traditional tonality over and over again in clearly audible terms. He liked to underscore large-scale musical and programmatic events, for instance, with elementary cadences from dominant to tonic with a bass progression down a fifth. The most pointed examples perhaps occur in *Ein Heldenleben*, when the victory of the hero over his opponents is celebrated with no less than two opulent cadences (at rehearsal number 77 and rehearsal number 79).

In addition to such effective written-out progressions, Strauss frequently used in his tone poems cadential progressions that are simple but artfully disguised; in this way, he could reach, quickly and elegantly, even the most remote keys and move away from them in the same fashion. The alienation effect is most frequently achieved by sliding the chords up or down by a half step.[36] "Normal" chord progressions such as E–A–D, for instance, are changed into E-flat–A–D, E–A-flat–D, E-flat–A-flat–D, and E–A–D-flat, or, expressed in programmatic terms, are *verrückt* (a pun meaning both "pushed out of their traditional positions" and "crazy"). The most well-known examples in the tone poems for such "crazy" progressions are the cadences in *Don Quixote*:[37]

EXAMPLE 4.3

It is clear that Strauss was fond of such procedures. They permitted him to indulge in harmonic shifts—unusual and surprising, sonorous and rhetorical—without abandoning the central cadential functions of harmony. In addition to being a method, both personal and modern, through which he stabilized the old system one more time, it was also a procedure that lent itself to a rich harvest in musical and programmatic terms.

Following this method, Strauss unfolded in his works a broad spectrum of chords and chord progressions based on simple and multiple leading tones. In principle, any sound can be followed by any other. Strauss preferred to use colorist sonorities, chordal shifts, or mixtures as ornamentation; in other instances, such passages served as tone painting. Such tone painting celebrates veritable triumphs in some tone poems (*Don Quixote, Eine Alpensinfonie*), but, on the whole, occupies a rather peripheral position. Some harmonic clashes, which have gained some notoriety, can be explained as being motivated by the program. The "Adversaries" section in *Ein Heldenleben* is a case in point with its quasi-atonal passages (6 measures before 14), which inspired Strauss later (at 41) even to a pointedly bitonal passage (combination of G minor and G-flat major). Another is the music of the bleating sheep in *Don Quixote*, which disturbed Strauss's contemporaries. After the Cologne premiere, the reviewer of the *Neue Zeitschrift für Musik* expressed indignation over the "absurd artistic manufacture that could not be described in any other terms but *Katzenmusik* (cat music)."[38]

Clearly, Strauss's harmonic language does not only serve programmatic ends, but also has musical and structural purposes. The grand cadences in *Ein Heldenleben* (mentioned earlier) do not only celebrate triumphs, they also introduce pointedly, after a long intensive development, the recapitulation of the sonata form that undergirds the entire work. In general, Strauss likes to prepare his listeners for recapitulations and reprise of the principal key by using dominant pedal points and connecting them with large-scale intensifications.

Still, there are other ways to utilize harmonic means—for instance, certain chords or brief successions of chords that are used as reference sonorities in the manner of Wagnerian leitmotivs. They further musical coherence and facilitate, at the same time (because they are linked to certain situations and characters), the communication of programmatic ideas. An example is the so-called *Überdruss* (weariness) motive of the winds in *Don Juan*, a succession of diminished seventh chord and "falsely" added minor triad ("false," because it lacks the leading-tone connection). We encounter the sounds for the first time in mm.53 and 55 and then, again and again, in the second half of the piece, as means to depict the increasing weariness of the hero about his life (mm.337, 375, 427, 434, 441, 598):

EXAMPLE 4.4

At the same time, these chord progressions link the conclusion of the piece closely to its stormy beginning.

Strauss intensified the use of reference sonorities (*Leitklänge*) in some tone poems to a degree that allows us to speak of reference tonalities (*Leittonarten*). In these cases, certain keys with their specific relationships determine not only the local harmonic but also the overall structural discourse. Of course, that had always been the case on the elementary level of the cadence. Even in the nineteenth century, tonic and dominant constituted the structurally significant pair of keys that impacted every work, even every movement. But, as mentioned before, its coherence-establishing power, including that of the cadence, had grown weaker over the course of time. It became more and more difficult to compose with tonic, subdominant, and dominant with their fifth progressions as principal keys. Strauss was not satisfied to continue this development, more or less passively. On the contrary, he resisted this development and tried to reconstitute principal keys from a fresh vantage point, musically as well as programmatically. He succeeded in this for the first time in *Also sprach Zarathustra*.

"From a musical perspective, Zarathustra is a conflict about two very remote keys (just a minor second apart)," noted Strauss in one of his diaries, and the Graz physician Anton Berger quoted in 1927 *Also sprach Zarathustra* commentary of the composer's as follows: "I was concerned simply to show that B minor and C major cannot be forced together; the entire piece shows all kinds of attempts, but it simply does not work. That's the sobering truth!"[39] In other words, Strauss attributed a substantial significance to the tonalities of C major and B minor in *Also sprach Zarathustra*. For the time being, this can be explained in programmatic terms. The tonality of C, represented immediately at the start by way of the elementary intervals of octave, fifth, and fourth (c'–g'–c'') symbolizes the Universe—eternal, everlasting Nature. "Theme c–g–c (universe): always unalterably rigid, unchangeable to the end"—that is what is written in the sketches.[40] Human life, on the other hand, is characterized by change and development. The human being, "represented" by way of the tonality of B (in minor as well as major), strives to reach ever new goals, because humanity is not satisfied by those just achieved. This is an idea pondered not only by Nietzsche but also by Goethe's *Faust*. At the end, the human being, overcoming all earthly problems, seems to have conquered all obstacles. But Nature, "unchangeable to the end," cannot be disregarded. It has the last word—in the form of pizzicato tones in the double bass.

The programmatic scenario, of course, does not come close to doing justice to the sophisticated handling of the two tonalities. The focus on the C–B conflict conceals the fact that Strauss introduces another important pair of tonalities in *Also sprach Zarathustra*, namely, C minor and A-flat major, whose significance is already revealed at the beginning of the work. The slow cantabile section "Von den Hinterweltlern" (Of the Afterworldsmen) is in A-flat major, while the section "Freuden und Leidenschaften" (Joys and Passions) following later is composed in C minor. But this has structural consequences. Key relations and the characters connected with them—calm and cantabile versus passionate and impetuous—suggest a sonata exposition in which the secondary theme precedes the principal theme. (Strauss had experimented with this variant already in the first movement of *Aus Italien*.) Later he even confirms the impression of sonata form through a free recapitulation of themes. The cantabile second theme returns in the "Tanzlied" (Dance Song), but in A minor and a fast tempo; the solo violin transforms it into a waltz melody (m.469ff). When the principal theme comes back, the tempo of the exposition is reversed (as was the case with the secondary theme); now it is played in a slow rather than a fast tempo, and it appears, characteristically, in A-flat major, the key of the slow second theme in the exposition (m.629ff). Thus, Strauss has retained the impression of a reprise by bringing back themes and, in part, tonalities and tempi, whereby the exchange of tempi, in a way, substitutes for the traditional change of the secondary theme to the tonic key.

Strauss overlaid this rather conventional tonal disposition—it can be found, for instance, in the first movement of Beethoven's last piano sonata—with the conflict between the tonalities of C and B. The contrast evolves gradually in the first part of *Also sprach Zarathustra*. A presentiment is given at the beginning of the section "Von der Sehnsucht" (Of the Longing): The music strives bravely upward in B minor, but Nature (c'–g'–c'') and religious themes call a halt to this development after only a few measures. A renewed attempt in B minor occurs within the section "Von der Wissenschaft" (Of the Science) (m.239), but now it is transformed quickly into B major and a broadly flowing character, leading to a spirited dance-like theme in the woodwinds (mm.252ff). But again Nature interferes and silences the "Dance Song."

The conflict of B and C, of Man and Nature, reaches its culmination at the beginning of the second part of *Also sprach Zarathustra*. Again the "Dance Song" sounds in B major (mm.386ff), again it is open-ended, but now, one is almost tempted to say, the opposing key of C major wrestles itself free from Nature and tries to get hold of the "Dance Song." Strauss forces G major (the dominant of C major) and B major together in mm.400ff—a struggle in which C major seems to emerge victoriously. In mm.529ff and 569ff the "Dance Song" is played in C major and, for the first time, by the strings.

The battle, however, is still undecided. The grand intensifications of the concluding section of *Also sprach Zarathustra* culminate again in C major (mm.857ff). But the bass sounds a pedal point on E, the third of C major, and, at the same time, the root of the subdominant of B major. For a long time, the music wavers, then it turns to B major at what appears to be the definite goal (mm.946ff). Nature, however, cannot be thwarted; the final word has the tone C.

It probably is no coincidence that Strauss, in his statements about the music of *Also sprach Zarathustra*, brought up precisely the conflict between C and B. This harmonic disposition had generated controversy already before the premiere, even though initially it had been reduced to the unusual closure of the piece. Thus Strauss's friend, the music critic Richard Batka, reported early in 1897 that "Strauss's combination of disparate tonalities had been sufficient reason for many to expect an excess [nonplus ultra] of ugly dissonances."[41] Even Johannes Brahms entered the fray by criticizing the conclusion as unmotivated, because nothing had "happened" in these two keys before.[42] In truth, a lot had "happened," and Strauss wanted to call attention with his remarks about the conclusion not only to the programmatic but also to the musical logic of the preceding music.

The novel character of the work, however, consists not only in the combination of C and B, but also in Strauss's strategy of welding this conflict with the dualism of C minor and A-flat major. The relations between both tonalities represent, as it were, two aspects of *Also sprach Zarathustra*: a traditional relationship that meets the listening expectations of the audience at least in some rough measure and a novel relationship that follows entirely its own laws.

Strauss has often been characterized as a "mystery" man. On the surface, so goes the verdict, he resembled a businessman; nobody could have suspected in him the artist who created works such as *Salome* or *Der*

Rosenkavalier. He was a well-established figure in the system of court orchestras and court theaters of the Wilhelminian era and, certainly since the mid-1890s, moved from success to success. But, at the same time, he despised the leading musical taste of the bourgeoisie and composed tone poems with heroes who set everything in motion to prevail over narrow-minded Philistines—precisely those Philistines who were listening, with fascination or horror, to concerts with Strauss's music and who thus ultimately contributed to filling the composer's wallet. Like many of his colleagues, Strauss was of two minds in this respect: As an artist he was unconditionally on the side of progress; when it came to political and social issues, he preferred to be on the side of conservatives. But the Janus-faced Strauss could not hide his personality even in his modern tone poems. They, too, combine new and challenging as well as old and traditional concepts.

Exactly this ambivalence is behind the tonal disposition of *Also sprach Zarathustra.* Convention prevails in the first part of the piece: Strauss establishes a traditional pair of keys with A-flat major and C minor, the tonalities of the first extended coherent section of the work, thereby suggesting a free but still recognizable sonata form. Even the fugue "Von der Wissenschaft" fits into the sonata form mold; fugues as development sections were not unusual. The conflict C–B plays only a secondary role here. But it gains in importance in the second half after a grandiose breakdown (mm.338ff)—symbol of the failure of the plans of the imaginary hero as well as of conventional sonata form. Now the relations are reversed: The new and unusual replaces the old. The sonata form is abandoned; the recapitulation mentioned above is only of subordinate significance. Instead, the conflict between C and B moves into the foreground; after the "Tanzlied," all themes and motives are drawn into this conflict, until all energies are exhausted. At the end, there is no longer enough power for a grandiose conclusion, comparable to the radiant cadence at the beginning. A quiet ending replaces the triumph.

THE TONE POEMS BETWEEN TRADITION AND PROGRESS

Not only *Also sprach Zarathustra* is characterized by the juxtaposition of traditional and modern elements. All of Strauss's tone poems have this quality, albeit to different degrees. Tradition is strongest in the grandiosely staged harmonic cadences as well as in the established structures and categories of form; the young Strauss already knew what could be accomplished with them. The composition of "masculine" principal themes and "feminine" secondary themes, of conflict-ridden developments saturated with rich polyphony, of triumphal recapitulations and restful codas—these were his métier as well as the realization of typical symphonic characters, which he sharpened and intensified: the grotesque Scherzo, the exuberantly flowing Adagio, the heroic Allegro, and the pompous Finale.

In his compositional strategies Strauss did not proceed in an arbitrary fashion; he avoided certain topoi. The grand brass chorale is as rare in his tone poems as are the nature sounds favored so much by Mahler. Strauss distrusted religion in the form of Christian dogmas. Hymnlike characters occur in his music only after large-scale intensifications, when they are expected anyway, or, as is the case for instance in "Auf dem Gipfel" (On the Summit) in *Eine Alpensinfonie*, when they are motivated by the sublime grandeur of Nature. The rough, amorphous, and unformed character of Mahlerian nature sounds (however artfully treated) can hardly be found in Strauss's music despite his "reverence for eternal glorious Nature" (diary entry of May 1911) expressed in *Eine Alpensinfonie*. Strauss's métier was compositional craft. He could express himself in his tone poems only in an advanced, sophisticated, and highly differentiated musical language; simplicity was not his thing.

But Strauss would have been the last to advance all musical means to the same degree. He feared the risk of remaining misunderstood, and he had been able to learn what compositional economy meant from his great models, especially from classical composers, namely, to establish a meaningful balance between complication and simplification of musical parameters. Strauss pointedly advanced instrumentation, the handling of texture as well as thematic, harmonic, and rhythmic aspects of music, but limited himself to surprisingly simple structures in terms of metric organization. Quite frequently his themes appear divided into regular, square-cut phrases. The stormy theme of the "Freuden und Leidenschaften" section of *Also sprach Zarathustra* is a case in point. Strauss domesticated his complicated polyphony, which still drives any untrained score reader to despair, by way of a simple metric organization; he abstained from musical prose and free irregular structures. One would not have expected such abstinence from a potential successor of Wagner. Strauss, however, was also an heir to Classical composers, and he knew all too well that instrumental and operatic music were two different things. Even a program could not replace a scenic representation.

The only tone poem featuring musical prose to a significant degree (if we disregard the beginning of the music of the "Companion" section in *Ein Heldenleben* or passages in the "Summit" music in *Eine Alpensinfonie*) is *Don Quixote*—an exceptional work in many ways. Unusual is not only the use of solo instruments (violoncello, viola), which brings the work close to the genre of the concerto, but unusual also is the entire conception. Since Strauss was of the opinion that only crazy composers could still write variations at the end of the nineteenth century, *Don Quixote* was to serve as a way to reveal the absurdity of the form by parodying it. For this reason he loaded his variation composition with all kinds of features that he usually did not use or used only sparingly in other works: a primitive way of composing with intentional errors (the theme of Sancho Panza), an excess of drastic tone painting, sequences that only feign development, and melodies consisting of formulas strung together; it even has a "religioso" passage. And part of this inventory of absurdities—seen from the perspective of the composer—are also the musical prose sections at the end of variation 1, at the beginning of variation 3, and in variation 5.

With *Don Quixote*—a work that may be understood as a satire on used-up forms and a critique of the popular conception of reducing program music to tone painting—Strauss emphatically pointed out what mattered for him in the composition of tone poems. A subject alone was not enough; what was needed for the purpose of shaping music into meaningful structures was compositional potency. Traditional and novel means were to be combined and related to each other in ever new ways. Programmatic ideas could aid in this process, but a composer could not rely on them.

The last tone poems reveal the dangers lurking when the balance between old and new, between music and program was imprecisely measured. Their large dimensions required especially strong scaffolds. Tradition protrudes massively at the end in *Symphonia domestica* in the form of a pompous coda that does not just contradict the composer's many statements against "empty" formulas; even worse is that Strauss, by and large, abandons in the coda the structural idea of the evolution of the third theme. A musically satisfactory conception is made difficult in *Eine Alpensinfonie* through the extreme proliferation of subheadings referring largely to nature images. In other words, the programmatic model prevails over the musical composition.

But *Eine Alpensinfonie* had already become for Strauss a secondary endeavor. In 1915 he was no longer interested in tone poems, only in operas. And this did not change in the years ahead. True, now and then Strauss still composed larger programmatic instrumental works. But almost always these were occasional compositions, clearly ranking behind his operas. This is true for his two piano concertos (1925 and 1927) as well as for the *Japanische Festmusik* (1940), but it also true for the instrumental pieces composed after his last opera *Capriccio* (1942). Most of them, (for example, *Metamorphosen*) were inspired by the programmatic idea of honoring great traditions with which Strauss felt connected. The time of the tone poems, of large-scale instrumental works with innovative conceptions and dramatic programs, was long passed.

NOTES

This chapter was translated by Jürgen Thym.

1. The term was coined by Rudolf Stephan to designate music between high art and entertainment.

2. Bülow's verdict on Strauss's Bläserserenade in E-flat, Op. 7, is found in a letter to Eugen Spitzweg, Strauss's publisher; the letter is housed in the Münchner Stadtbibliothek.

3. Franz Trenner, ed., *Richard Strauss–Ludwig Thuille: Ein Briefwechsel,* Veröffentlichungen der Richard-Strauss-Gesellschaft München, Bd. 4 (Tutzing: Hans Schneider, 1978), 78.

4. Letter to his sister dated 6 November 1890 in Bayerische Staatsbibliothek.

5. Walter Werbeck, *Die Tondichtungen von Richard Strauss,* Dokumente und Studien zu Richard Strauss, Bd. 2 (Tutzing: Hans Schneider, 1996), 528.

6. Franz Zagiba, *Johann L. Bella (1843–1936) und das Wiener Musikleben* (Vienna: Notringes der wissenschaftlichen Verbände Österreichs, 1955), 48; and Werbeck, *Tondichtungen,* 27n. 11.

7. Emphasis added. Charles Youmans, "Ten Letters from Alexander Ritter to Richard Strauss, 1887–1894," *Richard Strauss Blätter* 35 (1996): 15.

8. Franz Grasberger, ed., *Der Strom der Töne trug mich fort: Die Welt um Richard Strauss in Briefen* (Tutzing: Hans Schneider, 1967), 41.

9. Willi Schuh, ed., *Richard Strauss: Betrachtungen und Erinnerungen* (Zurich: Atlantis Verlag, 1981), 211.

10. Franz Trenner and Gabrielle Strauss, eds., *Cosima Wagner–Richard Strauss: Ein Briefwechsel,* Veröffentlichungen der Richard-Strauss-Gesellschaft München, Bd. 2 (Tutzing: Hans Schneider, 1978), 36.

11. Werbeck, *Die Tondichtungen,* 538.

12. Ibid., 69n. 19.

13. Grasberger, *Der Strom der Töne,* 56.

14. Werbeck, *Die Tondichtungen,* 245ff.

15. Dietrich Kämper, ed., *Richard Strauss und Franz Wüllner im Briefwechsel,* Beiträge zur rheinischen Musikgeschichte (Cologne: A. Volk, 1963), 25.

16. Werbeck, *Die Tondichtungen,* 153n. 213.

17. Ibid., 158.

18. Ibid., 33.

19. Willi Schuh, ed., "Hans von Bülow–Richard Strauss: Briefwechsel," in *Richard Strauss Jahrbuch* 1954 (Bonn: Boosey and Hawkes, 1953), 70.

20. David Ewen, ed., *The Book of Modern Composers,* 2d exp. ed. (New York: Knopf, 1950), 55.

21. Herwarth Walden, ed., *Richard Strauss: Symphonien und Tondichtungen*, Erläutert von G. Brecher, A. Hahn, W. Klatte, W. Mauke, A. Schattmann, H. Teibler, H. Walden, Meisterführer Nr. 6 (Berlin: Schlesinger'sche Buch- und Musikhandlung, 1908), 95.

22. Norman Del Mar, *Richard Strauss: A Critical Commentary on His Life and Works* (Ithaca, N.Y.: Cornell University Press, 1986), 1:126.

23. Richard Strauss, *Briefe an die Eltern, 1882–1906*, ed. Willi Schuh (Zurich: Atlantis Verlag, 1954), 128ff.

24. Hermann Kretzschmar, *Führer durch den Konzertsaal* (Leipzig: Breitkopf and Härtel, 1930–33).

25. Wilhelm Klatte, "Die Symphonia Domestica," *Die Musik* 4, no. 8 (1904–05): 124.

26. Ibid., 125.

27. Werbeck, *Die Tondichtungen*, 27n. 11.

28. Carl Dahlhaus, *Johannes Brahms: Klavierkonzert Nr. 1 in d-moll, op. 15* (Munich: W. Fink, 1965), 21.

29. Werbeck, *Die Tondichtungen*, 167.

30. Natalie Bauer-Lechner, *Recollections of Gustav Mahler*, ed. Peter Franklin, trans. Dika Newin (London: Faber and Faber, 1980), 203.

31. Carl Dahlhaus, *Nineteenth-Century Music*, trans. J. Bradford Robinson (Berkeley: University of California Press, 1989), 331.

32. Richard Strauss, *Briefe an die Eltern*, 119.

33. Robert Schumann, *Gesammelte Schriften über Musik und Musiker*, ed. Heinrich Simon (Leipzig: Breitkopf and Härtel, [n.d.]), 3:8.

34. Eduard Hanslick, *On the Musically Beautiful: A Contribution towards the Revision of the Aesthetics of Music*, trans. Geoffrey Payzant (Indianapolis, Ind.: Hackett, 1986), 8.

35. Ibid., 101.

36. Del Mar, *Richard Strauss*, 1:150. Del Mar spoke of "harmonic side-slips."

37. Roland Tenschert, "Die Wandlunger einer Kadenz. Absonderlichkeiten der Harmonik in 'Don Quixote' von Richard Strauss," *Die Musik* 26, no. 9 (1933/34): 667.

38. Werbeck, *Die Tondichtungen*, 267n. 697.

39. Ibid., 61.

40. Ibid., 136n. 150.

41. Ibid., 254.

42. Otto Biba, "Richard Strauss und Johannes Brahms," *Musikblätter der Wiener Philharmoniker* 37, no. 7 (February 1983): 195ff.

5

The Early Reception of Richard Strauss's Tone Poems

Mark-Daniel Schmid

By the end of the first decade of the twentieth century, Richard Strauss had firmly established himself with his tone poems as an internationally recognized and lauded orchestral composer and could with full confidence direct his creative attention toward the genre of opera. Had Strauss never written anything after *Symphonia domestica* (1903)—no more operas or Lieder—these technically demanding programmatic compositions alone would have guaranteed him a secure position among the foremost composers of all time. The popularity—or even notoriety—of these works had been actualized and seemed impervious, especially when one takes into account the shrinking number of negative opinions by antagonistic critics and opponents, which by this time had little impact on Strauss's reputation among musicians and the concertgoing public.

The tone poems have long been regarded as the musical arena in which Strauss honed his skills as a precocious composer of a basically romantic bent in preparation for the string of mostly successfully received operas he would begin composing after 1904.[1] Responses by critics (writing for local newspapers or music journals), artists of every discipline, amateur writers, and members of the audiences—those who were present at the early performances of Strauss's tone poems—give us a glimpse of the disparate impression these works made. In their colorful and varied expressions these verbal reactions form an integral component in tracing and highlighting the various curves of popularity each of these works underwent in its early stages. Ultimately, they elucidate Strauss's position as early as 1890 as one of the leading avant-garde composers of the time. Commentary poured in from every city or town where orchestras played any one of the tone poems, creating a body of fascinating literature—some of which is still in dire need of being made available to the English-speaking reader—and supplying a valuable barometer for the disparate range of emotions and sets of opinions these works elicited. The overall reception ultimately gives a sense of the prevailing attitudes and tastes of the time.

Viewpoints on the musical and technical merits of the tone poems, discussions about their compositional features and indebtedness to earlier composers, and evaluations regarding the quality of their performances by orchestras often changed from one geographical location to another. They even differed within one single, generally larger, city in which several powerful men of the pen ruled, casting their written assessments of musical works in a kaleidoscopic and persuasive discourse. Of course, there were differences in reception from one tone poem to the next, since critics and audiences did not always perceive a new work as equally successful as the previous one. A major factor that determined the course of a value judgment regarding a tone poem was brought about by the experience of several hearings of a particular work, often within a few years. As the public grew increasingly familiar with the tone poems, the reception of Strauss gradually shifted away from this body of work, and, after the premiere of *Salome* (in December of 1905), focused on his "stage tone poems."[2]

The path that each tone poem traveled to become part of the orchestral repertoire differs as one looks at Strauss's reception history in terms of where concerts were held. Performances of these works in the 1890s were given in North America as well as in a variety of European countries, led in frequency by Germany, Austria, Switzerland, and Great Britain but extending to the Netherlands, Belgium, France, Spain, Italy, Sweden, Denmark, and Russia. Except for the *Symphonia domestica*, the world premieres of all the tone poems occurred in German cities, in which a second performance of that particular work frequently did not take place until years later. First performances—in larger cities and smaller towns— were reviewed quite extensively in local and out-of-town newspapers, and music writers, to prepare audiences adequately, often discussed these works ahead of time.

Another, more popular, form of preparing an audience for a particular new work and, according to Leon Botstein, "to encourage a sense of competence" in them was to publish a guidebook containing detailed descriptions of instrumental works, such as Strauss's tone poems, resembling a substantially augmented set of program notes. However, these written analyses of particular works were intended for reading at home prior to attending a concert and were often available only through limited commercial venues. They required that readers draw connections between musical expressions and feelings of mood and emotion, that they focus on brief yet catchy melodies and motives, and that they be acquainted with the basic musical terminology of harmony and theory. For the growing number of concertgoers in the last two decades of the nineteenth century who lacked the skill of reading full scores or playing from piano reductions, these musical guides became the single literary means to familiarize themselves with newly emerging works. By studying the guides, a layperson could now go to a concert—often a "much-coveted social occasion"—equipped with some prior knowledge and be confident enough to partake in an intelligent musical conversation about the work with one's social peers.[3]

Guidebooks to accompany Strauss's tone poems were mostly written in German and published in collections with such titles as *Der Musikführer* (The Musical Guide) or *Symphonien und Tondichtungen*.[4] Although Strauss did not write the descriptions of the programs of his tone poems, he encouraged and authorized others close to him to write them.[5] Often used by critics in their concert reviews as references for discussing the intricacies of the tone poems, musical guides not only figured prominently in helping popularize Strauss's works, but also became highly influential in shaping the written commentary surrounding them.

Larger essays within a book on composers, such as "character sketches" and biographies, were also an important source of Strauss's reception. In 1896 the German music writers and critics Arthur Seidl (1863–1928) and Wilhelm Klatte (1870–1930) became the first to chronicle the composer's reception in a so-called *Charakterskizze* (character sketch). The authors traced the compositional style of Strauss beginning with his early works and then focused on the tone poems through *Also sprach Zarathustra*.[6] Four years later Gustav Brecher (1879–1940), a German conductor and writer on music, followed suit with a monograph in which he first acquainted the general listener with Strauss's life before presenting each tone poem in chronological order through *Ein Heldenleben* and combining analysis with criticism.[7] In a scholarly compilation of writings by different authors, *Moderne Essays zur Kunst und Litteratur*, the German music writer Erich Urban published an essay emphasizing Strauss's status as the most prominent avant-garde composer of the fin-de-siècle.[8]

Newspaper reviews of tone poem performances, in several instances preceded by a general description of the composer's role in musical society at the time, form perhaps the most sweeping and insightful documentation of Strauss reception. The reviews were issued everywhere: from Berlin to Vienna, Zurich to London, and across the ocean, from New York to Boston to Chicago. In their comprehensive overview, these critiques, often written by some of the most prominent musical scholars and writers of their time, generated a multifaceted picture of Strauss and assembled the unique trademarks and intricate characteristics of his colorful and provocative compositions. In the final analysis, they revealed a composer who has always eluded easy classification.

The most abundant criticisms came, of course, from German-speaking countries—Germany, Austria, and Switzerland—and countries with English as the main language—Great Britain and the United States. Drawing examples predominantly from these sources, this discussion will divide the reception history of Strauss's tone poems into the five aforementioned countries—with Austria being limited to reviews from Vienna, and London singled out as the most representative city for Great Britain—and will focus on the years 1887 to 1908, when Strauss reception shifted toward the composer's operas.

GERMANY

The widest and fastest circulation of Strauss tone poems occurred in Germany, with performances in numerous larger cities as well as smaller ones. This should not come as a surprise, considering that Strauss was born there, and beginning in the late 1880s quickly emerged as Germany's leading composer, continuing the legacy of Franz Liszt and Richard Wagner. Holding important conducting posts in several major German cultural centers, such as Meiningen, Munich, and Weimar, and relentlessly guest conducting his own works in every city in which he could secure a performance—an undertaking he carried on more than any other composer before him—helped Strauss bolster his reputation and capture his audience in countless cities. With his programmatic compositions he appealed to an audience conditioned by 1890 to orchestral music of Liszt and others based on literary, historical, and descriptive subject matter, and Strauss expanded the listeners' horizons by adding works that derived their inspiration from philosophical as well as autobiographical and biographical themes. With his keen sense of business acumen he also knew how to sell his music to publishers—as the famous case of *Macbeth* shows—and was instrumental as the driving force of the Genossenschaft Deutscher tonsetzer founded in 1903 in establishing new copyright laws for composers.[9]

Some cities, of course, behaved in a more friendly manner toward Strauss than others did. Likewise, certain conductors scheduled his works repeatedly and certain critics wrote favorably about them. A major proponent of Strauss in Germany was Gustav Kogel (1849–1921) and the Frankfurt City Orchestra.[10] Their first association began in 1887 when the orchestra invited Strauss to conduct his Symphony in F Minor on 7 January in one of their concerts, which earned the composer rave reviews from a critic of the *Freie Presse*: "Already a master despite his youth, he knows that he must wear his mastery with modesty, for its springs are not voluntary but imperative."[11] Kogel and the Museum Society began to schedule Strauss's descriptive orchestral works regularly in 1891, initially with one performance per season and eventually increasing the number to three and then five annually. In the city that experienced the world premieres of *Also sprach Zarathustra* and *Ein Heldenleben*, both under the baton of their composer, this trend did not change when the Austrian conductor and composer Siegmund von Hausegger (1872–1948) succeeded Kogel in 1904, while the latter took on an engagement with the Berlin Philharmonic Orchestra and continued his support for Strauss there.

The world premiere by the Frankfurt City Orchestra of *Also sprach Zarathustra* on 27 November 1896, under Strauss's direction, resulted in a "reception [that] was enthusiastic and expressed in tumultuous applause." Documenting the views critics held of the work and of Strauss in general, the anonymous critic of the Berlin-based *Musikalisches Wochenblatt* kept his review brief, mentioning that the work's orchestration was "treated masterfully," and perceiving "the great original thrust charging through the *Zarathustra* composition."[12] For the performance of the work, with which he had originally included the subtitle "Symphonic Optimism in Fin de Siècle Form, Dedicated to the Twentieth Century," Strauss explicitly directed that none of the work's subheadings, not even the word "Zarathustra," be included in the concert program. It was not until after the performance that many concertgoers learned of the philosophical origins of the tone poem.

Following the world premiere of *Ein Heldenleben* in 1899 in Frankfurt, the anonymous critic of the *Frankfurter Zeitung* acknowledged the heated debate that was raging over the issue of programmatic music. Nevertheless, he avoided stating his own stance and cheered the "heroic work, lavishly and significantly endowed with motives, truly ingeniously conceived over and over in its extraordinarily complex thematic elaboration." The critic particularly stressed two aspects of the work: "the absolute autonomy of musical ideas" from any nonmusical reference—despite a descriptive analysis by Wilhelm Klatte, sanctioned by Strauss and handed out prior to the concert—and Strauss's "tremendous skill in arranging them." Then again, he did not hesitate to list two of the work's weaknesses. First, the presence of too many "motives and dissonances of previously unheard of audacity," seemed to go beyond the harmonic language to which the average listener was accustomed. Second, the critic perceived the work's "unusual length" (somewhere between thirty-two and thirty-four minutes) as stretching the limit of the average listener. Obviously this aspect did not concern Strauss who expected to be "understood by his audience in all of his intentions, and [to keep] interest alive to the end."[13]

On the other hand, the length of *Don Quixote* did not arouse much controversy among critics; aspects such as instrumentation, harmonic treatment, rhythm, form, and the underlying program gave rise to an array of colorful responses following the first performance of the work in Cologne on 8 March 1898 by Franz Wüllner (1832–1902) and the Gürzenich Orchestra. One critic from the *Frankfurter Zeitung* called the fantastic variations on a theme of knightly character the "total disintegration of all musical thought" that made his previous two tone poems—*Till Eulenspiegel* and *Also sprach Zarathustra*—look mild in comparison. While instrumentation was Strauss's most recognized and admired trademark so far, with *Don Quixote* the utilized effects of a wind machine and muted brass imitating sheep became "particularly strange."[14]

Rudolf Louis (1870–1914), the influential music critic of Munich, took the issue further, calling the work's instrumentation "mired in more than one place, in unsuccessful experiments" and thus preventing it "from becoming a masterpiece that is just as perfect, in its own way, as *Till Eulenspiegel*."[15] With *Don Quixote*, Louis felt that Strauss had "developed the ideal [and] elevated gestures of the tonal language of Liszt into a gestural language of great specificity that undertakes quite seriously not only interpreting the events of an external plot in tone but also drawing them until they are recognizable to the inner eye."[16] Louis's matter-of-fact review appears rather favorably inclined toward Strauss compared to the majority of commentary by other critics of Munich.

Strauss had already forged an initial reputation as a composer of orchestral music during the first tenure in his hometown of Munich—a three-year appointment at the Munich Court Opera (1886–89) as third conductor behind Hermann Levi (1839–1900) and Franz Fischer (1849–1918), a stint that left the composer disillusioned and frustrated.[18] With the local Hofkapelle Strauss gave the world premiere of his first programmatic attempt for large orchestra, the symphonic fantasy *Aus Italien*, on 2 March 1887 in the Odeonsaal. Strauss's father Franz played all of the French horn solos in s work Michael Kennedy calls a "halfway house between his youthful classicism and the originality of the tone poems."[18] This assessment seems to resemble rather closely what Oskar Merz, main critic of the city's leading newspaper *Münchner Neueste Nachrichten*, had formulated after the premiere of the work in which the young Strauss, under the increasing influence of Liszt's symphonic poems, had for the first time openly revealed his progressive tendencies and no doubt "has become better acquainted with modern music and now wishes to reflect the impressions it has made on him in an individual manner. It is not surprising that on his first sortie into the realm of programme music he has not yet altogether succeeded in reaching the goal he has set himself."[19]

Hans von Bülow (1830–94), the famous pianist and conductor of the Meiningen Orchestra, who took Strauss under his wing advised him in different matters and arranged his first conducting post in Meiningen in the fall of 1885. Bülow, who, in return for these favors, was to become the dedicatee of *Aus Italien,* had a slightly more critical view of the work by an author he called "a genius." Bülow wrote to Alexander Ritter (1853–96), another of Strauss's influential mentors, on 30 December of that year, "I find he [Strauss] has gone to the utmost limit of what is musically possible (within the bounds of beauty) and has often, indeed gone beyond the limit without any really pressing need for it."[20]

Just like Bülow, many others in the city of Munich had seen in Strauss their greatest hope for the future, a hope that after the performance of *Aus Italien* was abruptly shattered. After the first work of the subscription concert on 2 March—Joseph Rheinberger's *The Taming of the Shrew* Overture, Op. 18—the audience was still unified and responding positively, but a "unanimity of opinion was no longer present" at the conclusion of Strauss's tone poem, as Otto Lessmann (1844–1918) observed in his review for the Leipzig newspaper *Neue Zeitschrift für Musik.*[21] Part of the audience shook their heads in disgust while the liberal faction—in German parliamentary fashion—signaled a jubilant "yes." If the audience greeted the first three movements of *Aus Italien* with applause, the hall quickly became filled with hisses and other utterances of disapproval after the last movement, which describes a *Neapolitanisches Volksleben,* and which already had been jeered by the orchestra during the rehearsal.[22] In another review of the same work one year later, Lessmann called it "from a technical, rhythmic, and harmonic standpoint the hardest thing a composer has ever demanded of an orchestra"; however, he commended the beautiful and broadly conceived themes and was surprised by the poetic moods the music was able to evoke.[23] Strauss's response to the antagonistic appraisals of his latest work shows the type of argument Strauss was to apply vis-à-vis any kind of controversy regarding his programmatic works in general, aiming straight at what he felt was the heart of the matter: "With the horrifying lack of judgment and understanding typical of a large proportion of today's pen-pushers, many of them, like a large proportion of the public, have allowed some of the external features of my work, which may be dazzling but are of *purely sec-ondary importance*, to deceive them as to its real *content*, indeed to overlook it altogether."[24]

Although the Bavarian capital and its critics had ample opportunity to review Strauss's work not only as a composer but also as a conductor, Munich refrained for several decades from fully acknowledging its own *Landsmann* (compatriot). Only a dozen performances of Strauss's tone poems through 1898, most of them conducted by Strauss leading either the Munich Hofkapelle or the Kaim Orchestra, gave audiences little ex-posure to the oeuvre of its most illustrious citizen.[25] During the 1899–1900 season four concerts by the Kaim Orchestra, three of them under the baton of Strauss and one by Hausegger, featured all of his tone poems from *Macbeth* through *Ein Heldenleben*, a trend maintained, how-ever, for only two more seasons. During this season Strauss was to have another vexing experience with his hometown when he offered to conduct the Court Orchestra in a performance of *Also sprach Zarathustra* on 17 March, but the intendant Karl Freiherr von Perfall (1824–1907) de-clined, choosing Franz Fischer instead. Thus, Strauss had to wait until 16 March 1900 to conduct it there for the first time. Perfall's decision came in response to Strauss's blocking any performances of the work at the local academy concerts in the 1897–98 season, the year during which the work was written, as a payback for having been fired there as a con-ductor in October 1896, two years after he had taken over their leadership in November 1894. It was not until 1910 that Strauss recaptured the favor of Munich concert promoters, critics, and audiences when the city or-ganized an elaborate Strauss-*Woche*, an event discussed in many different German newspapers.[26]

In contrast to Munich, Berlin was the city where Strauss had the most intense and longest-lasting professional association, which began at a time when he was just starting to make a name for himself as a composer. Fol-lowing one brief season in 1885, first as assistant conductor to Hans von Bülow and a month later taking over as the principal conductor of the Meiningen Orchestra, Strauss accepted the aforementioned position of third conductor in Munich beginning in August 1886. In the middle of a rather busy season Strauss was able to secure, on 23 and 25 January 1888, his first engagement in Berlin, leading the Berlin Philharmonic Orchestra in a pair of concerts that featured *Aus Italien* less than eleven months after the work's world premiere.[27] On 4 February 1890—in the midst of his first season as assistant conductor of the Weimar Court Orchestra—Strauss and the Berlin Philharmonic Orchestra presented *Don Juan*, which Hans von Bülow had premiered there with great success only five days earlier.[28] The following year Strauss again led the Berlin Philharmonic, on 23 and 24 February 1891, in two concerts, which included the city's first performance of *Tod und Verklärung* eight months after the world premiere in Eisenach on 21 June 1890.[29] And then, a year later, on 29 February 1892, Strauss and the orchestra also gave the Berlin debut of the revised version of *Macbeth*, which was received enthusiastically. Bülow, who was shocked by the dissonance of the first version, now accepted it "in spite of all its acerbities and the monstrosities of its material."[30] Strauss's relationship with the orchestra intensified dramatically in the 1894–95 season, when he was appointed principal conductor of the Berlin Philharmonic following Bülow's death; he conducted them in ten seasonal concerts, none of which included any of his tone poems. Much to Strauss's chagrin, the offer was not extended for a second season and instead went to Arthur Nikisch (1855–1922).

Leipzig, which Strauss initially visited in 1883, and where in 1887 he first met Gustav Mahler, was another city able to boast a similar number of tone poem performances to those in Berlin. Renowned musical ensembles such as the Gewandhaus Orchestra and the less familiar Winderstein Orchestra, both responsible for 25 percent of the performances in Germany, as well as several guest orchestras from nearby cities, produced over thirty-five such performances by 1908.[31] And the statistics again show that Strauss participated actively, conducting one-fourth of the concerts himself.

Overall, Frankfurt (55 concerts), Berlin (40 concerts), Leipzig (35 concerts), and Munich (30 concerts) were the most instrumental in the propagation of these symphonic works while other cities, such as Cologne, Hamburg, Düsseldorf, Dresden, and Bremen witnessed only a fair number of performances between the years 1887–1908. In the last decade of the nineteenth century, Frankfurt, Berlin, Leipzig, and Munich contributed to an average of sixteen concerts annually featuring Strauss's tone poems; this figure is doubled in the first decade of the twentieth century. Between 1900–10 some four hundred concerts featuring one or more of Strauss's tone poems were given in Germany by almost one hundred different conductors of various nationalities. Not surprisingly, Strauss conducted the most (120), more than one-fourth of the total number, followed by Kogel (27); Nikisch (16); and Wüllner, Hausegger, Max Fiedler, and Julius Buths (10+ each). Most frequently scheduled was *Tod und Verklärung* (130), followed by *Don Juan* and *Till Eulenspiegel* (both around 90); and *Ein Heldenleben* and *Symphonia domestica* (both around 50). Strauss most frequently conducted his favorite work, *Tod und Verklärung* (36), followed by *Don Juan, Till Eulenspiegel, Ein Heldenleben*, and *Macbeth* least of all. *Tod*

TABLE 5.1
Approximate Number of Performances in Germany by Tone Poem, 1887–1908

Tone Poem	Number of Performances	Strauss Conducting
Tod und Verklärung	130	36
Don Juan	90	27
Till Eulenspiegel	90	14
Ein Heldenleben	50	19
Symphonia domestica	50	11
Aus Italien	45	16
Also sprach Zarathustra	40	13
Don Quixote	30	10
Macbeth	20	7

und Verklärung also emerges as the front-runner in terms of total performances in Germany between 1887 and 1908 and is trailed by *Don Juan* and
Till Eulenspiegel (see Table 5.1).

Strauss's stature as Germany's foremost composer of his time, his relentless self-marketing, and an unmatched work ethic in bringing his
compositions to the concert stage on a continuing basis provided the foundation for these works to remain at the orchestral forefront in his home
country. By 1910 the tone poems had been circulated far and wide, and performed frequently enough, by the leading orchestras and conductors of the
time, to have secured a permanent place in Germany's concert repertoire.
Likewise, the Austro–Hungarian Empire, represented by its capital, Vienna,
would also play a role in the transmission of the tone poems, despite the
long-lasting tradition of negative criticism leveled against the representatives of the New German School, including Strauss, who endorsed Liszt's
philosophy that "new ideas must be expressed in new forms."

AUSTRIA

Throughout his life Austria held a special place in Richard Strauss's
heart—he even considered the country his *seelische Wahlheimat* (country of
choice).[32] Although nothing could replace the *heimische* (native) atmosphere

and quaint surroundings of his villa in Garmisch at the foot of the Bavarian Alps, in which he lived beginning in June 1908, it was Austria's cultural energy and musical tradition that never ceased to fascinate him. Three of Strauss's works were inspired by the Austrian sentiment and depicted elements of Viennese life: *Der Rosenkavalier, Arabella,* and the ballet *Schlagobers.* In Vienna, which for him became synonymous with Austria itself, Strauss even owned a house for several years at the Belvedere in the Jacquingasse.

The importance that the imperial capital already played after 1911 in Strauss's musical career, comparable only to that of Berlin, was paramount after the composer signed a contract as conductor of the local Court Opera. It was Vienna's intimate link to the bygone period of Mozart's classicism and the waltz as its main artistic expression that truly fascinated the Bavarian composer.[33] The city's well-defined cultural upper class—endorsing side by side such unorthodox extremes as the provincial and the global, the conventional and the modern—generated an ideal environment for testing new ideas in all artistic domains, including music.[34] Interested throughout his life in the arts, Strauss was attracted to a city that more than any other cosmopolitan cultural center provided him with artistic inspiration and intellectual exchange.[36] Vienna "became a decisive metaphor for Strauss's artistic energies," and through the acquaintance of Hugo von Hofmannsthal, one of the city's major literary figures, the creative impulses of the composer were unleashed in what became the longest and most prolific collaboration of his life.[36] The relationship between the two artists resulted in some six operatic masterworks and numerous other artistic projects.

Despite this veneration, the conservative city on the Danube always marked a particularly challenging territory for the German *Neutöner* (modernist), and not just in terms of gaining acceptance as a composer of programmatic music—tone poems and operas alike.[37] The ambiguity of his relationship with the capital of the former Habsburg Monarchy culminated in the difficulties he experienced when his proposed appointment as the codirector of the Vienna Court Opera by the late summer of 1918 was jeopardized by a formal yet unsuccessful protest lodged against him by the staff members of the opera company, although he was finally able to take the post in May 1919. He was to last there only five years, resigning in 1924 over insurmountable political intrigue; nevertheless, he continued to conduct the Vienna Opera as well as the Vienna Philharmonic Orchestra until his death in 1949.

As early as 1892, the first disparaging reviews from Vienna came in response to performances of Strauss's early set of tone poems—*Macbeth, Don Juan,* and *Tod und Verklärung.* Compared to other cities of the Habsburg Empire, including its second capital Budapest, Vienna boasted the largest number of concerts that featured Strauss, more than in the cities of Graz, Linz, Salzburg, and others. More significant, it was in Vienna where newspaper critics leveled the most colorful, extensive, and diverse criticism against Strauss's works. Who were these mighty men of the pen who could make or break a performer or composer and, who, along with the Viennese performing institutions and audience, could determine just how successful someone's career might be?

The Viennese critics were the most influential cultural judges who nurtured Vienna's intellectual and artistic climate with their written commentary. Gustav Schoenaich (1841–1906) wrote primarily for the *Wiener Allgemeine Zeitung* and the *Wiener Tagblatt*, while Robert Hirschfeld (1858–1914), writing for the *Neue Musikalische Presse*, had acquired notoriety as a writer of theater reviews and scholarly articles.[38] Eduard Hanslick (1825–1904) was the chief music critic of the *Neue Freie Presse*, Vienna's most prestigious paper; after Hanslick's death Julius Korngold (1860–1945) took over that position.[39]

Reviews of musical works directed at the general public figured prominently in daily Viennese newspapers and appeared in the so-called feuilleton, along with other news to entertain the general reader, on the first page of the newspaper and often continued on the second page.[40] A reflection of the type of discourse conducted between critics and audiences, these feuilletons were also a pulse of the sardonic climate in which the performing arts were discussed. Almost all of the reviews by either Hanslick or Korngold of the Viennese premieres of Strauss's tone poems appeared there.[41] Strauss, like Wagner before him, received his share of penetrating assaults from several Viennese writers, which generally came in adverse and often lengthy criticisms.[42] These assessments did not, however, hinder in any way a heightening interest in Strauss; a steadily growing number of performances of his works—including the tone poems—would reach its climax in the 1940s.

The first acquaintance of the Viennese public with a Strauss tone poem occurred on 10 January 1892, fairly late, considering that three of the composer's works of that genre had already been performed for between fifteen and twenty-six months throughout Europe.[43] Under the direction of Hans Richter (1843–1916), the Vienna Philharmonic presented *Don Juan* for the first time to an Austrian audience twenty-six months after the work's world premiere had taken place in Weimar.[44] None other than the mighty Eduard Hanslick reviewed the concert, and his commentary of this work has long been considered among the archetypes of its genre. Influenced in different ways by the triumvirate of programmatic composers Berlioz, Liszt, and Wagner, Strauss had created a work not worthy of the title "'tone paint-

ing' but rather a tumult of brilliant daubs, a faltering tonal orgy, half bacchanale, half witches' Sabbath," Hanslick argued, pushing the agenda that
he and Johannes Brahms endorsed: that "absolute music" claims superior
status over "programmatic music." In 1892 Strauss belonged to a group of
younger composers who were convincingly setting philosophy, poetry, and
painting into music, the "mother tongue" of the arts. In the process, according to Hanslick, he was only able "to translate badly, unintelligibly,
tastelessly, with exaggeration," making his tone poem one of these "out-
wardly brilliant compositions" and carrying the listener "to the dissolute
ecstasy of a Don Juan."[45] Almost predictably Hanslick was to repeat this
argument every time his discussions centered on a fresh work of Strauss or
any composer belonging to the New German School.

A case in point is Strauss's next tone poem, *Tod und Verklärung*, which
Hanslick reviewed after its Austrian premiere by Richter and the Vienna
Philharmonic on 15 January 1893, as part of the fifth Philharmonic Concert, two-and-a-half years after its world premiere in Eisenach on 21 June
1890. Again the critic was busily spreading the gospel of the superiority of
absolute over programmatic music: that "the realism [of *Tod und Verklärung*] lacks only the final step: the dimly lighted sickroom with the dying
man upon a real stage." There was no question that Strauss was a dazzling
orchestrator, who "illustrated with brilliant virtuosity, sometimes even with
really new color combinations"—but as a translator of musical ideas he was
rather unsuccessful because "he composes with poetic rather than with musical elements."[46] Robert Hirschfeld echoed Hanslick's objections
concerning "programmatic music, which in its degeneracy does not require
that additional step from the sublime to the derisive—it carries both of
them within itself." Furthermore, he felt the work's inflated instrumentation distracted the listener from discovering anything important, and that
the penetrating radiance of the orchestral colors erased any sense of formal
coherence, failing to justify the tone poem's rather "paltry motive."[47]

Three months passed between the world premiere of *Till Eulenspiegel*,
which took place on 5 November 1895 in Cologne, and its Austrian premiere in Vienna, when Richter and the Vienna Philharmonic gave a reading
of the work as part of a pension fund concert on 5 January 1896.[48] Schoenaich, writing for the *Neue Musikalische Presse*, perceived rather positively in
the eccentric yet technically versatile Strauss, whose "individual language"
of composition was steeped in the solid classical tradition of his predecessors, the leader of a modernist movement, able not to be "crushed under the
weight of the phenomenon of Richard Wagner." The recent performance of
Till Eulenspiegel was also proof to Schoenaich that the composer's sophisticated control of form and savvy treatment of subject matter was at a level

"considered permissible."[49] In his general evaluation of Strauss and his orchestral works, the critic of the *Neues Wiener Tagblatt,* Max Kalbeck (1850–1921),[50] in a vein similar to Hanslick, provided a sarcastic evaluation of a tone poem, "with a laborious and affected title of an orchestral work, which is only associated with rondo form insofar as it is a supposedly comical two-measure melody, but which in truth is meager and complicated, repeatedly returning in different form." Not only was *Till Eulenspiegel* loaded with "amassed dissonances by the orchestra gone crazy," but Kalbeck further believed that "as a prime example of musical ugliness, the score, heavily burdened with instruments, may perhaps have a pedagogical value or may also stand out as curious testimony to the corruptness of taste which finds pleasure in evoking with artistic means as inartistic an impression as possible."[51]

Only slightly more time—five months to be exact—elapsed between the world and the Viennese premieres of another tone poem, *Also sprach Zarathustra,* which received a first performance in the Habsburg capital soon after its world premiere in Frankfurt on 27 November 1896 with the composer himself conducting. Less than four months later, on 21 March 1897, Richter reunited with the Vienna Philharmonic players "who let Richard Strauss's anarchic music-bomb explode in their last concert" of the season.[52] More than any other tone poem, *Also sprach Zarathustra* had to weather the criticism of incompatibility between the philosophical ideas set forth by Nietzsche's original account and its musical depiction by Strauss. As Hirschfeld succinctly noted, "[O]ne can lead the tone poem to infinity and finally bring musical composition to the point at which it plays several volumes of Kant or Hegel into our hands, with musical footnotes, and as explanations of the philosopher, the motives 'pure reason' or 'immanent negativity' are identified in [musical] notes."[53] Hirschfeld also aimed his fierce attack at other issues such as instrumentation, form, the work's concluding collision of B major and C major (referred to by Strauss as the "World Riddle"), and the composer's inflated use of counterpoint. Strauss's reputation was seemingly at stake, if one is to believe the majority of Viennese critics.

Even with Strauss conducting his works, the Viennese critics were rarely, if ever, appeased. Strauss gave his debut as a conductor in Vienna's Grosser Musikvereinssaal on 23 January 1901 with the Munich Kaim Orchestra in a concert, which, according to Hanslick, "was well attended by an extremely attentive audience that was not sparing with applause and laurels" and that featured *Till Eulenspiegel* and *Ein Heldenleben* in its Vienna premiere. The critic allowed a few words about the former work, musically unable to stand on its own—"he who does not read uninterruptedly in the 'guide' will have no clue what this is all supposed to represent"—since audiences were already familiar with *Till Eulenspiegel* and its critical reception in the press from an earlier performance in Vienna. Thus, Hanslick's commentary centered exclusively on the latter work and its accompanying *Erläuterungsschrift* (explanatory pamphlet) by Gustav Brecher and Friedrich Rösch (1862–1925), authorized by the composer. Their analysis certainly provided enough debatable material to lash out indirectly at "truly ugly music . . . which fascinates neither through clear and coherent form nor by independent musical beauty." Was there anything to which Hanslick did not object? Despite "its splendid orchestration and several inspired, bold or tender ideas," the critic suggested "that fifteen years from now nobody will ask about his hero's life anymore."[54]

The following two years found Strauss again in Vienna several times with the Berlin Tonkünstler Orchestra, bringing back to the challenging Viennese audiences not only three of his own early tone poems but *Ein Heldenleben* as well, its fourth appearance since 1901.[55] Despite the work's initially frequent scheduling on concert programs and Strauss's personal involvement in promoting it whenever he was in Austria, performances of the work were not as numerous as the composer's most popular tone poem, *Till Eulenspiegel*—a work that perhaps most eloquently captured the particular idiosyncratic nature of the Viennese citizen and which eventually, by the beginning of the second decade of the twentieth century, was to emerge as Strauss's most celebrated tone poem.[56]

SWITZERLAND

In Switzerland, Strauss's tone poems began to be disseminated approximately five years later than in Germany and Austria but quickly proved that the attention they attracted at first hearing was a result of their intriguing qualities. Perhaps because these works were so technically demanding (or perhaps in spite of it) over one hundred years ago—pushing the level of orchestral playing to new heights—orchestras all over Europe regarded the tone poems as a welcome challenge, and Swiss conductors from Zurich to Geneva began programming them regularly. In a matter of a few years, several found their way into the permanent repertoire of major Swiss orchestras, who featured them on a rotating basis.

Generally thought to be on the more conservative side of musical tastes, the Swiss audience had been accustomed to hearing works from the classic and romantic period, but if conductors included contemporary compositions in a concert program, they did not object to a work by a

Swiss composer. When a conductor decided not to choose a modern Swiss work, he frequently chose something by Strauss or another German or Austrian composer such as Reger, Wolf, or Mahler. This was particularly true for several of the German conductors employed by a Swiss orchestra, many of whom, such as Oscar Jüttner, had a penchant for Strauss and his compatriots.

As a conductor, Strauss learned to understand his audiences only too well and over time developed a successful strategy of promoting his works and finding ways of getting them heard. Throughout his life he was his own best advocate; he appeared frequently as a guest conductor—an event that was billed as a "special concert" and added to his already busy concert schedule. In addition to his many conducting appearances throughout Europe, Strauss also took his orchestras on regular tours, an additional venue for him to promote his works, which ultimately brought him hard-earned cash. Twice during the first decade of the twentieth century, Strauss went on tour in Switzerland.

On his first rather short Swiss tour, which began in early 1903, Strauss headed the Berlin Tonkünstler Orchestra. The first stop on 19 March was Geneva, the largest city of the French part of Switzerland. Their concert there, advertised as *Un Seul Concert* (a single concert), opened with the symphonic fantasy *Aus Italien*, a forerunner to the composer's "real" tone poems and which a Swiss audience could finally hear for the first time, sixteen years after its creation.[57] *Aus Italien* became the only larger orchestral work by Strauss to receive a Swiss premiere in a city where only *Don Juan*, *Tod und Verklärung*, and *Till Eulenspiegel* had appeared in subscription concerts. Ed. C.'s program notes, available prior to the concert for perusal, first informed the concertgoer of Strauss's position among the leading conductors of his time—Nikisch, Felix Mottl (1856–1911), and Felix von Weingartner (1863–1942). He then went on to bemoan the lack of exposure that this youthful work had received to date as he believed "it is nevertheless of a maturity which astonishes and can be classified among the best compositions of a young master." Concluding his discussion, he felt that in *Aus Italien* "although youthful exuberance is indeed somewhat in evidence, nonetheless, everything is fresh and spontaneous."[58]

The tour's second and last stop was Zurich, located in the German part of the country. No other city witnessed as many Swiss premieres of Strauss tone poems or programmed more concerts in which these were repeatedly performed than Zurich. By 1903 concertgoers in Zurich had already had the opportunity—in fifteen different subscription, benefit, pension fund, and popular concerts yearly since 1895—to become acquainted with Strauss's tone poems save *Macbeth*, which was not heard there until 1911.

Consequently, when Strauss and the Berlin Tonkünstler Orchestra visited Zurich to give two concerts there, the first on 20 March, featuring *Aus Italien* in its Zurich premiere, the second on 21 March with *Tod und Verklärung* and *Don Juan* on the program, they found a well-prepared and eagerly awaiting audience. Strauss's concerts in Switzerland for 1903, however, were not over yet. Only three days later, on 24 March, Strauss appeared in Basel at the thirty-eighth Tonkünstlerfest of the Allgemeiner Deutscher Musikverein, whose president he had been since 1901, and led the Orchester der Allgemeinen Musikgesellschaft in a performance of *Don Juan* and *Ein Heldenleben*.[59]

Five years later (in May 1908) Strauss returned to Swiss soil to conduct a concert that featured his own orchestral works. This time Strauss traveled with the other famous Berlin orchestra, the Berlin Philharmonic, which was celebrating its twenty-fifth anniversary and whose principal conductor he had been during the 1894–95 season. Lausanne was the first destination and on 22 May enthusiastically embraced *Tod und Verklärung*, which by that time had been performed eighteen times in Switzerland in every one of its major cities, more than any other Strauss tone poem thus far. The Cathédrale de Lausanne was the site of this first concert, which also included works by four of Strauss's favorite composers—Mozart, Weber, Liszt, and Wagner.[60] The commentary of an anonymous critic writing for the local *Gazette de Musicale* named Strauss "the greatest composer of Germany today," one who could claim a considerable musical knowledge that "is always spontaneous and impulsive."[61] Three days after the concert a review appeared in the *Gazette de Lausanne* in which possibly the same critic rather briefly took stock of the concert and of *Tod und Verklärung*, in particular, which was heard only for the second time in that city. After suggesting that a cathedral may not be the ideal locale for a heroic symphonic poem such as *Les Préludes* or an elegant work such as Mozart's *Jupiter* Symphony, he concluded that at least *Tod und Verklärung* was given full justice as "the realism (realistic environment of the cathedral) is put to the service of a higher ideal."[62] Other critics had similar apprehensions about the cathedral's acoustical proprieties for a symphony concert by such a large ensemble as the Berlin Philharmonic, and, in general, found "a church being almost as unfavorable in this respect as the outdoors. But if we were expecting from the brass too strong a resonance under the arches, we were surprised by the opposite." The perfect performance of *Tod und Verklärung* was not surprising to this critic, considering that Strauss and his orchestra had been playing their repertoire for more than two months. Nonetheless, the critic raised the question "Will it be permitted to regret that its composer has not continued on his path and that he has allowed himself to be carried away by musical caprices and witticisms whose technical refinement is all the greater even as spirit and inspiration are absent from it? This symphonic poem, already eighteen years old and composed by a young man of twenty-six, is still of poignant intensity and incomparable beauty."[63] For the concert in Geneva the following day, Strauss programmed overtures and symphonies by Wagner, Beethoven, Berlioz, and his own *Don Juan*. This was to become the sixteenth performance of the work in Switzerland in eighteen years—second only to *Tod und Verklärung*—and the third time it was given in Geneva; it was also the second appearance of an orchestra from Berlin under Strauss's baton.[64]

Following a day of rest, Strauss and the Berlin Philharmonic, back in the German-speaking part of the country, continued on to Basel and Bern where they performed *Till Eulenspiegel* on 25 and 27 May, respectively, raising the work's number of performances in Switzerland since 1897 to thirteen.[65] In *La Vie Musicale*, a journal that on a weekly basis provided highlights of concerts in all major Swiss cities, the critic using the initials U. T. assessed both concerts, each time focusing on different aspects relevant to the concert. For example, in his discussion of the Basel concert, the reviewer sidestepped the characterization of *Till Eulenspiegel*, instead centering his discussion on Strauss the conductor: "Richard Strauss has conquered his audience by the simplicity with which he conducts; an exaggerated gesture never diverts from the work the attention of the listener, who is able to forget about the artists in order to think of nothing but the music itself." Similarly lacking analysis, his review of the Bern concert was mostly about the orchestra: "What tranquility reigns in this large orchestra, even in the most animated passages; the greatest difficulties are tossed off with ease, and one does not have the troublesome impression one feels with small orchestras of the fierce struggle of a musician who wants to produce more sound than his colleague."[66] A reading of *Don Juan* in Neuchâtel on 30 May in the Temple de Bas concluded the successful five-city tour. Trying not to be redundant in his commentary, the critic U. T. kept it short but nevertheless could not help but notice that "*Don Juan* strikes us with its elevated science and by its brilliant instrumentation."[67]

From 1895—when the Swiss conductor Friedrich Hegar (1841–1927) first introduced a Swiss audience in Zurich to *Don Juan*—until 1908 not a single concert season went by during which a Swiss orchestra did not perform one of Strauss's tone poems somewhere in one of the cities of this small but musically active country. For ten of them, Strauss was the conductor, as his proclivity to promote his own compositions throughout his long career also applied to Switzerland. No doubt, his efforts in disseminating his works there were surprisingly sizable, and probably had something to do with the country's proximity to Strauss's native country, common German language, and its wealth of cultural institutions.

Likewise, one cannot underestimate the personal zeal conductors and their particular orchestras brought to the challenge of making Strauss's works known throughout Switzerland. There is always that one individual conductor in each country who stands out as having contributed more than others in establishing a tradition of performing Strauss, a tradition often carried on by his successor(s).[68] Conducting Swiss premieres of *Don Juan, Tod und Verklärung, Till Eulenspiegel, Don Quixote, Ein Heldenleben,* and *Symphonia domestica,* Hegar was the first to make a name for himself as a tireless advocate of Strauss. With his talent of "hiring the best soloists for the concerts, putting excellent programs together, featuring seldom heard and new works," Hegar was able to build in a rather short time Switzerland's most renowned orchestra, the Zurich Tonhalle Orchestra.[69]

Despite the singular position of the Tonhalle Orchestra in the decades before the First World War, there were other musical forces in Switzerland that helped disseminate works by Strauss. With seven documented performances between 1899 and 1905, the Spa Orchestra of Montreux, under its first conductor, the Prussian-born Oscar Jüttner (1863–1905), also participated in the dissemination of Strauss's tone poems.[70] Beginning in 1899, Jüttner programmed at least one tone poem per season until he relinquished the post shortly before his death in 1905 to Julius Lange (1866–1939).[71] In Basel, the German-born Alfred Volkland (1841–1905) and the Basel Subscription Orchestra programmed Strauss tone poems with constant regularity, leaning toward the early popular tone poems. These and other Swiss conductors not only favored Strauss's orchestral works for their musical quality but also believed that they pointedly showed off the virtuosic skills of their orchestras.

In the first thirteen years (1895–1908), the reception of Strauss in Switzerland can be considered overall as favorable. While the focus of a critical discussion in Switzerland of the composer's work after 1906 also shifted toward his operas, the first ten years left behind a great amount of written testimony that elucidates in sufficient detail how and why the tone poems paved the reputation of Strauss as one of the most innovative and controversial composers of his generation. Despite the fact that over the years the tone poems experienced multiple exposures in most Swiss cities, newspaper critics never grew tired of commenting on some aspect of these works in their reviews, even if that meant sounding daringly similar to each other.

For example, in the German-speaking city of Bern, which had a rich Strauss tradition, two critics seemed particularly to affect one another's commentary.[72] Each of them produced for their newspaper a review of the fourth subscription concert given by the Bern City Orchestra on 19 January 1904 in the local city theater, a concert that included the Bern premiere of *Don Juan*. Two days after the concert, the critic L. of the *Intelligenzblatt*, decided not to analyze the work because of the guidebooks that were already handed out to audiences prior to the concert, and thus restricted his commentary to the singular statement that "the impression it produced was great."[73] One day later, on 23 January, the anonymous critic of the rival *Berner Tagblatt* argued that it was not the composer who was to blame for a prevailing skepticism toward program music such as *Don Juan*,[74] but rather the overly zealous music critics and authors of guidebooks who, unable to control their urge to *tisteln* (gossip), concocted flowery prose saturated with overrated adjectives and alliterations. In his own description of the tone poem, however, the author proved only that he, too, had succumbed to the same pitfall he so assiduously attacked, touched by its "burning passion, heightened sensuousness, combined with an amazing amount of detailed musical depiction, that goes by only too quickly." He also left unanswered exactly where and how Strauss's musical representation of the character of Don Juan "skirts only here and there the limits of what has been considered up to now to be musically legitimate."[75] Even for an adversary of programmatic music, the work had to be interesting and captivating, he strongly believed, if only the antagonist was able to enjoy it as a whole rather than search for incoherent individual effects.

Munzinger and the Bern Symphony Orchestra repeated the tone poem less than two months later, on 15 March, in the sixth subscription concert of the season, and while the critic from the *Berner Tagblatt* did not dwell on any aspect of the work, the *Intelligenzblatt* critic did make a few noteworthy comments.[76] His characterization sounded suspiciously similar to the one his colleague had issued in January after the work's Bern premiere: "The burning passion which permeates the entire work, the elemental force of its trappings, competing motives wildly wrestling with each other, incomprehensible creative imagination captivate the listener so much in their effect that he only sees before his inner eye the hero, permeated by a thirst for beauty, hurrying towards his downfall."[77] The long-winded sentence barely disguises its distinction from the previous review and reveals quite noticeably the verboseness of critical newspaper commentary so prominent in German- and English-speaking countries.

Between 1895 and the end of the 1907–8 regular concert season, approximately seventy-one concerts of tone poems were recorded, ten conducted by Strauss. Among them was the Swiss premiere of *Macbeth*, perhaps the least popular of the composer's works of that genre, on 15 November 1908 in Basel under Volkland and the Basel Subscription

TABLE 5.2

Years of World and Swiss Premieres of Tone Poems, 1887–1908

Tone Poem	World Premiere	Swiss Premiere
Aus Italien	1887	1903
Don Juan	1889	1895
Macbeth	1890/1892	1908
Tod und Verklärung	1890	1895
Till Eulenspiegel	1895	1897
Also sprach Zarathustra	1896	1898
Don Quixote	1898	1900
Ein Heldenleben	1899	1900
Symphonia domestica	1904	1904

Orchestra—eighteen and sixteen-and-a-half years after the world premieres of its first version in Weimar and its second version in Berlin, respectively. *Don Juan* fared better, as it remained unknown to Swiss audiences for approximately six years, one year more than *Tod und Verklärung*. Only two years elapsed between world and Swiss premieres in the cases of *Till Eulenspiegel*, *Also sprach Zarathustra*, and *Don Quixote*, while this gap was further reduced to one year with *Ein Heldenleben*. The *Symphonia domestica* remained the only tone poem premiered by Basel's Subscription Orchestra under the direction of Hermann Suter (1870–1926) in the same year of its March 1904 New York world premiere (see Table 5.2).

GREAT BRITAIN

Great Britain always welcomed Richard Strauss the conductor and the composer. This is evident in the frequent visits Strauss paid to that country to conduct his compositions during his lifetime. He visited London for the first time on 7 December 1897 when he and the Queen's Hall Orchestra presented the English premiere of *Tod und Verklärung* in a Grand Wagner concert, which had opened with works by Mozart and Wagner and concluded with *Till Eulenspiegel*. A tradition of regular London appearances was not inaugurated, however, until 1902, when on 4 June the Queen's Hall

Orchestra under Strauss gave their first all-Strauss concert at the Queen's Hall. To impress his British audience Strauss had chosen for the program his three most successful tone poems to date—*Don Juan, Tod und Verklärung*, and *Till Eulenspiegel*—all of which had already been introduced to the city in the late 1890s in individual performances. The impact these three tone poems made reinforced the English audience's affinity to the orchestral works of the composer, and London eventually emerged as the city that could claim more performances of Strauss tone poems in the first decade of the twentieth century than any other European or American city, approximately a dozen per year on average. In comparison, during that same time period, Great Britian as a whole witnessed over one hundred such concerts, averaging about ten per season.

The aforementioned concert also strengthened Strauss's association with the Queen's Hall Orchestra and led to a lasting relationship with its conductor Henry J. Wood (1869–1944). The influence Strauss exerted on his British conducting colleagues, who in turn were often instrumental in disseminating his tone poems in Great Britain, was particularly evident in his friendship with Wood, founder of the legendary Promenade Concerts in 1897 and the long-standing conductor of the Queen's Hall Orchestra.[78] When visiting London, Strauss would frequently stay at Wood's house in the wealthy section of Mayfair.

During one of these visits to London in the winter of 1902, Strauss again presided over the Queen's Hall Orchestra on 6 December in the first British performance of *Ein Heldenleben*. Wood sat in the audience and watched his older colleague Strauss with great admiration and respect: "I have always modeled my Strauss on Strauss himself as I was fortunate in hearing him rehearse and produce all his important works for a period of years. He was always most complimentary to me over my direction of his tone-poems which he heard me conduct on several occasions as a member of the audience."[79]

The English press was predominantly enthusiastic, despite a few isolated negative reactions. One of these critics, Ernest Newman, in his landmark article containing a summary of all English reviews issued after the performance of *Ein Heldenleben*, made a valid observation about the English criticisms, considering them "all too much of the one type, that they discuss the work too intelligently" but then continued with a tirade about critics, "that they are too generous toward a startlingly new composer [such as Strauss], and that no one has indulged in imbecility or impertinence." He then deplored the vanishing of the "ancient fighting spirit [of] English musical criticism," which "instead of saying brickbats at Strauss and retailing all kinds of scandal about his personal habits and domestic ethics, greet him with open arms and tell him he is a fine, big fellow." Most of Newman's commentary on Strauss's tone poems is intermingled with and in response to the various newspaper reviews, which he evaluated in several instances as "fine in its union of enthusiasm and discretion." In conclusion he then characterized the work as one

you cannot treat respectfully or patronizingly, no matter how much you disagree with it; that its painting of a hero is for the most part extremely vigorous, consistent and convincing; that the music is occasionally a trifle too realistic in its manner, and that the battle scene is a flaw in the picture; that the love scene and the ending are among the noblest things in the library of music; that the merely musical handling of the themes, their combination and contrasts, is sheer joy to the musical sense; that only the unevenness in the psychology of the work—mainly due to the battle scene—prevents it being one of the supreme pieces of tonal architecture in the world; and that the English critics on the whole are to be congratulated on their openness of mind and the soundness of their taste.[80]

The Queen's Hall Orchestra under Wood was also responsible for another British tone poem premiere. On 25 February 1905—after seventeen rehearsals that had to be held because the score was so difficult—they gave the first reading of *Symphonia domestica* with acclaim from both audience and critics. For the critic of the *Musical Standard*, J. H. G. B., Strauss's latest work was "absolutely a new departure," as convincing as any of the earlier tone poems, displaying "a mellower handling of the orchestra [as well as] technically an increased adroitness." The work's thematic material was not as fresh and captivating as in earlier works, the critic noted, but was made up by a treatment, which "is a miracle of skill and inspiration."[81] After briefly explaining the symphony's most pertinent programmatic events and musical themes, J. A. Fuller Maitland of the *Times* piquantly observed that "there are a good many pages where the hearer has just to wait under an avalanche of noise as patiently as he can until something recognizable as music greets his ear."[82] While Maitland was accused by one of his colleagues to have written "in a somewhat mixed way"[83]—in one section of his review laughing at the work and in another part praising it—he considered the work's themes fairly easy to remember but lacking in "beauty or distinction of actual invention."[84] Instead, Maitland wished for more appealing themes rather than cleverness of conception, which created "all possible discords" in their consequent development. He did, however, praise the "masterly manner" of instrumentation, despite the lack of effectiveness in employing an oboe d'amore and a quartet of saxophones.[85] Placing himself halfway between those listeners who "again relish the almost diabolical ingenuity" of Strauss's thematic treatment and those exasperated by it, the critic of the *Daily*

Telegraph, Lionel Monckton, noted that despite the many "sounds that defy the ear to analyze them satisfactorily, we have music whose absolute beauty is undeniable." With repeated hearings, the critic predicted, the work's "structures will not lose [the audience's] interest and fascination."[86] Most of the reviews acknowledged that Strauss had learned his craft well as a composer despite their objection to the quality of his musical inspiration.

Strauss gave a repeat performance of *Symphonia domestica* at the Queen's Hall on 1 April 1905, once more leading the Queen's Hall Orchestra. The composer could not hide his astonishment regarding the high quality of this famous ensemble in a letter to the orchestra's concert manager, Edgar Speyer: "I cannot leave London without an expression of admiration for the splendid Orchestra which Henry Wood's master hand has created in so incredibly short a time. He can be proud indeed of this little colony of artists, who represent both discipline and quality of the highest order."[87] Years later Wood remembered Strauss's laudation when in 1912 the former tried to describe his own orchestra's ability to produce a superb performance of *Five Orchestral Pieces*, were its composer, Arnold Schoenberg, willing to come to London and conduct them.[88] Extremely satisfied with the orchestra's rendition of the work—among the best he had conducted as of late—Strauss praised "the amount of hard work, expert knowledge, and sympathetic comprehension of [his] intentions [which] have been expended on this performance."[89] Strauss almost always applauded an orchestra when it was able to deliver a good interpretation of his work.

Another of Strauss's tone poems—*Till Eulenspiegel*—was particularly loved by those concertgoers who frequented the Promenade Concerts.[90] It appeared in three Promenade Concert lineups in September 1905, was programmed on a Saturday Night Popular Concert on 7 October, and surfaced a fifth time the following Friday.[91] The work, first heard in London on 21 March 1896 in a performance by August Friedrich Manns (1825–1907) and the Crystal Palace Orchestra, immediately became an audience favorite and was repeated only a couple of months later, on 1 June, in a powerful performance by Hans Richter and the London Symphony Orchestra. Both Manns and Richter with the Manchester Hallé Orchestra went on to fervently promulgate Strauss in Great Britain.

In early June 1903, as a response to Strauss's pivotal visit in 1902, London organized the first British Richard Strauss Festival, to which they invited the Amsterdam Concertgebouw Orchestra, who over a three-day period played all of the composer's tone poems. Willem Mengelberg (1871–1951), the orchestra's regular conductor, shared the conducting duties with his colleague and friend Strauss, whose works he was to conduct frequently throughout his long tenure with The Netherland's primary orchestral ensemble.[92] Even before the beginning of the festival, English newspapers were flooded by a wave of articles and essays in which rivaling critics scrutinized each other's artistic views on the tone poems, particularly in a discourse carried out between the *Times* and the *Musical Standard*. In the course of the festival *Also sprach Zarathustra* became the only work to be rendered twice, six years after it was first given in the country on 6 March 1897 by Manns and the Crystal Palace Orchestra. Strauss was in such good spirits after the festival that during a brief holiday on the Isle of Wight he completed the final bars of *Symphonia domestica* with ease, and spoke of "Bubi [nickname of Strauss's son] running about all day in the hot sand and going in and out of the sea."[93]

When it came to introducing and promoting Strauss's programmatic music in Great Britain, the London Symphony Orchestra also played an important role. Under the directorship of Englishman George Henschel (1850–1934) it gave the first British performance of *Aus Italien* on 28 November 1889. Seven years later, on 24 May 1897, the orchestra, which meanwhile had appointed Hans Richter as principal conductor, performed *Don Juan* for the first time. Furthermore, the orchestra launched a noticeable increase in concerts featuring the composer's other tone poems, eight such concerts in the 1905–6 season alone. This led to a public availability of Strauss's music of between five and fourteen annual concerts by different local as well as visiting orchestras and conductors. Other British cities, including Birmingham, Manchester, Liverpool, and Sheffield, equally participated in performing Strauss with their own orchestras or those visiting from London.

UNITED STATES

There is no question that today the works of Richard Strauss form an integral component of the classical repertoire of all major American orchestras alongside those of Beethoven, Brahms, Wagner, Tchaikovsky, and others.[94] Furthermore, at auditions for those coveted open spots in professional orchestras, excerpts from Strauss's tone poems have for years formed part of the basic repertoire that brass, woodwind, and string players are required to play to demonstrate their musicality, stylistic understanding, and technical skill. Strauss's orchestral works were not always so established in the standard repertoire of an orchestra, however, and looking back to the turn of the nineteenth century, a different picture emerges.

The rapid ascent of Strauss's popularity, which began in the 1890s, was due to the six major American orchestras in existence in 1900. Neither the New York Philharmonic Society Orchestra, founded in 1842, nor the orchestra of the New York Symphony Society, founded in 1878, was among the more active Strauss proponents.[95] The Boston Symphony Orchestra, founded in 1881, and the Chicago Symphony Orchestra, founded in 1891, rapidly surfaced as two ensembles which quickly and frequently programmed Strauss into their annual concerts. Statistically, the Cincinnati Symphony Orchestra, founded in 1895, and the Philadelphia Orchestra, founded in 1900, rank somewhere between the two New York orchestras and those of Boston and Chicago in terms of including tone poems of Strauss in their concert programs. By the time the nineteenth century came to a close, over seventy performances of tone poems in some sixty concerts had been given—the first three concerts in the second half of the 1887–88 season and last five in the first half of the 1899–1900 season—an average of six concerts per season. With twenty-nine and twenty-two concerts, respectively (three-quarters of the total number), the orchestras of Boston and Chicago took the lion's share.[96] Tracing the number of concerts which included tone poems over an additional period of years, the Boston Symphony Orchestra and the Chicago Symphony Orchestra emerge even more markedly as the musical forces advocating Strauss and his works.

Nonetheless, it is the Chicago Orchestra together with its charismatic founder Theodore Thomas who can really claim to have promoted Strauss most effectively and persistently throughout the United States in local Chicago subscription concerts and on extended concert tours throughout North America and elsewhere.[97] But the dissemination of Strauss's orchestral works throughout the first half of the twentieth century was also expedited by a host of other conductors—including Frederick Stock in Chicago; Ernst Kunwald in Cincinnati; Alfred Hertz in San Francisco; Artur Rodzinski in Chicago, Cleveland, and Los Angeles; Leopold Stokowski both in Cincinnati and Philadelphia; and Eugene Ormandy in Philadelphia and Minneapolis—who championed the composer's tone poems in their seasonal concerts. However, for the first twenty years of performances of tone poems, Thomas and the Chicago Orchestra had perhaps the largest effect on the dissemination of these orchestral works.

Thomas and the Chicago Orchestra also gave the American premieres of two-thirds of the tone poems in the Windy City and forged a Strauss tradition, which continued with Thomas's successor Stock and has remained to this day.[98] From the mid-1880s, when Thomas's relentless advocacy for Strauss began with his own full-time Thomas Orchestra in New York, until he resigned as the principal conductor of the Chicago Orchestra in December 1904, Thomas championed the works of Richard Strauss like no one else.[99] While an American audience was just "reeling from the onslaught of Wagner . . . and beginning to relax to the less strenuous strains of

Tchaikovsky," Thomas and the Chicago Orchestra, along with a few other American orchestras, increased the demand for Strauss's music, paving the way for its widespread popularity and helping the tone poems to become integrated rather speedily into the permanent literature of other musical ensembles as well.[100]

By the end of the Chicago Orchestra's first season (1891–92), the composer's first three tone poems—*Macbeth, Don Juan,* and *Tod und Verklärung*—and *Aus Italien* had already been heard several times in various European cities, totaling more than fifty performances. In comparison, audiences in America during the same time period had experienced them in only twelve instances altogether: four performances of both *Aus Italien* and *Don Juan* and two each of *Macbeth* and *Tod und Verklärung.* While many of Strauss's tone poems had become staples in the repertoire of European orchestras by the last decade of the nineteenth century, the presence of Strauss's works in the American symphonic repertoire—with a share of between 4 and 5 percent—did not occur until the onset of the twentieth century. What made Strauss an increasingly popular composer in the United States was also the fact that it never took his latest works very long after their world premiere—which in all but one case took place in Germany—to receive its American premiere and to be enthusiastically embraced by audiences in cities around the country.

Till Eulenspiegel can be cited as the most telling example of how little time passed between a tone poem's world premiere and its introduction to the United States. On 5 November 1895 Franz Wüllner and the Gürzenich Orchestra had given the very first performance of the work in Cologne as part of the second Gürzenich concert, gathering rave reviews. Barely two weeks later, on 16 November, Thomas and the Chicago Orchestra introduced the tone poem at the local Auditorium Theater in downtown Chicago for the first time to an American audience. A concert on Friday afternoon, a day before the official premiere—a long-standing tradition with many American orchestras—gave several anonymous Chicago critics the opportunity to review the concert prior to the regular subscription concert. Their commentaries share many similarities regarding various aspects of *Till Eulenspiegel,* which the *Chicago Herald* critic, whose review appeared first, called a "fantastic piece of musical horde play" because it was marked by "eccentricity run mad; bedlam expressed in musical numbers." He viewed Strauss's program—which depicted the old German jester showing off all of his comical pranks in the form of a musical farce—as a failure, and expressed surprise at discovering the "audience in a state of hilarity [despite] the amount of bizarre musical or unmusical sound to be extracted from an orchestra."[101] Along the same lines, the critic of the

Inter-Ocean spoke of an "extraordinary farrago of discords and harmony" in a "satire of Wagnerian tendencies" endowed with a marvelous orchestration. Despite having heard the work only once, the critic observed a "semblance of coherency [although more] absurdities than we ever heard before in a sane composition," which left the question unanswered if this was a composition by a genius or a maniac.[102] *Till Eulenspiegel* "is the essence of fun in a high art medium," the anonymous critic from the *Chicago Record* concluded in his review, and noted further that the "intricacy of the score is extraordinary, the ingenious devices resorted to for effect amazing."[103] And in a fourth review in the *Chicago Daily Tribune* on 17 November the commentator praised Strauss as a composer with "an imagination now fantastic to the verge of riot, whose treatment of the orchestra leaves no room for doubt of ability, although his choice of subjects not infrequently do. Young, opposed to exciting traditions, and led to an exaggeration of his own ideas through that opposition, this new evidence of it is one of the most hopeful, as far as his future is concerned."[104]

When *Till Eulenspiegel* was heard in Chicago, Strauss's reputation was slowly beginning to grow in North America, but by the end of 1895 only fifteen concerts containing a tone poem had occurred in the four cities with large orchestras: Philadelphia, New York, Boston, and Chicago. Inquisitive audiences and eager critics had to wait nine more years to experience in person the composer of these eccentric orchestral soundscapes and form their own judgments about both. Nonetheless, between 1896 and 1904, in over one hundred additional concerts that took place across the United States, audiences increased their familiarity with Strauss's works and amply prepared for the composer to make his first acquaintance with the American people.

Strauss visited the United States on two occasions, the first time in the early months of 1904, almost a year after he and the Berlin Tonkünstler Orchestra had gone on a tour of Switzerland. For the two months that the composer remained in the United States—the piano firm of Steinway had arranged all of the concerts he gave there—Strauss made thirty-five appearances in various cities, accompanying his wife in numerous Lieder recitals and leading several different orchestras. New York City, where Strauss started his concert tour, organized a festival in his honor and hosted some ten concerts with all of the major local orchestras.[105]

On Saturday, 27 February—three days after arriving in New York on board the liner *Moltke*—Strauss made his American debut at Carnegie Hall as a conductor and as "the prophet of a new evangel in art."[106] He shared the directing duties with Hermann Hans Wetzler, who had organized the Strauss Festival and conducted the concert's opening work, *Also sprach*

Zarathustra.[107] "There was a very large and uncommonly distinguished audience present last evening; it gave Dr. Strauss an enthusiastic welcome befitting the distinguished position he occupies," the anonymous *New York Times* critic observed. Indeed, the audience applauded for several minutes following *Also sprach Zarathustra*, after which Strauss was brought out on stage. For the second half of the concert he took up the baton to lead the Wetzler Orchestra in *Ein Heldenleben* and thoroughly impressed the critic who called the work Strauss's "most difficult composition [to date], in which all the manifold voices were flexibly treated." Then he centered his observations on aspects of interpretation and style, citing, for example, the violin passage in the section "The Hero's Adversaries"—representing the hero's companion—which he described as "enormously difficult, ungrateful, and frequently ugly." With these comments the critic had exhausted his rather brief observations of the semibiographical work. He was more specific about compositional features relevant to *Also sprach Zarathustra*. Although he admitted that several passages of this work, which he left unspecified, were indeed convincing in their "vividly picturesque" setting, the critic stressed that the "larger purpose he [Strauss] had in view cannot at present be successfully maintained." In other words, "the philosophy of the philosophical piece, the psychology of the psychological one do not make their success as such," he argued, questioning the fitness of a philosophical subject matter for musical treatment, an aspect of this tone poem many others had already challenged at length before him.[108]

The second Richard Strauss Festival Concert at Carnegie Hall on 3 March featured three more tone poems that had not yet been heard in the United States.[109] *Don Juan*, under Wetzler's execution, impressed with "its themes [which] are well defined, plastic, and worked with a much greater regard for the limitations of euphony hitherto prevailing than Dr. Strauss has shown" with his later works, that is, *Don Quixote* and *Ein Heldenleben*. Strauss then took over and conducted *Tod und Verklärung* as well as *Don Quixote*, which the anonymous *New York Times* critic felt "represents some of the most daring adventures into the domain of realistic music, [and] some of the most relentless attempts to make music a medium of crassly materialistic prose."[110] Six days later, on 9 March, Strauss made his fourth appearance at Carnegie Hall at a packed afternoon concert, which initially was to include the world premiere of *Symphonia domestica*. Interestingly, the premiere had to be postponed due to "the late arrival from Europe of the orchestral parts," leaving Strauss with "a lack of sufficient time for rehearsal" for a polished performance of this rather difficult work.[111] Thus the composer presented another reading of *Don Quixote*, the love scene from his second opera *Feuersnot*, seven songs rendered by his wife Pauline, and, for the first time under his baton in New York, the comedic rondo *Till Eu-lenspiegel*.[112] Praised as one of the tone poems "in which [Strauss's] enormous technical skill has not obscured or overlaid the spirit in which he has gone to work," *Till Eulenspiegel* inspired one *New York Times* critic to marvel that the composer "never deliberately abandons music in his search for expression."[113]

Finally, on 21 March, for the fourth and last festival concert, Strauss and the Wetzler Orchestra joined forces once more in the world premiere of the *Symphonia domestica* at Carnegie Hall.[114] What a coincidence it must have been for Strauss, that seventeen years after his F Minor Symphony had received its very first public performance on 13 December 1887 under Theodore Thomas, his next "symphony" was to become the only other work to receive its world premiere in the United States, not in Germany. Over a dozen rehearsals were needed before Strauss was pleased with the sound by the "band of anarchists," as he lovingly described the orchestra. Already as early as 6 March the *New York Times* columnist and music critic Robert Aldrich furnished a lengthy article about the work, replete with its chief themes as transcribed by the composer himself. Two weeks prior to the concert, the columnist tried to make up for the lack of a publicly available "description of what [Strauss] has sought to express" in the work, and ignored the composer's explicit directive: "This time I wish my music to be listened to purely as music." Ultimately, Aldrich agreed with Strauss that the latest venture into the realm of programmatic music "is better able to stand on its own merits simply as music, [and] is less dependent for intelligibility in the mind of the listener upon explanation" than most of the composer's other tone poems.[115]

Even before American and other critics could present their first impression to the public, the German–Italian composer Ferruccio Busoni (1866–1924), while on the boat to the United States, wrote to his wife after repeatedly studying a score of the work that he finally realized that one "gains nothing from renewed acquaintance." While he did not object to the work's program, he concluded that Strauss's "orchestration—in spite of unusual virtuosity—is not 'sonorous' because his style of composing is opposed to his orchestral writing. It branches out too much."[116] There was not enough sincere musical thought contained in the *Symphonia domestica*, according to Busoni, but instead too much attention-grabbing, shallow polyphony. However, the composer's appraisal of the work was not shared by the New York audience who received it so enthusiastically that two additional performances had to be added on 16 and 18 April. They were arranged by the department store Wanamaker, who cleared an entire floor and converted it into a temporary concert hall, a move Strauss embraced without hesitation. Later the composer was severely chastised for it by the German press who called this type of event a "prostitution of art." Strauss's response was simple and matter-of-fact, "[E]arning money for [my] wife and child is no disgrace, even for an artist" and only reinforced a commonly held view of Strauss, that of a money grubber.

Concert managers and conductors in Europe and the United States could not have cared less about such accusations and Strauss's commercially oriented sagacity. They programmed the *Symphonia domestica* more times in the first three seasons of its existence than any other previous work by Strauss. With a seasonal average of twenty-one performances, it ranked ahead of the boisterous *Till Eulenspiegel*, which only by the end of the twentieth century was to emerge as Strauss's most frequently performed tone poem overall.

Although a large audience in New York greeted the work with much excitement, its overall reception in the United States was rather modest by comparison with earlier tone poems: a total of a dozen performances in the first four seasons.[117] An ensuing review of the premiere in the *New York Times* disclosed some of the "most intimate details [of the work] and the succession of pictures" with explicit permission granted by Strauss. A depiction in tones of one's private family life did not strike the critic as an appropriate subject for a musical composition, nor did Strauss's assumed comedic approach help to persuade him otherwise, because the composer's "humor of it is very elaborately and sometimes very strenuously voiced, and the gentlemen of the orchestra, as well as most of the audience, doubtless found it a most serious matter." Even the composer's compositional savvy was called into question in the third section of the work in which a dispute between papa and mamma over how to raise their child Bubi ignites in the form of a double fugue, "one at which [Johann Joseph] Fux and [Johann Georg] Albrechtsberger would have torn their hair, and which [is] likely to give pause to theorists of much more modern tendencies." As the work's various subjects and countersubjects culminate in a traditional fugal stretto, "there is an incoherent tossing about of all the themes, apparently in every key, in every interlocking rhythm, and with an effect that can only be described as a bedlam of sound." Continuing his assault on the work, the critic further argued that "the cacophony upon which the harmony sometimes enters is recklessness" and even attacked Strauss's treatment of themes, "while they are plastic and yield amazing results under his manipulation, [they] have little potency of their own, little characteristic physiognomy." Ultimately, the reviewer called the *Symphonia domestica* "incredibly out of proportion" and concluded that there was "little justification in the subject and the treatment of it for all this expenditure of tremendous orchestral resources and the composer's transcendent technique."[118] Was it surprising the work was to embark on an initially slow journey of dissemination?

Between New York appearances Strauss traveled to Philadelphia to conduct *Tod und Verklärung* with the Philadelphia Orchestra on 4 March and later visited Pittsburgh, where he appeared in a pair of concerts on 11 and 12 March presenting *Till Eulenspiegel* and *Tod und Verklärung* with the Pittsburgh Symphony Orchestra. Back in New York again Strauss led the New York Philharmonic Society Orchestra in its eighth and last subscription concert of the season, which included Mozart's *Jupiter* Symphony, a short love scene from *Feuersnot*, and *Tod und Verklärung*.[119] This marked the third New York performance of the latter work, which by the end of Strauss's American tour had been performed no less than nine times, more than any of the other tone poems.[120]

The penultimate leg of Strauss's welcome tour of America was Chicago. Thomas had invited him to conduct the Chicago Orchestra on 2 April in an all-Strauss evening. The town was buzzing with excitement, eagerly anticipating the first guest conductor in the orchestra's history. Strauss was known for holding more than the usual number of rehearsals, and left the musicians of the orchestra quite surprised when, after only one rehearsal, he jovially and in a complimentary manner addressed them:

Gentlemen, I came here in the pleasant expectation of finding a superior orchestra, but you have far surpassed my expectations, and I can say to you that I am delighted to know you as an orchestra of artists in whom beauty of tone, technical perfection and discipline are found in the highest degree. Gentlemen, such a rehearsal as that which we have held this morning is no labor but a great pleasure, and I thank you all for the hearty goodwill you have shown toward me.[121]

Prior to the twentieth subscription concert on Saturday in the Auditorium Theater, audiences and critics were invited to the traditional Friday afternoon preview performance.[122] Among them was Mr. Boersianer, the critic for the *Chicago Daily News*, providing his general impression. In his review, featured in the Saturday edition of the paper on the day of the regular Saturday evening concert,[123] he treated *Also sprach Zarathustra* rather unsympathetically, echoing views of other American critics. Boersianer not only accused Strauss of lacking melodic talent but also of exhibiting a Nietzschean dichotomy: "Precisely as Nietzsche—with all his immense learning and facility of expression—is destitute of sweetness and light, Strauss—with his wonderful resources and masterful technique—is devoid of melody and beauty."[124] Nevertheless, Strauss was pleased overall with the concert and the outcome of the tour and promised to return to America in the near future.[125]

CONCLUSION

When the twenty-three-year old Richard Strauss first conducted *Aus Italien* in 1887, critics and audience members alike experienced a full range of emotion, not to mention an overwhelming curiosity about the young composer. Some twenty-one years later, Strauss had completed eight of his nine different tone poems, not to mention four operas, and the reception concerning these works remained controversial. Perhaps the only consistent perception among the critics was the uncertainty with which they heard the tone poems even after repeated listenings. Although they might have hated the idea of a musical composition based on a philosophical work, the use of the muted brass imitating the sound of the sheep, a biographical self-glorification, or a tone poem depicting the act of lovemaking, they could not have helped but to respect—secretly at times—Strauss's bold orchestral innovations.

And thanks not only to Strauss's confidence and persistence in seeing his works performed but also to the conductors and orchestras who believed in the validity of the tone poems, critics in some cities were able to formulate their opinions over and over again. This was particularly true of the major European and American cities, which also saw the largest number of concerts featuring Strauss tone poems given either by their own local orchestras or those visiting during a period of approximately two decades from 1887–1908 (see Table 5.3). Smaller cities, however, also contributed their share of concerts. In that way sixty-eight German cities shared in some 460 concerts, whereas in the United States it took twenty-three cities to accrue 275. Ten cities in Great Britain scheduled ninety concerts, while only seven Swiss cities witnessed seventy-five; and Vienna experienced twenty-five concerts. Primarily responsible for programming Strauss tone poems was, of course, the conductor with his orchestra, who, in larger cities was frequently competing with another local ensemble.

Of approximately 150 conductors who performed tone poems in some 930 concerts in 110 cities between 1887 and 1908, Strauss clearly emerges as the most active, as he conducted almost all of the major European and American orchestras in a total of 170 concerts. Likewise, the sixty concerts of Thomas seem even more impressive, considering he worked almost exclusively with the Chicago Orchestra in Chicago and in other American cities for less than ten seasons. Frederick Stock, who took over the orchestra after the death of Thomas in 1905, added twenty-eight more, raising the overall number of concerts to eighty-eight and making the Chicago Orchestra the second most Strauss-oriented ensemble. Only the Boston Symphony Orchestra, under Wilhelm Gericke (forty-five), Emil Paur

TABLE 5.3

Approximate Number of Concerts Featuring Strauss
Tone Poems by City, 1887–1908

City	Number of Concerts
New York	70+
London	60+
Boston	50
Chicago	50
Frankfurt	50
Leipzig	35
Berlin	30
Munich	20
Vienna	20
Zurich	20

(thirty), Karl Muck (twenty-five), Arthur Fiedler (ten), and Arthur Nikisch
(five), could claim more performances of tone poems (ninety-four).[126]

Among the German orchestras the Frankfurt Museum Society programmed the most concerts (fifty-five), followed by the Berlin Philharmonic
(twenty-six), the Munich Kaim Orchestra (seventeen), and the Berlin
Tonkünstler Orchestra (ten), the latter three mostly under Strauss's baton.
In Great Britain two orchestras took the lion's share with some twenty-five
concerts: the London Symphony Orchestra under Richter's directorship and
the Queen's Hall Orchestra led most frequently by Wood. Although Arthur
Fiedler had conducted ten concerts in Hamburg beginning in 1899 that featured tone poems, his penchant for Strauss soared to new heights when he
replaced Gericke as the principal conductor of the Boston Symphony Orchestra in 1906. One encounters a similar situation in Zurich where Hegar
established a Strauss tradition with nineteen tone poem concerts, a number Volkmar Andreae doubled. All in all, close to fifty different orchestras
performed Strauss's tone poems over this twenty-one-year period. For a
long time, the most popular tone poem among conductors (including
Strauss), orchestras, critics, and audiences alike (and certainly the most frequently performed) was *Tod und Verklärung* (see Table 5.4). In the decades
following 1908 and leading up to the twenty-first century *Tod und Ver-*

TABLE 5.4

Approximate Number of Performances by Tone Poem in Germany, Austria, Switzerland, Great Britain, and the United States, 1887–1908

Tone Poem	Number of Performances	Strauss Conducting
Tod und Verklärung	238	59
Till Eulenspiegel	186	27
Don Juan	128	42
Aus Italien	77	18
Macbeth	23	9
Also sprach Zarathustra	75	17
Don Quixote	43	14
Ein Heldenleben	90	26
Symphonia domestica	75	14

klärung, Till Eulenspiegel, and Don Juan have maintained their undiminished popularity. For Richard Strauss, however, Tod und Verklärung always remained his favorite tone poem.

On 13 August, as Strauss lay bedridden, he said to his daughter-in-law, "I hear so much music." He was then brought some music paper to jot down new ideas as he would usually do, but he replied, "No, I wrote it 60 years ago in Tod und Verklärung. This is just like that." Strauss died less than four weeks later, on 8 September 1949. By then his legacy was assured and his tone poems had long been integrated into the standard repertoire of every major orchestra. They continue to captivate audiences, young and old alike, and have become so familiar and easy to listen to that it is enlightening to contemplate the discordant ways listeners over one hundred years ago reacted to them.

NOTES

1. I will explore eight of Strauss's nine tone poems, leaving out Eine Alpensinfonie (1915) and trace their dissemination only from 1887 to 1908, due to the shift in Strauss reception toward opera beginning with Salome in 1904. This discussion, however, will include Aus Italien.

2. Norman Del Mar, *Richard Strauss: A Critical Commentary on His Life and Works* (Ithaca, N.Y.: Cornell University Press, 1986), 1:239ff.

3. Leon Botstein, "Music and Its Public: Habits of Listening and the Crisis of Musical Modernism in Vienna, 1870–1914" (Ph.D. diss., Harvard University, 1985), 957, 964. Botstein provides a detailed and insightful description of the content, format, and intention of concert guides.

4. Hermann Kretzschmar's *Führer durch den Konzertsaal*, prose descriptions of orchestral works illustrated by musical examples, first published in 1886, became the most widely read and respected guidebook serving as an early model for later ones.

5. The writers were either biographers, conducting colleagues, or music historians: Gustav Brecher, Arthur Hahn, Wilhelm Klatte, Wilhelm Mauke, Hans Merian, Friedrich Rösch, Leopold Schmidt, A. Schattenmann, E. Siegfried, Hermann Teibler, and Herwarth Walden. Strauss did write one analysis—for *Aus Italien*—which first appeared in 1889 in the *Allgemeine musikalische Zeitung*; it is reproduced in Erich H. Müller von Asow, *Richard Strauss: Thematisches Verzeichnis* (Vienna: Doblinger, 1959), 1:66–68.

6. Arthur Seidl and Wilhelm Klatte, *Richard Strauss: Eine Charakterskizze* (Prague: Otto Payer, 1896).

7. Gustav Brecher, "Richard Strauss: Eine monographische Skizze" in *Moderne Musiker* (Leipzig: H. Seemann Nachfolger, n.d. [1900]), 1–57.

8. Erich Urban, "Richard Strauss," in *Moderne Essays zur Kunst und Litteratur*, vol. 1, ed. Hans Landsberg (Berlin: Gose and Tetzlaff, 1900), 21–38.

9. Scott Warfield, "The Genesis of Richard Strauss's *Macbeth*" (Ph.D. diss., University of North Carolina at Chapel Hill, 1995), 204. Although Eugen Spitzweg, Strauss's first publisher, was not interested in *Macbeth* and initially tried to convince his client not to have the tone poem printed, fearing it might interfere with the predictable success of *Don Juan*, Strauss cleverly continued to negotiate using Carl Friedrich Peters and other rivaling publishers interested in the publication of the work by withholding *Tod und Verklärung*. Finally Spitzweg gave in and—as can be gleaned from a letter dated 27 November 1890—Strauss agreed to publish all three tone poems: *Don Juan*, *Macbeth*, and *Tod und Verklärung*.

10. Founded in 1808 by a group of local Frankfurt citizens, the "Museum"— intended to bring literature, painting and sculpture, and music together for the elevation of culture—was expanded fifty years later into a full-fledged concert establishment and renamed Museums-Gesellschaft (Museum Society). The orchestra providing the concerts is and has always been the Opera Orchestra and is still called Städtisches Frankfurter Opernhaus- und Museumsorchester, although it is frequently referred to as the Frankfurt City Orchestra. Kogel served as its conductor (1891–1903) and established the Museum Concerts as one of the foremost concert series in Germany.

11. Willi Schuh, ed., *Richard Strauss: A Chronicle of the Early Years, 1864–1898*, trans. Mary Whittall (Cambridge: Cambridge University Press, 1982), 124.

12. *Musikalisches Wochenblatt*, 21 January 1897, p. 47: "die Aufnahme eine enthusiastische war und in stürmischem Beifall sich äusserte"; "mit Meisterschaft

behandelt"; "der grosse, geniale Zug, der durch die *Zarathustra*-Tondichtung geht." Unless noted, all translations are by the author.

13. "Kleines Feuilleton," *Frankfurter Zeitung*, 3 March 1899, p. 1, col. 1: "heldisches Stück, motivisch verschwenderisch und bedeutend ausgestattet, in der wiederum außerordentlich komplizirten thematischen Verarbeitung wahrhaft genial concipirt"; "die absolute Selbständigkeit der musikalischen Gedanken"; "das gewaltige Können in der Ausgestaltung"; "Motiven und Dissonanzen von bisher unerhörter Kühnheit"; "außerordentliche Ausdehnung"; "von seinen Hörern in allen seinen Absichten richtig verstanden zu werden und das Interesse bis zum Schlusse wach zu halten."

14. "Kleines Feuilleton," *Frankfurter Zeitung*, 11 March 1898, p. 1: "vollkommene Auflösung alles musikalischen Denkens" and "höchst merkwürdig."

15. Rudolf Louis, "On the Tone Poems of Richard Strauss: Rudolf Louis," trans. Susan Gillespie, in *Richard Strauss and His World*, ed. Bryan Gilliam (Princeton, N.J.: Princeton University Press, 1992), 306–7.

16. Ibid., 309.

17. As a third conductor Strauss was relegated to conducting only a limited number of operas and felt his abilities were not used to their full potential.

18. Michael Kennedy, *Richard Strauss: Man, Musician, Enigma* (Cambridge: Cambridge University Press, 1999), 50–51.

19. Schuh, *Richard Strauss*, 135.

20. Ibid.

21. Otto Lessmann, "Aus München," *Neue Zeitschrift für Musik*, 27 April 1887, p. 184: "Einhelligkeit im Urtheile war aber nicht mehr vorhanden." Lessmann was the main editor of the *Allgemeine Musik-Zeitung* in Berlin.

22. Strauss was under the assumption that the movement's main theme was the "well-known Neapolitan folksong" and only later found out that it was a popular song, by Luigi Denza with the title "Funiculì, funiculà."

23. Otto Lessmann, "Aus dem Conzertsaal," *Allgemeine Musik-Zeitung*, 27 January 1888, p. 38: "in technischer, rhythmischer und harmonischer Beziehung das schwerste ist, was je ein Komponist einem Orchester zugemuthet hat" and "breit legen die Themen aus, wie schön gelingt es dem Komponisten, poetische Stimmungen zu erwecken und festzuhalten."

24. Schuh, *Richard Strauss*, 136.

25. In Stuttgart, another southern German city, approximately 200 km northwest of Munich, and the capital of the state of Baden-Württemberg, Aloys Obrist (1867–1910) presented *Till Eulenspiegel* as the first Strauss tone poem played for a Swabian audience on 7 December 1897 leading the Stuttgarter Hofkapelle in the Königsbau Saal. Although three seasons can be cited during which two tone poems by Strauss were performed, the seasonal average for Stuttgart was only one every other year.

26. The Strauss Week (23–28 June) featured the operas *Feuersnot*, *Salome*, and *Elektra*, all tone poems conducted by Strauss, and several chamber music and vocal concerts.

27. The only other performance of *Aus Italien* prior to the Berlin concerts took place in Cologne on 8 January where Strauss and the Berlin Philharmonic Orchestra gave a first reading of the work in one of the Gürzenich concerts.

28. On 29 October, Kogel guest-conducted the Berlin Philharmonic in a concert that included *Don Juan*, marking only the second of nine concerts of Strauss tone poems in Berlin that the composer did not conduct.

29. The work was premiered in the fifth concert of the twenty-seventh Tonkünstlerversammlung des Allgemeinen Deutschen Musikvereins.

30. Schuh, *Richard Strauss*, 248.

31. Nikisch was the principal conductor of the Leipzig Gewandhaus Orchestra from 1895 to 1906. The German conductor Hans Winderstein (1856–1925) led the Nürnberg Philharmonic Orchestra and the Kaim Orchestra before he moved to Leipzig and founded the Winderstein Orchestra in 1896.

32. Franz Grasberger, *Richard Strauss und die Wiener Oper* (Tutzing: Hans Schneider, 1969), 10. This phrase is perhaps best translated as "the place where his soul felt most at home."

33. Leon Botstein, "Strauss and the Viennese Critics (1896–1924): Reviews by Gustav Schoenaich, Robert Hirschfeld, Guido Adler, Max Kalbeck, Julius Korngold, and Karl Kraus," in *"Richard Strauss and His World*, ed. Bryan Gilliam (Princeton, N.J.: Princeton University Press, 1992), 311. Botstein also speaks here of a "particular affinity with Vienna" that artists from Catholic Bavaria, such as Strauss, developed because of cultural and historical communications that can be traced back to the Middle Ages.

34. Carl E. Schorske, *Fin-de-siècle Vienna: Politics and Culture* (New York: Vintage, 1981), xxvii.

35. Vienna's primary attraction for Strauss prior to the First World War was its abundant elements reminiscent of the baroque found in buildings and museums.

36. Botstein, "Strauss and the Viennese Critics," 312.

37. Ibid., 311–71. "Recognition in Vienna often marked the difference between an international career and a provincial one."

38. Hirschfeld was a professor of aesthetics at the Vienna Conservatory and was responsible for modern performing editions of stage works by Haydn and Schubert.

39. Hanslick was the musicology chair of the Music Historical Institute, which was part of the University of Vienna. Korngold, father of the composer Erich Korngold, eventually immigrated to the United States where he published his memoirs.

40. The style of writing found in these feuilletons was either fiction or any type of criticism. Today, feuilletons are a permanent section of many European newspapers.

41. Except for *Symphonia domestica*, premiered after his death, Hanslick wrote reviews of all of Strauss's tone poems.

42. Even Mahler was appalled by the strong negative influence Viennese critics had on its audience during the preparations leading to the performance of Strauss's second opera *Feuersnot* on 29 January 1902: "I am so disgusted with the attitude of the Viennese critics, and I can't get over the fact that the audience goes for it all" (Ich bin so angeekelt von der Haltung der Wiener Presse, und vor allem, daß sich das Publikum so ganz ins Schlepptau nehmen ließ, daß ich gar nicht darüber wegkomme). See Grasberger, *Richard Strauss*, 13.

43. Strauss's first contact with Vienna dates back to 1882, when on 5 December he gave his debut at the Bösendorfer Hall in a concert featuring his Violin Concerto, Op. 8, the piano reduction of which he played himself. Hanslick reviewed the concert rather favorably.

44. Richter was the principal conductor of the Vienna Philharmonic Orchestra from 1875 to 1882 and the Vienna Court Opera Orchestra from 1875 to 1900. For a period of twenty-four years he organized the Vienna Philharmonic Concerts.

45. Eduard Hanslick, *Vienna's Golden Years of Music: 1850–1900*, trans. Henry Pleasants III (New York: Simon and Schuster, 1950), 292.

46. Ibid., 292, 312–13.

47. Robert Hirschfeld, "Concerte," *Die Presse*, 24 January 1893, pp. 1–2: "Die Programm-Musik in ihrer Entartung braucht auch den einen Schritt vom Erhabenen zum Lächerlichen nicht—sie trägt beides in sich" and "dürftigen Motive."

48. The concert began with a Mozart symphony, followed by *Till Eulenspiegel*, Mendelssohn's *Hebrides* Overture, and concluded with the first performance of Bruckner's Fourth Symphony.

49. Susan Gillespie, "Opera and Concert Reports," in *Richard Strauss and His World*," ed. Bryan Gilliam (Princeton, N.J.: Princeton University Press, 1992), 321–22.

50. Botstein, "Strauss and the Viennes Critics," 318–19. Kalbeck also wrote poetry and on other subjects than music and translated some of Mozart's Italian operas into German.

51. Max Kalbeck, "Concerte," *Neues Wiener Tagblatt*, 3 January 1896, p. 1, col. 1: "umständliche und affectirte Titel eines Orchesterstückes, das nur insoferne mit der Rondoform zusammenhängt als es eine angeblich komische, in Wahrheit dürftige und verzwickte, zwei Tacte lange Melodie in veränderter Gestalt immer wieder bringt" and "aufgehäuften Mißklängen des tollgewordenen Orchesters." "Als Musterbeispiel des Musikalisch-Häßlichen hat die schwer mit Instrumenten belastete Partitur vielleicht einen didaktischen Werth oder auch als curioses Zeugniß für die Verderbtheit eines Geschmacks, der sich darin gefällt, daß er mit künstlerischen Mitteln eine möglichst unkünstlerische Wirkung hervorbringt."

52. Gillespie, "Opera and Concert Reports," 323.

53. Ibid., 324.

54. Eduard Hanslick, "Concerte," *Neue Freie Presse*, 27 January 1901, pp. 1–2: "war gut besetzt von einer äußerst aufmerksamen, mit Beifall und Lorbeerkränzen nicht sparsamen Hörerschaft"; "wer nicht unausgesetzt im 'Führer' nachliest, hat keine Ahnung, was das alles vorstellen soll"; "wahrhaft scheußliche Musik . . . welche weder durch klare, übersichtliche Form noch durch selbstständige musikalische Schönheit fesselt"; "seiner glanzvollen Orchestrirung, und mancher genialen, kühnen oder zarten Gedanken"; "daß nach fünfzehn Jahren kein Mensch mehr nach seinem Heldenleben fragt."

55. The first of three concerts in 1902 took place on 21 June and included *Till Eulenspiegel*; the second followed on 25 June with *Tod und Verklärung* and *Ein Heldenleben*, a program that was repeated for the last concert on 28 June—the fifth time the former work was heard in Vienna since 1896, an average of once a year.

In 1903, prior to participating in the London Strauss Festival, Strauss and the Berlin Tonkünstler Orchestra performed *Aus Italien* and *Tod und Verklärung*, marking only the second and fourth appearances of the two works in Vienna since 1899 and 1893, respectively.

56. By the end of 1908 *Tod und Verklärung* was still clearly leading the list of Strauss's most frequently performed tone poems with *Till Eulenspiegel* in second place and *Don Juan* in third.

57. Sandwiched between *Aus Italien* and *Don Juan* were Liszt's *Mazeppa*, a scene from Alfred Bruneau's opera *Messidor*, and a premiere of Tchaikovsky's *Der Woywode*, a symphonic ballad based on a poem by the German poet Ludwig Uhland.

58. Ed. C., Program notes to *Un Seul Concert* on 19 March 1903 at Victoria Hall in Geneva, p. 3: "Elle est néanmoins d'une maturité qui étonne et peut être classée parmi les meilleurs compositions de jeune maître"; "L'exubérance de la jeunesse s'y fait bien un peu sentir, mais par contre, tout y est frais, spontané."

59. These annual musical events were initially called "Tonkünstlerversammlungen," but were renamed in 1901 "Tonkünstlerfeste." The Allgemeiner Deutscher Musikverein, founded in 1861 by Franz Liszt (1811–1886) and Franz Brendel (1811–1868), organized the first of these musicians' festivals in Weimar in 1861 and continued them until 1937. However, there were already Tonkünstlerversammlungen in 1859 and 1860, which then led to the founding of the Allgemeiner Deutscher Musikverein. For the only authoritative discussion of this organization and Strauss's association with it, see Irina Kaminiarz, ed., *Richard Strauss: Briefe aus dem Archiv des Allgemeinen Deutschen Musikvereins, 1888–1909*, Veröffentlichungen der Hochschule "Franz Liszt," Bd. 1 (Weimar: H. Böhlau Verlag, 1995).

60. The concert opened with Carl Maria von Weber's *Oberon* Overture, followed by Liszt's symphonic poem *Les Préludes*, Mozart's *Jupiter* Symphony, *Tod und Verklärung*, and concluded with Wagner's overture to *Tannhäuser*.

61. Advertisement of Cathédrale de Lausanne concert, 1908, p. 3: "le plus grand compositeur de l'Allemagne d'aujourd'hui"; "est toujours spontanée et impulsive."

62. "Le Philharmonique de Berlin," *Gazette de Lausanne* (25 May 1908), 2: "le réalisme est mis au service d'un idéalisme supérieur."

63. U. T., "La Music en Suisse," *La Vie Musicale* 1, no. 19 (1908): 323, 325: "une église étant presque aussi défavorable sous ce rapport que le plein air. Mais si nous nous attendions à une resonance trop forte des cuivres sous les voûtes, nous avons été surpris de contraire"; "Sera-t-il permis de regretter que son auteur n'ait pas continué dans cette voie et qu'il se soit laissé entraîner à des jeux d'esprit et à des boutades musicales dont le raffinenement technique est d'autant plus grand que l'âme et l'inspiration en sont absentes? Toujours est-il que ce poème symphonique, vieux déjà de dix-huit ans et composé par un jeune homme de 26 ans, est d'une intensité poignante et d'une beauté incomparable."

64. The works on the program in Geneva were the *Meistersinger* Overture, the Bacchanale to *Tannhäuser*, Beethoven's Eighth Symphony, the overture to Berlioz's *Benvenuto Cellini*, and *Don Juan*.

65. The Basel concert opened with Wagner's *Meistersinger* Overture, followed by *Till Eulenspiegel*, Beethoven's Eighth Symphony, a scene from Wagner's *Tannhäuser*, and concluded with the overture to Berlioz's *Benvenuto Cellini*. The concert in Bern featured almost the same composers, but different works: the overture to *King Lear* by Berlioz, *Till Eulenspiegel*, Beethoven's Fifth Symphony, fragments from Wagner's *Parsifal*, and Liszt's First Rhapsody.

66. U. T., "La Music en Suisse": "Richard Strauss a conquis son auditoire par la simplicité avec laquelle il dirige, jamais un geste exagéré ne vient détourner de l'œuvre l'attention de l'auditeur qui peut oublier les interprètes pour ne plus penser qu'à la musique elle-même"; "Quelle tranquillité règne dans ce grand orchestre, même dans les passages les plus mouvementés; les grandes difficultés sont enlevées avec souplesse et l'on n'a pas cette impression pénible, que l'on restent dans de petits orchestras, d'une lutte acharnée du musicien qui veut produire plus de son que son collègue."

67. Ibid., 326. The concert began with the Bacchanale from Wagner's *Tannhäuser*, continued with Beethoven's Eighth Symphony, *Don Juan*, the overture to Wagner's *The Flying Dutchman*, and closed with Berlioz's *Benvenuto Cellini*; "nous a frappés par sa science élevée et par sa brillante instrumentation."

68. Volkmar Andreae (1879–1962), also of Swiss birth, and the Zurich Tonhalle Orchestra undoubtedly paralleled what Theodore Thomas and the Chicago Orchestra meant for Strauss in the United States, certainly when it comes to the number of concerts he conducted during his forty-three-year career as a conductor. With 108 concerts Andreae clearly outnumbered all other conductors, placing Hegar with 19 performances in a distant second place. Interestingly, both Hegar and Andreae, who succeeded the former in January 1907 as principal conductor, were associated with the same Zurich Tonhalle Orchestra and together were responsible for 150 concerts. This amounts to approximately 60 percent or clearly over half of all tone poem performances recorded in Switzerland.

69. Rudolf Schoch, *Hundert Jahre Tonhalle Zurich* (Zurich: Atlantis Verlag, 1968), 57: "beste Solisten für die Konzerte zu verpflichten, ausgezeichnete Programme zusammenzustellen, selten Gehörtes und Neues einzubauen." Andreae not only followed in Hegar's footsteps by continuing his tradition of programming a healthy combination of traditional and newly composed works, but, more important, increased the frequency of Strauss works, performing between one and seven tone poems every year.

70. The first musical ensemble that existed in this picturesque town nestled at the foot of Lake Geneva was the Chapelle de Montreux, founded in 1872. Jean Tabaglio became its first permanent conductor in 1873. Eight years later the orchestra had grown substantially, providing musical entertainment for the many prominent guests who frequented this town. That year it was renamed the Spa Orchestra of Montreux and in 1889 Oscar Jüttner became its principal conductor. Under his leadership the orchestra produced a staggering number of concerts—thirty in one winter—often performing twice a day, in the morning and the evening. After leading the orchestra for sixteen years he was succeeded by Julius Lange, who conducted from 1905 to 1907. See Jacques Burdet, L'Orchestre

du Kursaal de Montreux: 1881–1914, Extrait de la *Revue historique vaudoise* (1969–1974), 7ff.

71. Francisco de Lacerda, who replaced Lange in 1907, scheduled all major Strauss tone poems during his tenure in Montreux (1908–1912), a tradition Ernest Ansermet continued while principal conductor of the orchestra from 1912 to 1914.

72. An index of performances of larger orchestral works by Strauss and his contemporaries from 1915 to 1932 by the Orchestra of the Bernische Musikgesellschaft lists Strauss with fourteen performances, behind Max Reger and the Swiss composer Othmar Schoeck both with seventeen but ahead of Stravinsky and Debussy with twelve apiece. In comparison, Mahler and Hindemith only show for four performances each.

73. L., "Viertes Abonnementskonzert," *Intelligenzblatt*, 21 January 1904, p. 2, col. 4: "Der Eindruck den es hervorrief war gross."

74. Tchaikovsky's overture to *Romeo and Juliet*, and Chabrier's *Prelude of Gwendoline*, preceded Strauss's tone poem, all of which were the aim of this probing defense of program music.

75. "Lokales: Abonnementskonzert," *Berner Tagblatt*, 22 January 1904, evening ed., p. 1, cols. 3–4: "Glühende Leidenschaftlichkeit, gesteigerte Sinnlichkeit, verbunden mit einer erstaunlichen Fülle nur zu rasch vorüberschwebender musikalischer Detailschilderung"; "die nur hie und da die Grenzen des bisher als musikalisch erlaubt Geltenden streift."

76. "Lokales: 6. Abonnementskonzert," *Berner Tagblatt*, 19 March 1904, evening edition, p. 1, col. 2. In his review of the repeat of *Don Juan* on 15 March of the same year, the anonymous critic focused his report solely on Brahms's Fourth Symphony, which preceded the tone poem; the sixth Subscription Concert ended with Mendelssohn's overture to *Fingal's Cave*.

77. Gvs., "6. Abonnementskonzert im Stadttheater," *Intelligenzblatt*, 18 March 1904, p. 1, col. 2: "Die brennende Leidenschaft, die das ganze Werk durchglüht, die elementare Wucht der Einkleidung, die wild miteinander ringenden, feindlichen Motive, die unbegreifliche Gestaltungskraft bannen den Zuhörer ganz in ihren Wirkungskreis, so dass er vor seinem inneren Auge nur noch den von Schönheitsdurst durchglühten Helden seinem Untergange entgegeneilen sieht."

78. The first Promenade Concert—of three that were planned—occurred on 30 January and was so successful that a fourth and a fifth had to be added.

79. Arthur Jacobs, *Henry J. Wood: The Maker of the Proms* (London: Methuen, 1994), 87. Strauss went on to conduct *Ein Heldenleben* on 1 January and 29 March 1903 for which he was allotted a total of seventeen rehearsals.

80. Ernest Newman, "*Ein Heldenleben* and Its English Critics," *Musical Courier*, 1 December 1902, p. 24, col. 1 and p. 25, col. 3. In his lengthy article Newman analyzed reviews by the following newspapers: *Daily Chronicle, Daily Express, Outlook, Referee, Daily News, Daily Telegraph, Manchester Guardian, Westminster Gazette, Sunday Times, Morning Leader, Pall Mall Gazette, Saturday Review, Morning Post, Times,* and *Times Literary Supplement*. Until Ernest Newman made a point in revealing his name after a review, music critics generally wrote anonymously.

81. J. H. G. B., "Strauss," *Musical Standard*, 4 March 1905, pp. 133, 132.

82. J. A. Fuller Maitland, "Musikberichte: London," *Zeitschrift der Internationalen Musikgesellschaft*, 6, no. 7 (1905): 294.

83. J. H. G. B., "Richard Strauss's: *Symphonia Domestica*," *Musical Standard*, 4 March 1905, p. 132.

84. Maitland, "Musikberichte," 295.

85. Ibid., 294

86. Lionel Monckton, "Musikberichte: London," *Zeitschrift der Internationalen Musikgesellschaft*, 6, no.7 (1905): 296.

87. Jacobs, *Henry J. Wood*, 102.

88. Initially Schoenberg had offered to conduct an entire program of his own music, a proposal that was turned down.

89. Jacobs, *Henry J. Wood*, 102.

90. The program announcements of Promenade Concerts were made only about a week ahead of time and thus heightened the audience's excitement.

91. On Wednesday, 11 October, *Ein Heldenleben* was performed as part of a new concert series called "Tchaikovsky–Brahms–Richard Strauss Night."

92. The first concert on 3 June featured *Till Eulenspiegel* (conducted by Mengelberg) and *Also sprach Zarathustra* (Strauss); the second concert on 4 June featured *Don Juan* (Strauss), *Don Quixote* (Mengelberg), and *Tod und Verklärung* (Strauss); and the third concert on 5 June featured *Macbeth* (Strauss), *Also sprach Zarathustra* (Strauss), and *Ein Heldenleben* (Mengelberg). Four days later Mengelberg and Strauss shared another concert together, in which the former conducted *Aus Italien* and *Ein Heldenleben*. The friendship between Mengelberg and Strauss went back to October 1897 when Strauss had visited Amsterdam to conduct the Concertgebouw Orchestra in two programs, which were sparsely attended and indifferently received. Despite the orchestra members' opinion that Strauss could not conduct, he nevertheless chose Mengelberg as the dedicatee of *Ein Heldenleben*.

93. Del Mar, *Richard Strauss*, 182.

94. By the end of the 1996–97 season a list of the most frequently performed works by the Chicago Symphony Orchestra found Strauss's *Don Juan* in tenth place with sixty-six performances; Beethoven's Seventh Symphony is at the top of the list (seventy-nine), followed by Brahms's First Symphony (seventy-four), Beethoven's Fifth Symphony (seventy-three), Schubert's *Unfinished* Symphony and Wagner's Prelude to *Die Meistersinger von Nürnberg* (seventy-two each), Beethoven's Third Symphony and Tchaikovsky's Fifth Symphony (seventy each), and Brahms's Second and Fourth Symphonies (sixty-nine each). In a list with most frequently recorded works by the Chicago Symphony Orchestra, Strauss's *Also sprach Zarathustra* shares a place with Bartok's Concerto for Orchestra and Beethoven's Fifth Symphony (all with six recordings) topped only by Mussorgsky's *Pictures at an Exhibition* (with seven recordings).

95. Nonetheless, in January 1891 Strauss turned down a post with the New York Symphony Orchestra, who had offered him a two-year conducting contract.

96. On 13 May 1862 Theodore Thomas (1835–1904) assembled his own orchestra of forty players, hired several soloists and an amateur choir, rented the two-year-old Irving Hall, and organized his first concert in New York. The Thomas

Orchestra, which gave three concerts featuring *Aus Italien* in 1888, was a third New York orchestra. It dissolved, however, when Thomas accepted the post in Chicago in 1891. The orchestras of the New York Philharmonic Society and the New York Symphony Society each contributed with two concerts; the Cincinnati Orchestra, of which Thomas became its principal conductor in 1878, performed one concert in 1899.

97. In 1891 Chicago invited Thomas to found his own orchestra, the Chicago Orchestra, which consisted of sixty musicians, thirty of whom Thomas had brought with him from New York, and which was supplemented by an additional thirty players from Chicago.

98. American premiere performances not by Thomas were *Don Juan* by Arthur Nikisch and the Boston Philharmonic Orchestra (30 October 1891), *Tod und Verklärung* by Anton Seidl and the New York Philharmonic Society Orchestra (9 January 1892), and *Symphonia domestica* by Strauss and Wetzler Symphony Orchestra (31 March 1904).

99. Already on 13 December 1884, as the opening work of the Second Subscription Concert of the forty-third season, Thomas and the New York Philharmonic Society Orchestra gave the world premiere of Strauss's Second Symphony in F Minor, Op. 12, from a manuscript given to Thomas by the composer at a meeting which probably took place in Munich between the beginning of June and mid-October 1880; Thomas had left New York for an extended visit to Europe on 26 May 1880.

100. John H. Mueller, *The American Symphony Orchestra* (Bloomington: Indiana University Press, 1951). Lacking in this list is the Pittsburgh Symphony Orchestra, which was founded in 1896 but was dissolved in 1910.

101. "Popular Orchestra Concert," *Chicago Herald*, 15 November 1895, [n.p.].

102. "Favorite Orchestra Concert," *Inter-Ocean*, 16 November 1895, [n.p.].

103. "Orchestra Concert Yesterday," *Chicago Record*, 16 November 1895, [n.p.].

104. "Chicago Orchestra Concert,"*Chicago Daily Tribune*, 17 November 1895, p. 42.

105. Because their principal conductor of the 1902–3 season, the German-American conductor Walter Damrosch (1862–1950), signed on with the rival New York Symphony Society Orchestra, the New York Philharmonic Society, lacking permanent leadership, divided the conducting responsibilities of the 1903–4 season among seven guest conductors, hoping at the same time to increase concert attendance again. Strauss was the fifth guest conductor, preceded by Wood from London, Edouard Colonne from Paris, Kogel from Frankfurt, and Weingartner from Munich, and followed by Vasily Safonov from Moscow and the composer Victor Herbert from Pittsburgh. Safonov became the orchestra's principal conductor during the 1905–6 season.

106. "Richard Strauss Appears: The Famous German Composer at Carnegie Hall: He Conducts One of His Own Works and Is Greeted Enthusiastically," *New York Times*, 28 February 1904, p. 7, col. 1.

107. This concert was the last in a series of five concerts given by the German expatriate Wetzler and his short-lived orchestra, formed at the beginning of the

1902–3 season. For the concert the Wetzler Orchestra—an ensemble of loosely as-sembled musicians often lacking adequate training—was temporarily augmented to include 110 players. Strauss appeared three more times with this orchestra in the following three weeks.

108. "The Famous German Composer at Carnegie Hall (: He Conducts One of His Own Works and Is Greeted Enthusiastically by a Large Audience)," *New York Times*, 28 February 1904, p. 7, col. 1. Prior to the last work David Bispham sang "Die Ulme zu Birsam," "Nachtgang," and "Das Lied des Steinklopfers."

109. On Tuesday afternoon, 1 March 1904, Strauss appeared at Carnegie Hall in the capacity of a pianist, accompanying his wife Pauline in the first half of the concert and in the second half executing the piano part of the melodrama *Enoch Arden*, based on Lord Tennyson's poem.

110. "Second Strauss Concert," *New York Times*, 4 March 1904, p. 9, col. 3. *Tod und Verklärung* under Strauss's baton followed and the composer's wife concluded the concert with four songs: "Das Rosenband," "Liebeshymnus," "Morgen," and "Cä-cilie," all in their orchestral versions.

111. "*Symphonia Domestica* Postponed," *New York Times*, 8 March 1904, p. 9, col. 3; and "Dr. Strauss Again Conducts: His *Don Quixote* and *Till Eulenspiegel* Played," *New York Times*, 10 March 1904, p. 9, col. 1.

112. Pauline sang orchestral versions of "Meinem Kinde," "Muttertändelei," "Wiegenlied"; and "Allerseelen," "Befreit," O Süsser Mai," and "Kling" with piano accompaniment provided by her husband. On 18 March Strauss gave his debut as a chamber musician accompanying the Mannes Quartet in Mendelssohn Hall with several of his own compositions.

113. "Dr. Strauss Again Conducts: His *Don Quixote* and *Till Eulenspiegel* Played," *New York Times*, 10 March 1904, p. 9, col. 1.

114. The concert began with *Also sprach Zarathustra* and concluded with *Don Juan*, two of the four tone poems Strauss conducted twice during his American visit; *Don Quixote* and *Tod und Verklärung* were the other two; *Aus Italien* and *Mac-beth* were left out entirely.

115. Robert Aldrich, "Strauss's *Symphonia Domestica*," *New York Times*, 6 March 1904, p. 5, cols. 3–4.

116. Rosamund Ley, ed. and trans., *Ferruccio Busoni: Letters to His Wife* (New York: Da Capo, 1975), 78.

117. The Boston Symphony Orchestra claimed the lead with six perform-ances, followed by the orchestras in Chicago and Philadelphia.

118. "*Symphonia Domestica* with Composer Leading," *New York Times*, 22 March 1904, p. 5, col. 1.

119. David Bispham also sang the Strauss songs "Hymnus" and "Pilger's Mor-genlied," both with orchestral accompaniment, and "Liebeshymnus," "Sehnsucht," and "Lied des Steinklopfers," with Strauss at the piano.

120. Mark-Daniel Schmid, "*Tod und Verklärung*: Debt and Transubstantiation in the Reception of Richard Strauss's Tone Poem" (paper read at a local chapter meeting of the American Musicological Society at DePaul University, Chicago, Ill., 1996). By the end of the regular 1907–8 season *Tod und Verklärung* had been the

most frequently heard tone poem in Europe and the United States with over 270 performances over a period of eighteen years between 21 June 1890 and May 1908, clearly outnumbering *Till Eulenspiegel* and *Don Juan*. Strauss was responsible for one-fourth of all performances of *Tod und Verklärung*, perhaps his favorite work.

121. Rose Faye Thomas, *Memoirs of Theodore Thomas* (Freeport, N.Y.: Books for Libraries Press, 1971), 503.

122. Friday afternoon concerts, generally scheduled at 2 P.M., were billed as regular concerts for a paying audience and attended by the critics, but they were actually somewhat of a "public rehearsal" of a program featured the next evening. Easily over three-quarters of the audience attending these Friday matinee concerts were women, from Chicago and its surroundings.

123. The concert began with *Tod und Verklärung* and ended with *Till Eulenspiegel*, both Strauss staples for Chicago audiences; the former they had heard already six times and the latter seven times.

124. Mr. Boersianer, "Chicago Orchestra Review," *Chicago Daily News*, 12 March 1904, p. 172.

125. Strauss visited the United States one more time, in 1921–22 when it was not in the best interest of concert managers to schedule works by "contemporary enemy composers." Patrons were extremely sensitive to hearing German music and even more so if it was written by a living composer like Richard Strauss. This had resulted in a total absence of the composer's works during the 1917–18 season, a scenario Strauss had apparently anticipated but one that did not deter him from returning. With a reversal in public sentiment, Strauss was received by New York's mayor John F. Hylan (1896–1936) as a "reconciliation ambassador." At the conclusion of his first concert in Carnegie Hall in October 1921, the city of New York presented the fifty-seven-year-old composer with a sumptuous wreath decorated with a black–red–gold ribbon, the colors of the German flag. Surpassing the concert schedule of his first tour seventeen years earlier, Strauss managed a staggering forty concerts during a fifty-day visit, leading over twenty different orchestras in nineteen cities. They ranged from New Haven, Connecticut, to as far west as Kansas City, Missouri, a musical undertaking that earned him an estimated $50,000, a hefty sum for the first quarter of the twentieth century.

126. When analyzing these statistics, numbers may seem inconsistent between cities, orchestras, and conductors. These statistics reflect concert tours by orchestras as well as guest apearances by conductors with various orchestras.

6

From "Too Many Works" to "Wrist Exercises": The Abstract Instrumental Compositions of Richard Strauss

Scott Warfield

Because the oeuvre of Richard Strauss is dominated by vocal music—fifteen operas, most of which remain in the repertoire, and over two hundred Lieder, several dozen of which are staples of vocal recitals everywhere—one might be surprised to learn that instrumental works account for well over one-third of the 298 entries in Franz Trenner's *Richard Strauss Werkverzeichnis*.[1] To be sure, most of the tone poems from *Don Juan* (1888) to *Eine Alpensinfonie* (1915) are as well-known as the best of the vocal music, but even those nine major orchestral works are outweighed—both in number and in sheer quantity of measures—by the ninety-nine "abstract" instrumental pieces and twenty-one fragments that Strauss composed in his nearly eighty-year career.[2]

In fact, Strauss composed in nearly every instrumental genre of his day. His output includes two symphonies; several concert overtures and miscellaneous orchestral pieces; concerted works for the horn, violin, cello, clarinet, and piano; solo sonatas for the violin, cello, and horn; numerous pieces for many of the standard chamber ensembles; and a large body of piano music. More than a few of these compositions have remained in the repertoire, either as central works known widely, for example, the *Metamorphosen*, or as "niche" pieces favored by certain instrumentalists to expand their particular repertoires, for example, the Cello Sonata, Op. 6. Moreover, the interest in Strauss's nonprogrammatic works has been growing in recent years, and a few of his abstract pieces that had not been heard in over a century have been revived in the years since 1980.[3] Presumably, some of this attention came about simply because of Strauss's status as a major composer, but it is equally obvious that such works would not have been played and published unless there was some sense of quality about them.

Beyond the intrinsic worth that might be found in any of Strauss's abstract instrumental compositions is their value as a record of his development as a composer. Not all of Strauss's early works are the negligible efforts of a boy learning the craft of composition. Before his twentieth birthday he had composed a number of well-received works; and had he not fallen under the influence of the Wagnerian Alexander Ritter, there can be no doubt that Strauss would have had a significant career as one of the natural successors to Brahms. Strauss's decision to follow the path of the New German School, however, did not result in a clean break with the direction set by his earliest compositions. Rather, the essence of Strauss's tone poems resides in his ability to realize an extramusical program through the traditional formal devices and procedures found in his earlier works. The late works of his "Indian Summer" are likewise less a regression, that is, a "going back," than a retrospection, that is, a "looking back," to older styles through modern eyes. Thus the instrumental works are central to an understanding of Strauss's musical style, tracing his career from its very beginning to nearly his last work.

THE EARLIEST EFFORTS (1870–80)

Strauss's earliest compositions came about as a natural outgrowth of both his father's career and the musical activities of his extended family. His father, Franz Strauss, was one of the nineteenth century's greatest horn virtuosos and a member of the Munich Court Orchestra for forty-one years. His own musical tastes were orthodox and conservative, with a strong bias against Wagner, Liszt, and other "progressive" composers. Even the late works of Beethoven and Schumann exceeded the bounds of what Franz Strauss thought was appropriate for music, and he saw that his son was impressed with these same values. Naturally, the younger Strauss was exposed to music at an early age. He delighted in frequent walks with his father to the Munich city square where they heard a military band accompany the daily changing of the guard, and at the age of about seven, he began to attend some of the operas and concerts in which his father performed. Richard began piano lessons when he was four-and-a-half years old, and he also took up the violin by his eighth birthday. In addition to his father's professional example, many members of the extended Pschorr family (Strauss's maternal relatives) were active in various forms of amateur music making, and when Richard became proficient enough—he was able to play Mozart piano sonatas by his ninth year—he joined in those private family performances. There, the young Strauss was exposed to a large body of conservative chamber music, including such works as the quartets of Haydn, Mozart, and even early Beethoven.[4]

These family ensembles also provided both an outlet and an impetus for Richard Strauss's initial efforts at composition. In fact, his very first work was a piece for piano called the *Schneiderpolka* (TrV 1) that Strauss created in 1870, shortly after his sixth birthday.[5] To say that it was "composed" in the traditional sense may stretch the point, since the young Strauss was not yet capable of writing out the notes. Doubtless, Richard had improvised the work by simply following the style of pieces he had played, and his father then wrote down the modest sixteen-measure polka with its four-measure introduction and eight-measure trio. Franz Strauss later orchestrated the work for a small ensemble, which Richard "conducted" at a Carnival Concert on 23 February 1873. In 1872 Franz orchestrated a second piano piece by his son, the *Panzenburg Polka* (TrV 11), for an amateur ensemble of family and friends known as the Harbni Orchestra. All of this arranging was done with a father's pride and with no intention to deceive. Nevertheless, one must wonder what sort of innocent corrections Franz made to his son's work, since there is later evidence that he did revise a few of his son's compositions.[6] Moreover, there are at least fifty works by Strauss that are known only by manuscripts in unidentified hands. These copies presumably were made by and for family members, since most of those manuscripts are from Strauss's youth and many carry dedications to his relatives.

Over the next ten years, the young Strauss proved to be quite a prolific composer, with over one hundred works to his credit before his sixteenth birthday. One-half of these are songs and other vocal works, about one-third are piano pieces, and one dozen are movements for small chamber ensembles, all made without the benefit of formal instruction in composition. The boy probably chose to compose whatever struck his fancy, modeling his pieces on works that he heard played in the family's frequent sessions of music making or in his own music lessons. So long as Richard limited himself to small forms, the casual help of his father—whose own formal musical education was limited in many ways—or the Pschorr cousins was sufficient to assist the young composer.

In 1873, however, Richard made his first attempt at composing a large-scale orchestral work, an overture to a singspiel entitled *Hochlands Treue* (TrV 17). There is no evidence that Strauss ever completed any more of his intended theatrical work than this overture, but even an overture was an audacious step for an untutored eight-year-old. The pencil score is clearly a working draft, with many erasures and revisions, and is written entirely in the hand of a child with no evidence of any adult's help. The handling of the overture's form, a simple sonata-allegro movement with an adagio section replacing the development, is surprisingly competent, but it is the orchestration that betrays the boy's lack of training in and understanding of both the medium and the genre. Frequent mistakes in transposed parts and a page layout that changes several times are only the most obvious errors. More important, there is no sense of orchestral style. The scoring in tutti sections is adequate, but in thinly scored passages there are some odd voicings. Individual parts are far from idiomatic, and the incessant homophonic textures suggest both a work conceived on the keyboard and a composer lacking in contrapuntal training.

As a child attempting an adult project, the young Strauss probably had little idea of what an orchestral score required from a composer, but the fact that the boy did not immediately abandon the overture and appears to have worked on the score for some time suggests his earnest desire to compose. Although Franz did not act immediately, he must have recognized his son's growing interest in composition. If the boy were to become a serious composer, he would need a thorough grounding in all aspects of music theory, counterpoint, and orchestration. Franz's own patchwork education had gaps in the more advanced areas of music, and so a better-educated teacher was required.[7] Thus, in 1875 Franz engaged Friedrich Wilhelm Meyer (1818–93), second conductor at the Munich Court Opera, as Richard's teacher of music theory, counterpoint, orchestration, and composition. The boy studied with Meyer for five years, from the age of eleven to sixteen, during which time he received his only formal training in composition in his life. Franz's choice of Meyer as his son's teacher might seem curious, given Meyer's relative anonymity (both then and now) and the availability of more prestigious teachers in Munich. On the other hand, Franz had known and worked with Meyer for nearly two decades, and thus he could be sure of the man's character and musical tastes. Franz would have had no fears that Meyer, an ordinary musician of conventional and conservative training, might poison young Richard's mind with radical ideas.[8]

Meyer's teaching doubtless mirrored his own work as a composer, and he surely stressed to Richard the importance of simple, traditional solutions in whatever harmony or composition problems on which the boy might be working. Meyer apparently also agreed with Franz Strauss's distrust of musical knowledge learned strictly from a book.[9] Whatever his own musical education had entailed, Meyer seems to have used only one brief textbook, Ernst Friedrich Richter's *Die Grundzüge der musikalischen Formen* (The Fundamentals of Musical Forms) in his work with the young Richard

Strauss.[10] Unlike many music theory books of the nineteenth century, Richter's *Grundzüge* is brief, only fifty-two pages long. Richter stated in the book's foreword that it was not his intention to provide as comprehensive a treatment of musical forms as others had done. Rather, he aimed only to introduce the basics of musical form as a foundation for further study. Moreover, his book did not join form with any of the other branches of music theory, even though Richter stated that a strong grounding in those other areas was important for the study of musical form. Presumably, it was up to a teacher to show a student how these connections were made in specific compositions.

Richter's architectonic approach to form is readily apparent and also consistent with the general tenets of *Formenlehre* (theory of musical forms) by earlier theorists like Koch, Reicha, Czerny, and Marx, among others. For Richter, all compositions are made by joining smaller closed units into larger ones. In longer works, the basic unit is the period, which is marked by its strong final cadence. In his discussion, Richter says almost nothing about the melodic elements of periods, save for a few general remarks on the necessity of "symmetrical contents," which are presumably demonstrated by the frequent four-measure phrases in antecedent–consequent pairs used in his examples. Instead, Richter is more interested in the cadences of a period, and he stresses the proper placement and weighting of internal cadences in relation to a period's final cadence.

The second half of Richter's book deals with "Larger Musical Forms," beginning with "The Forms of the Sonata." As before, his explanation is simple and to the point. The first part of a sonata's initial movement, that is, the exposition of a sonata-allegro movement (Richter never uses these terms), is based on harmonic motion from the tonic to the dominant or, in minor, to the relative major. Moreover, due to the greater length of a sonata movement, each key area has its own thematic material, which should provide melodic contrast. Richter then summarizes the first part of the movement (the exposition) as four discrete periods: first period, or first main ideas; second period, or connecting–transitional periods; third period, the second main ideas; and fourth period, or closing phrase. In his following analysis of the initial movement of Mozart's Sonata in F, K. 533, Richter explains for the first time how the remainder of a sonata-allegro movement is formed. He views the entire movement as a two-part form, with the second half also divided in two. Richter's discussion passes over the first part of this second half (the development) in only one sentence, while the recapitulation is explained in just one paragraph.

The other movements of a sonata are discussed in even more general terms than is the first movement. Richter notes that the slow movement is basically in the same form as the first, but says nothing specific about any differences between the two. He merely describes the scherzo as a two-part form to which a trio is usually appended. Richter notes that the fourth movement is often in the same form as the first, although finales may also be rondos, but his discussion is so general that it is of no real use to a composition student. The remainder of Richter's book passes quickly over the string quartet, the symphony, and the overture by briefly noting their particular affinities to the forms used in the sonata. In a more practical vein, Richter suggests the study of works by Haydn, Mozart, Beethoven, Mendelssohn, and Schumann for students of those genres, and in the concluding section of his book, he finally mentions the expansion and elaboration of musical ideas. Unfortunately, he merely describes the development in the last movement of Beethoven's Fifth Symphony and offers to a student little that can be applied to other works.

Although the discussion of musical form in *Grundzüge* was quite simple, it was doubtless well suited to the needs of an eleven-year-old boy who was just beginning the formal study of music theory and composition. Richter's instructions, stripped to the basics with no mention of the many subtleties and complexities inherent in a larger composition, eliminated any aesthetic dilemmas that might have overwhelmed a child. Presumably, Meyer could introduce such issues at the appropriate time. Meanwhile, his pupil's attention would remain focused on the basics. In fact, Strauss did produce about three dozen instrumental works while studying with Meyer, most of which were based on Richter's paradigm of the sonata.

One of the first works that Strauss composed after beginning his studies was a *Concertouvertüre* in B minor (TrV 41) that he presented as a gift to Franz Strauss on his name day in the fall of 1876. Although Richard drafted a full score (with significant help from Meyer), there is no evidence that the setting for full orchestra was ever performed. Instead, the overture was probably played only in its keyboard version in the Strauss and Pschorr households. Formally, the work is a sonata-allegro movement without a development, which follows Richter's advice for an overture, and both the exposition and the recapitulation also follow Richter's plans to the letter. Each of the four basic subsections is a closed period of regular construction, and the importance of harmony in determining form at all levels is confirmed by the way in which Strauss builds his periods. The first theme, for instance, is a sixteen-measure unit, divided by clear half cadences into phrases of four, four, and eight measures. The entire period is then repeated before an elided full cadence joins it to a twenty-four-measure transition that contains no melodic material whatsoever; rather, it is a simple modulation to V of III. The level of inspiration in the second theme is scarcely higher, with a melody that consists of nothing but chord outlines, while the closing material is just routine filler.

The ways in which Strauss constructed these periods and the phrases contained within them reflect the same mechanical approach that governs the work's form on a larger scale. The phrases of the first theme, for instance, are formed by repetitions of a one-measure motive that is little more than a thinly disguised appoggiatura, molded to fit the harmonic plan of the first period. Harmony is also obviously the controlling factor in the melodically empty transition, although Strauss did take care to maintain regular four-measure phrases. Indeed, much of the compass of this period seems contrived, with single chords extended to entire phrases merely to expand the harmonic progression to a length suitable for a symphonic work. Above all, Strauss's respect for symmetrical periods and correct musical structure determines the shape of this work. The result is far from a masterpiece, but after the undisciplined *Hochlands Treue*, the composer's father must have been pleased with this proper, if unimaginative, overture.

Although Richard now had a formal teacher of composition, Franz Strauss continued to exert his own influence over his son's development, even to the point of silently improving his son's works. The younger Strauss's next orchestral work was the *Festmarsch* (TrV 43), composed in 1876 and published five years later by Breitkopf und Härtel as Strauss's Op. 1, albeit strictly because the composer's uncle underwrote the cost of publication.[11] The *Festmarsch* became one of Strauss's earliest works to be played in public when his father programmed the piece on a concert (3 March 1881) by the Wilde Gung'l, an amateur orchestra that Franz conducted. Since the published version was not ready by that date, Franz copied out parts by hand, adjusting his son's orchestration to fit the unique instrumentation of the Wilde Gung'l. Franz also added contrapuntal flourishes to fill some inactive spots in Richard's melodies.

The four-movement Serenade (TrV 52), composed by the younger Strauss in 1877, also carries signs of Franz's influence. This Haydnesque work was likely the first of Richard's to be played by the Wilde Gung'l, and as Franz later did with the *Festmarsch*, he prepared a neat ink copy from his son's rough pencil score for a performance in 1878.[12] Again, the putative impetus was to adapt Richard's standard double-wind orchestration to the particular needs of the Wilde Gung'l, but Franz also took the opportunity to make numerous improvements in his son's score. Many changes are just obvious corrections, such as the key signatures of transposed parts or the revoicing of parts that are too high or too low for certain instruments. In some cases, however, Franz went so far as to change melodic and contrapuntal details, and thereby transformed Richard's minimally competent material into evocations of eighteenth-century masters.

The Serenade's four movements resemble a symphony in broad outline. Indeed, the slow second movement, the scherzo, and the finale could pass for symphonic movements, while only the first movement falls a bit short of a true symphonic allegro. As with his earlier works, Strauss built his movements out of independent, self-contained periods. The finale is a textbook example of Richter's sonata-allegro form, while the first movement is less so, but with an exposition that fits the mold precisely. Its development is slight, however, and the recapitulation omits the first theme, beginning instead at the transition. Even the second movement owes something to the sonata paradigm, as Richter's textbook suggested. Although it can be analyzed broadly as a ternary structure—a typical form for a slow symphonic movement—the outer sections also follow the harmonic plan of a sonata-allegro movement with a pair of closed themes connected by brief transitions.

The phrase structure within these periods is still regular, with very predictable cadences, but the quality of Strauss's material, although still formulaic, is better than before. Short, harmonically based motives are again his favorite starting point. Some, like the second theme of the fourth movement or the first theme of the second movement, seem to wander with little purpose. Others, like the first theme of the fourth movement or the first theme of the scherzo, are infused with a rhythmic drive of real potential. In these latter two cases, however, Strauss simply repeats these ideas over and over, which eventually reveals their short-winded quality as well as the boy's inability to develop his material. In fact, Strauss's development of his material in the Serenade consists of little more than a few complete repetitions of his themes. In the first movement, for instance, the "development" takes up barely twenty of the entire movement's more than two hundred measures. The second theme is merely repeated four times in two pairs of antecedent–consequent phrases, first in F major and then in A minor. Strauss shows a bit more ingenuity in the fourth movement by combining his two chordally based themes in the development, but again, he simply repeats the entire four-measure phrase sequentially four times before a one-measure fragment of the first theme leads back to the recapitulation.

Richard doubtless knew of his father's modifications, and he was probably present when the Wilde Gung'l played the Serenade. Perhaps more important than Franz's superficial, but still useful, changes in the orchestration was the fact that Franz did not alter Richard's forms, melodies, or harmonies. Such a tacit acknowledgment was tantamount to praise from Franz. Although elements of the Serenade were often the product of ordinary inspiration or even mechanical invention, the boy was beginning to master the craft of composition.

The majority of Strauss's compositions in the years 1877 to 1880 were probably intended for use by the Pschorr family. Of the next forty works listed in Trenner's *Richard Strauss Werkverzeichnis* after the Serenade (TrV 52), fully half of them are songs, many with dedications to relatives. More than a dozen other pieces might be classified as *Hausmusik*. There are two Trios for piano, violin, and cello (TrV 53 and TrV 71), a set of variations for the horn (TrV 50), and several piano pieces, the most important of which is probably the Grosse Sonate II (TrV 79).[13] Another of these piano pieces, *Aus alter Zeit* (TrV 72), a gavotte composed early in 1879, became the first work by Richard Strauss ever published when it appeared in the initial (and only) volume of Lothar Meggendorfer's *Musikalisches Bilderbuch* later that same year.[14]

Works for orchestra occupy a small but increasingly important place in Strauss's output during these years. There are two incomplete movements for orchestra (TrV 55 and TrV 56) from 1877, and in the next year Strauss composed an Overture in E major (TrV 69). Only a pencil score was completed, and the work, which carries no dedication, was never performed. One unusual feature of this overture is the way in which Strauss effects the retransition out of the slim development into the recapitulation. Rather than approach the tonic through the expected dominant harmony on B, Strauss moves to the single pitch F-natural by way of its own dominant. After thirteen measures on this lone F, one measure of B—again, a single pitch and not a chord—acts as a pickup note to the first theme, and thereby reinterprets the F as an implied Neapolitan harmony. To the ear, the moment is more confusing than convincing; nevertheless it presages similar unorthodox or deceptive transitions between sections in otherwise standard forms by Strauss.

The Gavotte (TrV 82/5), composed in 1879 and orchestrated later that same year, is of interest only because it was probably the very first of Strauss's works to be performed in public.[15] Its slightly unusual instrumentation, notably the use of a piccolo, only one flute, and also just a single trombone, implies that it was scored specifically for the Wilde Gung'l, and in this case Franz Strauss apparently copied his son's orchestration with no changes. Not surprisingly, the strings carry the bulk of the load, and even in the tutti passages the wind and brass lines merely double the strings. The string parts themselves are conservative, with cello and bass doubling each other at the octave for virtually the entire piece. Occasional passages for solo winds and a contrasting Pastorale section provide some relief from this bland, if correct, texture.

About that same time, the ever busy Strauss also finished a second orchestral score, an Overture in A minor (TrV 83) that he dedicated to Meyer
in honor of his teacher's twenty-five years of service in Munich. Again, the
work shows only modest advancement over Strauss's previous efforts, with
numerous empty passages that merely fill up blocks in Richter's mold. For
example, the first sixteen measures of the twenty-four-measure transition
between the first and second themes simply marks time with four alternating phrases (i–V–i–V), before the last eight measures carry out the actual
modulation to the second key area, and the closing group is merely a sixty-
measure prolongation of the dominant using more meaningless filler. As in
some earlier works, Strauss replaced the development with an insertion of
unrelated material in a new meter (6/8) and a new key (E-flat). The unpre-
pared leap from the B that ended the exposition to this new key, as well as
the surprising harmony that began the overture, an F-sharp fully diminished seventh chord, suggests that Strauss's interest was now focusing on the
points of transition within his standard form, but the form itself remained
inviolate.

In 1895, in reply to a questionnaire about his compositional process,
Strauss remarked that he had composed "too many works" uncritically in
his early years.[16] Certainly his youthful enthusiasm had led him to rely on
the most facile solutions to any compositional problems. Nevertheless, these
works composed by Strauss in his adolescence gave him a fluent technique
in a conservative idiom on which he could build in the next few years.

FIRST MATURITY (1880–86)

Strauss completed his studies with Meyer in February 1880 with a "vale-
dictory" five-voice double fugue for violin and piano (TrV 91). Within a
month he was at work on a Symphony in D minor (TrV 94), which he completed on 17 October 1880. Despite its successful premiere on 30 March
1881 in a Musical Academy Concert under the baton of Hermann Levi, first
conductor of the Munich Court Opera, the symphony was only rarely heard
in later performances. Compared to Strauss's earlier efforts, however, this
symphony can stand up to scrutiny without apologies for the youthfulness
of its composer. An anonymous reviewer for the *Münchner Neueste
Nachrichten* wrote on 3 April 1881, "The symphony in D minor by . . . this
still very young composer . . . shows considerable competence in the treatment of form as well as remarkable skill in orchestration. It must be said
that the work cannot lay claim to true originality, but it demonstrates
throughout a fertile musical imagination, to which composition comes eas-

ily."[17] More than a century later that assessment of Strauss's Symphony in D minor is still an equitable one.

Strauss's "considerable competence in the treatment of form" should have been no surprise to anyone who knew his earlier works, since the Symphony in D minor follows the same formal plans that Strauss had been studying and using for nearly five years. The outer movements are real sonata-allegro movements, now complete with true developments, and, as in the Serenade, the slow second movement draws on that same model. The Scherzo follows the standard binary form. In contrast to his earlier adolescent technique of simply connecting periods of unrelated material to fill out a static form, for the first time, Strauss demonstrates an awareness of generative aspects of musical form. This is most apparent in the first movement.

The symphony opens with a fifty-measure slow introduction that unveils several motives that will be used in the movement. The first is a unison statement of a simple five-note motive that will serve as the basis of the first theme. Next, two ideas, both derived from chord outlines, are presented simultaneously in the horns and strings. Both will appear in the transition and closing areas of the exposition. Finally, a lyric solo for flute that will also figure in the transition is heard. The exposition proper begins with a shift to triple meter. In contrast to the static antecedent–consequent themes in many of Strauss's earlier works, this movement's first theme has a more dynamic and open-ended construction (four plus four plus eight measures) supported by an underlying I–IV–V progression, and its momentum carries over into a transition made of fragments from both the introduction and the first theme. This transition also shows Strauss's awareness of the possibilities of standard forms, and his ability to play with those options. After using the transition to establish that the dominant (A major) will be the apparent key of the impending second theme—an unusual, but not unlikely, choice in a minor-key movement—an unexpected F appears in the bass in the first measure of the second theme, simultaneously revealing the true key of the theme (mediant) and the ruse of the transition. Unlike the misjudged retransition of the Overture (TrV 69), the effect here is much more convincing, demonstrating Strauss's progress as a composer in only one year.

This opening movement also contains the first genuine development section in any symphonic work by Strauss. His technique for development in this lengthy subsection (188 measures) consists primarily of repeating his material in its original four- and eight-measure phrases or of building new, similarly regular units out of this same material. Once a model phrase has been established, it seldom changes as it sequences mechanically through various harmonic levels within its own subsection. Although this harmonic motion takes place under regular four- and eight-measure phrases, Strauss has no large-scale tonal plans for this development and seems intent merely on avoiding harmonic stasis. Still, this section marks the first time in an orchestral work that Strauss went beyond the safety of a codified formal plan. At the same time he revealed the limits of his ability to plan beyond a single period. The strong V–I progressions that mark the beginning of each subsection suggest that Strauss also applied the same architectonic methods to this development that normally guided his composition of an exposition or a recapitulation.

As in all of Strauss's earlier sonata-allegro movements, the recapitulation is nearly an exact reiteration of the exposition, even to the details in the orchestration. One significant alteration is a slight abbreviation of the transition and the cutting of the first eight measures of the second theme. Another change is the transformation of the closing group into a coda. Moreover, the expected V–I cadence joining the second theme to the coda is replaced with a deceptive cadence that leads back into a series of cadential progressions in D minor. The result of these small adjustments is to weaken the structural joints and to maintain forward motion in these obligatory sections. As with all of the other improvements in Strauss's handling of sonata form, none of these is particularly original when viewed in isolation, but the sum of these modest changes is a movement far above the level of anything he had previously composed.

The remaining three movements all show similar improvements over his earlier efforts in the same forms. There are no changes in the formal plans themselves, only in Strauss's execution of them. The slow second movement in A major, for instance, follows an abbreviated sonata-allegro plan similar to that of the Serenade's second movement. In the Symphony, however, the slow movement has a wider variety in the lengths of phrases, as opposed to the extreme regularity in the Serenade's second movement. Strauss also gives this movement greater unity by deriving all of its connecting and closing material from the first transition. The first part of the D-minor Scherzo has an engaging rhythmic vitality that comes from the simple two-measure motive that dominates the movement. The Trio offers a nice contrast, with a theme that is relatively calm. Moreover, its orchestration, which is initially for winds alone, offers a refreshing change from the string-dominated textures that characterize the rest of the Symphony. The Finale offers another example of Strauss's academic sonata-allegro form. One notable feature is the fugal episode in G minor that concludes the development. The first eighteen measures of this subsection are a textbook exposition of a fugue in four parts, and the two ensuing attempts at stretto display Strauss's solid command of counterpoint, something he obviously owed to Meyer's tutelage.

Despite its evident advances, in the end, this symphony's weaknesses outweigh its strong points and mark it as a work of uneven inspiration. Certainly there are many fine moments, including much of the first movement and the Scherzo. On the other hand, the slow movement lacks true depth of feeling, while the themes in the Finale are short-winded, a fault that becomes increasingly obvious with their frequent repetition, and that same movement's fugue has an air of academic self-consciousness about it. Nevertheless, it is a measure of how far Strauss had come by his sixteenth birthday that this symphony need not be excused as a "student" work.

Strauss's First Symphony was not the only one of his works to premiere in March 1881. On the fourteenth, the Benno Walter Quartet played a String Quartet (TrV 95) by Strauss, and two days later, Cornelia Meysenheym sang three of his songs on texts by Emmanuel Geibel (TrV 75) in a recital. The cumulative effect of these public performances, doubtless abetted by some gentle persuasion from Franz Strauss, was the beginning of an arrangement with the Munich publishing firm of Aibl to issue Richard's compositions. The agreement would last for nearly twenty years, during which time thirty works by Strauss—including eleven instrumental pieces and his first seven tone poems—appeared in the Joseph Aibl catalog. The majority of these abstract instrumental works are not well-known today, although most of them are competent and occasionally interesting pieces in conservative idioms. More important, these published works are the ones by which Strauss became known to the world beyond his Munich home.

The first of Strauss's compositions in the catalog of the Aibl Verlag was the String Quartet in A, which was given the opus number "2" when it appeared late in 1881. Even at the time of its premiere the quartet was viewed as an almost reactionary work, one that looked back to Mozart and Haydn for inspiration. Its most successful movement is the scherzo, which may be due to the brevity of its form. The other three fully developed sonata-allegro movements rely on their melodic charm to hold the listener's attention, but Strauss's old habit of repeating rather than developing his material tests the patience of even the most indulgent listener.

Strauss's next published compositions were piano works: first, a set of *Fünf Klavierstücke*, Op. 3 (TrV 105), and a Sonata in B minor, Op. 5 (TrV 103), and a bit later, a set of five *Stimmungsbilder*, Op. 9 (TrV 127). When the piano pieces were offered to Aibl, Eugen Spitzweg, son of the firm's owner, was unsure of their potential, so he turned to an old friend, the conductor and pianist Hans von Bülow, for advice. Bülow replied to the inquiry in memorable fashion in a letter dated 22 October 1881, "I do not care at all for the piano pieces by Richard Strauss—immature and over-done. Lachner has the imagination of Chopin in contrast. I fail to see the youth in his invention. No genius according to my innermost convictions, but rather at best a talent."[18] Despite Bülow's negative assessment, Spitzweg published the *Fünf Klavierstücke* late in 1881. These competent, if ordinary works continue the direction of Strauss's earlier keyboard pieces by mimicking the styles of Schumann, Mendelssohn, and Bee-thoven. The Sonata has a slightly higher reputation, due in part to the dramatic urgency of a first movement whose principal theme was cribbed from Beethoven's Fifth Symphony.

The *Stimmungsbilder* (literally, impressionistic pictures) are the best of these early piano works. Despite their atmospheric titles, they have little in common with Strauss's later programmatic works. As *Charakterstücke*, they "express" nothing beyond a general mood and remain grounded in an aesthetic that valued melody and feeling over abstract design and musical argument. From a formal standpoint, there are no surprises. Phrasing is reg-ular, tonal plans are clear, and there is a preference for ternary forms. The second piece of the set ("At a Lonely Spring") imitates moving water to achieve its effect, while the last ("Portrait of the Moor") uses open fifths in the left hand to evoke the misty Scottish highlands. The first ("On a Quiet Wooded Path") and fourth ("Dreaming") are more in the manner of a Mendelssohn *Song without Words* or a Schumann character piece, but both are just as effective as the more mimetic pieces. The "Intermezzo" is the only work in this collection without a scene to paint, but its evocative principal theme makes it the most interesting of the set.

Easily the best known and most successful of Strauss's earliest pub-lished works is the Serenade, Op. 7 (TrV 106). Composed in 1881 and published a year later, this piece for thirteen wind instruments attracted little interest until Hans von Bülow included it in the touring repertoire of the Meiningen Court Orchestra in the winter of 1883–84. Played by Germany's leading orchestra, it soon became the first of Strauss's compo-sitions to win widespread praise. Years later, Strauss referred to his Serenade as "nothing more than the respectable work of a music student." His self-deprecating manner aside, the Serenade remains one of Strauss's most attractive early works, with more than a hint of Mozart's influence in it. Its form is a straightforward sonata-allegro movement with a brief developmental episode at its center. The two principal themes are both quite appealing, even in their very regular phrase structures, while the var-iegated orchestration is the Serenade's strongest point. Each instrument has its own moments, but it is Strauss's ability to combine and change timbres that is most striking in this work, and those variations in the orchestration make up for the lack of melodic and harmonic variety in the development.

The success of the Serenade soon led Bülow to ask Strauss for another showpiece for winds. In fact, Strauss had already begun work on the Suite, Op. 4 (TrV 132). The winds of the Meiningen Orchestra gave the premiere on 18 November 1884 while on tour in Munich, an occasion made all the more memorable because it was Strauss's formal conducting debut. Pleasant though it may be in spots, much of the Suite lacks the spontaneous charm of the Serenade. The first two movements follow Strauss's usual sonata-allegro form, but without developments of any kind. The Praeludium's martial character stems in part from the opening triplet theme and prominent horns, although the initially static harmonies prevent the movement from gaining any real momentum. The Romanze has an interesting modal quality, but like the first movement it lacks a long line. The Gavotte is the gem of this suite, with a bubbling first theme that never grows tiresome. Its contrasting Pastorale section, complete with a drone bass, also employs a modal melody, and the retransition to the main theme is one of Strauss's best to this point in his career. The concluding Introduction and Fugue round out the Suite by borrowing a theme from the Romanze for the beginning and adapting the Pastorale theme for the fugue subject. In the Fugue, however, Strauss reveals his occasional tendency to go on a bit too long when he starts the fugue anew for no apparent purpose after bringing the movement to a fortissimo climax.

Before 1878, Strauss never completed any works for solo instruments, save the piano, but in that year he made his first attempt with a piece for his father on his name day, the Introduction, Theme, and Variations for the valveless natural horn (the instrument favored by Franz Strauss) and piano (TrV 70). Less than a year later, Strauss repeated the genre with a similar work for flute and piano (TrV 76), and a few months after that, he composed a Romanze for solo clarinet and orchestra (TrV 80) that was performed as part of the closing exercises for his Gymnasium in the summer of 1879. As their titles imply, these works were limited forms that allowed Strauss to experiment with writing in idiomatic styles as preparation for more expansive solo works. After entering into his arrangement with Aibl Verlag, Strauss tried his luck with works for three different solo instruments and achieved varying degrees of success.

The first of these, the Concerto for Violin, Op. 8 (TrV 110), was composed in 1882 for Strauss's uncle and violin teacher, Benno Walter. It has never found a secure place in the repertoire for at least two good reasons. First, Strauss's thematic material is uneven at best. While there are many bravura passages for the soloist, there are also many ideas that seem better suited to a more intimate work than to a concerto. The shifts from one type of material to the other are thus quite noticeable and even occasionally disconcerting. Second, Strauss's lack of experience with the concerto form is obvious from the way the first movement progresses from one obligatory section to the next. Far too often, the piece simply grinds to a halt and a new section begins, which draws attention to the seams in the structure as well as to the lack of a genuine symphonic argument. This problem is most evident in the development section, where Strauss resorts to three cadenzas for the soloist, each introduced by a complete stop, in place of a more symphonic reworking of his materials. With no real momentum in this section, the moment of recapitulation becomes a hollow, formulaic gesture, which is further emphasized by the full return of the entire exposition. The second and third movements likewise fall short of the genre's demands. The somber second movement lacks a true contrasting middle section, and the concluding rondo never quite captures the spirit of Mendelssohn's Violin Concerto that Strauss seems to be emulating.

In contrast to the disappointing Concerto for Violin, Strauss's next concerted work, a Concerto for Waldhorn, Op. 11 (TrV 117), is one of the finest compositions of his formative years, and to this day it remains a favorite of audiences and soloists alike. Although the title implies a work for valveless horn, many passages can be played only on a modern valved instrument. Several of the primarily triadic and unmistakably idiomatic melodies, notably the principal theme of the first movement and the rondo theme, are clearly related to one another, which emphasizes the structural innovations of this work. Rather than follow the outdated classical plan of three separate movements, Strauss employs a more compact design of three movements compressed into one, which eliminates the purely formulaic returns of material that mar too many of his earliest works. The first section, with only a few brief orchestral tutti passages between the solo's themes, serves as the exposition, while the slow middle movement takes the place of a development (another potentially weak area for Strauss in those years). The concluding rondo then does double duty as both a finale and a recapitulation, thanks to the close resemblance between the principal themes of the rondo and the first movement. Strauss plays a small joke with this similarity by having the soloist begin one return of the rondo theme as if it might revert to the Concerto's opening theme, only to have the orchestra "correct" the error. Franz Strauss's own Concerto for Horn, Op. 8, was the likely source of this formal plan, and several of Richard's themes possess more than a passing resemblance to his father's.[19] Richard's solo lines are more daring than his father's, however, as well as more interesting. In fact,

Franz never played his son's Concerto in public, chiefly because he found the high notes too treacherous.

Strauss's other solo works from the early 1880s were composed for the cello and were inspired by Hans Wihan, a distinguished Czech cellist who was a colleague of Franz Strauss in the Munich Court Orchestra. Wihan's wife, Dora, was a close friend of Richard's sister and a frequent guest in the Strauss home. Through these relationships, Strauss doubtless came to know Wihan and his instrument's idiomatic possibilities. The first work Strauss composed for Wihan was a Sonata for Cello and Piano, Op. 6 (TrV 115), in 1881. In the winter of 1883, Strauss revised the first movement, and a few months after that he also composed a single-movement Romanze (TrV 118) for cello and orchestra. The strengths in both of these works lie in their melodic ideas, which are superior to the mechanically contrived themes found in many of Strauss's earlier works. The flowing first theme of the sonata's opening movement is especially noteworthy in that regard. The developments in the outer movements, however, still reveal a weakness in the handling of that section.

Through the early 1880s, Strauss's evolving style never consistently reflects the influence of any one composer, although it is quite possible to point to specific moments and even to whole pieces that mimic individual composers ranging from Haydn, Mozart, and early Beethoven up to Mendelssohn and Schumann. In fact, Strauss spoke the common, conservative musical language of mid-nineteenth-century Germany, since he knew little else. In 1880, Wagner's *Der Ring des Nibelungen* was barely four years old and had been heard in its entirety just a handful of times, and only one of those performances had been outside of Bayreuth. Admittedly, Strauss had heard all of Wagner's works by 1879. At the age of seventeen (in 1881), he had even begun to study the score of *Tristan und Isolde*, against his father's express wishes, but according to Strauss's own recollections it was not until several years after his first acquaintance with that score that he began to fully appreciate Wagner's methods. As to the potential influence of Liszt's symphonic poems, it is doubtful if the young Strauss ever heard any of them in Munich since they were so rarely performed anywhere well into the 1890s.[20]

Around 1882–83, however, Strauss began to emulate a more contemporary composer, in fact, the first living composer whose music seemed to interest Strauss: Johannes Brahms. That attraction would lead in 1885–86 to what Strauss would call his "*Brahmsschwärmerei*" (literally, worship of Brahms). That phase would pass within a year or so, and by 1891, Bülow would describe Strauss as "almost fanatically anti-Brahms."[21] Locating the beginning of Strauss's enthusiasm for Brahms, however, is more difficult.

As late as January 1884, Strauss seems to have had little understanding of Brahms's music, as revealed in a letter he wrote to his father from Berlin, where Strauss heard several early performances of Brahms's Third Symphony. Within a month, however, Strauss had changed his mind completely and had written gushingly of his admiration for the music of Brahms.[22] Even before this relatively short period of professed fascination, there are suggestions in Strauss's music that he was moving toward an affinity with Brahms's style. It is impossible to say whether this was a conscious decision on Strauss's part, but it is not unreasonable to assume that as a composer of *Hausmusik* in his early years, Strauss knew and had studied the chamber works of Brahms, virtually the only major figure active in those traditional genres at the time.[23] One element of Brahms's "sound" is evident already in the thicker textures of Strauss's Cello Sonata and the heavier orchestration of his *Concertouvertüre* (TrV 125), and slightly later works would adopt other Brahmsian techniques.

Although it was never published in Strauss's lifetime, the *Concertouvertüre* was one of his more successful works from the early 1880s, yet it also shows the limitations of Strauss's style at that time. Strauss had completed the work sometime in 1883, and it was premiered later that year (28 November) under Hermann Levi's direction in another Musical Academy Concert similar to the one in which the Symphony in D minor was first heard. As with the Symphony, the *Münchner Neueste Nachrichten*'s critic praised the overture, although he also complained modestly of orchestration that seemed a bit heavy in parts.[24] Almost immediately after the concert, Strauss left for a four-month visit to Berlin by way of Leipzig and Dresden. It was his first extended trip away from home alone, but more important, this journey was an opportunity for Strauss to meet the leading figures of German musical life and to show them his music in the hopes of winning performances and gaining publication.[25]

The recently premiered *Concertouvertüre* was the showpiece in Strauss's portfolio on this trip, and it was pulled out at nearly every opportunity. Strauss did manage to secure performances of it in Berlin and Innsbruck, but more frequently, conductors and concert promoters declined to program the work. Publishers also had no interest in the overture, since it had not yet proven itself in the concert hall. Hugo Bock went so far as to pronounce it not "saleable," although he did promise to discuss the possibility of publishing other works by Strauss later that year.[26] In the following years, the *Concertouvertüre* was performed a few times, including once as late as 1886 in Meiningen under Strauss's leadership, but soon thereafter it disappeared from the repertoire until it was published, primarily as a historical document, a century later.

A close look at the *Concertouvertüre*'s score confirms the judgments of his contemporaries. The work's imposing primary theme clearly owes its inspiration to Beethoven's *Coriolanus* Overture, although Strauss's treatment of the material is still his own. The overall sense of forward motion is easily the best to date in a large-scale work by Strauss, and his approaches to several of the climaxes are well judged. But as before, Strauss continues to rely primarily on the mechanical sequencing of regular phrases to make the development section, and the energy level slumps without apparent reason at a few structural joints. Both of these shortcomings draw attention to Strauss's safe and unimaginative approach to sonata-allegro form, and also explain why conductors and publishers were not especially interested in this work.

The influences of Brahms are even more noticeable in the Quartet for Piano and Strings, Op. 13 (TrV 137), and the *Burleske* in D minor (TrV 145). In both, the debt to Brahms is evident chiefly in the overall "sound," that is, the disposition of the individual parts, and in the ways in which Strauss creates and manipulates his material at the level of the motive and phrase.[27] Each thematic area flows effortlessly into the next; the Quartet's opening Allegro is particularly notable in this regard. At the same time, its opening theme and subsidiary ideas lend themselves well to variation, making the development and extended coda far superior to Strauss's earlier efforts in this section of a sonata-allegro movement.

In the *Burleske*, a work Strauss described as the consequence of his enthusiasm for Brahms, Strauss actually parodied elements from both of Brahms's piano concertos by cleverly juxtaposing them with reminiscences of Wagner's *Tristan und Isolde* and *Die Walküre*. The difficult solo part is thick with Brahmsian octaves filled with sixths or thirds, and it requires such frequent shifts of hand positions that even as fine a pianist as Bülow declared the piece "unplayable." In contrast, the orchestral accompaniment includes many lightly scored passages and a clever part for solo timpani. One other aspect of Brahms's technique that Strauss adopts is the use of an elemental three-note cell as a unifying device. The only failing of this work is its length. The recapitulation of this sonata-allegro movement is exact, and the long final cadenza, which merely elaborates a dominant ninth chord, only emphasizes this problem.

In contrast to the *Concertouvertüre* and the *Burleske*, Strauss's last traditional symphonic essay, the Symphony in F minor, Op. 12 (TrV 126), was also his first truly successful work in an orchestral genre and even eclipsed the Serenade, Op. 7, in popularity and the estimation of most contemporary critics. Strauss began his second symphony late in 1883 and completed it in Berlin on 25 January 1884, just in time for it to be shown to various publishers and conductors there. Nevertheless, the first performance was

given by the New York Philharmonic Orchestra under the baton of
Theodore Thomas on 13 December 1884, thanks primarily to Franz
Strauss's friendship with Thomas. The German premiere took place exactly
a month later in Cologne, and before the end of 1885, Meiningen, Munich,
and Berlin also heard the Symphony. In light of these successful performances, Spitzweg quickly agreed to publish it as Strauss's Op. 12, provided
Franz Strauss paid the printing costs of one thousand marks. Franz's gen-
erosity was soon repaid out of the royalties generated by the Symphony as
the work began to enter the German orchestral repertoire. Critics were
impressed with the Symphony, particularly in view of the composer's age
(Strauss had completed the Symphony before his twentieth birthday). They
generally approved of his handling of musical form and often singled out
the Scherzo for praise, even though they also noted that the forms and musical language of the Symphony were not original.

Despite any minor reservations they might have had, there were good
reasons for Strauss's contemporaries to admire this work on its own merits. For the first time, Strauss tempered his traditional forms with several
progressive features, albeit without violating the spirit of their classical
models. As in his previous multimovement works, three of the four movements are in sonata-allegro form, while the Scherzo is in its usual rounded
binary form. The two inner movements are switched, a structural novelty
with numerous precedents, and another new feature is an attempt at cyclical form in the coda of the final movement, based on thematic interrelationships among three of the four movements. The real essence of
Strauss's newfound maturity, when compared to his earlier works, however,
is a less dogmatic approach to musical form.

The Symphony's slow third movement offers a rudimentary example of
this new manner. As in the slow (second) movements of the early Serenade
and the Symphony in D minor, the Symphony's third movement is a
sonata-allegro form reduced to its basic elements, but now also with an abbreviated, rather than an exact, return of the opening section. The
recapitulation is shortened by the omission of the unnecessary transition,
which allows the first theme—itself reduced from four phrases (in the exposition) to only two and with its final cadence also excised—to lead
directly into the second theme without an obvious break. In an era in which
listeners knew the sonata paradigm well, Strauss finally recognized that only
a partial return of previous material, in place of a mechanical, full return,
was sufficient to fulfill the dictates of classical form. Each of the outer movements has a similar solution to this same problem.

In a manner that looks to the style of Brahms, the seams between the
constituent parts of movements are often elegantly hidden. In the opening

movement, for instance, the first theme begins as an antecedent–consequent pair of phrases, a customary shape for such a theme in one of Strauss's early works. A third phrase (atypical for Strauss) is then appended to the otherwise self-sufficient pair through a deceptive cadence. This extra phrase is scored for full orchestra, which falsely appears to signal the start of the transition, when, in fact, the cadence that closes the first theme is not reached until the end of the third phrase.

Similarly, the beginning of the second theme is obscured through a bit of harmonic subterfuge. The theme itself is a ternary form (a–b–a') in the submediant (D-flat) instead of the more usual mediant (A-flat). Strauss prepares this area with the expected secondary dominant in the transition but delays the resolution until after the second theme has begun. Additionally, the harmonies here are in inversion, which further masks their function and leaves the listener in doubt as to the formal boundaries at this point. Only with the return of the a' material, can one recognize in retrospect what was the start of the second theme. Both the choice of key and the shape of this second theme strongly suggest that the music of Brahms served as a model for this passage.[28]

Strauss obscured these structural joints even further in the recapitulation. As in the slow movement, the first theme returns without its final cadence, and the entire transition is cut as well. In its place are three new measures that join the first theme to the second in the middle of its initial phrase. The remainder of the second area, transposed up a fifth, follows exactly as before until a full cadence on A-flat brings the theme to a close. A new, extended closing group then serves as the movement's coda, where the F-minor tonic is finally reached with melodic material in the bass that bears a strong resemblance to the second theme. This delay of the second theme's return in the tonic—the essence of the sonata principle—until virtually the last possible moment denies the perfunctory character of Strauss's earlier recapitulations. Moreover, these subtle changes in the structure contribute to a sense of ambiguity that holds the listener's interest to the very end of the movement. In the fourth movement the recapitulation of the second theme is handled in a similar fashion, delaying the expected triumph of the tonic at the beginning of the second theme until the end of the theme.

Strauss also attempted to throw more emphasis onto the end of the finale with brief recalls of themes from earlier in the symphony. On the surface, there is no compelling reason to bring back material at that point, and that gesture has drawn criticism to this otherwise well-made work. In fact, the similarities among the work's individual themes—a characteristic seen as a weakness ever since Brahms's oft-repeated criticism—suggest that Strauss was attempting to unite the four movements through a web of interrelationships centered on the opening movement's first theme.[29] Strauss did not handle these cyclic interconnections quite as subtly as Brahms might have, however. Material from the Scherzo is missing from this nexus of relationships, probably because of the work's compositional history. Strauss completed the Scherzo in June 1883, and then composed the rest of the Symphony between October 1883 and January 1884. The idea of uniting the work through its thematic material probably did not occur to Strauss until long after the Scherzo was done. The inclusion of the Scherzo's unrelated theme in the finale then led commentators to view the coda of the fourth movement as an isolated effect and not as the culmination of the entire symphony.

In its day, the F-minor Symphony was praised both as a work of quality in its own right and as a harbinger of even better things to come, but over the years the work has fallen into disrepute to one degree or another in the eyes of most critics. The problem is undoubtedly one of perspective, as the Symphony is usually compared unfavorably to Strauss's later tone poems. The Symphony, Op. 12, is a far-from-inconsequential work, however, and critics in the 1880s were correct to praise it as one of the best works of the decade, as only the symphonies of Brahms were superior to it. Moreover, it was the work that marked the emergence of Strauss as a significant new voice in German concert halls. For a more equitable assessment of the Symphony, we need to change our point of view. Rather than regard the Symphony as a work overshadowed by the later tone poems, we should consider the Symphony as the work that marks the end of Strauss's apprenticeship.

By 1885 Strauss was poised on the threshold of a promising career, due in large part to the success of his instrumental compositions. The Serenade, Op. 7, and the Symphony, Op. 12, had established his credentials as a composer with a promising future, and critics of the time described Strauss as a "master of form," which usually meant the sonata-allegro design. Nevertheless, Strauss's tendency to rely on purely mechanical recapitulations was a weakness that weighed down many an otherwise successful work. Strauss had begun to address that shortcoming in the Symphony, with movements that altered the expected tonal plans, particularly in the recapitulations, and with an attempt at cyclical form. The solution to this problem, however, would come less than a year later from a quite unexpected source.

In the spring of 1885, Franz Mannstädt, the second conductor and Bülow's assistant in Meiningen, resigned his post to accept an appointment in Berlin. The chance to work with Bülow was an exceptional one, and at least a dozen well-qualified candidates inquired about the vacancy in Meiningen. For reasons that are not entirely clear, Bülow ignored the applications of such experienced young conductors as Felix Weingartner and Gustav Mahler, and instead used Spitzweg as an intermediary to ask whether Strauss, who had no practical experience as a Kapellmeister, would accept the position as an educational opportunity. Strauss assented, and in the fall of 1885 he began his career as an apprentice music director. Watching the exacting Bülow's rehearsals and conducting the court orchestra himself gave Strauss an education in practical music making that he could never have gotten in any other way. Even more important for Strauss's future than this hands-on experience, however, was the complete reorientation of his aesthetic compass under the initial guidance of Alexander Ritter, a string player in the Meiningen orchestra and a fervent disciple of Richard Wagner.

Strauss met Ritter only days after arriving in Meiningen, and during the following year, the two spent many evenings together talking about music and philosophy. While it is impossible to know exactly what they discussed or even the degree to which Ritter actually influenced the young composer, from that winter on, Strauss would turn away from the conservative path on which he had begun his career as a composer.[30] As Strauss explained many years later in his own reminiscences, Ritter patiently tutored him in the music and writings of Wagner and especially the tone poems of Franz Liszt, influences that ran completely contrary to the education that he had received up to that point in his life. From Ritter's Wagnerian viewpoint, Beethoven's last compositions were the source of all musical progress in the nineteenth century, and they led inevitably to works with overtly expressive contents, such as Liszt's tone poems. Opposite this "Music of the Future" were epigonal composers like Brahms whose works merely reiterated the already used up sonata forms in meaningless displays of compositional technique.[31] Despite his upbringing, these ideas appealed to the young composer. Strauss quickly became one of the most fervent and vocal supporters of Wagner's music, and he soon adopted a musical credo that echoed Wagner's: "New ideas must seek out new forms for themselves—this was the fundamental principle of Liszt's symphonic works, in which the poetic idea was in fact also the form-creating element—became for me from then on the guiding principle of my own symphonic works."[32]

While Strauss had shifted his allegiance to this new aesthetic viewpoint in a relatively short period of time, the process of putting those ideas into practice took a bit longer. For all of their philosophical importance, Wagner's voluminous writings said almost nothing specific about how to compose programmatic music, and thus it was up to Strauss alone to find his own new compositional voice. In fact, his next major orchestral work would be only a partial step toward that goal. In a letter of 11 June 1888 to his uncle, Carl Hörburger, Strauss called *Aus Italien*, Op. 16 (TrV 147), the "bridge" that led from the conservative works of his early years to his tone poems.[33] In retrospect, the transitional nature of *Aus Italien* is fairly evident from the disparity between contemporaneous reports of the work's tumultuous early reception and the lukewarm response that the music engenders today. The premiere in Munich on 2 March 1887 split the audience into opposing factions—in an imitation of the German Reichstag, according to one critic—which delighted Strauss. Subsequent performances were closely scrutinized by the press, who were quick to mark *Aus Italien* as one of the most difficult and demanding scores in the repertoire, and as one of the most important new works of the era.[34] Nowadays, however, audiences hardly raise their collective eyebrows at Strauss's "Symphonic Fantasy" (the composer's own subtitle), when the work even finds a place on a concert program. The reason for this simple dichotomy is the difference between intention and execution.

Strauss left Meiningen in the spring of 1886 with a contract for a three-year term as third conductor at the Munich Opera. Before returning home, however, he headed south for a holiday in Italy, although he did not leave his sketchbook at home. In a letter of 11 May 1886 from Rome, Strauss told his mother that he was busily working on some musical ideas, and after his return from Italy, he wrote to Bülow that he was now capable of composing works based on external inspiration: "I have never really believed in inspiration through the beauty of Nature, [but] in the Roman ruins, I was set right, for ideas simply came flying to me. Perhaps it will interest you that on a drive on the Appian Way, one glorious afternoon, I suddenly caught myself unconsciously humming the D-major trio of the Scherzo of [Beethoven's] Seventh Symphony, it expressed so completely the mood of this wonderful Campagna."[35] Such an admission demonstrates the remarkable change in Strauss's compositional aesthetic in only a few months. At the same time, the musical work engendered by the sights of Italy was relatively conventional, as one might expect from a composer who had spent over a decade honing his technique with traditional forms.

More than two years after the premiere, Strauss published his own "analysis" of *Aus Italien* in the *Allgemeine Musikzeitung*, a Berlin-based journal edited by the sympathetic critic Otto Lessmann.[36] Strauss's brief exegesis is far shorter and simpler than any of the detailed concert guides that would be published by various writers after each of Strauss's tone poems appeared, but the purpose of his summary was surely not an in-depth analysis. Rather, it was probably intended as a public relations maneuver to outflank any critics who might claim that *Aus Italien* lacked a coherent form. Strauss's descriptions begin with a sentence or two elaborating on each of the evocative titles of the four movements. The musical analysis that follows consists merely of identifying a few important themes with musical examples. Although this information was probably only modestly helpful to novice listeners, it is noteworthy that Strauss identified his themes with technical terms usually associated with abstract forms, for example, *Hauptthema* (main theme), *Seitenthema* (secondary theme), and so on, which suggests in his mind the affinity of the forms in *Aus Italien* with traditional models.

Strauss described "In Roms Ruinen," the second movement of *Aus Italien*, as a great symphonic first movement, that is, as a sonata-allegro movement. Its chief progressive feature is the recapitulation of the second theme outside of the tonic, a gesture Strauss had already used in the Symphony, Op. 12. The third movement, "Am Strand von Sorrent," like Strauss's previous slow movements, combines ternary form with the tonal plan of a sonata-allegro movement; and the thematic material is also rearranged in the recapitulation. The fourth movement, "Neapolitanisches Volksleben," is a loose sonata-rondo form with reminiscences of the first movement near the end. The first movement is the most ambiguous of the four; rather than a standard symphonic form, "Auf der Campagna" is a process of thematic clarification, in which the principal theme is revealed at the high point of the movement. The movement is far from incoherent, however, as the seeds of most of its material can be found in the first few measures. Unusual harmonic progressions, notably the opening move from major tonic to minor dominant, and unique orchestral effects contribute to the movement's atmospheric sound.

The traditional techniques of Strauss's earlier works are also evident throughout *Aus Italien*. Tonal areas are almost never in doubt, and most of the thematic material is organized in regular units, although less rigidly so than in many of the earlier works. For instance, the beginning of "Auf der Campagna," a section in which Strauss seems determined to obscure the rhythmic flow through irregular changes in exotic-sounding harmonies, is nothing more than two parallel phrases. "In Roms Ruinen" also begins with a balanced, parallel construction in C major, but in the second phrase the symmetrical form is distorted by an insertion that deflects the harmonic progression to E-flat and then A-flat before returning to the original key. Similarly, the plethora of orchestral effects in the third movement and the breakneck pace and kaleidoscopic changes in the fourth movement overshadow the generally regular rhythms of these movements.

Consequently, even though *Aus Italien* seemed to press the bounds of the possible for orchestras and audiences used to pre-Wagnerian scores, the demands of Strauss's new style were primarily on the orchestral musicians who had to execute their individual parts and not on the audiences who merely had to follow the progress of the work's four movements. While brass players might have complained that Strauss's parts were too high and too exposed and lacked sufficient rests—a legitimate complaint for a hornist or trumpeter used to playing only cadential passages and supporting lines in works from an earlier and more conservative repertoire—in truth, no intelligent listener familiar with the standard symphonic forms was (or is) ever in danger of becoming lost in *Aus Italien*. Strauss's training in and adherence to traditional forms were simply too much a part of his technique for him to abandon them in one fell swoop. In his next work, his first tone poem, *Macbeth*, Op. 23, Strauss would struggle even more to loose himself from the grip that sonata form seemed to have on his symphonic works,[37] but it would not be until *Don Juan* that Strauss would be able to compose a programmatic piece that did not automatically follow a classical form.

OCCASIONAL WORKS (1900–1940)

Although Strauss's reputation was transformed forever in less than a year from that of a promising young assistant Kapellmeister to Germany's most avant-garde composer by the extraordinary premieres of *Don Juan* (11 November 1889) and *Tod und Verklärung* (21 June 1890), he did continue to compose traditional, nonprogrammatic instrumental works when the circumstances demanded. Many of these arose out of requests for a *pièce d'occasion* or as directed commissions, and thus Strauss's craftsmanship often took precedence over his inspiration in these works. Moreover, after his two initial flurries of tone poems came to an end with *Ein Heldenleben* in 1898, Strauss's interest in programmatic instrumental music declined and eventually died—it would be almost five years until *Symphonia domestica* and another decade after that work until *Eine Alpensinfonie*—to be replaced by his enthusiasm for the stage. It is thus not surprising that most of Strauss's instrumental works from the first four decades of the twentieth century languish in obscurity.

Among the most representative of Strauss's "duty" pieces are the six marches (TrV 213, 214, 217, 221 [I and II], and 222) that he composed in 1905–7 for his employer, the Kaiser, who cared more for military music than for his famous court conductor's shockingly modern operas.[38] A similar royal request in 1909 led to the composition of the *Feierliche Einzug* (TrV 224) for the investiture ceremonies of the Prussian Order of St. John, whose chief patron was the Kaiser's son. These unremarkable trifles are scarcely recognizable as the work of the same hand that created *Salome* and *Elektra*, but they do say much about Strauss's own surprisingly archaic view of himself as a court functionary.

Strauss's later association with the Vienna Opera likewise led to a series of ceremonial pieces for that city. Even before he moved there, he supplied a massive *Festliches Präludium*, Op. 61 (TrV 229), for the 1913 dedication of Vienna's new concert hall. The work employs such a large orchestra that it is virtually never performed. Moreover, its substance is nothing but the sort of empty bombast that Strauss's detractors are quick to deride. Strauss later composed four fanfares for brass ensembles to play at festivals in Vienna, which are effective for their purposes but have little use outside of ceremonial settings.[39] Finally, the wedding of his son Franz in 1924 inspired a modest *Hochzeitspräludium* (TrV 247) for two harmoniums, based on themes from *Symphonia domestica*, *Guntram*, and *Der Rosenkavalier*.

During the early years of the century Strauss occasionally visited the Vienna home of industrialist Karl Wittgenstein, where he sometimes played piano duets with Karl's son Paul, a budding virtuoso. Tragically, Paul lost his right arm in the First World War, but he still retained his desire for a career in music. After the war Wittgenstein commissioned a series of works for piano left-hand. Strauss initially declined Wittgenstein's request before changing his mind after his own son made a successful recovery from a life-threatening illness in 1924. The resulting work, *Paragon zur Symphonia Domestica*, Op. 73 (TrV 209a), is a cross between a piano concerto and a tone poem. To portray Franz's illness, the F-major child's theme from the tone poem is plagued in various ways throughout the work by a C-sharp. As a showpiece for Wittgenstein, the *Paragon* was fairly well received, although Strauss overestimated the ability of a one-armed pianist to compete with a large orchestra, which forced Wittgenstein to thin out the accompaniment. Strauss later wrote a second work for Wittgenstein, the *Panathenäenzug*, Op. 74 (TrV 254), but this series of variations on a passacaglia bass was not a success. As the literal property of one man, neither work has made much of an impact in the years since their premieres.[40]

In 1939, Strauss interrupted work on his penultimate opera, *Die Liebe der Danae*, to compose the *Japanische Festmusik* (TrV 277), a work that commemorates (inaccurately) the twenty-six-hundredth anniversary of the Mikado dynasty. While one might first assume that he accepted the commission primarily for its honorarium of ten thousand Reichmarks, in fact Strauss's motives were anything but pecuniary. By the end of the 1930s Strauss was in a precarious position with the Third Reich. In 1935, he had been forced to resign the presidency of the Reichsmusikkammer, publicly for reasons of "ill health," but in actuality because he had naively (and quite incorrectly) assumed that his celebrity placed him above politics. With the disclosure of his indiscreet letter to Stefan Zweig just before the premiere of *Die schweigsame Frau*, the Nazi elite turned on Strauss, and he would spend the remaining decade of their rule attempting to curry favor with any officials who might provide some measure of protection for his family—specifically his Jewish daughter-in-law Alice and his two half-Jewish grandchildren. In 1936, for instance, and without any official impetus, Strauss had composed and conducted the *Olympic Hymn* for the Berlin Olympic Games as a gesture that he hoped might win him some bit of approval.[41]

Strauss thus accepted the Japanese ambassador's commission—and even declined the fee—in the hopes of guaranteeing his family's safety.[42] Strauss's artistic interest in the project may be best judged from his disinclination to start the work afresh. Instead, he turned to some old "generic" symphonic sketches from several decades earlier for the work's basic material, rather than compose something more specifically "Japanese." The piece itself is in five continuous sections, labeled in the composer's draft but not the published score as "Seascape," "Cherry-blossom Festival," "Volcanic Eruption," "Attack of the Samurai," and "Hymn to the Emperor." Despite these potential cues, the work is far from programmatic, with only the middle section exhibiting a bit of tone painting in the manner of Strauss's tone poems from the 1890s. The large orchestra also included Japanese tuned gongs in a gesture obviously intended to please the Japanese ambassador who first requested the work. Ultimately, the political value of the *Japanische Festmusik* clearly outweighed its musical importance, and Strauss's ceremonial presentation of the manuscript to the Japanese ambassador was well covered in the German press.[43]

In many ways, the *Japanische Festmusik* is quite typical of Strauss's abstract instrumental music in the first four decades of the twentieth century. None of these works was composed out of any inner artistic need. Rather, virtually all were written to fill commissions or as personal gifts, and thus the musical results were seldom inspired, although never incompetent. Strauss's command of traditional techniques remained as strong as ever through these years, and all of these works were supplied efficiently and without fanfare. It is also worth remembering that Strauss lost a fortune when England confiscated his holdings there during the First World War, and thus when he was well beyond the age at which most men would have been considering retirement, Strauss was still concerned about securing his family's future. Thus, while these modest instrumental works often did not earn huge sums, they did keep his name before the public and in some cases they may have even helped to ensure his (and his family's) physical safety, if only briefly. Not surprisingly, Strauss's best instrumental music in this era came from his stage works as excerpts for the concert hall, although those transcriptions hardly count as "abstract instrumental music."[44]

"INDIAN SUMMER" (1942–47)

Strauss's decision to lay down his pen after the premiere of *Capriccio* in 1942 must have been a difficult one. His fifteenth opera was a masterpiece that showed no diminishing of his compositional powers. But at the same time, the Allied war effort was beginning its destruction of Munich with nightly bombing raids, while the privations of war were being felt even in well-off households like Strauss's. Moreover, in that same year the Nazi's "final solution" first touched Strauss when some of his daughter-in-law's kin were sent to Theresienstadt.[45] For a man in his late seventies, who considered himself a cultured German, the looming destruction of his homeland—both from without and from within—along with the intimations of his own mortality that came with his declining health, were doubtless more than enough to stifle any hopes for the future and to still his compositional urge. In October 1943, Strauss seemingly confirmed the end of his career in a letter to his future biographer Willi Schuh: "With *Capriccio*, my life's work is complete, and the notes that I now scribble down for my heirs as wrist exercises (as Hermann Bahr called his daily dictation) have absolutely no importance in music history, even less so than the scores of all the other symphonists and composers. It is only to banish the boredom of idle hours, since one cannot read Wieland and play skat all day."[46] For Strauss, a composer who had ever been occupied with new projects and a man who had always welcomed hard work, the complete cessation of all composition was probably impossible. Still, as Strauss told Schuh, any work in his final years was just a means of passing the time.[47]

In fact, initially, Strauss seemed incapable of completing anything substantial after his final opera. An attempt in 1942 to compose something for the centennial of the Vienna Philharmonic Orchestra led to naught. After struggling for some time with a projected tone poem about the Danube (TrV 284), Strauss had to settle for sending them a congratulatory letter. A few years later he gave the orchestra the unfinished sketches, which he signed "A few drops from the dried-up source of the Danube." Despite this one setback, Strauss had no difficulties with abstract works, which seemed to serve a useful and very necessary purpose for him. As Tim Ashley has noted, Strauss's turn to abstract musical forms in his final years allowed this programmatic composer, who had relied for over fifty years on words to inspire his tone poems and operas, to disconnect himself from a reality that he did not want to face. By restricting himself to the realm of abstract composition, Strauss could express himself freely and without fear of being misunderstood.[48]

In fact, there can be no question of the meaning of Strauss's first important abstract instrumental work in over fifty years. With the Second Concerto for Horn and Orchestra (TrV 283), Strauss retreated symbolically into the nineteenth century, as the inscription on the autograph—"To the memory of my father"—makes clear. The orchestra, comprised of only double winds, a pair of horns, a pair of trumpets, timpani, and strings, is the smallest called for by Strauss since the 1880s, and his treatment of it like a nimble classical ensemble stands in marked contrast to the lush timbres and virtuosic handling of the large orchestras in his tone poems and operas. At the same time, Strauss's chromatically colored harmonic language is still evident, as are the extended dominant pedals, although both are scaled back to the more modest dimensions of this retrospective work. Structurally, the work's three movements are less rigid than the classical models they seem to evoke. The first movement opens with a long, rhapsodic solo for the horn that never quite settles into the regularity of a theme. The rest of the movement is filled with perpetual variations of the material, which may account for the brevity of both the development section and the recapitulation. The second movement, which connects directly to the first without pause, is more of an orchestral Romanze with obbligato horn than a showcase for the soloist. It also allows the soloist a bit of rest before the finale, a rollicking rondo with a principal theme that spans two octaves with widely spaced leaps. The last return of that theme, a harmonized statement by the soloist and the two orchestral horns, is only one of many well-judged moments. As a whole, the concerto is a marvelously youthful work from a composer nearly eighty years old, yet at the same time it is totally unconnected to the era in which it was written. The vitality of this concerto is perhaps a measure of how completely Strauss was able to disassociate himself from a present he did not understand.

In only a few days in January 1943, Strauss complied with a request from the city of Vienna for a brass fanfare, which he then conducted on 9 April 1943. This opportunity to work with members of the orchestra he had conducted two decades earlier, along with the pleasure he undoubtedly felt with the successful completion of the Second Horn Concerto, encouraged Strauss to tackle a musical problem that had bothered him—at least a bit—since the 1880s. His two early pieces for small wind ensembles, Op. 7 and Op. 4, had each been composed for four horns and nine woodwinds, an imbalance, in Strauss's opinion, that required more woodwinds. Thus, in the summer of 1943, while convalescing from a medical procedure, Strauss composed his

First Sonatina in F (TrV 288) for sixteen winds, a score he subtitled "From the Workshop of an Invalid." He was so invigorated after completing the three-movement Sonatina that he set to work almost immediately on a separate Introduction and Allegro for the same combination of instruments. Substantial as that new movement was, Strauss nevertheless composed another Allegro to precede it. These two movements were too weighty to stand alone, however, so in June 1945, Strauss completed an Andante and a Minuet that became the second and third movements between the Allegro and the Introduction and Allegro. That four-movement work was published posthumously with the misleading title "Symphony for Winds," even though Strauss had entitled his manuscript "Second Sonatina for Sixteen Winds" (TrV 291) and added the nostalgic dedication "To the eternal spirit of Mozart at the end of a thankful life."

These two works testify to Strauss's declining power of inspiration, which was nevertheless compensated for and complemented by his still undiminished ability to discover all of an idea's potential. Neither work's basic materials are more than ordinary, and many ideas are so short or fragmentary that they are better described as "figures" than as "themes." Strauss had always admitted that his gift for melody lay not in the long line, but in his ability to invent short motives that he could then extend and develop into full-fledged themes,[49] and this was surely something that he learned from both Meyer and his own father. Nowhere is that skill more evident than in these pieces. In nearly every one of these seven movements, the texture is invigorated by constant motion and an almost nervous contrapuntal energy, as Strauss seeks to extract all that he can from his terse motives through perpetual reharmonizations, melodic reshapings, and ever-changing contrapuntal combinations. The effect is almost that of an improvisation, literally the spontaneous "making of music."[50] For some listeners, such a sound can grow tiresome, as each of these sonatinas goes on for about a half hour or even more. One must remember, however, that Strauss composed these works for himself and not for any public audience.

As the war ground to its inevitable conclusion, the Allied bombing eventually penetrated Strauss's apparent indifference to the hostilities through the ruin of Germany's great centers of culture, including the opera houses in Dresden, Vienna, and Munich. The destruction of Munich's Nationaltheater, where Strauss's father had performed for nearly fifty years and where Strauss himself had first heard so many works and then later served as a conductor, was an especially grievous blow. Strauss's musical response to the end of his world was a pair of works, *München* (TrV 274 and 274a) and the *Metamorphosen* (TrV 290), whose intertwined histories have only recently been disentangled. *München* was originally composed for a 1939 documentary film about Munich that was banned by the Nazis before its release. That waltz then lay dormant until Strauss revised it five years later as an outlet for his grief after the near annihilation of his birthplace.

The original version of *München* borrowed from Strauss's second opera, *Feuersnot*, which was set in medieval Munich. As an expression of pride in the new Germany of the 1930s, Strauss had quoted a passage from the opera that corresponded to the restoration of the city's fires. In the revised version of *München*, Strauss added a section in minor labeled "In Memoriam" and, in an obvious allusion, he quoted additional music from *Feuersnot* that described the extinguishing of Munich's fires. At the same time, the *Rosenkavalier*-like sweetness of the first version was tempered with an elegiac, mournful tone better suited to the "memorial waltz" that this work had become. The proximity of the revised *München* to the *Metamorphosen*, both temporally and in Strauss's sketchbooks, encouraged the belief that both works memorialized the decimated Munich.

In fact, a careful analysis of the sketch material by Timothy L. Jackson establishes separate points of origin for these two works.[51] In contrast to the public mourning of *München*, the *Metamorphosen* had a more private beginning. In his reading of Goethe during the war years, Strauss came across a poem, "Niemand wird sich selber kennen" (No One Can Know Himself), which he sketched in an incomplete setting for four male voices. The crux of the poem is the importance of striving for self-knowledge and the realization of who one truly is. In August 1944, Strauss received a commission for a work for string orchestra from Paul Sacher. It was about at that time that Strauss may have finally recognized the culpability that emanated from his own earlier involvement with the Nazis. His piece for Sacher then became a reworking of the incomplete "Niemand" setting and thereby a musical confession of his self-perceived guilt. The title undoubtedly refers to Goethe's *The Metamorphosis of Plants* and *The Metamorphosis of Animals*. In both, the philosopher optimistically conceives of that process as "order in motion."

Strauss's *Metamorphosen* turns Goethe's concept on its head. In the musical work, self-knowledge does not elevate man; rather, it reveals his bestial nature. To symbolize the inversion of Goethe's noble concept, Strauss reworks a basic motive from his "Niemand" sketch in the *Metamorphosen*. In the vocal piece, the C-major tonic is initially undermined by either E-minor or C-minor harmonies, either of which may easily be transformed into C major by the shift of a single pitch. Jackson equates those slippery harmonic relationships, which he calls the *Metamorphosenmotiv*, with the elusiveness of Goethe's unknowable self. In "Niemand wird sich selber kennen" the poet asserts that self-knowledge is the way in which man elevates himself, a concept that Strauss supports in his vocal setting through the triumph of C major over the E-minor and C-minor harmonies. In the *Metamorphosen*, however, Strauss's transformations of the *Metamorphosenmotiv* determine the work's underlying harmonic structure and symbolically contradict Goethe. C major is defeated by C minor, self-knowledge is not redemptive, and only man's most degenerate nature is revealed. For a musical form, Strauss employs a loose sonata-allegro design in which the recapitulation necessarily emphasizes the triumph—or in this case, the defeat—of one tonality by another. To focus attention on this background tonal conflict, the six surface motives remain unchanged throughout the work, while the orchestration for twenty-three solo strings imparts a rich and solemn tone well suited to the serious subject matter. Alan Jefferson, viewing it only as a memorial to Munich, called the *Metamorphosen* "possibly the saddest piece of music ever written."[52] One might add, however, that Strauss's sadness came not simply from the loss of buildings, but from his belated realization of the evil that brought on the destruction. In contrast to the many nostalgic works of Strauss's last years, the *Metamorphosen* is a masterpiece fully grounded in its own time.

The end of the war brought American soldiers to the doorstep of Strauss's Garmisch villa. Among them was John de Lancie, an oboist with the Pittsburgh Symphony Orchestra before the war, who would later become solo oboist of the Philadelphia Orchestra. During one of his visits, de Lancie asked if Strauss had ever considered writing a concerto for the oboe. The answer was a curt "no," and the subject was dropped.[53] That brief exchange lit a spark in Strauss, however, since less than two months later he wrote to Schuh that he was "concocting an oboe concerto in his workshop at the request of an oboist from Chicago."[54] The short score was finished on 14 September 1945, making it his last work composed in Garmisch, and the full score was completed six weeks later, shortly after he and his wife entered into exile in Switzerland.

The Concerto for Oboe and Small Orchestra (TrV 292) has a three-movements-in-one design, similar to that of the First Horn Concerto from the 1880s, but in this later piece the thematic interrelationships across the three sections are treated much more freely. Additionally, unlike in the earlier work, each of the Oboe Concerto's sections could stand as a virtually independent movement, since each adheres more closely to traditional designs. The first section is a modest sonata-allegro movement, whose only exceptional features are a very brief development and a second theme that is recapitulated in the submediant rather than the tonic. The middle section is likewise an easily heard ternary form, while the concluding third section has some traits of a rondo, but clings less dogmatically to a textbook scheme than the preceding movements. Thematically, each movement's primary materials are independent of those in the others, but in the second movement, Strauss begins to recall ideas heard previously. By the middle of the third movement, most of the work's principal themes have resurfaced—many several times. Thus, when the opening idea of the first movement brings the concerto to a close, the moment seems inevitable and confirms the unity of the mood that pervades the whole work.

Although the Concerto suggests a lifetime of experience in the seemingly effortless way in which Strauss combines and manipulates its various ideas, the sketch materials, including one recently discovered item, show that in some ways Strauss's conception of musical form had not changed all that much from what he had been taught as a youth. The revealing document represents an intermediate stage of composition, somewhere between raw sketches and a final draft. The most interesting aspect of this leaf is that it contains several passages that are virtually identical with their final forms, yet on the sketch leaf these segments are completely out of the order in which they would appear in the finished concerto.[55] Even to the end of his career, then, it appears that Strauss conceived of abstract works as concatenations of smaller units, just as Meyer had taught him.

While in exile Strauss continued to compose, filling sketchbooks with ideas, as his thoughts turned to old friends. One such acquaintance was Hugo Burghauser, a bassoonist in the prewar Vienna Philharmonic who had since emigrated to New York. There he later helped to facilitate the sale of some Strauss manuscripts to generate some much-needed funds for the composer during his first year in Switzerland. Strauss was obviously grateful when he wrote to his former colleague in October 1946 that he was "busy with an idea for a double concerto for clarinet and bassoon, thinking especially of your beautiful tone." A sketchbook from that time reveals a possible programmatic foundation for that work: a musical representation of the "Beggar's Tale." After the Duett-Concertino for Clarinet and Bassoon (TrV 293) was completed in December 1947, Strauss hinted that Hans Christian Andersen's "The Princess and the Swineherd" was his inspiration, but he also wrote to Burghauser that the clarinet and bassoon represented a princess and a dancing bear, further confusing the issue. Tellingly, Strauss never answered a request from Willi Schuh for a more precise indication of the program, which seems not to have influenced the composition beyond a few incipient ideas.

The score carries no verbal cues, and the musical form contains no irregularities that can be traced to a program. The Duett-Concertino is cut from much the same cloth as Strauss's other recent concerted works. The opening cantilena for the solo clarinet is an obvious cousin to the wide-spaced opening solo statements in the works for horn or oboe, and the reduced orchestra assumes the same unobtrusive supporting role. Structurally, the three movements are also run together as one, although here the first two movements are collectively shorter than the concluding Rondo. The first movement is dominated by the clarinet's long, spun-out melody, whose serene mood is rudely broken by the entrance of the bassoon. Thereafter the clarinet's line takes on a more agitated quality. This interaction between the soloists is the only vestige of the original program, suggesting the princess (clarinet) upset by the swineherd (bassoon). The middle Andante at first favors the bassoon over the clarinet, although the segment soon becomes a dialogue and then a cadenza for both. A sprightly five-note motive—based on the very first notes of the work's opening[56]—dominates the concluding Rondo, and its manipulation in sequence, inversion, and similar devices reveals a composer whose own roots reach deep into the eighteenth century. All in all, the Duett-Concertino is a fitting farewell from a composer who revered Mozart above all others.

In the seventy-seven years between the composition of the *Schneiderpolka* and the Duett-Concertino, Western classical music passed from the last vestiges of nineteenth-century Romanticism to the second generation of serial composers. At both ends of his life, Richard Strauss lagged behind the leading trends of the day, even as he stood at the head of the avant-garde for about two decades (1890–1910) between those times. Such a career trajectory suggests a musician who did not simply bend to fashion, but rather pursued his own course while history followed another. For Strauss, the foundation of all music was the great Austro–Germanic tradition that began for him with Mozart, and at the heart of that tradition were two fundamentals: tonality and time-honored forms. Indeed, there is an admirable consistency to Strauss's instrumental works, with the conservative foundations laid down for him by his father and by his composition teacher Meyer serving him well from the beginning to the end of his life.

What is perhaps most remarkable about Strauss's adherence to those supposedly exhausted resources was his capacity to see new possibilities in old ways. At the beginning of his professional career, he seldom repeated himself and usually composed only one of a genre—one string quartet, one piano sonata, one violin concerto, and so on—before moving on to another. Even at the end of his life, when he returned to abstract forms such as the concerto, he approached each of his three final concerted works as a new challenge, and each time he solved the genre's "problem" in a slightly different manner. In that way, Strauss's instrumental music upholds his personal dictum: "New ideas must seek out new forms for themselves."[57]

Surely one reason for Strauss's ability to remain a creative tonal composer throughout his entire life was his complete mastery of traditional forms and techniques. For Strauss, the challenge was in the conception of a piece and not its execution. One of the most often repeated stories about Strauss involves a remark that he made to the Philharmonia Orchestra during the rehearsals for the final concert on his 1947 visit to London. When the ensemble did not execute a passage to his liking, he chided them gently, "No, I know what I want, and I know what I meant when I wrote this. After all, I may not be a first-rate composer, but I *am* a first-class second-rate composer."[58] As with so many other anecdotes about Strauss's life and work, there is more than a grain of truth in what he said. Most critics read that statement only as an admission from Strauss of the mediocre quality of some of his less well respected works. In fact, the emphasis in Strauss's comment is on compositional technique—in knowing how to put one's musical intentions on paper for performers—and in that regard, Strauss was correct to imply that he had few equals. Moreover, it was primarily in abstract instrumental forms that Strauss first learned his technique, and it is his faith in and reliance on traditional forms that provides his listeners a secure starting point for understanding much of his output.

NOTES

1. Franz Trenner, *Richard Strauss Werkverzeichnis*, Veröffentlichungen der Richard-Strauss-Gesellschaft München, Bd. 12 (Munich: W. Ludwig Verlag, 1993). In the catalog, many of the songs are subsumed under single entries in groups that correspond to their published collections.

2. The term *abstract work* is used here in the sense of a composition without an explicit extramusical apparatus necessary for the explication of the work. For that reason, pieces like *Aus Italien*, Op. 16, and the *Metamorphosen*—both of which may have external reference points—are included under this category in Strauss's oeuvre and are discussed in this chapter.

3. The *Romanze* for Clarinet and Orchestra (TrV 80), the First Symphony in D minor (TrV 94), the *Romanze* for Cello and Orchestra (TrV 118), and the Concert Overture in C minor (TrV 125) have all been "repremiered" and then published since 1980. ("TrV" numbers refer to the chronological order of Strauss's compositions in Trenner's *Werkverzeichnis*.)

4. On Strauss's family background, his first musical experiences, and domestic music making within the Pschorr family, see Willi Schuh, *Richard Strauss: A Chronicle of the Early Years, 1864–1898*, trans. Mary Whittall (Cambridge: Cambridge University Press, 1982), 6–42.

5. The *Schneiderpolka*, as well as the Serenade (TrV 52), the Gavotte IV (TrV 82/5), and the (third) *Festmarsch* in C (TrV 157), were recorded in 1994 by the

Wilde Gung'l Orchestra from manuscript copies in the hand of Franz Strauss, and those performances were issued on Koch 3–1533–2. Franz's manuscript copies of the Serenade and the *Festmarsch* differ slightly from Richard's originals.

6. At least seven works by Richard Strauss exist for which there are two extant manuscripts: one by the composer and a second, altered copy in the hand of Franz Strauss. For a description of the last such pair of manuscripts and the differences between them, see Scott Warfield, "The Autograph of Strauss's *Festmarsch*, o. Op. 87 (T 157)," *Richard Strauss-Blätter* 27 (June 1992): 60–79.

7. For biographical information on Franz Strauss and his limited formal musical training, see Schuh, *Richard Strauss*, 1–11, which is drawn primarily from Franz Trenner, "Franz Strauss (1822–1905)," in *Richard Strauss-Jahrbuch 1959–60* (Bonn: Boosey and Hawkes, 1960), 31–41.

8. For a biographical sketch of Meyer and descriptions of his few extant compositions, see Scott Warfield, "Friedrich Wilhelm Meyer (1818–1893)," *Richard Strauss-Blätter* 37 (June 1997): 54–72.

9. In a letter of 31 December 1877 to Ludwig Thuille, Strauss wrote, "In regard to learning instrumental music, I can only give you the good advice not to learn it out of a book, since this, as my Papa would say, would be the absolutely worst." Slightly over a year later, in a letter of 22 February 1879 and after noting that he had not yet replaced a copy of Richter's *Die Grundzüge der musikalischen Formen*, which he had previously sent to Thuille, Strauss wrote, "You see I am learning everything almost without a book." See Franz Trenner, ed., *Richard Strauss–Ludwig Thuille, Ein Briefwechsel*, Veröffentlichungen der Richard-Strauss-Gesellschaft München, Bd. 4 (Tutzing: Hans Schneider, 1980), 30, 60. Selected English translations by Susan Gillespie from the early Strauss-Thuille letters, including these two extracts, may be found in *Richard Strauss and His World*, ed. Bryan Gilliam, (Princeton, N.J.: Princeton University Press, 1992), 193–296.

10. Ernst Friedrich Richter, *Die Grundzüge der musikalischen Formen* (Leipzig: Georg Wigard, 1852). Although there is no evidence that Richter and Meyer ever met, the two were in close proximity in Leipzig for several years. Richter arrived first as a student at Leipzig University in 1831, while Meyer matriculated there in 1838. Both were active in the city's musical life in the late 1830s. Meyer left Leipzig around 1840 to assume a position in Trier, while Richter remained in the city until 1847 as a conductor of the Singakademie and as a teacher of harmony and counterpoint at the newly founded conservatory. Richter's texts on harmony, counterpoint, and form were standard works to the end of the nineteenth century, and even if Meyer never met Richter, it is not surprising that Meyer used his texts.

11. The sixteen-year-old Richard Strauss himself offered the work to Breitkopf and Härtel in a letter of 8 February 1881. (See Erich H. Mueller von Asow, *Richard Strauss: Thematishes Verzeichnis* [Vienna: Doblinger Verlag, 1959], 1:4–5). In fact, the *Schneiderpolka*, which was lithographed and circulated among Strauss's relatives, and *Aus alter Zeit* (TrV 72), a gavotte for piano composed in 1879, appeared in print before the *Festmarsch*.

12. The Wilde Gung'l apparently differed from the standard double-wind orchestra of the nineteenth century in several ways that were most noticeable in the

wind and brass sections. First, the ensemble used a piccolo and one flute instead of a pair of flutes, and the brass section always included a single trombone. Moreover, many of the players appear to have been of lesser ability or were older individuals who had learned to play instruments that were gradually becoming obsolete toward the end of the century. For instance, the trumpet players apparently played on the older six-foot trumpets in F, and the clarinetists may have used simple-system Mueller instruments. For evidence of these and other suppositions, see Warfield, "The Autograph of Strauss's *Festmarsch*," passim.

13. For a descriptive analysis of the Grosse Sonate, see Craig DeWilde, "The Compositions of Richard Strauss from 1871–1886: The Emergence of a 'Mad Extremist'" (Ph.D. diss., University of California at Santa Barbara, 1991), 128–48.

14. A facsimile of both the print and the autograph has been issued as Richard Strauss, *Aus alter Zeit: Gavotte, Faksimile der handschriftlichen Vorlagen sowie des Erstdrucks,* ed. Stephan Kohler, Faksimile-Drucke des Richard-Strauss-Instituts München, Bd. 1 (Tutzing: Hans Schneider, 1985).

15. Franz Trenner, "Richard Strauss und die 'Wilde Gung'l,'" *Schweizerische Musikzeitung* 90 (1950): 403. The first performance of the Gavotte was by the Wilde Gung'l with Franz Strauss conducting on 29 May 1880. Both the piano and the orchestrated versions of the Gavotte were completed on 16 July 1879.

16. Friedrich von Hausegger, "Aus dem Jenseits des Künstlers," in *Gedanken eines Schauenden: Gesammelte Aufsätze,* ed. Siegmund von Hausegger (Munich: Verlagsanstalt F. Bruckmann, 1903), 394–99.

17. Cited in Schuh, *Richard Strauss,* 52.

18. Marie von Bülow, ed., *Briefe und Schriften* (Leipzig: Breitkopf and Härtel, 1908), 8:112–13. Bülow implied a similar assessment in a slightly later letter of 31 March 1882 to Spitzweg, who had asked for an opinion of a manuscript by Phillip Wolfrum. Bülow did not care at all for that work and in his reply wrote that "if you have money to lose, it can happen in a proper way by printing this opus, or by means of the green young Strauss or the gray old [Max] Zenger" (Bülow, *Briefe und Schriften* (1907), 7:150–51).

19. For a comparison of these two works, see Peter Damm, "Gedanken zu den Hornkonzerten von Richard Strauss," *Richard Strauss-Blätter* 4 (1980): 31–41.

20. Although Franz Liszt had completed all of his major symphonic works by 1857, the scores and performing materials for them remained unavailable for many years, except in manuscripts controlled by Liszt. Breitkopf and Härtel issued study scores to only six of the twelve tone poems in 1856, and published orchestral parts were not made available until 1864–84. (Alan Walker, *Franz Liszt,* vol. 2, *The Weimar Years, 1848–61* [New York: Knopf, 1989], 304–5.) In fact, performances of Liszt's symphonic poems were so infrequent in the second half of the nineteenth century that they were usually listed in German musical periodicals in the columns that identified performances of new works, for example, "Aufgeführte Novitäten" in the *Musikalisches Wochenblatt.*

21. Bülow made the comment in a letter to Eugen Spitzweg (14 January 1891), with the precise phrase "a decidedly, almost fanatical Brahms-Thersites" (Bülow, *Briefe,* 8:326n.). Bülow, in his typical fashion, used a grand metaphor to

make his point. Thersites, a figure from ancient mythology, was the ugliest man in the Greek army at Troy. He was malicious, slanderous, and celebrated for his sharp tongue, and he even dared to abuse the commander in chief of the army. As an example of the comments Strauss routinely made against Brahms's music, see the extract from his letter to Jean Louis Nicodé (14 December 1888) in Schuh, *Richard Strauss*, 137.

22. The two letters from Strauss to his father are dated 6 January 1884 and 1 February 1884. The original German texts are published in Richard Strauss, *Briefe an die Eltern: 1882–1906*, ed. Willi Schuh (Zurich: Atlantis Verlag, 1954), 33–35, 37–40. A summary of Strauss's views on Brahms and extracts from these same letters may be found in Schuh, *Richard Strauss*, 66–69.

23. R. Larry Todd, "Strauss before Liszt and Wagner: Some Observations," in *Richard Strauss: New Perspectives on the Composer and His Work*, ed. Bryan Gilliam (Durham, N.C.: Duke University Press, 1992), 5.

24. The relevant portion of the review is given in Schuh, *Richard Strauss*, 60.

25. For an overview of this trip and Strauss's business dealings in Berlin and elsewhere on that trip, see ibid., "The Berlin Winter, 1883–84," chap. 3; and Strauss, *Briefe an die Eltern*, 22–54.

26. Hugo Bock (1848–1932) was director of the Berlin publishing house of Bote and Bock.

27. Todd, "Strauss before Liszt and Wagner," especially 5–13.

28. Such ternary-form themes, particularly in second theme areas, were used often by Schubert and later by Brahms. See James Webster, "Schubert's Sonata Forms and Brahms's First Maturity," *Nineteenth-Century Music* 2 (1978): 18–35 and 3 (1979): 52–71. As to the choice of key, Brahms's well-known Piano Quintet in F minor, Op. 34 (composed in 1864), has a ternary-form second theme in D-flat (albeit in minor mode) in its first movement.

29. Brahms criticized Strauss's Symphony by saying, "[A]ll that piling-up of a large number of themes on a triad, with only rhythmic contrast between them, has no value whatsoever." For similarities among the themes of this work, see Theodore Bloomfield, "A Case of Neglect: Richard Strauss' Symphony in F minor," *Music and Musicians* 22 (1974): 25–28; Helan Hon-Lun Yang, "From Symphony to Symphonic Poem: A Study of Richard Strauss's Two Early Symphonic Works" (Master's thesis, University of Texas at Austin, 1989), 11–13; and Norman Del Mar, *Richard Strauss: A Critical Commentary on His Life and Works* (Ithaca, N.Y.: Cornell University Press, 1986), 1:21. For a more thorough discussion of the specific ways in which the themes of this symphony relate, see Scott Allan Warfield, "The Genesis of Richard Strauss's *Macbeth*" (Ph.D. diss., University of North Carolina at Chapel Hill, 1995), 70–82.

30. For an overview of Ritter's influence on Strauss, see Charles Dowell Youmans, "Richard Strauss's *Guntram* and the Dismantling of Wagnerian Musical Metaphysics" (Ph.D. diss., Duke University, 1996), especially chap. 2: "Strauss's Reception of Schopenhauer."

31. The term *Music of the Future* (*Zukunftsmusik* in the original German) was frequently associated with Franz Liszt and the group of progressive composers

around him and Wagner. Credit for the coining of the term itself probably should go to Liszt's companion Carolyne Sayn-Wittgenstein. See Walker, *Franz Liszt*, 336–37.

32. Richard Strauss, *Betrachtungen und Erinnerungen*, ed. Willi Schuh (Zurich: Atlantis Verlag, 1949), 168. Quote is from Schuh, *Richard Strauss*, 118–19.

33. Franz Grasberger, ed. *Die Strom der Töne trug mich fort: Die Welt um Richard Strauss in Briefen*, with the cooperation of Franz and Alice Strauss (Tutzing: Hans Schneider, 1967), 42.

34. For extracts and translations of criticism of the premiere and other early performances of *Aus Italien*, see Warfield, "Genesis of *Macbeth*," 421–27.

35. Willi Schuh and Franz Trenner, "Hans von Bülow/Richard Strauss: Briefwechsel," in *Richard Strauss Jahrbuch 1954*, ed. Willi Schuh (Bonn: Boosey and Hawkes, 1953), 32. (My translation.)

36. Strauss's analysis appeared in vol. 16 (28 June 1889): 263, 265–66, complete with musical examples. It is reprinted in its entirety in Mueller von Asow, *Richard Strauss*, 1:66–68, while the text only appears in Schuh, *Richard Strauss*, 139–40.

37. In its initial version of January 1888, *Macbeth* contained at least a portion of a literal recapitulation of its first thematic area, a fact confirmed by a facsimile of the excised leaf in an antiquarian catalog. For a detailed description of the leaf and its significance, see Warfield, "Genesis of *Macbeth*," 284–86, 293–351.

38. Kurt Wilhelm (*Richard Strauss: An Intimate Portrait*, trans. Mary Whittall [New York: Rizzoli, 1989], 77–78) recounts the story of how the Kaiser had two military bands parade around for three hours so that Strauss, who claimed to know nothing of marches, could learn the genre.

39. For descriptive analyses of these works (TrV 248, 250, 286, and 287) and also of the *Feierliche Einzug*, see Karl Kramer, "The Symphonic Brass Music of Richard Strauss," *Richard Strauss-Blätter* 16 (1986): 36–53.

40. See E. Fred Flindell, "Paul Wittgenstein (1887–1961): Patron and Pianist," *Music Review* 32 (1971): 107–27, for a discussion of Wittgenstein's life and career, and especially 121–22 for his relationship with Strauss. This article also includes a facsimile of a manuscript of exercises composed by Strauss in 1926 for Wittgenstein that are not cited in the standard catalogs of Strauss's works.

41. Bryan Gilliam, *The Life of Richard Strauss* (Cambridge: Cambridge University Press, 1999), 151.

42. Wilhelm, *Richard Strauss*, 251; on the decline of the fee, see Michael Kater, *Composers of the Nazi Era: Eight Portraits* (New York: Oxford University Press, 2000), 367n. 317.

43. One such notice is "Japanischer Kompositionsauftrag für Richard Strauss," *Die Musik* 32 (1940): 349–50.

44. The instrumental works extracted from Strauss's operas in the years 1900 to 1940 include three orchestral suites from *Der Rosenkavalier* (TrV 227 a, c, and d), the "Bürger als Edelmann" Suite (TrV 228c) rescued from the first version of *Ariadne auf Naxos*, the Symphonic Fragment from "Josephslegende" (TrV 231a),

the Symphonic Fantasy from "Die Frau ohne Schatten" (TrV 234a), the Orchestral Suite from the Ballet "Schlagobers" (TrV 243a), and the Four Symphonic Interludes from "Intermezzo" (TrV 246a).

45. Michael Kennedy, *Richard Strauss: Man, Musician, Enigma* (Cambridge: Cambridge University Press, 1999), 339. Strauss and his immediate family were generally ignorant of the purpose of concentration camps like Theresienstadt. Initially, they assumed it was a transfer point on the way to resettlement for Jews, and Strauss even presented himself once at the gates of the camp and asked to see one of his in-laws.

46. Strauss to Willi Schuh (8 October 1943) in Willi Schuh, ed., *Richard Strauss: Briefwechsel mit Willi Schuh* (Zurich: Atlantis Verlag, 1969), 50.

47. In other letters to Schuh, Strauss referred to his composition in those years as "for the estate" (10 December 1942), "helping me to escape many gloomy hours" (31 May 1943), and "workshop trifling" (15 August 1943) (ibid., 38, 40, and 43).

48. Tim Ashley, *Richard Strauss* (London: Phaidon Press, 1999), 191.

49. Richard Strauss, "Vom melodischen Einfall," in *Betrachtungen und Erinnerungen*, ed. Willi Schuh (Zurich: Atlantis Verlag, 1949), 134–40.

50. Del Mar describes this sound with the German word *musizieren*, which means "to make music" (in the sense of "to perform"), see his *Richard Strauss*, 3:415.

51. Timothy L. Jackson, "The Metamorphosis of the *Metamorphosen*: New Analytical and Source-Critical Discoveries," in *Richard Strauss: New Perspectives on the Composer and His Work*, ed. Bryan Gilliam (Durham, N.C.: Duke University Press, 1992),193–241.

52. Alan Jefferson, *The Lieder of Richard Strauss* (New York: Praeger, 1971), 11.

53. For de Lancie's recollections of those meetings, see "John de Lancie: Im Gespräch mit Richard Strauss," ed. Stephan Kohler, *Richard Strauss-Blätter* 11 (1984): 36–42. A detailed photographic record of their meetings can be found in Wilhelm, *Richard Strauss*, 270–73.

54. Strauss, *Briefwechsel mit Willi Schuh*, 84. The letter to Schuh is dated 6 July 1945.

55. For a complete discussion of these sources, see Günter Brosche, "The Concerto for Oboe and Small Orchestra (1945): Remarks about the Origin of the Work Based on a Newly Discovered Source," in *Richard Strauss: New Perspectives on the Composer and His Work*, ed. Bryan Gilliam (Durham, N.C.: Duke University Press, 1992), 177–92. This essay appeared earlier as "Das Konzert für Oboe und Kleines Orchester (1945) von Richard Strauss: Bemerkungen zur Entstehung des Werkes an Hand einer neu bekannt gewordenen Quelle," *Richard Strauss-Blätter* 24 (1990): 80–103.

56. A very similar motive figured prominently in the Second Horn Concerto, which, as Del Mar notes, bears a close resemblance to some of the "Skat-playing" music of *Intermezzo* (see his *Richard Strauss*, 3:408).

57. Strauss, *Betrachtungen und Erinnerungen*, 168. 139. Quote is from Schuh, *Richard Strauss*, 118–19.

58. Del Mar, *Richard Strauss*, 1:xii.

Part III
Vocal Works

7

Richard Strauss before *Salome*: The Early Operas and Unfinished Stage Works

Morten Kristiansen

While Richard Strauss's operas now loom at least as large in the musical landscape as his tone poems, this was not the case before *Salome* (1905), the watershed work that put Strauss on the map as an opera composer and allowed him to build his villa in Garmisch.[1] When Strauss continued to write operas, the course of events seemed clear: He had abandoned the tone poem in favor of opera. Since *Salome* was the first among Strauss's operas to earn a solid place in the repertoire, the facile notion that this opera followed *Symphonia domestica* of 1903, the last in an unbroken series of tone poems, may have given rise to the idea of *Salome* as the direct "continuation" of the tone poems—especially since many commentators have viewed Strauss's one-act operas as "tone poems for the stage." Thus, it has been too easy for scholars to ignore the crucial role of Strauss's first two operas *Guntram* (1893) and *Feuersnot* (1901) in the development of his early modernist aesthetic, especially through their rejection of Wagner's musical metaphysics, a lacuna that two recent dissertations have begun to bridge.[2] Similarly, commentators have paid little attention to Strauss's unfinished stage works of the 1890s, ones that show several crucial aspects of his aesthetics and musical style to have developed before 1900: his penchant for comic or "light" subjects and his constant need for variety of subject and style, which renders futile attempts to trace his stylistic development in linear terms.

EARLY OPERATIC DRAFTS

Willi Schuh has transcribed the essential portions of Strauss's operatic plans and drafts from the composer's diaries of the 1890s, so a brief discussion of these should suffice here.[3] While the drafts of the early 1890s emphasized serious issues, those of the later 1890s would focus on comic subjects. Several of the plans, conceived more or less concurrently with the later stages of the *Guntram* libretto in 1892–93, contained strong autobiographical and philosophical components. Although *Das erhabene Leid der Könige* (The Sublime Suffering of Kings) contained no philosophy but, rather, politics, nationalism, intrigue, and heroism, the other two subjects dealt with current issues in Strauss's life that he worked out simultaneously in *Guntram*: art, philosophy, and personal relationships. Thus, the sketches for *Don Juan* displayed Strauss's preoccupation with the central issues of contemporary opera, redemption, and renunciation (discussed below), issues worked out in *Guntram*, and those for *Der Reichstag zu Mainz* (The Imperial Diet at Mainz) treated other *Guntram* elements such as physical love, Schopenhauerian philosophy, and art. Although the drafts for *Das erhabene Leid der Könige* may well represent a failed attempt on Strauss's part to divert himself from those personal and philosophical issues that occupied him during the early 1890s and especially during his extended trip as a convalescent (November 1892–July 1893), these issues all found their (temporary) resolution in *Guntram*.

GUNTRAM

Although scholars have shown little interest in Strauss's first opera *Guntram*, the work that Gustav Mahler called "the most important opera since *Parsifal*," detailed discussions of the work are available in English.[4] Willi Schuh has carefully chronicled the difficult genesis of the work, using primary sources from the Richard-Strauss-Archiv (RSA) in Garmisch; Norman Del Mar and William Mann have discussed text and music in some detail; and Charles Youmans has reevaluated the two most significant issues in the reception of the opera: its relationship to Wagner and the perceived transition from a Schopenhauerian or "Romantic" metaphysics to a Nietzschean or "modern" worldview in the third act.[5] In my brief discussion of *Guntram* I will seek to augment their work by locating it in the context of the Germanic libretto of the 1890s and thereby assess its precarious balancing act between tradition and rebellion.

German opera after Wagner emulated his aesthetic and musical features to such an extreme extent that the opera libretto of the late 1880s through 1900 and beyond seemed to congeal in its rigid deployment of idealistic themes derived from Wagner's pseudo-Schopenhauerian metaphysics. Foremost among these themes was Wagner's favorite concept of redemption through love/compassion (*Erlösung durch Mitleid*), one to which other significant idealistic topoi such as *Entsagung* or renunciation, *Mitleid* or compassion, the "power of love," physical versus ideal love, and the metaphysics of art became subordinate. Thus, in the serious operas of Strauss's most prominent contemporaries—Max von Schillings (1868–1933), Eugen d'Albert (1864–1932), Wilhelm Kienzl (1857–1941), Felix von Weingartner (1863–1942), and Hans Pfitzner (1869–1949)—the predominance of these themes constituted a post-Wagnerian operatic tradition bordering on doctrine.[6]

When seen in the context of contemporary music drama, *Guntram* fits in surprisingly well, but minor differences in treatment become crucial in appreciating the rebellious tendencies of the work. Thus, *Guntram* contains virtually all the Wagner-derived elements: *Mitleid*, *Entsagung*, physical versus ideal love, the metaphysical power of music, and possibly *Erlösung*. The theme of *Mitleid* dominates large portions of the plot, and Strauss introduces it in the very first scene when the fugitives tell of Freihild's compassion.[7] Later in that scene Guntram introduces the theme of sinful passion, to which he himself succumbs later on, when he speaks of "the sinful human being under the spell of passion,"[8] and here the religious mission of his brotherhood of minnesingers, the "Streiter der Liebe" (Champions of Love), becomes explicit: "Savior, my Lord . . . You who suffered death on the cross to bring back love to human beings, you planted the solemn urge in my heart: to preach your word in ardent song!"[9] He now invokes his lyre and thus adds the metaphysical power of music to the list of contemporary themes. Soon after this Guntram encounters Freihild, daughter of the king and wife of the evil Duke Robert. She waxes romantic about death, but Guntram counters by doing the same about life (28–35)—much like Cain and Abel in d'Albert's *Kain* (1900)—and prevents her from committing suicide. At the court Guntram later sings of peace and compassion in the so-called *Friedenserzählung* (peace narration; 94–123), thereby offending Robert—whom he kills in self-defense—and ending up in jail.

Reflecting on his moral dilemma, Guntram realizes that he has done the right thing for the wrong reason: killing the evil Robert was no bad deed in itself, but his physical attraction to Freihild—Robert's wife—acted as a fateful catalyst and makes the act condemnable from his own moral and religious standpoint. Although Guntram rightly reproaches Robert for not heeding "the call of compassion" (*des Mitleids Ruf*) and "love's decree" (*der Liebe Gebot*; 168), Freihild expresses Guntram's predicament: "ardent love guided your sword."[10] When a representative of his brotherhood, Friedhold, appears to mete out the punishment, Guntram decides that he alone must atone his guilt through solitary reflection and the *Entsagung* of all worldly things, including Freihild, he smashes his lyre (190), and denies the "Streiter der Liebe" the right to punish him. Rejecting the idealistic philosophy of the brotherhood as "a beautiful dream" (*ein schöner Traum*; 197), Guntram identifies his true enemy as physical love—"Vain illusion to preach redemption, myself unredeemed! Oh, horrible compulsion of loathsome senses, most agonizing urge of the sweetest yearning. The only enemy of the desire for redemption!"[11]—and pronounces that only Freihild's renunciation of him can fully redeem him (210, 228). Upon the king's death Freihild will now become a compassionate ruler, and this knowledge accompanied by her heroic *Entsagung*—her rejection of him—sends the now disillusioned Guntram on his way to his presumed eventual *Erlösung*.

In many ways this is an extremely Wagnerian concoction very much in line with the serious operas of Strauss's contemporaries, but the ways in which Strauss's treatment of a few themes differs from theirs are essential to an understanding of the subtle, in some ways, aesthetic rebellion of *Guntram*. One such crucial (but not very subtle) difference is Guntram's destruction of his lyre out of disillusionment with the metaphysical aims of the brotherhood, an apparent rejection of music/art as a viable means of *Erlösung*—truly a radical statement within the post-Wagnerian operatic climate. Surprisingly perhaps, contemporary reception did not take note of this, but such a blatant dismissal of music's metaphysical qualities certainly flew in the face of orthodox Bayreuth ideology. As I will show, Strauss argued this point with his mentor Alexander Ritter.

Strauss's approach to the concept of *Erlösung* also differs from that taken by his fellow opera composers.[12] Oddly enough, we must first ask if *Guntram* actually contains an *Erlösung*, for Strauss's libretto treats the issue with deliberate imprecision. Although Eugen Schmitz believed that Guntram does indeed obtain his redemption through a genuinely Wagnerian and Schopenhauerian *Entsagung* and *Verneinung* (denial), the text itself only partly supports this reading.[13] Guntram clearly states that only Freihild's *Entsagung* can effect his complete *Erlösung*, but that is an imprecise statement in that he also makes it very clear—through the rejection of the brotherhood and his insistence on solitary contemplation—that only he himself can atone for his crime. Eugen von Ziegler pointed out this inconsistency, arguing that Freihild's renunciation of Guntram is an inconsequential afterthought that plays no role in Guntram's redemption, that Guntram had made up his mind before the appearance of Friedhold, and that his character is so selfishly individualistic that he could leave Freihild out of the picture altogether.[14] However we assess Freihild's role in Guntram's redemption, the fact remains that Strauss placed the *Erlösung* outside of the opera itself and thereby skirted the issue through noncommitment. The fact that the *Mitleid* and death of the female protagonist are not required to redeem her male counterpart further underscores Strauss's unconventional treatment of *Erlösung*. In preventing Freihild's suicide Guntram sings the praises of life and rejects her Schopenhauerian *Verneinung* of existence, thus opposing the morbid glorification of death found in Wagner's *Tristan* and contemporary operas such as Felix von Weingartner's *Genesius* (1892) and Waldemar von Baussnern's *Dichter und Welt* (1897).

A final theme of which Strauss avoids the customary Wagnerian treatment is that of love. Although Guntram's conflict between physical and ideal love is entirely conventional, its resolution does not conform to Wagner's two related conceptions of love. In his writings of the 1850s Wagner treated basic or instinctual emotions such as love and hate as the highest possible motivators under the heading of *das Reinmenschliche* (the purely human), and his interpretation of the Oedipus myth in *Oper und Drama* (pt. 2, sec. 3) is a good example of this. Here Wagner sings the praises of Antigone's love for her brother as instinctual, selfless, redemptive, and transcendent of societal norms—a type of love best exemplified by Brünnhilde in *Der Ring*. In other works Wagner's conception of ideal love is that of Christian *Mitleid* (*Tannhäuser, Parsifal*). *Guntram* reflects neither, however. Unlike most Wagnerian characters, as Ziegler noted, Guntram lets neither instinctual love nor Christian *Mitleid* be his guiding principle.[15] In spite of his initial devotion to *Mitleid*, Guntram ends up rejecting its relevance in his self-imposed solitude, and the love between Guntram and Freihild is framed as sinful, not transcendental or redemptive, and remains unresolved in any traditional sense.

This unconventionality amid tradition takes on added significance when viewed in comparison with Pfitzner's more conventional first opera *Der arme Heinrich*, completed in 1893, the year of Strauss's completion of *Guntram*. A number of parallels between the two plots makes this comparison especially interesting, the crucial difference being their contrasting solutions to the problem of guilt and penance. Adapted by librettist James Grun from the verse legend by Hartmann von Aue, *Der arme Heinrich* tells the story of a knight redeemed by a virgin. The young Agnes is watching over the sick Heinrich, whom only the willing sacrifice of a virgin can save. We learn that his disease is a punishment from God for his attachment to worldly glory: "You thrived in the glory and splendor of the world! Now God's hand weighs down [on you] with iron severity!"[16] Agnes wishes to redeem Heinrich, but her parents refuse to allow it, her father arguing— significantly—that a sinner should do penance for his own sins (act 2, scene 2; 83). Using the example of Christ's sacrifice, however, Agnes is able to persuade her parents and Heinrich. As she is about to suffer her "most blissful love-death" (*seligster Liebestod*), Heinrich retracts his consent in the pivotal line, "no more will I be saved!" (*nicht mehr will ich gerettet sein!*), a bolt of lightning heals him, and he prevents the sacrifice of Agnes. A chorus of monks interprets the event for us: "In you spoke the love of Jesus Christ, whose compassion is so wondrous."[17] Predictably, his newfound *Mitleid* has converted him from a worldly knight to a devout Christian: "He whom the Redeemer's wondrous power, bleeding anew, has brought eternal salvation desires not vain splendor; on foot with humility I shall wander, forever bearing witness to Him."[18] Heinrich's *Erlösung*, then, results from his *Entsagung* of his own redemption through the discovery of Christian *Mitleid*.[19]

The parallels between *Der arme Heinrich* and *Guntram* are obvious: In both operas the central issue is a struggle between the worldly and the ideal (Heinrich's disease as punishment for his pursuit of worldly glory and Guntram's slaying of Robert as inspired by his physical attraction to Freihild); the solution comes about through a double *Entsagung* (Agnes's renunciation of life itself and Heinrich's renunciation of salvation through Agnes versus the mutual renunciation of Guntram and Freihild); no one dies in the process; and the male protagonist becomes the primary agent of his own salvation. Despite the great similarities between the two plots, a few crucial differences outweigh these parallels. The most obvious difference is, of course, that the *Erlösung* occurs as the climax of the opera in *Der arme Heinrich*, whereas Strauss evades this contemporary inevitability by placing it outside the opera. Equally important, Heinrich completes his conversion to the Christian ideals of *Mitleid* and *Erlösung* and even intends to dedicate his life to preaching them, whereas Guntram starts out as a Christian singer in a brotherhood and winds up rejecting that brotherhood—representing conventional Christianity in the form of a community of believers—and music/art along with it. Thus, Guntram's unconventional and crucial assertion of individualism stands in stark contrast to Heinrich's submission to the goals of the faith community, and this individualism is precisely what estranged Guntram and Strauss from their more orthodox surroundings.

In his unorthodox treatment of music/art as a metaphysical agent, redemption, and Christian *Mitleid*, Strauss attempted to create a compromise between his own worldview and that of his mentor Ritter, one that was destined to fail. In what is probably the most fascinating document in the genesis of *Guntram*, a stirring fifteen-page letter of 17 January 1893, Ritter called the new ending the most painful experience of the last decade and implored Strauss to redo the entire third act.[20] In this vehement indictment Ritter charged Strauss with robbing the drama of tragedy, artistic unity, and morality and called Guntram a psychological impossibility. Ritter further argued that Guntram is a devout Christian in the first act but finds himself "on the rocky ground of confused Stirnerism" in the third, and asked if perhaps someone slipped Guntram Max Stirner's book or Nietzsche's *Beyond Good and Evil* (1886) during the night.[21] On 3 February Strauss defended himself in a twelve-page letter in which he attempted to justify Guntram's rejection of the brotherhood's authority and maintained that Guntram is neither immoral nor un-Christian.[22] Strauss also professed that he had not finished Stirner's book, that he had never read Nietzsche's work, and that he had been reading only Wagner, Goethe, and Schopenhauer for the past four months. While this, strictly speaking, may have been true, we know that Strauss had made the acquaintance of Stirner's biographer and notorious author of *Die Anarchisten* (The Anarchists, 1891), Scottish poet John Henry Mackay (1864–1933), in 1892; that Stirner figured prominently in Strauss's subsequent drafts for a Don Juan opera (March 1892); and that Strauss had read *Beyond Good and Evil* by April 1893 at the very latest.[23] Although Strauss may well have read Nietzsche before 1893, we have no direct evidence to support this, but it has become very clear that Strauss made a crucial ideological transition from Schopenhauer to Nietzsche during and immediately following the composition of *Guntram*, a transition that Youmans has chronicled and that brings us to a central issue in the early reception of *Guntram*: the supposedly Nietzschean ending.[24]

With respect to philosophical orientation, the overwhelming majority of contemporary commentators viewed *Guntram* as an odd mix of Schopenhauer and Nietzsche, a strange blend of traditional and "modern" traits. Specifically, they interpreted Guntram's rejection of the brotherhood and insistence on determining his own punishment to be a direct reflection of Nietzsche's advocacy of a radical "individualism," perhaps the most prominent Nietzschean buzzword of the 1890s. Arthur Seidl, for example, expressed this view and saw Strauss as standing with one leg each in the Schopenhauerian and Nietzschean camps, as it were.[25] Seidl considered individualism to be the very essence of the modern spirit, and in *Guntram* he saw this modern ideal of "self-determination" (*Selbstbestimmung*) asserting itself, at least up to a certain point, against the Romantic "redemption tragedy" (*Erlösungstragik*).[26] As Schmitz noted—perhaps the only commentator to do so—Guntram's moral and ascetic goals conflict oddly with Nietzsche's idea of the *Herrenmensch* (superior human being) and hardly qualify him as a Nietzschean character.[27] In this regard it is noteworthy that Strauss, in an important letter to Ludwig Thuille of 13 February 1893 (ten days after his response to Ritter), wrote that he had now found support for his ending in Schopenhauer's *Die Welt als Wille und Vorstellung* (The World as Will and Idea) and thus ammunition for his defense against Ritter's accusations.[28] Youmans has fleshed out Strauss's rebuttal, arguing that the *Guntram* libretto carefully follows the progression of ideas in *Die Welt als Wille*, with Schopenhauer's assertion at the end of book 3 that art can only temporarily quiet the Will and his positing of solitary "sainthood" as the more promising solution in book 4, and that Guntram's actions are thus utterly antithetical to Nietzsche's ideas.[29] In this view *Guntram* is, in fact, much more Schopenhauerian than the works of Wagner and his followers, who, of course, had no use for Schopenhauer's reservations about art.

Regardless of his very un-Nietzschean asceticism and moral quest, Guntram's individualism—his decision to be his own moral arbiter—was virtually synonymous with an embrace of Nietzsche's philosophy in the eyes of contemporaries, even a sophisticated thinker such as Seidl, and there can be no doubt that Guntram's rejection of the brotherhood is bound up significantly with one result of Strauss's own individualism: his exit from the Bayreuth circle. In retrospect, Strauss emphasized the pivotal significance of this rejection to his career and compositional aesthetic. In an unsent letter written in 1945 to Joseph Gregor he stated that his operas from the third act of *Guntram* to *Capriccio* deserve a modest place beside those of Wagner, thus implying that his life's work (at least for the stage) and perhaps his compositional maturity began with the last act of *Guntram*, and specified the significance of Guntram's individualism to his career: "After the rejection of tradition: 'my spirit's decree determines my life; my god speaks to me solely through myself!', which even estranged my faithful friend (Friedhold) Alexander Ritter from the work that he long supported and approved of, the road was clear for unimpededly independent work."[30] Here he clearly identified Guntram's withdrawal of the brotherhood as his own rejection of "tradition," meaning the Wagnerian aesthetic tradition that Pfitzner's *Der arme Heinrich* represented and that Ritter had felt Strauss to be abandoning in the third act of *Guntram*. Strauss was now free to compose as he desired after liberating himself from the constrictive grip of Bayreuth conservatism.

Other statements by Strauss have indicated his preference for the personal over the universal, the specific over the general. If Strauss's well-known comment to Hofmannsthal in a letter of 12 July 1927—"I would always prefer to compose myself"—was the most obvious statement of his preference for autobiographical subject matter, other comments would supplement this frank declaration.[31] In another letter to Hofmannsthal of 1 November 1928, for example, Strauss emphasized the value of the personal or characteristic:

For 2000 years always the same: murder and killing, intrigue of the servant against the hero, betrothals with overcoming of obstacles or divorce—that is all uninteresting and seen so often. New, however, is—as Goethe already says when he recommends every person to write his memoirs—every individuality: never seen like this before, never returning, and therefore I find a character portrayal so nicely and consistently carried through as in *Intermezzo* more interesting than any so-called plot.[32]

Along the same lines he praised "self-fulfillment" (*Selbstvollendung*) in a letter to Clemens Krauss of 8 October 1935: "But this medieval heroism, this 'communal dying' etc. etc. found its final transfiguring conclusion in Siegfried's funeral march—one would think! Instead of self-torment—self-fulfillment. Instead of Napoleon—Goethe!"[33] As I will show, Kunrad in *Feuersnot* is the ultimate expression of Strauss's particular brand of individualism, or what he referred to as "subjectivity." This individualism involved a rejection of the traditional subject matter of contemporary opera along with the adherence to a specific school of thought (Bayreuth), a desire to treat subjects that are personally relevant, and a strong autobiographical component for which Strauss found support in the writings of Goethe.

LATER OPERATIC DRAFTS AND *KYTHERE*

Given the neat separation of serious and comic subjects in Strauss's operatic development with *Guntram* as the pivotal work, we may suppose that he found some degree of resolution and clarification in the latter. Perhaps the most interesting and significant aspects of the operatic drafts between *Guntram* and *Feuersnot*—the various incarnations of the *Till Eulenspiegel* project of 1893–97, the *Lila* "collaboration" with Cosima Wagner in 1895–96, and Strauss's own *Ekke und Schnittlein* of 1899—are that they are all comic or *volkstümlich* (popular or folklike) and almost all feature characters on the fringes of society who have "renounced collectivism," to borrow Strauss's phrase.[34] Although conventional wisdom attributes Richard Strauss's own Till-like desire to fly in the face of the bourgeois collective beginning with the orchestral *Till Eulenspiegel* to the failure rather than the subject matter of *Guntram*, we must remember that Strauss had begun his *Till Eulenspiegel* plans long before the premiere of that opera in May 1894, at least as early as June 1893.[35] Even if we cannot prove that a direct connection existed between the ideas for the *Till Eulenspiegel* project and Guntram's rejection of the brotherhood, the persistence of the anti-collective theme in *Ekke und Schnittlein* and *Feuersnot* supports this interpretation. Based on the "Novela de Rinconete y Cortadillo" (Story of Rinconete and Cortadillo, 1613) by Cervantes, *Ekke und Schnittlein* tells the story of two boys who join a thieves' guild.[36] Whereas the original had a moralizing ending, Strauss's boys end up rejecting all forms of collective authority, much like Guntram and Till. In *Feuersnot* Kunrad's extracollective existence and affront to majority values continues this pattern, and Kurt Wilhelm has pointed out that the opposition of the philistines of Munich and Kunrad recalls that of Schilda and Till.[37] Their spirit of opposition, however, appears to stem from the personal and philosophical clarification that Strauss achieved in the revisions of his *Guntram* libretto completed in November 1892 rather than the bitterness caused by the failure of the opera, although this disappointment certainly must have amplified any feelings of opposition. This also suggests that Strauss's desire to write a comic opera—a desire that culminated in *Feuersnot*—did not result from the failure of his serious opera, but probably from the desire to remove himself as far as possible from the very Romantic, Wagnerian, and philosophical world that he had sought to purge from his system in *Guntram*.

Strauss's apparent attempt to rediscover the simplicity of an earlier age in his work on *Lila*, based on Goethe's Singspiel of 1788 (final version), seems odd when seen in the context of the surrounding tone poems: *Till Eulenspiegel* and *Also sprach Zarathustra*.[38] Although Strauss told his temporary collaborator Cosima Wagner that he would set it to "modern" music (using quotation marks), he nonetheless insisted on maintaining the spoken dialogue for the sake of historical and stylistic correctness and composing the music as if "the works" (of Wagner) had never existed.[39] While the music sketched in 1895–96 is a good deal more complex than the two arias composed for *Lila* in 1878, it does not approach the style of *Also sprach Zarathustra* so far as one can judge from the facsimiles published by Stephan Kohler.[40] Strauss's comments to Cosima and the relative simplicity of the sketches suggest that Strauss wished to break the ties with his own immediate past and experiment with different subjects and styles than those practiced by the metaphysical post-Wagnerians. His desire to write the music as if Wagner had never existed reveals an objective musical mind willing and able to create isolated musical environments that best suit a given text or dramatic framework. In his comments on the musical style of *Lila*, Kohler made the important observation about its anticipation of *Feuersnot*, *Der Rosenkavalier*, and other works that "the 'nerve counterpoint' of *Salme* and the pastoral nature of a Rococo-like classicism were simultaneously available to Strauss from the outset," and thus that the nonlinearity of Strauss's stylistic development invalidates the argument for a sharp stylistic divide separating *Elektra* and *Der Rosenkavalier*.[41] I have discussed this crucial principle of constant variety and objective stylistic selection under the heading of "Stilkunst" (style art) elsewhere.[42]

Continuing this search for variety of subject and style, now within the same work, Strauss conceived and partially composed the rather bizarre ballet *Kythere* (1900), set on Cythera, the mythical island of love and birthplace of Venus (Cytherea) according to one tradition, and based it in part on Watteau's famous painting *L'Embarquement pour Cythère* (The Embarkation for Cythera) (1717).[43] A key component of Strauss's very long and complicated scenario, later published by Willi Schuh, is the stark contrast between two radically different cultures—in Strauss's own words, that between the "most overripe culture" (*überreifster Cultur*) of the eighteenth-century French aristocracy and the still natural "animal drives" (*tierischen Triebe*) of the island's indigenous peasant population.[44] Adding Classical Antiquity in the second act, the ballet featured three very different cultures within one work, a motley blend reflected in the music. Ranging from simple dance numbers to canons to more chromatic music, the sketches display some of the stylistic pluralism found in *Feuersnot* and demonstrate Strauss's desire to select styles and forms based on the subject at hand.[45]

FEUERSNOT

Strauss's second opera of 1901—a work that has received little attention although Debussy called it "something truly new," Mahler noted that it elicited "the astonishment of German critics and the envy of German opera composers," and Adorno appraised it as "perhaps the most Straussian" and worthy of performance—represents the culmination of his individualism and rejection of Bayreuth idealism.[46] In his final diary entry of 19 June 1949, the so-called *Letzte Aufzeichnung* (last entry), Strauss identified at least three central features of the *Feuersnot* libretto that contemporary scholarship had failed to recognize: its deliberate mockery of the contemporary opera libretto, the novelty of its personal or individualistic approach as seen in the context of the pervasive Wagner emulation of the day, and the proper meaning of the libretto in general—and, by extension, the role of its librettist.[47]

The story is set on Midsummer's Day, traditionally celebrated with a huge bonfire. The loner Kunrad represents Strauss and lives in the house of his evicted master, the old sorcerer representing Wagner. When a group of children knocks on his door asking for firewood, Kunrad suddenly rejects his gloomy broodings, embraces life and light, and begins to tear pieces of wood from his house, leaving it (and, figuratively, his past) demolished. Kunrad now causes an uproar when he brazenly kisses the mayor's daughter Diemut in public. Although he is seemingly able to win her affection, a trap set by Diemut and her three girlfriends soon has him dangling in mid-air in a basket on his way up to Diemut's balcony, making him the laughing stock of the town. Kunrad now summons the sorcerer's magic, extinguishes all fires ("Feuersnot" meaning "fire deprivation"), and begins a monologue in which he establishes himself as the sorcerer's heir and scolds the people of Munich for evicting Wagner as well as for scorning the power of his love for Diemut. She must now sacrifice her virginity in order for the city to have its fires relit and thereby "redeems" the city in what amounts to an irreverent parody of Wagner's favorite concept of redemption through love/compassion in the finale.

Strauss's librettist and equal partner in this endeavor was Ernst von Wolzogen (1855–1934), half brother of Hans von Wolzogen (1848–1938), the infamous editor of the *Bayreuther Blätter*. Born to descendants of Austrian nobility that had long since lost its estates, Wolzogen lived a long and prolific life as a writer, director, producer, translator, orator, biographer, and even librettist and composer. From 1881 to 1905 he was a freelance writer in Munich and Berlin but withdrew from the public eye in 1905 following the failure of several ventures, including his pioneering and infamous Berlin cabaret *Das Überbrettl* (The Superstage) founded in 1901, the year of the *Feuersnot* premiere—a circumstance that seriously impacted the early reception of the opera. Although his legacy is now reduced to his early introduction of cabaret into Germany, an examination of his essays and literary works reveals close intellectual parallels with Richard Strauss—such as the rejection of Wagner's concept of redemption, espousal of a Nietzschean individualism, and interest in comic opera—and thus that Wolzogen was an equal and ideal partner for this project.[48]

Collaboration and Libretto

Despite the fact that *Feuersnot* was Strauss's first collaboration with a librettist, the first serious treatment of the subject was an essay of 1954 by Franz Trenner.[49] He extracted all salient passages from the letters from Wolzogen to Strauss at the RSA and included comments on *Feuersnot* from Wolz-ogen's autobiography, but he was apparently unaware of the existence of Wolzogen's handwritten libretto with Strauss's annotations, also at the RSA and the best source of information on Strauss's alterations since it documents his interaction with the text in the planning stages. Trenner's comparison of the printed libretto with the vocal score, however, is quite complete in its inventory of the minor changes Strauss made to Wolzogen's text.

Following this essay it would be twenty-five years before Stephan Kohler provided a needed augmentation by studying the annotated libretto and by publishing the correspondence between Strauss and Wolzogen (now including a few letters from Strauss to Wolzogen), the correct text as based on the autograph score (the first printed libretto contained alterations due to censorship and many mistakes that continued to be repeated), and the full text of the one-act opera projected as their next collaboration: *Coabbradibosimpur oder Die bösen Buben von Sevilla* (Coabbradibosimpur or The Bad Boys of Seville) based on the manuscript at the RSA.[50] As documented by Trenner and Kohler, most of the changes that Strauss made were of minor significance and of a linguistic nature. He changed a few words to more-correct Bavarian dialect, deleted a few instances of Stabreim, added personality traits to some characters in the stage directions, and inserted a few jokes of his own.

Most scholars have placed Strauss's acquaintance with Wolzogen during 1898–99, primarily based on Wolzogen's earliest extant letter to Strauss of 18 March 1899,[51] but Kohler has pointed out that the published correspondence between Strauss and Cosima Wagner shows that Strauss and Wolzogen in fact became acquainted at a concert in Leipzig as early as 1892.[52] Although both lived in Munich during Strauss's second term there (1894–98), we do not know of any contact between them during this time. In November 1898 Strauss began his tenure in Berlin, and just a few months later Wolzogen moved to Berlin as well.

Not surprisingly, scholarly attention has focused on Strauss's reasons for seeking revenge on Munich, not those of his partner, and only Kohler appears to have consulted Wolzogen's autobiography rather than merely passing along the two passages relating specifically to *Feuersnot*.[53] Franz Trenner, for example, stated that Wolzogen's bitterness resulted from a lack of support for his idea of transferring French cabaret to Germany—an assertion that William Mann would later repeat, even adding that Wolzogen had wanted to transfer French cabaret to Munich before succeeding with it in Berlin.[54] As I will show, there is little or no basis for this assertion. Still more fictitious is the scenario of Norman Del Mar, who posited Wolzogen as the instigator of this operatic revenge.[55]

Wolzogen's answer to the question, as he outlined in his autobiography of 1922, was straightforward.[56] When he founded the Freie literarische Gesellschaft in 1897, he pointed to the writer Ludwig Ganghofer as chairman. Following the failure of Wolzogen's revival of Shakespeare's *Troilus and Cressida* in 1898, Ganghofer conspired to have Wolzogen thrown out of his own society, or so the latter claimed. The subsequent decline in Wolzogen's reputation and inability to find support for other projects caused his bitterness toward Munich and his desire to leave the city.

Willi Schuh has carefully chronicled Strauss's dissatisfactions with Munich and his decision to leave that city in favor of Berlin.[57] The following factors all played a role: conflicts with colleagues and superiors at the opera house, lack of respect on the part of the orchestra and the press alike, increasing realization of the provinciality of Munich, the devastating reception of *Guntram*, tempting job offers (Hamburg, New York, Berlin), and the presence of good friends in the Berlin musical press. Interestingly, both Strauss and Wolzogen emphasized the poor reception of *Guntram* as Strauss's central motivation.[58]

Their next project was to be the one-act comic opera *Coabbradibosimpur oder Die bösen Buben von Sevilla* based on Strauss's own draft *Ekke und Schnittlein*, but since Strauss had already begun his work on *Salome* when he received the text in 1903, the project was stranded and their collaboration appeared to end there.[59] Although we do not know of any further contact between them, my research has revealed an interesting late blossom of the collaboration: a later, rewritten, and extended version of this story.[60] The later version, dated 1932–33, titled *Die bösen Buben von Sevilla*, and labeled Op. 67 by Wolzogen, preserves the general features of the earlier version but is now expanded to three acts with a comic plot of intrigue and deception. Even more interesting than the text itself is the fact that Wolzogen began setting it to music. The 211-page full score of act 1 is dated 11 November 1933, but the rest is missing, and we do not know if he ever completed the score.[61]

The Cabaret Connection

The one issue that colored the early reception of *Feuersnot* in a most unfortunate manner was that of cabaret. In the time between the opening of Wolzogen's *Überbrettl* in Berlin in January 1901 and the Dresden premiere of the opera in November, Wolzogen's name had become virtually synonymous with the concept of cabaret, and reviewers of the Dresden premiere did not fail to criticize the allegedly overt connection between the libretto and Wolzogen's *Überbrettl*. Carl Söhle, for example, saw too much *Überbrettl* in the text, and Georg Richter called Wolzogen the "*Überbrettlli-brettist.*"[62] Indeed, it was Wolzogen's greatest regret that he was unable to shed the *Überbrettl* label and regain his reputation as a serious artist.[63]

As I have noted, Franz Trenner and William Mann attributed Wolzo-gen's bitterness toward Munich to a failure to transplant French cabaret to Munich, but the actual chronology does not support this assertion. Al-though Wolzogen did indeed write a few so-called "Brettl-Lieder" for the satirical journal *Simplicissimus* while in Munich, this hardly suffices as evi-dence of cabaret aspirations. In fact, having a contribution published by that journal was a matter of prestige even among serious writers at the time. Stephan Kohler went so far as to state that Wolzogen was trying to create a reputation for himself through the "Brettl-Lieder" and described Wolzo-gen's decision to move to Berlin as if his intention to found a cabaret was already clear at that time,[64] but Wolzogen himself, in the essay "Das Über-brettl" (1900), had a very different slant on the same events, describing his cabaret aspirations as a latent desire awakened by the prodding of others.[65] Nonetheless, there are some indications that Wolzogen did indeed have cabaret aspirations while still living in Munich. In his *Verse zu meinem Leben* (Verses about My Life, 1906) he described his intention to form a touring company of sorts while still in Munich, but he dated any active involvement with cabaret plans *after* his move to Berlin and again placed the initiative in the hands of others.[66]

Despite arguments to the contrary, the available evidence seems to sup-port Wolzogen's claims. The most important corroboration comes from the correspondence of the writer Frank Wedekind, who already in 1895 had wished to found a literary cabaret in collaboration with Otto Julius Bier-baum and who would later perform his own material at the Munich cabaret Die Elf Scharfrichter (The Eleven Executioners).[67] While Wedekind was serv-ing a jail sentence from August or September 1899 to February 1900, Ernst von Wolzogen, Otto Erich Hartleben, and Martin Zickel sought his collab-oration for the cabaret that they intended to open in Berlin. While Wedekind mentions Wolzogen only once in the jail letters (28 December 1899), a re-mark in a postincarceration letter of 20 March 1900 reveals that Wolzogen was now soliciting assistance for his *Überbrettl* on his own, but also that he had *not* been in charge of the project earlier on.[68] Clearly, then, others ap-proached Wolzogen during the winter of 1899–1900 to enlist him in a Berlin cabaret project of which he assumed leadership within two to three months.

From a purely chronological perspective Wolzogen's early cabaret plan-ning activities did overlap with the writing of the libretto, but not with its initial planning. Wolzogen's first letter to Strauss of 18 March 1899, which outlined Wolzogen's suggestions for alterations of the literary source and included his interpretation of the text-to-be, predates his initial exposure to concrete cabaret plans by eight months or so. Moreover, the letter shows that the core elements of the text were already in place at this point, including the "offensive" idea of the female protagonist sacrificing her virginity to the male protagonist at the end of the opera. The actual writing of the libretto, however, did not take place until more than a year later. In his autobiography Wolzogen recalls writing the libretto on the island of Rügen in 1900, but does not say when during that year.[69] From Strauss's first reaction to the libretto, documented in his letter to Wolzogen of 7 September 1900, we may infer that Wolzogen wrote the libretto sometime during the summer of 1900. While it might seem strange that more than a year would pass between Wolzogen's initial scenario and its realization, we can only assume that Strauss and Wolzogen met to discuss changes to this scenario in the interim, since they were now both living in Berlin.

Although Wolzogen's *Überbrettl* and the *Feuersnot* libretto share some important elements—satire, parody, erotic freedom, and dialect—it is not difficult to show that these features were essential to the *Zeitgeist* and not peculiar to cabaret or other "light" entertainment. Eugen Schmitz was perhaps the only commentator willing to admit that *Überbrettl* had become an umbrella term for certain cultural tendencies:

The old saga has assumed a modern spirit in the libretto; if one so desires one may use the catchword "Überbrettl" to characterize this type of "modern spirit." Two characteristic sides of the "modern spirit" are especially prevalent in the "Überbrettl": first of all the tendency towards *satire* unique to any age standing on the brink of a superculture, and in intimate connection with this a tendency towards the most free and uninhibited treatment of the *sexual problem* at the center of all life. These two elements also make up the internal basis of the *Feuersnot* libretto.[70]

The satirical and parodistic qualities of the libretto had its roots in the spirit of the journals *Jugend* and *Simplicissimus*, both founded in Munich in 1896, and the erotic freedom of some cabaret texts had long since been a trait of contemporary literature and drama.

The Literary Source

Opinions have differed as to the route from saga to libretto of the Flemish saga *Das erloschene Feuer zu Audenaerde* (The Extinguished Fire of Audenaerde) upon which *Feuersnot* is based, although the only solid piece of evidence is Strauss's oft-quoted comment from his memoirs: "Then I happened upon the Flemish saga *Das erloschene Feuer zu Audenaerde* which gave me [the] idea to write a little intermezzo *against* the theater, with personal themes and a minor revenge on my dear home town where, as the great Richard I thirty years ago, now also the lesser Richard III (there is no "II," Hans von Bülow said once) had such unpleasant experiences."[71] While the phrase "I happened upon" is rather vague, this brief passage gives us no reason to believe that Wolzogen drew Strauss's attention to the saga. Max Steinitzer reported that Strauss had found the saga years earlier, but Strauss's correspondence and diaries contain no corroborative mention of the saga.[72]

The original story, taken from a volume of Dutch sagas and reprinted in the libretto, may be briefly summarized.[73] A young man has long been in love with a woman who scorns his love. The plot unfolds as in the libretto: She appears to soften, he gets in the basket, she lets him dangle in midair, and the town ridicules him. But now the young man, not himself a sorcerer, relates the incident to an old sorcerer who extinguishes all light in the town and demands a sacrifice if the town is to regain its light: The young virgin must publicly undress and allow everyone to light their candles on a flame shooting out from her back. In summary, Wolzogen merely made the young man a sorcerer's apprentice and allowed him to handle his own revenge, made the sorcerer a background figure who does not appear, altered the virgin's plight to a sacrifice of her virginity behind closed doors, and added a "happy ending" where the boy "gets the girl."

In determining which ideas stem from Wolzogen and Strauss, respectively, Wolzogen's frequently quoted first letter to Strauss is the only direct evidence, and from this letter we can only conclude with certainty that Strauss had given Wolzogen the saga, and that they had discussed possible changes. Prefaced by "I now have the following idea" Wolzogen outlined the plot changes and stylistic features that would all be preserved in the final libretto: the young hero as sorcerer, the excision of the old sorcerer himself, the virgin's sacrifice of her virginity to the hero, and an archaic language using dialect.[74] From this letter it seems clear that Wolzogen came up with the excision of the old sorcerer and the use of dialect, but other features appear to be already agreed on.

Key Interpretive Issues

The essential issues for our understanding of this "rebellion within adulation" are the Nietzschean characteristics of Kunrad and the critique of the Wagnerian concept of *Erlösung* along with other idealistic residue. In

Feuersnot Kunrad displays all the individualist exuberance of Nietzsche's popularized *Übermensch*, blatantly disregards the *Sklavenmoral* (slave morality) of the townsfolk, making the Nietzschean connection explicit by declaring that he is "too good for virtue" (*für die Tugend zu gut*), and sings the praises of *Lebensphilosophie* in rejecting his own previous bookish broodings. Among early commentators Eugen Schmitz understood Kunrad's statement about virtue as a reference to Nietzsche, an interpretation that Roland Tenschert would later echo.[75] Wishing to emphasize Kunrad's impertinence and arrogance, Strauss asked the conductor of the premiere, Ernst von Schuch, in a letter of 17 November 1901 (four days before the premiere), to tell the singer "that he must give his entire monologue in a very arrogant, superior tone and generally emphasize the burlesque, impudent, rude, parodistic element throughout the entire work."[76] Even if Strauss did not explicitly associate Kunrad's haughtiness with Nietzsche, he revealingly called himself a "naughty Nietzsche comrade" (*schlimmer Nietzschebruder*) in a letter to Cosima Wagner of 30 October 1901 in which he encouraged her to attend a performance of the opera.[77]

As mentioned earlier, the finale is an outright mockery of Wagner's concept of *Erlösung*, with Diemut sacrificing her virginity to "redeem" the city, something only Schmitz appears to have noticed.[78] Significantly, both Strauss and Wolzogen rejected *Erlösung* on the basis of their (Nietzsche-inspired) critique of Catholic confession and absolution, their belief that the individual must take full responsibility for his or her actions (as Guntram had insisted).[79] In advancing their sexual conception of love they also debunked the Wagnerian and contemporary exaltation of the (metaphysical) "power of love"—here *Minnegebot* (love's decree or command). While Kunrad appears to follow tradition in his desire to punish Diemut and the townsfolk for their affront to *Minnegebot*, his physical conception of love turns out to differ drastically from that of Wagner and Strauss's fellow opera composers. Christopher Morris has put it: "Wagner's lovers [in *Tristan* und Isolde] never quite lose sight of their metaphysical perch, but Kunrad seems to have put aside the mantle of the master and replaced mystical sermonizing with some very down-to-earth pleasure."[80]

Wolzogen's *Feuersnot*

Wolzogen's intentions had already crystallized in his very first letter to Strauss of 18 March 1899: "When love unites with the magic of genius, even the most ingrained philistine must be clued in!"[81] Although Wolzogen did not mention art directly, it seems obvious that he intended *Feuersnot* to be an "allegory of creative force and its inspiration," as William Mann has suggested.[82] In his autobiography Wolzogen elaborated on this:

All creative power springs from sensuality. The creative spirit possesses the magic ability to create something living from nothing. When this magic now becomes animated by the fire of the senses, I have every right to seize it wherever I find it. I gave poetic expression to this artistic conceit in the singing poem *Feuersnot*. . . . Every true artist is a Prometheus who creates human beings in the image of God. But he does not need to steal the distant light of heaven for his creatures; he can take the fire from earth.[83]

In addition to the idea of sexuality as a source of artistic inspiration, his fanciful yet conventional image of the Promethean artist shows his allegiance to the antimetaphysical principles of Realism. The artist needs no metaphysics for his creation, but can derive it all from his sexuality. In the passage of his memoirs following the one cited above Wolzogen spoke of paying "loving" attention to "the beast within us," a pseudo-Nietzschean view of instincts that makes Wolzogen sound like a writer unafraid of putting our instinctual drives on display in his literary works, but an examination of these show that his concept of morality was quite old-fashioned for a writer who considered himself "modern." Significantly, this suggests that the sexual emphasis of the *Feuersnot* plot came from Strauss rather than Wolzogen.

GENRE AND STYLE IN *FEUERSNOT*

To gain a better understanding of the oppositional attitude of *Feuersnot* we must confront the problem of its genre. Not surprisingly, scholars have not agreed on the genre of the opera, some opting for *Märchenoper* (fairy-tale opera) and others for comic opera. Clearly, the opera as a whole refuses to commit to a specific genre and pokes fun at the contemporary genres of *Märchenoper* and music drama in the process. Despite this refusal, however, the opera shows Strauss's penchant for comic opera, and in this regard a comparison with the potential model of *Feuersnot*—Wagner's *Die Meistersinger von Nürnberg*—becomes a crucial ingredient in understanding Strauss's attempt to "modernize" comic opera. This clear espousal of a "new" comic, or at least nonpathetic or nonmetaphysical, opera is evident in Strauss's pre-*Feuersnot* operatic projects, as we saw, and his letters.

With respect to the general character of the opera, Strauss's comments are contradictory. In letters to his parents written during the composition of the opera in 1900, Strauss emphasized that the style of *Feuersnot* would be "simple," "melodic," and "pure Lortzing," called it "highly popular," and reassured his father—who continually lectured his son on the need for melodies rather than intricate counterpoint—that his preaching had borne fruit in *Feuersnot*.[84] While these adjectives and the reference to Lortzing suggested a comic opera, a letter of 6 March 1902 to the Berlin intendant Graf von Hochberg, in which Strauss asked for postponement of the Berlin premiere of *Feuersnot*, offered a radically different characterization: "But the end of April is so inconvenient for a serious work, which is *primarily* directed at true art connoisseurs and musical epicures and—if at all—can only gradually attract a wider audience, that I would like to submit the most humble request that your Excellency postpone the performance of my opera until next fall."[85] Here Strauss drew attention to the serious nature and lack of mass appeal of the opera and thus squarely contradicted the parental description. Although here he surely exaggerated these aspects to strengthen his case, this letter revealed Strauss's awareness of the deeper levels of meaning in *Feuersnot*, intertextual levels that only "connoisseurs" of the opera scene would be able to appreciate. Although most listeners would view *Feuersnot* as an unusual comic opera with admixtures of fairy-tale and music drama, more "informed" observers would, at least ideally, recognize the opera as a commentary on post-Wagnerian opera.

Four decades later, in the unsent letter to Joseph Gregor quoted in part previously, Strauss offered a few comments on the novel features of *Feuersnot*:

The new elements (at least as compared to the standard opera tradition with its knights, bandits, gypsies, Turks, Sicilian peasants, troubadours, court jesters) mainly consisted in the new genre of a dialect opera, in the courage to make a personal and polemical confession of the composer, in its lightly satirical nature. . . . *Feuersnot* has always been accused of stylistic intermingling of the harmless farce with Kunrad's reprimanding sermon. Admitting the truth in this objection—without it the whole thing would just have been too simple, and to me Kunrad's speech was clearly the main thing and the rest of the story an amusing addition.[86]

In addition to emphasizing the novel elements of dialect, satire, and personal polemic in *Feuersnot*, Strauss admitted to the incongruity of the comic and serious portions of the plot, emphasizing the latter as the essence of the opera and almost dismissing the former as mere "amusing additions," an assessment clearly in line with the letter to Hochberg. This apparent inconsistency merely underscores the difficulty of assigning *Feuersnot* to a specific genre.

Text and Music

The subtitle of the opera and the indication of time and place preceding the text itself provide the first clues to its potential genre—or lack of it—and the oppositional attitude of Strauss and Wolzogen. By using the neutral subtitle "ein Singgedicht," meaning "a poem to be sung" or "a poem for singing," the authors deliberately veiled the genre of the opera and emphasized its unique status. Although the apparently innocent label *Singgedicht* could apply to any opera, it is significant that Strauss and Wolzogen avoided standard labels and chose one that refused to commit *Feuersnot* to a specific genre. The indication that the opera plays in Munich *zu fabelhafter Unzeit*, meaning something like "in legendary nontime," augments this initial uncertainty. While the word *fabelhaft* appears to indicate that we are dealing with a simple legend, saga, or fairy tale, the nonsensical word *Unzeit* negates any sense that the innocent word *fabelhaft* might have made, adds an enigmatic flavor to the time indication, and highlights the nonconformist attitude of Strauss and Wolzogen.

Of the three genres with which *Feuersnot* most obviously interacts—*Märchenoper*, music drama, and comic opera—the subversion of the *Märchenoper* is perhaps the most striking and effective. The plot of *Feuersnot* contains most of the basic elements of the fairy tale: the element of "wonder," simple or naive characters and moral, happy ending, and unspecified time. Thus, the element of magic is prominent in the story, most of the characters—with the notable exceptions of Kunrad, Diemut, and the girlfriends—represent simple or naive views of life, Kunrad gets the girl in the end, and the action plays in *fabelhafter Unzeit*. By setting up a clear *Märchen* expectation and framework, Strauss and Wolzogen were able to augment the effect of shattering this framework through Kunrad's anything but naive behavior.

Indeed, the lack of naiveté of Diemut, the three girlfriends, and especially Kunrad shatters the boundaries of the imaginative fairy-tale form and thrusts it into a world of sexual Realism. When Kunrad discovers "real life" and kisses Diemut, he disrupts the normal expectations of this presumed fairy-tale world. Although the clear erotic undertone of the girlfriends' teasing, the antics of the basket scene, Diemut's complex emotional course between revenge and attraction, and Kunrad's overtly Nietzschean demeanor also have no place in a fairy-tale universe, the story does not completely shatter the fairy-tale potential until Kunrad demands Diemut's virtue as his price for restoring the fires. Even if many fairy tales incorporate sexual symbolism at various levels, the genre hardly allows for such directness. Erich Urban, for example, noted in his review of the Dresden premiere that Kunrad's qualities are decidedly un-*Märchen*-like as compared to the original saga, and Fritz Gysi pointed out in 1934 that the sexual candor of the opera breaks the boundaries of the *Märchen* form, rightly calling Kunrad's ultimatum "inimical to the fairy tale" (*märchenwidrig*).[87] The naiveté of the *Märchenoper* was simply incompatible with Strauss's erotic directness or his satirical and polemical bent. Kunrad's brutal dismissal of fairy-tale innocence thus stands as an emblem of Strauss's anti-Romantic aesthetic.

Kunrad and his views, drawing on the contemporary operatic dogma of the "power of love" (here *Minnegebot*), are also the key to the way in which *Feuersnot* engages the genre of music drama. As the sole representative of music drama Kunrad seems quite out of place in this setting, one otherwise populated with characters from comic opera. Although Kunrad is able to assert dominance for the ideas of music drama through his magical powers, one passage in particular places his ramblings in an exaggerated and satirical light. Reacting with incomprehension to Kunrad's most Stabreim-filled and Tristanesque ravings, the Burgvogt sings "Hey, this fellow is haunted! I am getting out of here; this place is getting rather eerie."[88] Kunrad effects a similar dichotomy of musical style by importing some of the grand gestures of music drama into this "lighter" environment. His very first entrance signals Kunrad's more "elevated" musical status especially well (26–27). Up to this point most of the music has moved along in a lively tempo, much of it in a "light" vein, but Kunrad's entrance effects a drastic if temporary change in musical style (a mere sixteen bars), with its suddenly slow tempo and rate of harmonic change, chordal sequences, and diminished chords (see Example 7.1).

After Kunrad's initial entrance, however, the musical passages imported from music drama do not separate themselves from their surroundings so neatly. Instead, they often contribute a mélange of rapidly or "nervously" changing styles that I have discussed under the heading of "Stilkunst" elsewhere.[89] In 1902, speaking specifically of *Feuersnot*, Ernst Otto Nodnagel accused Strauss of "playing" with style and art itself, even claiming that this attitude signaled "the end of music."[90] In *Feuersnot* we may distinguish at least three basic categories, although these do no exhaust the stylistic diversity of the work: older or "light" styles, Wagnerian textures and quotations, and waltzes. While the opening scene and the children's choruses exemplify the first category, Kunrad's entrance and some Wagnerian or simply "music-dramatic" moments in the love duet (92–96) and Kunrad's monologue (152–55) represent the second, and the waltzes prefiguring those of Baron Ochs in *Der Rosenkavalier* make up the third (60–68, 158–59). In my view, this dehierarchized stylistic pluralism stems from

EXAMPLE 7.1
Kunrad's Entrance (27)

Strauss's objective selection of styles to suit a given subject and constitutes a musical analogue to the many "isms" into which European cultural life of early Modernism fragmented during the 1890s.

The most prominent genre appealed to in *Feuersnot* is comic opera. Although some scholars have preferred a different classification for the opera, most commentators view it as a comic opera with an admixture of other elements. Max Steinitzer, for example, referred to the work as comic in 1911, and Werner Bitter included it in his 1932 study of the genre.[91] Similarly, Erich Urban noted in 1901 that Strauss was following the contemporary trend toward *volkstümliche* opera, Oscar Bie stated in 1906 that "now one could . . . mock tragedy . . . and sing cheerful songs of midsummer," and in 1907 Eugen Schmitz related *Feuersnot* and the general resurgence of comic opera to the desire of Strauss and some of his contemporaries to escape the Schopenhauerian "redemption fog" (*Erlösungsnebel*) that had enveloped the genre of music drama.[92] More important, however, the text and the music themselves support the view of *Feuersnot* as a comic opera. In employing the historical conventions of comedy and comic opera alike, the work establishes itself as an example of a "modern" comic opera that does not view the concept of genre as a fixed element but manipulates it to submit the contemporary, static view of genre to a stinging critique.

Both the plot structure and the setting of *Feuersnot* help identify it as a comic opera. Its general structure follows the generic outline and historical precedent of countless comedies preceding it: A "wrong" situation moves through obstacles or intrigue to its resolution, typically marriage or engagement. In *Feuersnot* Kunrad's improper proposal or courtship (the kiss) creates the "wrong" situation: the separation of Kunrad and Diemut, who are destined to end up together. Diemut and her three friends now plan out the intrigue, the basket trap, intended to teach Kunrad a lesson and possibly encourage him to court Diemut in the "right" way. Had Wolzogen followed a conventional scheme here, Kunrad would have learned his lesson, reformed his ways, and he and Diemut would have ended up engaged following a "proper" courtship. Although the eventual result—Kunrad and Diemut ending up together—remains the same, Kunrad's Nietzschean views and command of magic enables him to overthrow this scheme and achieve his ends in a drastically different way. This interruption of the expected resolution of the comedy involves the "intrusion" of Kunrad's serious sermon and use of magic, elements stemming from *Märchenoper* and music drama and alien to the genre of comedy, which relies mainly on Realism for its effect. Despite this alteration, however, the general structure of the *Feuersnot* plot remains that of a comedy, albeit one that manipulates the idea of genre to make its points.

The general setting of the opera and details of the plot also help identify *Feuersnot* as a comic opera. Although the setting is Munich, it breathes the atmosphere of a small town—hardly a typical setting for a fairy tale or a music drama but very much so for a comedy. Similarly, the cast consists of ordinary people, the type of people who populated most operatic comedies of the period, as opposed to the knights, royalty, and gods of fairy-tale operas or music dramas. A set of such idiosyncratic characters is typical of comedy or comic opera.

Apart from Kunrad's sermon and other outbursts, the atmosphere of the opera remains "light" in the sense of comic opera, with the basket scene bordering on the farcical. Although Kunrad does his utmost to quell this lighthearted and naive atmosphere and lead the townsfolk to a more elevated mode of thinking, their concerns remain quite earthbound and simple-minded—as after the extinguishing when they expect the involvement of the Devil himself but are more terrified at the thought of having to eat cold soup in the absence of fire than dealing with Satan (120–27). This contrast between Kunrad and the townsfolk in level of sophistication is, of course, a time-honored comic effect.

The music also plays a significant role in classifying *Feuersnot* as a comic opera. In addition to the significant presence of "light" music, especially for the simple townsfolk and the children's choruses, the most important factor in this regard is the unusual prominence of choruses and ensembles, one of the distinguishing features of Germanic comic opera but hardly of post-Wagnerian fairy-tale opera or music drama. Strauss's admiration for Peter Cornelius's *Der Barbier von Bagdad* (1858), with its impressive ensembles and choruses, establishes a potential parentage for *Feuersnot*.[93] In a letter of 1 July 1905 to Georg von Hülsen, Generalintendant of the Berlin theaters from 1903, Strauss reported from a guest performance in Cologne on the success of *Feuersnot* and *Der Barbier von Bagdad* in a way that displayed his admiration for the latter and suggested a kinship between the two operas: "The people of Cologne had not seen anything like our servant choruses from *Der Barbier von Bagdad* and the great darkness chorus from *Feuersnot* in their theater before."[94] Already around 1885, as Steinitzer reported, Strauss had, in fact, sung and played the entire *Barbier von Bagdad* at his Uncle Pschorr's house.[95]

The *Meistersinger* Connection

Yet another significant factor in the interpretation of *Feuersnot* is its relationship to Wagner's *Die Meistersinger*. Although Strauss and Wolzogen deliberately entered into a dialogue with Wagner's "comic" masterpiece in choosing *Johannisnacht* as the setting of *Feuersnot*, only Stephan Kohler among more recent commentators appears to have given the question serious consideration. He drew parallels between Reichhart (the old sorcerer) and Sachs, noting that they are both "masters," as well as between the names of the Meistersinger and those of the Munich townsfolk in *Feuersnot* (Pöschel, Hämerlein, Kofel, Kunz Gilgenstock, and Ortlieb Tulbeck).[96] He also aptly noted that Walther's act of leaving his safe castle to explore life in Nuremberg closely resembles Kunrad's spontaneous abandonment of his house upon his discovery of "real life," and he pointed out several textual allusions.

The comparison of Walther and Kunrad is perhaps the most fruitful aspect of investigating the similarities between the two operas. Although there are some important differences between the two characters, Kunrad is, in fact, a "modernized" Walther. The plots offer an obvious parallel besides those noted by Kohler: Both Walther and Kunrad must pass through a rite of passage of sorts—the humiliation of the trial singing and the basket scene, respectively—before they may unite with the objects of their love or desire. In fact, the *Feuersnot* libretto bears out this parallel through a clear textual allusion: In *Die Meistersinger von Nürnberg* Walther asks, "*Hier in den Stuhl?*" (Here in this chair?; act 1, scene 3), when asked to sit in the *Singestuhl* (singing chair) for his trial song, and in *Feuersnot* Kunrad poses the almost identical question, "*Hier in den Korb?*" (Into this basket?), when Diemut prompts him to climb into the basket (98). A curious and apparently unnoticed circumstance is the fact that Walther's name was Konrad von Stolzing in Wagner's second draft of *Die Meistersinger von Nürnberg* of 1861.[97] While Strauss could hardly have known this in 1899, Wolzogen may have learned it while still a part of the Bayreuth circle.

The differences between Walther and Kunrad are as important as their similarities, however. First of all, the solutions to their respective dilemmas, "securing" Eva and Diemut, differ drastically: While Walther relies on the help of Sachs and his own artistic abilities, Kunrad takes matters into his own hands and acts as anything but a knight in doing so. Second, the feelings between Walther and Eva are explicit and mutual, whereas Kunrad is going to "secure" Diemut's "love" with or without her consent. Where Walther's love for Eva is courtly and reverent, Kunrad's "love" for Diemut manifests itself openly as physical desire and thus "updates" Walther's source of inspiration to *Eros*. Thereby, Kunrad follows cultural trends of the 1890s—in this case an open attitude toward sexuality, Nietzsche's critique of *Sklavenmoral*, and one manifestation of the philosopher's *Übermensch*—and distances himself from the old-fashioned Walther by becoming his "modern" alter ego.

The Larger Perspective: Strauss and Comic Opera

To appreciate the significance of *Feuersnot*—in its primary capacity as comic opera—in Strauss's oeuvre we must step back and briefly investigate the crucial role of comic opera in his career. As we saw earlier, Strauss's operatic drafts after *Guntram* pointed ahead to *Feuersnot*, which many later commentators have viewed as the natural realization of his search for light or comic subjects. The composer's published correspondence completes the picture of a composer always in search of light subjects—but rarely finding them.

The evidence from his correspondence with respect to comic or non-Romantic opera is unequivocal. Although the two operas separating the comic *Feuersnot* and *Der Rosenkavalier*—*Salome* and *Elektra*—were anything but comic, their "nervous" and psychological focus had to do with Strauss's objective selection of subjects and constant need for variety and represented only a brief interruption in Strauss's quest for comic, light, and Realistic subjects. Although Strauss expressed no particular desire for comic opera in his correspondence around 1900, a significant comment of 1 March 1900 from the diary of Romain Rolland—noting that Strauss felt tragedy to have been exhausted by Wagner and that he attended small Parisian theaters in search of comedy and buffoonery—shows that Strauss was looking for relief from the tragic post-Wagnerian opera around the time of *Feuersnot*.[98]

Although Strauss never had any success in persuading Hofmannsthal to write comic or Realistic librettos, their correspondence reveals Strauss's continued attempts to elicit "his" kind of libretto from his collaborator. Clearly, Strauss had no reason to complain during the early years of the collaboration, which yielded *Der Rosenkavalier*—a work about which Strauss complained that commentators had not viewed as the "long-awaited musical comedy of our time"—and *Ariadne auf Naxos*, a work that Strauss believed would "lead comic opera onto a new path."[99] Until the much later *Arabella*, however, Strauss was unable to persuade Hofmannsthal to write another comic and/or Realistic opera. In the famous letter of 5 June 1916, for example, Strauss confessed his calling to become the "Offenbach of the twentieth-century" and once again solicited a comic text from his collaborator, ending with the enthusiastic exclamation: "Long live the political-satirical-parodistic operetta!"[100] A few weeks prior to this Strauss had asked Hofmannsthal for "a *completely modern*, absolutely Realistic character- and nerve-comedy" featuring a female spy and filled with intrigue and deception and had emphasized the talent of Eugène Scribe in this direction, and about three months later Strauss asked more specifically for librettos "à la 'Schwarzer Domino,' 'Maurer und Schlosser,' 'Wildschütz,' 'Zar und Zimmermann,' 'Teufels Anteil,' à la Offenbach," stressing that he now wanted to move "entirely into the domain of the un-Wagnerian opera of comedy, sentiment, and human beings."[101] Although *Wildschütz* and *Zar und Zimmermann* are, of course, by Lortzing, the other three are all by Scribe (with music by Daniel-François-Esprit Auber); indeed, it hardly surprises that Strauss favored librettos by Scribe and later products of French opera, for comic and/or Realistic operas with elements of suspense, intrigue, satire, and politics—precisely what Strauss solicited from Hofmannsthal—were a specialty of nineteenth-century French opera in general and Eugène Scribe in particular.[102] Unfortunately for Strauss, however, it also is not surprising that Hofmannsthal would have nothing to do with such projects, for he openly told Strauss that he was against Realism on principle.[103] This statement goes a long way toward explaining the essential incompatibility of these two artists.

Strauss continued his quest for comic librettos throughout his long career. Thus, during his collaboration with Stefan Zweig he once again expressed his desire to create the female figures of "the woman as con artist or the sophisticated lady as spy," and although Zweig showed no interest in this, Strauss was overjoyed when Zweig suggested what would become *Die schweigsame Frau*, calling it "the born comic opera."[104] In spite of this opera, however, Strauss continued his quest for comic opera in his (somewhat unfruitful and reluctant) collaboration with Joseph Gregor. Thus, Strauss wanted *Die Liebe der Danae* to become a "light mythological operetta," but even before completing this work he asked Gregor for the next libretto: "How about an amusing comic one?"[105]

Strauss, then, never ceased to propose comic subjects to his various collaborators, and it was only fitting for him to end his career with *Capriccio*. While many are probably happy that Strauss did not succeed in eliciting spy stories and other light fare from his librettists, his constant desire for comic and/or Realistic subjects formed a red thread through his career, one that began with the *Till Eulenspiegel* drafts of the 1890s and documents Strauss's continuing desire for un-Wagnerian subjects devoid of metaphysics and all-too heroic gestures.

ANALYTICAL ISSUES: ASSOCIATIVE TONALITY AND LEITMOTIV

The term *associative tonality*—the process of associating certain keys with specific characters, objects, events, or emotions—appears to have been coined by Robert Bailey in his well-known article on Wagner's *Der Ring des Nibelungen*, and recent discussions of Strauss's operas have placed his pervasive use of this method at the fore.[106] Although the term seems to imply that a referential passage must be a tonality per se—that is, a stable tonal area confirmed by a cadence—I prefer to frame the notion as a fluid continuum of differing degrees of tonal presence or stability. Thus, we might think of these associative "events" as harmonic "markers" or "colors" that may be fleetingly touched on or actually prolonged, confirmed, and stabilized as genuine keys occupying a stretch of music. Although leitmotivic exegesis was always more prominent, Strauss scholars began exploring the composer's associative use of keys early on, beginning with the work of Edmund Wachten[107] in the 1930s and continuing with that of Willi Schuh, Eva-Maria Axt,[108] Kenneth Birkin, Derrick Puffett, Bryan Gilliam, and Charles Youmans in more recent times.[109] Whereas Wachten, Schuh, and Axt focused on key associations across Strauss's works, the others have been more cautious in their claims, confining themselves to the interaction of keys within a single opera.

As the studies of Willi Schuh, Charlotte Erwin, and Bryan Gilliam have shown, Strauss's practice of annotating the librettos prior to composition consistently favored harmonic annotations over other types, and the *Feuersnot* libretto—to my knowledge the most pervasively annotated of all the extant librettos—confirms their findings.[110] A study of this document reveals, among other things, that Strauss originally intended to end *Feuersnot* in D major, the key of the Munich people in which it began, rather than B-flat major, the key of Diemut. Since the finale is a mass scene involving the people with Kunrad and Diemut singing offstage, D major would seem a logical choice, but it would not reflect the psychological transformation of the two main characters.

With respect to the operas, Youmans has shown that Strauss's employment of associative tonality was already in full bloom in his first opera.[111] Although the key associations in *Feuersnot* are less focused than those of the surrounding operas *Guntram* and *Salome*, several keys act as tonal symbols: In order of strength of association, D major is associated with the Munich people, D minor with Diemut's humiliation, B-flat major with Diemut, A major with Kunrad's love, F-sharp minor/major with the power of love (*Minnegebot*), and A-flat major with the love duet (*Mittsommernacht*). Furthermore, F major initially associates itself with Kunrad and E major periodically with Diemut's three girlfriends. It is noteworthy that E major, the key that most scholars agree represents *Eros* in many of Strauss's works, must yield to A and F-sharp major as the keys of Kunrad's erotic exuberance.[112]

Although *Feuersnot* may not be the most unalloyed example of Strauss's use of associative tonality, it does contain examples of most of his techniques, ranging in abstraction from the use of key signatures to signify the strength of a key association to single chords as fleeting "markers" referring back to earlier events. An example of the most abstract technique involves what I call the "entrance effect," the sudden change of key signature (and usually also of key) caused by the entrance of an important character. In *Feuersnot* only Diemut's entrance is able to effect such a change, an abrupt move to B-flat major with no harmonic transition or modulation (7–8; see Example 7.2).

EXAMPLE 7.2
Diemut's Entrance (7–8)

Exemplifying Strauss's associative use of brief passages, the association of D minor with Diemut's humiliation and later with Kunrad's extinguishing of the fires is the most focused and pervasive in *Feuersnot*. Characteristically, the first appearance of the D minor key signature following Kunrad's brazen kiss is a clue to the potentially associative role of the key, and this section establishes D minor as a referential key (50; see Example 7.3). Two later referential excerpts contain brief occurrences of D minor within other keys, both expressing Diemut's furious indignation and clearly deriving their key association from the kiss episode (56, 82; see

EXAMPLE 7.3
The Kiss (50)

Example 7.4 for the first of these). Interestingly, Kunrad now appropriates D minor for the extinguishing of the fires and thus turns it against Diemut and the crowd mocking him (121). For the remainder of the opera D minor mainly expresses the people's plight in reference to the extinguishing (134, 136–39, 174, 181). Although the associative usage of a single harmony is rare, B-flat major chords appear as references to Diemut scattered throughout the opera. Thus, the music suddenly turns to B-flat major when the three friends tease, *Diemut, die hats!* (Diemut is in love!; 40), and in other instances Strauss uses a B-flat major chord for references to Diemut's "golden hair" (80, 85, 109–10).

The comparatively great number of motives clinging almost exclusively to one pitch level in this opera are a crucial element in Strauss's

EXAMPLE 7.4
D-minor Humiliation Reference (56)

extraordinary attention to pitch. *Feuersnot* contains at least six such pitch-fixed motives: the "Subendfeuer" chords (see Example 7.5 pages 269–270); the "Maja, maja, mia, mö" children's chorus, always in D major; the two motives associated with Kunrad; Diemut's Infuriated Theme (see Example 7.5.10), almost always in D minor; and the "Kätzlein" motive (Example 7.5.4).[113] Moreover, Kunrad's "Minnegebot" motive tends to appear in F-sharp minor, the quotations from other operas appear at pitch, and even the two pitches for "Kyrieleis" reappear later for that word.[114]

When Youmans posited Strauss's use of associative tonality as the composer's "positive identity" with the purpose of emphasizing Strauss's individuality against the influence of Wagner, he may have overstated his case.[115] Wagner's frequent use of the "entrance effect," for example, suggests a Wagnerian source for this technique.[116] Wagner also used passages ranging in length from stable key areas down to very brief passages and the rarer single chords referentially. In *Das Rheingold*, for example, Wagner establishes the association of C major with the gold (in its natural state) in the ensemble "Rheingold! Rheingold!" of the Rhine maidens about midway into the first scene. In the middle of the second scene Loge calls forth a brief episode in C major when he sings of the return of the gold to the Rhine, and Wotan's reference to the Rhine maidens and their gold toward the beginning of the fourth scene makes use of C major for just a few bars. The beginning of the third scene of act 3 of *Tannhäuser* in which the music turns briefly to E major on the word *Venusberg* shows an example of the associative use of a single chord. With respect to pitch-specific motives, we know from Bailey that Wagner used a number of them in the *Ring* (Curse, Tarnhelm, Valhalla, Sword, Siegfried's Horn Call).[117]

While many more examples could be cited, even these few suggest that Strauss adopted, or at least adapted, these techniques from Wagner, and thus that the connection between the two composers with respect to associative tonality and pitch is much closer and more derivative than demonstrated thus far. This does not relegate Strauss's music to an inferior status of emulation, however, just as it does not compromise the strongly individual nature of his musical language and aesthetics. The fact that Strauss adopted Wagnerian musical techniques does not make his musical *style* derivative, and the styles of the two composers obviously differ widely. Although most of Strauss's contemporaries copied the slithering chromaticism of *Tristan und Isolde* and the cursory application of a network of leitmotivs, Strauss sought a deeper and less cosmetic connection with Wagner, and he apparently seized on Wagner's close attention to pitch along with its significative potential, adapting and extending the technique to suit his own purposes.

Leitmotiv

Strauss's extensive use of the leitmotiv, in his tone poems as well as his operas, is a more outward sign of his connection with Wagner.[118] Needless to say, Strauss was far from unique in employing the leitmotiv, a technique that had become virtually obligatory during the 1880s and 1890s. Most scholars hold Strauss's leitmotivs to be less clearly referential than those of Wagner, less closely tied to specific words of the text and more "symphonic" in nature. Although the leitmotivs of *Feuersnot* display a wide range of referentiality and include quite text-dependent motives, the bulk of the motives are only referential in a general sense.

Although early as well as more recent commentaries on or "guides" to Strauss's operas do concern themselves with determining the semantic associations of the various motives, they almost never resort to labeling in the manner of Hans von Wolzogen's guides to Wagner's works, and few if any Straussian leitmotivs are universally referred to by a label to the extent of, say, Wagner's Sword or Valhalla motives.[119] This fact alone seems to support the idea that Strauss's motives have appeared less clearly referential than those of Wagner. Thus, the early discussions of *Guntram* and *Feuersnot* by Wolfgang Jordan, Arthur Smolian, Eugen von Ziegler, and Eugen Schmitz did focus on leitmotivs, but without the rigidity of Wolzogen.[120]

The later "guide" to *Der Rosenkavalier* by Alfred Schattmann, however, adopted a seemingly more dogmatic approach in that it presented no fewer than 118 motives, labeling some motives and merely citing others with their text.[121] This elaborate labeling procedure would not be so interesting were it not for Schattmann's note stating that Strauss approved of most of these labels.[122] Here Schattmann also noted that he settled for citing some motives with their text—and thus without fixed labels—since Strauss specifically wished to avoid a "schematic stamping" (*schematische Abstempelung*) of the motives. Significantly, then, we see Strauss both approving of and resisting a rigid system of fixed labels, showing that he acknowledged the clearly referential nature of only some motives while disavowing it for others.

In more recent Strauss scholarship Carolyn Abbate and Derrick Puffett have revisited Strauss's use of the leitmotiv. In his essay "*Salome* as Music Drama" (1989) Puffett criticized the "literalist" view of Mann and Del Mar and held up the "relativist" view of Dahlhaus as the "modern" view of the leitmotiv.[123] While observing that Strauss's sketches display a "simplistic" conception (with labels) of the leitmotiv, he noted that Strauss's practice was more complex, and that most of the *Salome* motives lie somewhere between the extremes in the continuum of pure music and meaning.

With respect to the operas, Charles Youmans has recently shown that Strauss treated the *Guntram* leitmotivs much in the manner of Wagner, drawing on the full range of Wagner's techniques.[124] Speaking of Strauss's first three operas, Ernst Krause stated that *Guntram* used Wagner's technique, *Feuersnot* was transitional, and *Salome* completed the transition to motives of "psychological characterization."[125] This is probably a fair assessment, although we should not take it to mean that all of Strauss's leitmotivs are "symphonic" or "psychological" after *Salome*. Example 7.5 provides the *Feuersnot* leitmotivs labeled by Strauss.

EXAMPLE 7.5

Feuersnot (Leit)motivs Labeled by Strauss

---

1. *"Flammenlodern"*
   (Flames Blazing):

2. *"Feuer" (Fire):*

3. *"Kikiriki, Kikiriki" (Rooster Sound):*

4. *"Kätzlein (Cat):*

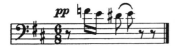

5. *"Die Mütter toben" (The Mothers Rage):*

6. *"Subend[feuer]" (Midsummer Fire):*

Su - - bend - Feu - er

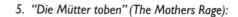

(continued)

EXAMPLE 7.5
Feuersnot (Leit)motivs Labeled by Strauss (*continued*)

---

7. *"Satansthema"* (*Satan Theme*):

8. *"Liebesthema"* (*Love Theme*):

9. *"Sehnsuchtsmotiv"* (*Yearning Motive*):

10. *"Diemuts ärgerliches Thema"* (*Diemut's Infuriated Theme*):

Since we cannot discuss all the leitmotivs here, I will focus on new information brought to light by my research: the motives directly labeled or otherwise named by Strauss in the particell (P) and the annotated libretto (AL).[126] Strauss employed labels for motives that are merely used for text painting, some imitating natural sounds and used only once or twice in the opera, and for "proper" leitmotivs serving a symbolic function. Half of

Strauss's ten extant labels, all from the particell, apply to the simpler, descriptive type of motive (VS=vocal score; R=rehearsal number):

1. "Flammenlodern" (Flames Blazing) [P 1, VS 4 at R 2/–2]
2. "Feuer" (Fire) [P 2, VS 6 at R 7/–4]
3. "Kikiriki, Kikiriki" (Rooster Sound) [P 5–6, VS 15 at R 18]
4. "Kätzlein!" (Cat) [P 60, VS 130 at R 166/–5]
5. "Die Mütter toben" (The Mothers Rage) [P 60, VS 130 at R 166]

Thus, the trills of "Flammenlodern" and the rapidly undulating "Feuer" depict the licking of flames, the children's "Kikiriki, Kikiriki" imitates the sound of a rooster (as stated in the stage direction) and "Kätzlein" that of a cat, and "Die Mütter toben" depicts the raging of the mothers through a rapid bass line in the bassoons.

The other set of labels stem predominantly from the annotated libretto and apply to "proper" leitmotivs of symbolic import (here listed in order of appearance in the score):

6. "Subend" (Midsummer) [AL 26; VS 81 at R 110/–7, but not present at this point]
7. "Satansthema" (Satan Theme) [P 56, VS 119 at R 155]
8. "Liebesthema" (Love Theme) [AL 50, not present in score at this point]
9. "Sehnsuchtsmotiv" (Yearning Motive) [AL 32, VS 104 at R 137/–4]
10. "Diemuts ärgerliches Thema" (Diemut's Infuriated Theme) [AL 23, VS 71 at R 94/2]

Importantly, these are not labels in the manner of Wolzogen's motivic guides; only the "Sehnsuchtsmotiv" appears as a motivic sketch with a label written above (see Example 7.6).

The first label on the list, "Subend," refers to the "Subendfeuer" chords discussed earlier. The "Satansthema" is another very text-dependent leitmotiv that Mann and Del Mar have connected specifically with the menace of evil.[127] Strauss's reference to the "Satansthema" in the particell occurs where Kunrad calls on his master's powers to come to his aid (119), but a much earlier occurrence is more interesting in that Strauss's private joke rather than the text itself calls forth the motive. When Tulbeck tells his tall tale of Onuphrius (supposed ancestor of the sorcerer), he notes that no one knows how the giant died (*weiss Niemand, wie er gestorben ist*; 21), and here the "Satansthema" sets in. Despite the reference to death and the potentially diabolical nature of Onuphrius, Strauss's joking remark in the particell— "*Der Teufel hat ihn aber geholt!*" (The Devil took him!)—is what summons the motive. While this does not really undermine the meaning of the motive, it shows Strauss "playing" with the notion of motivic referentiality by setting a private joke to music, as it were.

Although Strauss's "Liebesthema" label confirms the analysis of most commentators, we now move into vaguer referential territory. In the score the motive first appears toward the beginning of Kunrad's discovery-of-life monologue (30), where it could be referring to any number of things, such as Midsummer, fire, or magic—all of which, however, converge in the concept of love. Nonetheless, the motive associates itself with various things before being used for Kunrad's wooing in particular and love in general: the teasing of Diemut's friends (39), Kunrad's enthusiastic demolition of his own house (45), and daylight/sun (49, 87). Later appearances connect the motive more directly with Kunrad's wooing (107, 163, 185, 191, 196).

The "Sehnsuchtsmotiv" is probably more clear-cut in meaning than the "Liebesthema," but its descriptive qualities contribute significantly to its referential content. Norman Del Mar correctly described the leap of a major seventh always dropping down and never quite reaching the octave as symbolic or descriptive of Kunrad's yearning to reach the balcony,[128] for this is precisely the point at which Strauss first sketched and labeled the motive (AL 32)—with its text "*Ach, an den Söller reich' ich noch nicht*" (Oh, I still cannot reach the balcony):

EXAMPLE 7.6
"Sehnsuchtsmotiv" (Yearning Motive) as Sketched in Annotated Libretto (32)

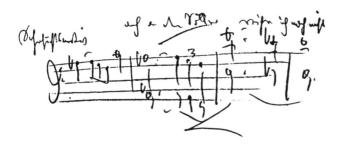

Were it not for its descriptive qualities, however, it would be much more difficult to assign the motive to the specific "Sehnsucht" as opposed to the more general "Passion."[129] Not until the descriptive instance sketched in the annotated libretto does the idea of "Sehnsucht" suggest itself as a convincing label, although later appearances reinforce a more general context of "Passion." The last item on the list, "Diemuts ärgerliches Thema," is another very clear-cut motive in terms of referential meaning, and most commentators agree that it represents Diemut's humiliation and anger, just as Strauss would have it.

The motives labeled by Strauss, then, represent various types of motives and degrees of referentiality. Since these motives include only those to which Strauss assigned a specific meaning, however, they do not represent the full spectrum of referentiality of the *Feuersnot* leitmotivs, but only the semantically most distinct. It stands to reason that we would discover Straussian labels for the more "traditional" leitmotivs with fairly clear referential contents rather than for the vaguer or more "symphonic" ones, but many of the opera's other motives belong in the latter category. Overall, the *Feuersnot* leitmotivs display a substantial emphasis on the indistinctly referential end of the spectrum and thus support the widely held belief that Strauss's leitmotivs are generally vaguer in meaning than those of Wagner.

To summarize briefly, a closer look at Strauss's early operas and unfinished stage works before *Salome* reveals fundamental components of his mature aesthetic: a compositional principle of constant variety in subject matter and style that negates efforts to construe the trajectory of Strauss's career in conventionally linear terms, the search for and discovery of comic or "light" subjects that would distance him from the tragic pathos and metaphysical still-Romanticism of the post-Wagnerians, and, especially, the rejection of Wagner's musical idealism along with an interest in prominent features of the early modernist culture of the 1890s such as Realism, Nietzschean philosophy, sexual freedom, satire, and nervousness. Although incipient or only selectively present in *Guntram* and the incomplete stage works, these features all converged in *Feuersnot* in 1901, Strauss's first operatic success and the work that gave him the necessary confidence to write *Salome*.

NOTES

1. We may trace the change in Strauss's status as an opera composer in the second and third editions of Richard Streatfeild's, *The Opera* (Philadelphia: Lippincott, 1896, 1902, 1907), for example. While the second edition gave only a few comments on *Guntram* and *Feuersnot*, Strauss received his own subheading in the table of contents in the third edition, showing the impact of *Salome* on his reputation as an opera composer.

2. See Charles D. Youmans, "Richard Strauss's *Guntram* and the Dismantling of Wagnerian Musical Metaphysics" (Ph.D. diss., Duke University, 1996); and Morten Kristiansen, "Richard Strauss's 'Feuersnot' in Its Aesthetic and Cultural Context: A Modernist Critique of Musical Idealism" (Ph.D. diss., Yale University, 2000).

3. See Willi Schuh, *Richard Strauss: Jugend und frühe Meisterjahre: Lebenschronik 1864–1898* (Zurich: Atlantis, 1976). Published in English as *Richard Strauss: A Chronicle of the Early Years, 1864–1898*, trans. Mary Whittall (Cambridge: Cambridge University Press, 1982), 258–63, 297–98, 306–8, 324. (Succeeding citations will be to the English version.)

4. See letter from Mahler to Strauss of 24 March 1894, in Herta Blaukopf, ed., *Gustav Mahler–Richard Strauss: Briefwechsel, 1888–1911*, exp. 2d ed. (Munich: Piper, 1988), 32. Although Mahler had praised *Guntram* to Bernhard Pollini, director of the Hamburg Opera, his efforts to get it performed were unsuccessful and his belief in the significance of *Guntram* surely insincere.

5. See Schuh, *Richard Strauss*, 269–325; Norman Del Mar, *Richard Strauss: A Critical Commentary on His Life and Works* (Ithaca, N.Y.: Cornell University Press, 1986), 1:87–120; William Mann, *Richard Strauss: A Critical Study of the Operas* (London: Cassell, 1964), 23–38; and Youmans, "Richard Strauss's *Guntram*."

6. For a detailed discussion of the post-Wagnerian libretto, see Kristiansen, "Richard Strauss's 'Feuersnot,'" 95–172.

7. Page numbers in parentheses in text and notes refer to the vocal score of the original version of the opera published by Fürstner in 1894. As opposed to the newer and more widely available vocal score published by Boosey and Hawkes, which is based on Strauss's later revision of the opera, this vocal score contains the unabbreviated version of the opera and thus the complete text.

8. "der sündige Mensch in der Leidenschaft Bann" (23).

9. "Heiland, mein Herr . . . Der du gelitten den Tod am Kreuze, den Menschen die Liebe wieder zu wecken, du legtest in's Herz mir den weihvollen Drang: dein Wort zu künden in begeistertem Sang!" (23–24).

10. "glühende Minne führte dein Schwert" (181).

11. "Eitler Wahn Erlösung zu künden, selbst unerlöst! O grässlicher Zwang verruchter Sinne, süssesten Sehnens qualvollster Trieb. Erlöstseinwollens einziger Feind!" (212–13).

12. For a discussion tracing Strauss's rejection of *Erlösung* through his early career, see Morten Kristiansen, "Parallel Lives: Richard Strauss, Ernst von Wolzogen, Arthur Seidl, and the Rejection of *Erlösung* (Redemption) in *Feuersnot*," in *Strauss Studies*, ed. Timothy L. Jackson and Graham Phipps (Cambridge: Cambridge University Press, forthcoming).

13. Eugen Schmitz, *Richard Strauss als Musikdramatiker* (Munich: Dr. Heinrich Lewy, 1907), 22–23.

14. Eugen von Ziegler, *Richard Strauss in seinen dramatischen Dichtungen: Guntram, Feuersnot, Salome* (Munich: Theodor Ackermann, 1907), 11.

15. Ibid., 13–16.

16. "Euch blühte Ruhm und Herrlichkeit der Welt! Nun wuchtet eisern schwer

die Gotteshand!" (act 1, scene 2; 26). Page numbers in parentheses in the text and notes refer to the vocal score.

17. "In dir sprach liebend Jesu Christ, dess' Mitleid so voll Wunder ist" (act 3, scene 6; 149–50).

18. "Wem des Erlösers Wunderkraft neu blutend ew'ges Heil gebracht, der will nicht eitle Pracht; zu Fuss in Demut will ich zieh'n, voll Dank nun ewig künden ihn" (act 3, scene 6; 158–59).

19. Pfitzner confirmed that Heinrich's redemption occurs primarily through the experience of the "agony of acknowledging the suffering of others as more intense than one's own" (*Qual des Zugebens des Leidens anderer stärker als das eigene Leiden*). See Hans Pfitzner, "Zur Grundfrage der Operndichtung" (1908–15), in *Vom musikalischen Drama: Gesammelte Aufsätze* (Munich: Süddeutsche Monatshefte, 1915), 180.

20. In the first version Guntram submitted to the punishment of the brotherhood. For the recently published extant correspondence from Ritter to Strauss, see Charles Youmans, "Ten Letters from Alexander Ritter to Richard Strauss, 1887–1894," *Richard Strauss-Blätter* 35 (1996), 3–24. The letter in question is quoted and translated in full in Youmans, "Richard Strauss's *Guntram*," 383–98, and a brief excerpt appears in Schuh, *Richard Strauss*, 282.

21. "auf dem wackligen Boden confuser Stirnerei" (Youmans, "Ten Letters," 12). Max Stirner (1806–56) espoused absolute egoism and anarchy in his *Der Einzige und sein Eigenthum* (The Ego and His Own) (Leipzig: Verlag von Otto Wigand, 1845).

22. The original of this letter is lost, but a surviving excerpt appears in Schuh, *Richard Strauss*, 284–85. Schuh's source was "Richard Strauss und sein Guntram," *Allgemeine Musikzeitung* 67, no. 42 (1940): 337–38 (see Youmans, "Richard Strauss's *Guntram*," 99n. 22).

23. On 7 April 1892 Strauss wrote his father of the meeting with Mackay (see Schuh, *Richard Strauss*, 258–59), and on 10 April 1893 he mentioned reading *Beyond Good and Evil* in a letter to Cosima Wagner (see Franz Trenner and Gabrielle Strauss, eds., *Cosima Wagner–Richard Strauss: Ein Briefwechsel*, Veröffentlichungen der Richard-Strauss-Gesellschaft München, Bd. 2 [Tutzing: Hans Schneider, 1978], 155).

24. See Youmans's "Richard Strauss's *Guntram*," 90–241, for a detailed discussion of Strauss's reception of Schopenhauer and Nietzsche, and his "The Private Intellectual Context of Richard Strauss's *Also sprach Zarathustra*," *Nineteenth-Century Music* 22 (1998):101–26, especially 106–10, for a convenient summary.

25. Arthur Seidl, "Richard Strauss—eine Charakterskizze" (1896), in *Straussiana: Aufsätze zur Richard Strauss-Frage aus drei Jahrzehnten* (Regensburg: Gustav Bosse, n.d. [foreword dated 1913]), 43–46. This essay, the first biographical sketch of Strauss, is an important source of information on Strauss's interest in Nietzsche. Specifically, Seidl noted that Strauss read passages from Nietzsche's major works aloud to him in the fall of 1893, and that Mackay's *Die Anarchisten* lay open when Seidl visited Strauss in Weimar on the day of the *Guntram* premiere (10 May 1893) (33–34).

26. See Arthur Seidl, "Moderner Geist in der dramatischen und instrumentalen Tonkunst," *Moderner Geist in der deutschen Tonkunst: Gedanken eines Kulturpsychologen um des Jahrhunderts Wende 1899/1900*, 2d ed. (Regensburg: Gustav Bosse, 1920), 104–15.

27. See Schmitz, *Richard Strauss*, 23–24.

28. See Franz Trenner, ed., *Richard Strauss–Ludwig Thuille: Ein Briefwechsel*, Veröffentlichungen der Richard-Strauss-Gesellschaft München, Bd. 4 (Tutzing: Hans Schneider, 1980), 128. The relevant excerpts are translated in Schuh, *Richard Strauss*, 287–88.

29. See Youmans, "Richard Strauss's *Guntram*," 114–67, 189–202.

30. "Nach der Absage an die Tradition: 'mein Leben bestimmt meines Geistes Gesetz; mein Gott spricht durch mich selbst zu mir!,' die selbst den treuen Freund (Friedhold) Alexander Ritter dem von ihm lange geförderten und gebilligten Werke entfremdete, war eben doch der Weg frei für unbehindert selbständiges Schaffen"; see Richard Strauss, "Betrachtungen zu Joseph Gregors 'Weltgeschichte des Theaters,'" in *Richard Strauss: Betrachtungen und Erinnerungen*, 2d ed., ed. Willi Schuh (Zurich: Atlantis, 1957), 176, 179.

31. "Ich möchte am liebsten immer mich selber komponieren"; see Willi Schuh, ed., *Richard Strauss/Hugo von Hofmannsthal: Briefwechsel* (Munich: Piper, 1990), 579.

32. "Seit 2000 Jahren immer das gleiche: Mord und Totschlag, Intrige des Subalternen gegen den Helden, Verlobung mit überwundenen Hindernissen oder Scheidung—das ist doch alles nicht interessant und so oft dagewesen. Neu aber ist—wie schon Goethe sagt, als er jedem Menschen empfiehlt, seine Memoiren zu schreiben—jede Individualität: nie in dieser Art dagewesen, nie mehr wiederkommend, und somit finde ich eine so hübsch und konsequent durchgeführte Charakterschilderung wie im *Intermezzo* interessanter als jede sogenannte Handlung" (see ibid., 670).

33. "Dieser mittelalterliche Heroismus: dies 'gemeinschaftliche Sterben' etc. etc. hat halt doch in Siegfrieds Trauermarsch seinen endgültigen verklärenden Abschluß gefunden—sollte man meinen! Statt Selbstzerfleischung—Selbstvollendung. Statt Napoleon—Goethe!"; see Willi Schuh and G. K. Kende, eds., *Richard Strauss–Clemens Krauss: Briefwechsel* (Munich: C. H. Beck, 1963), 36.

34. For a discussion of the *Till Eulenspiegel* drafts, see Kurt Wilhelm, "Die geplante Volksoper 'Till Eulenspiegel,'" in *Richard Strauss Jahrbuch* 1954, ed. Willi Schuh (Bonn: Boosey and Hawkes, 1953), 102–9 (abridged translation in Schuh, *Richard Strauss*, 503–8).

35. See letter of 14 June 1893 in Richard Strauss, *Briefe an die Eltern, 1882–1906*, ed. Willi Schuh (Zurich: Atlantis Verlag, 1954), 181–82.

36. For a discussion of the sources of *Ekke und Schnittlein*, see Stephan Kohler, "'Ein prachtvolles maul voll Klang': Bemerkungen zu Ernst von Wolzogens Operntext 'Coabbradibosimpur' nach einem Entwurf von Richard Strauss," in *Richard Strauss: Feuersnot* [program booklet for the 1980 production of the Bayerische Staatsoper], ed. Klaus Schultz and Stephan Kohler (Munich: Bayerische Staatsoper, 1980), 70–74.

37. Wilhelm, "Die geplante Volksoper," 102.

38. For an in-depth study of the three versions of Goethe's *Lila*, see Gottfried Diener, *Goethes "Lila": Heilung eines "Wahnsinns" durch "psychische Kur"* (Frankfurt: Athenäum, 1971).

39. See letters of 3 and 30 September 1895 in Trenner and Strauss, *Cosima Wagner–Richard Strauss*, 211, 215. See Schuh, *Richard Strauss*, 409–10, for excerpts, and 407–13, for a summary of the *Lila* project.

40. See Stephan Kohler, "'Glück auf zum Veralteten, Modernden, Rokokohaften!': Richard Strauss und Cosima Wagner als Bearbeiter von Goethes Singspiel 'Lila,'" *Jahrbuch der Bayerischen Staatsoper* 5 (1981/82):100–20.

41. Ibid., 106.

42. See Kristiansen, "Richard Strauss's 'Feuersnot,'" 400–60.

43. Strauss admired this painting at the Louvre in Paris on 9 March 1900, calling it a "fairy-tale painting" (*Märchenmalerei*) of sorts; see Rollo Myers, ed., *Richard Strauss and Romain Rolland: Correspondence, Diary, and Essays* (London: Calder and Boyars, 1968), 130. For a short summary of the plot, see Lyle F. Perusse, "*Der Rosenkavalier* and Watteau," *Musical Times* 119, no. 1630 (1978), 1042–44. Interestingly, Perusse sought to demonstrate that significant plot elements of *Der Rosenkavalier* are derived from the *Kythere* scenario and the literary sources of Watteau's painting.

44. Richard Strauss, "Kythere Ballettentwurf," ed. Willi Schuh, *Richard Strauss Jahrbuch* 1959–60 (Bonn: Boosey and Hawkes, 1960), 59–83 (here 62).

45. For transcriptions from the sketches, see Willi Schuh, "Das Szenarium und die musikalischen Skizzen zum Ballett 'Kythere,'" in *Richard Strauss Jahrbuch 1959–60* (Bonn: Boosey and Hawkes, 1960), 88–97.

46. See Claude Debussy, concert review in *Gil Bla*s of 30 March 1903, cited as "Plädoyer für Feuersnot" in *Richard Strauss: Feuersnot*, ed. Klaus Schultz and Stephan Kohler (Munich: Bayerische Staatsoper, 1980), 50; letter dated 6 June 1905 from Gustav to Alma Mahler, in Henry-Louis De La Grange and Günther Weiß, eds., *Ein Glück ohne Ruh': Die Briefe Gustav Mahlers an Alma* (Berlin: Wolf Jobst Siedler, 1995), 249; and Theodor W. Adorno, "Richard Strauss, Born June 11, 1864," trans. Samuel and Shierry Weber, *Perspectives of New Music* 2 (spring/summer 1966), 113–29.

47. See Richard Strauss, "Letzte Aufzeichnung," *Betrachtungen und Erinnerungen*, 2d ed., ed. Willi Schuh (Zurich: Atlantis, 1957), 180. Del Mar gave a partial translation in his *Richard Strauss*, 1:233–34.

48. For a detailed discussion of Wolzogen's ideas, see Kristiansen, "Richard Strauss's 'Feuersnot,'" 173–217; and for a summary of his stake in *Feuersnot*, see Kristiansen, "Parallel Lives."

49. Franz Trenner, "Richard Strauss und Ernst von Wolzogen," in *Richard Strauss Jahrbuch 1954*, ed. Willi Schuh (Bonn: Boosey and Hawkes, 1953), 110–21.

50. See Stephan Kohler, "Der Vater des 'Überbrettl': Ernst von Wolzogen im Briefwechsel mit Richard Strauss," *Jahrbuch der Bayerischen Staatsoper* 3 (1979–80), 100–22.

51. William Mann has made the stunning assertion that Wolzogen misdated his letter by a year, and that he and Strauss actually began their collaboration in March 1900, not 1899 (Mann, *Richard Strauss*, 24). The basis of this assertion is the

further assertion that *Also sprach Zarathustra* was not performed in Munich until 1900, thus making it impossible for Wolzogen to describe his reaction to a Munich *Also sprach Zarathustra* performance of 17 March 1899. Mann's information proves to be false, however, for *Also sprach Zarathustra* did indeed have its Munich premiere on 17 March 1899 under Franz Fischer as described by Wolzogen. A brief notice in the *Münchner Neueste Nachrichten* on 16 March 1899 (p. 2) announced the first Munich performance of the tone poem, and the review of the concert in the same paper on 19 March (p. 2) corroborates this.

52. Kohler, "Der Vater des 'Überbrettl,'" 102. See also Trenner and Strauss, *Cosima Wagner–Richard Strauss*, 118.

53. See Kohler, "Der Vater des 'Überbrettl,'" 101–3.

54. Trenner, "Richard Strauss und Ernst von Wolzogen," 111; and Mann, *Richard Strauss*, 23.

55. Del Mar, *Richard Strauss*, 1:202.

56. See Ernst von Wolzogen, *Wie ich mich ums Leben brachte: Erinnerungen und Erfahrungen* (Braunschweig: Georg Westermann, 1922), 153–65.

57. See Schuh, *Richard Strauss*, 423, 465–69, 473–77, 493–500.

58. See the oft-cited essay Richard Strauss, "Reminiscences of the First Performance of my Operas" (1942), in *Richard Strauss: Recollections and Reflections*, ed. Willi Schuh, trans. L. J. Lawrence (London: Boosey and Hawkes, 1953), 149; and Wolzogen, *Wie ich mich ums Leben brachte*, 165.

59. Kohler published the *Coabbradibosimpur* libretto (see Schultz and Kohler, *Richard Strauss: Feuersnot*, 75–107).

60. The libretto is in Wolzogen's *Nachlaß* (Ana 316) in the Handschriftenabteilung of the Bayerische Staatsbibliothek in Munich.

61. The score is located at the Musikbibliothek of the Bayerische Staatsbibliothek under the signature Mus. Ms. 15901. Since Wolzogen died in August 1934, he may simply not have had the requisite energy to complete the work.

62. See Carl Söhle's and Georg Richter's reviews of the Dresden premiere on 21 November 1901 in *Kritiken zu den Uraufführungen der Bühnenwerke von Richard Strauss*, ed. Franzpeter Messmer, Veröffentlichungen der Richard-Strauss-Gesellschaft München, Bd. 11 (Pfaffenhofen: W. Ludwig, 1989), 22, 20. For the reception of the Viennese premiere under Gustav Mahler on 29 January 1902, see Julie Dorn Morrison, "Mahler, Strauss, and *Feuersnot*: Emblems of Modernity at the Vienna Court Opera," *Opera Quarterly* 15, no. 3 (1999): 377–89; and for reviews of the Munich premiere on 23 December 1905, see Schultz and Kohler, *Richard Strauss: Feuersnot*, 43–53.

63. Ernst von Wolzogen, *Ansichten und Aussichten–Ein Erntebuch: Gesammelte Studien über Musik, Literatur und Theater* (Berlin: F. Fontane and Co., 1908), xiii.

64. Kohler, "Der Vater des 'Überbrettl,'" 101–2.

65. This essay was originally published in *Vossische Zeitung*, 16 December 1900; see also Wolzogen, *Ansichten und Aussichten*, 224–25. For a summary of the roles of Drachmann, Bierbaum, and others in anticipating or inspiring Wolzogen's cabaret, see Harold B. Segel, *Turn-of-the-Century Cabaret* (New York: Columbia University Press, 1987), 119–23.

66. Ernst von Wolzogen, *Verse zu meinem Leben* (Berlin: F. Fontane and Co., 1906), 133–34. Two decades after the end of the *Überbrettl*, in his autobiography, Wolzogen again emphasized that he did not take the initiative in the early stages, expressed surprise at being "selected" for such a project, and placed his first contact with it during the winter of 1899–1900—more than six months after leaving Munich (see Wolzogen, *Wie ich mich ums Leben brachte*, 194).

67. See Edward P. Harris, "Freedom and Degradation: Frank Wedekind's Career as Kabarettist," in *The Turn of the Century: German Literature and Art, 1890–1915*, ed. Gerald Chapple and Hans H. Schulte (Bonn: Bouvier, 1981), 493–506.

68. Fritz Strich, *Frank Wedekind: Gesammelte Briefe*, 2 vols. (Munich: G. Müller, 1924), 2:33, 2:45.

69. Wolzogen, *Wie ich mich ums Leben brachte*, 146.

70. "Die alte Sage hat in der Operndichtung modernen Geist angenommen; wenn man will, kann man ja die Art dieses 'modernen Geistes' mit dem Schlagwort 'Überbrettl' kennzeichnen. Zwei charakteristische Seiten des 'modernen Geistes' kommen im 'Überbrettl' speziell zur Geltung: einmal der jedem an der Grenze der Überkultur stehenden Zeitalter eigene Hang zur *Satyre*, und im engsten Zusammenhang damit eine Neigung zur freiesten und ungeniertesten Behandlung des im Mittelpunkt alles Lebens stehenden *sexuellen Problems*. Diese beiden Punkte bilden auch die innere Grundlage der Dichtung zur 'Feuersnot'" (Schmitz, *Richard Strauss*, 35).

71. "Da fiel mir die flämische Sage 'Das erloschene Feuer von Audenarde' [*sic*] in die Hand und gab mir die Idee, ein kleines Intermezzo *gegen* das Theater zu schreiben, mit persönlichen Motiven und kleiner Rache an der lieben Vaterstadt, wo, wie vor dreißig Jahren der große Richard I., nunmehr auch der kleine Richard III. (einen 'Zweiten' gibt es nicht, hat Hans von Bülow einmal gesagt) so wenig erfreuliche Erfahrungen gemacht hatte" (Strauss, "Reminiscences of the First Performance of my Operas," 149).

72. See Max Steinitzer, *Richard Strauss* (Berlin: Schuster and Loeffler, 1911), 84.

73. Johann Wilhelm Wolf, ed., *Niederländische Sagen* (Leipzig: Brockhaus, 1843), no. 407.

74. See Del Mar, *Richard Strauss*, 1:203–4, for a translation of this letter.

75. Schmitz, *Richard Strauss*, 37. See also Roland Tenschert, "Autobiographisches im Schaffen von Richard Strauss" [1939], in *Straussiana aus vier Jahrzehnten*, ed. Jürgen Schaarwächter (Tutzing: Hans Schneider, 1994), 119.

76. "daß er seinen ganzen Monolog in recht übermütigem, überlegenen Tone halten soll, überhaupt das Burleske, freche, unverschämte, parodistische Element im ganzen Werke recht zu betonen." See Friedrich von Schuch, *Richard Strauss, Ernst von Schuch, und Dresdens Oper* (Leipzig: Breitkopf and Härtel, 1952), 61.

77. Trenner and Strauss, *Cosima Wagner–Richard Strauss*, 243.

78. See Schmitz, *Richard Strauss*, 37. See Kristiansen, "Parallel Lives" for a more detailed discussion of this and other anti-idealistic issues.

79. See Richard Strauss, "Reminiscences of My Youth and Years of Apprenticeship," in *Richard Strauss: Recollections and Reflections*, ed. Willi Schuh, trans. L. J.

Lawrence (London: Boosey and Hawkes, 1953), 140; and Wolzogen, *Wie ich mich ums Leben brachte*, 48.

80. Christopher Morris, "What the Conductor Saw: Sex, Fantasy, and the Orchestra in Strauss's *Feuersnot*," *Journal of Musicological Research* 16, no. 2 (1996): 91.

81. "Wenn die liebe sich mit dem zauber des genius vereint, dann muß auch dem ärgsten philister ein licht aufgehen!" (Kohler, "Der Vater des 'Überbrettl,'" 104).

82. Mann, *Richard Strauss*, 37.

83. "Alle schöpferische Kraft entspringt der Sinnlichkeit. Der schöpferische Geist besitzt die Zauberkraft, aus nichts etwas Lebendiges zu gestalten. Wenn nun dieser Zauber durch das Feuer der Sinne wirksam wird, so habe ich das gute Recht, dieses Feuer an mich zu reißen, wo immer ich es finde. Ich habe diesem künstlerischen Übermut dichterischen Ausdruck gegeben in dem Singgedicht 'Feuersnot.' . . . Jeder ächte Künstler ist ein Prometheus, der Menschen schafft nach dem Ebenbilde Gottes. Aber er braucht seinen Geschöpfen nicht das ferne Himmelslicht zu stehlen, er kann das Feuer von der Erde nehmen" (Wolzogen, *Wie ich mich ums Leben brachte*, 146–47).

84. See letters of 14 October, 26 November, and 18 December 1900 in Strauss, *Briefe an die Eltern*, 236–40.

85. "Ende April ist aber für ein ernstes Werk, das sich *vorerst* doch noch mehr an wirkliche Kunstkenner und musikalische Feinschmecker wendet und wenn überhaupt, doch nur allmählich ein breiteres Publikum sich gewinnen kann, derart ungünstig, daß ich an Euer Exzellenz die ergebenste Bitte richten möchte, die Aufführung meiner Oper auf den nächsten Herbst zu verschieben." See Julius Kapp, "Richard Strauss und die Berliner Oper," in *Die Staatsoper Berlin 1919 bis 1925: Ein Almanach*, ed. Julius Kapp (Stuttgart: Deutsche Verlags-Anstalt, 1925), 80.

86. "Die neuen Momente (wenigstens gegenüber der normalen Operntradition mit ihren Rittern, Banditen, Zigeunern, Türken, sicilianischen Bauern, Troubadours, Hofnarren) lagen zuerst im neuen Genre einer Dialektoper, im Mut, darin persönliches, polemisches Bekenntnis des Autors abzulegen, in ihrem leicht satirischen Charakter. . . . Man hat der 'Feuersnot' stets die Stilvermischung der harmlosen Posse mit Kunrads Strafpredigt zum Vorwurf [gemacht]. Die Richtigkeit dieses Einwandes zugegeben—ohne diese wäre das Ganze doch zu simpel geworden, und mir war doch die Kunradrede die Hauptsache und die übrige Handlung lustiges Beiwerk" (Strauss, "Betrachtungen zu Joseph Gregors 'Weltgeschichte des Theaters,'" 179–80).

87. See Erich Urban's review in *Kritiken zu den Uraufführungen der Bühnenwerke von Richard Strauss*, ed. Franzpeter Messmer, Veröffentlichungen der Richard-Strauss-Gesellschaft München, Bd. 11 (Pfaffenhofen: W. Ludwig, 1989), 23; and Fritz Gysi, *Richard Strauss* (Potsdam: Athenaion, 1934), 82–83.

88. "Heio! da spukts! Da heb' ich mich fort, dünkt mich nicht ganz geheuer am Ort" (78).

89. See Kristiansen, "Richard Strauss's 'Feuersnot,'" 400–60. Nervousness (*Nervosität*) was a central topic in the cultural debate of the 1890s and beyond. Arthur Seidl, for example, spoke of a "nerve culture" (Nervenkultur) around 1900

(see his "Was ist modern?" in *Moderner Geist in der deutschen Tonkunst: Gedanken eines Kulturpsychologen um des Jahrhunderts Wende 1899/1900*, 2d ed. [Regensburg: Gustav Bosse, 1926], 14).

90. Ernst Otto Nodnagel, *Jenseits von Wagner und Liszt: Profile und Perspektiven* (Königsberg: Druck und Verlag der Ostpreußischen Druckerei und Verlagsanstalt, 1902), 126, 186.

91. See Steinitzer, *Richard Strauss*, 84; and Werner Bitter, "Studien zur Entwicklung der deutschen komischen Oper im 20. Jahrhundert" (Ph.D. diss., University of Leipzig, 1932), 78, 119, 125, 135, 141.

92. See Urban, "Review of *Feuersnot*," 25; Oscar Bie, *Die moderne Musik und Richard Strauss* (Berlin: Bard Marquardt and Co., 1906), 65; and Schmitz, *Richard Strauss*, 56.

93. *Der Barbier von Bagdad* premiered with Liszt's help in Weimar in 1858. Failing there due to intrigue, it lay dormant until Felix Mottl revived it in his own Wagnerian reorchestration in 1884, after which it slowly became a staple of the repertoire. Cornelius's original version did not reappear until 1904. Most commentators consider the work to be the birth of modern comic opera, as it was the first to abandon the number principle and use the chromatic harmony of the New Germans.

94. "So etwas wie unsere Dienerchöre aus dem Barbier von Bagdad, die Kinderchöre und den großen Dunkelchor in Feuersnot hatten die Cölner auf ihrem Theater noch nicht erlebt" (Kapp, "Richard Strauss und die Berliner Oper," 83–84).

95. Steinitzer, *Richard Strauss*, 151.

96. Stephan Kohler, "'Ein Operntext ist keine Kinderfibel': Zur Geschichte des 'Feuersnot'-Librettos," in *Richard Strauss: Feuersnot*, ed. Klaus Schultz and Stephan Kohler (Munich: Bayerische Staatsoper, 1980), 30–34.

97. See John Warrack, "The Sources and Genesis of the Text," in *Richard Wagner: Die Meistersinger von Nürnberg*, ed. John Warrack (Cambridge: Cambridge University Press, 1994), 12.

98. See Myers, *Richard Strauss and Romain Rolland*, 125.

99. "seit langer Zeit erwartete musikalische Lustspiel unserer Zeit"; "einen neuen Weg der Spieloper weisen" (see letters of 15 December 1913 and 20 June 1912 in Franz Strauss and Alice Strauss, with Willi Schuh, eds., *Richard Strauss und Hugo von Hofmannsthal, Briefwechsel: Gesamtausgabe* [Zurich: Atlantis Verlag, 1952], 249, 184).

100. "Es lebe die politisch-satirisch-parodistische Operette!" (ibid., 344–45).

101. "eine *ganz moderne*, absolut realistische Charakter- und Nervenkomödie"; "ganz ins Gebiet der unwagnerschen Spiel- Gemüts- und Menschenoper" (see letters of 25 May and 16 August 1916 in ibid., 342, and 358–59). The titles *Schwarzer Domino*, *Maurer und Schlosser*, and *Teufels Anteil* are the German translations of *Le Domino noir*, *Le Maçon*, and *La Part du diable*, all products of the Auber–Scribe partnership.

102. See, for example, Hellmuth Christian Wolff, *Geschichte der komischen Oper von den Anfängen bis zur Gegenwart* (Wilhelmshaven: Heinrichshofen, 1981), 119–79.

103. See letter of 4 September 1917 in Strauss and Strauss, *Richard Strauss und Hugo von Hofmannsthal*, 391.

104. "die Frau als Hochstaplerin oder die Grande Dame als Spion"; "die geborne komische Oper" (see letters of 31 October 1931 and 24 June 1932 in Willi Schuh, ed., *Richard Strauss, Stefan Zweig: Briefwechsel* [Frankfurt am Main: Fischer, 1957], 8, 18.

105. "leichte mythologische Operette"; "Wie wär's mit einer lustigen komischen?" (see letters of 15 February 1937 and 8 March 1939 in Roland Tenschert, ed., *Richard Strauss und Joseph Gregor: Briefwechsel, 1934–1949* (Salzburg: O. Müller, 1955), 79, 174.

106. See Robert Bailey, "The Structure of the *Ring* and its Evolution," *Nineteenth-Century Music* 1 (1977):48–61.

107. Edmund Wachten, "Das Formproblem in den sinfonischen Dichtungen von Richard Strauss—mit besonderer Berücksichtigung seiner Bühnenwerke" (Ph.D. diss., University of Berlin, 1933). For another excerpt from Wachten's dissertation see "Der einheitliche Grundzug der Straußschen Formgestaltung," *Zeitschrift für Musikwissenschaft* 16, no. 5–6 (1934), 257–74. Despite his thorough treatment of Strauss's key associations, Wachten's dissertation receives only a footnote in modern treatments of the topic, a circumstance explained by the work's publication history and overgeneralizing claims. In the preface to the published portion, Wachten explained that the publication consists only of selective parts of the first half of his dissertation, whereas the second half—now lost—had provided detailed analyses of the works. Wachten's overly ambitious claim consists of a list of one or two associative meanings for each of the twenty-four keys—or what he calls the "Straussian system of key determination" (System der Strauss'schen Tonartenbestimmung).

108. Willi Schuh, *Hugo von Hofmannsthal und Richard Strauss: Legende und Wirklichkeit* (Munich: Carl Hanser, 1964), 15–35; and Eva-Maria Axt, "Das Ineinanderwirken von Bewusstem und Unbewusstem—Zum Stimmungs- und Symbolcharakter der Tonarten bei Richard Strauss," *Richard Strauss-Blätter* 29 (1993): 7–21.

109. See Kenneth Birkin, *Richard Strauss: Arabella*, Cambridge Opera Handbooks (Cambridge: Cambridge University Press, 1989), 75–90; Derrick Puffett, "The Music of *Elektra*: Some Preliminary Thoughts," in *Richard Strauss: Elektra*, ed. Derrick Puffett, Cambridge Opera Handbooks (Cambridge: Cambridge University Press, 1990), 33–43; his postscript to Roland Tenschert's "Strauss as Librettist," in *Richard Strauss: Salome*, ed. Derrick Puffett Cambridge Opera Handbooks (Cambridge: Cambridge University Press, 1989), 45–50; and "'Lass Er die Musi, wo sie ist': Pitch Specificity in Strauss," in *Richard Strauss and His World*, ed. Bryan Gilliam (Princeton, N.J.: Princeton University Press, 1992), 138–63, especially 148–52; Bryan Gilliam, *Richard Strauss's Elektra*, Studies in Musical Genesis and Structure (Oxford: Clarendon Press, 1991), 67–106; and Youmans, "Richard Strauss's *Guntram*," 343–66.

110. See Schuh, *Hugo von Hofmannsthal und Richard Strauss*, 15–20 and appendix (facsimile of four pages of Strauss's annotations in a fragment of the

Rosenkavalier text); Charlotte Erwin, "Richard Strauss's Presketch Planning for *Ariadne auf Naxos*," *Musical Quarterly* 67 (1981): 348–65; and Bryan Gilliam, "Strauss's Preliminary Opera Sketches: Thematic Fragments and Symphonic Continuity," *Nineteenth-Century Music* 9, no. 3 (1986): 176–88, and *Richard Strauss's Elektra*, 107–63. Furthermore, Richard Specht reported seeing Strauss's annotations in the *Die Frau ohne Schatten* libretto, which were almost all keys (see his *Richard Strauss und sein Werk*, 2 vols. [Leipzig: E. P. Tal, 1921], 1:81).

111. See Youmans, "Richard Strauss's *Guntram*," 343–66.

112. Nonetheless, conspicuous appearances of E major for amorous purposes, frequently as an isolated harmony, seem almost habitual to Strauss already at this point. Thus, the harmony appears at the words *Flammensprung* (leap through the flames; 38–39), *Hochzeit* (wedding; 56), and *Mittsommernacht* (midsummer night; 88).

113. For the "Subendfeuer" chords see pages 3, 6, 8, 30, 32, 36, 43, 44, 45, 64–65, 66, 70, 71, 75, 88, 96, 132, 148–49, 198, 200–01; for the children's chorus pages 5, 30, 33, 59, 69, 73, 116, 200–01; for D-minor instances of Diemut's motive see pages 50, 56, 61, 71, 82, 109, 113, 193–95.

114. For quotations from other operas see page 152 (the Valhalla motive in D-flat major from *Das Rheingold*), pages 155–56 (the Dutchman motive in D minor from *Der fliegende Holländer*), and page 156 (the war motive in C minor from *Guntram*). For a brief overview of Strauss's treatment of quotations, see Puffett, "'Lass Er die Musi, wo sie ist,'" 140–47. For "Kyrieleis," see pages 19, 127; for the "Kätzlein" motive, see pages 101–2, 107, 130–32.

115. For discussions of Wagner's use of associative tonality besides that of Bailey see Patrick McCreless, *Wagner's Siegfried: Its Drama, History, and Music* (Ann Arbor, Mich.: UMI Research Press, 1982), "Ernst Kurth and the Analysis of the Chromatic Music of the Late Nineteenth Century," *Music Theory Spectrum* 5 (1983): 56–75, and "Schenker and the Norns," in *Analyzing Opera: Verdi and Wagner*, ed. Carolyn Abbate and Roger Parker (Berkeley: University of California Press, 1989), 276–97; and Warren Darcy, *Wagner's Das Rheingold* (Oxford: Oxford University Press, 1993), 218; and see 45–58 for a convenient summary of the various analytical positions on tonality and leitmotiv.

116. Examples of associatively loaded entrances in Wagner include those of Elsa and Lohengrin in *Lohengrin* (A-flat and A major); the giants, Loge, and Erda in *Das Rheingold* (F major/minor, F-sharp major/minor, and C-sharp minor, respectively); Brünnhilde in *Die Walküre* (B minor); Gutrune in *Götterdämmerung* (G major); and Parsifal (B-flat major).

117. See Bailey, "The Structure of the *Ring* and Its Evolution," 53.

118. For a history and discussion of the term, see Thomas Grey, "*Wie ein rother Faden*: On the Origins of 'Leitmotif' as Critical Construct and Musical Practice," in *Music Theory in the Age of Romanticism*, ed. Ian Bent (Cambridge: Cambridge University Press, 1996), 187–210.

119. Early guides to the tone poems, on the other hand, did label motives à la Wolzogen. The idea of motives representing characters, emotions, or events was, of course, central to the genre of the tone poem, as countless commentaries on these

works have demonstrated. As John Williamson noted in his study of *Also sprach Zarathustra*, Hans Merian stated in 1899 that Strauss had transferred the leitmotiv from music drama to the tone poem, and leitmotivic accounts of this repertoire soon became standard. See Williamson, *Strauss: "Also sprach Zarathustra"* (Cambridge: Cambridge University Press, 1993), 73; and Hans Merian, *Richard Strauss' Tondichtung "Also sprach Zarathustra": Eine Studie über die moderne Programmsymphonie* (Leipzig: Carl Meyers graphisches Institut, 1899), 10–13.

120. See Wolfgang Jordan, "Guntram: Musikdrama in drei Akten," 11–48, and Arthur Smolian, "Feuersnot," 49–77, in *Richard Strauss: Musikdramen*, ed. Georg Gräner (Berlin: Schlesingersche Buch- und Musikhandlung; n.d. [circa 1912–13]); and Ziegler, *Richard Strauss*, 3–55; and Schmitz, *Richard Strauss*, 19–43. Richard Specht included elaborate motivic catalogues with his biography. Curiously, the motivic tables for *Guntram, Feuersnot, Salome,* and *Ariadne* use no labels, whereas those for *Elektra, Der Rosenkavalier,* and *Die Frau ohne Schatten* do. Specht's analyses, however, uniformly attach semantic tags to motives. (*Thementafeln* enclosed as separate booklets)

121. Alfred Schattmann, *Richard Strauss: Der Rosenkavalier* (Berlin: A. Fürstner, 1911).

122. Ibid., ix.

123. Derrick Puffett, "*Salome* as Music Drama," in *Richard Strauss: Salome*, ed. Derrick Puffett, Cambridge Opera Handbooks (Cambridge: Cambridge University Press, 1989), 58–87.

124. See Youmans, "Richard Strauss's *Guntram*," 289, 294, 301.

125. Ernst Krause, *Richard Strauss: Gestalt und Werk*, 5th ed. (Leipzig: Breitkopf and Härtel, 1975), 150.

126. The particell is at the Münchner Stadtbibliothek along with the autograph score, and the annotated libretto is at the RSA.

127. See Mann, *Richard Strauss*, 28; and Del Mar, *Richard Strauss*, 1:207. For all occurrences, see pages 7, 16, 19, 21–23, 28, 119–20, 123, 126, 132–33, 156.

128. See Del Mar, *Richard Strauss*, 1:224.

129. For the motive and its variants, see pages 76–78, 81–82, 85, 93–95, 104–5, 109–11, 153, 161, 179–80, 193–94.

8

The Late Operas of Richard Strauss

James L. Zichowicz

Compared to many other composers, Richard Strauss stands out because of his long career that extended from the late nineteenth century to the mid-twentieth century and encompassed several changes in musical style and taste. From the Wagnerian affinities of his early years, Strauss evolved his own style with his mature operas. During the first quarter of the twentieth century, he composed at a time when musical style faced various innovations, including reactions against the fundamental tonal syntax that had been the lingua franca of Western-European music culture since the eighteenth century. Although Strauss absorbed some of these stylistic innovations in his own music, at some point he chose to go no further and continued to write in the idiom that is uniquely his own.

As a result, assessments of Strauss's late operas should not necessarily emphasize the growth or maturing of a style that found its flowering at the end of his life, but rather an extended maturity in which the composer faced other, personal challenges in continuing to compose in a style that obviously continued to please him and his audiences over many decades. This differs from the situation that exists for other composers, for whom musicologists might speculate what might have happened had Mozart or Weber or Debussy lived longer to compose further works. Rather, Strauss's long career offers a unique glimpse of a composer who faced various shifts in musical taste and style, waves of innovation, and other, often competing trends, and responded to such forces in his own way.

At a time when he could have remained content with his reputation and the legacy of his earlier compositions, Strauss continued to compose new works. At the beginning of the 1930s, Strauss was the preeminent opera composer in Germany, and his works were known throughout the world. Unlike the obstacles he faced earlier in his career, when it seemed that he set out to shock audiences with operas based on the violent stories of Salome and Elektra, he faced other kinds of challenges later in his life because of his almost iconic status in culture. As a composer whose new works were anticipated as national events, Strauss needed to reinvent himself with each new composition. Whether he succeeded is another matter. Yet his later years are marked by an ongoing quest to find the proper subjects for opera. For years, this had been an issue, even when Strauss had as his librettist one of the finest authors of the time, Hugo von Hofmannsthal. Yet the search for a suitable subject for opera and its optimal presentation in the libretto intensified even further later in Strauss's career. Without a reliable collaborator like Hofmannsthal, Strauss was critical of his later librettists; and with Joseph Gregor, Strauss became more deeply involved in arriving at the librettos that he was setting than occurred with his earlier operas. The situation resembles that which existed between Verdi and several of his librettists, such as Piave, and it shows how sensitive Strauss was at the nature of the sung text. At the same time, Strauss continually sought to address the proper balance between music and text, and this otherwise internal struggle of an opera composer became the overt substance of his last opera, *Capriccio.*

Unlike Strauss's earlier operas, especially works like *Salome, Elektra, Der Rosenkavalier,* and, to a degree, *Ariadne auf Naxos,* the later ones are neither as well-known nor performed as regularly. One element that arises in the assessments of Strauss's late works is his complicity with the Nazi regime and the taint of Nazism that became associated with music Strauss composed at that time. For some, the fact that Strauss held a post in the Nazi government and did not flee the country becomes intertwined with the criticism of the music he wrote during the Third Reich. The matter sometimes becomes simplified in the question of whether Strauss was a Nazi;[1] however, this line of discussion should not color considerations of the musical content of the works he composed during Hitler's regime.[2]

The late operas to be considered here (see Figure 8.1) include all the works in this genre that Strauss completed after *Arabella* (1929–32) his last collaboration with Hugo von Hofmannsthal: *Die schweigsame Frau* (1933–35); *Friedenstag* (1935–36); *Daphne* (1936–37); *Die Liebe der Danae* (1938–40); and *Capriccio* (1940–41). The late operas differ from each other in style and subject matter, but they have in common the absence of Strauss's longtime collaborator, Hofmannsthal.[3] This element is critical when it comes to understanding Strauss's efforts late in his career. At this point in his career, the onus was on Strauss to diligently seek out suitable

FIGURE 8.1
The Late Operas of Richard Strauss

Title	Librettist	Source	Composed	Premiere
Arabella	Hugo von Hofmannsthal	Original libretto	1929–32; rev. 1939	1933
Die schweigsame Frau	Stefan Zweig	Ben Jonson, *Epicene*	1933–35	1935
Friedenstag	Joseph Gregor	Pedro Calderón de la Barca, *El sitio de Breda* (as adapated by Stefan Zweig)	1935–36	1938
Daphne	Joseph Gregor	Classical mythology	1936–37	1938
Die Liebe der Danae	Joseph Gregor	Classical mythology	1938–40	(1944); 1952
Capriccio	Clemens Krauss and Richard Strauss	Antonio Salieri, *Prima la musica e poi le parole*	1940–41	1942

subjects for his operas. No longer the rebel, innovator, and Wunderkind, Strauss was clearly the embodiment of the old guard in the 1930s and 1940s. He did not pursue the modernist trends of his day by composing *Zeitoper* (contemporary opera) like those of Hindemith or cabaret-influenced stage works like those of Weill or by otherwise using avant-garde approaches to opera. Rather, Strauss adhered to the traditions that had taken opera to the twentieth century in lieu of striking out in completely new directions, as he had when he had begun his career as a composer and shocked the world with such works as *Salome* and *Elektra*.

STRAUSS AFTER HOFMANNSTHAL

Strauss's collaboration with Hofmannsthal began with *Elektra* (1906–8), which was given its premiere in 1909. Their working relationship resulted in many fine works, especially *Der Rosenkavalier* (1909–11), which is, perhaps, his most successful opera. In fact, various commentators call attention to the efforts of Strauss and Hofmannsthal in the 1920s as being an attempt to repeat, if not surpass, the success they experienced with *Der Rosenkavalier*. With *Arabella* (1929–32), the pair returned to the Viennese milieu of the earlier opera, albeit at a later period, and hoped to create in *Arabella* a work as appealing as *Der Rosenkavalier*. Notwithstanding the succès d'estime of *Arabella,* which Strauss completed after Hofmannsthal's death, Strauss set out to find a suitable talented author with whom he could work.

These efforts at first resulted in the collaboration with Stefan Zweig, which was in itself promising. When Hofmannsthal died in July 1929, Strauss had sketched most of the first act of *Arabella*, but the composer had not worked through the text of the last two acts with the librettist. The idea of revising the text emerged, but Strauss essentially retained the libretto as Hofmannsthal had left it rather than pursue a drastically revised text in the hands of another writer.

Even while he was completing work on *Arabella*, Strauss began to look for a librettist for his next opera. In 1931, Strauss met with Zweig, who already had attained some prestige as a dramatist but was mainly known as a novelist and writer of biographical studies, and they talked about several ideas for operas. During their discussion Zweig mentioned the possibility of adapting Ben Jonson's play *Epicene, or the Silent Woman*, and Strauss was responsive to the idea. They quickly came to agree on this project, and Zweig began to work on the libretto while Strauss proceeded with completing the final details on the last collaboration between himself and Hofmannsthal, of *Arabella*. While the works overlap, as occurred with other operas of Strauss, the styles and themes did not blur into each other. The tone of the latter comedy is hardly derivative of the earlier work, but has its own identity. Moreover, it is one of the more successful comic operas of the twentieth century.

Die schweigsame Frau is the kind of comedy involving love and deception that has a long history in opera. By choosing Jonson's play as the source for this opera, Strauss and Zweig agreed on a story that had essentially been set by Gaetano Donizetti in *Don Pasquale.*[4] In adapting the play, Zweig refrained from making it contemporaneous, choosing instead to retain a historical setting. He did move the work from the seventeenth century to the eighteenth, which gave Strauss some latitude for enhancing the locale musically. At the same time, this aspect of *Die schweigsame Frau* recalls the predilection Hofmannsthal had for the same period, especially as found with *Ariadne auf Naxos.*

Of Strauss's late operas, the genuine comedy at the heart of *Die schweigsame Frau* sets it apart from the other works, which have at their core more earnest aesthetics. Even with Jonson's ribald humor toned down in this adaptation, Zweig's libretto is a human comedy that concerns the expressed desires of a curmudgeon and challenges the all-too-common tendency of prejudging situations that are new and different. It is a charming opera that finds Strauss picking up where he had left off with Hofmannsthal and producing a worthy successor to the other operas he had composed.

The collaboration with Zweig boded well for what would have been a natural partnership, but the political situation in Germany soon had its effect. When Hitler took power in 1933, the chances of successfully producing *Die schweigsame Frau* were compromised, since Strauss had collaborated with a Jew. Despite his status as the preeminent opera composer in Germany, it was a struggle for Strauss to bring this work to the stage, and this was complicated further by Strauss's role as head of the Reichsmusikkammer. Strauss eventually succeeded in having *Die schweigsame Frau* performed—but for only three performances—and other projects he had discussed with Zweig were essentially suspended. In the course of the premiere of *Die schweigsame Frau,* even the inclusion of Zweig's name on the playbill caused the dismissal of a member of the theater staff, and Strauss's involvement with Zweig became more controversial. Although it may seem circumspect, Strauss urged his colleague not to publicly acknowledge his work on opera librettos with him, and Zweig offered to contribute librettos for Strauss's operas under the name of a known and accepted individual whose involvement would not be questioned by the Third Reich. This essentially ended a promising partnership, including any future operas.

In working on this opera with Zweig, Strauss did, however, rise to the occasion and completed a score that rivaled his work on *Arabella* in vivifying the drama. Strauss also composed the opera almost as quickly as *Der Rosenkavalier*, and if this was his response to a libretto by Zweig, the cessation of their collaboration is even more tragic. The opera failed to secure a place on the stage anywhere in Europe in those troubled times, despite its exuberant music and excellent libretto. Nevertheless, *Die schweigsame Frau* stands as testimony to a partnership that might have rivaled that of Strauss and Hofmannsthal.

STRAUSS AFTER ZWEIG

Strauss's subsequent work owes a debt to his work with Zweig. Soon after completing *Die schweigsame Frau,* Strauss was interested in pursuing another project he had discussed with Zweig, an adaptation of Giovanni Battista Casti's libretto for Antonio Salieri's opera *Prima la musica e poi le parole*. While Strauss would only take this up a decade later in the opera *Capriccio*, another suggestion of Zweig's caught his attention, an adaptation of a play by Pedro Calderón de la Barca,[5] which became the basis for *Friedenstag*. Zweig produced the first version of the libretto for *Friedenstag*, and Gregor worked with him behind the scenes on the revisions. Strauss composed this work between 1935 and 1936, and *Friedenstag* received its premiere in 1938.

In choosing the Calderón play Strauss found a historical setting to escape contemporary political concerns and to provide a vehicle for Zweig's pacifist leanings. In adapting the drama about the Thirty Years' War as an opera, Strauss asked Zweig to integrate a love story into Calderón's plot, and the result should have been a story that is typical—and timeless—for opera. By the time he was ready to work on it, however, Strauss had been forced to sever his relationship with Zweig and had found another writer to work on the project, the Austrian theater historian Joseph Gregor.

Gregor was not nearly the dramatist that Zweig was, but Strauss found ways to work with him. In pursuing work on *Friedenstag*, Strauss rewrote Gregor's dialogue and even had Zweig read the new version. Work occupied Strauss from 1934 through 1936. It did not receive its premiere until 1938, and at that time Strauss planned to have the single-act *Friedenstag* performed on the same program with his next opera, *Daphne*, another one-act work.

The latter intention was not fully realized, and after the initial double-bill, the operas were left to be performed separately. *Friedenstag* was left to stand on its own. Perhaps this is why *Friedenstag* was never appreciated as strongly as Strauss's other works. Stylistically, it is a departure from Strauss's other late operas, since it does not retain the conversational idiom usually associated with those works. At the same time, the harmonic language is more static and less colorful than usually found with Strauss's mature works. It is not clear whether Strauss used this idiom to evoke a starker setting, but the dark and somber tone through much of the work remains one of the weaker aspects of this opera. At the same time, the political situation at the time made this work seem more like a piece of propaganda than anything else.

In comparison, Strauss's *Daphne* is markedly different and seems to be a return to the style one often associates with the composer, and *Daphne* is a far stronger opera than *Friedenstag*. Although opinions differ about the quality of the libretto, it is clear that Strauss had to work harder with Gregor than with either Hofmannsthal or Zweig. Gregor submitted his draft of the libretto to Zweig before showing it to Strauss, and even with Zweig's intervention, Strauss rejected the first version. Gregor's second version failed to please Strauss, who worked with the author on yet another draft of the libretto. Gregor's conception of *Daphne* as the second part of a double-bill with *Friedenstag* undoubtedly influenced his thoughts about the work. Likewise, the idea of putting *Daphne* on the same program as *Friedenstag* prompted Gregor to insist on a choral finale, similar to the one that he used to conclude *Friedenstag*. In dealing with this matter, Strauss sought the advice of the conductor Clemens Krauss, and Krauss confirmed Strauss's conception of the ending as an instrumental number rather than a choral piece. While short on words, the finale of *Daphne* is one of Strauss's more effective scenes. Without a single line of text, he uses the orchestra to depict the transformation of the beautiful Daphne into a tree in an ending that elicits the skillful tone painting that was Strauss's stock-in-trade and yet seems fresh and new in this late work. This scene seems to serve as a summing up of Strauss's creative work. Here the consummate composer of opera uses his skill as a composer of tone poems to evoke in an instrumental milieu what could only be suggested with words, and the deft command of the orchestra allowed him to transform Daphne into a tree without relying entirely on any artifice of stagecraft to create the illusion.

On the whole, *Daphne* is regarded as one of Strauss's finest works.[6] In retelling the story of Daphne, Strauss and Gregor combined various strands of myth into a single narrative. At the core of *Daphne* is the story of the shepherd Leukippos's infatuation with Daphne, whom the god Apollo also loves. When Apollo makes himself known to the worshipers of Dionysius—a god whose cult rivals his own—he is ready to reveal his divinity to the mortals, and this leads into the scene in which Daphne recognizes Apollo in his glory, which culminates in the duet in which they express their infatuation for each other. Daphne is steadfast in her love for the human, Leukippos, and Apollo eventually kills the mortal in order to possess Daphne. Daphne does not yield to Apollo, and she is ultimately changed into a tree to become part of nature, which she had also adored. In the ensuing scene, Strauss is clearly mastering the drama and the text, and he continues to sustain the mood through the final scene, in which Daphne is transformed into a tree. In this work Strauss's experience in both tone poems and opera merge, and the result is an extraordinary opera. At an age when other composers would rest on their laurels, Strauss created an opera that stands among his best.

At its premiere in 1938 *Daphne* enjoyed more acclaim than its companion piece *Friedenstag*, and Strauss continued to compose in this genre. Again relying on Greek myth for inspiration, he worked with Gregor on a project that Hofmannsthal had proposed years before: a conflation of the myths of Danae and Midas. In this work, they attempted to combine the two stories into a single text, with the image of gold binding it together. The shower of gold with which Zeus visited the beautiful Danae has its parallel in the golden touch granted to King Midas, and the human beings must deal with the consequences of both situations in the opera *Die Liebe der Danae*. It is uncertain how strongly Strauss felt compelled to complete a work he had once considered with Hofmannsthal or if he remembered it at all.

Strauss asked Gregor to use Hofmannsthal's scenario as the basis for the libretto, and Gregor produced a text that combined his own ideas with those of Strauss's earlier collaborator. This did not meet Strauss's approval and, as had occurred with *Daphne*, the composer required substantial revisions. It is as though he wanted to complete the work fully in Hofmannsthal's spirit, and this almost sacrificed the working relationship with Gregor. He rejected Gregor's first version of the libretto and criticized the writer about the form of the work and the quality of the language used in it. As with *Daphne*, Strauss wanted to sharpen the focus of Gregor's libretto for *Die Liebe der Danae*, but he must have had something in mind that he did not express clearly to Gregor or that simply did not coincide with Gregor's conception of the work. No matter what the reasons were, Strauss and Gregor clashed, and the sensitive Gregor avoided contact with the composer by absenting himself from the premiere of *Daphne* in 1938 in Dresden. To complete work on *Die Liebe der Danae,* however, Strauss even went so far as to draw the conductor Clemens Krauss into the matter. Strauss eventually completed the score of *Die Liebe der Danae* in 1940.

Despite its difficult gestation, *Die Liebe der Danae* ranks high among Strauss's late works. It is an effective opera for its blending of fantastic mythic elements with the depiction of purely human emotion. While the convention in opera of the deus ex machina was often used to resolve an otherwise difficult or twisted situation, Strauss reversed the norm and presented the god Zeus as one of the problematic elements in the plot, and it is his departure from the human sphere that helps to resolve the plot satisfactorily. In fact, Zeus's farewell to the human world is one of the supreme moments of the opera. It simultaneously echoes the departure of Wotan in Richard Wagner's *Siegfried* and functions, in a sense, as the composer's own farewell to opera. The scene, which occurs late in the opera, is one of its strongest elements, and in using it, Strauss allowed the various strands of the plot to resolve, if not happily, then at least satisfactorily, with the character of Danae having the final word in the story.

As to the music itself, *Die Liebe der Danae* remains one of Strauss's finer efforts, and the force of Strauss's musical imagination is as strong in this work as it was two decades earlier. Strauss's compositional skill never weakened late in his career, and the score to this opera is clear evidence of its vigor as he used his command of the orchestra to depict the descent of Zeus and, likewise, contributed to his portrayal of the human characters through musical, as well as textual, elements.

In some respects this opera represents Strauss's farewell to composing, since it was his last large-scale work. It could have been that it was apparent to Strauss that this would be his final opera. In a self-referential gesture toward opera repertoire, Strauss depicted Zeus in a way that resembles Wagner's portrayal of Wotan in *Siegfried*. Although Wagner did not depict Wotan as consciously taking leave of the world of *Der Ring des Nibelungen*, Strauss shows Zeus bidding farewell to the human world in the latter part of *Die Liebe der Danae*, and this portrayal has connotations that may be attached to the composer himself. While Strauss lived long enough to compose another opera and to consider other subjects for operas, *Die Liebe der Danae* is his last traditional opera—*Capriccio* is not the same kind of work, but rather an opera about the nature of the genre itself.

Nevertheless, *Die Liebe der Danae* is a work that should command the stage, and recent efforts at concert performances suggest the strength of the score itself and the potential for equally strong results when the work is fully staged. While it seems unlikely that *Die Liebe der Danae* will become part of the standard opera repertoire as has occurred with Strauss's earlier operas, like *Salome* or *Der Rosenkavalier*, it contains equally fine music. As with the other works of Strauss's maturity, the musical language has not extended beyond the dissonances found in *Elektra*, but Strauss used an idiom suitable to his text and the dramaturgy of the work. Rather, it is Strauss's contexts that create the melodic and harmonic tension of *Die Liebe der Danae*, and they are accentuated in the careful and precise orchestration found in this work.

THE OPERA ABOUT THE NATURE OF OPERA

Strauss's last completed opera is *Capriccio* (1940–41), a work that he conceived with the conductor Clemens Krauss as an inspired "conversation piece" on the relative importance of words and music in opera. As a subject for an opera, this work has an antecedent in Salieri's opera *Prima la musica, e poi la parola* (1786), with its libretto by Giovanni Battista Casti that concerns the philosophical debate about the primacy of text over music in opera. Notwithstanding this antecedent, the subject seems to be a natural one for Strauss, who was often as concerned about the text he was setting as the way he composed the music for it.[7] In responding to this perennial concern, Strauss created in *Capriccio* a fascinating work that succeeds in bringing the issues to the forefront without becoming pedantic. In fact, the result is one of his strongest operas.

In *Capriccio*, Strauss personified the rivalry between words and music by a poet and a composer who are vying for the love of a widowed countess, who purports to choose between the two. The entire text is a conversation that envelops her and the guests at her chateau, and just as the countess never commits to either lover, so too Strauss leaves the conflict between words and music unresolved at the end of the work. Nevertheless, the episodes found in this text provide useful points of reference for this potentially lofty debate, and the situation inspired Strauss to underscore the text with musical quotations that contribute another level of meaning to the music.[8] In doing so, Strauss subtly wove the quotations into the fabric of the music. Where quotations occur, the musical structure does not rely on the citation for its meaning, and Strauss allowed the allusions to exist without a priori knowledge of the source. For those who know the music, though, this makes the text of the opera all the more meaningful, since most of the works cited belong to the period in which he set the work.

Within the historical setting of *Capriccio* Strauss created an opera that is also timeless. It is a work that also stands as testimony to his own lifelong search for the proper balance between text and music in opera, and the lack of an absolute and fixed resolution suggests Strauss's lifelong search for the impossible—the perfect opera. Only a master like Strauss could compose a work like this, which is essentially a sophisticated dialogue about the nature of opera that avoids pretension without becoming arch. Rather, the skill that

Strauss brought to the composition conveys a sure style in which the music moves from motive to arioso, with allusions to other works and quotations of others intersecting freely. *Capriccio* is a subtle work that lacks the overt action and drama of traditional opera. Yet it is effective in conveying the ideas behind the work in a kind of fable. Strauss's masterful hand is evident in the fluid musical lines and deft orchestration. Instead of a formal prelude for full orchestra, *Capriccio* opens with a string sextet and this, in turn, takes the listener directly into the opening scene of the guests listening to chamber music in the chateau. As facile and light as the result may be, *Capriccio* remains a testimony to the art of composing opera, and the evidence of the late works makes it clear that Strauss was the master of the genre in the early part of the century.

Capriccio is a kind of summing up, Strauss's opera about opera itself. As obvious and self-referential as that may sound, it is also a masterful gesture that only a composer as experienced and long-lived as Strauss could do. It reaches back, in a sense, to the opening of *Ariadne auf Naxos*, with the composer who dominates the prelude. Yet in *Capriccio* Strauss goes further to make this final opera a testimony to opera itself by connecting his own music with that of previous generations.

THE SEARCH FOR SUBJECT: CLASSICAL MYTH AND CONTEMPORARY DRAMA

Taken as a whole, the late operas of Strauss have two themes in common which recur throughout the works: the composer's ongoing search, a proper, or appropriate, subject for an opera, and the composer's attempt to achieve a balance between words and music. Even though these ideas are most prominent in his final opera, *Capriccio*, they may be traced to almost all of his works in this genre. Whether he succeeded is another matter, yet the presence of these elements in his music is significant for what Strauss attempted to convey in his operas.

Strauss's efforts in *Capriccio* are notable for the attention he continually paid to the libretto in his search for an ideal balance between text and music. Throughout his life he sought a proper attention to text or music without allowing either to dominate a work. He avoided emphasizing the sheerly musical elements that typify the bel canto style, and simultaneously developed an idiom that is Wagnerian in approaching without slavishly imitating the earlier composer's style. Thus, he could make use of set pieces and vocal pyrotechnics in some parts of a work like *Ariadne auf Naxos* and at the same time allow a more conversational musical idiom as a vehicle for setting the text in other parts of the same work. Although the distinctions between such elements are more pronounced in some of the earlier operas, by the time he composed *Arabella* Strauss was able to move in and out of such elements deftly, and the style of the late operas is typified by such fluid, almost cinematic style.

Yet the operatic idiom itself must fit the subject of the work, and Strauss spent much time selecting the appropriate story to present on stage. Not one to use stock-in-trade libretti as had occurred in the eighteenth century, Strauss worked directly with almost all his librettists, with the exception being Oscar Wilde. In the course of these collaborations, the composer worked with his librettists to shape the texts that he was setting. This does not mean that he thought he knew more than the librettists, but he preferred to have texts that evolved along with his conception of the resulting work.

Influenced by Wagner, his early operas betray the medieval and late-medieval milieu that may be found in works like *Die Meistersinger von Nürnberg*. Yet he abandoned such settings with *Salome* by basing his libretto on Oscar Wilde's controversial play, and he went further in his attempts at modernism in *Elektra,* which set Hofmannthal's adaptation of Sophocles's play. In *Elektra*, Strauss found Greek myth a rich source for opera and worked with Hofmannsthal on various operas that rely on mythic topics. The fantastic plot of *Die ägyptische Helena* is firmly rooted in stories from classical antiquity, and *Daphne* has a similar basis. With *Die Liebe der Danae* Strauss composed an opera that has at its core two myths, and the libretto he chose to use is particularly effective in its fresh retelling of traditional myths to create a memorable work.

But Strauss and his collaborators were not entirely dependent on myths for their inspiration. Hofmannsthal's ideas that led to *Der Rosenkavalier* were a departure from their earlier work and with their novelty helped ensure its popularity. Strauss was keenly aware of the success of *Der Rosenkavalier* and attempted to capture the same kind of result with other works, especially *Arabella*. While none of Strauss's later operas ever supplanted *Der Rosenkavalier* in popularity, the attempts to recapture the blending of romantic and comic elements found in that work resulted in such an inspired collaboration as *Die schweigsame Frau*. Yet other collaborations sometimes failed to meet with similar acclaim. Despite the laudable sentiment behind the libretto of *Friedenstag*, for example, the finished work simply does not rise to the same level as most of Strauss's other operas.

In arriving at an appropriate subject for opera, though, Strauss relied on librettists whom he could trust and respect. For years Strauss had such a collaborator in Hofmannsthal, and his death marked the end of a successful partnership. The operas that emerged from the latter part of Strauss's career are marked by the composer's search for a suitable successor. Although Ste-

fan Zweig showed promise, circumstances did not allow them to work together for long; given more time, they could have developed a dynamic
working relationship. Similarly, Gregor's qualifications did not result in what
could be regarded as an easy working relationship. His background as a theater historian did not guarantee that he could be an adept librettist. Strauss
intervened strongly in Gregor's librettos and eventually brought in Clemens
Krauss to collaborate on the text for his last opera, *Capriccio*. Gregor certainly
contributed to Strauss's late operas, but he never truly replaced Hofmannsthal
as the same kind of creative partner for the works with which he was involved.

OTHER PLANNED OPERAS

It may be that Gregor's shortcomings as a librettist limited the working
relationship, and Strauss may have found it just as difficult to work with
Gregor as he did to take on such a large-scale project as an opera during his
last years. Nevertheless, in January 1945 Strauss suggested an idea for opera
by referring to a dream he reportedly had in which Hofmannsthal mentioned a one-act opera with nymphs.[9] What eventually emerged in Gregor's
hands was a ballet treatment dealing with "Die Rache der Aphrodite"
(Aphrodite's Rage), but Strauss did not pursue the work.

A couple of years later, in 1947, Strauss again mentioned to Gregor the
prospect of collaborating on an opera after he received a request from the
school in Ettal that his eldest grandson attended. Gregor responded by suggesting a story from classical antiquity based on Christoph Wieland's *Die
Abderiten* (The Abderites). Wieland's story is essentially a retelling of a classic fable about an argument about the ownership of something as
insubstantial as the shade of a donkey's shadow. The story culminates in a
trial that becomes so drawn out that the ass in question dies before it is resolved. Gregor proposed a libretto entitled "Des Esels Schatten," and the two
spent some time on it. This could have become a satisfying little work, but
the interchange between Strauss and Gregor failed to develop into anything
substantial, and the piece was never completed.

Strauss did leave some sketches for the work that were posthumously
brought to performance by Karl Haussner, and the posthumous collaboration was given its premiere in 1964 at the school in Ettal to commemorate
the centenary of Strauss's birth. This is by no means the work that Strauss
would have completed, by Haussner's efforts to make something of the
sketches the composer left. Ethically, it is difficult to condone the posthumous completion of a work that a composer chose not to complete. Even
though "Des Esels Schatten" has been performed at various times and even

recorded, it is more a curiosity than a work that can be regarded as one of Strauss's completed operas.

Nevertheless, these later efforts with Gregor suggest something of the composer's fascination with classical mythology for his operas. Although nothing came of these later impulses, they show that Strauss was at least interested in composing large-scale works. Yet the almost proverbial farewell that Strauss expressed through the character of Zeus in *Die Liebe der Danae* and the valediction to opera in *Capriccio* seem to have taken Strauss as far as he wanted to go with the genre. Anything else would certainly seem trivial.

CONCLUSION

Despite the problems that existed with finding a suitable librettist after Hofmannsthal's death, the operas that Strauss composed in the 1930s and 1940s are impressive works that stand well beside his earlier and, perhaps for some audiences, better-known works. The later operas bear attention for many reasons, not the least of which is the mature and unflagging skill of the composer in creating some of his more expressive and poignant scores. They include music by a consummate man of the theater, whose sense of drama and understanding of the balance between text and music was still strong. In a sense these operas are also a testament to Strauss's ability to compose under the most difficult conditions. In those works created during the Third Reich, Strauss did not compose in strict adherence to the guidelines issued by the government. Rather, these works are, for the most part, reflective of the mature Strauss and contain some of his finest music. Moreover, in these works Strauss transcends the political situation he faced. It may be that he used composition to escape the vicissitudes of the Third Reich and the Second World War, since the works are hardly topical. In fact, Strauss's final opera, *Capriccio*, is essentially a meditation on the nature of opera and art itself that expresses his own artistic beliefs. *Capriccio* stands as testimony to a life devoted to opera and as a legacy for future generations to contemplate as they experience Strauss's own works in this genre and those of other composers.

NOTES

1. For a balanced and insightful treatment of Strauss's Nazi associations, see Pamela M. Potter, "Strauss and the Nationalist Socialists: The Debate and Its Relevance," in *Richard Strauss: New Perspectives on the Composer and His Work*, ed. Bryan Gilliam (Durham, N.C.: Duke University Press, 1992), 93–113.

2. Recent discussions by the historian Michael H. Kater bear some consideration, including *The Twisted Music: Musicians and Their Music in the Third Reich* (New York: Oxford University Press, 1997). Although Kater mentions Strauss throughout the book, it is especially useful to consider the section on Strauss and Pfitzner (203–21). In his later book on the subject, *Composers of the Nazi Era: Eight Portraits* (New York: Oxford University Press, 2000), Kater devoted one chapter to the composer (211–63). The information that Kater brings to light in both studies points out the complexity of the situation in which Strauss survived.

3. In his overview of Strauss's operas, Michael Kennedy devotes one chapter to the works up to and including *Arabella*, Strauss's last collaboration with Hofmannsthal, and another to the rest, thus separating the early operas from the late ones. See Michael Kennedy, *Richard Strauss,* 2d ed., The Master Musicians (New York: Schirmer Books, 1995), 162–74.

4. Norman Del Mar traces the use of this story as the basis for an opera not only to Donizetti's *Don Pasquale,* but also to Antonio Salieri's *Angiolina, ossia Il matrimnio per susurro* (1800). See Norman Del Mar, *Richard Strauss: A Critical Commentary on His Life and Works,* 3 vols. (Ithaca, N.Y.: Cornell University Press, 1986), 3:3–5.

5. For a discussion of the adaptation, see Del Mar, *Richard Strauss* 3:54–56. Del Mar gives the title as *La Redención de Breda,* while the corresponding play among Calderón's works is rendered as *El sitio de Breda.* See also Bruce W. Wardropper, *Siglos de oro: Barroco* (Barcelona: Editorial Crítica, 1983), 744.

6. Bryan Gilliam calls attention to the outstanding qualities of this opera in "Daphne Transformed," in *Richard Strauss and His World,* ed. Bryan Gilliam (Princeton, N.J.: Princeton University Press, 1992), 33–66.

7. As to Strauss's concern about the libretto, his work with Hofmannsthal on the final scene of *Elektra* is a case in point. See Bryan Gilliam, *Richard Strauss: Elektra,* Studies in Musical Genesis and Structure (Oxford: Clarendon Press, 1991), especially 217–23.

8. Reinhold Schlötterer discusses some of the quotations in his article "Ironic Allusions to Italian Opera in the Musical Comedies of Richard Strauss," in *Richard Strauss: New Perspectives on the Composer and His Work*, ed. Bryan Gilliam (Durham, N.C.: Duke University Press, 1992), 56–92, especially 79–89.

9. Del Mar, *Richard Strauss,* 3:451–53.

Richard Strauss's Poetic Imagination

Pierre Marc Bellemare

THE MAN WHO NEEDED PICTURES
FOR MUSIC MAKING

In 1969, Otto Klemperer granted a series of in-depth interviews to Peter Heyworth later published in book form as *Conversations with Klemperer*.[1] It was unavoidable, in a comprehensive review of his career, that Klemperer would want to talk at some length of the towering figure of Richard Strauss, just as it was inevitable, as a refugee from Nazi persecution, that he would feel a need to censure the latter's behavior under Hitler. All the same, the dour Klemperer was an honest man who could not but express his admiration for Strauss, both as a composer and a conductor, and, indeed, his authoritative assessment of Strauss's mastery on the podium is one of the most appreciative that we have:

You see, the difference between a conductor like, say, Nikisch on the one hand and Strauss and Mahler on the other is that Strauss and Mahler were composers, first composers and then conductors. The creative was also evident in Strauss' conducting. When he conducted Mozart it was particularly splendid, because Strauss was also apparent in it. And the way in which Strauss conducted his own music was miraculous. For instance, under him *Elektra* sounded like an opera by Lortzing. He really understood how to let an orchestra breathe. *He* didn't throw himself around like a madman, but the orchestra played as though *it* was possessed.[2]

That admiration was almost boundless, except for a tiny doubt raised in his mind by a candid confession that he had once heard from Strauss:

Have I told you about Strauss and Beethoven's Fifth Symphony? In the summer of 1928 he and I were both staying at the Waldhaus Hotel in Sils Maria and we sometimes went for walks. On one of those occasions he said to me, "You know, I can't conduct a Beethoven symphony unless I have some sort of picture before me." "Really," I said, "and what sort of a picture?" "Well now, for instance, the second movement of the Fifth is the farewell from the beloved, and when the trumpets enter that is onward to higher goals." Isn't that incredible? I couldn't believe my ears.[3]

It is perhaps surprising that Klemperer would have been baffled by that statement, for it constitutes the perfect demonstration of his own contention that Strauss conducted *as a composer*. Norman Del Mar seems to have had a better grasp of the composer's peculiar creative genius when he quotes him: "I have long recognized that when composing I am unable to set anything down without a program to guide me."[4] This is not to say, however, that we should follow Del Mar when, following that quote, he claims that Strauss "only found himself as a composer when his imagination was stimulated by literary and other external influences, and it is arguable that had he not, through the encouragement of some Alexander Ritter, found emancipation away from the classical forms of Absolute Music in which he had grown up, he might never have blossomed into an outstanding genius at all."

The point is indeed arguable, even if, as will be noted, Del Mar is careful to refer to "*some* Alexander Ritter," as if to acknowledge that as powerful a creative force as Strauss's poetic imagination could not have been breathed into him from the outside, but only awakened in his soul by some Socratic midwife. In truth, the approach to music making to which both Klemperer, bemusedly, and Strauss himself, without any complex, are bearing testimony is so childlike, even childish, that it is hard to believe that it was not present in him from the beginning, when, as a boy, he was learning his trade through the study of the classical forms. How could it be that, as a child, he might have had an ability to compose without the help of "pictures" that he would have lost as a mature artist? It is true that none of his early works are programmatic, but then conception is not the same as publication, and, even at the height of his glory as a composer of tone poems, Strauss would sometimes show himself reticent to disclose his full programs, and would do so only after some of the details had been leaked to the public by friends or publicists. In that light, it would appear that what Ritter did for Strauss was convince him that those private images that he needed in order to compose were not to be kept as secrets, but should be divulged as an integral part of the work itself. That revelation was decisive, but, if the spark had not come from "that Ritter," Strauss would have owed it to "some other Ritter," for such is evidently the kind of music that he was meant to compose.[5]

But what were those pictures that would fashion Strauss's poetic imagination throughout his career? The issue, which constitutes the proper object of this chapter, is not a simple one. In the case of the operas, the librettos can serve as guides, but the mental images that actually enabled Strauss to compose his instrumental works at the time when he composed them are irretrievably lost. All that we have, and have to be satisfied with, are the published programs or, more rightly put, whatever the composer may have chosen to tell us about the poetic images that guided him in the compositional process.[6] Also, Strauss had an inordinately long career. From the day in 1870, when, at age five or six, he was composing at the piano a *Schneiderpolka* that he was, as yet, unable to note down himself, to the day, precisely dated (12 August 1949), when he finally laid down his pen on his last, unfinished, manuscript of a song, nearly eight decades had elapsed. Such a time span necessarily entails a complex evolution in an artist's imaginary landscape. Finally, Strauss's catalog of works is both enormous and varied: it is therefore necessary to make a selection of "the major works," tone poems and operas, to the detriment of most of the rest, including all of the songs.

The methodology to follow is clearer: To measure any evolution, we must start by comparing its beginning and its end. But where to start? With the tone poems or with the operas? The dilemma is, to a certain extent, meaningless, considering the essential unity of the composer's poetic imagination. All the same, it is prudent to define the issue within the confines of one genre alone. In establishing a starting point, considerations of long duration should lead us. The chronology of Strauss's works reveals that he began working on *Aus Italien* in 1886 and that he completed *Eine Alpensinfonie* in 1915—in all a period of nearly thirty years. On the other hand, he began working on *Guntram* in 1888 and completed *Capriccio* in 1941—in all a period of some fifty-three years. It thus appears that we should begin by comparing *Guntram* and *Capriccio*.

FROM *GUNTRAM* TO *CAPRICCIO*

It is hard to conceive of two operas more different than *Guntram* and *Capriccio*. Its subtitle defines *Capriccio* (1940–41) as a *Konversationsstück*, an expression that constitutes both a translation into German and an import into the realm of music of the "Conversation Piece," a pictorial genre very popular in the eighteenth-century English-speaking world.[7] Conversation pieces are portraits of aristocrats or grand bourgeois surrounded by friends and relations who are enjoying a pleasurable and quiet day in each other's company. And this is exactly what *Capriccio* is meant to be: Set in the eighteenth century, it consists in a sophisticated depiction of polite society, the celebration, on the musical stage, of sociable humanity at its most civilized, in friendly intercourse and pleasant conversation. The work is practically unique in the annals of the musical theater. Opera thrives on conflicts, but, while conflicts are not entirely absent from *Capriccio*, they are treated metaphorically and never truly resolved, and the work, notoriously, ends on a note of affected indecisiveness.

Now, if we reach back half a century earlier (1892–93) to *Guntram*, we find ourselves in a world in turmoil defined by sharp and violent conflicts: the conflict for justice that pits Guntram against Robert; the inner conflicts of Guntram's soul, torn between his knightly duty and his culpable attraction to Freihild; and, finally, the ideological conflict that forces him either to submit to the code of the League of the Champions of Love or to reject it. In the end, Guntram resolves all of those conflicts by killing Robert and by making two fateful decisions: First, renouncing Freihild's love, he announces his departure on a solitary journey; and second, repudiating the League's authority and, through it, all authority, he solemnly proclaims that from now on he will not recognize any law but the decrees of his own conscience.

To see how much *Guntram*, and its gospel of radical individualism, can be said to be typical of Strauss's poetic imagination at this early stage in his career, we must now consider the works, all of them tone poems, that he composed during the same period of his creative life.

THE MAGNIFICENT LONER

His first programmatic work *Aus Italien* (1886) is only a postcard pack, an exercise that the composer set to himself to demonstrate that he could translate a series of four unconnected poetic visions into a four-movement symphony suite, or as he calls it "a symphonic fantasy." With the next four tone poems, however, we strike gold, for all of them, and each one in its own way, conform to the "loner" pattern of *Guntram*. *Macbeth* (1886–88) is the story of a man whose crimes outlaw him from humanity. *Don Juan* (1888), the hedonist, has embarked on a quest for the ideal woman during which he wreaks havoc with the lives of everyone he comes in contact with. Ostracized by all, he eventually finds himself all by himself walking down the path to self-destruction. Nothing is even suggested of the attitude to society of the hero, an artist, of *Tod und Verklärung* (1888–89), but, in the face of death, he stands in absolute solitude. As he waits for the end and the splendid, but solitary, transfiguration to follow, he relives the great moments of his career, rich in achievements, but remarkably devoid of references to other people. The hero of *Till Eulenspiegel* (1894–95) is a prankster extraordinaire who respects no one and to whom nothing is sacred. That twerp has a field day making fun of everybody until people are fed up with him and they have him executed.

The pattern of the young Strauss's fascination for various social misfits—noble knights, egotistic sensualists, mischief makers, self-absorbed artists—could not be more solidly established. But what could have led him from such beginnings to the celebration of human society in *Capriccio*?

His second opera, *Feuersnot* (1900–01), offers a first clue. Its main character, Kunrad, presents both important affinities and differences with Till. He too is a nonconformist with special skills who, after running against opposition, resolves to play a trick, of humongous proportion, on his fellow citizens. However, unlike Till, Kunrad is also an integral member of the community, the town's cabinetmaker. And, in any event, far from being excluded from the group, he triumphs over all and even gets the girl in the end. *Feuersnot* thus opens a new path to the composer's imagination, that of the loner's integration into society, but on his own terms.

This emerging pattern will be readily confirmed by an examination of the next two tone poems, beginning with *Also sprach Zarathustra* (1896). The opening lines of Nietzsche's poem, which Strauss chose to inscribe on the first page of his score, are emblematic of his then obsession with solitary loners: "When Zarathustra was thirty years old, he left his home and the lake of his home and went to the mountain. There, he reveled in his spirit and his solitude, and for ten years was not weary of it."[8] But Zarathustra does not remain forever in the solitude. After the ten years have elapsed, he returns from the desert to fulfill his mission, which is to address the people as a prophet. This move constitutes a form of social integration, for, while a prophet remains an exceptional individual set apart from the rest of society, he needs an audience to whom to deliver his prophetic message.

Don Quixote (1897) may seem to be the ultimate loner, constantly joining imaginary battles with whomsoever is unfortunate enough to cross his path, but, in reality, the knight of the sorrowful countenance is never alone. Sancho Panza faithfully remains at his side and together they form a society of sorts, an odd couple to which Strauss devotes many a lovely passage, especially in variation 3, "Conversations between a Knight and his Squire" (*Gespräche zwischen Ritter und Knappe*).[9]

This novel pattern of integration of the hero, the magnificent outsider within humanity, is not only confirmed but conferred a greatly enriched and unexpected meaning in the three grandiose symphonic scores that conclude the series of the composer's tone poems.

In a sense, *Ein Heldenleben* (1898) is a compendium of all that fascinated Strauss in the unique individual—his uncompromising self-assertion, his irresistible drive to reinvent the world, his victorious triumph over all opposition. But this portrait of the hero also presents two new elements of great significance. For one, he, an artist, is no longer pitted against the whole world, but only battling specific enemies, the critics who carp at his music and on whom he inflicts a crushing defeat at the head of his own army. More important, he now has a companion who is much more to him than Sancho could ever be to the Don: She is the ideal woman, his wife, and as much of a heroine as he is a hero. For, not content with making an appearance in the tone poem, she, endowed with her own theme and instrument, the solo violin, takes it over, at least for a while. Her section is a long one, in which their complicated courtship is described in intriguing detail and in the conclusion of which he does not conquer her as much as she captures him, and the tone poem itself, never to leave her husband's side until the final coda.

The hero is thus no longer unique, but has become the male half of a couple. All that remains for the couple is to find fulfillment in parenthood, and that of course is the object of the *Symphonia domestica* (1903). A score that critics have often dubbed vulgar, that work remains popular with the public, which, however, tends to regard it as some sort of a musical joke. But Strauss had little patience with either view and insisted that the *Symphonia domestica* be taken seriously as a testimony on one of the most important aspects of human life:

The symphony is meant to give a musical picture of married life. I know that some people believe that the work is a jocular exposé of happiness in the home, but I own that I did not mean to make fun when I composed it. What can be more serious a matter than married life? Marriage is the most serious happening in life, and the holy joy over such a union is intensified through the arrival of a child.[10]

When one compares the program drawn from Lenau for *Don Juan* to the statement just quoted, it seems that the interval of fifteen years separating the two works is one of light years rather than calendar years. They differ most remarkably with regard to the composer's attitude toward sex. *Don Juan*'s outlook can only be characterized as pornographic: the hero's quest for the ideal woman is unashamedly sensual, and any reference to procreation in that context would be laughable. The depiction of sexual intercourse in the *Symphonia domestica* is, if anything, even more graphic and explicit, but, this time it refers to an authentic act of human love, the love of a couple of which a child is already the living fruit.

The composer's signature rhetoric of heroic grandiloquence had not changed, only the use to which he was putting it. Commenting on the "frightful" evolution of German dramatic music since 1876, the conductor Hans Richter was to pleasantly remark, when the *Symphonia domestica* was the latest sensation: "All the cataclysms of the downfall of the gods in burning Valhalla do not make a quarter of the noise of one Bavarian baby in his bath."[11] Nothing can totally dissipate the incongruous contrast between the language and the program of that work, but that program itself is the culmination of a gradual process of the opening of Strauss's poetic imagination to the inclusion of "the other" into the life of his hero. Is the boudoir of the *Capriccio*'s Countess Madeleine in sight? Perhaps, but if it can be seen, it is but faintly, and from the faraway summits of the Alps.

Eine Alpensinfonie has both a public and a private program. Its public program is the series of twenty-two sections, clearly marked in the score, that describe the progress of the climber from the foot to the top of the mountain. Its private program consists in a few weighty sentences that the composer jotted down in his diary upon hearing the news of Mahler's death. They summarize the work's intended message under three headings or slogans: *sittliche Reinigung aus eigener Kraft* (moral purification by means of one's own strength), *Befreiung durch die Arbeit* (liberation through work), and *Anbetung der ewigen herrlichen Natur* (worship of eternal, glorious nature).[12] Nowhere in the public program is it explicitly stated that there is more than one person on the mountain. However, the inference that Strauss's poetic vision is meant to engage a group follows readily. To begin with, it is widely known that such expeditions are not to be attempted by an isolated individual. Therefore, it is natural to assume, and is, in fact, generally assumed,[13] that the outing involves a team of mountain climbers. Furthermore, the work's private program makes it clear that its intended message is prophetic, as in *Also sprach Zarathustra*, with, however, a significant difference. In *Eine Alpensinfonie*, Strauss, with a simpler message to convey and more concrete poetic metaphors to use as a matrix for the musical expression of its key concepts, is much more effective in sermonizing his fellow humans, on the liberating virtues of sustained work, the spectacle of Nature and so on, than he had been in translating Nietzsche's philosophy into music. Once the various musical sections of *Eine Alpensinfonie* have been cross-referenced with the titles that make up its program, they become their perfect sonic translation, so much so that if the listener so wishes he can actually "see" the intended sequence of poetic images and then relate those pictures to the main components of the work's message, which quite naturally proceeds from them.

FROM THE TONE POEMS TO THE OPERAS: THE MUTATION OF STRAUSS'S IMAGINATION

Having reached such heights, one might have perhaps hoped that Strauss would come down from his mountain and gradually deepen his appreciation of the value of human society, just as he had previously evolved out of his initial fascination for rebellious misfits into an opening to "significant others." This, however, was not to be, at least not in the ideal, straightforward way that one might have wished for. Among the composer's works, *Capriccio* stands practically alone.[14]

Strauss's failure on that account is largely due to one of his serious limitations, not as an artist but as a human being. It is sad to say, but true, that he could never completely shed his deep-seated contempt for the common run of humanity. Thus, even after *Capriccio*, one sees him take a passing interest in *Des Esels Schatten*, a project of an opera based on a satirical novel whose point is precisely that the vast majority of humankind is made up of imbeciles. From *Feuersnot*, in which stupid Bavarians are trying to "catch moonbeams in mousetraps," to *Des Esels Schatten*, in which stupid Abderitans are dragging each other to court over a donkey's shadow, there is hardly a sign of a positive evolution in the composer's "superior attitude" to the man of the street.

More significant, there is this incontrovertible fact that, after Strauss discovered the other, he began to see him, or rather *hear her*, in a new way that would both expand and specialize his outlook on human relationships. And here we are confronted with a paradox. To the concertgoing public, on the one hand, Strauss is the composer of tone poems in which the hero is invariably male and from which women are absent, with but two exceptions. To the operagoing public, on the other hand, he is a composer who, in all of his stage works but two, favors women to the detriment of their male counterparts, most notably tenors. As for those who take an interest in his whole musical legacy, they have to conclude that, at some point in his creative life, the composer underwent a spectacular conversion, from a male-oriented to a female-oriented imagination.

It is tempting to define that period as the decade between the *Symphonia domestica* and *Eine Alpensinfonie*, when Strauss composed the four operas that remain the pillars of his popularity on the operatic stage. Of those, three (*Salome, Elektra, Ariadne auf Naxos*) are named after their central female character. *Der Rosenkavalier* is the sole exception, inasmuch as the *character* of the *Kavalier* (knight) of the title is undeniably male, but only the character, for the *role* itself is actually sung by a female who, incidentally, spends about half of "his" time on stage in drag. In fact, in that period, Strauss was so taken by female voices, that, shortly afterward, when, setting the prologue to *Ariadne*, he had to decide on a *Fach* for the role of the composer, and operatic conventions offered him a choice between a light tenor or a high baritone, he went for a woman's voice again, to the utter bafflement of his librettist and much of posterity after him.[15]

In reality, though, this spectacular shift from the male- to a female-oriented imagination, even as it manifests itself most spectacularly in the time of *Salome* and *Elektra*, had preceded those works by a number of years. Thus, in the series of the operas, the real turning point would seem to lie between *Guntram* (begun in 1892), in which the female lead Freihild is so admirably *unreal*, and *Feuersnot* (begun in 1900), in which the maiden prize Dietmut is flesh-and-blood, and hot-blooded too. A consideration of the tone poems makes it possible to pinpoint the date with even greater accuracy, to 1898, and *Ein Heldenleben*, the first major work in which a female figure not only appears, but asserts herself with great forcefulness.

Those familiar with Strauss's biography will readily relate this development to contemporary events. In 1887, as he was working on *Don Juan*, he had become acquainted with the willful young soprano Pauline de Ahna. A long courtship ensued, with the tempestuous Pauline, slowly, but resolutely, inching her way from the margins of the young maestro's life into its very heart. Eventually, the two became engaged and married, in 1894—an event that sparked the composition of many a love Lied, some dedicated to Pauline, all inspired by her. Section 3 of *Ein Heldenleben* is a monument to their love, just as the *Symphonia domestica* is meant to immortalize the coming into their life their only child Franz or "Bubi," born in the third year of their union.

It is evidently Pauline who, early in their married life, inspired her husband to embark on a new career as an explorer of womanhood. The object of that quest was not womanhood in the abstract, successive portraits of essentially different women, but the essence of womanhood in the concrete and in all of its diversity as incarnated in the remarkable Pauline. On the subject of the identity of the "hero's companion" in *Ein Heldenleben*, Romain Rolland in his diary[16] quotes Strauss as having said, "It's my wife I wanted to show. She is very complex, very feminine, a little perverse, a little coquettish, never like herself, at every minute different from how she had been the moment before."

It is notorious that, beyond *Ein Heldenleben* and the *Symphonia domestica*, two of the main figures of women in Strauss's operas are explicit portraits of Pauline. One is the formidable Christine in *Intermezzo*, or the composer's wife as seen through the eyes of her husband and of no one else, for, in that instance, Strauss acted as his own librettist. The other is the bitter Dyer's wife of *Die Frau ohne Schatten*, or Pauline as seen by Hofmannsthal—who could hardly stand the sight of her—but mercifully in a text set to music by her loving husband. However, it is safe to assume that there is something of the kaleidoscopic Pauline in all of her husband's operas. From Dietmut to Madeleine by way of the not-so-silent Aminta, Strauss's ladies are much too true to life not to owe part of their soul to the one woman with whom he remained in love for so many years.[17] And that might even include the trousers roles, considering that he had once coached his wife to be the first Hänsel.[18]

Strauss's "conversion" to womanhood involved a reversal of attitude not only to women, but to men as well, and that raises another paradox. How could it be that, once so deeply immersed in male heroism, he could change so much that, at times, men seem to vanish from his works? But perhaps the question should be taken from the opposite end: How could he have been so infatuated with men in the first place?

As is often the case with paradoxes, this one is more apparent than real and one rewarding to dissipate. To begin with, while there is no denying that Strauss the opera composer was to take a deeper interest in women than in men, he did nonetheless make a number of worthy additions to the male repertory, notably in the baritone department (Ochs, Barak, Mandryka). Also, he could, on occasion, overcome his bias, as in *Capriccio*, in which, by the measure of the number of main roles, men actually predominate, in the ratio of four (Count, Olivier, Flamand, LaRoche) to two (Countess, Clairon).

Second, and more important, the notion that he was ever that obsessed with men is questionable. Rather, what a closer review of his early works reveals is that, the young Strauss was inordinately fond of one man, and of one man alone: himself. Three of those works (*Ein Heldenleben*, *Feuersnot*, *Symphonia domestica*) are ostentatiously autobiographical, and the others suspected to be, to a certain extent, and rarely less than to some extent. Thus, that there was something of mischievous Till in the composer of the *Krämerspiegel* is not a point that the publishers Bote and Bock would have disputed. Similar arguments could be made for *Don Juan* and *Guntram*, even for *Also sprach Zarathustra*. While it would be going too far to suggest that Strauss's gallery of heroes is, in fact, a collection of self-portraits, most of those heroes seem, at any rate, to have functioned as "alternate selves." In that light, the transition from the first to the second Strauss appears less of a gender issue than a epochal shift from self-centeredness to marital and parental love.

But that transition also involved a change of medium, from the tone poem, in which Strauss was sole master of his programs, to opera, which would, most of the time, force him to contend with librettists driven by their own creative dreams. In any event, he would be more fortunate than most opera composers in his dealings with librettists. An eminent conductor, he did not have to compose for a living, and, unlike Verdi in his galley years, he was never compelled to deal with indifferent texts. Besides, as the undisputed giant of German music in in his time, he had the literary world at his feet and the roster of his librettists would include two of the foremost writers of the age. All the same, no one works all the time under ideal conditions, and Strauss would occasionally have to adapt to the visions of his collaborators, with variable results.

Following *Guntram*, *Feuersnot* was his first opera set on a text by someone else. By all accounts the venture was a smooth affair, for, regardless of the artistic worth of the end product, both he and Wolzogen were quite satisfied with it. This ideal situation would present itself again at least twice in the compsoser's later career. Once would be with Krauss and *Capriccio*— an opera whose subject matter is precisely the problem of the difficult equilibrium between words and music in musical drama. The success in that case is hardly surprising, given that Strauss was to contribute to the libretto as much as a composer can do so while remaining able to graciously attribute the merit of its actual writing to someone else. Until politics began to complicate his relationship with Zweig, *Die schweigsame Frau* had also been a success story, although one must note that, in his eagerness to win Zweig over, he chose to settle for a libretto adapted from a preexisting stage play. This may sound trivial, for such librettos are plentiful in opera (*Rigoletto*, *La Traviata*, *Il Trovatore*), but, in point of fact, Strauss had never accepted that sort of arrangement before nor would he ever do so again, for an apparent lack of willingness to accommodate the vision of some other creative genius with whom he could not engage in dialogue.

Contrary perhaps to appearances, the librettos of the two works, *Salome* and *Elektra*, with which he conquered the lyric stage do not quite belong in that category. In the making of those operas, Strauss never felt a need to reshape Oscar Wilde's or Sophocles's texts like Zweig would have to do with Ben Jonson's play. He was content with adopting the German translations to his purpose, through judicious cuts and a few modifications. The two plays had taken hold of his imagination and it was not long before he knew exactly how he would deal with them.

Del Mar is at his most insightful when he defines those works as "staged tone poems." Strauss's aesthetic objective with them was the same as with *Macbeth* or *Don Juan*; he wanted to fuse highly inspired musical moments into an organic whole—a quality notoriously lacking in his first two operatic scores. And the method he used to achieve his goal, his poetic matrix, was just about the same; he would focus on one individual possessed with a larger-than-life passion, an obsession, an *idée fixe*, resulting in an increasingly acute conflict with everyone else. The tragedy culminates in the individual's frenzied, ecstatic death. The parallel with *Don Juan* is remarkable.

In poetic terms, those operas are thus a throwback to earlier times when the composer was obsessed with the magnificent isolation of exceptional individuals. Musically, however, the move proved to be justified, as it enabled Strauss to establish himself as Wagner's foremost successor. And then he found himself trapped because, as suggested by the strong resemblances between the two works, such powerful dramatic effects could be achieved only with a specific type of subject, and, after *Elektra*, he was unwilling to go further in that direction, if that had even been possible. Instead, he decided to specialize in the depiction of quieter women.

In this endeavor, he would have to count on mainly two men: Hugo von Hofmannsthal (for five works) and Joseph Gregor (for three). Neither would completely succeed in matching Strauss own vision of opera, but for opposite reasons. Gregor, a fine scholar but an indifferent writer, would fail to rise up to the composer's expectations and, while consistently doing his best, could only present him with usable, but not superlative, librettos. The highly gifted Hofmannsthal, on the other hand, would offer him the most marvelous texts, literary masterpieces, but also problematic gifts, deeply imbued with the peculiar forms of the writer's own poetic imagination which, at times, would tend to overwhelm the musician. In both cases, Strauss would have to set to music stretches of text that did not inspire him. Overall, however, his collaboration with Hofmannsthal would prove to be a much more fruitful venture because the poetic visions to which he would have to adapt himself would often end up enriching his own.

FAIRY-TALE ROMANCES

For the purpose of this chapter, I will distinguish two groups within the Hofmannsthal operas. The first is comprised of *Der Rosenkavalier*, *Ariadne*, and *Arabella*. To those, one can add the Zweig opera *Die schweigsame Frau*, which follows the same pattern, the simple and familiar pattern of fairy-tale romances: Boy and girl meet and fall in love; obstacles stand in the way of their happiness, but they succeed in overcoming them; in the end, they are about to marry and live happily ever after.

Such stories are common in popular literature, but not as much in opera, at least not in nineteenth-century opera. Previously, happy endings were often *de rigueur* on the lyric stage, even in works adapted from the myths and tragedies of antiquity: even Gluck's *Orfeo* concludes joyfully. But that situation changed with the passing of aristocratic culture. Thus, only two of Verdi's twenty-three serious works end on a merry matrimonial note,[19] and, in both cases, the optimistic development is only the conclusion of a subplot, for the fate of the young couples (Fenena and Ismaele, Amelia and Gabriele) is hardly the main focus of interest in *Nabucco* and *Simon Boccanegra*, respectively. In comedy, on the other hand, fairy-tale endings remained a nearly indispensable cliché. Verdi wrote only two comic operas, *Un Giorno di Regno* and *Falstaff*, and they both conclude with a marriage. Even Wagner, who had so masterfully turned the old fairy-tale romance archetype on its head in *Lohengrin*, had no choice but to fall back on it in *Die Meistersinger von Nürnberg*.

For the occasion, however, Wagner had managed to work out a fairly original variation on the hoary pattern and Hofmannsthal would steal a few leaves from him for *Der Rosenkavalier*. The librettos of the two works, at any rate, present striking similarities. In each case, much emphasis is put on the presence of a third party who keeps a watchful eye on the events surrounding the young couple. That person can both play a key role in removing the obstacles that stand in the lovers's path and make a claim on one of them. And the two plots are resolved in the same way when the party in question both gracefully renounces that claim and benevolently sees to it that the couple obtain the paternal consent needed for their union.

The essential difference between *Rosenkavalier* and *Die Meistersinger von Nürnberg* lies in the casting, by Hofmannsthal, of a woman as the noble third party and, more generally, his definition of the relationship between the Marschallin and Oktavian. Whereas Sachs is merely a friend of Eva's family and he is renouncing only the possibility of marrying the girl after winning her hand at the Meistersingers's contest, the Marschallin is very much in love with Octavian and breaking an emotionally and physically rewarding relationship with him. For her, it is a heartrending choice between preserving her selfish interests or generously helping her lover to marry the girl he loves. And, then, in the highly moral terms in which Hofmannsthal defines her decision, the nature of the marriage itself is changed, for, in renouncing Octavian, the Marschallin is acting not only out of love for him, but for the sake of Sophie as well, because she wants the girl to be happier in life than she was. The fairy tale thus acquires a depth unusual in conventional romance, where, as in Rossini's *Il Barbiere di Siviglia*, more emphasis is normally put on the fun inherent in the overcoming of the obstacles ("Una voce poco fa") than on the love affair itself. There is something of that fun in *Rosenkavalier* too, notably in the first half of act 3. But, from the moment when the Marschallin makes her entrance in the latter part of the same act, a tone of quasi-sacred gravity prevails, as she proceeds to transsubstantiate marriage, from a legal contract and a social convention into a nearly mystical union of two into one.

The amused but fond and sympathetic depiction of social interactions which accounts for so much of the pleasure that *Ariadne auf Naxos* has to offer represents a new departure for Strauss. As we have seen, outside of the mountaineers of *Eine Alpensinfonie*, who remain shadowy figures, the tone poems were remarkably devoid of positive references to society beyond the couple and the nuclear family. More ominous, in *Salome* and *Elektra*, society is presented as the strange "world out there" where the uncomprehending and threatening "others" dwell. In *Feuersnot*, the outlook on society is not as bleak, but still bitingly satirical and hardly sympathetic. It is only with the early Hofmannsthal operas that Strauss's music begins to depict humans as social animals in a favorable light, if always in the comic vein. This happens first with the levee (act 1) and the conspiracy (act 3) scenes of *Rosenkavalier*, and then, and a great deal more, through most of *Ariadne*. Although these were the only times when Hofmannsthal would provide him with such material, Strauss had evidently developed a taste for it, as witnessed by much of *Die schweigsame Frau* and the whole of *Capriccio*.

So there is, after all, a thread leading from the Alps to the country seat of the Countess Madeleine. That thread, however, remains rather slim, compared to the theme of matrimony, in which Strauss was more truly and more generally interested.

Ariadne's connection to that theme is ambiguous. To begin with, in the telling of the rather conventional fairy-tale romance on which it is based, the emphasis is put on the initial kindling of love, as in the first half of act 2 in *Rosenkavalier*, but without a Marschallin to take a long-term positive view of that nascent love. Instead, we have Zerbinetta, whose views on the subject are markedly pessimistic and cynical. She is there to suggest that Ariadne, the survivor of an unhappy relationship, may be in for further disappointments. Hers is the skeptic philosophy of *Così fan tutte*. As much as Strauss worshiped Mozart's masterpiece, those are not views for which he would have more room in any other of his works.

As a variation on the comedic romance stereotype, the libretto of *Arabella* appears as an update of a form of aristocratic comedy popular in the eighteenth century. Such comedies, of which Marivaux was the undisputed master, are centered on the search for the ideal sexual partner. The plots typically involve two or more mismatched couples (like A–D and B–C) whose members, by the end of the story, would have been rematched to more suitable partners (as A–B and C–D). The potential weakness of such plots lies in the contrivances and complications (such as false and mistaken identities, lies and disguises, and so forth) that they necessarily entail. Mozart, who had cultivated the genre in his youth (*La Finta Giardiniera*), would have had a field day "deconstructing" it in—of course—*Così fan tutte*.

Hofmannsthal's stroke of genius was to revive that genre in a streamlined form, with only two couples and just enough implausible ploys to keep the story going while keeping a semblance of verisimilitude. He also chose to set his aristocratic story within the framework of bourgeois comedy, that of Molière's *L'Avare* or Beaumarchais's *Le Barbier de Séville*, or, for that matter, his own *Rosenkavalier*. In that very different type of comedy, the obstacles set in the path of the lovers arise from the down-to-earth values of a class that regards marriage, not love, as the proper object of courtship and defines it as a contract dealing primarily with matters of hard cash and property. What would the history of comedy have been without the peculiar institution of the dowry?

In *Arabella*, the matter of the dowry is not only an important element of the action, as in *Rosenkavalier*, but its mainspring, for it defines the absurd situation in which the two sisters find themselves at the beginning of the opera, and from which proceeds all the rest of the action. When the opera ends, it is not with the triumph of love over money, but of love *with* money and as a poor girl's dream comes true: that one day, Mr. Right—handsome, kind, loving, *and well-off*—will ask for her hand, but without insisting on a dowry. In other words, if *Arabella* ends happily, this is not only because both sisters have found love, but also because that love has also brought along with it the resolution of the family's cash-flow problems. To dwell too much on the financial aspects of the tale would be to miss its poetic point—for, after all, this is a love story—and, yet, Strauss was evidently not indifferent to the material aspects of marriage. At any rate, in his entire oeuvre, he shows but little or no interest in star-crossed lovers promised to an early death, so common in nineteenth-century opera. Instead, he evinces a distinct preference for serious and levelheaded types with honest and long-ranging views of family life and/or some guarantee of an establishment. Arabella and Mandryka certainly fit the description, as did Octavian and Sophie.

The last of the four romantic fairy-tale operas, *Die schweigsame Frau*, tells exactly the same tale, with the difference that this time the dramatic framework is purely bourgeois. The story is very similar to that of Donizetti's *Don Pasquale*, and not by accident, because the librettos of both works ultimately derive from the same literary source, Ben Jonson's *Epicoene*, directly for Strauss and through some intermediaries for Donizetti. Zweig has made a skillful job of the adaptation by transposing the action into the eighteenth century, a period of considerable appeal to Strauss; by taking a leaf or two from his Italian predecessors, notably in his design of the role of Aminta—not a woman, but a boy in drag in the original play; and especially by emphasizing the eminently operatic elements of music and noise, in the hope, amply rewarded, that Strauss would turn them to good effect.

But the key characteristic of the libretto's originality was the decision to turn Henry and Aminta into a duly married couple right from the beginning of the opera—duly married but penniless.[20] Henry's uncle Morosus has money, but, scandalized at his nephew's union with a singer and the couple's association with an opera company, he has disowned him and is now threatening to marry a young woman, a silent bride, who might give him an alternate heir. The story of the comedy is that of the elaborate charade that Henry, in cahoots with Aminta and their performer friends, devises to successfully trick his uncle out of his ominous matrimonial project. Here again, the happy ending does not consist in a triumph of love over money, as romantic conventions would dictate, but in the acquisition, by the loving couple, of excellent prospects of eventually coming into the money that they need to "live happily ever after."

THE RESOLUTION OF MARITAL CRISIS

The four Hofmannsthal operas considered so far have led us only to the threshold of marital happiness. Those which make up the second group will take us further, into marital life itself and the difficulties inherent in it. They are *Die Frau ohne Schatten* and *Die ägyptische Helena*, to which one must add *Intermezzo*, which Strauss composed on a libretto of his own, as an interlude (hence its title) in between the two other operas.

While composers tend to find unmarried lovers more interesting, married couples are not uncommon in opera, where they appear in a variety of situations, ranging from a partnership in crime, as in *Macbeth*, to a joint struggle for freedom, as in *Fidelio*. Operas in which couples are going through a marital crisis are not rare either. A common situation occurs when one of the two spouses is having an affair, carnal or platonic, with a third party, as in *Tristan und Isolde*, or Strauss's *Guntram*, in which case the attention will usually be focused on the amorous affair rather than on the marital crisis between one of the lovers and a boring or repulsive third party. In the less common instances, in which part of the focus is on the crisis itself, it usually results in tragedy, as in *Un Ballo in Maschera* or *Othello* or *Pelléas et Mélisande*. Much scarcer are the operas in which the crisis is happily resolved when as, for instance, in *Stiffelio* or *Le Nozze di Figaro*, it results from adultery, whether actual or intended, and the offended spouse forgives the culpable one. But cases of operas in which husband and wife succeed in pulling out of a marital crisis together are quite rare. A fine, if little-known, example is that of Eugen d'Albert's one-act opera *Die Abreise* (1898) in which the estranged spouses are easily reconciled after discovering that they have been manipulated into an artificial quarrel by a scheming "friend." That work, needless to say, is a light *comédie de moeurs*, for only humor, it would seem, could ever make such tedious material, as the development and subsequent patching up of a marital feud, work on the operatic stage.

Thus, it is remarkable to see Strauss, in between *Ariadne* and *Arabella*, devoting no fewer than three operas, or one-fifth of his operatic production, to precisely that theme. Moreover, only one of those works, *Intermezzo*, is a comedy, just as only one, *Helena*, deals with an actual adultery, although it is true that another, *Intermezzo* again, draws considerable mileage out of the appearance of one. Finally, the most successful of the three works, *Die Frau ohne Schatten*, is also the most daring in its approach to the theme of marital fall-out and reconciliation, for neither is it a comedy nor does it involve any adulterous relationship.

Through that unusual choice of subject, Strauss confirms what *Salome* and *Elektra* had already demonstrated, namely, that he is a twentieth-century opera composer. That century, the fourth in the history of the art form, would bring about an extraordinary blossoming in the variety of dramatic material deemed worthy of exploration on the operatic stage. From *Wozzeck* and *Lulu* to *Le Grand Macabre* and *Nixon in China*, many of the major works from that period would break with past conventions. At the same time, there would be a price to pay for that freedom. The period (1914–27) when Strauss was occupied with *Die Frau ohne Schatten*, *Intermezzo*, and *Helena*, would also witness the triumph of cinema and the beginning of the decline of opera, and of theater itself, within mainstream culture. In that context, composers' choices of dramatic subjects no longer matters that much because the public interested in operatic novelties has become smaller and continues to shrink.

Of these three works, the most revealing is *Intermezzo*. Unlike most of Strauss's operas, it is based on one of his original ideas and in which he believed so much that he ended up writing his own libretto, after

Hofmannsthal and others had declined to deal with it. The idea was of a burning interest to him because it was based on an event of his own biography, a memorable rough spot in his life with Pauline from the first decade of their marriage. Not unexpectedly, the resulting opera is intimately connected with the *Symphonia domestica*, from the same period in the history of the couple. Indeed, one could even say of *Intermezzo* that it is the elaboration, on the operatic stage, of a particular section from the tone poem, the double fugue "Merry Arguments—Reconciliation—Happy Ending." There would, however, be an important difference: While merry arguments bear on trifles, the matter at stake here is nothing short of the very survival of the couple—a potentially fatal crisis, but consistently treated in a light mode. In the opera, Christine Storch, also known as Pauline Strauss, the temperamental wife of the Kapellmeister Robert Storch, also known as Richard Strauss, having obtained what she thinks is an incontrovertible proof of her husband's infidelity, is now threatening him with divorce. But Storch is, in fact, innocent and, although he has a hard time defending himself, he is finally "forgiven" and the couple is reconciled.

Intermezzo and *Symphonia domestica* are the two main pieces of what could be called Strauss's "Family Album." That album also contains two minor works composed at about the same time as the composer was working on *Intermezzo*. One is the 1924 *Hochzeitspräludium* (Wedding Prelude) for two harmoniums written for Strauss's son Bubi's marriage to Alice Grab. The other is the 1925 *Parergon* (complement) to the *Domestica* (*Parergon zur Symphonia Domestica*), a programmatic concertante piece for piano and orchestra celebrating Bubi's recovery from a grave illness during his honeymoon.[21] In each wrok, Strauss makes use of previously existing material of intimate significance, notably from the *Symphonia domestica*, in both cases, and—most appropriately—from the trio of *Der Rosenkavalier,* in the *Präludium*. Taken together, those four works summarize Strauss's philosophy of marriage, as the proper end of human love, and of parenthood, as the fulfillment of marriage itself.

That philosophy, evidently close to the composer's heart, is a sound one in most people's book, but his own outlook on it strikes one as more sincere than profound. *Intermezzo* is a delightful work, and one that deserves more exposure, but it is also a rather naive piece, and a limited one in its outlook, in view, precisely, of what makes it so charming: it is much too personal to strike a universal chord. To deepen his perspectives, Strauss needed outside help. So, before and then after *Intermezzo*, he and Hofmannsthal made two attempts to grapple with marital crises. One, *Die Frau ohne Schatten*, was to be one of their greatest collaborative efforts, while the other, *Die ägyptische Helena*, would be a comparative failure.

There are various reasons for that failure but, in the perspective of Strauss's poetic imagination, two of those stand out. One is that Strauss, the impeccably faithful husband, would naturally find it difficult to relate to adulterer, and Helen happens to be the most notorious adulteress in history. As proof of his bias against such offenders, one only needs to be reminded of Guntram's utter horror at his desire for another man's wife or again remember the adulterous couples from his other operas: Egisth and Clytemnestra in *Elektra*, Herod and Herodias in *Salome*—dreadful people in all instances. It is true that Strauss did develop a passion for the Marschallin, an adulteress too, but then what makes her story so moving? Is it not that it concludes when she puts an end to her extramarital affair so that rightful marriage might triumph? As shown by *Intermezzo*, it is the thought of marital fidelity—*unblemished* marital fidelity—that Strauss found appealing, obviously because it corresponded so well to his own circumstances. But the painful life experiences of the likes of Helen and Menelas were the opposite to his own and the fact that he was unable to relate to them is hardly surprising.

The other major problem with *Die ägyptische Helena* is structural: there is simply not enough dramatic material in it to sustain interest throughout a work of such length. In *Don Giovanni*, Mozart needed only one aria ("Batti, batti, o bel Masetto") for Zerlina to turn her husband's anger to kinder feelings, and even less than an aria, a mere arioso, for the Count to seek and obtain forgiveness in the final scene of *Le Nozze di Figaro*. That moment is effective because it comes at the conclusion of a story that we have been following for a long time. *Helena*, on the other hand, results from a bizarre attempt to construct a full opera out of the resolution of a long-standing marital crisis that has already run most of its course— over more than twenty years—by the time the action begins. Hofmannsthal, evidently, did not see that as a problem, but as an opportunity to construct a clever story of marital reconciliation. But the libretto as he actually wrote it is perhaps too clever and all of the imaginative ploys with which he loaded it only serve to complicate his basic dramatic premise without contributing much to its development.

Die ägyptische Helena is an opera that bears a superficial resemblance to *Intermezzo*, but the two works, in fact, have practically nothing in common. *Die Frau ohne Schatten*, on the other hand, is a work that does not seem to resemble *Intermezzo* in the least and yet the connections between them and, indeed, between it and the whole "Family Album," go very deep.

On the face of it, the two librettos bear but little resemblance beyond the common theme of the ultimately happy resolution of a marital crisis. The action of *Intermezzo* is as simple and straightforward as that of *Die Frau*

ohne Schatten is convoluted and clogged with symbolism—all of it Hofmannsthal's very own. Furthermore, *Intermezzo*, like *Symphonia domestica*
and *Helena*, and most stories of married people in bliss or in trouble, only
involves one couple, whereas *Die Frau ohne Schatten* features two. In a
French *comédie de moeurs*—a theatrical genre with which *Intermezzo* presents clear affinities—this would almost inevitably entail some goings-on of
a sexual nature, but in *Die Frau ohne Schatten*, the two couples never inter-
act at that level. In fact, they do not even belong in the same world. Only
one, made up of Barak the Dyer and his wife, is human. The other, comprised of the Emperor and the Empress, inhabits a superior world,
intermediate between ours and the higher realm of the spirits, from which
the Empress, incidentally, originates, being the daughter of Keikobad, its
ruler. The conflictual situations dealt with in each opera are even more incomparable. While the Storchs' marital problem is punctual and banal, the
couples in *Die Frau ohne Schatten* are experiencing an existential crisis of
metaphysical proportions and on which their future, even their lives, depends. At the heart of that crisis, there is yet another difference between
them and the Storchs, and one that makes all of the difference: the Storchs
have a son, whereas they are childless.

The whole of *Die Frau ohne Schatten* proceeds from this fact, or double
fact, because the two couples are childless for quite different reasons. The
human couple does not have children because the wife, most unhappy with
her life, does not want any. The superhuman couple remains without issue
because the Empress is barren—or shadowless, in Hofmannsthal's peculiar
symbolism. The paths of the two couples cross after the Empress is warned,
by a messenger from her father, that if she does not manage to acquire a
shadow in short order, her husband will be turned into stone. She can get
the required shadow from a mortal—not steal it but obtain it from a
woman willing to yield hers. The Empress then travels down to the human
world in search of a miserable soul whom she can trick into surrendering
her fertility, and she finds her in the person of the Dyer's wife.

The message of *Die Frau ohne Schatten*, that "the purpose of marriage
is procreation," could not be more traditional and, yet, it is easy to misun-
derstand. Some will interpret it as an exhortation to raise large families,
assorted with a moral condemnation of sexual intercourse when not aimed
at procreation. Needless to say, those are views to which neither Hofmannsthal nor Strauss subscribed. What they meant to say, instead, is that
marriage remains incomplete for as long as it does not result in parenthood.
Strauss was deeply convinced of that. Is not his son Bubi the only "character" who can be found in all of the four works that make up the "Family
Album?" Admittedly, only one of those had been composed at the time, but

that one, the *Symphonia domestica*, was more than sufficient evidence for the composer's intense personal interest in parenthood. Later, after *Intermezzo*, Hofmannsthal would be careful to introduce the theme even in *Helena*, in the final scene, where Hermione, the only child of the royal couple, suddenly appears out of the blue, to seal, as it were, the reconciliation of her parents.

But there is more of Strauss's "Family Album" in *Die Frau ohne Schatten* than the coming of the child considered as the fulfillment of the marital union. As already mentioned, the composer's own wife was used as a model for the *Färberin* by Hofmannsthal, an idea seized upon by Strauss, but from an utterly different viewpoint. Thus, while the librettist saw Pauline as a shrew, and so depicted her, the composer saw her through a lover's eyes, as an essentially good person, and so depicted her in his own medium. Would it be going too far to suggest that the character of Barak was patterned on Pauline's husband? At any rate, it is tempting to regard the Dyer as an alter ego of a composer who saw himself as a craftsman, and one especially gifted in the art of lending color to music.

The miracle of *Die Frau ohne Schatten* lies in the organic, if not absolutely seamless, integration of two very different poetic visions. One, the poet's, considers the story and the values embodied in its *sub specie aeternitatis* and as universal truths as it were. The other one, the composer's, presents them from the concrete angle of their human interest. Hofmannsthal's genius was to construct his literary legend in his own poetic language, intellectual and indirect, quite foreign to that of Strauss, and yet with a sufficient transparency of purpose that the latter could grasp its message and translate it into his own sensual and immediate musical language. It greatly helped that the composer, then at the peak of his technical proficiency, could clothe the fruit of the poet's inspiration in the most opulent orchestral garb, worthy of the gorgeous "Arabian Nights" imagery of the text.

All the same, for the miracle to happen, Strauss had to relate the essence of Hofmannsthal's tale to the world of *Intermezzo* and his own domestic life. While it does not appear that he and Pauline ever went through a crisis quite like the one experienced by Barak and his wife, the resemblance between the latter and the alter egos of the Strausses, the Storches, is unmistakable. Those are couples in which it is the wife who plays the most visibly active role, takes the initiative, makes a display of her emotions. Her husband, on the other hand, is a quiet, lovingly patient man. There is nothing that he would not do for his wife, but, for the most part, his role is limited to wait for her to make the decisive move, in her own way and in her own time. In both instances, his patience is rewarded.

RENUNCIATION

Beyond marital affairs, another conception of Hofmannsthal's that moved Strauss to invest the best of himself in *Die Frau ohne Schatten* is the particular way the drama is resolved. The decisive moment comes, in the next-to-last scene of the opera, when it now only depends on the Empress to take possession of the shadow of Barak's wife. But, as she is to utter the word, the human couple's wailing laments can be heard, and, moved, she refuses to sacrifice them to her own happiness. At this point, we are unmistakably reminded of the ethical dilemma of *Rosenkavalier*, where the Marschallin is offered a similar choice, and makes exactly the same decision. In the Empress's case, however, the stakes are much higher. By renouncing Octavian's love for his sake and that of Sophie, the Marschallin was not only putting an end to an affair, a pleasant one no doubt, but still only an affair, "like she had several before and will have others again," but she was gaining the satisfaction of having done "the right thing." This is no small gain if we have to take her inner life seriously, as Hofmannsthal certainly would like us to do, but still that represents only a stage, and not necessarily a decisive one, in her spiritual development. The Empress, on the other hand, is making the tragic choice of her life, for it seems that, by doing the right thing, she will lose everything. But, in the end, there is no tragedy, for although she is unaware of that at the moment of making her fateful decision, her father only wanted to put her to a test. And so, at the point when she appears to be sacrificing everything, all that was hers, and more, is unexpectedly restored to her and she receives a shadow all her own. The opera concludes as we hear the chorus of the unborn children of the two couples, jubilating in anticipation of the gift of life that their parents' love for one another is about to confer on them.

Hofmannsthal's intention in both instances was to explore another form of love than the one proceeding from the natural attraction between the sexes, the traditional subject matter of most operas. This is the form of love, of unmistakably Christian origin, through which a person negates himself for the sake of someone else, often at a cost to himself and without expecting anything tangible in return. That theme of "altruistic renunciation" is an original contribution of Hofmannsthal to Strauss's imagination, nowhere to be found in the latter works prior to *Rosenkavalier*. All that remotely resembles it in the pre-Hofmannsthal period is the last section of *Ein Heldenleben*, where the hero turns his back on the world, but in truth, that is more of a gesture of retiring from the world than of renouncing it. The composer, however, was evidently moved by this new theme, as it would reemerge in two of his later operas, first, in a muted fashion, in the final scene of *Die schweigsame Frau*, and, then, more emphatically, in the final scene of act 3 of *Die Liebe der Danae*.

That renunciation scene from *Die Liebe der Danae* could pass for a repeat of those of *Der Rosenkavalier* and *Die Frau ohne Schatten*, if it were not that Jupiter, like Morosus, and the composer himself, is male and older, whereas both the Marschallin and the Empress were young and female. Those differences are crucial, for they determine what is at stake in the decisions that each one of those various characters is called to make. For both the Marschallin and the Empress, those decisions involve a costly sacrifice, even, in the latter's case, an immeasurable one. The two men, on the other hand, are merely invited to take stock of their age and begin considering bidding farewell to the pleasures of this world. The young ladies whom the two elderly men thus "renounce"—the false bride in Morosus's case, the amorous conquest-to-be for Jupiter—are hardly more than symbols of the joys and desires of their younger days, while the sacrifices of the two noble ladies are made for specific individuals, whose characters, incidentally, are more sharply delineated, in Strauss's music, than those of Aminta and Danae. Morosus's and Jupiter's acts of renunciation are thus more akin to the move to retirement of the aging hero of *Ein Heldenleben* than to the abnegation of the heroines of the two Hofmannsthal operas, just as they adumbrate Strauss's own farewell to this life in his *Vier letzte Lieder* from a few years later.

VERKLÄRUNG, VERWANDLUNG, METAMORPHOSEN

Of the five operas that Strauss composed after Hofmannsthal's death, two, *Capriccio* and *Die schweigsame Frau*, have already been discussed. The remaining three—*Friedenstag, Daphne, Die Liebe der Danae*—are the fruit of his ill-fated collaboration with Joseph Gregor. Gregor was an unfortunate historian of literature on whom the composer entrusted the impossible task of being as good as Hofmannsthal and Zweig while not allowing him to be original in the elaboration of projects inherited from them. This bizarre situation accounts for much of the shortcomings of the first and the third of those works. *Friedenstag* is an oddity for Strauss, an opera with a "military" subject in which all of its roles of any length but one are cast for male voices and which, not unexpectedly, finds the composer at his most uninspired. As for *Die Liebe der Danae*, already mentioned, and more inspired, but only in certain of its moments, it is a pleasant exercise in bogus mythology that owes much less to Homer and Hesiod than to Crémieux and Halévy, Offenbach's librettists for *Orphée aux Enfers*.

Of the Gregor operas, the sole *Daphne* has retained a foothold on the fringes of the repertory. Even though Strauss commonly passes for a specialist of mythological subjects, that opera and *Ariadne* are, in fact, the only two of his stage works to be based on actual Greek myths, as opposed to a comic fantasy in mythological disguise (*Danae*) or episodes from the Trojan Cycle (*Elektra, Helena*). The story, which tells how the beautiful Daphne was transformed into the archetypal laurel tree, is one of the many "metamorphosis" myths of the Greeks. To construct a full opera on such material, Gregor, like his early baroque predecessor Rinuccini,[22] had to fill it out with borrowals from variants of the legend, subplots and secondary characters, such as Leukippos, Daphne's love interest, who spends much of the opera dressed as a girl. That extraneous material is of little relevance to this chapter compared to the celebrated *Verwandlung* (Transformation Scene), one of the most glorious moments in the whole of Strauss. But what is it that the composer found so inspiring about the notion of a woman turned into a tree? And why is it that, a few years and a world war later, he was to compose a piece for twenty-three solo strings to which he would also entitle "Transformations," or *Metamorphosen*? Raising that issue is to enquire about Strauss's attitude toward death and the afterlife.

Death is noticeably absent from most of Strauss's operas. This may sound surprising when one remembers *Salome* and *Elektra*, where violent deaths are common occurrences, but the fact is that when one considers those two works within the entire Straussian canon, they appear as exceptions. All told, in the rest of the operas, there are only three instances of people meeting their end on the stage: Robert in *Guntram*, Da-ud in *Helena*, and Leukippos in *Daphne*. Even in *Friedenstag*, where the threat of death is hanging over everyone's head until the end, no one actually dies and the tense drama concludes on a joyful celebration of life and peace.

When it comes to the tone poems, on the other hand, the situation is the opposite. More than half of those feature "death scenes." Four (*Macbeth, Don Juan, Till Eulenspiegel, Don Quixote*) are based on previously existing literary models in which the action concluded with the death of the main character. *Tod und Verklärung*, on the other hand, is based on an original program, and death, evidently, is not only one of its episodes but its subject matter. While not strictly autobiographical, the work describes the kind of death—the death of an artist rich in accomplishments—that the composer wished for himself. As evidence, we have the inclusion, nearly sixty years later, of one of its key motifs in the musical fabric of "Im Abendrot" (sunset), the first of his *Vier letzte Lieder*. And then there is the story of the composer on his death bed, remarking that there was nothing more for him to compose because dying was "just the way I described it in *Tod und Verklärung*."[23]

So much for *Tod*, but what about *Verklärung*? What did Strauss exactly mean when he decided first to call, and then to describe in music, the aftermath of the artist's death as a "transfiguration"?

Wahrig's Deutsches Wörterbuch[24] defines the verb *verklären* as "to make something appear more beautiful, more brilliant," and indicates that it applies primarily to immaterial objects, for example, "the past transfigured by memory" or the "transfigured night," the *verklärte Nacht* of Dehmel's poem that inspired Schoenberg. When applied to persons, the participle *verklärt* can be used as a synonym of *beseligt*, *glückselig*, meaning "blissful," "made happy." The corresponding substantive *Verklärung*, however, properly belongs in the field of religion and in the sense of *Erhöhung ins Überirdische* (elevation above this world), it almost exclusively refers to the mysterious biblical episode of the Transfiguration of Christ.[25]

There is a suggestion of a blasphematory intent here, suspicion confirmed by an examination of the thick file of anti-Christian pronouncements in which Strauss indulged over the years, and especially as a younger man. Not all of those statements are impromptu remarks. Some do actually refer to the intended meaning of his musical works. Thus, in the "private" program of *Eine Alpensinfonie*, he ventures the hope that the work would be known as "The Antichrist," as its message would greatly help the German people to purify itself from Christianity. Already in his teenage years, he had decided to renounce Christianity and its promises of salvation—or at least most of those promises for, as we shall see, the idea of an afterlife never ceased to hold some appeal for him, at least as an artist.

A man still longing for a life everlasting after turning his back on all religion would find himself in a tragic quandary, but that was not the case with Strauss. Never an agnostic, let alone a materialistic atheist, he always retained some faith in a higher power, Whom (or more likely Which) he "humbly" acknowledged as the ultimate source of his existence, and inspiration. As he was to confide to an American journalist, in his Weimar years, "When in my most inspired moods, I have definite compelling visions, involving a higher selfhood. I feel at such moments that I am tapping the source of Infinite and Eternal energy from which you and I and all things proceed. Religion calls it God. I am at present very much interested in the personal experiences of the great Swedish mystic Swedenborg."[26] This is something that Strauss said before he discovered Nietzsche, but even after giving up on heterodox Christian mysticism, he remained a pious man by the standards of his personal brand of natural religion. This piety would manifest itself in a number of texts in which he attempts to reappropriate religious language for paganism, thus proclaiming Wagner not only a saint, but even "The Almighty."[27] At another level, both in words and in music, he would celebrate the holiness of matrimony and parenthood (but then the Catholic priest who married him and Pauline in church would hardly have found fault with that) as well as invite us to climb the Alps and worship "the source of Infinite and Eternal energy from which you and I and all things proceed." All in all, this spirituality that he devised for himself would prove its usefulness in helping him confer meaning on his life and provide nourishment to his art.

Even after it has become known that "Great Pan is dead,"[28] paganism may still contribute to foster happiness, but there are limits to the hopes that it can hold for its devotees. Confronted with the prospect of his own death, the modern pagan remains tragically unable to completely resolve the contradiction between his desire for everlasting life and the shortness of the time imparted to him on earth. Only religion and philosophy can provide credible answers, and Strauss, who refused to adhere to any religious creed and whose grasp of philosophical arguments was limited, had to content himself with the formulation of poetic responses, with mixed results.

The first of his responses, the *Verklärung*, is also the least satisfactory. Intellectually, first, it is hard to see how one could make use of such a specifically Christian notion in any other spiritual context than the one from which it originated. Aesthetically, then, no one among the few who are said to have been transfigured has ever provided a subjective description of that state, so that our only reports on it come from external witnesses; hence, a striking contrast between the two parts of *Tod und Verklärung*. In the first (*Tod*) Strauss's point of view is subjective, as the composer is drawing on his experience of illness and suffering, reminiscence, and so on, which is both personal and common to all. When it comes to the second part (*Verklärung*), however, the tone poem becomes an exercise in the objective, and conventional, depiction of the vision of the blessed, a rather fine exercise one may add, but one that does not proceed from anything more existential than a careful study of the rhetoric of ecstasy in Christian religious music, as in the final pages of *Parsifal*, then still a novelty.

In the final section of *Ein Heldenleben*, the composer succeeds in giving us a more concrete sense of the object of his longing by enriching it with elements borrowed from life itself. For one, here is a paradise to which he expects to be able to take his wife with him and this is a brilliant idea, for her musical presence in that section (as the solo violin) contributes to enliven it. Moreover, death itself is depicted as nothing but the final stage of a progressive retirement or withdrawal from life and the world (*Weltflucht*), which is expressed by the music as the slow extinction of both the melody and the orchestra itself. Finally, the moment of death's coming is one of bliss and satisfaction, the natural conclusion of a process of fulfillment (*Vollen-*

dung) of a long and rewarding existence, symbolized by a final tutti, powerful but gentle, and laden with both contentment and nostalgia.

It is remarkable that, already by his mid-thirties, Strauss was in possession of the poetic imagery of the end of human existence that would sustain him until his own death: a serene and consoling wisdom of the gradual diminishment of life and the quiet acceptance of the natural conclusion of his earthly journey. That philosophy was to reappear in the works of his old age, unchanged it would seem in the series of his gorgeous farewells to life that begins with Morosus's "slumbering" monologue and concludes with "Beim Schlafengehen" and "the slow closing of summer's eyes" in "September."

At the same time, that wisdom could only take Strauss to the gates of Hades and not a step farther. All that it could do for him was to call the dream of supernal bliss previously invested in the fantasy of the *Verklärung* back to this earth and concentrate them into life's final moment. But life's final moment still remains part of life and outside of the realm of death, so that Hades itself remains a mystery, and the question of what lies beyond remains unanswered. But Strauss, possessed with a curiosity for the afterlife, would still need an answer and he had to go a step farther, if only in his imagination. To that end, and on three occasions, he would draw on ancient paganism.

The first time was with *Ariadne*, which concludes when Ariadne, a mortal woman, is invited by a god smitten by love for her to ascend with him into the heavens and become a goddess in her turn. That process of absorption of the human into the divine is what the ancients knew as an apotheosis.[29] Strauss's impression of one is magnificent, but not any more convincing, intellectually or spiritually, than the *Verklärung* had been. It remains within the register of beatific vision, as in the finale of Mahler's Eighth Symphony.

Next, Strauss's imagination would fasten on the theme of the *Verwandlung* (Transformation), which makes its first appearance in *Daphne*. Even within mythology, as documented by Ovid among others, the notion of Transformation is twofold. It may refer to the metamorphoses of the gods, who could assume various shapes to consort with mortals, as Zeus (Jupiter) did when he wanted to seduce Semele, Europa, Alcmene, and Leda, the four queens in *Die Liebe der Danae*. A transformation in that sense is a mere change of external appearance, a disguise that does not in any way affect the god who is only temporarily assuming it. Transformation in another sense, of greater relevance to our purpose, is a permanent change of nature. In myths, the gods use such transformations to confer an immortality of sorts on a deserving human being. He may be a person who has died and whom they want to resurrect, but in a new, everlasting, form. This is what

Apollo did when, after accidentally killing the boy Hyacinthus, he made flowers of a new species—the hyacinth—spring from his blood. Or again the person who is transformed may be a mortal whose fate has moved the gods' hearts to pity. This is what happened to the boy Cyparissos when, heartbroken for having accidentally killed his cherished pet, he was begging them to turn him into an eternal symbol of unrelenting grief, and they transformed him into the cypress.

The tale of Daphne belongs in the same category, but, curiously, more so in Gregor's reworking of it than in its original form. In the Greek myth, Daphne is already, to begin with, a divine being, the daughter of the river god Peneios and, when she is transformed into the laurel tree, by her father, or, according to some sources, by Zeus, it is at her own request, because she wants to escape the unwanted amorous advances of the god. In Gregor's version, Daphne, her father demoted to the humble station of a fisherman, is a mortal to whom Apollo takes a fancy and it is at *his* request that Zeus transforms her. His reworking of the legend is brilliant, for it meaningfully sets the key moment of Apollo's consecration of the laurel tree as a prize for the most deserving of mortals in a new light. Whereas, in the myth, the consecrating act comes only as an afterthought, a consolation prize as it were, for the god who has lost the girl, in the opera, the creation of the new form of life becomes the specific object of his request to Zeus. Thus, it is not only Daphne herself who is transformed, but Apollo's love for her, from a short-lived infatuation to a passion for excellence destined to endure forever.

This accords perfectly with the spirit of the transformation myths of the ancients, which are tales of rebirth into immortality. In them is already contained the kernel of the cosmologies of the early Greek philosophers. For those, death, to a large extent, was an illusion because even as everything is destined to perish, everything that dies is also destined to be reborn in some other form. Through a myriad of metamorphoses, the One is incessantly recycled into the Other.

That mythical philosophy of an eternal triumph of life over death could not but appeal to Strauss. However, there was nothing in it to confer any substance on his dreams of personal immortality, or *Verklärung*. All the same, in his later days, he would occasionally find repose in that gentle paganism, and draw inspiration from it for his *Metamorphosen*.

As is widely known, the composition of that piece was prompted by the destruction, in Allied bombing raids, of Germany's foremost opera houses. But what connection can we establish between Strauss's response to those events and the notion of transformation?

The beginning of the answer can be found, not in the piece's program, for there is not any, but in two of Goethe's *Zahme Xenien* that Strauss copied

in his manuscript of the score.[30] Those poems, written by an old man, deal
with the proper use of one's time on earth. In one, the reader is advised
not to look for meaning in the confusion of the world. Instead, he should
live one day at a time and, always conducting himself with understanding
(*mit Verstand*), never cease to reflect on the time imparted to him to convince himself that "(if) it's gone all right till now, it may well go on to the
end."[31] In the other poem, the reader is invited not to try to reach a perfect
understanding of his inner being, which is impossible, but to strive to know
himself more clearly by meditating daily on "what he is and what he was,
what he can do and what he cares for."[32]

Neither poem contains the word *metamorphosis*, but the term is found
elsewhere in Goethe, and it happens that, at the time of composing *Metamorphosen*, Strauss had embarked on a traversal of the poet's complete
works.[33] The exception is revealing, not so much in itself as a limitation, for
others would have skipped the rest of Goethe's "scientific" writings as well,
most of which deal with biology and geology. Not so with Strauss, though.
Indeed, he must have read those with a particular interest, for it is precisely in them that he found the key notion of *metamorphosis*.

The notion is central to Goethe's projected theory of physical life. It is
while the poet was traveling in Italy in 1786–88 that his vision of the essential unity of all terrestrial life forms had taken hold of his imagination.
He had then gained the precious insight that all those forms—humans, animals, plants, even crystals—might derive from the same simple original
organism, through a constantly renewed process of transformation (*Metamorphose*). That insight, he had first expressed it in his poetic *Die
Metamorphose der Pflanzen* (Metamorphose of the Plants) and *Die Metamorphose der Tiere* (Metamorphose of the Animals) written after his return
aus Italien. In their duality, those two poems are indicative of one of the
three fundamental problems, or *gaps to bridge*, that the author of *Faust*
would have to contend with in his subsequent attempts, in prose, to work
out his insight into a viable scientific theory. Those are the gap between
mineral and plant life, or the search for the original plant (*Ur-Pflanze*); the
gap between plant and animal life, or the search for the original animal (*Ur-
Tier*); and the gap between animal and human life, or the search for the
original human (*Ur-Mensch*).

In his lifetime, Goethe had been told by the scientific community that it
had no use for his metaphorical approach to nature, just as Strauss, in his
days, would be served a warning from the critical faculty that his works composed after *Elektra* were irrelevant to the development of music. But neither
creative genius could have cared less, and so, in his old age, increasingly
detached from literature, the poet would find himself devoting more and

more of his time to what he felt were valuable scientific pursuits, just as the composer would continue composing "the only music that he knew to compose" to the end of his long life. And eventually, in one of Germany's darkest hours, the old composer would revisit the old poet's "flawed" scientific writings and extract meaning out of them, seizing on the fundamental insight of "the metamorphoses," not with enthusiasm, for such was not the mood of the day, but with hope, or a fervent desire for hope. In those texts, he would find a *Weltanschauung*, more than a theory, akin to that which the thinkers of the pre-Socratic age had developed out of the ancient transformation myths. That wisdom would both confirm him in his pessimism—for it proclaims the inevitable passing of all beings—and offer him a promise of rebirth, out of the ashes of the destroyed cities, of the noble German culture that he held so dear. Moody and meditative as *Metamorphosen* may be, they bear an optimistic title. Within weeks of composing it, Strauss would find himself eagerly planning for the long-term future of the German opera houses that temporarily lay in ruins.

Thus, in the sunset of his life, the composer, a man generally pleased with himself and blessed with a long career and both marital and parental happiness, did find, if not the promise of personal immortality that he was pining for, at least a certain wisdom that would renew his confidence in the divine resiliency of life.

NOTES

1. Peter Heyworth, ed., *Conversations with Klemperer*, 2d rev. ed. (London: Faber and Faber, 1985).

2. Ibid., 47.

3. Ibid., 48.

4. Norman Del Mar, *Richard Strauss: A Critical Commentary on His Life and Works* (London: Barrie and Rockliff, 1969), 2:272.

5. In fairness to Del Mar, Strauss was not stingy in expressing his debt to Ritter, the man whose influence on him had been "in the nature of the whirlwind" and who had "urged him toward the poetic and the expressive in music" (see Del Mar, *Richard Strauss*, 1:40). On the other hand, he seems to be making short shrift of Strauss's well-attested use of Hans Christian Andersen's tale "The Swineherd" as a source of poetic inspiration for the late Duett-Concertino, going so far as to claim that, by then, Strauss found "illustrative composition no longer interesting" (3:447).

6. And this within the limits clearly set by Strauss in his correspondance with Romain Rolland: "In my opinion, a poetic programme is nothing but a pretext for a purely musical expression and development of my emotions, and not a simple *musical description* of concrete everyday facts." Strauss to Rolland, 5 July 1905, in

Rollo Myers, *Richard Strauss and Romain Rolland, Correspondence* (London: Calder and Boyars, 1968), 29.

7. Later in the century, the theme of the Conversation Piece would resurface in Luchino Visconti's next-to-last film entitled *Gruppo di Famiglia in un Intero* (Conversation Piece; 1974). That film tells the story of a scholar who, disgusted with the times, turns his back on them and finds refuge in eighteenth-century art, but to no avail for, as Visconti argues, one cannot escape from one's own historical context. The parallel with Strauss is striking and almost certainly intentional.

8. "Als Zarathustra dreissig Jahr alt war, verliess er seine Heimat und den See seiner Heimat und ging in das Gebirge. Hier genoss er seines Geistes und seiner Einsamkeit und wurde dessen zehn Jahr nicht müde" (my translation).

9. Complete title: *Gespräche zwischen Ritter und Knappe. Forderungen, Fragen und Sprichwörter Sanchos, Belehrungen, Beschwichtigungen und Verheißungen Don Quixottes* (Conversations between Knight and Squire. Sancho's Claims, Questions and Sayings; Don Quixote's Advice, Blandishments and Promises). Quite a program!

10. "Die Heirat ist das ernsteste Ereignis im Leben, und die heilige Freude einer solchen Vereinigung wird durch die Ankunft eines Kindes erhöht" (translated by Del Mar; see his *Richard Strauss*, 1:198).

11. "Alle Zerstörung, die das brennende Walhall beim Sturz der Götter erlebt habe, sei auch nicht annähernd so laut wie das Geschrei eines bayerischen Kleinkindes im Bade" (translated by Del Mar; see his *Richard Strauss*, 1:188–89). This famous *bon mot*, *bon* as it may be, is perhaps apocryphal.

12. Kurt Wilhelm, *Richard Strauss Persönlich* (Munich: Kindler Verlag, 1984), 129. (translated by Del Mar; see his *Richard Strauss*, 1:188–89).

13. By Del Mar, among others. (see Del Mar, *Richard Strauss*, 2:110 ("the moutaineers plunge into a wooded part of their climb"), 111 ("The climbers are at an agreeable part of their journey"), and so forth.

14. But not altogether alone. As the title of its original version (1923) clearly indicates, the suite of dances after Couperin belongs in the same world: *François Couperin: Gesellschaft und Theatertänze im Stile Ludwig XV* (François Couperin: Society and Theater Dances in the Style of Louis XV). That resemblance was later accentuated, at the time of the composition of *Capriccio*, and in collaboration with its librettist, the conductor Clemens Krauss, when a new version of the ballet, set in eighteenth-century France, was given the title *Verklungene Feste*, that is, in Del Mar's periphrastic translation (*Richard Strauss*, 2:276), "Bygone Festivities the sounds of which have faded away" [*sic*].

15. And then, in the late 1920s, when they were working together on *Ariadne auf Naxos*, the same librettist had to work very hard to talk him out of the proposition to turn the young Daoud into a mezzo in his turn.

16. Myers, *Strauss and Rolland* 133.

17. Excerpt from a letter to her, dated 1930, when they had been married for more than thirty-five years: "I don't know if it's the same with you—my inner belonging to you grows greater all the time. I think of you and the children all day long. I am wholly happy only with you. With our family!" See Kurt Wilhelm,

Richard Strauss: An Intimate Portrait, trans Mary Whittal (London: Thames and Hudson, 1989), 6.

18. In the event, Pauline did not sing at the premiere of *Hänsel und Gretel* because she had taken ill a few days earlier. There is, however, a fine picture of her as the boy Hänsel (and not looking indisposed at all) in ibid., 45.

19. A third, *I Vespri Siciliani*, ends during the marriage ceremony, just as the groom and his friends are about to be massacred.

20. In *Don Pasquale*, the more conventional situation is that the lovers are not yet married and their objective is to both convince the uncle to renounce his matrimonial plans and obtain his consent to their union.

21. Strauss's sketches for that work and its score provide an eloquent testimony of his deep concern for his only child. In Wilhelm's words, "[F]or a time his (i.e. Franz Strauss) life was in danger. His father's anxiety came out in music he sketched at the time, in which the child's theme from the symphony [is] reworked in passages of a heart-breaking despair, alternating with the idyllic recall of the past. Tragedy is never far away, until the danger is banished at the end. The harmonic writing [in] the *Parergon* goes as close to polytonality and atonality as *Elektra*, and rarely did Strauss express such desperation" (see *Richard Strauss*, 92).

22. Ottavio Rinuccini (1562–1621) used the legend of Daphne as the basis for his libretto of Peri's *Dafne*, the first opera ever composed (1598). Peri's opera is no longer extant, but an opera of the same title by Marco da Gagliano (1608), set on a revised version of the same text, has survived. Incidentally, the first German opera ever composed (now lost) was also a *Dafne* (1627), music by Heinrich Schütz, libretto by Martin Opitz.

23. Wilhelm, *Richard Strauss*, 425: "Ich hab's schon vor 60 Jahren geschrieben, in *Tod und Verklärung*. Es ist genau so."

24. Gerhard Wahrig, *Deutsches Wörterbuch* (Munich: Mosaik Verlag, Neuausgabe 1980), 3971.

25. Witness the Luther Bible: Matt.17.2: "Und er wurde verklärt vor ihnen, und sein Angesicht leuchtete wie die Sonne." Mark 9.2: "Und er wurde vor ihnen verklärt." Luke 9.32: "Als sie aber aufwachten, sahen sie, wie er verklärt war, und die zwei Männer [that is, Moses and Elijah], die bei ihm standen."

26. Arthur M. Abell, *Talks with Great Composers* (New York: Philosophical Library, 1955), 86. The interview took place in 1890.

27. The short score, completed on 24 December 1892 in Cairo, is inscribed "Deo gratias (und dem heiligen Wagner)." At that date, God was still part of the picture, but by the time that Strauss finished *Feuersnot* on 22 May 1901—*des Meisters Geburtstag*—He had disappeared and Wagner was promoted in His stead as "den Allmächtigen" in the score's completion note. For the first text, see Wilhelm, *Richard Strauss*, 60; for the second one, see Del Mar, *Richard Strauss*, 204.

28. The mysterious announcement of the deah of the god Pan, an event supposed to have occurred under the reign of the Roman emperor Tiberius, symbolically marks the end of classical paganism. See Plutarch, *De defectu oraculorum*, 419A–E.

29. Leukippos's "transfer" to Olympus in *Daphne* belongs in the same category, but Strauss does not make nearly as much musically out of it as he does with Ariadne's apotheosis.

30. Del Mar, *Richard Strauss*, 3:426.

31. "Denk immer: 'Ist's gegangen bis jetzt. / So wird es auch wohl gehen zuletzt."

32. "Doch probier' er jeden Tag. / Was nach aussen endlich, klar. / Was er ist und was es war, / Was er kann und was er mag."

33. Wilhelm, *Richard Strauss*, 390.

10

The Lieder of Richard Strauss

Christine Getz

STRAUSS AS A LIEDER COMPOSER

Richard Strauss's interest in Lieder composition spanned the entirety of his career. Yet his approach to the genre, particularly in terms of tonal and harmonic style, appears to have changed surprisingly little during the sixty-seven years following the publication of his earliest published song set, the universally admired Op. 10 (1882–83). Over half of Strauss's Lieder, and, indeed, the majority of the best-loved songs, were composed during the late nineteenth century. As a result, the entire canon usually suffers comparison with the Lieder of Hugo Wolf, a phenomenon which suggests that even the late Lieder are myopically viewed as nineteenth-century compositions. In fact, as early as 1905, it was remarked that Strauss's songs were considered old-fashioned and outdated.[1] Although fin de siècle Germany was marked by extensive social, artistic, and literary upheaval, Strauss's Lied style reflects only the beginnings of that upheaval, for he rejected, for the most part, the pessimistic and dissonant poetic and musical language of the dominant German Expressionist School.

Many scholars have grappled with the issue of compositional style in the hopes of identifying a means by which Strauss's persistent attachment to a post-Romantic Lied style might be explained. Some have attributed Strauss's dated approach to Lieder composition, particularly during the latter years of his life, to his bourgeois family background.[2] The problems of the German working class in post–First World War Germany were, admittedly, far removed from his social experience, and, consequently, of little interest to him. Strauss's naive, if egocentric, refusal to face fundamental moral and political issues in Nazi Germany, as well as his attendant acceptance of the appointment as president of the Reichsmusikkammer, betray a certain disregard for social responsibility that is somewhat uncommon in modern artists.[3] Leon Botstein has suggested that Strauss, who was infected with both a high degree of self-centeredness and the social cynicism of the late-nineteenth-century bourgeoisie, possessed the uncanny ability to mold both his personality and his music to his current political and social aims.[4] In an attempt to ensure the isolation of his musical environment amid the swirl of the social and moral conflict that engulfed many German intellectuals during the first half of the twentieth century, Strauss seems to have intentionally directed his Lieder toward a privileged German social class unintimidated by "the skat-playing Bavarian musician with vulgar tastes."[5]

Although Strauss's late Lieder feature a tonal and harmonic style that is reminiscent of much music composed during the late nineteenth century, they also demonstrate that his approach to text setting, conception of form, and treatment of the accompaniment did mature during the course of his career. The melodic lines of Strauss's lieder, which are characterized by plastic melodies in which rhythm and pitch serve both to underscore and to heighten the natural inflection of the text, became increasingly free of metrical constrictions. The forms of the later lieder are increasingly dependent on complex variation procedures that allow continual reshaping of the vocal line and recasting of accompanimental materials. The accompaniments themselves are increasingly orchestral in conception, and clearly demonstrate the influence, initially, of the tone poems and, later, of the operas that occupied so much of Strauss's compositional attention.

Strauss emerged as a Lieder composer during the heyday of the genre, but outlived its decline as a principal form of concert entertainment. Although Lieder were often performed in concerts featuring mixed genres after 1833,[6] the *Liederabend* was not a successful concert venue during the middle decades of the nineteenth century. Thanks to the efforts of several advocates of salon performance such as tenor Gustav Walter, however, it gradually gained acceptance. Between 1880 and 1920, concerts dedicated solely to the Lied became extremely fashionable.[7] As might be expected, the *Liederabend* provided a natural and inexpensive concertizing and touring vehicle for the composer, who performed Lieder recitals regularly with his spouse, soprano Pauline Strauss-de Ahna, between the years 1894 and 1905. Strauss appears to have preferred Pauline's renditions of his Lieder to those of all other singers associated with him, and the reviews of their performances of several orchestral Lieder with the Philadelphia Orchestra at Symphony Hall in Boston, like the surviving assessments offered by German reviewers of the period, suggest that while her voice was mediocre, her interpretive abilities were unsurpassable: "Mme De Ahna is an expressive singer, but not above some of the many Strauss Lieder singers that we have already heard. We must not forget that there was Strauss worship in Boston long before Buddha himself came. The singer's voice would be at its best in a small hall or drawing-room, but it seemed forced and thin in Symphony Hall."[8] And "Her singing, while as accentric [*sic*] as before in the matters of tone production and phrasing, made its effect, for it was, at all events, strong in dramatic feeling."[9] Therefore, it is noteworthy that Strauss composed and published numerous Lieder between 1882 and 1905, but ceased production of the genre when Pauline retired from the concert stage in 1906.[10] However, his abandonment of the genre, which actually begins around the year 1901, may owe less to her retirement than it does to his preoccupation with the composition of *Salome*. Moreover, Strauss's failure to produce new Lieder was motivated, in part, by attempts to avoid fulfilling certain contractual obligations to his publishers.[11] Strauss published no Lieder between 1906 and 1918,[12] and when he reentered Lieder circles in 1918 alongside such composers as Schoenberg and Berg, the character of the genre had already been greatly altered by the rise of the Expressionist movement. Although Strauss returned periodically to the genre after 1918, his compositional output reflects an increasing interest in larger projects.

Among the most widely criticized characteristics of Strauss's Lieder are the texts themselves. Fundamental to an understanding of the composer's approach to the genre, however, are his own claims that he selected texts on the basis of their immediate inspirational value: "Many songs owe their origin to the circumstance that the composer looks for a poem which will match a fine melodic idea and the poetically musical atmosphere."[13] And "I open a book of poems; I turn over the leaves casually; one of the poems arrests my attention, and in many cases, before I have read over it carefully, a musical idea comes to me. I sit down and in ten minutes the complete song is done."[14] For Strauss, the primary qualification of a potential Lied text was that it suggests immediate musical images.[15] This mode of thinking often led Strauss to select poetry that is not well-known today, and, as a result, numerous critics and scholars have judged many of the texts to be of poorer quality than those used by other Lied composers active during the same period. In an attempt to defend Strauss on this point, Barbara Petersen has demonstrated that numerous texts set by Strauss were also chosen by his contemporaries, a fact that has eluded scholars because many of Strauss's Lieder are not indexed in nineteenth-century Lieder catalogs that list the Lieder by title. In a number of instances, Strauss's Lieder are omitted from such catalogues simply because they were composed outside the historical parameters, such as dating, set for the items included. Even when Strauss's songs are catalogued, however, their textual concordance to Lieder by other composers is not easily recognized because the Lieder themselves bear different titles than did the original texts.[16]

Although there is some truth to the assertion that much of the poetry selected by Strauss does not occupy a position of importance in the German literary canon, many of the songs based on these so-called second-rate poems are among Strauss's best-loved Lieder. In fact, the songs of Op. 10, Op. 21, and Op. 27 bear witness to the fact that the supposed literary quality or prestige of the text of a Strauss Lied had little to do with its actual success as a composition. A similar case can be made for a number of the famous Lieder of Schubert and Brahms that are based on texts by secondary poets, including Schubert's "Seligkeit" and "Die Forelle" and Brahms's "Botschaft," "Erinnerung," and "Juchhe!" Unfortunately, several factors that greatly influenced Strauss's poetic preferences are often either brushed aside or entirely ignored. One of the most important of these is his aforementioned attachment to texts that immediately evoke musical images. Another is Strauss's strong connection to the Munich-centered German literary style known as *Jugendstil*.

Strauss's connection to the artistic and literary developments of the *Jugendstil* in turn-of-the-century Munich was observed as early as 1904–05,[17] but the impact of these trends on both his poetic tastes and his compositional style has only recently been fully recognized.[18] Norman Del Mar, who has published the most thorough chronological study of Strauss's lieder, discussed Strauss's relationship with the *Jugendstil* poets, but he merely brushed the tip of the iceberg in observing that in Munich "the reaction was against the soft-grained sentimental poetry of the mid-nineteenth century culminating in the verses of poets such as Geibel and Heyse (favored by Hugo Wolf) and including mock medieval or folk poetry, such as the *Des Knaben Wunderhorn* collection, or the work of Rudolf Baumbach."[19] *Jugendstil*, which parallels Art Nouveau, featured a return to simplicity, an emphasis on diction and construction, and the extensive use of symbolism. Strauss set a number of poems by figures associated with this movement, including Gilm, Dehmel, Schack, Bierbaum, Mackay, and Dahn. From 1894 to 1898, moreover, Strauss was engaged at the opera in Munich, the city regarded as the literary center of this movement. There he came into contact with a number of poets and artists active in the *Jugendstil* movement, including the founders of the movement's journal *Jugend*. Several of his Lieder were published in the journal, including "Wir beide wollen springen" (1896) and "Wenn" (1895).[20]

Ludwig Finscher has suggested that two aspects of the *Jugendstil*—constructivism and ornamental writing—converged in Strauss's post-*Jugendstil* Lieder.[21] Finscher's definition of the latter of these two characteristics is self-evident, while that of the former is more elusive, and appears to include such characteristics as the musical reinforcement of aspects of the poetic form, the ongoing development of singular motives, and a careful attention to overall musical architecture. Finscher seems to view "Stiller Gang" (Op. 31, no. 4) as the epitome of Strauss's *Jugendstil* composition, and observes that this setting of Dehmel's text is freely declamatory, featuring both rhythmic and harmonic adherence to the poetic inflection. In addition, the work's declamation is musically halted and broken, in keeping with the tradition of *Jugendstil* texts. Finally, its primary thematic development takes place in the accompaniment, where a single motive is continuously developed as a ritornello that clarifies the overall architectural structure.[22]

EXAMPLE 10.1
"Stiller Gang," Op. 31, no. 4

Mässig langsam

Finscher points to "Wiegenlied" (Op. 41, no. 1), also based on a text by Dehmel, as another fine example of *Jugendstil* in Strauss's Lieder. He cites both the ornamental style of the arpeggiated accompaniment and the melodic symmetry of the setting's three stanzas as evidence of the *Jugendstil* influence.[23] Interestingly enough, however, "Wiegenlied" is stylistically modeled on Schubert's textually similar "Nacht und Träume," which also features a strophic setting, arching sustained melodies, and a broken-chord accompaniment. The imitation of existing models, a technique shunned by the poets of the *Jugendstil* movement, was an important feature of Strauss's style throughout his lifetime, and it is likely that the composer, who enjoyed performing the Lieder of his predecessors,[24] was exploring the symbolic association between the two texts. Such conflicts between *Jugendstil* philosophies and Strauss's own compositional habits seem to suggest that while he favored *Jugendstil* poetry, he may not have embraced their compositional philosophies as his own.

Whether Strauss's association with the *Jugendstil* poets, as well as his frequent use of their texts, had an impact on the actual quality of the lieder is difficult to determine. Although a number of his songs on texts by poets associated with the *Jugendstil* circle have fallen into obscurity, others, such as "Zueignung" (Gilm), "Allerseelen" (Gilm), "Ständchen" (Schack), "Ach Lieb, ich muss nun scheiden!" (Dahn), "Morgen!" (Mackay), and "Befreit" (Dehmel), are among his best-known Lieder. An analogous situation, moreover, arises in applying a similar hypothesis to the Lieder of Hugo Wolf. Mörike and Goethe provided the texts for several of Wolf's most famous Lieder, but his settings of texts by the more obscure poets Geibel and Heyse have been equally successful in the concert repertoire.

STRAUSS'S DECLAMATORY STYLE

It is likely that Strauss was drawn to the *Jugendstil* circle partly because its philosophies regarding declamation most closely adhered to his own. The foreshadowing of a style that some scholars regard as full-blown musical *Jugendstil* can be detected in Strauss's published vocal works as early as Op. 10, which is comprised of eight settings of texts by Hermann von Gilm. The text of the seventh song, "Die Zeitlose" (Op. 10, no. 7), features numerous references to traditional symbolic images from the visual and literary arts, including the lily, the rose (both symbols of purity), and the cup (the "sacrament"). The text itself is well suited to a declamatory presentation, for it is characterized by simple, halting poetic lines. Strauss establishes the stylistic tone of the setting in the opening lines of the Lied, which feature short, jagged phrases that directly mirror the inflections of speech. These are declaimed against a chordal sighing figure provided by the piano accompaniment. When the thesis line of the text—"*doch es ist Gift, was aus dem Kelch, dem reinen, blinkt so rötlich*" (yet it is poison that glimmers so pure and red in the cup)—is presented, however, the rhythm of the sighing figure is transferred to the vocal line, where it is incorporated into the single expansive phrase of the Lied. The importance of this phrase is further underscored by the accelerated rhythm and harmonically colorful accompaniment, which features several unresolved diminished-seventh chords that are chained together through chromatic voice leading.

EXAMPLE 10.2
"Die Zeitlose," Op. 10, no. 7

The thesis phrase is then extended by several fleeting phrases that further reflect on it, at the close of which the sighing figure returns. The rhythmic care
with which Strauss set the text of "Die Zeitlose" is immediately apparent. Yet
the Lied also reveals Strauss's ability to offset melodically awkward phrasing
by manipulating the harmony. What could have easily become a rhythmi-
cally redundant and unyielding setting of the thesis line is rendered natural
by the chromatic counterpoint and syncopations of the accompaniment.
Strauss's preoccupation with the union of natural poetic inflection and a
finely chiseled melody is further evident in the fact that he was haunted later
in life by what he viewed as an inability to marry these two characteristics in
the popular "Ständchen."[25] Yet modern analyses of the piece unveil a number of rhythmic and harmonic devices that offset the very problems with
which Strauss was so concerned.[26] Moreover, Strauss recognized that such
difficulties could not be solved through manipulation of the melodic line
alone. In his search for the unification of text and music, Strauss increasingly
relied on the balanced incorporation of specific compositional devices,
including declamatory melodic writing, systematic utilization of key symbolism and text painting, shifting melodic and harmonic accents,
evolutionary musical forms, and unifying ritornelli. Although such compositional devices were applied by other successful Lieder composers,
including Schubert, Schumann, Wolf, and Mahler, the manner in which they
are simultaneously employed is a distinguishing feature of Strauss's Lieder.

One of the most fundamental compositional techniques frequented by
Strauss was an operatically inspired declamatory style similar to that found
in "Die Zeitlose." Two other songs from Op. 10 also feature declamatory
passages, and can be regarded as evidence of both Strauss's interest in clarity of declamation and familiarity with the Lieder of Hugo Wolf. In
"Nichts" (Op. 10, no. 2), the declamatory style dominates only the opening

eight measures of the vocal line, probably because the text stated there introduces the song's subject of discourse "should I name my lover so unabashedly in song?" As the text unfolds, the regular musical accent established in the Prelude is gradually displaced by the musically irregular inflection of the text, a characteristic often evidenced in the Lieder of Wolf. However, the musical material introduced in the Prelude, which functions as the song's ritornello, returns, and subsequently serves to reestablish the effect of rhythmic regularity. The remainder of the text, which is devoted to reflection on the opening question, is presented in an aria style. The entire song is formally united by the lively ritornello that arises from its Prelude. "Die Verschwiegenen" (Op. 10, no. 6), which features a charming text extolling the hidden virtues of the simple violet, is set as a dramatic accompanied recitative that sometimes gives way to arioso passages. As in many of the Wolf Lieder, the melodic accents of the vocal line shift freely in order to accommodate the natural inflections of the text. At first glance, the chordal accompaniment serves primarily to support the voice. However, its opening motive, which recurs several times throughout, additionally provides the thematic unification absent from the vocal line.

Op. 10 marks a period of great experimentation with the declamatory style as a viable means of melodically manipulating language inflection. In the published song sets that immediately follow, the technique is used more selectively. For example, Op. 15 and Op. 21 feature songs in which the declamatory passages are reserved primarily for the most significant phrases of the text. "Du meines Herzens Krönelein" (Op. 21, no. 2) features several declamatory passages that gradually unfold into expansive melodies. These not only reflect the protagonist's halting, yet unabashed declaration of love, but also serve to contrast the falsity of his previous lovers with the innocent honesty of the dedicatee. Recitative appears only in the opening and the final measures of "Lob des Leidens" (Op. 15, no. 3). The text that is set in recitative style—"*als wer für ewig scheiden muss*"—is actually part of the larger phrase "*und keiner küsst so heissen Kuss, als wer für ewig scheiden muss*" (and no one kisses so passionately as he who forever must part). The latter phrase is accorded several driving melodic repetitions, but is pulled to a gradual halt by the interference of the declamatory style accorded "*als wer für ewig scheiden muss.*" The resulting sensation is one of inconsolable despair. The declamatory passage in "Ach Lieb, ich muss nun scheiden" (Op. 21, no. 3) is also placed at the close of the work. In this case, it is created by the insertion of rests into the ultimate melodic line, thus forcing the singer to execute the text in a halting manner that resembles speaking while sobbing.

EXAMPLE 10.3
"Die Zeitlose," Op. 10, no. 7

KEY CHARACTERISTICS

It has recently been observed that Strauss further underscored the meaning of certain passages of text through the use of keys that held a specific meaning for him. Several scholars, including Willi Schuh, Edmund Wachten, Kurt Overhoff,[27] Bryan Gilliam,[28] Tethys Carpenter,[29] and Derrick Puffett,[30] have detected such use of key symbolism in the operas, where key characteristics serve not only to convey either the emotional content of the drama or the psychological condition of a given character, but also as a unifying feature of the dramatic form. In *Elektra* (1909), for example, the key of E major, which most scholars have interpreted as Strauss's "love" key, is a part of Elektra's polytonal chord, but does not assert itself until the end of the opera, at which time Elektra performs a dance in celebration of the avenging of Agamemnon's murder. Certain individuals are also assigned keys; D minor, for instance, is assigned to Orestes, while E-flat major represents Chrysothemis.[31] Gilliam further observes that although Elektra is symbolized by a chord, she is given no representative key, thus illustrating her sacrifice of both self-identity and life in the present.[32] Most scholars agree that the entire work revolves around the symbolic tonal relationships established in Elektra's monologue, namely, B-flat major/minor and C major/minor, but they do not always agree on the relative importance assigned to subsidiary keys, the affective interpretation of a given key, and the way in which various keys are tonally related to one another.[33]

Interestingly enough, the recent divergence of opinion regarding the symbolic significance of certain keys in Strauss's works has not yet led Strauss scholars to reconsider generalizations regarding the affective attributes assigned to various keys that were frequently utilized by Strauss. After all, Strauss's comments regarding key symbolism found in the letters, sketches, and autograph scores, motivated much of the preliminary research regarding this issue. Consequently, the notion that E major is the key of passion, E-flat the tonal region of heroic and noble behavior, A-flat the realm of childhood memories, and the tritone the interval of parental conflict has not disappeared from the literature on Strauss.[34] In actuality, these generalizations can be applied to the song literature with only a moderate degree of success. For example, the interpretation of E major as the key of passion and eroticism works fairly well for "Heimkehr" (Op. 15, no. 5) and "All mein Gedanken" (Op. 21, no. 1), since the texts of both songs are introspective, yet passionate in their approach to love. That both songs similarly feature harmonic inflection of the flatted submediant C major) may also be worthy of note, since this key is often interpreted as Strauss's key of triumph. However, the application of generally accepted key characteristics is less successful when considering "Winterweihe" (Op. 48, no. 4), a Lied that celebrates the victory of immortal love over human mortality. Strauss's choice of E-flat for this song is not indicative of any attempt to symbolize heroism, but rather a desire to invoke tranquillity, solidity, and emotional maturity. It is particularly significant, nonetheless, that "Im Abendrot" (*Vier letzte Lieder*), which features a very similar text, is also set in the key of E-flat. Moreover, a number of the songs with hymnlike texts are set in the key of D-flat. Such parallels suggest that certain keys did hold symbolic associations for Strauss, but that these keys must be interpreted according to a matrix of specific emotions, rather than a single emotional state.

John Kissler has suggested that the systematic application of key characteristics is also present in the *Vier letzte Lieder*, for he has discovered that the form of each song is dependent not only on motivic development, but also on symbolic keys or pairs of keys that function as tonal centerpieces. In Kissler's analysis, however, the symbolic interpretation of a given key is determined primarily by its concurrence with the text, rather than by any preexisting associations suggested in other Strauss works. For example, Kissler notes that "September" is cast in an A–B–A form that is determined by both the layout of the text and the interplay between the "garden" key of D major and the "summer" key of G major. Moreover, he notes that the tonal descent by a fifth that occurs in the latter half of the song symbolizes the arrival of autumn, and, thus, the passing of life.[35] If the evidence presented by Kissler is considered in the light of the studies devoted to key characteristics in Strauss's operas, it would seem clear that keys do not necessarily convey the same meaning from one work to another, despite the fact that a few tenuous relationships can be drawn.[36] Kissler's interpretation of the keys in the *Vier letzte Lieder*, in contrast to that pursued by several of the opera scholars, is more referential than systematic, and, perhaps, suggests a more practical approach to the study of key characteristics in Strauss's works. Such an approach would embrace other pertinent considerations that are often ignored, including major/minor polarities, the employment of increasingly sharp or flat tonalities, harmonic structure, and tonal directionality.

APPROACH TO TEXT PAINTING

Text painting serves much the same purposes in Strauss's hands that it did in those of the madrigalists and earlier German Lied composers: it either underlines key textual words and phrases or serves as a backdrop for the unfolding of the musical drama. The former is generally achieved through madrigalistic treatment of individual words in the melody or the accompaniment, while the latter is effected primarily through either recurring thematic material or referential stylistic devices found in the accompaniment. Strauss's approach to specific words and phrases is not unlike that of the sixteenth-century madrigalist, since significant words or phrases in a Strauss song are either illustrated melodically or emphasized through textual and harmonic contrasts. Moreover, the melodic illustration of individual words and phrases, like that of the madrigalists, is often blatantly obvious. Note, for example, the gradually rising line preceding the word *Himmel* (heaven) in "Wiegenlied" (Op. 41, no. 1); it seems to stretch the voice toward its limits. "Sie trugen ihn" (Op. 67, no. 3) features a falling melisma on the word *Sonne* (sun) that illustrates the warm, soft glow of a ray of sunlight, while the syncopated, lilting *Vogelsang* (bird song) in "Frühling" (*Vier letzte Lieder*) recalls the distant cry of the nightingale. Perhaps the most picturesque madrigalisms found in Strauss's writing appear in "Amor" (Op. 68, no. 5), "Beim Schlafengehn" (*Vier letzte Lieder*), and "Im Abendrot" (*Vier letzte Lieder*). The leaping arpeggios, falling scales, and trills of "Amor" not only are the trappings of a coloratura showpiece, but also serve to illustrate the fiery passion and hysterical joy of love (see Example 10.4). The slightly syncopated, leaping motive that appears to struggle free from its unseen captor provides the principal thematic material of "Beim Schlafengehn" (*Vier letzte Lieder*), where it appears to symbolize the release of the soul (see Example 10.5). This concept, incidentally, is further underscored in the close of "Im Abendrot" (*Vier letzte Lieder*), which features a quotation from Strauss's tone poem *Tod und Verklärung*. The trilling countermelody played by the flutes in "Im Abendrot" appears to represent the symbolic larks soaring into eternity (see Example 10.6).

Like a number of sixteenth-century madrigal composers, including Cipriano de Rore, Adrian Willaert, Luca Marenzio, and Carlo Gesualdo, Strauss often relies on chromaticism and changes in texture for the musical depiction of text. In "Traum durch die Dämmerung" (Op. 29, no. 1), for instance, Strauss draws attention to the final line of text "*in ein mildes,*

EXAMPLE 10.4
"Die Zeitlose," Op. 10, no. 7

chelt in die Flam - - - - - - - - men - er und

lä   chelt,

EXAMPLE 10.5
"Die Zeitlose," Op. 10, no. 7

EXAMPLE 10.6
"Die Zeitlose," Op. 10, no. 7

I

Fl.

II

blaues Licht" (in a mild, blue light), which refers to the seeming endlessness of twilight, by replacing the triplet sixteenth-note pattern that persists throughout the song with an eighth-note pattern, thus augmenting the pervading rhythmic subdivision of the beat. Despite this slowing of the rhythmic motion, however, the intervallic relationships previously established in the sixteenth-note accompaniment are retained in the soprano line of the accompaniment, which is itself harmonized by the colorful progression I–(IV substitute)–#IVG (#4 in the bass)–I⁶–V⁷–I.

EXAMPLE 10.7
"Die Zeitlose," Op. 10, no. 7

The chromatic voice leading that effects this progression, when combined with the slowing of the rhythmic motion, serves to illustrate the sensation of traveling through the endless gray mist toward a light. The harmonic underscoring of the text of "Freundliche Vision" (Op. 48, no. 1) is less localized, and, instead, features fluctuation between long passages of nontonic harmonization and harmonization of the tonic. The first nontonic section is found in the song's opening measures, and emphasizes the key of C-sharp major, the seventh degree of the song's tonic D major. The upward movement from C-sharp to the tonic D major that follows effects the sensation of emerging from a dream into reality, as is described in the text. When a later reference to realization of the dream occurs, the accompaniment plunges into a section of chromatic counterpoint that eventually returns to the tonic D major. At one point during this chromatic passage the tritone relationships E#–B and G#–D are fully exposed, probably for the ironic purpose of underscoring the "coolness" (*Kühle*) and "peacefulness" (*Friede*) of the white house in the thicket, which, in this text, appears as a symbol for requited love. The general motivic outline and rhythmic motion of the accompaniment remain unchanged throughout the entire song, perhaps because Strauss intended to veil the sense of division between dreams and reality.

The use of pictorial motivic material in the accompaniment also assists in determining the overall essence of a given Lied, and Strauss's approach to this device differed somewhat from that of his contemporaries. His pictorial accompaniments are usually generated by a single motive that is introduced at the outset and developed during the remainder of the piece. Finscher appears to view the intensive formal integration of an initial motivic idea as a "constructivist" trademark of *Jugendstil* writing,[37] but it should be noted that numerous examples of such an approach can be found across the entire canon of German Lieder. Some of Schubert's most famous Lieder, including "Erlkönig," "Die Forelle," "Gretchen am Spinnrade," and "Auf dem Wasser zu singen," feature a similar approach to motivic development in the accompaniment. However, Strauss carries Schubert's approach to accompanimental motivic development one step further by treating short, tightly constructed motives to greater melodic and harmonic variation during the course of the work. The flirtatious, mocking trill motif that opens "Mohnblumen" (Op. 22, no. 2), for example, persists throughout the entire Lied, albeit reharmonized and sounded at differing pitch levels. The rocking, arpeggiated sixteenths that illustrate the suspended dream state of "An Sie" (Op. 43, no. 1) are retained across all four melodically and harmonically varied strophes. The storm motif that opens "Schlechtes Wetter" (Op. 69, no. 5) is unrelentingly varied both harmonically and melodically during the course of the work, and the unstable harmonic motion effected by the repeated chromatic graces and continuously pivoting seventh chords of "Ruhe, meine Seele!" (Op. 27, no. 1) threatens to destroy the listener's grasp of tonic. Development of a solitary rhythmic idea serves an ironic purpose in "Geduld" (Op. 10, no. 5) where the exasperation of the lover is revealed in the pervasive quarter–eighth pattern that is repeated continually in the accompaniment.

EXAMPLE 10.8
"Geduld," Op. 10, no. 5

MODELING AS A FORM OF TEXT PAINTING

The introduction and development of thematic materials that assist in setting the stage for the text is sometimes extended to include stylistic references to preexisting compositions. For instance, the gently rolling, arpeggiated accompaniment of Strauss's "Wiegenlied" is modeled on that of Schubert's similarly texted "Nacht und Träume." A stylistic parallel can also be detected between Strauss's ironic "Geduld" (Op. 10, no. 5) and Schubert's "Ungeduld." Both songs are in a similar meter, feature related accompanimental rhythms, and coloristic use of major–minor shifts. The impatience of the speaker in Gilm's text thus recalls the impatience of the lover of *Die schöne Müllerin*. Strauss draws on such stylistic associations not only when he wishes to symbolically underscore the theme of a poem, but also when he wishes to underline the stylistic milieu of a given text. For example, his setting of Heine's "Mit deinen blauen Augen" (Op. 56, no. 4) recalls the melodic and harmonic language of Schumann, and even features a Schumannesque postlude. His treatment of Bürger's "Muttertändelei" (Op. 43, no. 2) and Arnim's "Einerlei" (Op. 69, no. 3) appropriately mirror the folk style of Mahler's *Des Knaben Wunderhorn* Lieder, while both "Das Rosenband" (Op. 36, no. 1) and "Das Bächlein" (Op. 88, no. 1), which were composed on the texts of Klopstock and Goethe, respectively, are thematically and stylistically modeled on the corresponding settings of Schubert. Such stylistic modeling can be considered an equally valid, though less obvious, form of text painting, for it provides a pictorial reference that leads to the discovery of abstract concepts inherent in a given Lied's text.

"Morgenrot" (Op. 46, no. 4), which is composed on a text by Rückert, is especially interesting, for it not only reveals that Strauss was adept at structural imitation, but also offers insight into the formal procedures that will be incorporated into the late Lieder. The Lied is modeled on those of Strauss's contemporary Gustav Mahler, who also set several of Rückert's texts around the year 1900. Mahler's penchant for thematic complexes that can be simultaneously rearranged and varied throughout is well-known,[38] and Strauss, in apparent emulation of Mahler, makes use of similar procedures in setting Rückert's text. The melody of the song's initial strophe is gradually transformed across the two successive strophes against a thematic complex comprised of three alternating accompanimental patterns. These accompanimental patterns are themselves simultaneously reordered and varied thematically and harmonically throughout the course of the work. As is characteristic of numerous Lieder of both Strauss and Mahler, each strophe opens in a firmly grounded key center—the first in C, the second in E-flat, and the last in E-flat, and the deviation from these tonal centers occurring during the course of each strophe is guided by the variation process. The song, like many of Mahler's Lieder, is a tour de force in continuous variation procedure.

STRUCTURAL DEFINITION THROUGH VARIATION PROCEDURES

The relationship between motivic development and formal procedures such as continuous variation in Strauss's Lieder is especially significant, for motivic development not only assists in determining the formal designs, but also in clarifying the textual images. Strauss repeats themes in their original or nearly original form infrequently in the Lieder, and, as a result, clear repetitions of melodic material lend special significance to the text with which they are associated. This is particularly true when such repetitions in the vocal part are accompanied by the simultaneous restatement of text, since such repetitions not only provide the work thematic and tonal closure, but also indicate that the thesis presented in connection with the repeated material is still intact. For example, "Wie sollten wir geheim sie halten" (Op. 19, no. 4) and "Ich trage meine Minne" (Op. 32, no. 1), both of which celebrate the simple ecstasy of love, feature an opening strophe of text that is repeated in conjunction with its musical material at the close of the song. In both cases, the repeated text and music indicate that the lover's original point of view has not been substantially altered during the course of the poetic event. The first two lines of "Meinem Kinde" (Op. 37, no. 3) similarly return at its close, but the musical material that accompanies it is slightly varied during the repetition. The text and music of the last two lines of "Einerlei" (Op. 69, no. 3) are also repeated, but are contracted for the second statement through elimination and slight rearrangement of text and thematic material. The varied repetitions found in both "Meinem Kinde" and "Einerlei" effect a sense of emotional maturation and relaxation that parallels the events described in their texts. "Wie sollten wir geheim sie halten," "Ich trage meine Minne," and "Meinem Kinde" are rendered ternary forms by the repeated music and text that close them, but the impetus for musical closure arises from the composer's desire to musically impose a given interpretation of the text. Similarly, the folk character of the Lied "Einerlei" is reinforced by the refrain treatment accorded its final text "*Einerlei, mancherlei, o du liebes Einerlei!*" (O beloved uniformity, how diverse you are!), but the varied refrain itself serves to illustrate the "diversity in uniformity" that is the subject of the text.

Unless there is a clear textual demand for the literal repetition of themes, however, Strauss instead prefers constant variation of them. This approach automatically provides for increased harmonic diversity, since any repetition of melodic materials need only follow a vague outline of the original. Experimentation with basic variation procedures can be found in the published songs as early as "Die Nacht" (Op. 10, no. 3), which features a vocal part comprised of four varied statements of the same thematic material. The thematic unity of "Die Nacht" is further assured by the persistently repeated eighth-note pattern that characterizes its accompaniment. The resulting miniature is tightly constructed, but at the same time allows for a great deal of harmonic fluctuation around the tonal centers of D major, B minor, F-sharp minor, and D minor. A similar approach can be detected in "Ach Lieb, ich muss nun scheiden" (Op. 21, no. 3), but in this case the varied theme alternates with two others so that the following thematic complex results:

Prelude   a   a1   b   b1   a2   c (recital) Postlude
(1–3)   (3–7)   (7–11) (11–15) (15–19) (20–24) (25–29)   (29–32)

Though the entire song remains well grounded in the key of f minor, both the introduction of diverse material and the variation of repeated themes allows for some limited chromaticism and interplay of the submediant and subdominant keys.

The variation of the long musical strophes of "Die Georgine" (Op. 10, no. 4) foreshadows the continuous variation techniques found in Strauss's mature Lied style. The song is characterized by a high degree of melodic and harmonic variation from one musical strophe to the next, for each of its three vocal sections is significantly altered to accommodate both the shifting inflections of the text and the motivic development of a repetitious accompanimental figure that lends itself to some chromatic counterpoint.

EXAMPLE 10.9
"Die Georgine," Op. 10, no. 4

The diversity of the three vocal sections further results from the grouping of a larger number of text lines for the second and third complexes, thus decreasing the possibility of structural symmetry. The song's Prelude introduces the repeated motive that is developed in the accompaniment, and, consequently, the Prelude is also treated to variation during each of the Interludes and the Postlude, the latter of which is punctuated with vocal declamation. The famous "Wiegenlied" (Op. 41, no. 1) features variation of a larger complex as well, but its melodic variants, unlike those of "Die Georgine," are limited to minor rhythmic and intervallic adjustments of the vocal line. Consequently, each of the strophes in "Wiegenlied" is more symmetrically arranged, and its accompaniment features little actual development of motivic material.

Both "Schlagende Herzen" (Op. 29, no. 2) and "Muttertändelei" (Op. 43, no. 2) are characterized by more complex variation of the musical strophes. In "Schlagende Herzen" the melodic motives introduced in the first strophe are simultaneously reordered and varied for the latter two, thus leaving the listener with only a vague impression that repetition has taken place. Strauss compensates for this lack of a strong aural conception of formal symmetry by reinforcing a perception of textual and melodic recapitulation through repetition of the "Kling klang, schlug ihm das Herz" motive. The Wunderhorn-style *ländler* "Muttertänderlei" features a gradual progression of alterations across its five strophes. The most striking variants are introduced in the second and third strophes, and then are incorporated and reworked in the fourth and fifth strophes. Because the process of melodic variation occurs gradually and the original thematic material is never entirely transformed, a strong sense of strophicism is maintained. This impression is reinforced by the principal theme of the Interludes and the Postlude, which is directly derived from measures five to ten of the first strophe.

The continuous variation process found in the later songs systematically evolved from a combination of the variation techniques evidenced in Strauss's earlier Lieder. "Die Allmächtige" (Op. 77, no. 4), for example, is cast in a ternary format, but even its contrasting central section features development of motives introduced in the opening strophe:

Prelude	a	Interlude	a1	Interlude	b	a2	Postlude
	2 lines		2 lines		4 lines	3 lines	
(1–2)	(2–11)	(12–14)	(14–23)	(24–25)	(25–45)	(45–59)	(60–64)

"Der Stern" (Op. 69, no. 1) also features a formal plan that might be described as ternary, but in this instance as well the second thematic group follows immediately after the first, and subsequently assists in generating the variant materials found in the return of the first thematic group:

a	b	a+b1	a+b2	Postlude
(1–4)	(5–11)	(12–19)	(20–27)	(28–31)

Close scrutiny of Strauss's variation procedures reveals that he often manipulates the rhythmic and harmonic content so that important points of textual, harmonic, and rhythmic tension coincide. As a result, moments of musical climax usually depend, in part, on the expansion or contraction of the song's characteristic rhythms at the desired point of coincision. As the elongation or shortening of the characteristic rhythms occur, however, the basic text rhythm suggested by the poetic meter is retained. A comparison of the settings of the final line of text in strophes one and two of "Zueignung" (Op. 10, no. 1) reveals that Strauss heightens the tension at the close of the second strophe by simultaneously displacing the original rhythm, varying the melodic line, and changing the harmonic direction suggested by the accompaniment (see Example 10.10.1 and 10.10.2). However, the most emotionally charged moment in "Zueignung" occurs during the final line of the third musical strophe. Here the vocal line is transposed up a third, albeit intervallically altered. The density and character of the accompaniment are simultaneously transformed by the abandonment of arpeggiated chords for repeated ones, thus placing the chromatic voice leading in bold relief. Most important, the original rhythmic patterns are again treated to variation, and the closing *"habe Dank"* (give thanks) is displaced by one measure. The resulting coincidence of rhythmic, harmonic, and melodic tension, as well as its subsequent release, illustrates the unrestrained passion suggested by the text (see Example 10.11). Such effects appear in numerous Strauss Lieder, and are generally associated with points of particular poetic significance and closure, as well as with musical codas. For example, the final strophe of "Allerseelen" (Op. 10, no. 8) is marked by simultaneous pitch variation and rhythmic contraction of the recurring phrase *"wie einst in Mai"* (as once in May), which, in this instance, is harmonized by chromatic counterpoint progressing from the secondary dominant to the dominant. Following a two-measure interlude, the phrase is repeated in its original rhythm, but with further pitch variation of the original motive. This setting of the phrase is differently harmonized, featuring chromatic movement from a German sixth chord (#4 in the bass) to an authentic cadence. The resulting effect is that of a gradual, yet halting release of tension (see Example 10.12).

EXAMPLE 10.10.1
"Zueignung," Op. 10, no. 1

EXAMPLE 10.10.2

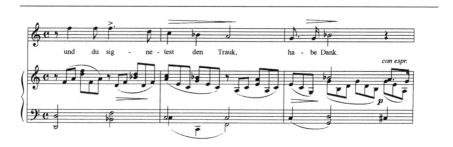

EXAMPLE 10.11
"Zueignung," Op. 10, no. 1

EXAMPLE 10.12
"Allerseelen," Op. 10, no. 8

STRUCTURAL DEFINITION THROUGH TONAL UNDERPINNING OF THE POETIC FORM

In addition to relying on variation procedures as a vehicle for controlling musical tension, many of the Lieder feature a tonal plan that mirrors the structure of the texts on which they were composed. Such tonal underpinning of the poetic structure is particularly significant in those songs that are basically through composed, for it provides a sense of formal grounding in the absence of substantial melodic or melodic/harmonic repetition. "Lob des Leidens" (Op. 15, no. 3), for example, is a through-composed song featuring two six-line strophes arranged in the simple rhyming pattern ababcc:

O schmäht des Lebens Leiden nicht!
seht ihr die Blätter, wenn sie sterben,
Sich in des Herbstes goldenem Licht
Nicht reicher, als im Frühling färben?
Was gleicht der Blüte des Vergehens
Im Hauche des Oktoberwehens?

Krystallner als die klarste Flut
Erglänzt des Auges Tränenquelle,
Tief dunkler flammt die Abendglut
Als hoch am Tag die Sonnenhelle.
Und keiner küsst so heissen Kuss,
Als wer für ewig scheiden muss.[39]

The opening strophe, which comprises the first seventeen measures of
music, is clearly set in the key of B-flat minor, although the key of g minor
is foreshadowed throughout. The second strophe, which occupies the last
twenty-six measures of music, is grounded in B-flat major, but features exploration of both g minor and D-flat major, as well a reestablishment of
B-flat minor at its close. The key exploration that occurs in the second strophe, which is accompanied by an expansion of the characteristic rhythmic
values of the vocal line, partly accounts for its musical elongation by nine
measures, since two additional measures are required for the first line of its
six-line strophe. The other additional seven measures, however, result from
the declamatory-style repetition of the final line of text. Although the musical elongation of the second strophe creates a "lopsidedness" that further
obscures a form already lacking in repetition, the individual harmonic underpinning given each strophe assists in clarifying the textual plan. The
resulting tonal structure not only is grounded formally, but also is driven
programmatically, for the fluctuation between B-flat minor and B-flat
major represents the bittersweet farewell suggested by the text. Although the
pain of the farewell (B-flat minor) is temporarily replaced by the memory
of the passionate moment of parting (B-flat major), the gnawing ache of
separation persists.

In through-composed songs featuring numerous textual complexes, the
synchronization of key movement and text plays an even more important
role in delineating textual form. In "Im Abendrot" (*Vier letzte Lieder*), key
changes sometimes occur within the progress of a single strophe, but every
strophe begins in a well-established key area. An overview of the song's tex-
tual/tonal plan might be sketched as follows:

Measures	*Section*	*Principal Key Area(s)*
1–20	Prelude	Eb–Cb–Eb
21–35	Strophe 1	Eb–Bb
36–44	Strophe 2	Bb–Gb–f#–c#–Db
45–55	Strophe 3	Db–Bb–Eb–Bb
56–76	Strophe 4	Bb–Eb/eb–surprise cadence on Cb6/4
76–96	Postlude	reestablishes Eb[40]

If E-flat major is viewed as the key of resignation in this piece (rather than as the key of heroics, as is sometimes suggested), then the fluctuation between E-flat and the subsidiary keys, including B-flat, C-flat, and D-flat (the key of freedom in "Beim Schlafengehn"), might be viewed as symbolic of the resignation process itself. This interpretation is particularly appropriate if one accepts the assertion that the key of C-flat, which is the tonality also associated with the *Tod und Verklärung* theme, is Strauss's "death" key.[41] The coloristic use of the parallel minor keys of D-flat and E-flat major may serve to underscore the bittersweet duality of the emotions associated with resignation and release in the face of death.

Some songs featuring a basic tonal outline that mirrors poetic format actually contain a hidden "tonal agenda" that serves to underscore significant textual points embedded within the poetic stanza as well. In such cases the tonal underlining of the embedded text often takes on more importance than that of the stanzaic formula itself. This is an especially noteworthy feature of "Befreit" (Op. 39, no. 4), a strophic song characterized by constant melodic and harmonic variation. A cursory glance at the text of "Befreit" suggests that either melodic repetition or harmonic underscoring should be allotted the final line "o Glück!" (oh happiness!) closing each of its three stanzas:

> Du wirst nicht weinen. Leise, leise
> wirst du lächeln und wie zur Reise
> geb' ich dir Blick und Kuss zurück.
> Unsre lieben vier Wände, du hast sie bereitet,
> ich habe sie dir zur Welt geweitet;
> o Glück!
>
> Dann wirst du heiss meine Hände fassen
> und wirst mir deine Seele lassen,
> lässt unsern Kindern mich zurück.
> Du schenktest mir dein ganzes Leben,
> Ich will es ihnen wiedergeben;
> o Glück!
>
> Es wird sehr bald sein, wir wissen's Beide,
> wir haben einander befreit vom Leide,
> so gab' ich Dich der Welt zurück.
> Dann wirst du mir nur noch im Traum erscheinen
> und mich segnen und mit mir weinen;
> o Glück![42]

Strauss maintained the rhythmic content of this melodic line with each repetition; however, he varied its intervallic content and delayed its expected harmonic resolution. Moreover, although each of the three stanzas does open in a fairly well-grounded key center—the first in E minor, the second in B major, and the third in A minor—the most prominent points of tonal resolution are actually found on the word *zurück* (return) that closes the third line of each stanza. The first resolution of *zurück* occurs in E major, the second in E major, and the third in D major. The tonal shift downward that occurs in the third stanza creates a sense of release from the brighter key of E major, and probably serves to illustrate not only grim resolution in the face of death, but also a sense of consolation. The strong tonal resolution of the word *zurück* temporarily draws attention away from the phrase *o Glück* in order to highlight the principal theme of the text—the release of the soul of the loved one. As a result, the delay of the expected tonal resolution on the final line of each strophe (*o Glück*) can be interpreted as symbolizing both the anticipation of the inevitable loss of the loved one and the ambivalent feelings that accompany such a loss. The anticipation of loss is already emphasized in the text through frequent use of the future tense.

Tonal underscoring plays a similar role in the song "Beim Schlafengehn," which is traditionally performed third in the set of *Vier letzte Lieder*. Its three strophes of text by Hermann Hesse joyfully anticipate a death that will free the soul from the exhausted body encumbering it. The Prelude and first two strophes of text occupy only the first twenty-four measures of music, while the final strophe is allotted the remaining forty-seven measures, thus upsetting the balance of measured time in favor of the final strophe. This uneven balance of measured time arises primarily from the application of continuous variation procedure during the final strophe, for the obligato-style melody introduced by the violin in measures 24 through 37 is repeated in variation by the voice in measures 38 through 60. The resulting emphasis on the final strophe of text is reinforced by the song's tonal plan, which during the first twenty-two measures is characterized by the virtual establishment and immediate obliteration of various tonal centers, after which the emergence of the obligato violin part and the introduction of the key of D-flat major coincide. The key of D-flat major remains firmly rooted for the entirety of the third strophe, perhaps as a symbol of the peace of the soul as it takes flight.

The role of tonal movement in defining textual context is crucial to the success of "Zueignung" (Op. 10, no. 1). Although essentially strophic, this song does feature some limited melodic variation that serves to accentuate important phrases of the text. The most obvious alterations of melody fall on the third line of each strophe, and in each case momentarily redirect the harmonic motion of the accompaniment, thus drawing attention to the text. The more important melodic changes, however, are rhythmic, and not only allow for correct linguistic inflection, but also heighten the dramatic impression.

EXAMPLE 10.13
"Zueignung," Op. 10, no. 1

The emotional impact of the piece is primarily dependent on what appears to be a slight lack of coordination between text and tonality that is corrected at the opening of the final strophe. This sense of tonal irregularity results from overemphasis of the mediant key in harmonizing the opening of the first two strophes. As a result, the tonic, although present throughout, seems tentative until the opening of the third strophe, at which time it strongly asserts itself. The aural sensation is one of tonal satisfaction, and it cleverly mirrors the romantic satisfaction suggested by the text.

Careful attention to text declamation, effective text painting, and the utilization of tonal movement to underscore the symbolism of the text are unified to create a miniature dramatic scene in "Schlechtes Wetter" (Op. 69, no. 5). The text of this song, which was taken from Heine's folk collection entitled *Die Heimkehr*, describes an onlooker watching a woman from his window that he imagines to be a mother trudging through the darkness carrying the flour, eggs, and butter with which she will make a cake for her daughter, who is at home lounging in the warmth and light. Heine's poem, which some literary scholars suggest was modeled on both Rückert's "Edelstein und Perle," no. 7, and Müller's "Italienisches Ständchen in Ritornellen," no. 11,[43] is a study in poetic chiaroscuro, for the dark stormy night is contrasted with the safety and security of light throughout.

Strauss set the poem to a recurring waltz theme that not only under-scores the simple folk character of the text, but also serves to illustrate the security of the narrator and imagined daughter, both of whom are sitting at home in the warmth and light. However, the inviolable nature of the waltz theme is obscured at the outset by a storm motif that is introduced in the piano prelude.

EXAMPLE 10.14
"Schlechtes Wetter," Op. 69, no. 5

As the waltz theme gradually emerges and is merged with the storm motif, the storm motif is transformed into cascading arpeggios that represent both the golden locks of the reclining daughter and the light that bathes them. The transformation of the storm motif occurs in two principal stages. In the first, the arpeggio in the soprano and the grace note figure of the bass ex-change places, and the grace note figure is repeated so that it not only appears to resemble both the sound of falling rain and the flickering of the mother's lantern, but also better incorporates the waltz theme.

EXAMPLE 10.15
"Schlechtes Wetter," Op. 69, no. 5

In the second stage the materials of the storm motif appear in the bass against the waltz theme, which is presented in the treble.

The vocal line is set against this colorful backdrop in a quasi-declamatory fashion that gradually gives way to aria style. Painstaking attention to the inflection of the text can be observed in the rhythmic writing of the vocal line throughout. Despite the emphasis on text inflection, madrigalisms are incorporated into the vocal line as well, and include such obvious figures as the dotted rising half step on the word *rains* ("regnet"), which suggests the splashing of the raindrops (see Example 10.15), and the falling scale that symbolizes the "cascading locks."

EXAMPLE 10.16
"Schlechtes Wetter," Op. 69, no. 5

Although the text painting of the vocal line does include the blatant illustration of other words and phrases, it focuses primarily on the various images of light that are set against the dark and stormy night. In the second strophe, for instance, the chromatic graces from the piano part, which evoke the image of the flickering lantern carried by the mother as she trods through the darkness, are incorporated into the repetitive quarter-eighth pattern of the vocal line, thus causing the vocal line to flicker. The grace figures return at the opening of the final strophe in connection with the image of the daughter blinking drowsily in the lamplight, and are succeeded by a strong tonic resolution on the word *light*.

EXAMPLE 10.17
"Schlechtes Wetter," Op. 69, no. 5

In this manner, the cascading golden locks of the daughter that are depicted by the falling arpeggio are picturesquely "bathed" in the lamplight.

The emphasis on light is also reflected tonally in the utter deflection of various key centers suggested by both the melodic direction of the vocal line and the harmonic motion supplied by the piano accompaniment. The only relatively stable key area is F major/minor, which can be interpreted as the chiaroscuro key center. Other keys are suggested or momentarily passed through, but none offer the level of stability allotted F major/minor. An outline of the primary tonal areas as they relate to the text clearly indicates that Strauss viewed Heine's "light" as an image of safety and security:

Section	Measures	Visual/Textual Image	Key Centers(s)
Prelude	1–3	Dark, stormy night	F/f
Strophe 1	3–31	Narrator looks out on stormy night	f–bb–f
Strophe 2	32–51	Mother trudges through dark with lantern	f/F
Strophe 3	52–69	Imaginings of the cake that mother will bake	Db–(D)–F
Strophe 4	69–94	The daughter drowsing at home in the light	F
Postlude	94–107	Light illuminates the sleeping daughter's face	F

The amount of musical time allotted each of the above sections is also worthy of note, for it corresponds directly to the dramatic action occurring in a given strophe. As the dramatic tension increases, the amount of musical time required for the setting of the strophe decreases. Conversely, as the dramatic tension decreases, the amount of musical time used for setting texts of corresponding length increases. Thus, as the mother nears home (strophe 3) the number of measures assigned the poetic strophe contracts from thirty to seventeen. After she has "stepped" through the door and into the light that surrounds her sleeping daughter, the number of measures required for the poetic strophe expands from seventeen to twenty-five, thereby signifying the relief that she experiences upon arrival.

THE ORCHESTRATED LIEDER

In the year 1896 Strauss became interested in orchestrating a number of Lieder composed earlier in his career. It is, of course, significant that Wolf and Mahler, the other leading Lieder composers of the period, also produced a number of orchestral Lieder during this time, for the coincidence suggests that orchestrated songs were gaining increased popularity as concert items during the late nineteenth century. The sudden interest in this genre probably stemmed primarily from the fact that Lieder with piano accompaniments were still often introduced into concerts featuring orchestral compositions, but the halls in which these concerts were performed were so large that orchestral accompaniment of the Lieder was found preferable for acoustical reasons. Moreover, the logistics of the performance situation itself must have been simplified by the omission of major breaks in the program for the changes in staging and personnel that would have been required when chamber music and large orchestral works were juxtaposed for a single concert. However, it is noteworthy that Richard Strauss and Pauline Strauss-de Ahna continued to perform Lieder for voice and piano at a number of concerts that also featured large-scale orchestral works. Their devotion to the voice–piano Lied during an age in which the Lied was being forced into the large hall may have been influenced by the derision with which some purists viewed the orchestral Lied.[44] It is equally likely, however, that Strauss simply did not find the time to orchestrate a number of the songs that he enjoyed performing, and, as a result, continued to program the voice–piano versions of them.

The songs for voice and piano that Strauss rearranged for orchestral performance fall, for the most part, into three distinct groups that are clearly aligned with the periods in which he was most active as a performer of his

Lieder (see Table 10.1).[45] Strauss's first encounter with the orchestral Lied occurred between the years 1896 and 1900, at which time he was touring
extensively with Pauline Strauss-de Ahna as an accompanist and conductor
of his own works. Aside from a few of Strauss's colleagues at the Munich and
Berlin Operas, Pauline was the principal performer of her husband's Lieder
between the years 1894 and 1906. She was said to have had a pleasing, though
technically uneven soprano voice, and was generally regarded as a better interpreter than she was a vocal technician.[46] That a large number of the Lieder
from the years 1894 to 1906 not specifically intended for another singer are
best suited to a soprano is not at all surprising, given the fact that during that
time Strauss considered Pauline the best interpreter of his Lieder. Between
1894 and 1906 the Strausses kept a busy concert schedule, and their 1904
agenda even included an American tour with the Wetzler Symphony Orchestra. Among the thirty-five orchestral concerts and Lieder recitals
comprising the American trip were two concerts at Wanamaker's New York
department store that included several Lieder sung by Pauline.[47] At least five
of the orchestral arrangements composed between 1896 and 1900 are known
to have been sung often by her—"Cäcilie" (Op. 27, no. 2), "Morgen" (Op. 27,
no. 4), "Wiegenlied" (Op. 41, no. 1), "Meinem Kinde" (Op. 37, no. 3), and
"Muttertänderlei" (Op. 43, no. 2). In fact, the latter three of these constituted
the group known as the "Mutterlieder," and Pauline performed them quite
frequently on concerts scheduled during the years 1900–01.[48]

When Strauss ceased composing Lieder for voice and piano in 1906, he
also stopped orchestrating preexisting ones. However, another brief period
of great activity in orchestrating the Lieder can be identified for the year
1918, at which time Strauss returned to composing for the genre. In 1918 the
performance and composition of Lieder may have been his quickest source
of cash, since a number of the European opera houses were closed for several years following the First World War. In arranging the publication of his
Op. 56 songs in 1906, moreover, Strauss had contractually obligated himself
to sign his next group of songs over to publishers Bote and Bock. Because
Strauss was one of the leading representatives of the Genossenschaft zur Ver-
wendung musikalischer Aufführungsrechte, a then recently established
organization that championed the rights of German composers in their dealings with publishers, he came to feel morally obligated to fight the Bote and
Bock contract, which denied him all rights to royalties earned through the
sales. Strauss dodged this contractual obligation for as long as possible, but
the issue of the promised set of songs came to a head in 1918 when Strauss
offered Bote and Bock the satirical *Krämerspiegel*, Op. 66. Strauss had also
completed two of the six Brentano Lieder (Op. 68) by early 1918, but evidently withheld them, perhaps hoping to offer them to a publisher who

TABLE 10.1

Lieder for Voice and Piano Orchestrated by Strauss

Orchestrated 1896–1900

Cäcilie (Op. 27, no. 1), 1897
Morgen! (Op. 27, no. 2), 1897
Liebeshymnus (Op. 32, no. 3), 1897
Verführung (Op. 33, no.1), 1896
Gesang der Apollopriesterin (Op. 33, no. 2), 1896
Hymnus (Op. 33, no. 3), 1897
Pilgers Morgenlied (Op. 33, no. 4), 1897
Das Rosenband (Op. 36, no. 1), 1897
Meinem Kinde (Op. 37, no. 3), 1897–1900
Wiegenlied (Op. 41, no. 1), 1899–1900
Muttertändelei (Op. 43, no. 2), 1900

Orchestrated 1918

Der Arbeitsman (Op. 39, no. 3)
Des Dichters Abendgang (Op. 47, no. 2)
Freundliche Vision (Op. 48, no. 1)
Winterweihe (Op. 48, no. 4)
Winterliebe (Op. 48, no. 5)
Waldseligkeit (Op. 49, no. 1)

Orchestrated 1933

Mein Auge (Op. 37, no. 4)
Befreit (Op. 39, no. 4)
Frühlingsfeier (Op. 56, no. 5)

Orchestrated 1940

Zueignung (Op. 10, no. 1)
An die Nacht (Op. 68, no. 1)
Ich wollt ein Sträusslein binden (Op. 68, no. 2)
Säusle, liebe Myrthe (Op. 68, no. 3)
Als mir dein Lied erklang (Op. 68, no. 4)
Amor (Op. 68, no. 5)
Lied der Frauen (Op. 68, no 6)

Orchestrated Singly

Ruhe, meine Seele! (Op. 27, no. 1), 1948
Ich liebe dich (Op. 37, no. 2), 1943
Die heiligen drei Könige (Op. 56, no. 6), 1906
Das Bächlein (Op. 88, no. 1), 1935

would allow him rights to the royalties. In any case, Bote and Bock refused to accept the *Krämerspiegel*, the texts of which directly attacked the German publishing industry. The firm retaliated by pursuing their earlier threat of legal action, and Strauss hastily prepared the six songs of Op. 67, which he offered in place of the offensive *Krämerspiegel*.[49] After matters were settled, Strauss was able to return to song composition free of potential legal difficulties. Around that same time, he also again began appearing in recitals with a number of his closest associates, including singers Elisabeth Schumann, Franz Steiner, and Elena Gerhardt. As a result of this renewed activity in Lieder performance, Strauss orchestrated a number of Lieder for concert presentation. In fact, several of the Lieder orchestrated in 1918 were intended specifically for Schumann, including "Freundliche Vision" (Op. 48, no. 1), "Winterweihe" (Op. 48, no. 4), and "Winterliebe" (Op. 49, no. 5).

The subsequent years are marked by two other brief periods of interest in the preparation of orchestral Lieder. The preexisting Lieder orchestrated in 1933, which include Op. 68, no. 6, were prepared specifically for soprano Viorica Ursuleac, who first performed them under Strauss's baton in Berlin on 13 October 1933 and subsequently sang them on numerous *Lieder-abende* accompanied by Clemens Krauss. Another flurry of activity marks the year 1840, at which time Strauss was primarily occupied with the preparation of the score of *Capriccio*. It is possible that Strauss briefly turned to the orchestral Lied in 1940 because his thoughts were occupied by the conflict between the poet and the musician that is reflected in the opera. However, such a notion seems a bit foreign to Strauss's practical personality. The 1940 orchestration of "Zueignung" was also prepared especially for Ursuleac, and it is much more likely that Strauss orchestrated the remaining five Op. 68 songs at this time as well simply because he wished to have Ursuleac and Krauss perform them.[50]

Strauss's orchestrated arrangements of his voice–piano Lieder often provide insight into the composer's affective conception of a given song because the orchestral palette allowed him a truer shading of the various accompanimental details that comprise the backdrop for the vocal drama. For example, although the style of the piano accompaniment of "Wiegenlied" (Op. 41, no. 1) suggests that it is a lullaby sung at night near a body of water, the orchestral version evokes an Italian serenade sung by some street musicians or gondoliers in the heart of Venice. The gentle rocking of the boats, the lapping of the water, the soft vibration of the stringed instruments, and the pumping of the accordion are invoked by the harmonics, heavy vibrato, and pizzicato assigned the strings, as well as by the changing kaleidoscope of woodwind timbres (see Table 10.2). The orchestral timbres thereby clarify the details of the scene suggested by the piano accompaniment.

The orchestral arrangements also reveal the extent to which Strauss reconsidered the compositional details of a given song. Although a number of minor alterations in rhythm of the vocal line, some small changes in the design of the Prelude, Postlude, and Interludes, and the addition of figural

TABLE 10.2
Special Features of Orchestration of Wiegenlied

Instrumentation	Material Derived from Piano	Effects Added in Orchestral Version
Strophe 1 (measures 1–34)		
Harp, viola, cello	Short chords on strong beats	Pizzicato
Solo celli	Sustained chords on strong beats	Harmonics, played with heavy vibrato
Solo violins	Arpeggiated accompanimental figure	
Violins	Long, sustained chords on strong beats	
Strophe 2 (measures 35–56)		
Harp, violin, viola, basses	Short chords on strong beats	Pizzicato
Solo violin(s), solo viola(s)	Arpeggiated accompanimental figure	
Celli, horns, clarinets, bassoon	Long, sustained chords on strong beats	
English horn		Melody in unison with voice
Strophe 3 (measures 57–86)		
Harp, celli, basses	Short chords on strong beats	Pizzicato
Solo violins, solo viola	Arpegggiated accompanimental figure	
Violins, viola, horn, bassoon	Long, sustained chords on strong beats	
Flute, oboe, English horn, clarinet	Long held chords in prelude and postlude	Cadential punctuation of vocal theme
Flute		Arpeggiated countermelody

details that are idiomatic to the instruments used can be found when a given Lied is transferred from the piano to the orchestra, the original melodic and harmonic conception of the Lied itself remains largely unchanged. In fact, the orchestration of "Ruhe, meine Seele!" (Op. 27, no. 1), which was completed more than fifty years after the song's first publication, reveals that the composer's original conception of the work remained intact, despite the fact that he had composed many Lieder since the time of its inception. Strauss's alterations for the orchestral score of "Ruhe, meine Seele!" consist primarily of added measures that result from the orchestra's superior ability to sustain pitch, fairly inconsequential rhythmic adjustments of the vocal line, and the addition of figuration idiomatic to the instrument to which it is assigned (see Table 10.3). It has recently been

TABLE 10.3

Revisions to "Ruhe, meine Seele!" for the Orchestral Score

Measure	Revision	Possible Reasoning
5	One measure extension of Introduction	Sustaining power of strings, incorporation of motivic integration
5	Incorporation of three-note arpeggiated figure from measure 7 of piano score	
23	Quarter rest replaces tied quarter on beat one	Orchestral tremolo more clearly exposed
27	Accompanimental figuration reworked	Increased rhythmic motion; heightens drama
28	Vocal rhythm replaces piano on beat four	Adheres more closely to text inflection
31	Accompanimental figuration reworked	Rhythmic diversity; heightens drama
32	F# extended by one beat in vocal part	Sustaining power of orchestra affords vocal part added time
33	Added measure for extension of chord introduced in measure 32	Sustaining power of orchestra superior to that of piano
40	Orchestra enters on beat three instead of beat one	Effects stronger anticipation of final statement
41	Length of Postlude doubled, and three–note motive developed more extensively	Greater motivic integration

suggested that Strauss orchestrated "Ruhe, meine Seele!" with the intention of using it as a prelude to "Im Abendrot" in the cycle currently known as the *Vier letzte Lieder*. The two songs share both a common textual theme and a recurring Notmotiv.[51]

Although most of Strauss's orchestral Lieder are orchestrations of works originally conceived for voice and piano, a few of them actually originated as orchestral Lieder. These include Op. 33, Op. 44, Op. 51, and Op. 71, as well as the *Vier letzte Lieder*. Op. 44 and Op. 51 were composed specifically for baritone and bass voices, respectively, but the voice types intended for Op. 33 and Op. 71 seem open to some speculation. Op. 33 features two songs for high voice and two songs for low voice, and Norman Del Mar reports that when they were performed at the 1910 Munich Strauss festival under the composer's baton, soprano Edyth Walker sang the first two, while baritone Fritz Feinhals sang the last two.[52] Op. 71, the Hölderlin settings, are specified as a collection for high voice, and seem best suited to the soprano voice.

STRAUSS'S PERFORMANCE OF HIS OWN LIEDER

One of the most interesting aspects of the study of Strauss's Lieder is that of his performance of them on concert tours as both an accompanist and a conductor. Perusal of the two recently released compact disc recordings of the recitals given by Strauss on the Viennese radio during the years 1942 and 1943[53] verifies, as is often claimed,[54] that Strauss frequently did not play the accompaniments of the songs as they were written. Although it is highly likely that many of his emendations were due to his age and flagging technique, the liberties that he chose to take were remarkably consistent from one performance to the next. Among the frequently recurring deviations from the printed score are the following:

1. arpeggiation or rolling of chords;
2. elimination of chord rolls included in the published version;
3. alteration of the playing style of the final chord;
4. changes of registration and altered octave doublings;
5. slight harmonic alteration of chords;
6. slight rhythmic changes, especially in Preludes and Postludes;
7. dropping beats and/or measures in Interludes and Postludes, as well as under long, sustained pitches;

8. simplification of the bass part whenever the accompaniment be-
    comes too difficult;

9. speeding up repeated notes, repeated chords, eighth-note se-
    quences, and sixteenth-note sequences;

10. changes of tempo, especially during Preludes, Interludes, Postludes,
    as well as under long notes in the vocal part.

The first three habits appear to reflect Strauss's flexible attitude toward the notation of chords, since he freely interchanges block chords,
rolled chords, and arpeggiated chords in the accompaniments, and sometimes adds appoggiaturas to the final chord as well. As Barbara Petersen has
already suggested, it is possible that some of his decisions to alter the playing style of chords were guided by elements of the performance itself,
including the singer's ability to sustain the sound and the tempo selected
for a given performance.[55] The various methods of altering the playing style
of chords, as well as the changes of registration, octave doublings, and
minor chord alterations used by Strauss may also have been driven by attempts to create an orchestral sound on the keyboard.[56] Strauss's free
treatment of chords in the 1942 and 1943 performances suggests that some
limited alteration in playing style of the chords is permissible in modern
performance, provided that the alterations chosen are guided by those used
by Strauss himself. Other Lieder composers, in fact, similarly altered the accompaniments to their Lieder in performance. The 1938–39 recording of
Hans Pfitzner's Lieder made by Gerald Hüsch and the composer reveals that
Pfitzner utilized a number of comparable alterations when accompanying
his own Lieder, including the rolling of chords, the arpeggiation of chords,
the omission of rolled chords indicated in the printed score, the occasional
reiteration of chords, and slight rhythmic alterations of the bass line.[57]
    Strauss's habit of dropping beats and/or measures from the songs is
marked by less consistency, but again appears to be guided, at least in part,
by the abilities of the singer. This is particularly true when the beats or
measures dropped are those which appear under the sustained notes of
the vocal part. However, material is also deleted from the Interludes and
Postludes, thus suggesting that some alterations were intended as a means
of either saving air time or reducing the length of exposed passages he
found technically difficult. In the 1942 radio broadcast of "Wiegenlied"
(Op. 41, no. 1), for instance, Strauss drops a large number of beats and
measures. The passages eliminated occur under sustained sounds, as well as
in some of the Interludes. Unfortunately, the resulting impression is that
singer Maria Reining does not know the music well.

It is clear that Strauss's practice of simplifying the bass part in the Lieder was also driven by his technical inability to play the part well as written. Strauss was nearly eighty years old at the time of these recordings, and he likely no longer possessed the dexterity to play accompaniments that had once been a part of his performing repertoire. His alterations of the bass often include dropping material altogether, as in the 1943 performance of "Blick vom oberen Belvedere" (Op. 88, no. 2), where most of the triplets in the bass are eliminated, and "Du meines Herzens Krönelein" (Op. 21, no. 2), where some of the eighths in the bass are left out. In other cases, such as the 1942 performance of "Schlechtes Wetter" (Op. 69, no. 5), he attempts to simplify the material by condensing it. In the 1942 performance of "Schlechtes Wetter," the condensation is achieved by substituting chordal accompaniment for some of the thirty-second-note patterns. The harmonic outline suggested by the notated material is thus retained.

Strauss's declining technical skill may also have affected his performance on the 1942 and 1943 recordings in several other ways. In a number of fast-paced and difficult passages, such as those of "In goldener Fülle," "Glückes genug," and "Schlechtes Wetter," not all of the pitches in a given chord sound together, and a muddy sound results. This problem appears to arise, in part, from Strauss's inability to precisely coordinate the motion of either all the fingers in a given hand or the right and left hands themselves. Some of the passages requiring extensive technical facility are further riddled with rhythmic inaccuracies and metric inconsistencies that appear to be the byproducts of Strauss's failure to maintain control over the technical aspects of the accompaniment. In addition, a few glaring pitch errors occur, the most prominent of which can be found in the first 1942 performance of the last strophe of "Zueignung," a song that Strauss had been playing for almost fifty years. Other similar "slips" can be found in measures 51 and 57 of "Blick vom oberen Belvedere," measures 10–11 of "Heimkehr" (1943 performance), and measure 80 of "In goldener Fülle," to name a few. Yet Strauss apparently was never a stellar accompanist, at least by current standards. Petersen, who studied several recordings of Strauss conducting and accompanying the Lieder that were cut in the 1920s and 1940s, noted that foremost among his consistent accompanying habits were the playing of incorrect rhythms and "rushing" of the tempo. Although she suggests that the habits are indications of Strauss's deficiency as a pianist, she also admits that the fluctuations in tempo may arise from attempts to assist the singer in sustaining the vocal line.[58]

In fact, Petersen's examination of the recordings on which Strauss accompanied or conducted performances of the Lieder focused heavily on the issue of tempo. Although the results of her evaluation have yielded several pertinent observations, they do fail to take certain historical issues into consideration. In analyzing the recordings, she discovered not only that he allowed the tempo within individual songs to fluctuate rather freely, but also that the basic tempos selected for a given song often differed markedly from one performance to the next. She attributes this phenomenon primarily to the vocal qualities and interpretive approach of the various singers involved, as well as to Strauss's desire to improve on certain elements of the original composition. However, Petersen fails to observe that such tempo fluctuations were common in late-nineteenth-century Lieder, whether notated or added by the performer. The consistency with which Strauss speeds up repeated notes, repeated chords, eighth-note sequences, and sixteenth-note sequences from one song to the next, in fact, seems to suggest that such fluctuations in tempo were driven, at least in part, by Strauss's conception of tempo as an expressive element. This assertion is further supported by the number of tempo changes actually noted in the Lieder, as well as by modern research that examines the use of tempo as an expressive element in German Lieder dating from around the year 1900.[59] Equally controversial are Petersen's statistics regarding the basic tempos selected by the composer, which she compares to those utilized by other performers who have recorded the same Lieder. Although Petersen does note that all of the tempo measurements that she has provided must be regarded as approximations, the determination of metronome markings from a number of recordings engineered seventy years ago under differing studio conditions seems inherently impractical. Moreover, her adjuration of the performers' tempo decisions as "broadened" or "rushed" in certain passages of various songs is merely an opinion, and may divert the reader from the basic issues that she intends to emphasize. More significant is her observation that Strauss did not seem to oppose the application of differing tempos to the same song from one performance to the next.[60]

Perhaps it should be noted that Strauss's interpretive skills sometimes outweighed his lack of technical facility on the later recordings. The effectiveness of the 1943 performance of "All mein Gedanken," for instance, is largely due to Strauss's expressive treatment of the accompaniment. He takes slight fluctuations in tempo that enhance the text expression, but at the same time successfully supports the somewhat erratic rhythmic motion of the vocal line. Consequently, there is great temptation to regard Strauss's own performance practice as a license for free improvisatory treatment of his accompaniments. This temptation is further fueled by Strauss's own flexible attitude toward compositional intent with regard to his own works.[61] As Gabriella Hanke Knaus has recently demonstrated through study of the manuscripts used by Pauline Strauss-de Ahna in performance, Strauss viewed the performance of his Lieder as a collaborative and evolutionary process. He frequently altered the vocal line for the purposes of bringing out certain vocal qualities or heightening the text expression.[62] Interestingly enough, some suggestions for the alteration of Strauss's accompaniments in performance have already been made by scholars of the Strauss Lieder. For example, Paul Hamburger, perhaps speaking tongue in cheek, has advocated deleting or altering musical material, presumably because Strauss did so on occasion.[63] However, such suggestions are rather extreme in nature, and do not necessarily reflect the musical intentions of the composer, who often appeared as an accompanist amid a busy touring and conducting schedule.

CONCEPTIONS OF STRAUSS'S POSITION IN THE CANON

Ernest Newman, the leading Strauss biographer from the beginning of the century, did little to help the cause of Strauss's Lieder when he suggested that only about fifteen to twenty of the Strauss songs from Op. 10 to Op. 56 deserved a position of prominence in the canon.[64] A number of the songs that he cites as representative are among Strauss's best-known works, including "Zueignung," "Allerseelen," "Schlagende Herzen," and "Morgen!" However, neither Newman nor other critics who regard Strauss's Lieder unfavorably can be held responsible for the fact that so many of the composer's Lieder remain obscure to the concert audience.[65] The composer himself may be partially at fault, for the Lieder recital programs that Petersen reconstructed from reviews and records of Strauss's 1904 and 1921 American tours reveal that the composer tended to program most frequently those songs which are best known today (see Table 10.4). A number of the songs are duplicated from program to program, including "Ich trage meine Minne" (on four programs), "Heimliche Aufforderung" (four), "Zueignung" (three), "Freundliche Vision" (three), "Traum durch die Dämmerung" (three), "All mein Gedanken" (two), "Morgen!" (two), "Cäcilie" (two), and "Du meines Herzens Krönelein" (two). Many of the same pieces are also featured on the two recently released compact disc recordings of Strauss accompanying Lieder recitals on the Viennese radio in 1942 and 1943 (see Table 10.5). Among the songs that reappear on the 1942 and 1943 recordings are "Ich trage meine Minne" (one performance), "Heimliche Aufforderung" (two), "Zueignung" (three), "Freundliche Vision" (one), "Traum durch die Dämmerung" (one), "All mein Gedanken" (two), "Morgen!" (two), "Cäcilie" (one), and "Du meines Herzens Krönelein" (two). The frequency with which some of these songs were performed during Strauss's lifetime suggests that the composer was fond of them and felt that they best represented his Lieder

TABLE 10.4
Five American Concert Programs Reconstructed by Barbara Petersen

1904 Carnegie Hall Lieder Recital

Ich trage meine Minne
Ich schwebe
Freundliche Vision
Junghexenlied
Du meines Herzens Krönelein
Ach lieb, ich muss nun scheiden!
All mein Gedanken
Winterweihe
Ein Obdach gegen Sturm und Regen
Gefunden
Traum durch die Dämmerung
Heimliche Aufforderung

1904 National Theatre Recital

Ich trage meine Minne
Himmelsboten
Einkehr
Cäcilie
Morgen!
Traum durch die Dämmerung
Ein Obdach gegen Sturm und Regen
Heimliche Aufforderung

1921 Town Hall Recital I

Zueignung
Junghexenlied
Du meines Herzens Krönelein
All mein Gedanken
Traum durch die Dämmerung
Wiegenlied
Glückes genug
Muttertändelei
Einerlei
Der Stern
Schlechtes Wetter
Ich trage meine Minne
Ich schwebe
Schlagende Herzen

(continued)

Freundliche Vision
Ständchen

1921 Town Hall Recital II

Allerseelen
Frühlingsgedränge
Die Nacht
Hat gesagt—bleibt's nicht dabei
Zueignung
Gefunden
Wie sollten wir geheim sie halten
Mein Auge
Meinem Kinde
Cäcilie
Ruhe, meine Seele!
Anbetung
Schlagende Herzen
Morgen!
Heimliche Aufforderung

1921 Town Hall Recital III

Breit über mein Haupt
Mit deinen blauen Augen
Sie wissen's nicht
Zueignung
Kornblumen
Mohnblumen
Epheu
Wasserrose
Freundliche Vision
Wozu noch, Mädchen
Das Geheimnis
Nichts
Morgen!
Die Nacht
Ich trage meine Minne
Heimliche Aufforderung

Note: The two 1904 programs were sung by Pauline Strauss-de Ahna. The first of the three Town Hall recitals was given by Elisabeth Schumann on 15 December 1921, the second by Elena Gerhardt on 24 December 1921, and the third by George Meader on 31 December 1921. Richard Strauss accompanied all five recitals.

Source: Barbara Petersen, *Ton und Wart: The Lieder of Richard Strauss,* Studies in Musicology 15 (Ann Arbor, Mich.: UMI Research Press, 1980), 151–52, 177.

TABLE 10.5
The 1942 and 1943 Radio Broadcast Recitals

1942[1]

Zueignung (two times)
Traum durch die Dämmerung
Meinem Kind
Wiegenlied
Freundliche Vision
Cäcilie
Du meines Herzens Krönelein
Ich trage meine Minne
Die Nacht
Seitdem dein Aug' in meines schaute
Breit' über mein Haupt
Ich liebe dich
Heimliche Aufforderung
Heimkehr
All mein Gedanken
Ständchen
Schlagende Herzen
Ich schwebe
Kling!
Waldseligkeit

1943[2]

Heimkehr
Seitdem dein Aug' in meines schaute
All mein Gedanken
Glückes genug
In goldener Fülle
Sehnsucht
Schlechtes Wetter
Blick vom oberem Belvedere
Du meines Herzens Krönelein
Ach Lieb, ich muss nun scheiden!
Ach weh mir unglückhaftem Mann
Wozu nach, Mädchen
Das Rosenband
Winterliebe
Ruhe, meine Seele!
Heimliche Aufforderung

[1] Singers included Maria Reining (soprano), Anton Dermonta (tenor), and Lea Piltti (soprano).

[2] Singers included Anton Dermota (tenor), Hilde Konetzni (soprano), and Alfred Poll (baritone).

style. The fact that most of the songs performed on the 1921, 1942, and 1943 recitals were published prior to 1906 is equally significant, for it seems to indicate that Strauss was somewhat reluctant to program the songs composed between 1918 and 1921, which includes Op. 67 through Op. 71. It is possible that Strauss was filling his Lieder recitals with audience favorites so that the occasional rarity might be inserted with only passing notice, thus making possible the retention of a high level of audience appeal while introducing a few lesser known gems. In glancing over the aforementioned programs with this possibility in mind, one begins to note the occasional introduction of lesser-known Lieder, including "Ach weh mir unglückhaftem Mann," "Mit deinen blauen Augen," "Das Geheimnis," "Waldseligkeit," and "Blick vom oberen Belvedere."

The existence of several Lieder in arrangements for keyboard solo may also have contributed to the popularity of certain early Lieder. The solo piano transcriptions include twelve arranged by Max Reger, twenty-five arranged by Otto Taubmann, and five arranged by Walter Gieseking. Most of these are transcriptions of songs from Op. 10 through Op. 49, and include such beloved works as "Allerseelen," "Morgen!," "Traum durch die Dämmerung," "Freundliche Vision," and "Winterweihe," but they have received little scholarly attention. While it is obvious that some of them were intended as concert pieces, many seem better suited to salon performance.[66] A detailed study of the transcriptions of Reger would, perhaps, yield the most interesting results, for it would reveal the manner in which another Lieder composer dealt with the piano arrangement of Strauss's songs. Whether Strauss ever played any of these piano transcription remains open to question, but it is clear that the publication of them assisted in the dissemination of certain Lieder that now rank among the most popular.

Since Strauss's death in 1949, his Lieder have experienced a revival of sorts. They are frequently programmed on song recitals, and have been the subject of several recently issued scholarly studies. As a result, a wider variety of the Strauss Lieder are gradually receiving attention. Moreover, the role of Strauss's songs in both shaping and reflecting aspects of the composer's mature style is increasingly the subject of critical inquiry.[67]

NOTES

1. Alfred Guttman, "Richard Strauss als Lyricker," *Die Musik* 4 (1904–5): 101.

2. See the discussion in A. S. Garlington, "Vier letzte Lieder: The Ultimate *opus ultimum*," *Musical Quarterly* 73, no. 1 (1989): 79–93.

3. See Edward E. Lowinsky's preface to *A Confidential Matter: The Letters of Richard Strauss and Stefan Zweig, 1931–1935*, by Richard Strauss and Stefan Zweig, trans. Max Knight (Berkeley: University of California Press, 1977), xi–xxv.

4. Leon Botstein, "The Enigma of Richard Strauss: A Revisionist View," in *Richard Strauss and His World*, ed. Bryan Gilliam (Princeton, N.J.: Princeton University Press, 1992), 3–14.

5. Ibid., 6. Strauss supposedly described himself thus to Hugo von Hofmannstahl.

6. Edward T. Kravitt, "The Lied in 19th-Century Concert Life," *Journal of the American Musicological Society* 18 (1965): 207.

7. The *Liederabende* given by Gustav Walter between 1879 and 1880 were primarily responsible for the rising interest in this concert format. See ibid., 211–13.

8. Robert Breuer, "Richard Strauss in Amerika. Teil 1: 1904," *Richard Strauss-Blätter* 8 (1976): 8.

9. Ibid., 9.

10. See Barbara Petersen, *Ton und Wort: The Lieder of Richard Strauss*, Studies in Musicology 15 (Ann Arbor, Mich.: UMI Research Press, 1980), 141–55.

11. I will discuss this at length.

12. See the complete chronological list of Strauss's Lieder in Peterson, *Ton und Wort*, 186–200.

13. Quoted from a letter by Strauss in Norman Del Mar, *Richard Strauss* (London: Faber and Faber, 1986), 3:247.

14. Quoted in numerous German and English sources, including Petersen, *Ton und Wort*, 25. For additional commentary, see ibid., 25–29. Here Petersen also suggests that Strauss's poetic preferences were driven by the dedicatee for whom the song was intended.

15. Del Mar, *Richard Strauss*, 3:246–48.

16. Petersen, *Ton und Wort*, 19–20.

17. Guttman, "Richard Strauss als Lyriker," 96; and Wilhelm Mauke, "Liliencron als Befruchter der musikalischen Lyrik," *Die Musik* 3, no. 3 (1904): 435–38.

18. Ludwig Finscher, "Richard Strauss und Jugendstil—the Munich Years, 1894–1898," *Miscellanea Musicologica* 13 (1984): 169–80.

19. Del Mar, *Richard Strauss*, 3:284.

20. Finscher, "Richard Strauss und Jugendstil," 169–70. Del Mar notes that Bierbaum's text *Wir beide wollen* originally appeared in the illustrated almanac *Der Bunte Vogel* in 1897. As a result, the manuscript containing Strauss's setting of the poem was decorated with an Art Nouveau illustration depicting Aeolus, god of wind, as a larged black-winged bird, which can be interpreted as a direct reference to the opening line of *Wir beide wollen* (*Richard Strauss*, 3:299).

21. Finscher, "Richard Strauss und Jugendstil," 176–80.

22. Ibid., 173.

23. Ibid., 173–74.

24. Elena Gerhardt recalls that Strauss sometimes requested that she program a group of lieder by another composer in place of one featuring his own songs (see her "Strauss and His Lieder: A Personal Reminiscence," *Tempo* 12 [1949]: 9).

25. Del Mar, *Richard Strauss*, 3:271.

26. See, for example, Petersen, *Ton und Wort*, 72–76.

27. A brief summary of the contributions of Schuh, Wachten, and Overhoff can be found in Bryan Gilliam, *Richard Strauss's Elektra*, Studies in Musical Genesis and Structure (Oxford: Clarendon Press, 1991), 67–68; and Eva-Maria Axt, "Das Ineinanderwirken von Bewusstem und Unbewusstem: Zum Stimmungs- und Symbolcharakter der Tonarten bei Richard Strauss," *Richard Strauss-Blätter* 29 (1993): 7–21. Axt extends the principles to the symphonic literature.

28. See Gilliam, *Richard Strauss's Elektra*, 67–106.

29. Tethys Carpenter, "The Musical Language of *Elektra*," in *Richard Strauss: Elektra*, ed. Derrick Puffett, Cambridge Opera Handbooks (Cambridge: Cambridge University Press, 1990), 74–106.

30. Derrick Puffett approaches the issue differently from the others in that he focuses on how Strauss's pitch-specific conception of recurring motifs in the operas affects the compositional process (see "'Lass Er di Musi, wo sie ist': Pitch Specificity in Strauss," in *Richard Strauss and His World*, ed. Bryan Gilliam [Princeton, N.J.: Princeton University Press, 1992], 138–63).

31. See the discussion in Gilliam, *Richard Strauss's Elektra*, 68–72, as well as the chart in Carpenter, "The Musical Language," 76–77.

32. Gilliam, *Richard Strauss's Elektra*, 70–71.

33. A comparison of the aforementioned studies of Carpenter and Gilliam reveals that Gilliam places more emphasis on the B major/minor key area than does Carpenter. Moreover, each scholar's affective interpretation of the C major/minor, B-flat major/minor, and B major/minor key areas differs somewhat. In addition, the divergent analytical approach taken by each is worthy of note.

34. See, for example, Gilliam, *Richard Strauss's Elektra*, 67–106; and Bryan Gilliam, "Strauss's Preliminary Opera Sketches: Thematic Fragments and Symphonic Continuity," *Nineteenth-Century Music* 9, no. 3 (1986): 176–88.

35. John M. Kissler, "The Four Last Songs by Richard Strauss: A Formal and Tonal Pperspective," *Music Review* 50, no. 3–4 (1989): 234–35.

36. Ibid., 231–39.

37. Finscher, "Richard Strauss und Jugendstil," 171–80.

38. A brief study of Mahler's approach to this technique can be found in Zoltan Roman, "Structure as a Factor in the Genesis of Mahler's Songs," *The Music Review* 53, no. 2 (1974): 157–66.

39. Text by A. F. von Schack.

40. Measure numbers from the orchestral version.

41. The interpretation of C-flat as Strauss's death key has been suggested by a number of scholars. See, for example, the brief discussion in Kissler, "The Four Last Songs," 238, in which he notes that the E-flat key used here has a somber timbre, but does not elaborate on its importance to the interpretation of the song.

42. Text by Richard Dehmel.

43. See the discussion in Michael Perraudin, *Heinrich Heine: Poetry in Context* (Oxford: Berg, 1989), 206.

44. The data in Kravitt suggests that a number of late-nineteenth-century enthusiasts attempted to revive the salon atmosphere originally associated with the genre (see "The Lied in 19th-Century Concert Life," 213–18).

45. Several orchestrations of Strauss's Lieder were also prepared by others, including Robert Heger and Felix Mottl. Of these, the most frequently used is Heger's orchestration of "Zueignung." Heger also orchestrated four other Strauss Lieder.

46. See Gerhardt, "Strauss and His Lieder," 10; Alan Jefferson, *The Lieder of Richard Strauss* (London: Praeger, 1971), 16–17; and Petersen, *Ton und Wort*, 152–55. A short biographical sketch that discusses Pauline's personality as it relates to her performance of Strauss's Lieder appears in Ernst Roth, "Gerechtigkeit für Pauline Strauss," *Internationale Richard Strauss-Gesellschaft Mitteilungen* 36 (1963): 21–22.

47. The reports indicate that approximately six thousand people were in attendance at each of the two concerts. Several critics took Strauss to task for allowing his music to be cheapened by such a commercial venue, and the composer responded by assuring the public in writing that he had closely monitored the surroundings in which his work would be presented. See Linda L. Tyler, "'Commerce and Poetry Hand in Hand': Music in American Department Stores, 1880–1930," *Journal of the American Musicological Society* 45, no. 1 (1992): 80–81.

48. Del Mar, *Richard Strauss*, 3:318.

49. See ibid., 3:355–65. Petersen suggests that the Op. 68 songs were destined for the publisher Fürstner from the outset (see *Ton und Wort*, 120).

50. The orchestral score of "Zueignung" bears a dedication to Ursuleac. Ida Cook and Alfred Frankenstein point out that the soprano roles of Strauss's last four operas were written with Ursuleac in mind (see "Remembering Viorica Ursuleac," *Opera* 37, no. 1 [1986]: 27). She frequently performed Strauss's works under Krauss's baton. Petersen features a detailed study of the sketches for Op. 68 (see *Ton und Wort*, 117–39).

51. See Timothy L. Jackson, "*Ruhe, meine Seele!* and the *Letzte Orchesterlieder*," in *Richard Strauss and His World*, ed. Bryan Gilliam (Princeton, N.J.: Princeton University Press, 1992), 90–137. Alan Jefferson questions Jackson's theories, largely through anecdotal evidence that the cycle never consisted of other than four songs (see "Strauss's Last Song Cycle," *Richard Strauss-Blätter* 33 [1995]: 69–75). Jackson rightly notes that Jefferson's objections arise from a visceral reaction to the concept of a fifth song, rather than a thorough examination of the arguments advanced (see "Reply to Alan Jefferson," *Richard Strauss-Blätter* 34 [1995]: 135–40).

52. Del Mar, *Richard Strauss*, 3:304.

53. *Richard Strauss begleitet* (Preiser Records: Mono 93261; 1988) and *Richard Strauss begleitet* (Preiser Records: Mono 93262; 1991). The recordings are digitally remastered from tapes recorded by the Reichssender Wien in April 1942 and 1943.

54. For a survey of the literature devoted to this topic, see Peterson, *Ton und Wort*, 155–57.

55. Ibid., 157.

56. See Alfred Orel reports that Strauss made a number of similar alterations in accompanying Elisabeth Schumann (see "Richard Strauss als Begleiter seiner Lieder," *Schweizerische Musikzeitung* 92 [1952]:13).

57. Hans Pfitzner, *Lieder*, performed by Gerhard Hüsch and Hans Pfitzner (Lebendige Vergangenheit #208; 1938).

58. Petersen, *Ton und Wort*, 155–61.

59. See Edward F. Kravitt, "Tempo as an Expressive Element in the Late Romantic Lied," *Musical Quarterly* 59, no. 4 (1973): 497–518.

60. See Petersen, *Ton und Wort*, 157–61.

61. Despite the fact that soprano Maria Jeritza made such extensive cuts to the score of *Salome* that only the "torso of the opera" remained, for instance, Strauss was absolutely enchanted by her performance. See Kurt Wilhelm, *Richard Strauss: An Intimate Portrait*, trans. Mary Whittall (London: Thames and Hudson, 1989), 158–59.

62. Gabriella Hanke Knaus, "Neuschöpfung durch Interpretation: Richard Strauss' Eintragungen in die Handexemplare seiner Lieder aus dem Besitz von Pauline Strauss-de Ahna," *Musiktheorie* 11, no. 1 (1996): 17–30.

63. Paul Hamburger, "Strauss the Song Writer," *Music and Musicians* 12, no. 10 (1964): 14.

64. Ernst Newman, *Richard Strauss* (1908; reprint, New York: Books for Libraries Press, 1969), 99–100.

65. For an overview of the critical opinions advanced before 1980 regarding Strauss's Lieder, see Petersen, *Ton und Wort*, 163–83.

66. A brief survey of the extant piano transcriptions is found in ibid., 12–13, 22. Del Mar further mentions that arrangements for piano duet and salon orchestra also proliferated (see *Richard Strauss*, 3:271).

67. Consider, for example, Suzanne Marie Lodato, "Richard Strauss and the Modernists: A Contextual Study of Strauss's Fin-de-Siècle Song Style" (Ph.D. diss. Columbia University, 1999); and Richard A. Kaplan, "Tonality as Mannerism: Structure and Syntax in Richard Strauss's Orchestral Song *Frühling*," *Theory and Practice* 19 (1994): 19–29.

11

The Challenge of the Choral Works

Suzanne M. Lodato

Ah, if only my technique in writing for male choirs had been better. . . . My choral
writing never sounds the way I would like it to!

—Richard Strauss

I myself do not understand enough about choral singing.

—Richard Strauss

One can say without exaggeration, that as seen on paper, the work in its entirety
could probably never be sung by human voices.

—Critical commentary on Richard Strauss's *Deutsche Motette* Op. 62

Choral composition occupied Richard Strauss from his boyhood through
the twilight of his career. Within the realm of freestanding choral works
(that is, pieces not contained within a larger work such as an opera or ora-
torio), he explored both a cappella and accompanied styles and mixed- and
single-gender vocal forces. Poetry that he set ranged from the intimate, lyrical moment to the depiction of the bombastic historical event. The choral
writing itself could consist of a relatively straightforward unison or homophonic setting over an unusually large orchestra or a highly nuanced
vocalism consisting of intricate polyphony, rapid and subtle shifts in color,
and dense chromaticism. Yet despite Strauss's lifelong engagement with the
choral genre and the wide variety of effects that he wrought with vocal ensembles, his fifty-one freestanding choral works have been all but forgotten.

Why have musicians, critics, scholars, and audiences ignored this body
of work? Is it true that, as Strauss asserted in the two quotes that open this

chapter, he simply did not understand how to write for choral ensembles? Were his choral works nearly impossible to execute, as the third quotation implies?

Perhaps part of the reason lies in the fact that Strauss wrote many of his choral works when he was quite young or produced them in response to commissions to celebrate special occasions. In the first case, many of the early choral compositions were immature works that were never performed or assigned opus numbers. Some of these exist only as sketches or studies. It is significant that Strauss only assigned opus numbers to nine of his fifty-one choral works, meaning that he only considered this small group significant enough to be accorded an official place in his output. The lack of an opus number, however, does not necessarily signify a work of low quality. Two pieces that do not have opus number designations have sparked recent interest among choral conductors: *Die Göttin im Putzzimmer* (1935) and *An den Baum Daphne* (1943). Their great beauty and stunning effects certainly merit a revival of interest (I will discuss these pieces in more detail later).

Little has been written on Strauss's choral repertory. As a result, musicians and scholars know little if anything about Strauss's output in this genre. Heiner Wajemann's excellent monograph, *Die Chorkompositionen von Richard Strauss*, is the only book-length work on Strauss's choral music. It is unfortunate that it has never been translated into English. Those who are interested in performing the a cappella choral works would benefit greatly from reading Judith Blezzard's review article from 1991.[1] A number of other brief articles written in the early- and mid-twentieth-century deal only with individual works.

The nine works with opus numbers have prompted little more interest than the juvenilia, sketches, studies, and occasional works that make up the bulk of Strauss's choral production. In two cases—*Bardengesang* and *Taillefer*—the historical topics of the poetry that were of considerable interest to nineteenth-century audiences would hold little attraction for today's listeners—the formidable orchestral requirements could only be met by world-class orchestras, and the music, while thrilling, is not distinctive enough to justify the expense and effort that would be needed to produce these works. *Austria*, a patriotic hymn set for chorus and orchestra, is undistinguished. Perhaps large instrumental forces have also prevented the performance of two worthy works set to lyric poetry of quality: *Wandrers Sturmlied* and *Die Tageszeiten*.

The four a cappella choral works with opus numbers have fared slightly better in recent years, possibly because they do not require the collaboration of expensive, top-class orchestras. The mixed a cappella pieces *Zwei*

Gesänge and *Deutsche Motette*, along with the two "non-'opused'" works *Die Göttin im Putzzimmer* and *An den Baum Daphne* have been added to the repertories of distinguished choral ensembles such as the Danish National Radio Choir, the Swedish Radio Choir, Pro Arte Chamber Singers of Connecticut, the BBC Singers, and the Choristers of King's College, Cambridge, as evidenced by several recordings that have appeared since 1970. The works for a cappella men's choir remain seldom performed. Strauss's unaccompanied choral works, particularly those for men, were written for highly skilled ensembles like the Vienna and Cologne Men's Singing Associations (Wienermännersingerverein and Kölner Männer-Gesang-Verein). Kenneth Birkin asserts that the high degree of skill seen in these groups did not survive the two world wars.[2] Blezzard echoes this sentiment, writing that Strauss wrote his choral works for "large, extremely expert forces that are the vocal equivalents of highly-accomplished professional orchestras."[3] The popularity of choral ensembles, particularly male societies, is evident in the many prestigious choral competitions that were held in Europe in the late nineteenth and early twentieth centuries. At the massive tenth German "Sängerbundfest" in Vienna in 1928, 120,000 singers from all over the world participated.[4] Strauss judged many competitions of this type (discussed later) and thus was exposed to some of the best choral singing in Europe.

Strauss's choruses demand what is only available in the best professional organizations today—size, stamina (singers must sustain long phrases, often at extremes of their tessituras), top-notch musicianship (the dense chromaticism, nontraditional voice leading, and frequent tonal shifts make these pieces difficult to sing in tune), and vocal prowess (the vocal lines cover an unusually wide compass and involve frequent large leaps). In addition, his choral scores tend to be difficult to read because so many have never been published in piano–vocal reductions, and many contain alto and tenor clefs, with which many choristers, particularly amateur ones, are unfamiliar.

As can be seen from the first two quotations, Strauss was well aware of the difficulties that his choral works posed to performers. At one time, he asked the famed choral expert Viktor Keldorfer (1873–1959) to simplify the scores for a cappella male chorus. In a letter to Strauss written 22 February 1931, Keldorfer respectfully declined, asserting that it was precisely the harmonic and rhythmic complexities that gave these choral works Strauss's special "physiognomy."[5] Strauss's choral works have therefore remained intact, possibly at the price of remaining relatively obscure.

In light of the fact that the music community knows little or nothing of both the history and the musical characteristics of Strauss's choral works, I have devoted the rest of this chapter to a brief chronicle of the "opused" choral pieces, along with a few of interest that were never assigned opus numbers, which includes some of the circumstances under which they were composed and some remarks on their musical style and content.

WORKS FOR CHORUS AND ORCHESTRA

Wandrers Sturmlied, Op. 14. Composed in 1884 or 1885.[6] Poem by Johann Wolfgang von Goethe (1749–1832). Six-part mixed chorus (SSATB) and orchestra.

Wandrers Sturmlied is the first choral work of Strauss's maturity and the first choral piece he considered substantial enough to be assigned an opus number. As Strauss recalled, *Wandrers Sturmlied* was composed during a period in which he was strongly influenced by the compositional style of Johannes Brahms (1833–97), and critics have noted the similarity between *Wandrers Sturmlied* and Brahms's *Gesang der Parzen* (Op. 83; 1882) for six-part mixed chorus and orchestra, which was also set to a Goethe text.[7] Strauss had been struck by *Gesang der Parzen* when he heard the work at a rehearsal at the Leipzig Gewandhaus in December 1883. Brahms had also dedicated the piece to the Grand Duke Georg II of Meiningen, where Strauss was employed as assistant court conductor beginning in 1885.

The idea for the poem had come to Goethe in 1771, after the breakup of a love affair. The pain of the failed relationship prompted a period of wandering, during which he sang "strange hymns and dithyrambs" of his own making. The passionate song *Wandrers Sturmlied*—"this half-senseless piece" (*dieser Halbunsinn*), as he later called it—came to him during a storm that he encountered during his wanderings.[8] The poem contains 116 lines of text. Strauss set the first thirty-eight, which comprise six stanzas of unequal length. The first four stanzas begin with the line "The one whom you never abandon, Genius,"[9] which becomes the central idea of Strauss's composition, although he does not set this textual refrain with the same music each time that it recurs. These four stanzas tell of the comfort and protection that genius provides to one who must face the difficulties and dangers of life. In the fifth and sixth stanzas, the original refrain disappears, and the poet invokes the Muses and Graces, asking them to surround him as he hovers above the earth like a god. A new refrain appears at the ends of these two stanzas— "Godlike" (*Göttergleich*). According to Hungarian composer and conductor Johann L. Bella (1843–1936), who directed a performance of the piece in 1888, the poem carries the message that genius steels its possessor against the storms of life. For Goethe, wrote Bella, poetry was a "means of purification for his soul when it became tarnished by passion."[10]

Strauss's setting begins with an orchestral storm in D minor portrayed by the full complement of instruments, which are dominated by a large brass section of four horns, two trumpets, and three trombones. Brahms's influence can be seen in the use of a number of motives that recur throughout the piece in different voices, instruments, and combinations. Heavy instrumentation, dense polyphony and, in a few places, polymeter challenge not only the performers, but the audience as well. The polymeters (simultaneously triple and quadruple, at reh. H through four measures before reh. M) reinforce the first major climax of the piece at the end of stanza 2: "Killing the python, swift, great, Pythius Apollo."[11] Beginning at reh. M, the instrumentation lightens somewhat as the chorus sings in long, arching lines of the widespreading wings of genius, but the more tranquil mood does not last for long: the orchestral storm figures that had been heard in the beginning return as genius is shown providing shelter from the snow. At the end of this section, the tonality returns to D minor, and the chorus, which is basically unaccompanied, presents the Muses and Graces, who are attracted to the protective warmth of genius. This segment leads to the final section in D major. The D-major section eventually settles into a slow tempo and a tranquil mood, the storm figures disappear, and the chorus finishes with a climactic, fortissimo tonic chord on "Godlike" that slowly fades as the chorus repeats the word several times. Despite his use of large instrumental forces, Strauss intended that the chorus be audible at all times. Recognizing the potential of the large orchestra to overwhelm the choir, he told Bella, who was to conduct a performance of *Wandrers Sturmlied* in December 1888, that some brass could be removed or muted to allow the chorus to be heard.[12]

Strauss dedicated *Wandrers Sturmlied* to conductor Franz Wüllner, whom he had met in Cologne when he gave the German premiere of his F minor Symphony in January 1885. It was also in Cologne that Strauss conducted the City Orchestra and Choir in the premiere on 8 March 1887.

Taillefer, Op. 52. Composed in 1903. Ballad by Johann Ludwig Uhland (1787–1862). Soprano, tenor, and baritone solos, eight-part mixed chorus, and orchestra.

It was nineteen years after *Wandrers Sturmlied* before Strauss was to complete his next freestanding work for soli, chorus, and orchestra, *Taillefer*, a setting of Uhland's ballad of the Battle of Hastings (1066) and the Norman Conquest. Strauss began sketching *Taillefer* in April 1902 and composed the piece at approximately the same time that he was working on his tone poem *Symphonia domestica* (1903). Although Strauss conducted the premiere of *Taillefer* on 26 October 1903 to celebrate his receipt of an honorary doctoral degree from the University of Heidelberg, he had actually begun the composition before the Heidelberg commission was obtained or the degree awarded. A few months after he began composing the work, he wrote his friend, noted choral conductor and composer, Philipp Wolfrum (1854–1919) informing him that the piece— which was being "written in the grandest music festival style"—was in progress.[13] Wolfrum, who was a professor of music at the university as well as its music director, saw an opportunity for his friend: the city had just built a new town hall, and the university was to be celebrating its one-hundred-year jubilee with a music festival in 1903. Wolfrum not only arranged for *Taillefer* to be premiered in Heidelberg's new town hall as part of the festivities, but also for Strauss to receive the honorary doctorate from the university. Critics generally responded positively, although many objected to the oversized orchestra. Otto Julius Bierbaum (1865–1910), whose poems Strauss set as Lieder, gave a later *Taillefer* performance a particularly withering review, referring to the setting as a "huge orchestral sauce."[14] Another commentator found the Heidelberg premiere noteworthy for relatively new concert practices for the time that are common currency today, such as lowered hall lights, musicians made "invisible" by being relegated to an orchestra pit, and the shifting of Strauss's large brass section to the back of the orchestra.[15]

This massive eighteen-minute piece, which Strauss orchestrated using special forty-stave music paper,[16] calls for 145 players to graphically portray the Norman victory at Hastings. Uhland's fifteen-stanza ballad tells of a lowly vassal, Taillefer, whose singing inspires the army of William, Duke of Normandy (1027–87) to win the battle. As a result, William became the first Norman king of England. Given that Strauss composed *Taillefer* at the time he was working on one of his most controversial tone poems, *Symphonia domestica*, it is hardly surprising that in some parts of the score *Taillefer* sounds like an enormous orchestral tone poem that is merely augmented by solo and ensemble singing. Yet although the orchestra, dominated by an unusually large brass section colored by timpani and snare drums, brings the battle to life, the instruments never overwhelm the voices. The chorus, which narrates the story and comments on the action, holds its own in unison and homophonic textures that set it in relief to the dense, colorful, and often dissonant instrumental writing. As the action builds, the chorus takes on a bigger role, with William (baritone solo), William's sister (soprano solo), and Taillefer (tenor solo) gradually fading into the background until the end. *Taillefer* is never subtle or nuanced in its effects, but it is characterized by a gradual increase in intensity from the beginning, when the three main characters are introduced, to the bom-

bastic battle scene toward the end. As the listeners learn of Taillefer's devotion to William, his eagerness to fight, William's sister's attraction to
Taillefer, and Taillefer's ability to inspire the troops with his singing, the
chorus first interjects and responds, then eventually moves to the forefront
in the second half of the piece as it narrates the battle events. The action
culminates in a three-and-a-half minute instrumental battle scene (rehs.
36–50) that interrupts the thirteenth stanza of the poem after the line
"Whistling arrows, clanging sword blows!" to resume at the last line of the
stanza, "Until Harold [King of England] fell and his defiant army succumbed."[17] The work ends with the newly-crowned William's praise of
Taillefer, echoed homophonically by the chorus. A short, triumphant
orchestral prelude ends the piece.

Bardengesang, Op. 55. Composed in 1906. Poetry from Friedrich Gottlieb
Klopstock's (1724–1803) *Hermannsschlacht*. Twelve-part male chorus
(TBTBTB) and orchestra.

   Only two years after premiering *Taillefer*, Strauss composed *Bardengesang* (Bardic Song), his second published work for chorus and orchestra on
a historical battle, and also his second treatment of the same event. The subject of *Bardengesang* is Hermann or Arminius (18 B.C.E.–C.E. 19), chief of the
Cherusci or Cheruscans (a German tribe), who won a major battle against
the Romans at the Teutoburg Forest in northwest Germany in C.E. 9. Plays
dealing with the battle at Teutoburg Forest by two major German poets,
Heinrich von Kleist (1777–1811) and Klopstock, reflected a nineteenth-century revival of interest in Hermann. Kleist's *Hermannsschlacht* was
presented in 1886 in Meiningen, where Strauss served as court composer
from 1885 to 1886. The play contained a musical setting of the *Bardengesang*, which extolled the actions of Hermann and his troops. The Grand
Duke Georg II, who was displeased with the song, asked Strauss to recom-
pose it, as Strauss recounted in a 12 January 1886 letter to his parents.[18]
Strauss finished the piece in a month, and it was performed for the duke in
February 1886. Strauss never published it, and the manuscript was lost.

   Although it appears that Strauss preferred to forget his early *Bardengesang*, Hermann's battle at the Teutoburg Forest still captivated him. In 1905,
he composed the Bardic Song again, this time to the text by Klopstock. At
the time, Strauss was serving as Kaiser Wilhelm II's chief conductor of the
Royal Court Opera in Berlin and asked permission to dedicate the piece to
the Kaiser. Permission was not granted.[19] Instead, Strauss dedicated the
work, which was finished on 26 April 1906, to choral conductor Gustav
Wohlgemuth, whom he praised as active in promoting the artistic endeav-
ors of men's choral societies. On 6 February 1907, the Dresden Teachers

Singing Society (Lehrergesangverein), reinforced by instrumentalists from a Dresden Saxon grenadier regiment, premiered the piece.

Klopstock's Bardic Song is divided into three parts which are separated by prose passages in the play. Strauss set only the twelve-stanza song, which contains little of substance beyond the German's exultant triumph over the slain Romans. Commentators have roundly criticized the poor quality of Klopstock's verse, describing it as "bloodless, leathery text,"[20] "devoid of content,"[21] "boundlessly unmusical," "fossilized material," and an "ethnographic map."[22] The latter phrase refers to what Wajemann complains of as the "abstruse and absurd" enumeration of Roman tribes that lasts four stanzas.[23] One stanza suffices as an example:

> Ha, ye Cheruscans! Ye Chattees! Ye Marsians! Ye Semnonians!
> Ye names of our heroes, whose praise we sing.
> Ye Brukterians! Ye Warnians! Ye Gothonians! Ye Lewovians
> Ye names of our heroes, whose praise we sing.[24]

Although critics recognized that Klopstock's verses barely rise above doggerel, most admired Strauss's compositional prowess nonetheless. Some even surmised that it was precisely Klopstock's list of old German tribes that stimulated Strauss to produce the kind of graphic word painting for which he became known.[25] Another praised Strauss for "making the impossible possible" in setting the words so effectively.[26] As is the case with *Taillefer*, the large orchestra of *Bardengesang* is dominated by the "military" sounds of large brass and percussion sections. Four extra trumpets, trombones, and bass trombones play behind the scenes, separated from the rest of the orchestra. *Bardengesang* begins with the backstage brass playing fanfares of a rising fourth in different keys as they herald the approach of various German tribes to the battlefield. Precise instructions in the score indicate that the fanfares should sound farther off, then progressively closer as the troops gather. The chorus is divided into three sections consisting of tenor and bass. The first two choirs sing separately, then together with the third as the warriors assemble. Each section divides further into three or four parts, so that in some places, ten parts are heard. In keeping with the higher degree of complexity that generally characterized writing for male choruses, the choral parts contain more contrapuntal writing than is seen in *Taillefer*, although the vocal parts are not complex and present no unusual musical difficulties. Strauss depicts the battle and victory in a modulation from C minor to a heroic C major and colors the tumultuous score with a battle hymn sung by the chorus in the second part of the piece that has an almost folklike melody.[27]

Die Tageszeiten, Op. 76. Composed in 1927. Poetry by Joseph von Eichendorff (1778–1857), taken from his *Wanderlieder: Der Morgen, Mittagsruh,
Der Abend*, and *Die Nacht*. Lieder cycle for four-part men's chorus (TTBB)
and orchestra.[28]

Strauss did not compose his next published work for chorus and orchestra until twenty-two years after he completed *Bardengesang*, but
Bardengesang played a role in the genesis of this cycle in an ironic way. In
May 1924, Keldorfer, who was a noted choral composer and conductor,
brought members of the Vienna Schubert Society (Schubertbund) to the
street outside Strauss's Vienna house and serenaded him to celebrate
Strauss's upcoming sixtieth birthday. Keldorfer had led the society in a performance of *Bardengesang* in December 1922, and in a repeat performance,
Strauss had conducted. Two years later, he was made an honorary member
of the society. After the serenade, Keldorfer asked Strauss to write the society a choral piece. Strauss demurred at first, disparaging his own ability to
write well for male choirs, but he became captivated by the idea when Keldorfer, hoping to deter Strauss from again setting poetry as poor as
Klopstock's, suggested that he set some of Eichendorff's work. Strauss had
last set Eichendorff's poetry in 1876 and 1880, both times for unaccompanied, mixed choir.[29] Upon hearing this idea, Strauss exclaimed, "Good. Very
good! He is a full-blooded romanticist who is close to me."[30]

Strauss and Keldorfer did not discuss the commission again until the
fall of 1927 when Strauss invited Keldorfer to his Vienna home and surprised him with the partially finished score of a four-movement cycle,
Die Tageszeiten, the poems for which he had chosen from Eichendorff's
Wanderlieder. Three of the four movements were completed, with only
Der Abend remaining. Strauss amiably offered to make changes to the
score, but he was not immediately enthusiastic when Keldorfer asked that
a few a cappella bars be inserted at the beginning of the piece to depict
the beginning of the day when the rooster crows. Strauss had begun *Der
Morgen* with a short, glowing orchestral prelude to the second stanza of
the poem that begins "The first ray of morning flies / Through the silent
misty valley," omitting the first stanza, "When the cock crows on the
roof."[31] Strauss's resistance was understandable: His rival, Hans Pfitzner
(1869–1949) had set those four lines of the first stanza in his cantata *Von
deutscher Seele* (Op. 28, composed in 1921).[32] Nevertheless, after some
consideration, Strauss saw the wisdom of Keldorfer's suggestion and
added an eighteen-bar setting of the first stanza at the beginning. Except
for the eighteenth measure, the introduction is unaccompanied. When
Keldorfer received the printed score (*Der Abend*, the final movement, was
finished in the spring of 1928), he was pleased to see that Strauss had

dedicated the piece to him and the Schubert Society. But Strauss had slyly added something else to the printed score in his own hand, above the title of the first piece, *Morgen*: an eighteen-bar snippet, written a cappella in four parts, that graphically depicted the crowing of the rooster at dawn in a number of keys in rapid succession. Keldorfer delightedly referred to this as Strauss's "calling card."[33]

Die Tageszeiten was premiered on 21 July 1928 by the Vienna Schubert Society and the Vienna Symphony Orchestra during the Schubert centenary year. Keldorfer reports that the public interest in the premiere was so intense that three extra performances failed to satisfy demand for admission.[34] In *Die Tageszeiten*, Hugo Leichtentritt sees the style of a mature artist who husbanded his considerable talents to produce a work characterized by judicious use of tone painting embedded in the musical structure, the dominance of melody over the "bustling counterpoint of many motifs," and the generation of most of the musically expressive content by the orchestra rather than the chorus.[35]

Austria, Op. 78. Composed in 1929. Poem by Anton Wildgans (1881–1932) entitled *Österreichisches Lied*. Male chorus and orchestra.

Only seven months later, in February 1929, Strauss was presented with another opportunity to compose a choral work with orchestra when Anton Wildgans, who was working to promote Austrian nationalism, sent him a short poem—*Österreichisches Lied*—that he thought could become an unofficial national hymn for Austria. In less than three weeks, Strauss finished the score, which he dedicated to the Vienna Men's Choral Society, a friendly rival of the Schubert Society. The Men's Choral Society premiered *Österreichisches Lied* on 10 January 1930 with Strauss conducting. Toward the end of that year on 1 October, Strauss wrote Wildgans to ask him if he would approve of changing the name of the composition to *Austria*, which Bote and Bock, who were to publish it, judged to be a "more effective" title.[36] Wildgans agreed, and the piece was renamed *Austria*. Wajemann points out that *Austria* is almost never performed today, most likely because despite the strong patriotic sentiment of the text, it lacks musical substance.[37] The chorus sings entirely in unison, and, indeed, the title includes the notation "For large orchestra with male chorus" rather than "For male chorus with orchestra." A note made by Strauss in the autograph score states that the one-hundred-member choir should not drown out the orchestra, which, like the orchestras for *Taillefer* and *Bardengesang*, is dominated by a large brass section. In addition, the title page of the score notes that *Austria* can be performed without voices, in which case they would be replaced by additional horns and trumpets. Any musical events that are of interest occur in the orchestra, in which tone painting is used to depict specific words or phrases, particularly those representing action, color, or sound. Strauss even quotes parts of the first line from Austria's national anthem, Franz Joseph Haydn's *Gott erhalte unsern Kaiser*, in three places in the score: measures 5–7, 99–106, and 139–41.

Olympische Hymne, o. Op. AV 119.[38] Composed in 1934. Poem by Robert Lubahn (1903–74). Four-part mixed chorus and orchestra.

Olympische Hymne, which Strauss wrote for the 1936 Olympic games in Berlin, is tainted by the association of the Berlin games with the Third Reich, even though commentators have pointed out that the commission for the hymn came not from the National Socialists, but from the International Olympic Committee (IOC). In 1932, Theodor Lewald, who was state secretary, president of the German Imperial Committee for the Olympic games, and Germany's representative on the IOC, approached Strauss about composing the Olympic anthem. Strauss agreed to compose the piece in early 1933, but he needed a suitable text. When attempts to approach respected poets failed to produce a satisfactory text, the IOC held an open competition in which a prize would be awarded for the winning poem. The three thousand entries were paired down to four suitable texts that the IOC sent to Strauss, who chose Berlin actor Robert Lubahn's poem with the approval of Lewald. (Lubahn was unknown as a poet at the time and remains so today.) Strauss completed the hymn on 22 December 1934. The following year, he was dismissed from his position as president of the Reich Chamber of Musicians after Gestapo operatives intercepted correspondence between him and Austrian Jewish author Stefan Zweig (1881–1942) in which Strauss criticized the National Socialists. The piece premiered on 1 August 1936 in the Olympic Stadium in Berlin during the opening ceremonies of the eleventh Olympic games. Despite his ostracization by the Reich, Strauss conducted, probably because the National Socialists realized that it would not be wise to prevent a composer of his renown from conducting his own composition during the ceremonies.[39]

Strauss set the poem for four-part mixed chorus and orchestra of massive dimensions, as illustrated in Strauss's notation in the autograph: "4 trumpets, multiplied by four if possible, the rest of the orchestra doubled or quadrupled, according to the strength of the choir and the capacity of the hall."[40] It was reported that approximarwly four hundred musicians performed in the premiere.[41] Each of the three stanzas of the poem, which deals with positive relationships among nations, ends in the word *Olympia*, which Strauss set to a distinctive motive:

EXAMPLE 11.1
Olympiatheme

O - lym - pia!

It is this motive, stated by the trumpets in unison, that opens the hymn. Wajemann notes several characteristics of the hymn that make it particularly suitable for an Olympic ceremony: a "folklike" choral melody, incorporation into the melody of some of the fanfare figures that appear in the brass, and the homophonic and unison singing of the chorus that lends "simplicity and monumentality" to the piece.[42] The IOC had expressed interest in making *Olympische Hymne* the official anthem for all future Olympic Games, but the hymn has sunk into virtual obscurity. One obvious reason is its continued association with the National Socialist regime. Another is that, despite its many positive characteristics, the wide range and complexity of the melody make it too difficult for audiences attending the games to learn and sing.[43]

WORKS FOR UNACCOMPANIED CHOIR

Zwei Gesänge, Op. 34. Composed in 1897. Poems: *Der Abend* by Friedrich Schiller (1759–1805) and *Hymne* by Friedrich Rückert (1788–1866). Sixteen-part a cappella mixed choir.

Zwei Gesänge, Op. 34, represents Strauss's first foray into composing for a large a cappella choir. In April 1897, Strauss, having already composed *Der Abend*, wrote to choral conductor Franz Wüllner asking if he could show him the piece the next time he visited Cologne. Several months later, Wüllner asked if he could premiere the work with students at the Cologne Conservatory. The Conservatory Choir, conducted by Wüllner, premiered *Der Abend* on 2 May 1898 and *Hymne* on 9 March 1899. Apparently, the first performance of *Hymne* evidenced the difficulties with intonation with which Strauss's unaccompanied choral works would continue to challenge choirs: according to Wüllner, the students finished *Hymne* a half step too high. Nevertheless, the audience responded enthusiastically.[44]

Each of the two pieces employs a sixteen-part chorus, but the disposition of the voices is quite different in the two works. In *Der Abend*, each of the four sections is divided into four parts, while the forces of *Hymne* are divided into two choruses of different sizes: the first chorus into four parts (SATB), the second chorus into twelve (SSSAAATTTBBB). The instructions in the score regarding the number of singers that should perform each of the sixteen parts indicate that Strauss did not intend for *Hymne* to be sung by a chamber choir. Blezzard notes that if the proportions called for in the edition are observed, the choir for *Hymne* would comprise 220 singers.[45] Nor did Strauss intend for the first choir to act as a quasi-soloistic quartet or octet; he allocated seventy musicians (slightly under one-third of the total) to sing in the first choir.

The stunning beauty of *Der Abend* lies both in Schiller's lush text, in which the sunset is seen as the lovemaking of the gods, and Strauss's delicate word painting. Indeed, it was both the word painting and the complex contrapuntal writing that caused one critic to compare Strauss's style in this piece to that of the madrigal composers of the Renaissance.[46] The large complement of singers that Strauss calls for never overwhelms the listener. Rather, the sixteen-part distribution enables the choir to sustain a soft wash of sound through which filaments of imitative counterpoint can be heard. This wash of sound is not always easy for the singers to produce. At the beginning of the piece ("Come down, beaming God—the plains thirst"[47]), the first sopranos and first tenors must sustain a g'' for seven measures, pianissimo, at a languid tempo (marked *sehr ruhig*) while other voices enter equally softly with imitative motives or sustained pitches (see Example 11.2).

The entire first section, which covers the first stanza, repeats this pattern, with various parts taking turns sustaining pitches. The next two sections are dominated by long lines of triplets sung imitatively by various parts. The triplets are an extension of the primary middle-section theme, "See who beckons to you, smiling sweetly, from the crystal waves of the sea."[48] The expertise needed to maintain proper intonation in this piece is evidenced in another example of word painting: passages of chromaticized triplets, sung both imitatively and in close harmony, that depict the last line of stanza 3, "Drinking the cool tide"[49] (see Example 11.3, soprano and alto lines only). In the final stanza of this ten-minute piece, the choir returns to the soft, high, sustained singing of the beginning.

Hymne is less immediately accessible than *Der Abend* because the dense and busy counterpoint, shifting meters, and chromaticism make it difficult for the listener to perceive the piece's structure and organization. Strauss set six of Rückert's ten verses, which make up a hymn of deep comfort. Each stanza ends in a refrain, "O do not grieve,"[50] which Strauss uses

EXAMPLE 11.2

EXAMPLE 11.3

as a structuring device by assigning it to the first chorus. The refrain is set off from the verses, which are sung by the second choir, by its homophonic texture and a relaxation in tempo. As the piece progresses, the refrain alternates less often with the verses, gradually becoming interweaved with them until at the end, it becomes absorbed into the last verse, which has taken on the homophony of the refrain. *Hymne* is characterized by the extended ranges and passages of sustained, high singing seen in *Der Abend*, but one feature distinguishes it from the first piece of the opus: an extraordinary fugal section built on a lengthy, chromatic subject that begins in the second basses.

EXAMPLE 11.4

Strauss's word-painting technique is seen again here in the use of this fugue to set the sixth stanza lines: "Indeed disturbing is our path, / Where we turn, / Seeing no goal; / But such a path, however long, / Must end some time."[51]

Zwei Männerchöre, Op. 42; *Drei Männerchöre*, Op. 45. Composed in the summer of 1899. Poetry from *Stimmen der Völker in Liedern* (1778–79), compiled by Johann Gottfried von Herder (1744–1803), who collected folk songs. Op. 42: *Liebe* and *Altdeutsches Schlachtlied*. Op. 45: *Schlachtgesang*, *Lied der Freundschaft*, and *Der Brauttanz*. Four-part (TTBB) a cappella men's chorus. Strauss dedicated Op. 45 to his father, Franz Strauss, in honor of his birthday.

These five compositions represent Strauss's first significant efforts (except for two pieces written in the 1880s) in a genre that was to become the most significant part of his choral output—works for unaccompanied male choir. Wajemann notes that Strauss wrote twenty-one pieces that fall into this category, more than the number of works for unaccompanied mixed choir and for chorus and orchestra combined.[52] Most commentators attribute Strauss's interest in the a cappella male choir to his activities as a choral competition judge. In September 1898, Strauss began a position in Berlin as chief conductor of the Royal Court Opera. As one of his duties, he served as a judge at contests for male choirs that the Kaiser held in various German cities, including the first of the Kaiser's competitions in Kassel. This competition took place at the end of May 1899, immediately before Strauss wrote six works for unaccompanied male choir—the five in Op. 42 and Op. 45 plus *Soldatenlied*, o. Op. AV 93, a setting of a poem by August Kopisch (1799–1853). Wajemann proposes that the Kaiser could also have ordered Strauss to compose some unaccompanied works for male chorus.[53] At the Kaiser's request, Strauss arranged six more folksongs—*Sechs Volkslied-bearbeitungen*, o. Op. AV 101—for unaccompanied four-part male chorus (TTBB) in 1905 and 1906 that were published by Peters in 1906 as part of a larger collection called the *Volksliederbuch für Männerchor*.[54]

As is the case with Op. 34, these pieces for a cappella male chorus present a host of difficulties for the singers, such as extremes of range, large leaps, extensive chromaticism, nontraditional voice leading, and shifting meters. Singers must cover unusually wide ranges within a short time span, as seen in this passage for the basses from *Lied der Freundschaft*.[55]

EXAMPLE 11.5

In *Altdeutsches Schlachtlied* (Old German Battle Song), which Strauss was thought to describe as "devilishly difficult," Strauss depicted the chaos of battle by employing a short motive (see Example 11.6), that is rapidly imitated by beginning on pitches that move up all twelve tones of the chromatic scale.[56] *Brauttanz* is characterized by shifts between 3/8 and 4/8, as well as frequent syncopations. The drinking song *Soldatenlied* combines an extremely fast tempo with syllabic word setting to present formidable challenges in articulation to the singers. Other difficulties lie in the high tessitura for the tenors; frequent changes in tonality, dynamics, accent patterns, and meters; and chromaticism that permeates the score.[57]

EXAMPLE 11.6

Fal - let in sie!

Op. 42 was premiered on 8 December 1899 by the Vienna Schubert Society, conducted by Adolf Kirchl. The date of the first performance of op. 45 is unknown. The Munich People's Singers Guild (Bürger-Sänger-Zunft), directed by Richard Trunk (1879–1968), premiered a simplified version of *Soldatenlied* (arranged by Trunk) on 26 November 1910. Strauss's original score of *Soldatenlied* has never been performed. Apparently, the complexity of Strauss's writing for unaccompanied male choir was not unusual for its time. At one of the male chorus competitions held in Kassel (before 1914), the Kaiser gave the judges an address in which he urged them to encourage composers to simplify their writing for male chorus. Referring to Strauss, who was standing beside him, he said, "With him I have also nurtured a viper in my bosom."[58]

Deutsche Motette, Op. 62. Composed in 1913. Poem—*Die Schöpfung ist zur Ruh gegangen*—by Friedrich Rückert (1788–1866), published in his 1822 collection *Freimund.* Soprano, alto, tenor, and bass solos. Sixteen-part a cappella mixed chorus.

Sixteen years after the *Zwei Gesänge,* Op. 34, Strauss returned to the sixteen-part a cappella mixed choir, and to Rückert's poetry as a vehicle for a singing ensemble. Like Rückert's *Hymne* in Op. 32, *Die Schöpfung* expresses hope in the comfort of a higher power, but through "an atmosphere of rapt dedication," in the words of Norman Del Mar, who notes that *Deutsche Motette* is one of the few works by Strauss that contains what might be called "spiritual" or "religious" content.[59] Wajemann conjectures that in choosing the name for this piece, Strauss must have intended to invoke the deeply spiritual *Deutsches Requiem* (1868) by Brahms, but no direct evidence of this possibility exists, nor has any other information been found that would shed light on the genesis of this special work.[60]

Similarly to *Hymne*, *Die Schöpfung* is organized around a refrain, "keep watch in me!"[61] which occurs every two lines. But in *Deutsche Motette*, Strauss's extraordinary setting of *Die Schöpfung*, he does not use the refrain to structure the music, as he did in *Hymne*. Rather, he returns to the technique seen in *Der Abend*, in which the piece begins and ends with quiet, slow movement anchored by long, sustained pitches in both higher and lower voices, while the middle section (rehs. 19–38) is distinguished by quicker tempi and imitative polyphony, some of it fugal, built on the manipulation of thematic and motivic material from the fugal subject and main theme of the section, "O show me, refresh me"[62] in a manner reminiscent of the fugal section in *Hymne*.

EXAMPLE 11.7

Deutsche Motette is the most compelling and captivating of Strauss's freestanding choral works not because he employs novel vocal techniques or poses new vocal challenges—no musical or vocal device turns up in *Deutsche Motette* that has not been seen previously—but because the singers are pushed to new limits of effort and endurance. In some places, the sixteen voices expand to twenty when the soloists sing as a quartet. The vocal compass of the choir is stretched to over four octaves, with sopranos reaching a d-flat''' (three measures before reh. 37) and fourth basses singing a B-flat[1] (three measures before reh. 25). The tessitura for both the first sopranos and the fourth basses tends to lie toward the extremes of their ranges, often in unusually long phrases that involve sustained tones. This phrase in the first soprano line serves as a particularly strong example.

EXAMPLE 11.8

In another instance, the fourth basses must repeat a D-flat for twenty-four measures, sustaining it for the last ten (rehs. 35–38). Sometimes a pianissimo is added (for example, the seven-measure *ppp* g″ for the sopranos and C¹ for the fourth basses at reh. 39).

Deutsche Motette was premiered by the Court Theater Choir (Hoftheatersingchor) in Berlin and conducted by Hugo Rüdel (1868–1934), its director, on 2 December 1913. Strauss also dedicated the piece to Rüdel and the group. Rüdel was recognized as one of Germany's most important choral directors, and Strauss had come to know and admire the work of Rüdel and the Court Theater Choir during his tenure in Berlin.

Die Göttin im Putzzimmer, o. Op. AV 120. Composed in 1935. Poem by Friedrich Rückert (1788–1866). Eight-part unaccompanied mixed chorus.

Little is known of the genesis of this eight-minute, virtuosic work for mixed choir, which was neither performed nor published until after Strauss's death. Strauss biographer Willi Schuh wrote that Strauss had intended to compose a companion piece to *Göttin*, also set for eight-part unaccompanied choir, and publish the pair in one opus, but he never completed the second composition.[63] On 2 March 1952, conductor and noted Strauss interpreter Clemens Krauss conducted the Vienna State Opera chorus in the premiere; an arrangement for *Die Tageszeiten* for mixed choir shared the bill.[64] *Göttin* was finally published in 1958.

Rückert's charming poem describes the gentle chaos of a boudoir characterized by the "erotica of a thousand and one different things" scattered about the room.[65] Like Klopstock's Bardic Song, Rückert's poem contains long lists—this time of mundane toiletry and household items (powder puffs, hooks, heels, thread, stockings, and so on). But in Rückert's hands, this text has none of Klopstock's "leathery" quality. Alliterations, parallelisms, an abundance of crisp consonants, and the galloping textual rhythms give *Göttin* a verve and color that undoubtedly presented Strauss with interesting compositional possibilities. The first three stanzas serve as an example:

Welche chaotische	What disorder
Haushälterei!	in the household!
Welches erotische	What a riot
Tausenderlei!	of erotica!
Alle die Nischchen,	All those little niches,
Alle die Tischchen,	all those little tables,
Alle die Zellchen,	all those little crannies,
Alle die Gestellchen,	all those little shelves!
Fächelchen, Schreinchen,	Drawers, cupboards,
Alle voll Quästchen;	full of powder puffs,
Perlchen und Steinchen,	Pearls and gems
All' in den Kästchen!	in caskets all![66]

The housekeeper—the "goddess" of the title—then enters the room and sets it in order, but in "harmoniz[ing] all elements, perceiv[ing] totality in disparity," she reveals herself as both the poet's Muse and Love personified, both of whom "turn nothingness, chaos, into a raiment of celestial light."[67] Commentators have drawn relationships between the subject matter of the poem and Strauss's relationship with his wife, Pauline, whom Strauss viewed as his Muse, as well as his portrayal of his own domestic life in *Symphonia domestica* (1903).[68]

Strauss divided the poem into two parts. The first eleven stanzas, which render the boudoir in impressionistic detail, are set in a polyphonic texture dominated by quickly articulated triplets, sung piano or pianissimo. The second section (reh. 5), begins on the stanza "Suddenly, from top / to bottom she stands / quite encased / in colorful frippery," as the housekeeper gathers the baubles and other small items and tucks them away into their proper places.[69] In sharp contrast to the previous section, the word *suddenly* (*plötzlich*) appears on two forte block chords, and the texture of the rest of the section, which describes the goddess/housekeeper as harmonizer and creative inspiration, is primarily homophonic. The lively tempo of the entire piece sets formidable challenges for the singers, who must clearly articulate many consonants of the text and sing the fast-moving, chromatically colored harmonies in tune.

An den Baum Daphne, o. Op. AV 137. Composed in 1943. Text by Joseph Gregor (1888–1960). Nine-part unaccompanied mixed chorus, including boys choir.

Strauss had completed his one-act opera *Daphne*, Op. 82, in 1937, and it had premiered in 1938 in Dresden. Originally, the libretto to *Daphne* had included a cantata to be sung at the very end of the opera, but Strauss had rejected it in favor of a solo vocalise for Daphne after her transformation into a tree. But Strauss did not forget the cantata, the text of which is an apostrophe to Daphne as the transformed, divine being. In 1943, Viktor Maiwald, director of the Vienna State Opera Chorus Concerts Society, commissioned Strauss to compose an unaccompanied choral work for the group. Strauss asked Joseph Gregor, the librettist of *Daphne*, to rework the cantata, and he finished composing it in November 1943, dedicating it to the society. War prevented the piece from premiering until 5 January 1947, but the delay turned out to be fortunate, since 1947 was the twentieth anniversary year of the society. The Vienna Boys Choir, which sang the top line of the nine-part piece, joined the society in the premiere performance.

Although the work is subtitled "Epilogue to Daphne," it was never intended to be included in the opera. Yet *An den Baum Daphne* opens in

F-sharp major, in which key the opera ended, and the opening thematic material is taken from Daphne's final music and words, with her main motive
added as an extension.

EXAMPLE 11.9

Ge - lieb - ter   Baum!

Much of the first section following the opening theme is homophonic,
interwoven with fragments of the two Daphne motives. The next section,
"And behold: transfixed was the fugitive foot! Earth's might entered you
from below"[70] (ten measures after reh. 5) begins with a sudden, downward
unison leap of a minor tenth from E-flat to C on "And behold." A melisma
based on the Daphne theme colors the word *fugitive*. Then follow seventy-
two measures of polyphonic, wordless vocalization by the choir under the
voices of the boys, who sing a relatively simple but somewhat chromaticized melody to the lines that recall Daphne's transformation: "Arms,
raised to the almighty tenderly, beseechingly, behold, receive welcome!
Thus you returned to your companions, thus you entered their circle anew,
and thus you draw us also eternally to you!"[71] This second section is notated in three sharps, although it never settles into a key. There is little clear
evidence of either A major or F-sharp minor until the end of the section
(six measures after reh. 13), where the choir pauses on the dominant 7th
chord of F-sharp. The third section ("Greater was the glorious offering")[72]
is demarcated by a slightly faster tempo and another key change, this time
to a notation of no accidentals, although again, the section never settles
into a key for any length of time. However, the disappearance of the accidentals in the key signature invokes the "heroic" key of C major, in keeping
with the textual description of Daphne's service to Apollo, in crowning the
heads of fallen heroes with laurel leaves. The final section ("How silently
you beckon us")[73] returns to the original F-sharp major tonality, and the
boys' choir is heard once again over a combination of sustained pitches and
undulating lines based on the Daphne theme heard in the adult choir. The
four-minute coda, marked *sehr ruhig*, returns to the transcendent, wordless, vocalization heard in the second section. At the very end, all nine parts

sing "Beloved tree!" in block chords, ending with a perfect cadence on the tonic F-sharp major.

Strauss's choral output, while uneven in quality, reveals a rich and interesting history that would reward deeper study. From the historical standpoint, this repertory could serve particularly well as the starting point for investigations into the recent history of choral singing and practice. More important, all of the a cappella choral works discussed here should be more widely performed by professional choral groups and could be taken on by advanced college choirs. Singers would discover musical and vocal capacities they never knew they possessed, and listeners would see a fascinating and seldom-revealed facet of Strauss's special "physiognomy."

NOTES

The original version of the chapter opening quotes and their sources are as follows. "Ach, wenn ich nur die Technik des Männerchorsatzes besser los hätte. . . . Mein Chorsatz klingt halt immer nicht so, wie ichs gern hätt'!" From a conversation with Strauss on 1 May 1924 in Viktor Keldorfer, "*Die Tageszeiten* von Richard Strauss," *Österreichische Musikzeitschrift* 7, no. 4 (1952): 130. "Ich verstehe vom Chorgesang selbst zu wenig." From a letter written to Keldorfer by Strauss on 5 February 1948 in Keldorfer, "Richard Strauss und sein Verhältnis zum Männerchor. Nach eigenen Erlebnissen eines Chordirigenten," *Österreichische Sänger Zeitung* 5, no. 3/4 (1956): 4. "Man kann wohl ohne Übertreibung sagen, daß das Ganze, so wie es auf dem Papier steht, wohl nie wird von menschlichen Stimmen zum Erklingen gebracht werden können." See Emil Thilo, "Richard Strauss als Chorkomponist," *Die Musik* 13 (1913–14): 309, commenting on *Deutsche Motette*, Op. 62.

1. Judith H. Blezzard, "Richard Strauss A Cappella," *Tempo* 176 (March 1991): 21–28.

2. Kenneth Birkin, "[Review of] *Die Chorkompositionen von Richard Strauss*," *Music and Letters* 69, no. 1 (1988): 97.

3. Blezzard, "Richard Strauss A Cappella," 21.

4. Keldorfer, "*Die Tageszeiten* von Richard Strauss," 132.

5. Keldorfer, "Richard Strauss und sein Verhältnis zum Männerchor," 2.

6. Citing various pieces of evidence, Heiner Wajemann shows that it is unclear whether *Wandrers Sturmlied* was composed in 1884 or 1885. See Heiner Wajemann, *Die Chorkompositionen von Richard Strauss* (Tutzing: Hans Schneider, 1986), 178–79.

7. ibid., 179; and Thilo, "Richard Strauss als Chorkomponist," 305. Critics also see similarities between *Wandrers Sturmlied* and Brahms's *Nänie*, Op. 82, and *Schicksalslied*, Op. 54, both for chorus and orchestra.

8. Wajemann, *Die Chorkompositionen*, 180, quoting Johann Wolfgang von Goethe, *Dichtung und Wahrheit* (pt. 3), vol. 28, *Goethe's Werke* (Weimar: H. Böhlau, 1846), 118ff.

9. "Wen/den du nicht verlässest, Genius."

10. "ein Läuterungsmittel für seine Seele, wenn diese von Leidenschaft getrübt wurde"; see Franz Zagiba, *Johann L. Bella (1843–1936) und das Wiener Musikleben* (Vienna: Verlag des Notringes der wissenschaftlichen Verbände Österreichs, 1955), 50–51, quoting part of Bella's lengthy program note of December 1888.

11. "Python tötend, leicht, groß / Pythius Apollo."

12. Zagiba, *Johann L. Bella*, 48.

13. "es wird im allergrößten Musikfeststil geschrieben"; from Strauss's 25 August 1902 letter to Philipp Wolfrum in the Bavarian State Library, Munich, Manuscripts Department, Signatur: ANA 330 I; quoted in Wajemann, *Die Chorkompositionen*, 190.

14. "eine große Orchestersauce"; see Otto Julius Bierbaum: "Feuilleton. Ludwig Uhland à la Richard Strauß," *Allgemeine Zeitung* 106, no. 321 (1903): 1–2.

15. Reinhold C. Muschler, *Richard Strauss* (Hildesheim: Franz Borgmeyer, 1924), 388. Wagner had instituted these practices at Bayreuth, but it took a number of years for them to become widespread in concert performances.

16. Letter from Strauss to his parents of 4 September 1902, in Richard Strauss, *Briefe an die Eltern, 1882–1906,* ed. Willi Schuh (Zurich: Atlantis Verlag, 1954), 260.

17. "Hei, sausende Pfeile, klirrender Schwerterschlag!"; "Bis Harald fiel und sein trotziges Heer erlag."

18. Strauss, *Briefe an die Eltern*, 81.

19. Letter from Strauss to Count Hülsen-Haeseler of 24 August 1905. See Franz Grasberger, ed., *Der Strom der Töne trug mich fort: Die Welt um Richard Strauss in Briefen*, with the cooperation of Franz and Alice Strauss (Tutzing: Hans Schneider, 1967), 162.

20. "blutleerer, lederner Text"; see Keldorfer, "*Die Tageszeiten* von Richard Strauss," 129.

21. "inhaltlos"; see Thilo, "Richard Strauss als Chorkomponist," 308.

22. "grenzenlos unmusikalisch"; "verknöcherter Stoff"; "ethnographische Landkarte"; see Muschler, *Richard Strauss*, 430–32.

23. "abstrus und absurd"; see Wajemann, *Die Chorkompositionen*, 150–51.

24. "Ha, ihr Cherusker! Ihr Katten! Ihr Marsen! Ihr Semnonen! / Ihr festlichen Namen des Kriegsgesangs! / Ihr Brukterer! Ihr Warner! Ihr Gothonen! Ihr Lewover! / Ihr festlichen Namen des Kriegsgesangs!" See Richard Strauss, *Bardengesang op. 55*, piano vocal score, arr. Otto Singer, English trans. John Bernhoff (Berlin: Adolph Fürstner, 1906).

25. Keldorfer, "*Die Tageszeiten* von Richard Strauss," 129; and Thilo, "Richard Strauss als Chorkomponist," 308.

26. "das Unmögliche möglich zu machen"; see Muschler, *Richard Strauss*, 430.

27. These features of the piece are noted by Walter Werbeck, Introduction, trans. J. Bradford Robinson, in Richard Strauss, *Richard Strauss Edition*, vol. 30,

Werke für Chor und Orchester (Vienna: C. F. Peters [Verlag Dr. Richard Strauss], 1999), xiv; and Wajemann, *Die Chorkompositionen*, 152.

28. On 2 March 1952, Clemens Krauss led the Vienna State Opera chorus and orchestra in an arrangement of *Die Tageszeiten* for mixed choir and orchestra. The director of the opera chorus, Richard Rossmayer, wrote the arrangement.

29. *Zwei Lieder* o. Op. AV 25 (1876), for four-part a cappella mixed chorus: *Morgengesang* and *Frühlingsnacht*; and from *Sieben vierstimmige Lieder* o. Op. AV 67 (1880) for solo vocal quartet or four-part a cappella mixed choir, no. 1, *Winterlied*.

30. "Gut, sehr gut! Das ist ein Vollblutromantiker, der mir nahesteht"; see Keldorfer, "*Die Tageszeiten* von Richard Strauss," 130.

31. "Fliegt der erste Morgenstrahl / Durch das stille Nebeltal"; "Wenn der Hahn kräht auf dem Dache."

32. Like Strauss's work, Pfitzner's Eichendorff setting was for chorus and orchestra, although he employed mixed chorus and added soloists and organ.

33. Keldorfer, "*Die Tageszeiten* von Richard Strauss," 132, and "Richard Strauss und sein Verhältnis zum Männerchor," 2. See "Richard Strauss und sein Verhältnis zum Männerchor" for a reproduction of the eighteen-bar rooster call (3). The last eight bars are also reproduced in "Ehrentafel Österreichischer Tonkünstler," *Österreichische Musikzeitschrift* 13, no. 5 (1958): 232.

34. Keldorfer, "*Die Tageszeiten* von Richard Strauss," 132.

35. Hugo Leichtentritt, "Richard Strauss: *Die Tageszeiten*, op. 76," *Die Musik* 23, no. 5 (1930–31): 379–80.

36. "zugkräftiger"; see Strauss, *Der Strom der Töne,* 330f.

37. Wajemann, *Die Chorkompositionen*, 167.

38. The term "o. Op.," or *ohne Opuszahlen* (without an opus number) designates works unpublished during Strauss's lifetime. The accompanying designation "AV 119" indicates the number (in this case, 119) assigned to the work by Erich Hermann Müller von Asow in his catalog of Strauss's compositions; see Müller von Asow, ed., *Richard Strauss: Thematisches Verkverzeichnis*, 3 vols. (Vienna: Doblinger, 1959–74).

39. Wajemann, *Die Chorkompositionen*, 177.

40. "4 Trompeten möglichst vierfach, das übrige Orchester je nach der Stärke des Chores und nach Massgabe des Raumes zu verdoppeln oder zu vervierfachen." Wajemann, 176–77.

41. Franz Miller, *So kämpfe und siegte die Jugend der Welt. XI. Olympiade Berlin* (Munich: Knorr and Hirth, 1937), 12.

42. Wajemann, *Die Chorkompositionen*, 176.

43. Werbeck, "Introduction," xvi.

44. Wajemann, *Die Chorkompositionen*, 120–21.

45. Blezzard, "Richard Strauss," 23. The proportions are as follows: Choir 1: S (20), A (20), T (15), B (15); Choir 2: S (3×15), A (3×15), T (3×10), B (3×10).

46. Thilo, "Richard Strauss als Chorkomponist," 305.

47. "Senke, strahlender Gott—die Fluren dürsten."

48. "Siehe, wer aus des Meeres krystallner Woge / Lieblich lächelnd dir winkt."

49. "Trinken die kühlende Fluth."

50. "O gräme dich nicht!"

51. "Zwar bedenklich ist unser Gang, / Wohin wir uns wenden, / Kein Ziel zu sehn; / Aber ein jeder Weg, wie lang, / Muß einst enden."

52. Wajemann, *Die Chorkompositionen*, 80.

53. An article on Op. 42 written in late 1899 claimed that the Kaiser had commissioned those two works. See Carl Kipke, "Besprechung: Strauss, Richard, Op. 42/1 u. 2, *Liebe* und *Altdeutsches Schlachtlied*," *Die Sängerhalle* 39, no. 50 (1899): 593. Quoted in Wajemann, *Die Chorkompositionen*, 97. Cf. Norman Del Mar, *Richard Strauss: A Critical Commentary on His Life and Works* (Ithaca, N.Y.: Cornell University Press, 1986), 2:363; and Muschler, *Richard Strauss*, 364, for commentary on the influence of choral competitions on Strauss's writing for male choruses.

54. The six songs, which were not taken from Herder's collection, are *Geistlicher Maien, Mißlungene Liebesjagd, Tummler, Hüt' du dich, Wächterlied*, and *Kuckuck*. Op. 42/1, *Liebe*, was also included in the *Volksliederbuch* für Männerchor (Leipzig: C. F. Peters, 1906) because it was considered to be somewhat folklike in style.

55. Del Mar, *Richard Strauss*, 2:363.

56. Wajemann, *Die Chorkompositionen*, 98.

57. Ibid., 100–01.

58. "Mit dem habe ich mir auch eine Schlange an meinem Busen ernährt"; see Thilo, "Richard Strauss als Chorkomponist," 309. This statement of the Kaiser's, which was made sometime before 1914, has been quoted elsewhere as a reaction to the premiere of Strauss's opera *Salome* in 1905. Cf. John Williamson, "Critical Reception," in *Richard Strauss: Salome*, ed. Derrick Puffett, Cambridge Opera Handbooks (Cambridge: Cambridge University Press, 1989), 133, quoting Michael Balfour, *The Kaiser and His Times* (London: Cresset Press, 1964), 162: "That's a nice snake I've reared in my bosom." It is unclear whether the Kaiser made the same remark about Strauss on two different occasions, or whether one of the quotes is apocryphal.

59. Del Mar, *Richard Strauss*, 2:368.

60. Wajemann, *Die Chorkompositionen*, 122.

61. "o wach in mir!"

62. "O zeig mir, mich zu erquicken."

63. Willi Schuh, "*Die Göttin im Putzzimmer*: Richard-Strauss-Uraufführung in Wien," *Schweizerische Musikzeitung* 92 (May 1952): 228.

64. Leichtentritt, "Richard Strauss: *Die Tageszeiten*, op. 76."

65. "erotische Tausenderlei," from the first stanza of the poem.

66. English translation modified from translation by Mari Pračkauskas, liner notes, 23, for Richard Strauss, *Richard Strauss: Deutsche Motette (op. 62) [and other choral works]*, BBC Singers and Choristers of King's College Cambridge (Collins Classics; 14952: 1997).

67. "Die Elemente / Hat sie verbunden, / Hat ins Getrennte / Ganzes empfunden"; "Denn nur ihr beide / Wandelt das Nichts, / Chaos, zum Kleide / himmlischen Lichts"; see Pračkauskas, *Richard Strauss*, 24–25.

68. Blezzard, "Richard Strauss," 27; and Wajemann, *Die Chorkompositionen*, 132.

69. "Plötzlich von unten / Steht sie bis oben / All mit dem bunten / Flitter umwoben"; see Pračkauskas, *Richard Strauss*, 24.

70. Und sieh: Es erstarrte / Der flüchtige Fuß! / Die Kraft der Erde / Durchdrang dich von unten"; see ibid., 15.

71. "Arme, / die zum Höchsten gehoben, / Zart und flehend, / Siehe, sie werden begrüßt! / So kamst du wieder / Zu deinen Gespielen, / So tratst du aufs neue / In ihre Kreise, / So ziehest du auch uns / Ewig hinan zu dir!"; see ibid., 16.

72. "Größer ward / Die herrliche Gabe"; see ibid.

73. "Wie still du uns winkest!"; see ibid.

Selected Bibliography

Scott Warfield

The bibliography for Richard Strauss is vast, with well over thirty-five hundred items known to have been published up to the time of the 1964 centennial of his birth. Moreover, in the thirty-five years that led up to the fiftieth anniversary of the composer's death in 1999, Strauss studies emerged as a legitimate field of inquiry for musicology. Consequently, the rate of serious publication on Strauss's life, music, and career has increased significantly, and thus no selective bibliography like this one could hope to do justice to this ever-growing body of Strauss scholarship. What follows is therefore merely a sample of recent publications, as well as some of the more enduring works.

BASIC TOOLS

For anyone interested in the life, music, and career of Richard Strauss, there are a handful of standard resources that should be consulted first. The majority of these items have been produced by individuals who were either close to the composer himself or to his heirs and the archives and libraries in southern Germany where the vast majority of primary sources still reside.

Editions of Music

Richard Strauss Edition. Vols. 1–18, Mainz: Schott (Verlag Dr. Richard
      Strauss), 1996; and Vols. 19–30, Vienna: C. F. Peters (Verlag Dr.
      Richard Strauss), 1999. Although this is not a scholarly edition in
      the "*urtext*" tradition, this thirty-volume set, issued in two separate
      parts, contains all of Strauss's major stage works and instrumental
      works. In addition to reprinting virtually all of his published works,
      many lesser compositions, out-of-print scores, and previously un-
      published pieces are included. The first eighteen volumes on the
      theatrical works add materials on the staging and production de-
      signs, while the twelve instrumental volumes include a facsimile of
      an autograph score of *Till Eulenspiegel.*
Franz Trenner, ed. *Gesamtausgabe der Lieder.* 4 vols. London: Boosey and
      Hawkes, 1964. This edition contains all of Strauss's songs with opus
      numbers, nineteen *Jugendlieder*, and twenty songs without opus
      numbers (vols. 1–3), as well as twenty-one orchestral songs and
      Strauss's orchestrations of twenty other songs (vol. 4).

Catalogs and Indicies

Brosche, Günter, and Karl Dachs, eds. *Richard Strauss: Autographen in
      München und Wien, Verzeichnis.* Veröffentlichungen der Richard-
      Strauss-Gesellschaft München, Bd. 3. Tutzing: Hans Schneider,
      1979. This volume indexes the two locations richest in Strauss let-
      ters and includes coverage of multiple libraries in both cities. Users
      of this volume should know, however, that since its publication
      many additional Strauss letters have been added to collections in
      both cities.
Mueller von Asow, Erich H. *Richard Strauss: Thematisches Verzeichnis.*
      3 vols. Vienna: Doblinger, 1959–74. In 1942 Mueller von Asow pro-
      posed to catalog the complete oeuvre of Richard Strauss, but
      conditions in postwar Europe permitted him to complete only the
      first two volumes (1959, 1962) before his death in 1964. The third
      volume, covering works without opus numbers, unpublished works,
      fragments, and sketches was completed from Mueller von Asow's
      notes by Franz Trenner and Alfons Ott. Because of its long gestation,
      during which many new sources came to light, this catalog has lost
      much of its currency, and serious users would do better to consult
      the more recent Trenner *Werkverzeichnis* (see next entry). Despite

its waning value, the o. Op. and AV numbers assigned by Mueller von Asow are still frequently used to identify works without opus numbers.

Trenner, Franz. *Richard Strauss Werkverzeichnis*. Veröffentlichungen der Richard-Strauss-Gesellschaft München, Bd. 12. Munich: W. Ludwig Verlag, 1993. This definitive catalog of Richard Strauss's music, which supersedes the outdated catalog by Mueller von Asow, follows a purely chronological ordering that interfiles published and un-published works, and assigns each work a number (generally written nowadays as the "Tr." number) that indicates its absolute place in Strauss's oeuvre. Each entry includes a musical incipit, and the whole volume is thoroughly indexed, including a cross index with Mueller von Asow's earlier catalog. A preliminary version of Trenner's catalog was issued in 1985 by Doblinger. (See the review by Scott Warfield of the 1993 Trenner catalog in *Fontes Artis Musicae* 42 [1995]: 382–84, for the intertwined histories of the Mueller von Asow and Trenner catalogs.)

———. *Die Skizzenbücher von Richard Strauss aus dem Richard-Strauss-Archiv in Garmisch*. Veröffentlichungen der Richard-Strauss-Gesellschaft München, Bd. 1. Tutzing: Hans Schneider, 1977. A rough index of the 144 sketchbooks held by Strauss's heirs in the Garmisch archive. Note that Trenner does not include sketchbooks held elsewhere or any fragments, although some of those items are occasionally noted in his 1993 *Werkverzeichnis*.

Periodicals and Other Publications

Mitteilungen der Internationalen Richard-Strauss-Gesellschaft. Nos. 1–62/63 (1952–69). A series of occasional newsletters with a variety of arti-cles—including discographies, reviews, letters, and reminiscences, among other types—aimed at both the scholar and the nonspecialist.

Richard Strauss-Blätter. Neue Folge. (June 1979 to present) A biannual pe-riodical published in German and English by the Internationale Richard-Strauss-Gesellschaft of Vienna that includes a wide range of significant essays by Strauss scholars on both sides of the Atlantic. Facsimiles and photographs are frequently featured on the anniver-saries of Strauss's stage productions, and there is regular news of Strauss manuscripts, letters, and book reviews.

Veröffentlichungen der Richard-Strauss-Gesellschaft München. A series of oc-casional monographic publications known to Straussians as the

"Blaue Reihe" (blue series) because of their distinctive blue covers. To date the series has issued many basic tools for Strauss research, including catalogs, indices, letters, and documentary studies.

Bibliographies

Richard-Strauss-Bibliographie. Teil I: 1882–1944. Bearbeitet von Oswald Ortner und aus dem Nachlass herausgegeben von Franz Grasberger. Vienna: Georg Prachner Verlag, 1964. *Richard-Strauss-Bibliographie. Teil II: 1944–1964.* Bearbeitet von Günter Brosche. Vienna: Verlag Brüder Hollinek, 1973. "Beiträge zur Richard-Strauss-Bibliographie 1882–1964: Ergänzungen zu den erschienenen Verzeichnissen." In *Festschrift Hans Schneider zum 60. Geburtstage,* ed. Rudolf Elvers und Ernst Vögel. Munich: Verlag Ernst Vögel, 1981. The first systematic bibliography of the literature on Richard Strauss's life and music, issued in 1964 for the centennial of Strauss's birth, contains 1,743 items, including many early items from now obscure German periodicals. The second volume added another 1,700 items and carried the coverage forward to the centennial year itself, while the little-known "Ergänzungen" (additions) adds yet another 134 items.

Primary Sources and Fundamental Research

Richard Strauss Jahrbuch 1954. Ed. Willi Schuh. Bonn: Boosey & Hawkes, 1953. The first of two volumes—the second issued in 1959–60—of primary sources, notably the Strauss–Bülow correspondence, and scholarly essays by individuals close to the Strauss family.

Richard Strauss Jahrbuch 1959–60. Bonn: Boosey and Hawkes, 1960. A second volume of scholarly essays—including reminiscences by Strauss's sister and a biography of the composer's father by Franz Trenner—by individuals close to the Strauss family.

Steinitzer, Max. *Richard Strauss,* Berlin: Schuster and Loeffler, 1911. A primary source in that it was written by Strauss's Gymnasium classmate, who had access to numerous music manuscripts and documents, many of which no longer exist or whose whereabouts are unknown. Also published in several later editions.

Strauss, Richard. *Betrachtungen und Erinnerungen.* Ed. Willi Schuh. Zurich/Freiburg im Breisgau: Atlantis Verlag, 1949. Published in English as *Recollections and Reflections.* Ed. Willi Schuh. Trans. L. J.

Lawrence. London: Boosey and Hawkes, 1953. A collection of Strauss's most important writings, both published and unpublished, from throughout his career.

Trenner, Franz. *Richard Strauss: Dokumente seines Lebens und Schaffens. Auswahl und verbindender Text von Franz Trenner.* Munich: C. H. Beck, 1954. Essentially a biography in its chronological recounting of Strauss's life, Trenner quotes liberally from numerous primary documents, which makes this volume a basic source.

BIOGRAPHIES AND GENERAL STUDIES OF STRAUSS'S LIFE AND WORKS

As with any major figure, there has never been a shortage of biographies and other monographic studies of Richard Strauss, especially in recent years. Perhaps the first published description of his life and career was a two-column article by Bernhard Vogel—"Deutsche Komponisten der Gegenwart: Richard Strauss," *Neue Musik-Zeitung* 12, no. 7 (1891): 78—while Arthur Seidl and Wilhelm Klatte coauthored the first, albeit brief, book-length biography of Strauss in 1896. The majority of pre–Second World War biographies are useful primarily for what they reveal about contemporary attitudes toward Strauss during his lifetime, while the recent upsurge in Strauss studies, coupled with an ever-growing body of primary sources, has ensured a generally more evenhanded consideration of Strauss's life and music. Listed below are only a few of these, with some earlier useful items also included.

Abell, Arthur M. *Talks with Great Composers.* New York: Philosophical Library, 1955. Includes three chapters that are based on the author's visits and correspondence with Strauss. Abell gives no documentation for statements he ascribes to Strauss, however, and in writing over fifty years after the fact, he often misdates or conflates events. Nevertheless, this source retains value when read with a careful eye.

Adrián, Enrique Pérez. *Richard Strauss.* Barcelona: Ediciones Península, 2000. Apparently the first original biography of Strauss written in Spanish.

Ashley, Tim. *Richard Strauss.* London: Phaidon, 1999. An excellent and fair account of Strauss's life that is among the best of the many biographies issued for the fiftieth anniversary of Strauss's death.

Beci, Veronika. *Der ewig Moderne: Richard Strauss.* Düsseldorf: Droste, 1998. A biography that traces Strauss's life and career through his lesser-known works such as the solo songs, the cantata *Die Tageszeiten,* and the *Metamorphosen.* Beci's emphasis is on Strauss's continual search for new means of expression.

Del Mar, Norman. *Richard Strauss: A Critical Commentary on His Life and Works.* 3 vols. London: Jenkins and Barrie, 1962; reprint, Ithaca, N.Y.: Cornell University Press, 1986. A standard work that provides frequently lengthy narrative descriptions of virtually all published and many unpublished compositions by Strauss. The facts of Strauss's life are used primarily to bind the musical descriptions together.

Gilliam, Bryan. *The Life of Richard Strauss.* Cambridge: Cambridge University Press, 1999. This important study, written by the current leading American expert on Strauss, offers the best summary of the scholarly consensus about Strauss at the end of the twentieth century.

Kennedy, Michael. *Richard Strauss.* The Master Musicians. 2d ed. New York: Schirmer Books, 1995. Provides a standard study of the composer, broken into separate halves on the life and works, by one of Strauss's earliest and most enthusiastic advocates in England.

———. *Richard Strauss: Man, Musician, Enigma.* Cambridge: Cambridge University Press, 1999. Covers much of the same ground as the preceding item, but also includes significant information about the relationship between Strauss and his wife and a spirited defense of Strauss's actions during the Nazi era.

Krause, Ernst. *Richard Strauss: Gestalt und Werk.* Leipzig: Breitkopf and Härtel, 1955. Published in English as *Richard Strauss: The Man and His Work.* Boston: Crescendo, 1969. A widely read work in its original edition—and in the many translations and later editions—that offers an East German perspective on Strauss.

Messmer, Franzpeter. *Richard Strauss: Biographie eines Klangzauberers.* Zurich/St. Gallen: M&T Verlag, 1994. A general biography that seeks to "learn about the music of the composer in the context of its genesis" and that is particularly concerned with Strauss's music as a reflection of the "revolutionary beginning of the twentieth century."

Panofsky, Walter. *Richard Strauss: Partitur eines Lebens.* Munich: R. Piper, 1965. A reliable standard biography, written for the centennial of Strauss's birth.

Ross, Alex, "The Last Emperor." *The New Yorker,* 20 December 1999, 86–94. A commentary, made on the fiftieth anniversary of the composer's death, which suggests that "Richard Strauss, for better or for worse, is the composer of the [twentieth] century."

Schuh, Willi. *Richard Strauss: Jugend und frühe Meisterjahre: Lebenschronik, 1864–1898*. Zurich: Atlantis Verlag, 1976. Published in English as *Richard Strauss: A Chronicle of the Early Years, 1864–1898*. Trans. Mary Whittall. Cambridge: Cambridge University Press, 1982. Virtually a primary source, this volume represents the first part of a never-completed biography by the Swiss writer and critic handpicked by Strauss for the task. Schuh had unlimited access to the voluminous materials held by Strauss and his heirs, although Schuh's documentation is not as thorough as some might like. The original version is slightly better in this regard than the English translation, which often omits the dates of letters, for instance.

Specht, Richard. *Richard Strauss und sein Werk*. Bd. 1. *Der Künstler und sein Weg der Instrumentalkomponist*. Bd. 2. *Der Vokalkomponist/Der Dramatiker*. Leipzig: E. P. Tal, 1921. Similar in nature to Del Mar, these volumes offer some of the earliest (and still excellent) detailed narrative and analytical descriptions of Strauss's major compositions through *Die Alpensinfonie* and *Die Frau ohne Schatten*.

Walter, Michael. *Richard Strauss und seine Zeit*. Laaber: Laaber Verlag, 2000. Another of the many biographies written for the fiftieth anniversary of Strauss's death, this one by a German musicologist who specializes in music during the Third Reich.

Wilhelm, Kurt. *Richard Strauss: Persönlich*. Munich: Kinder Verlag, 1984. Published in English as *Richard Strauss: An Intimate Portrait*. Trans. Mary Whittall. London: Thames and Hudson, 1989. A copiously illustrated biography by an intimate of the Strauss family that offers perhaps the best "visual" biography of Strauss. (The English edition omits much from the original German edition.)

PUBLISHED CORRESPONDENCE

It has been estimated that Strauss may have written an average of more than ten business letters for every day of his adult life, and even though he lived well into the era of the telephone, the handwritten letter remained his preferred manner of communication to his final years. Literally thousands of letters from and to Strauss survive, offering one of the most immediate windows into both his personality and his working methods. The single largest collection of letters is undoubtedly that owned by the Strauss family in Garmisch, while libraries in Munich and Vienna also have significant holdings. Additionally, there are numerous important smaller groups of Strauss letters in both public and private collections throughout the world,

and the Strauss literature regularly includes announcements of newly uncovered letters. The publication of Strauss's correspondence has been
underway since well before his death with the appearance of many selectively edited letters and partial correspondence, but in recent years the
interest in fully documenting the lives of composers has led to numerous
"complete" editions that leave out almost nothing. To date, there are about
forty major collections of Strauss's letters, and what follows are only a few
of the most important.

Blaukopf, Herta, ed. *Gustav Mahler/Richard Strauss: Briefwechsel,*
    1888–1911. Munich: Piper, 1980. Published in English as *Gustav*
    Mahler/Richard Strauss: Correspondence, 1888–1911. Trans. Edmund
    Jephcott. Chicago: University of Chicago Press, 1984. This impor-
    tant, but incomplete, correspondence documents the era during
    which both composers first made their reputations. Since the first
    publication of these letters, some additional ones from this corre-
    spondence have appeared and have been published separately.
Brosche, Günter. *Richard Strauss—Clemens Krauss: Briefwechsel: Gesam-*
    tausgabe. Publikation des Instituts für Österreichische Musikdoku-
    mentation, Bd. 20. Tutzing: Hans Schneider, 1997. Krauss, Strauss's
    collaborator for *Capriccio,* conducted several premieres of Strauss's
    later operas, and his wife, Viorica Ursuleac, was Strauss's favorite so-
    prano in his later years. This complete edition supersedes an earlier
    selection of letters edited by Schuh and Kende.
————. *Richard Strauss—Franz Schalk: Ein Briefwechsel.* Veröffentlich-
    ungen der Richard-Strauss-Gesellschaft München, Bd. 6. Tutzing:
    Hans Schneider, 1983. Schalk was codirector with Strauss and, after
    Strauss's forced resignation in 1924, sole director of the Vienna
    State Opera.
————. "Richard Strauss—Franz Schneiderhan: Briefwechsel." *Richard*
    Strauss-Blätter 43 (2000): 3–115. Schneiderhan was general inten-
    dant of the Austrian State Theater in the 1920s, a period when
    Strauss was most active in Vienna. These letters, which cover the pe-
    riod 1924–36, are typical of the many smaller, but still important,
    correspondence awaiting publication.
Grasberger, Franz, ed. *Die Strom der Töne trug mich fort: Die Welt um*
    Richard Strauss in Briefen. With the cooperation of Franz and Alice
    Strauss. Tutzing: Hans Schneider, 1967. A large miscellany that in-
    cludes a broad sampling of letters from nearly every era in Strauss's
    life and many of his most important correspondents.

Hanke Knaus, Gabriella. *Richard Strauss—Ernst von Schuch: Ein Briefwechsel.* Veröffentlichungen der Richard-Strauss-Gesellschaft, Bd. 16. Berlin: Henschel, 1999. Schuch was conductor in Dresden until his death in 1914, and he conducted the premieres of *Feuersnot, Salome, Elektra,* and *Der Rosenkavalier.* This edition replaces an earlier one edited by Schuch's son.

Hülle-Keeding, Maria. *Richard Strauss—Romain Rolland: Briefwechsel und Tagebuchnotizen.* Veröffentlichungen der Richard-Strauss-Gesellschaft München, Bd. 13. Berlin: Henschel Verlag, 1994. Strauss corresponded with the French man of letters during the years 1899 to 1924, and their exchanges are often quite revelatory of Strauss's attitude in those years. This volume also includes diary entries and several essays that complement the letters.

Kaminiarz, Irina, ed. *Richard Strauss: Briefe aus dem Archiv des Allgemeinen Deutschen Musikvereins 1888–1909.* Veröffentlichungen der Hochschule "Franz Liszt," Bd. 1. Weimar: H. Böhlau, 1995. The Allgemeiner Deutscher Musikverein (ADMv), the society founded by Franz Liszt to promote new German music, was an important venue for some of Strauss's earliest orchestral premieres. In 1901 Strauss accepted his election as president of the ADMv, after having previously declined election to its committee, in order to work for composers' rights.

Konhauser, Marc. "Der Briefwechsel zwischen Alfred Kerr und Richard Strauss (Erstveröffentlichung)." *Richard Strauss-Blätter* 39 (1998): 34–51. Kerr was a theater critic, who supplied Strauss with the texts for *Krämerspiegel,* the notorious song cycle filled with biting puns and satirical references to Germany's leading music publishers.

Ott, Alfons. "Richard Strauss und sein Verlegerfreund Eugen Spitzweg." In *Musik und Verlag: Karl Vötterle zu 65. Geburtstag am 12. April 1968.* Ed. Richard Baum and Wolfgang Rehm. Kassel: Bärenreiter, 1968. This narrative, which includes many excerpts from the correspondence, traces Strauss's relationship with his first publisher, Eugen Spitzweg, the owner of Aibl Verlag.

Schuh, Willi, ed. *Richard Strauss: Briefwechsel mit Willi Schuh.* Zurich: Atlantis Verlag, 1969. During Strauss's final decade, the Swiss writer and critic Willi Schuh was one of Strauss's closest confidants. This selection of letters from their correspondence documents the difficulties of the final years for Strauss and his wife.

Steiger, Martina. *Richard Strauss/Karl Böhm: Briefwechsel 1921–1949.* Mainz: Schott, 1999. Böhm conducted the premieres of *Friedenstag* and *Daphne,* and he was also well-known for his performances of other works by Strauss.

Strauss, Franz, and Alice Strauss, with Willi Schuh, eds. *Richard Strauss und Hugo von Hofmannsthal: Briefwechsel: Gesamtausgabe.* Zurich: Atlantis Verlag, 1952. Published in English as *A Working Friendship: The Correspondence between Richard Strauss and Hugo von Hofmannsthal.* Trans. Hanns Hammelmann and Ewald Osers. New York: Random House, 1961. As early as 1925 Strauss had proposed to Hofmannsthal that their correspondence be published as a means of documenting "the seriousness of our joint labors." In his reply, Hofmannsthal suggested that only a judiciously edited selection from the years 1907 to 1918 appear in print, so as to withhold "ammunition" from spiteful critics. Thus, the first publication from this correspondence, edited by Strauss's son in 1925, scratched only the surface of the available materials. The 1952 edition (and the 1961 English translation) of the Strauss–Hofmannsthal correspondence was thus heralded as the first "complete" edition, even though it still contained various lacunae. Numerous editions in German and English have since restored many of the excised passages, but no truly complete edition has yet appeared in print. (Note: When using the English translation, readers should refer back to the German when possible, because letters are misdated, there are mistranslations, and excisions are made without ellipsis dots or other indications that material was cut.)

Strauss, Gabriele. *Lieber Collega!: Richard Strauss im Briefwechsel mit zeitgenössischen Komponisten und Dirigenten.* Veröffentlichungen der Richard-Strauss-Gesellschaft, Bd. 14. Berlin: Henschel, 1996. Strauss, Gabriele, and Monika Reger. *Richard Strauss im Briefwechsel mit zeitgenössischen Komponisten und Dirigenten. II: Ihr Aufrichtig Ergebener.* Veröffentlichungen der Richard-Strauss-Gesellschaft, Bd. 15. Berlin: Henschel, 1998. These two collections include virtually complete correspondences between Strauss and Hans von Bülow, Antonìn Dvořák, Giuseppe Verdi, Hans von Bronsart, Fritz Busch, Engelbert Humperdinck, Jean-Louis Nicodé, Eugen d'Albert, and Franz Wüllner in *Lieber Collega!,* and with Emil von Reznìck, Hermann Bischoff, Willem Mengelberg, and Gustav Brecher in the second volume. Those with Bülow and Wüllner simply reprint earlier publications, while the others are all new. A third volume of similar letters is anticipated for the near future.

Strauss, Richard. *Briefe an die Eltern: 1882–1906.* Ed. Willi Schuh. Zurich: Atlantis Verlag, 1954. This selection from Strauss's letters to his parents offers an important personal view of the events that shaped the early years of his professional career. Although drawn primarily from the composer's letters, some replies from his family are also included.

Strauss, Richard, and Stefan Zweig. *A Confidential Matter: The Letters of Richard Strauss and Stefan Zweig, 1931–1935.* Trans. Max Knight. Berkeley: University of California Press, 1977. Originally published as *Richard Strauss, Stefan Zweig: Briefwechsel.* Ed. Willi Schuh. Frankfurt am Main: Fischer, 1957. Strauss's attempt to ignore Nazi racial policies by collaborating with the Jewish writer Zweig on *Die schweigsame Frau* ended in an embarrassing episode that cost Strauss dearly. In addition to documenting their work together, the bluntness of Strauss's infamous letter of 17 June 1935 and some of those that preceded it demonstrate his naiveté about the realities of life in Germany in the mid-1930s.

Tenschert, Roland, ed. *Richard Strauss und Joseph Gregor: Briefwechsel, 1934–1949.* Salzburg: O. Müller, 1955. Selected English translations by Susan Gillespie appear in Bryan Gilliam, ed., *Richard Strauss and His World.* Princeton, N.J.: Princeton University Press, 1992, 193–236. Following Zweig's withdrawal as Strauss's librettist, Gregor, a theater historian, agreed to serve as Strauss's collaborator. Unfortunately, his literary talents were no match for Strauss's sense of the theater, and their working relationship degenerated into a one-sided partnership—documented in these letters—in which Strauss dominated Gregor.

Trenner, Franz, ed. *Richard Strauss–Ludwig Thuille: Ein Briefwechsel.* Veröffentlichungen der Richard-Strauss-Gesellschaft München, Bd. 4. Tutzing: Hans Schneider, 1980. Selected English translations by Susan Gillespie appear in Bryan Gilliam, ed., *Richard Strauss and His World* (Princeton, N.J.: Princeton Unviersity Press, 1992), 193–236. Ludwig Thuille, who would later become a professional composer, was an orphan whose musical talents led to his introduction to the young Richard Strauss in 1871. The two boys corresponded frequently during their adolescent years, and their letters have since become a primary source for information on Strauss's formative years. Strauss was later embarrassed by his anti-Wagnerian comments in some of these letters, but in fact, the comments are quite understandable in their contexts.

Trenner, Franz, and Gabriele Strauss, eds. *Cosima Wagner–Richard Strauss: Ein Briefwechsel.* Veröffentlichungen der Richard-Strauss-Gesellschaft München, Bd. 2. Tutzing: Hans Schneider, 1978. After Strauss declared his allegiance to Wagner's music, he quickly became a favorite of Wagner's widow, who then began to groom Strauss to be an acolyte for Bayreuth. Strauss never completely accepted that role, however, as he began to define his own musical persona, and Strauss's conflicts with Cosima's brand of Wagnerism are often quite apparent in these letters.

Turner, J. Rigbee. "Richard Strauss to Caecilie Wenzel: Twelve Unpublished Letters." *Nineteenth-Century Music* 9 (1985–86): 163–75. Franz Strauss frequently advised his son to be discreet in his dealings with the opposite sex during the early years of Richard's professional career. The relationship with Dora Wihan-Weis is usually the only one cited by biographers, but Strauss's friendship with an actress whom he first met in Meiningen is actually better documented with this correspondence.

Youmans, Charles. "Ten Letters from Alexander Ritter to Richard Strauss, 1887–1894." *Richard Strauss-Blätter* 35 (1996): 3–24. According to Strauss, his conversion from a conservative, molded chiefly by his father's influence, to a Wagnerian was effected primarily by Alexander Ritter—a string player, erstwhile composer, and husband of Wagner's niece—during Strauss's term in Meiningen. The most important contents of these letters deal with Ritter's almost desperate attempts to convince Strauss to reshape the libretto of *Guntram* in a way that would conform to Wagner's ideology.

SELECTED STUDIES

There is no shortage of quality writing on specific topics related to the life and music of Strauss, especially in recent years. Just as the 1964 centennial of Strauss's birth served as a catalyst for publication, so did the fiftieth anniversary of his death in 1999. The commentary on Strauss's operas has tended to concentrate on the handful of his most important works, with several useful guides to particular works appearing in the last two decades. Nevertheless, in recent years nearly every one of Strauss's lesser-known theatrical works has attracted some serious scholarly attention. Studies of the instrumental works have likewise begun to move beyond the early attempts simply to describe musical forms and match them with programs, into more nuanced approaches that combine careful source studies with more sophisticated analytical tools. Only work on the Lieder has seemed to lag behind, although the smaller number of studies in that area is offset by the quality of much of that work. Finally, the complexities and contradictions of Strauss's life and career, notably his relationship with the Third Reich, have begun to receive equitable and evenhanded treatment in the literature.

Conference Reports and Collected Essays

Brosche, Günter. "Richard Strauss und Wien: Symposium zum 50. Todestag von Richard Strauss" *Richard Strauss-Blätter* 42 (1999): 15–163. Another of the many symposia held to mark the fiftieth anniversary of Strauss's death, this one concerned with Strauss and his adopted city of Vienna.

————, ed. "Richard Strauss in der Musikgeschichte der 1920er Jahre: Symposium zum 50. Todestag von Richard Strauss." *Richard Strauss-Blätter* 45 (2001): 5–223. One of several different symposia held to mark the fiftieth anniversary of Strauss's death, this one focusing on the decade of the 1920s.

Edelmann, Bernd, Birgit Lodes, and Reinhold Schlötterer, eds. *Richard Strauss und die Moderne: Bericht über das internationale Symposium München, 21. bis 23. Juli 1999.* Veröffentlichungen der Richard-Strauss-Gesellschaft, Bd. 17. Berlin: Henschel, 2001. Still another symposium marking the fiftieth anniversary of Strauss's death, this one dealing with the question of "modernism."

Gilliam, Bryan, ed. *Richard Strauss and His World.* Princeton, N.J.: Princeton University Press, 1992. A selection of papers initially presented at the International Conference on Richard Strauss at Duke University, Durham, North Carolina, in 1990.

————. *Richard Strauss: New Perspectives on the Composer and His Work.* Durham, N.C.: Duke University Press, 1992. A mixture of original essays, translations of earlier studies, and a few primary sources in translation that was issued in association with the 1992 Bard Music Festival.

Hanke Knaus, Gabriella. *Aspekte der Schlussgestaltung in den sinfonischen Dichtungen und Bühnenwerken von Richard Strauss.* Dokumente und Studien zu Richard Strauss, Bd. 1. Tutzing: Hans Schneider, 1995. A revision of the author's doctoral dissertation that discusses the final sections and even final measures of seven works by Strauss, based on the importance and influence she ascribes of Wagner's *Der Ring des Nibelungen* to Strauss's compositional approach.

Heinemann, Michael, Matthias Herrmann, and Stefan Weiss, eds. *Richard Strauss: Essays zu Leben und Werk.* Laaber: Laaber Verlag, 2002. The most recent collection of German essays on Strauss written by seventeen different authors. The topics addressed in this 271-page book range from the composer's operas (*Feuersnot, Salome, Elektra, Ariadne auf Naxos, Frau ohne Schatten, Daphne*), his orchestral works (Concerto for Horn and Orchestra, Op. 11, the Piano Concertos, *Also sprach Zarathustra, Don Quixote, Metamorphosen*), his songs (Op. 10 and *Four Last Songs*) to discussions of Strauss's involvement with the copyright, his relationship to the city of Dresden, his association with the Nazi Regime, and his view of the artist and the world.

Krellmann, Hanspeter, ed. *Wer war Richard Strauss? Neunzehn Antworten.* Frankfurt am Main: Insel, 1999. A collection of essays by nineteen different authors on various aspects of Strauss's life and music.

Masur, Kurt, and Bernd Pachnicke. *Kongressbericht zum VI. Internationalen Gewandhaus-Symposium: Richard Strauss, Leben, Werk, Interpretation, Rezeption anlässlich der Gewandhaus-Festtage in Leipzig vom 29. September bis 1. Oktober 1989.* Leipzig: Gewandhaus zu Leipzig and Frankfurt am Main: C. F. Peters, 1991. A selection of papers presented at one of the first international conferences devoted to Richard Strauss.

Schuh, Willi. *Straussiana aus vier Jahrzehnten.* Tutzing: Hans Schneider, 1981. Selected essays by the Swiss critic, longtime admirer of Strauss, and eventually the composer's biographer.

Seidl, Arthur: *Straussiana: Aufsätze zur Richard Strauss-Frage aus drei Jahrzehnten.* Regensburg: Gustov Bosse, [n.d.] (foreword dated 1913]). A lifelong friend, who first met Strauss when both were students in Munich's Ludwigsgymnasium, Seidl would also write one of the first biographies and numerous other pieces about Strauss.

Opera

Anderson, David E. "Fritz Busch and Richard Strauss: The Strauss Scores in the Busch Nachlass." *Music Review* 49 (1988): 289–94. A brief look at the annotations in the scores owned by the conductor Fritz Busch and their implications for the performance of some Strauss operas.

Antokoletz, Elliott. "Strauss's *Elektra:* Toward Expressionism and the Transformation of Nineteenth-Century Chromatic Tonality." In *Musik und Dichtung: Neue Forschungsbeiträge, Viktor Poschl zum 80. Geburtstag gewidmet,* 443–68. Frankfurt am Main: Lang, 1990.

An examination of the harmonic language of Strauss's most dissonant work, with an emphasis on how symmetrical tonal relationships are used symbolically to express the psychological states of the characters.

Birkin, Kenneth. *Richard Strauss: Arabella.* Cambridge Opera Handbooks. Cambridge: Cambridge University Press, 1989. A general guide to the final Strauss–Hofmannsthal opera, including its origins, a plot synopsis, several analytical essays, and its reception history.

Daviau, Donald G., and George J. Buelow. *The* Ariadne auf Naxos *of Hugo von Hofmannsthal and Richard Strauss.* Chapel Hill: University of North Carolina Press, 1975. Cowritten by a literary specialist and a musicologist, this book offers a detailed history of the complex genesis of the third Strauss–Hofmannsthal collaboration, along with several chapters interpreting the opera.

Erwin, Charlotte E. "Richard Strauss's Presketch Planning for *Ariadne auf Naxos.*" *Musical Quarterly* 67 (1981): 348–65. A study of Strauss's annotations on Hofmannsthal's draft of the libretto, which demonstrates the degree to which Strauss determined such details of this opera as key areas, harmonic relationships, melodic ideas, tempos, and orchestration before beginning to sketch the work.

Gilliam, Bryan. "Daphne's Transformation." In *Richard Strauss and His World*, ed. Bryan Gilliam, 33–66. Princeton, N.J.: Princeton University Press, 1992. A study of the final scene of *Daphne,* which was a particular favorite of Strauss's in his later years, based in part on the author's 1984 doctoral dissertation.

———. *Richard Strauss's Elektra.* Studies in Musical Genesis and Structure. Oxford: Clarendon Press, 1991. A detailed study, including examinations of previously unknown sketches, of *Elektra* that emphasizes the tonal structures underlying the opera's dissonant surface.

———. "Strauss's *Intermezzo:* Innovation and Tradition." In *Richard Strauss: New Perspectives on the Composer and His Work,* ed. Bryan Gilliam, 259–83. Durham, N.C.: Duke University Press, 1992. *Intermezzo* marks a shift in Strauss's operatic output from the epic and mythological plots of its predecessors to a completely modern tale of marital squabbles. To parallel his realistic subject, Strauss set the libretto in a manner that resembles contemporary cinematic techniques.

Hartmann, Rudolf. *Die Bühnewerke von Uraufführung bis Heute.* Freiberg im Breisgau: Freiburger Graphische Betriebe, 1980. Published in English as *Richard Strauss: The Staging of His Operas and Ballets.* Ed. and Trans. Graham Davies. New York: Oxford University Press, 1981.

Written by a director who staged three Strauss premieres and later served as general director of the Bavarian State Opera, this well-illustrated volume aims to document Strauss's preferred approaches to the stagings of all his theatrical works, including the ballets.

Jefferson, Alan. *Richard Strauss: Der Rosenkavalier.* Cambridge Opera Handbooks. Cambridge: Cambridge University Press, 1985. A general guide to Strauss's most popular opera, with an analytical description and synopsis by Norman Del Mar.

Krebs, Wolfgang. *Der Wille zum Rausch: Aspekte der musikalischen Dramaturgie von Richard Strauss' Salome.* Munich: W. Fink, 1991. A study of *Salome* that analyses the opera as a Nietzschean critique of Christianity in fin-de-siècle culture.

Kristiansen, Morten. "Richard Strauss's 'Feuersnot' in Its Aesthetic and Cultural Context: A Modernist Critique of Musical Idealism." Ph.D. diss. Yale University, 2000. A study of Strauss's second opera that finds in this work his final break with Wagnerian metaphysics, a critique of opera librettos in the 1890s that carried on that Wagnerian aesthetic, and the assertion of Strauss's new "modernist" style.

Mann, William. *Richard Strauss: A Critical Study of the Operas.* London: Cassell, 1964. The first comprehensive English-language survey of Strauss's operas, complete with the history and background of early performances and a detailed analysis of all fifteen operas.

Messmer, Franzpeter, ed. *Kritiken zu den Uraufführungen der Bühnenwerke von Richard Strauss.* Veröffentlichungen der Richard-Strauss-Gesellschaft München, Bd. 11. Pfaffenhofen: W. Ludwig Verlag, 1989. A collection that gathers together much of the journalistic criticism that followed all of Strauss's theatrical works, including the revised versions of his operas and ballets.

Murphy, Edward. "Tonality and Form in *Salome.*" *Music Review* 50 (1989): 215–30. An analysis that emphasizes the traditional tonal aspects of this opera.

Osborne, Charles. *The Complete Operas of Richard Strauss.* North Pomfret, Vt.: Trafalgar Square, 1988. A comprehensive guide to all fifteen of Strauss's operas. Each chapter begins with the brief history of an individual opera's genesis, followed by a description of the work's action and music.

Potter, Pamela. "Strauss's *Friedenstag:* A Pacifist Attempt at Political Resistance." *Musical Quarterly* 69 (1983): 408–24. An essay by a leading American expert on music under the Third Reich that argues for Strauss's twelfth opera as an expression of his antiwar sentiments.

Puffett, Derrick, ed. *Richard Strauss: Elektra.* Cambridge Opera Handbooks. Cambridge: Cambridge University Press, 1990. The volume has a slightly more academic tone than other guides in this series, chiefly in the detailed analysis of the opera's use of referential motives. It also includes discussions of the Elektra story and Hofmannsthal's version of it, the opera's dramatic structure and tonal organization, the harmonic language, and the orchestration.

Puffett, Derrick. *Richard Strauss: Salome.* Cambridge Opera Handbooks. Cambridge: Cambridge University Press, 1989. A collection of various essays by several different authors, along with a plot synopsis and commentaries on the work's reception.

Seshadri, Anne Marie Lineback. "Richard Strauss, 'Salome,' and the 'Jewish question.'" Ph.D. diss, University of Maryland, 1998. An interdisciplinary study that argues that contemporary audiences saw and heard the premiere of *Salome* as a *Judenoper*, which served to reinforce antisemitic prejudices.

Splitt, Gerhard. "Oper als Politikum: *Friedenstag* (1938) von Richard Strauss." *Archiv für Musikwissenschaft* 55 (1998): 220–51. An analysis by a German scholar, generally critical of Strauss's cooperation with the Third Reich, who views *Friedenstag* as an expression of Nazi ideals.

Steiger, Martina. *"Die Liebe der Danae" von Richard Strauss: Mythos, Libretto, Musik.* Mainz: Schott, 1999. A history of the work's genesis, libretto, and wartime production, and a musical analysis.

Wilhelm, Kurt. *Fürs Wort brauche ich Hilfe: Die Geburt der Oper Capriccio von Richard Strauss und Clemens Krauss.* Munich: Nymphenburger, 1988. A documentary history of the genesis of Strauss's final opera, with facsimiles drawn from the working drafts of the libretto and the composer's sketchbooks.

Youmans, Charles Dowell. "Richard Strauss's *Guntram* and the Dismantling of Wagnerian Musical Metaphysics." Ph.D. diss. Duke University, 1996. A study of Strauss's first opera and the manner in which it marks the beginning of a shift in Strauss's aesthetic viewpoint from one grounded in Schopenhauer to one based on Nietzsche.

Lieder and Choral Music

Blezzard, Judith H. "Richard Strauss *A Cappella.*" *Tempo* 176 (March 1991): 21–28. A description of Strauss's works for larger, unaccompanied choral forces, including a handful of early works and a few operatic excerpts.

Jackson, Timothy L. "Ruhe, meine Seele! and the Letzte Orchesterlieder." In *Richard Strauss and His World*, ed. Bryan Gilliam, 90–137. Princeton, N.J.: Princeton University Press, 1992. Also published in German in *Richard Strauss-Blätter* 32 (1994): 84–130, with a response from Alan Jefferson ("Strauss's Last Song Cycle," *Richard Strauss-Blätter* 33 [1995]: 69–75) and a final reply from Jackson ("Reply to Alan Jefferson," *Richard Strauss-Blätter* 34 [1995]: 135–40). Based on a motivic connection between the orchestrated version of "Ruhe, meine Seele!" and the four last songs, as well as a careful analysis of the sketches, Jackson argues for the inclusion of that earlier Lied in the final group.

Kaplan, Richard A. "Tonality as Mannerism: Structure and Syntax in Richard Strauss's Orchestral Song *Frühling*." *Theory and Practice* 19 (1994): 19–29. An analysis of Strauss's late orchestral song *Frühling*, which compares its voice leading with passages from *Elektra* and concludes that "despite the obvious surface differences . . . Strauss's late style represents a refinement of, not a departure from, his most radical music."

Lodato, Suzanne Marie. "Richard Strauss and the Modernists: A Contextual Study of Strauss's Fin-de-siècle Song Style." Ph.D. diss. Columbia University, 1999. A study of the influences of late-nineteenth-century German literary modernists on the compositional style of Strauss's middle-period Lieder.

Petersen, Barbara A. "Richard Strauss: A Lifetime of Lied Composition." In *German Lieder in the Nineteenth Century*. Ed. Rufus Hallmark, 250–78. Studies in Musical Genres and Repertories. New York: Schirmer, 1996. An overview of Strauss's songs by the leading American expert on the topic.

————. *Ton und Wort: The Lieder of Richard Strauss*. Studies in Musicology 15. Ann Arbor: UMI Research Press, 1980. Published in German as *"Ton und Wort": Die Lieder von Richard Strauss*. Trans. Ulrike Steinhauser. Veröffentlichungen der Richard-Strauss-Gesellschaft München, Bd. 8. Munich: Pfaffenhofen, 1986. Although not a comprehensive study of Strauss's Lieder, this work, a revision of the author's Ph.D. dissertation, presents the first in-depth examinations of various aspects of his songs, concluding with a detailed examination of *Sechs Lieder nach Gedichten von Clemens Brentano*, Op. 68.

Schumann, Karl. "Richard Strauss vertont Friedrich Rückert." In *Festschrift Walter Wiora zum 90. Geburtstag (30. Dezember 1996)*, 417–25. Tutzing: Hans Schneider, 1997. An examination of Strauss's *Klavierlieder,* Op. 36, the a cappella *Hymne für gemischten Chor,* Op. 34, no. 2, and the three a cappella *Männerchöre* (TrV 230), all of which set texts by Rückert.

Serpa, Franco. "La Deutsche Motette di Richard Strauss." In *Novecento Studi in onore di Adriana Panni,* 9–14. Torino: Edizioni di Torino, 1996. A brief overview of Strauss's setting of a Rückert text for four soloists with a 16-voice a cappella choir.

Templet, Jill Marian. "Richard Strauss and Adolf Friedrich von Schack: Observations on the Poetry and Music of opp. 15, 17, and 19." DMA diss., University of Texas at Austin, 1996. A study of the songs based on the poetry of Schack, the single poet set most often by Strauss, which suggests that language, subject matter, and emotional content were what most attracted the composer to this poet's work.

Wajemann, Heiner. *Die Chorkompositionen von Richard Strauss.* Tutzing: Hans Schneider, 1986. A survey of Strauss's works for large choral ensembles, including those in his operas. This study also deals with issues of Strauss's compositional technique and musical style.

Tone Poems and Orchestral Music

Bayreuther, Rainer. "Naturalismus und biographische Struktur in den Tondichtungen *Symphonia domestica* und *Eine Alpensinfonie* von Richard Strauss." In *Biographische Konstellation und künstlerisches Handeln.* Ed. Giselher Schubert, 94–106. Mainz: Schott, 1997. A study of the sketches for *Symphonia domestica* that suggests that Strauss structured the tone poem not as a superficial tone painting of one day in Garmisch, but as a fictional biography of himself.

———. "Zur Entstehung der 'Alpensinfonie' von Richard Strauss." *Archiv für Musikwissenschaft* 51 (1994): 213–46. A study of the sketches for *Eine Alpensinfonie* that demonstrates that the original program of 1900–02 was concerned with the life of the Swiss portrait-painter Karl Stauffer. In 1910 Strauss used these sketches to draft a four-movement symphony, of which the first movement represented a hike in the mountains. In 1913, that first movement became the work known as *Eine Alpensinfonie.*

Bloomfield, Theodore. "A Case of Neglect: Richard Strauss' Symphony in F minor." *Music and Musicians* 22 (1974): 25–28. A descriptive analysis of Strauss's first published symphony that argues for the return of the work to the repertoire.

Brosche, Günter. "Das Konzert für Oboe und kleines Orchester (1945) von Richard Strauss: Bemerkungen zur Entstehung des Werkes anhand einer neu bekannt gewordenen Quelle." *Richard Strauss-Blätter* 24 (1990): 80–103. Published in English as "The Concerto for Oboe and Small Orchestra (1945): Remarks about the Origin of the Work Based on a Newly Discovered Source." In *Richard Strauss: New Perspectives on the Composer and His Work,* ed. Bryan Gilliam, 177–92. Durham, N.C.: Duke University Press, 1992. A brief history of the origins of the Oboe Concerto and a study of its sketches.

Cooper, John Michael. "The Hero Transformed: The Relationship between *Don Quixote* and *Ein Heldenleben* Reconsidered." *Richard Strauss-Blätter* 30 (1993): 3–21. An analysis of the two tone poems *Don Quixote* and *Ein Heldenleben*, their programs, and some sketch materials, which concludes that the theme of domestic love is the link between the two works.

Gerlach, Reinhard. "Die Orchesterkomposition als musikalisches Drama: Die Teil-Tonalitäten der 'Gestalten' und der bitonale Kontrapunkt in *Ein Heldenleben* von Richard Strauss." *Musiktheorie* 6 (1991): 55–78. This study analyzes selected passages in *Ein Heldenleben* as "collisions" of competing tonalities—each representative of particular characters or ideas in his narrative—that are motivated by the work's program and result in bitonal passages and other novel sounds.

Gilliam, Bryan. "Richard Strauss." In *The Nineteenth-Century Symphony.* Ed. D. Kern Holloman, 345–68. New York: Schirmer, 1997. A historical overview of and commentary on Strauss's programmatic orchestral music.

Harrison, Daniel. "Imagining *Tod und Verklärung*." *Richard Strauss-Blätter* 29 (1993): 22–52. A study of the relationship between the program and the music of *Tod und Verklärung* that offers a slightly revised version of the program.

Hepokoski, James. "Fiery-Pulsed Libertine or Domestic Hero? Strauss's *Don Juan* Reinvestigated." In *Richard Strauss: New Perspectives on the Composer and His Work,* ed. Bryan Gilliam, 135–75. Durham, N.C.: Duke University Press, 1992. A landmark essay in Strauss studies that reasserts the importance of the program in any analysis of a programmatic work. In this case the program is used to explain the tensions between sonata-allegro and rondo forms in Strauss's second tone poem.

———. "Structure and Program in *Macbeth:* A Proposed Reading of Strauss's First Symphonic Poem." In *Richard Strauss and His*

World, ed. Bryan Gilliam, 67–89. Princeton, N.J.: Princeton University Press, 1992. A close reading of Strauss's first tone poem that accounts for more of the work's unique features than any earlier study.

Jackson, Timothy L. "The Metamorphosis of the *Metamorphosen*: New Analytical and Source-Critical Discoveries." In *Richard Strauss: New Perspectives on the Composer and His Work*, ed. Bryan Gilliam, 193–241. Durham, N.C.: Duke University Press, 1992. Based on a careful study of the sketch materials, Jackson locates the origins of *Metamorphosen* in a sketch for a choral setting of Goethe's poem "Niemand wird sich selber kennen."

Kennedy, Michael. *Strauss Tone Poems*. BBC Music Guides. London: BBC, 1984. A general guide to Strauss's programmatic works, based chiefly on narrative descriptions of the individual programs.

Liebscher, Julia. *Richard Strauss, Also sprach Zarathustra: Tondichtung (frei nach Friedr. Nietzsche) für grosses Orchester, op. 30*. Meisterwerke der Musik, Bd. 62. Munich: Fink, 1994. A recent, detailed concert guide for the educated listener, including background on Nietzsche's philosophy as a potential program, a history of the earliest performances, and reprints of concert reviews.

Murphy, Edward. "Tonal Organization in Five Strauss Tone Poems." *Music Review* 44 (1983): 223–33. A series of analyses of *Don Juan, Tod und Verklärung, Till Eulenspiegel, Also sprach Zarathustra*, and *Ein Heldenleben* purely in terms of traditional symphonic forms.

Phipps, Graham H. "The Logic of Tonality in Strauss's *Don Quixote*: A Schoenbergian Evaluation." *Nineteenth-Century Music* 9 (1986): 189–205. A close harmonic reading, using Schenkerian techniques, and formal analysis of *Don Quixote*.

Schaarwächter, Jürgen. *Richard Strauss und die Sinfonie*. Cologne–Rheinkassel: Dohr Edition, 1994. A revision of the author's master's thesis that looks at Strauss's conception of the symphony, focusing chiefly on his two early traditional symphonies, as well as *Symphonia domestica* and *Eine Alpensinfonie*.

Schmid, Mark-Daniel. "The Tone Poems of Richard Strauss and Their Reception History from 1887–1908." Ph.D. diss., Northwestern University, 1997. A detailed study of the critical reception of Strauss's first nine programmatic works, from *Aus Italien* to *Symphonia domestica*, in the two decades straddling the turn of the twentieth century.

Walden, Herwarth, ed. *Richard Strauss: Symphonien und Tondichtungen*. Erläutert von G. Brecher, A. Hahn, W. Klatte, W. Mauke,

A. Schattmann, H. Teibler, H. Walden. Meisterführer Nr. 6. Berlin: Schlesinger'sche Buch- und Musikhandlung, 1908. A series of early concert guides whose importance lies in their origins with writers close to Richard Strauss.

Warfield, Scott. "The Autograph of Strauss's *Festmarsch,* o. Op. 87 (T 157)." *Richard Strauss-Blätter* 27 (1992): 60–79. A comparison of the recently discovered composer's autograph score with the revised copy made by Franz Strauss for use with the Wilde Gung'l Orchestra in Munich.

Warfield, Scott Allan. "The Genesis of Richard Strauss's *Macbeth.*" Ph.D. diss., University of North Carolina at Chapel Hill, 1995. A detailed study of Strauss's first tone poem, including its sketches, multiple versions, and program, as well as a documentary history of Strauss's emergence as the leading German composer after the death of Wagner.

Werbeck, Walter. *Die Tondichtungen von Richard Strauss.* Dokumente und Studien zu Richard Strauss, Bd. 2. Tutzing: Hans Schneider, 1996. An important and wide-ranging book that gathers together an impressive amount of primary and secondary materials on all of Strauss's nine tone poems and tackles the analytical issues for each of those works. Although far from a definitive study, this volume sets the stage for a new level of discourse about Strauss's programmatic music.

Wilde, Denis. *The Development of Melody in the Tone Poems of Richard Strauss: Motif, Figure and Theme.* Studies in the History and Interpretation of Music 32. Lewiston: Edwin Mellen Press, 1990. A revision of the author's doctoral dissertation that seeks to analyze and categorize the melodic ideas of Strauss's seven programmatic works from *Macbeth* to *Ein Heldenleben.*

Williamson, John. *Strauss: "Also sprach Zarathustra."* Cambridge: Cambridge University Press, 1993. A detailed study of Strauss's fifth tone poem, including the work's intellectual background, its reception history, and analyses of several aspects of Strauss's musical language.

Youmans, Charles. "The Private Intellectual Context of Richard Strauss's *Also sprach Zarathustra.*" *Nineteenth-Century Music* 22 (1998): 101–26. A study of *Also sprach Zarathustra* that demonstrates the fundamental role that Nietzsche's philosophy played in Strauss's conception of the work, with a convincing analysis of the work's programmatic structure.

———. "The Twentieth-Century Symphonies of Richard Strauss." *Musical Quarterly* 84 (2000): 238–58. A study of *Symphonia domestica* and

Eine Alpensinfonie that examines both works as Straussian critiques of nineteenth-century musical metaphysics.

Miscellaneous Works and Studies

Adorno, Theodor W. "Richard Strauss at Sixty." Trans. Susan Gillespie. In *Richard Strauss and His World*, ed. Bryan Gilliam, 406–15. Princeton, N.J.: Princeton University Press, 1992. Originally published in *Zeitschrift für Musik* (1924), this early assessment of Strauss's music by his leading twentieth-century critic is less well known than the following item, but follows the same path.

———. "Richard Strauss: Born June 11, 1864." Trans. Samuel and Shierry Weber. *Perspectives of New Music* 4 (fall–winter 1965): 14–32; 5 (spring–summer 1966): 113–29. One of the most scathing critiques of Richard Strauss, whose music Adorno views as mere musical commerce for its failure—as perceived by Adorno—to adhere to the line of development that led to Schoenberg's twelve-tone principles.

Berlioz, Hector. *Instrumentationslehre*. Ergänzt und revidiert von Richard Strauss. Leipzig: C. F. Peters, 1905. In 1902 Strauss was asked by the publisher C. F. Peters to revise and update Berlioz's famous *Treatise on Instrumentation*, which Strauss did by means of his own comments inserted into the original text. (Note: The English translation has been reissued by Dover.)

DeWilde, Craig. "The Compositions of Richard Strauss from 1871–1886: The Emergence of a 'Mad Extremist.'" Ph.D. diss., University of California at Santa Barbara, 1991. A study of the transformation of Strauss's early musical style, chiefly through descriptive analyses of the unpublished piano sonata in C minor (TrV 79), the Symphony in F minor, and *Aus Italien*.

Dümling, Albrecht. "Zwischen Autonomie und Fremdbestimmung: Die Olympische Hymne von Robert Lubahn und Richard Strauss." *Richard Strauss-Blätter* 38 (1997): 68–102. A detailed history of the origins of Strauss's *Olympic Hymn* that notes the relatively autonomous organization of the games, and thus the lack of Nazi influence on Strauss's work.

Grasberger, Franz. *Richard Strauss und die Wiener Oper*. Tutzing: Hans Schneider, 1969. Beginning in 1919, Strauss shared the directorship of the Vienna State Opera with Franz Schalk until 1924, at which time Strauss resigned before he could be dismissed. Grasberger covers the history of this era thoroughly with liberal quotations from numerous letters by all principals involved and documents from the opera's archives.

Kissler, John Michael. "Harmony and Tonality in Selected Late Works by Richard Strauss, 1940–1948." Ph.D. diss., University of Arizona, 1988. A study of four works from 1940 to 1948 (*Metamorphosen,* Oboe Concerto, and some vocal works) that stresses the traditional harmonic elements and organization in these pieces.

Lehman, Lotte. *Singing with Richard Strauss.* Trans. Ernst Pawel. London: Hamish Hamilton, 1964. A mixture of personal reminiscence and commentary on five Strauss operas closely associated with this singer.

Todd, R. Larry. "Strauss before Liszt and Wagner: Some Observations." In *Richard Strauss: New Perspectives on the Composer and His Work,* ed. Bryan Gilliam, 3–40. Durham, N.C.: Duke University Press, 1992. A discussion of the influences of Brahms and, to a lesser extent, of Mendelssohn and Schumann on Strauss's music in the early to mid-1880s.

Wattenberger, Richard Ernest. "Richard Strauss, Modernism, and the University: A Study of German-Language and American Academic Reception of Richard Strauss from 1900 to 1990." Ph.D. diss., University of Minnesota, 2000. A study of the scholarly reception of Strauss and his music in the twentieth century, with particular attention to the philosophical and political issues that conditioned the negative academic response to Strauss for much of the century.

STRAUSS AS CONDUCTOR

Although history remembers him primarily as a composer, in his lifetime Strauss earned his living chiefly as a conductor and music director, and even after his compositions entered the repertoire, Strauss continued to conduct as a means of ensuring some financial stability in his family's life. Although perhaps not as famous for his conducting as his contemporary Mahler, Strauss was nevertheless renowned for superb performances of his own works, as well as the works of Wagner, Mozart, Beethoven, and others. Having lived into the age of recording, many performances under Strauss's direction have been captured for posterity and rereleased in recent years.

Birkin, Kenneth. "Richard Strauss in Weimar. Part I: The Concert Hall." *Richard Strauss-Blätter* 33 (1995): 3–36; "Richard Strauss in Weimar.

Part II: The Opera House." *Richard Strauss-Blätter* 34 (1995): 3–54. A history of Strauss's five-year term in Weimar (1889–94) as a second conductor, with lists of concerts and operas he led and facsimiles of programs.

Holden, Raymond. "Richard Strauss: The Beethoven Recordings." *Richard Strauss-Blätter* 35 (1996): 57–70. A brief overview of Strauss's conducting of Beethoven, with a close examination of his recordings of the Fifth and Seventh Symphonies in the 1920s.

———. "Richard Strauss: The Mozart Recordings." *Richard Strauss-Blätter* 35 (1996): 39–56. A general study of Strauss as a performer of Mozart's music, with a detailed examination of several Mozart recordings led by Strauss in the 1920s.

Kende, Götz Klaus. "Was Richard Strauss in Wien dirigierte." *Richard Strauss-Blätter* 19 (1988): 29–41. An extended list of operas and concerts conducted by Strauss in Vienna.

Munster, Robert. "Richard Strauss als Dirigent von Mozarts *Così fan tutte:* Beobachtungen aus dem Aufführungsmaterial der Bayerischen Staatsoper." In *Festschrift Klaus Hortschansky zum 60. Geburtstag,* 497–504. Tutzing: Hans Schneider, 1995. This essay describes Strauss's own annotations in the copy of the score to Mozart's *Così fan tutte* used by Strauss to conduct performances in 1886, 1897, and 1925.

Wurmser, Leo. "Richard Strauss as an Opera Conductor." *Music and Letters* 45 (1964): 4–15. A personal reminiscence of Strauss's conducting, based on performances heard in Europe between the two world wars.

STRAUSS AND THE NAZIS

Strauss's reputation has long been colored by his association with the Third Reich as president of the Reichsmusikkammer under Joseph Goebbels's Propaganda Ministry in the years 1933 to 1935. Although Strauss was exonerated in the postwar years in a denazification trial, there were too many actions by Strauss during the years of Nazi rule that could be construed by some as pro-Nazi and by others as exigencies of self- and family preservation. The question of Strauss's culpability is not easily answered—and there are many who want a simple, absolute answer—and thus his reputation remains tainted to some degree. Despite the nature of this question, a small handful of scholars have begun to clear away the polemical baggage in recent years.

Kater, Michael H. "Richard Strauss: Jupiter Compromised." In *Composers of the Nazi Era: Eight Portraits*, 211–63. New York: Oxford University Press, 2000. The best detailed and most evenhanded account of Strauss's actions during the Third Reich, by one of the leading experts on the period.

————. *The Twisted Muse: Musicians and Their Music in the Third Reich.* New York: Oxford University Press, 1997. Larger than the preceding item, this study covers virtually the whole of musical life under the Nazis and includes several sections dealing directly with Strauss in his official capacity as Reichsmusikkammer president and otherwise.

Potter, Pamela. "Strauss and the National Socialists: The Debate and Its Relevance." In *Richard Strauss: New Perspectives on the Composer and His Work*, ed. Bryan Gilliam, 93–112. Durham, N.C.: Duke University Press, 1992. An excellent overview of the scholarly debate over Strauss's cooperation with the Nazis, which often points out the agendas of individual authors, while also giving them credit for honest revelations.

STRAUSS: BUSINESS DEALINGS AND PERSONALITY

Axt, Eva-Maria. "Das Ineinanderwirken von Bewusstem und Unbewusstem: Zum Stimmungs- und Symbolcharakter der Tonarten bei Richard Strauss." *Richard Strauss-Blätter* 29 (1993): 7–21. A discussion of the use of associative tonality in Strauss's operas and symphonic works, with an emphasis on the latter.

Oliveri, Dario. "Il wagneriano 'imperfetto': Richard Strauss e gli Dei di Bayreuth." In *Ceciliana, per Nino Pirrotta*, 399–417. Palermo: Flaccovio, 1994. A discussion of the relationship between Strauss and Wagner, beginning with the earliest influences of Hans von Bülow and Alexander Ritter, and extending through Strauss's participation in the 1933 Bayreuth Festival. The correspondence with Cosima Wagner serves as the chief source for the years up to their break over *Salome* in 1911.

Petersen, Barbara A. "Die Händler und die Kunst: Richard Strauss as Composers' Advocate." In *Richard Strauss: New Perspectives on the Composer and His Work*, ed., Bryan Gilliam, 115–32. Durham, N.C.: Duke University Press, 1992. An explanation of the business climate in which Strauss came of age as a composer, and how he worked within its confines and also to change copyright laws and licensing agreements to the benefit of all composers.

STRAUSS: FAMILY AND MILIEU

Rauchenberger-Strauss, Johanna von. "Jugenderinnerungen." In *Richard Strauss Jahrbuch 1959/60.* Ed. Willi Schuh, 7–30. Bonn: Boosey and Hawkes, 1960. Reminiscences by his sister of Strauss's earliest years in both his nuclear family and within the extended family of his Pschorr cousins.

Trenner, Franz. "Franz Strauss (1822–1905)." In *Richard Strauss Jahrbuch 1959/60.* Ed. Willi Schuh, 31–41. Bonn: Boosey and Hawkes, 1960. A biographical sketch of Strauss's father.

———. "Richard Strauss und die 'Wilde Gung'l.'" *Schweizerische Musikzeitung* 90 (1950): 403–5. An overview of the Munich amateur orchestra conducted by Franz Strauss, in which Richard, as a violinist, received his first practical orchestral experiences.

Warfield, Scott. "Friedrich Wilhelm Meyer (1818–1893)." *Richard Strauss-Blätter* 37 (1997): 54–72. A biographical sketch of Strauss's only formal teacher of composition.

Index of Musical Works

All works are referenced by their opus number (Op.) and Trenner (TrV) number, that is, the number assigned them by Franz Trenner in his *Richard Strauss: Werkverzeichnis*, Veröffentlichungen der Richard-Strauss-Gesellschaft München, Bd. 12 (Munich: W. Ludwig Verlag, 1993).

OPERAS

Op.	TrV	Title
25	168	Guntram (3, Strauss), 1892–93, rev. 1934–39
50	203	Feuersnot (Singgedicht, 1, E. von Wolzogen), 1900–01
d54	215	Salome (Musikdrama, 1, O. Wilde, trans. H. Lachmann), 1903–5
58	223	Elektra (Tragödie, 1, H. von Hofmannsthal), 1906–8
59	227	Der Rosenkavalier (Komödie für Musik, 3, Hofmannsthal), 1909–10
60	228	Ariadne auf Naxos (1, Hofmannsthal), 1911–12 (to be played after *Der Bürger als Edelmann*, see TrV 228b)
60	228a	Ariadne auf Naxos, 2d version (prologue, 1, Hofmannsthal), 1916
65	234	Die Frau ohne Schatten (3, Hofmannsthal), 1914–17
72	246	Intermezzo (bürgerliche Komödie mit sinfonischen Zwischenspielen, 2, Strauss), 1918–23
75	255	Die ägyptische Helena (2, Hofmannsthal), 1923–27, rev. 1932–33 (act 2), rev. 1940

Op.	TrV	Title
79	263	Arabella (lyrische Komödie, 3, Hofmannsthal), 1929–32
80	265	Die schweigsame Frau (komische Oper, 3, S. Zweig after B. Jonson), 1933–35
81	271	Friedenstag (1, J. Gregor, after Zweig, 1935–36
82	272	Daphne (bukolische Tragödie, 1, Gregor), 1936–37
83	278	Die Liebe der Danae (heitere Mythologie, 3, Gregor, after Hofmannsthal), 1938–40
85	279	Capriccio (Konversationsstück für Musik, 1, C. Krauss/Strauss), 1940–41
—	294	Des Esels Schatten, 1947–48, inc.

OTHER DRAMATIC WORKS

—	61	Lila (Singspiel, J. W. von Goethe), 1878, inc.
—	150	Romeo und Julia (incidental music, W. Shakespeare), 1887
—	167	Lebende Bilder (incidental music), 1892
—	201	Kythere (ballet, Strauss), 1900, inc.
60	228b	Der Bürger als Edelmann (incidental music, Hofmannsthal, after Molière: *Le bourgeois gentilhomme*), 1912 [including fragments from Lully], rev. 1917 (as ballet)
—	227b	Der Rosenkavalier (film score), 1925 [arr. from opera Der Rosenkavalier, and marches and dances from TrV 167, TrV 214, TrV 217, TrV 245]
63	231	Josephslegende (ballet, 1, H. G. Kessler/Hofmannsthal), 1912–14
70	243	Schlagobers (ballet, 2, Strauss), 1921–22
—	245a	Verklungene Feste (ballet), 1941 [including Tanzsuite nach F. Couperin, TrV 245, chamber orchestra, 1923, with 6 new numbers later included in Divertimento, op. 86, chamber orch. 1940–41]

SONGS

Solo Voice and Piano

—	2	Weihnachtslied (C. F. D. Schubart), 1870
—	3	Einkehr (J. L. Uhland), 1871
—	4	Winterreise (Uhland), 1871
—	5	Waldkonzert (J. N. Vogel), ?1871

Op.	TrV	Title
—	7	Der böhmische Musikant (O. Pletzsch), ?1871
—	8	Herz, mein Herz (E. Geibel), 1871
—	10	Gute Nacht (Geibel), 1871, inc.
—	13	Der Alpenhirten Abschied (F. von Schiller), ?1872, lost
—	16	Der müde Wanderer (A. H. Hoffmann von Fallersleben), ?1873
—	42	Husarenlied (Hoffmann von Fallersleben), ?1873
—	48	Der Fischer (J. W. von Goethe), 1877
—	49	Die Drossel (Uhland), 1877
—	50	Lass ruhn die Toten (A. von Chamisso), 1877
—	51	Lust und Qual (Goethe), 1877
—	58	Spielmann und Zither (T. Körner), 1878
—	59	Wiegenlied (Hoffmann von Fallersleben), 1878
—	60	Abend- und Morgenrot (Hoffmann von Fallersleben), 1878
—	62	Im Walde (Geibel), 1878
—	63	Der Spielmann und sein Kind (Hoffmann von Fallersleben), 1878 [also for soprano, orch.]
—	65	Nebel (N. Lenau), 1878
—	66	Soldatenlied (Hoffmann von Fallersleben), 1878
—	67	Ein Röslein zog ich mir im Garten (Hoffmann von Fallersleben), 1878
—	74	Für Musik (Geibel), 1879
—	75	Drei Lieder (Geibel): Waldgesang, O schneller mein Ross, Die Lilien glühn in Düften, 1879
—	77	Frühlingsanfang (Geibel), 1879
—	78	Das rote Laub (Geibel), 1879
—	87	Die drei Lieder (Uhland), 1879, lost
—	88	Im Vaters Garten heimlich steht ein Blümlein (H. Heine), 1879
—	89	Der Morgen (F. von Sallet), 1880, lost
—	90	Die erwachte Rose (Sallet), 1880
—	98	Begegnung (O. E. Gruppe), 1880
—	100	Mutter, o sing mir zur Ruh (F. von Hemans), 1880, lost
—	101	John Anderson, mein Lieb (R. Burns, trans. F. Freiligrath), 1880
—	107	Geheiligte Stätte (J. G. Fischer), 1881, lost
—	112	Waldesgang (K. Stieler), 1882, lost
—	113	Ballade (A. Becker), 1882, lost
—	119	Rote Rosen (Stieler), 1883
—	128	Mein Geist ist trüb (G. N. G. Lord Byron), 1884, lost

Voice and Orchestra

CHORAL

With Orchestra

Unaccompanied

OTHER CHORAL WORKS

Op.	TrV	Title
—	64	Ein Alphorn hör' ich schallen (J. Kerner), 1 voice, horn, piano, 1878
—	—	Utan scafvel och fosfor [From a Swedish matchbox], 2 tenor, 2 bass, 1889
38	181	Enoch Arden (A. Tennyson, trans. A. Strodtmann), melodrama, speaker, piano, 1897
—	191	Das Schloss am Meere (Uhland), melodrama, speaker, piano, 1899
—	—	Zwei Lieder aus Der Richter von Zalamea (P. Calderón de la Barca): Liebesliedchen, tenor, guitar, harp; Lied der Chispa, mezzo, unison male voices, guitar, 2 harp, 1904
—	—	Hymne auf das Haus Kohorn (Strauss), 2 tenor, 2 bass, 1925
—	—	Hab Dank, du güt'ger Weisheitspender (Strauss), bass, 1939
—	—	Notschrei aus den Gefilden Lapplands (Strauss), soprano/tenor, 1940
—	—	Wer tritt herein (Strauss), soprano/tenor, 1943

ORCHESTRAL

Op.	TrV	Title
—	17	Ouvertüre zum Singspiel Hochlands Treue, 1872–73
—	41	Concertouvertüre, b, 1876
1	43	Festmarsch, E-flat, 1876
—	45	Ouvertüre zu der geplanten Oper Ein Studentenstreich, E, 1876, inc.
—	46	Ouvertüre zu der geplanten Oper Dom Sebastian, E-flat, 1876, inc. (piano score only)
—	52	Serenade, G, 1877
—	55	Andante cantabile, D, 1877, inc.
—	56	Andante, B-flat, 1877, inc.
—	69	Ouvertüre, E, 1878
—	83	Ouvertüre, a, 1879
—	94	Symphony No. 1, d, 1880
—	124	Lied ohne Worte, E-flat, 1883
—	125	Concertouvertüre, c, 1883
12	126	Symphony No. 2, f, 1884
—	135	Festmarsch, D, 1884–85, rev. 1888
16	147	Aus Italien, Symphonische Fantasie, 1886
20	156	Don Juan, Tondichtung nach Nikolaus Lenau, 1888–89
—	157	Festmarsch, C, 1889
24	158	Tod und Verklärung, Tondichtung, 1888–89

With Soloists

Op.	TrV	Title
—	80	Romanze, E-flat, clarinet, orch., 1879
8	110	Violin Concerto, d, 1880–82
11	117	Horn Concerto No. 1, E-flat, 1882–83, arr. horn/piano 1883
—	118	Romanze, F, violoncello, orch., 1883
—	133	Der Zweikampf, polonaise, flute, bassoon, orch., 1884 [doubtful attribution]
—	145	Burleske, d, piano, orch., 1885–86
—	146	Rhapsody, c-sharp, piano, orch., 1886, inc.
35	184	Don Quixote, "Phantastische Variationen über ein Thema ritterlichen Charakters," violoncello, orch., 1897
73	209a	Parergon zur Symphonia domestica, piano left hand, orch., 1925
74	254	Panathenäenzug "symphonische Klavieretüden in Form einer Passacaglia," piano left hand, orch., 1927
—	283	Horn Concerto No. 2, E-flat, 1942
—	292	Oboe Concerto in (D Major), 1945, rev. 1948
—	293	Duett-Concertino, clarinet, bassoon, strings, harp, 1947

Brass and Wind

7	106	Serenade, E-flat, 13 wind, 1881
4	132	Suite, B-flat, 13 wind, 1884
—	224	Feierlicher Einzug der Ritter des Johanniter-Ordens, brass, timpani, 1909
—	248	Wiener Philharmoniker Fanfare, brass, timpani, 1924
—	250	Fanfare zur Eröffnung der Musikwoche der Stadt Wien im September 1924, brass, timpani, 1924
—	286	Festmusik der Stadt Wien, brass, timpani, 1942–43
—	287	Wiener Fanfare, brass, timpani, 1943
—	288	Sonatina No. 1 "Aus der Werkstatt eines Invaliden", F, 16 winds, 1943
—	291	Sonatina No. 2 "Fröhliche Werkstatt," E-flat, 16 winds, 1944–45

CHAMBER AND SOLO INSTRUMENTAL

—	15	Zwei Etuden, No. 1 for E-flat horn, No. 2 for E horn, ?1873
—	21	Zwei kleine Stücke, violin, piano, 1873, inc.

PIANO WORKS

Op.	TrV	Title
—	14	Polka, Walzer, und andere kleinere Kompositionen, ?1872, lost
—	18	Fünf kleine Stücke, ?1873
—	19	Sonatina No. 1, C, ?1873, lost
—	20	Sonatina No. 2, E, ?1873, lost
—	22–27	Six Sonatinas: C, F, B-flat, E, E-flat, D [TrV 25 inc., TrV 27 lost], 1874
—	29	Fantasie, C, ?1874
—	30	Zwei kleine Stücke, ?1874
—	—	Untitled composition, c, ?1874
—	34	Allegro assai, B-flat, 1875, inc.
—	47	Sonata, No. 1, E, 1877
—	68	Zwölf Variationen, D, 1878
—	72	Aus alter Zeit, eine kleine Gavotte, 1879
—	73	Andante, c, 1879
—	79	Sonata, No. 2 (Grosse Sonate), c, 1879
—	82	Skizzen, 5 pieces, 1879
—	86	Scherzo, b, ?1879
—	—	Four-part Fugue, C, 1879; Double Fugue, B-flat, 1880
—	93	Zwei kleine Stücke, 1879–80
—	—	Scherzando, G, 1880
—	99	Fugue on Four Themes, C, 1880
5	103	Sonata, b, 1880–81
3	105	Fünf Klavierstücke: Andante, Allegro vivace scherzando, Largo, Allegro molto, Allegro marcatissimo, 1881
—	111	Albumblatt, F, 1882
—	120	Largo, a, ?1883
—	121	Stiller Waldespfad, 1883
—	122	Melodie (Ruhig), G-flat, ?1883, inc.
9	127	Stimmungsbilder, 2 pianos: Auf stillem Waldespfad, An einsamer Quelle, Intermezzo, Träumerei, Heidebild, 1882–84
—	130	Improvisation und Fuge a-Moll über ein Originalthema, 1884 [only fugue survives]
—	138	Intermezzo, F, piano 4 hands
—	213	Parade-Marsch des Regiments Königs-Jäger zu Pferde No. 1, E-flat, 1905
—	214	De Brandenburgsche Mars, D, 1905, orch. 1905
—	217	Königsmarsch, E-flat, 1905, orch. as Militärischer Festmarsch, 1906
—	222	Parade Marsch für Kavallerie No. 2, D-flat, 1907

STUDIES AND EXCERCISES

Op.	TrV	Title
—	31	Four-voice exercise, B-flat, ?1875
—	32	Four-voice chorale exercise, B-flat, ?1875
—	38	Four-voice exercise, d, 1876
—	39	Four-voice exercise, A-flat, 1876
—	57	Contrapuntal Studies I (imitative exercises and canons), 1877–78
—	81	Contrapuntal Studies II (9 fugues), 1879
—	91	Contrapuntal Studies III (3 fugues), 1879–80

ARRANGEMENTS

—	108	F. Lachner: Nonett, F, piano 4 hands
—	139	W. A. Mozart: Piano Concerto, c, K491, 1885 lost [cadenza]
—	140	A. Ritter: Der faule Hans, 1886 [overture arr. for piano]
—	143	J. Raff: Bernhard von Weimar, 1885 [2 marches, arr. for piano]
—	161	C. W. Gluck: Iphigénie en Tauride, 1899
—	162	R. Wagner: Rienzi, 1890, lost
—	164	A. Ritter: Nun hält Frau Minne Liebeswacht, 1898 [song, op. 4/8 arr. for 1 voice, orch.]
—	227b	R. Wagner: Die Feen, 1888 [insertions for act 2]
—	242	A. Boieldieu: Johann von Paris, 1922 [revision of "Welche Lust gewährt das Reisen"]
—	249	L. van Beethoven: Die Ruinen von Athen [text rev. Hofmannsthal], 1924
—	262	W. A. Mozart: Idomeneo [text rev. L. Wallerstein], 1930
—	285	F. Schubert: Kupelwieser-Walzer, G-flat, 1943 [arr. for piano]

GENERAL INDEX

Adorno, Theodor W.: on R. S., 32–34, 40, 47, 51–52, 56
Aldrich, Robert, 174
Allgemeiner Deutscher Musikverein (ADMv), 38, 45, 108–9, 161, 184n. 59
Allgemeine Musikzeitung, 113, 214
Andersen, Hans Christian: "The Princess and the Swineherd," 224
Andreae, Volkmar, 178, 185n. 68
Auber, Daniel-François-Esprit, 36, 261
Ausdrucksmusik, 13
Austria, 154–59

Bach, Johann Sebastian, 56, 69, 95
Bahr, Hermann, 219
Bailey, Robert, 262
Basel, 161–65; Subscription Orchestra, 163
Batka, Richard, 139
Baumbach, Rudolf, 338
Bayreuth, 16–17, 44, 46, 50–51, 77–78, 105, 207, 245; *Bayreuther Blätter*, 246
Beethoven, Ludwig van, 13, 37, 77, 169, 213; influence on R. S., 5, 8, 113–14, 130, 192–93, 196, 207; symphonic

style, 74, 105. Works: *Coriolanus* Overture, 12, 106, 209; *Egmont* Overture, 12; *Fidelio*, 49; *Leonore* Overture, 12, 106; Piano Sonata, Op. 81a, 12–13; Piano Sonata, Op. 111, 138; Symphony No. 3, 106, 112; Symphony No. 5, 196, 204; Symphony No. 6, 9, 13, 106; Symphony No. 7, 214; Symphony No. 8, 48; Symphony No. 9, 12, 106
Bella, Johann Leopold, 14, 106, 122, 123
Berger, Anton, 137
Bergson, Henri, 127
Berlin, 48, 111, 120, 210, 250; concerts, 48, 120, 208, 210; Court Opera, 31, 48, 155; premieres, 111, 165; Philharmonic Orchestra, 50, 149, 152–53, 161–62, 178; R. S. posts, 152–53, 155, 247–49; Tonkünstler Orchestra, 159, 160, 172, 178
Berlioz, Hector, 5, 162; *idée fixe*, 13, 17; instrumentation, 22; program music, 13, 113; *Requiem*, 11; *Symphonie fantastique*, 13, 17, 118
Bern, 162–64; *Berner Tagblatt*, 164; City Orchestra, 164

About the Contributors

PIERRE MARC BELLEMARE is a Canadian philosopher and classicist and a published writer, both in English and in his native French, now residing in Ottawa where he teaches Latin at St. Paul University. Holder of a Ph.D. from the University of Montreal, he specializes in ancient philosophy and has published papers in that field, as well as in classical studies, notably ancient numismatics. He is also a passionate opera buff and has written articles on that subject for published and forthcoming collective books in which he deals with aspects of the life and/or works of Mascagni, Verdi, and Strauss. As a critic and essayist, he is also a regular contributor to *La Scena Musicale,* a monthly musical magazine published in Montreal. He is currently working on a novel.

PETER FRANKLIN is reader in music at the University of Oxford, where he is a Fellow of St. Catherine's College. His published work includes *The Idea of Music: Schoenberg and Others* (London: Palgrave Macmillian, 1985), *Mahler: Symphony No. 3* (Cambridge: Cambridge University Press, 1991), and *The Life of Mahler* (Cambridge: Cambridge University Press, 1997). He has contributed to the *New Grove Dictionary of Opera* and the *Revised New Grove Dictionary of Music and Musicians* and also writes on early-twentieth-century opera and Hollywood film music.

CHRISTINE GETZ, assistant professor of music at the University of Iowa, was formerly a member of the Music Faculty at Baylor University, where she was the director of the Collegium Musicum and the recipient of the

1999 Outstanding Teacher Award. Her research interests include Italian archival studies and sixteenth-century Italian polyphony, and focus specifically on the city of Milan. Dr. Getz has been the recipient of a Rotary Foundation Graduate Fellowship (1988–89), an NEH Summer Stipend (1993), an NEH Summer Seminar Fellowship (1994), and a Fullbright (1997–98). Her articles have appeared in *BACH* (Journal of the Riemenscheider-Bach Institute), *Explorations in Renaissance Culture, Musica Disciplina, Arte Lombarda, Early Music History, Studi musicali*, and the *Journal of the Royal Music Association*, and have recently been published in the *Atti del X Convegno internazionale di studi sul tema La musica e il sacro* (Cono: A.M.I.S.–Como, 2003).

MORTEN KRISTIANSEN, originally from Copenhagen, completed his doctorate at Yale University in 2000 with a dissertation on Strauss's *Feuersnot*. He currently teaches musicology at Truman State University in Kirksville, Missouri, and his essay "Parallel Lives: Richard Strauss, Ernst von Wolzogen, Arthur Seidl, and the Rejection of Erlösung (Redemption) in Feuersnot" is forthcoming in a volume of *Strauss Studies* from Cambridge University Press.

SUZANNE M. LODATO is associate program officer in the Scholarly Communications Program at the Andrew W. Mellon Foundation. Previously she was a Fellow in Music in the Society of Fellows in the Humanities at Columbia University and received her Ph.D. in musicology from Columbia. Her research focuses on word–music relationships and the music of late-nineteenth-century composer Richard Strauss, especially interrelations between modernist literary style and musical style in Strauss's songs. She is vice president of the International Association for Word and Music Studies.

MARK-DANIEL SCHMID is currently associate professor of music history and piano at Mansfield University in Pennsylvania. He received his Ph.D. from Northwestern University in 1997 with a dissertation on the early reception of Strauss's tone poems. He was a contributor for the *International Dictionary of Black Musicians*, ed. Samuel A. Floyd (Chicago: Fitzroy Dearborn, 2001). He is also an accomplished pianist and has accompanied recitals in Germany and Switzerland as well as throughout the United States.

JÜRGEN THYM is a professor at the Eastman School of Music (University of Rochester, New York). He is known as a cotranslator (together with David Beach and John Rothgeb, respectively) of music theory treatises (Kirnberger and Schenker), as an editor of several volumes in the Schoenberg Gesamtausgabe, and as an author of numerous articles about the German Lied and text–music relations. For eighteen years he was the chair of the musicology department at Eastman.

HEINER WAJEMANN is assistant professor at the Hochschule für Musik und Theater in Hannover, Germany, where he teaches in the areas of hymnology, liturgy, and theology. Since 1985 he has been the pastor at the Protestant-Lutheran City Church in Schneverdingen. He studied at the Johannes-Gutenberg University of Mainz from 1973 to 1978 and received his Ph.D. from the Catholic University Eichstätt in 1983. His dissertation centered on the choral compositions of Richard Strauss. On topics ranging from theology and church music to hymnology to general music history, his articles have appeared in several German publications including the *Richard Strauss-Blätter*.

SCOTT WARFIELD holds a Ph.D. from the University of North Carolina at Chapel Hill, where he wrote his dissertation on Richard Strauss's first tone poem, *Macbeth*. He has published articles and reviews in the *Richard Strauss-Blätter*, MLA *Notes*, and *Fontes Artis Musicae*. Warfield's research in Munich in 1988 uncovered several lost Strauss manuscripts, including the original version of the composer's third *Festmarsch* (T 157), which he edited for its first-ever performance by the North Carolina Symphony in 1991. In the fall of 2002, Warfield joined the faculty at the University of Central Florida in Orlando as assistant professor.

WALTER WERBECK is professor of musicology at the University of Greifs-wald, Germany. He received his Ph.D. from the University of Detmold/Paderborn in 1987 with a dissertation on the German *Moduslehre* in the first half of the sixteenth century. His *Habiliationsschrift* in 1995 centered on the tone poems of Richard Strauss and was published as *Die Tondich-tungen von Richard Strauss* (Tutzing: Hans Schneider, 1996). He has published articles in the *Schütz-Jahrbuch, Richard Strauss-Blätter,* the Bonner *Schriften zur Musikwissenschaft,* and the *Kieler Schriften zur Musikwis-senschaft,* and he wrote the entry "Instrumentalmusik" in the *Historisches Wörterbuch der Rhetorik*. He has also contributed several articles on Mahler, Schoenberg, Brahms, Strauss, and modernism. He is the principal editor of the *Neue Schütz-Ausgabe* and the *Schütz-Jahrbuch.*

CHARLES D. YOUMANS is assistant professor of musicology at Penn State University. He received his Ph.D. from Duke University in 1996 with a dissertation on musical and philosophical influences in Strauss's first opera,

Guntram. He has published articles in *Nineteenth-Century Music,* the *Musical Quarterly*, and elsewhere. Currently, he is writing a book on Strauss and the German intellectual tradition.

JAMES L. ZYCHOWICZ holds a Ph.D. in musicology from the University of Cincinnati, Ohio and was a Fulbright Scholar during his time there. He is the author of *Mahler's Fourth Symphony* (2000), a volume in the series of Studies in Musical Genesis and Structure published by Oxford University Press. His other publications include various articles as well as the two-volume critical edition of the opera *Die drei Pintos* (Recent Researches in the Music of the Nineteenth and Early Twentieth Centuries. [Middleton, Wis.: A-R Editions, 2000]), which Mahler completed from sketches and other music by Carl Maria von Weber.